black dog press

EAT & ART

EAT & ART

EAT & ART

CHEFS & ARTISTS

18 TIAGO BONITO
PEDRO TUDELA 33

34 NOÉLIA
NUNO NUNES FERREIRA 48

49 PEDRO LEMOS
ALBUQUERQUE MENDES 65

66 MARLENE VIEIRA
HUGO BRAZÃO 81

82 BERTÍLIO GOMES
FÁTIMA MENDONÇA 97

98 MIGUEL CASTRO E SILVA
ANA VIDIGAL 113

114 JOSÉ AVILLEZ
JÚLIA CÔTA 129

130 ALEXANDRE SILVA
LILIANA PORTER 145

146 VÍTOR SOBRAL
ANA TISCÓRNIA 161

162 MIGUEL LAFFAN / MAFALDA SANTOS 177

177 JOÃO RODRIGUES / SUSANNE S.D. THEMLITZ 191

192 MIGUEL ROCHA VIEIRA / GRAÇA PEREIRA COUTINHO 207

208 PEDRO PENA BASTOS / ALICE GEIRINHAS 224

225 JOÃO OLIVEIRA / RODRIGO OLIVEIRA 239

240 RICARDO COSTA / CRISTINA ATAÍDE 255

256 HENRIQUE SÁ PESSOA / MIGUEL PALMA 271

272 LEONEL PEREIRA / PEDRO GOMES 287

288 JOSÉ JÚLIO VINTÉM / ANTÓNIO NEVES NOBRE 303

306 TIMELINE 345

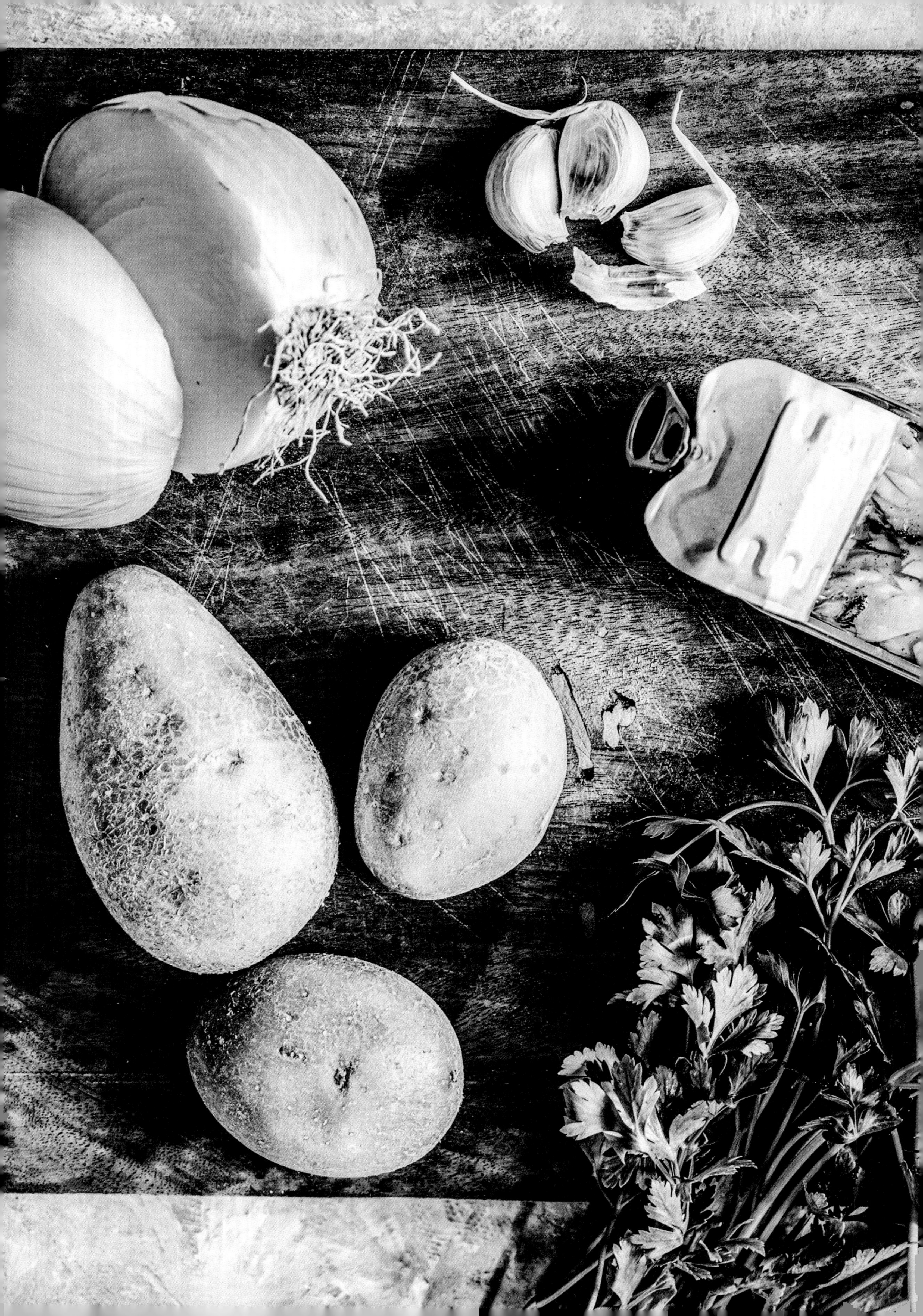

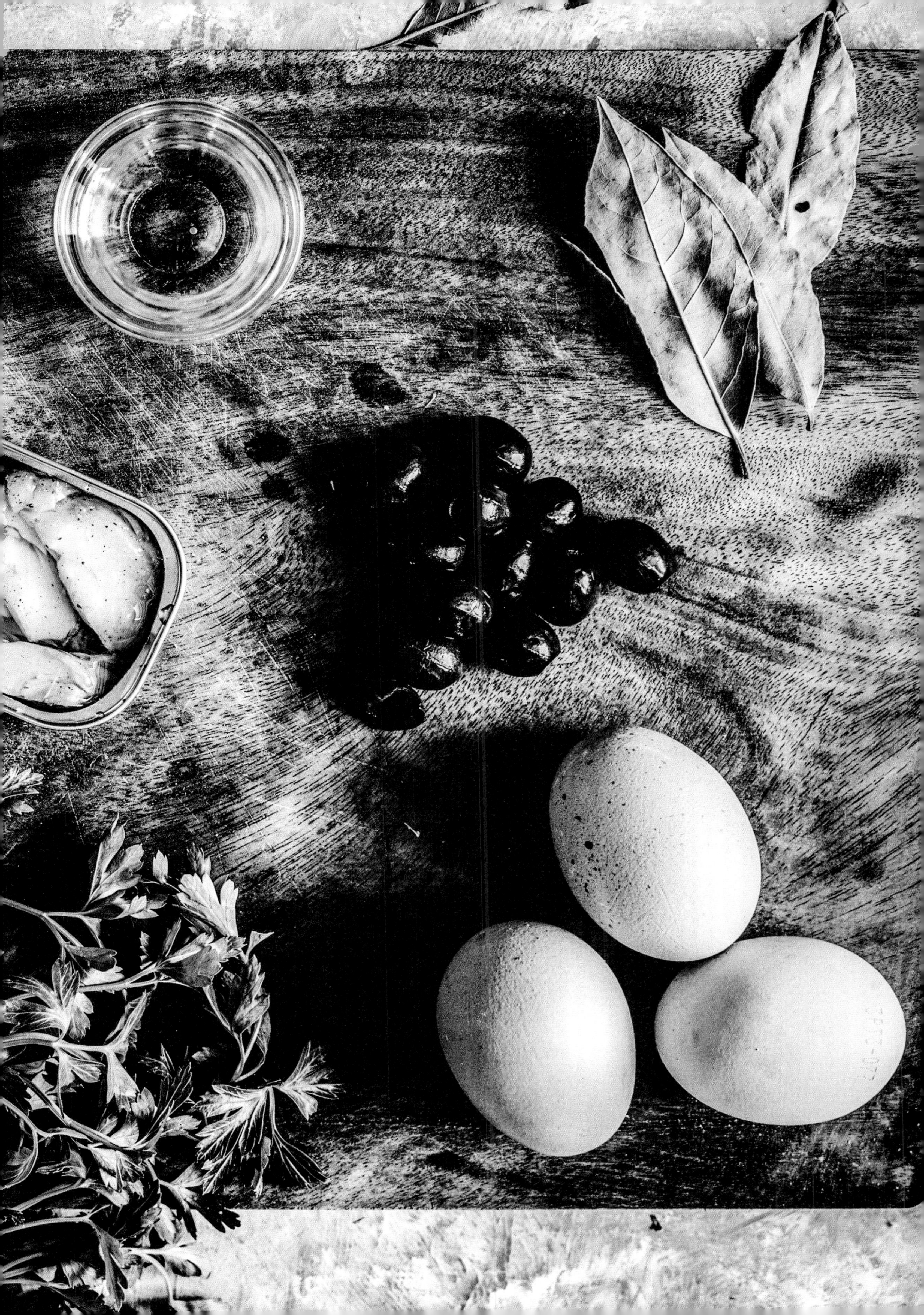

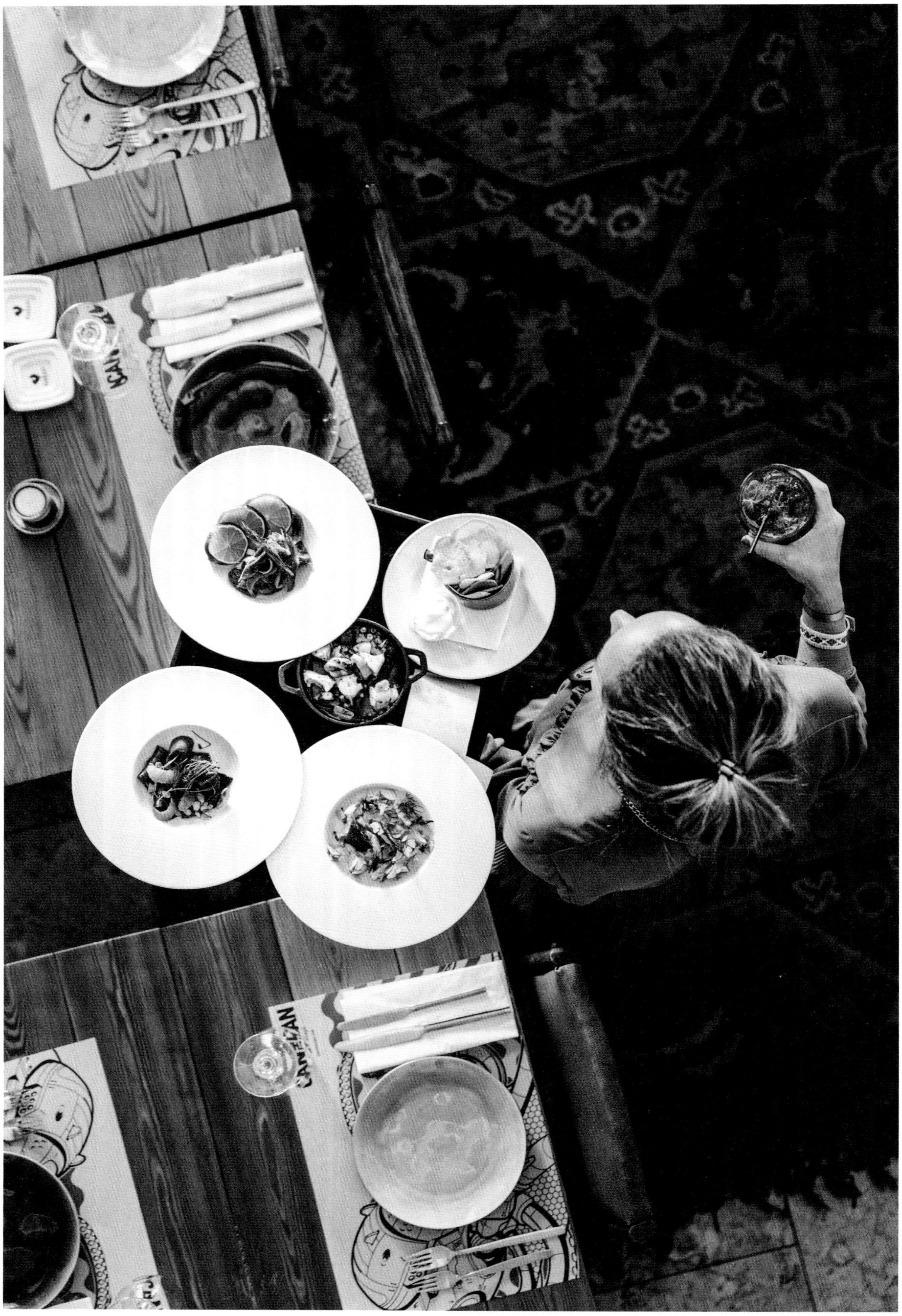

"Cooking must be seen as the oldest expression of world view and identity, long before the arrival of sculpture, painting, and even spoken language. Paleolithic cooking processes have already used concepts like analysis, synthesis, condensation, symbolism. Therefore cooking must also be seen as the ancestor of physics, chemistry and philosophy."

PETER KUBELKA

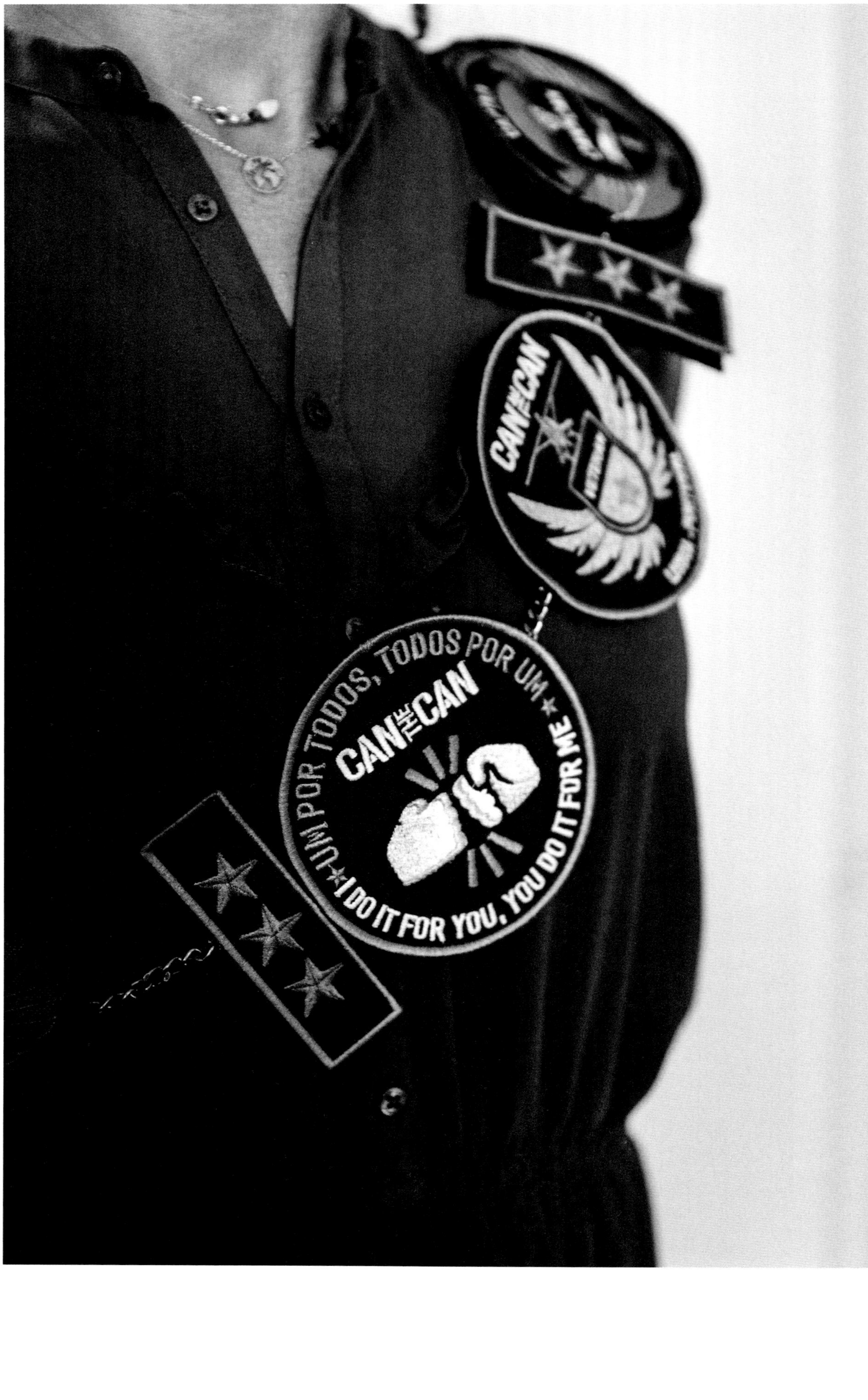
CAN THE CAN
UM POR TODOS, TODOS POR UM
CAN THE CAN
I DO IT FOR YOU, YOU DO IT FOR ME

Can the Can opened its doors in June 2012 in one of Europe's biggest and most impressive squares, Praça do Comércio, also known as Terreiro do Paço. This was once the location for Paço da Ribeira, the palace of Portuguese royalty for more than 200 years until its destruction in the huge earthquake that struck Lisbon in 1755. This history and a stunning vista over the Tagus compete to turn this into one of the most impressive squares in Europe.

Portugal has a long coastline which, from early days, led the Portuguese towards the sea in search of new horizons. So was born a maritime odyssey and a culture of seafood, helped by access to excellent fish. All of these factors – the extensive coastline, the abundance and high quality of its fish, and Portugal's excellence in the art of fishing – created conditions for the rapid growth of canning in Portugal from the 19th century onwards.

Can the Can was born of a fascination with this industry, and aims to dignify it and bring it to a wider audience. Our cuisine is typically Mediterranean, defined by the use of natural products and healthy ingredients. We strive to elevate tins into an exclusive product, and we are innovative with our recipes, trusting that quality of preparation and presentation can help promote the consumption of tinned fish.

More than just a restaurant, we want to be guardians of history. We want to investigate and promote the cultural heritage invested in the many people still working in this industry alongside consumers and, notably, the artists who know how to give it a unique and recognisable identity.

From the start we have been members of ANICP (Associação Nacional Industrial dos Conservas de Peixe, which translates as the National Association of Industrial Fish Canners), whose goal is to support and enhance the gastronomy of tinned fish.

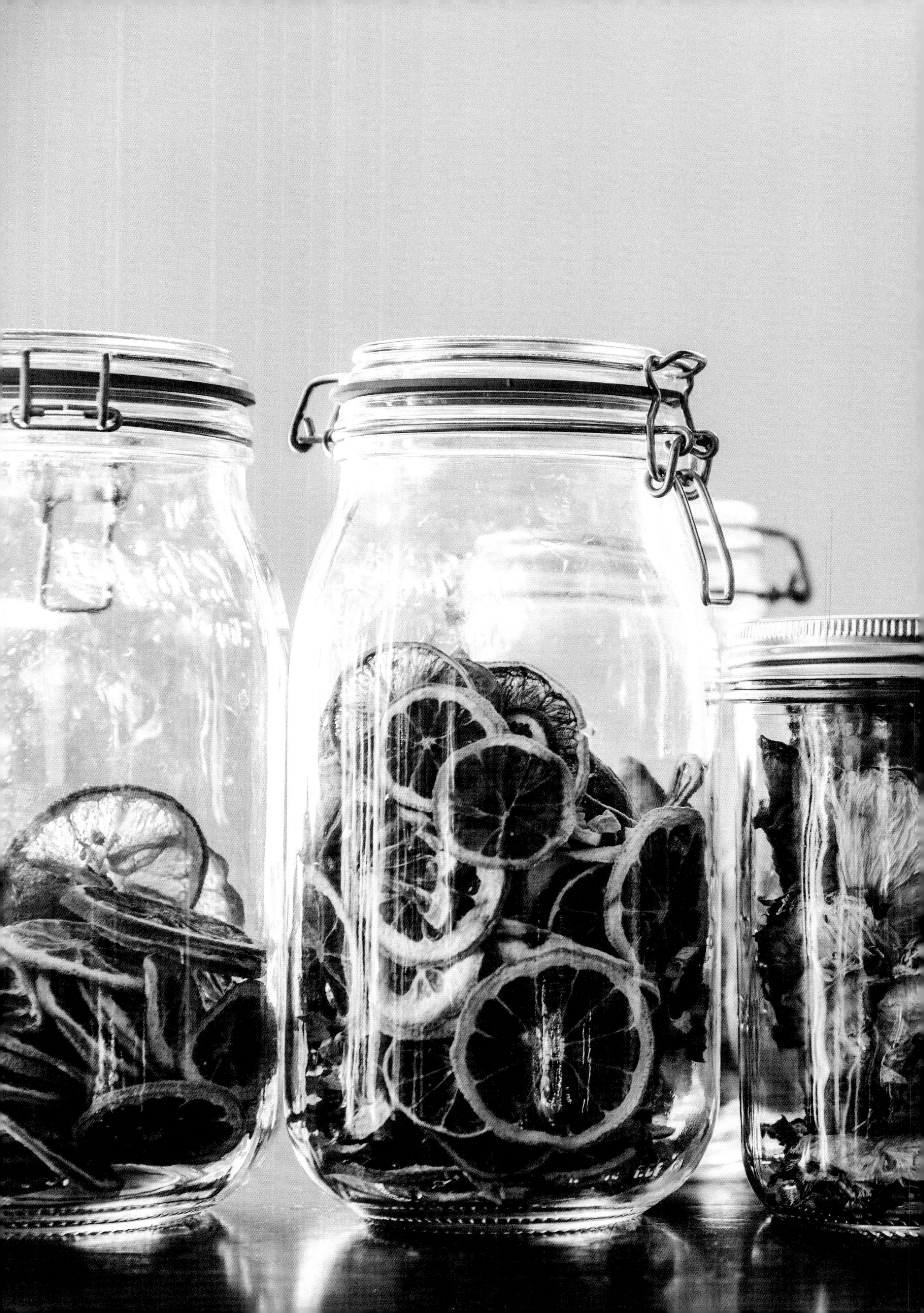

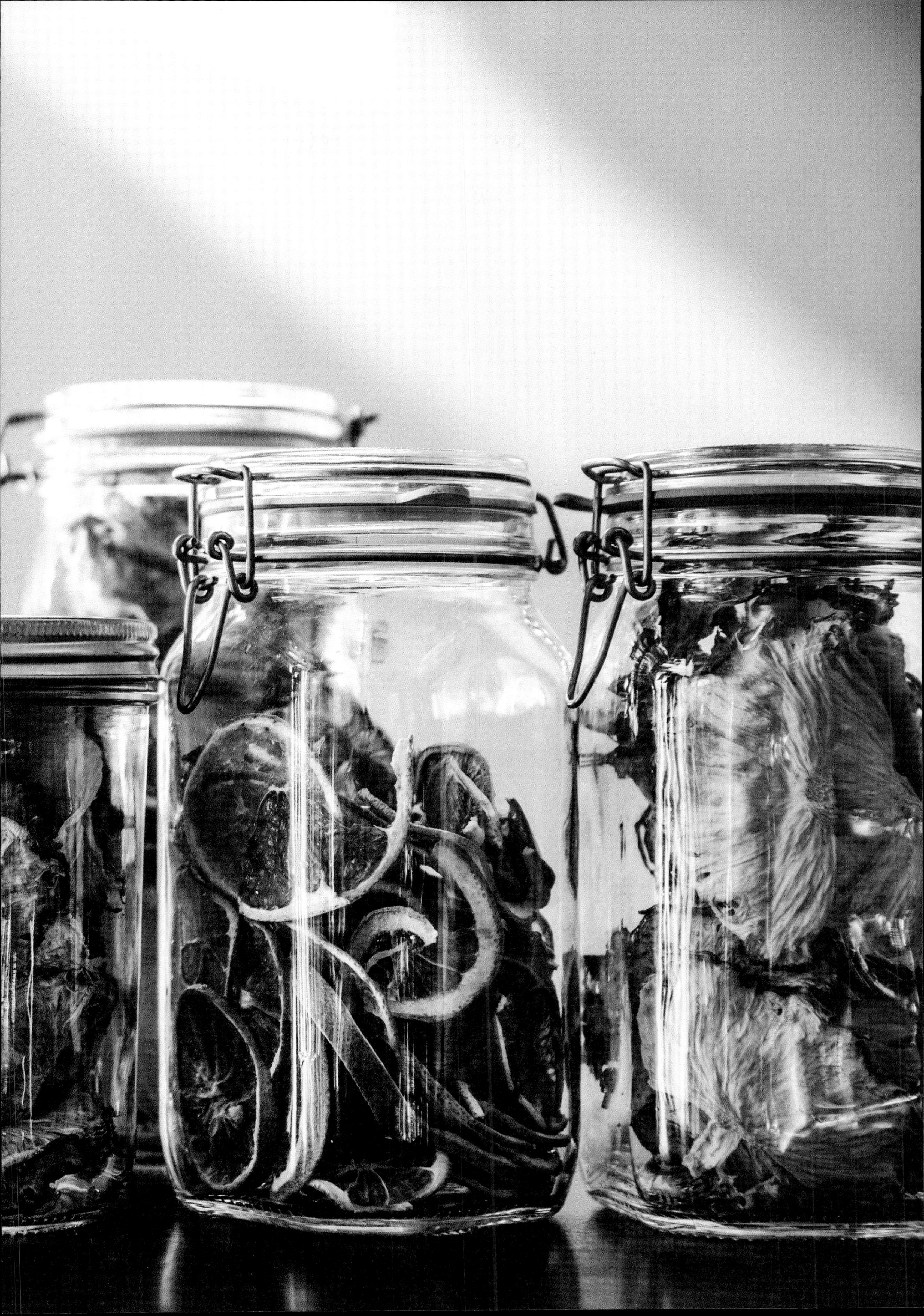

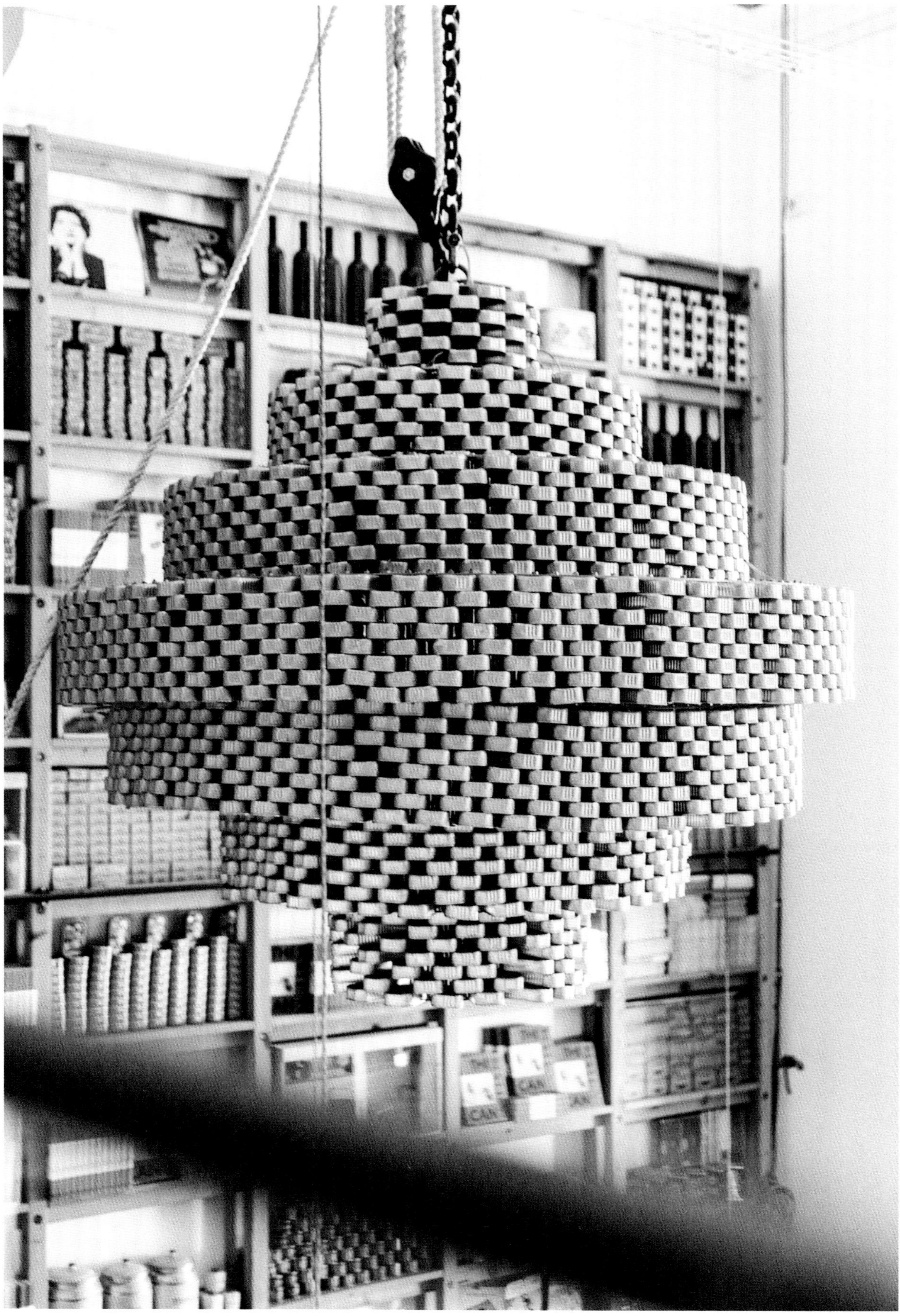

Eat & Art is all about exploring the affinities between the worlds of gastronomy and contemporary art through a project that aims to showcase the work of artists and chefs alike, with canned seafood products as a backdrop.

In this way, the nucleus of a potential future collection of Portuguese artworks is assembled – alongside an array of recipes conceived by star chefs that revisit Portuguese national cuisine and place canned fish front and centre. At the same time, the project explores the identity of our authors in each of these fields, bringing them together in a common dialogue.

People have been drawing, painting and carving animals since prehistory, as long as they have been hunting and cooking them. High points include the decorative art of ancient Egypt, the *asàratos òikos* of the Greeks and Romans, 16th-century Italian Mannerism, and Portuguese decorative tiles with their representations of fish.

The fascination that food exerts on artists – the way animals and vegetables used in the culinary field are represented, or the results of their elaboration – has been a constant over the centuries and is probably worth a treatise in itself. To approach the mutual influences of these two worlds, and the overlapping of their particular rules – to address Filippo Tommaso Marinetti's *Manifesto of Futurist Cooking*, the food-related 'snare pictures' of Swiss artist Daniel Spoerri, Gordon Matta-Clark's FOOD restaurant in New York, the performance-art cookery of Austrian film-maker Peter Kubelka, or the participation of the three-Michelin-star chef Ferran Adriá in the art event documenta 12 – is not to label the chef's activity as 'art'. At least not in the same way as the great art historian Giorgio Vasari, and later the Romantics, would understand artistic activity. All the same, creative cuisine is clearly and naturally *cosa mentale*, or a mental thing.

Returning to Ferran Adriá, the Catalan chef behind the award-winning elBulli restaurant, it's worth noting his words when he says that cuisine is not "museable" – that the interaction between kitchen and lounge, between the chef, his team and the diners, is an experience that takes place under unique circumstances in the restaurant, a space that has a similar historical background to the museum. Trying to translate the activities of some chefs in the performative field of cuisine into the art world, using the tired argument of creativity, would be like returning to the debate on the leading role of design in the industrial and capitalist culture of the last century. (According to George Steiner, redefining the modern grammars of creation.) We should simply note the progressive recognition of the so-called secondary arts and the high ratings given to the more technical arts, such as photography or cinema, architecture or technology. Even art forms as apparently distinct as fashion and gastronomy.

The act of preserving – i.e. preparing and conditioning vegetables, fruit or meat for later consumption – has been frequent throughout food history. A huge variety of products fall into this category, but our specific concern is with canned fish, and particularly tuna and sardines. These had an important role in the pre-fast-food cuisine of Mal Cozinhado da Ribeira das Naus, a big complex of sea-front eateries along the River Tagus, between Cais do Sodré and Praça do Comércio, referred to by 16th-century diarists as the dining area of Lisbon's most humble workers, who would go there for grilled sardines and bread. We are also interested in the many tinned by-products of the two principle species found and caught for centuries along the Portuguese coast, including clams and bivalves, mackerel, garfish, octopus, cod, anchovy, swordfish, mussels, razor clams, cockles, lamprey, eels and horse mackerel.

Besides the historic and financial value of canning in Portugal, there is also the memory of cans in our larders, reminding us of less plentiful days when this food source would assure a good protein supply at times when access to fresh fish was restricted. From those days we also remember canned goods always present in our holiday supplies, on family camping trips or with our teenage friends.

Despite its undeniable potential, the tin hasn't received relevant expression in the arts, or at least its due expression, considering all it can offer as a material for installations, as a medium or a theme. This might be a result of its association with less relevant social or economic environments, placing sea produce and its people at a less elevated level than inland producers. The same thing is implied by the numerous expressions that lend a negative connotation to activities or products associated with tin cans. Thus, the can as a container, a material, a theme, an object or a medium hasn't received due emphasis in national art production – nor, until recently, in haute cuisine.

We only know of two paintings by Arcimboldo where the fish appears in anthropomorphic figures. The tradition of *bodegones*, or Portuguese still life, led by Josefina de Óbidos's work, elevated confectionery and vegetable produce alongside hunting and furry animals rather than sea creatures, as if fearing their rapid deterioration on walls or in canvases. There are, however, some exceptions, such as the enormous *The Fish Seller*, assigned to the

Flemish baroque master Frans Snyders, which can be found in the Panel Room of Lisbon's Palacio da Foz, and which portrays the confrontation between a cat and a sea wolf, beneath a huge table featuring an array of giant fish.

In fact, comparing a physical space to a sardine can or calling a woman a fishmonger evokes nothing positive. It's true that iconography related to the national fishing industry has regularly been the target of appropriation, from modernism to graphic designs for marketing popular festivals, if always as caricature or touristic promotion. But things seem to be changing, as can be seen by the inclusion of props like sardine cans in the *mise en place* of haute cuisine in Portugal.

In any case, Portuguese examples of appropriation are a long way from what happens elsewhere. There are two historic examples of the use of tins as art objects: Piero Manzoni's edition, from 1961, of 90 small round cans with eschatological contents and trilingual subtitles, listed in the Arte Povera movement; and Andy Warhol's *Campbell's Soup Cans*, from 1962, which echo the *Air de Paris* by Marcel Duchamp from 1919. The first is the motif for an obsession of the protagonist of *30 Gramas*, a book from 2009 by Leonel Moura, where someone seeks to unveil the real contents of Manzoni's work. There are also more prosaic references, such as those in *Come Viaggiare Con Un Salmone* by Umberto Eco, with its references to the canned tuna the semiology specialist had to grudgingly eat with pasta in the canteen of the University of Turin in 1920, which marked him forever. The use of cans is also present in the memory of my generation, as seen in animated films from Eastern Europe presented by Vasco Granja at the end of the 1970s. More recently, there is Eugénio Ampudia's proposal of revisiting the mosaic *Chão Por Varrer*, after his residency in Vila do Bispo in 2016, and the series of embroidery work *Vivarium*, from 2018, by the mother of Miguel Barceló, Francisca Artigues, about some of the Catalan artist's drawings.

Considering all the above, we can only rejoice at this editorial initiative from Eat & Art, which places Portuguese cans at the centre of cultural activity, transforming this intrinsic component of everyday life, this delicacy so noble in its simplicity, into the motor of an inter-disciplinary dialogue from which can spring productions to satisfy the public heart, head and stomach. All we can do now is to dedicate some time to reading and enjoying the works by the artists invited and, who knows, to visiting some restaurants. For the more daring among us, it's time to follow the cooks' examples and make good use of the cans we all have in the cupboard...

D.ANDRÉ DE QUIROGA

PRESIDENTE DA ACADEMIA DE GASTRONOMIA DO CAMINHO PORTUGUÊS DE SANTIAGO DE COMPOSTELA

TIAGO
BONITO

PEDRO
TUDELA

PEDRO
TUDELA

TIAGO
BONITO

TIAGO BONITO
PEDRO TUDELA

ONE THING LEADS TO ANOTHER

There's no excuse for not knowing the north Portuguese city of Amarante. The place possesses an ancient beauty, with the River Tâmega's banks almost like something from a 19th-century novel, where people sigh of love and time passes as serenely as the waters flow. At the centre of the city stands a 16th-century palace, now converted into a charming hotel, going by the name of Casa da Calçada and featuring a Michelin-starred restaurant.

Tiago Bonito is the chef responsible for that star. With us, we have brought the artist Pedro Tudela. It's time for the two to get to know one another.

We wait in a French-style lounge, with patterned damask curtains and antique furniture. The chef, it seems, has his hands full, and while we wait we take the opportunity to drink in the view. Finally, we are called to the kitchen.

Tiago is working at his palette: numerous boxes containing aromatic herbs that he selects with tweezers and places on individual plates. He tells us of his artistic adventures: of how he used watercolours to disguise something as an olive; of the goose barnacles made of mousse; of the tuna, swordfish and sea bass roe sausages.

"You cook in trompe l'œil," says Pedro. And Tiago is quick to agree: "We try to pull the rug from under our clients' feet."

Both are believers in the power of association – between colours, flavours and scents. A creative synaesthesia that prompts crossovers and partnerships. In the end, that's what this is all about: in art as in cuisine, one thing leads to another.

Tiago's cooking is a constant debate between the old and the new, between traditional techniques and other ways he has learned. But where does his passion for cuisine come from?

"My godmother used to have a bakery," says Tiago. "My aunt was a butcher. My mother used to make and sell sweet rice, and I was responsible for the cooking. My mother wanted me to become a doctor of something – we were from Coimbra, the famous university town – but all I wanted was to cook."

Tiago pauses, as if passing again to that childhood. Then he smiles, and continues.

"I can't be a great sushi chef. I'm a Portuguese cook. I remember the smell of the freshly baked bread, of the lamb and the rooster. That's what I want to get across."

Pedro ponders his own formative years and admits that yes, they could have had some influence. All the same, none of his relatives was an artist or painter.

"I liked to paint, and had a knack for drawing," he says. "But what I really liked was to observe and consume things in all sorts of different ways. It's funny, I've already put on exhibitions with all the senses except taste...

"Right from when I was small I had an interest in electronics, and used to repair everything that was electrical in my home. I was so proud of my electrical tools. These days, I don't know... I like to mix materials, and I'm never held hostage by traditional techniques."

And we're back among the mixtures, the crossovers and the tensions between tradition and innovation.

Meanwhile, it's already approaching lunchtime and, just as we're preparing to leave, Tiago invites us to the table. "What, you came all the way here and were going to leave without tasting my food?"

It's the best conclusion to our discussion. And if we could describe it, we would. When you go to Amarante, just ask for Casa da Calçada. And send our best to Tiago.

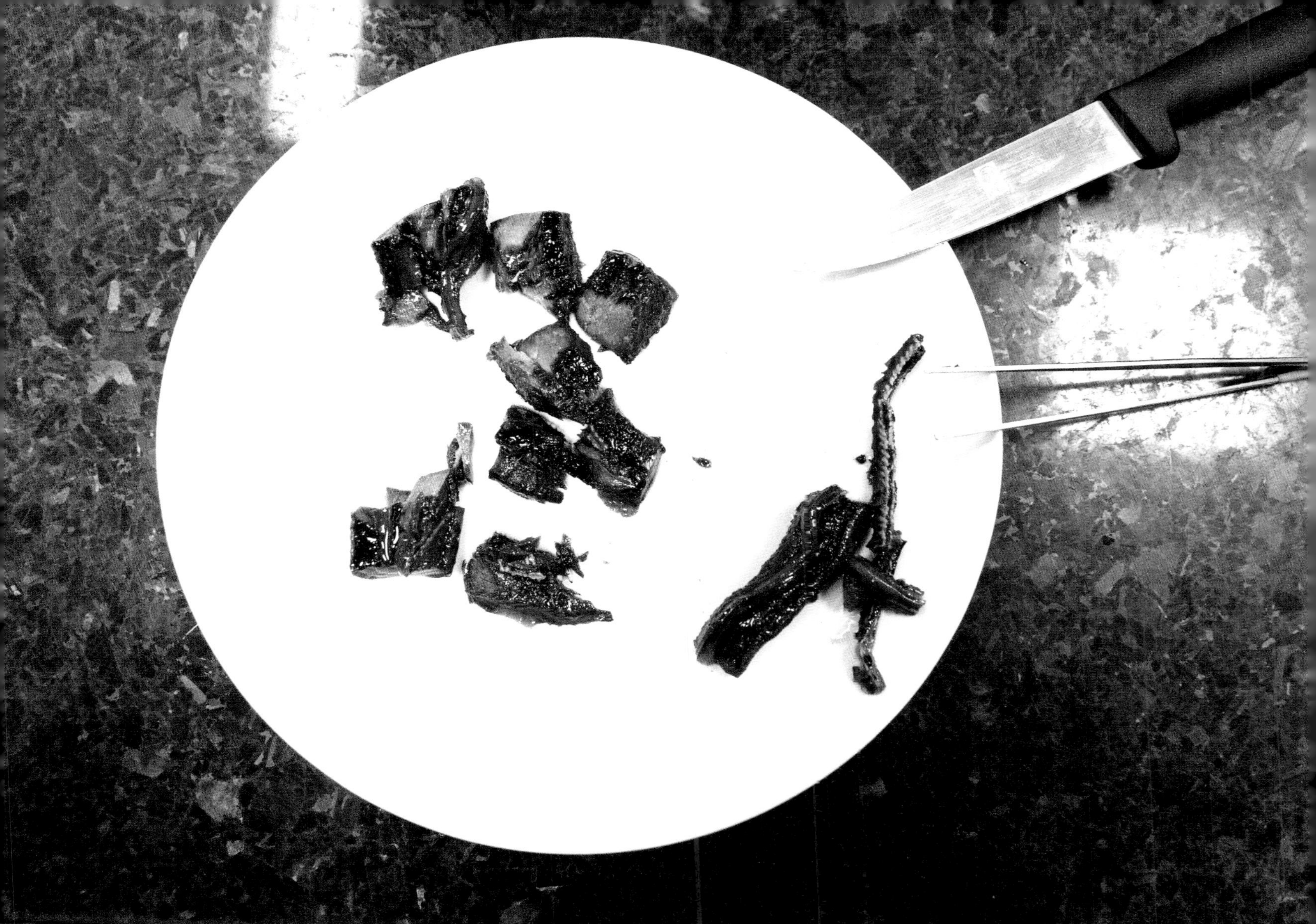

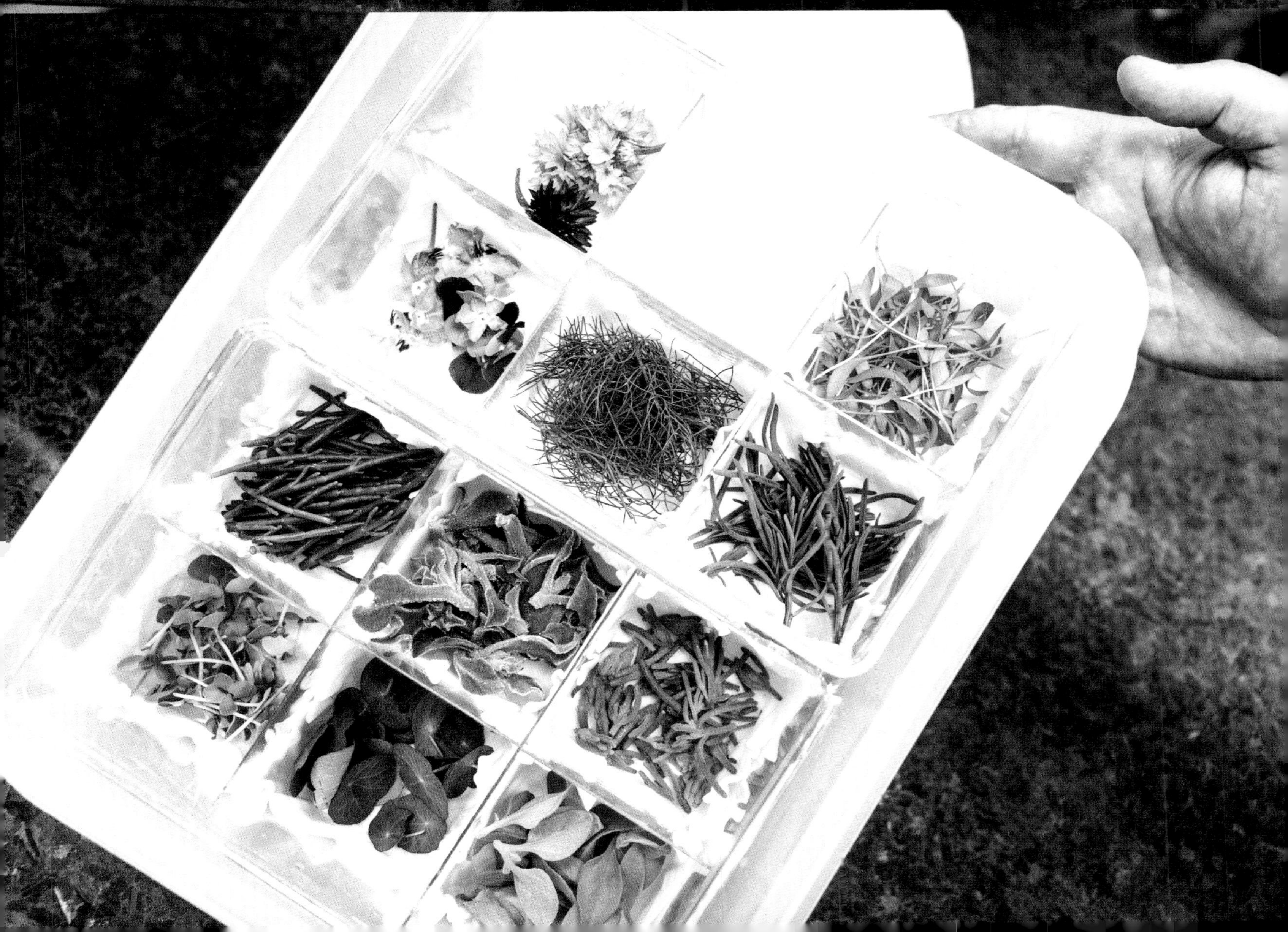

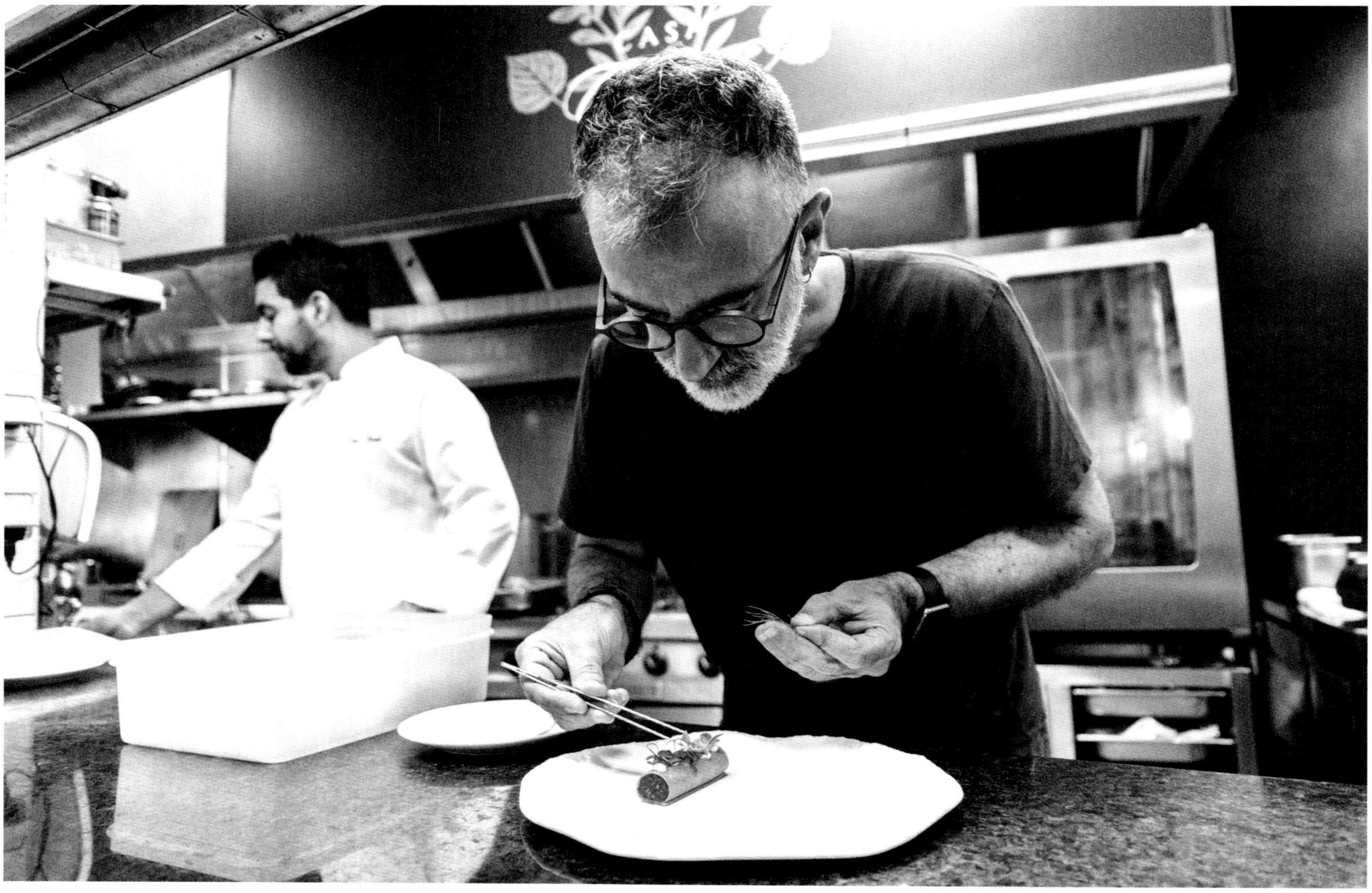

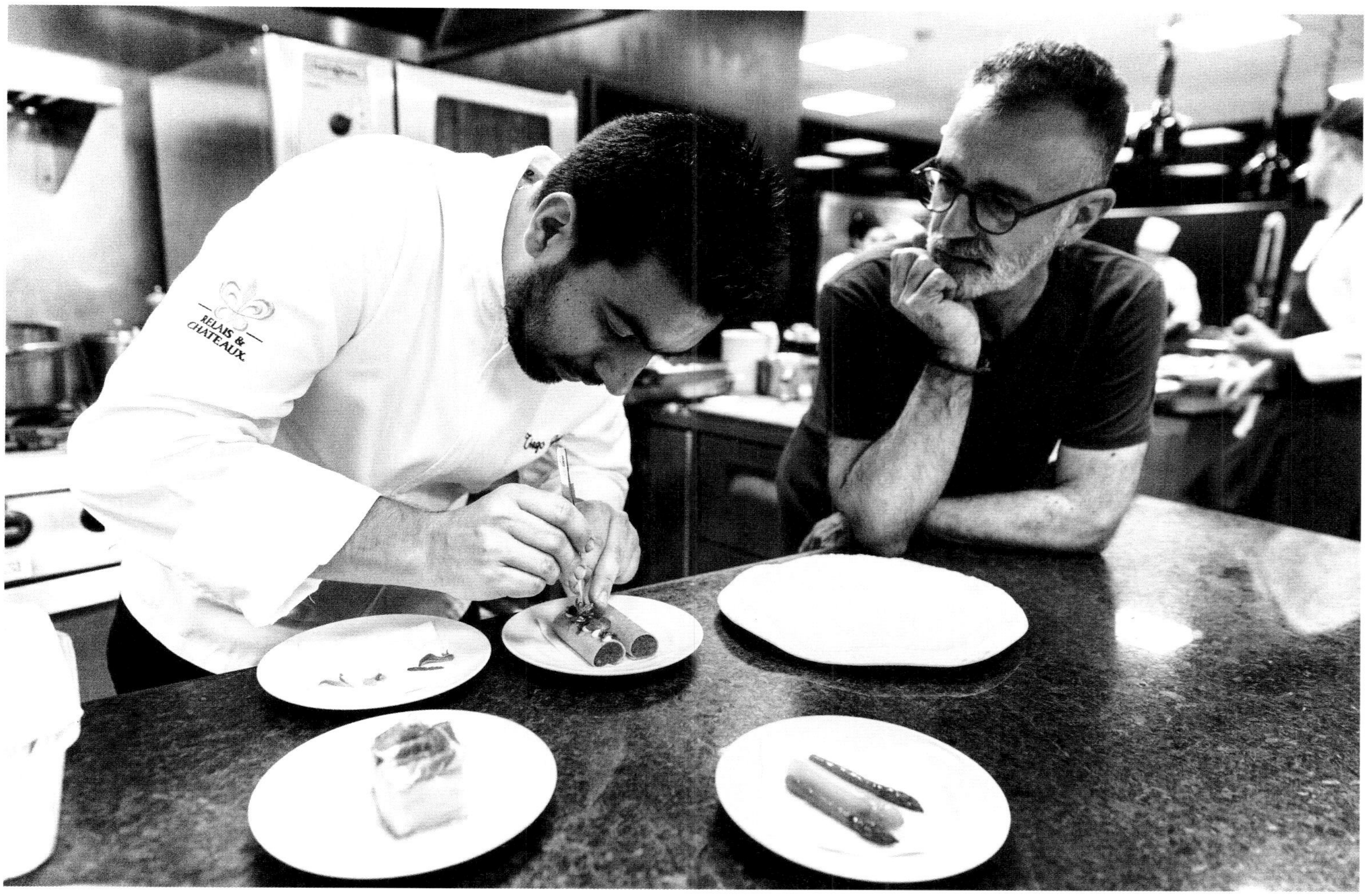
RELAIS & CHATEAUX

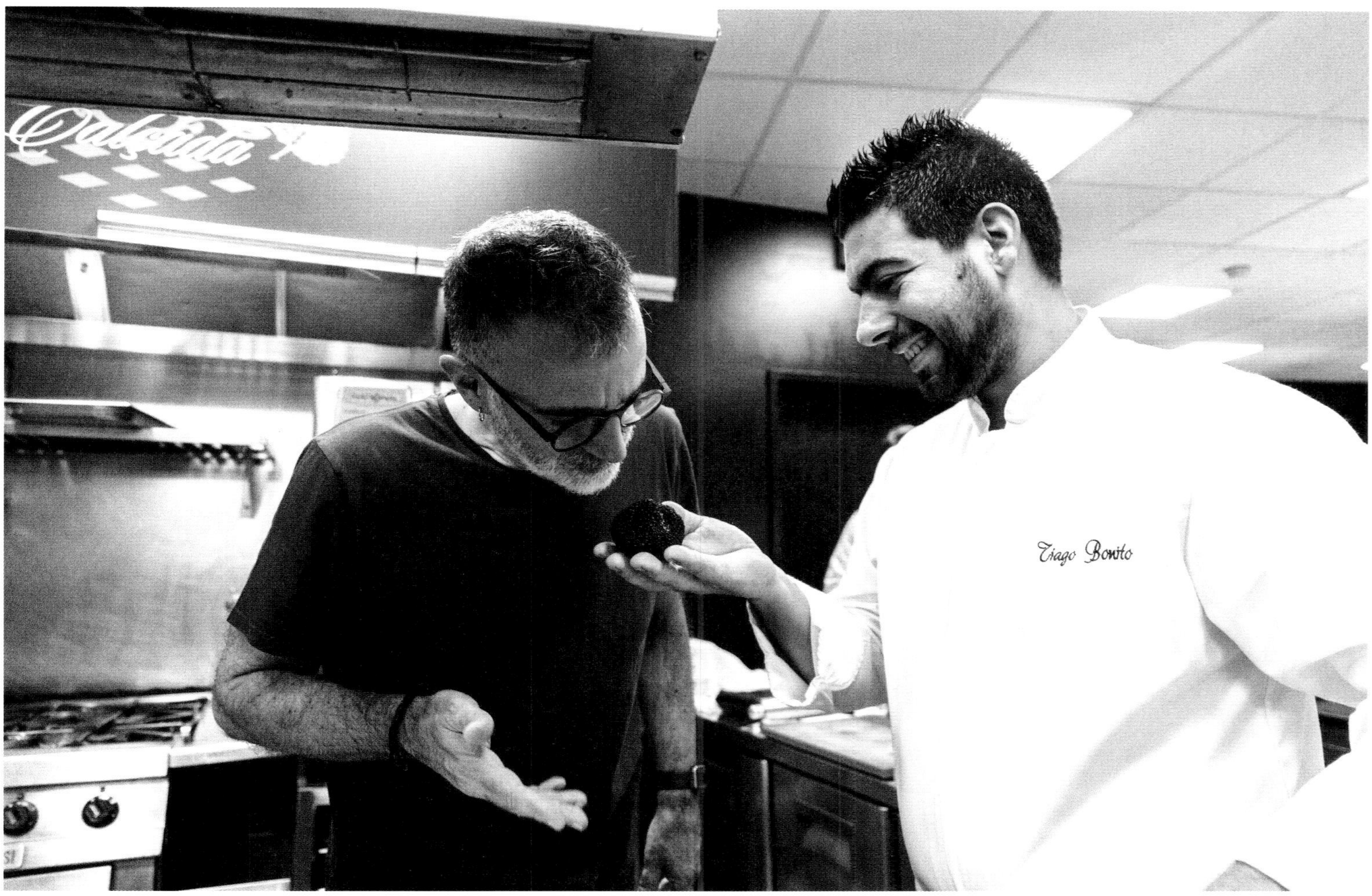
Tiago Bonito

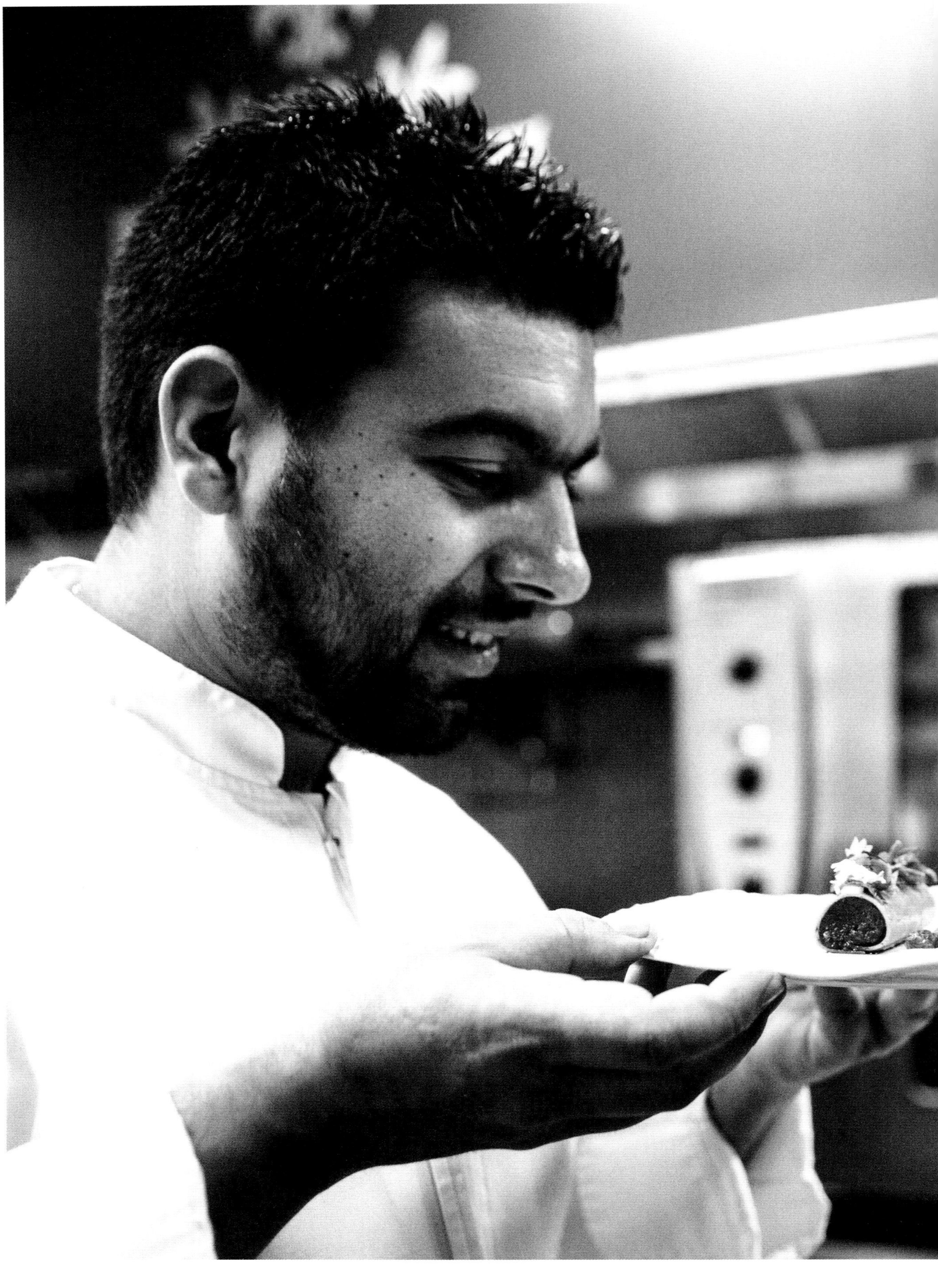

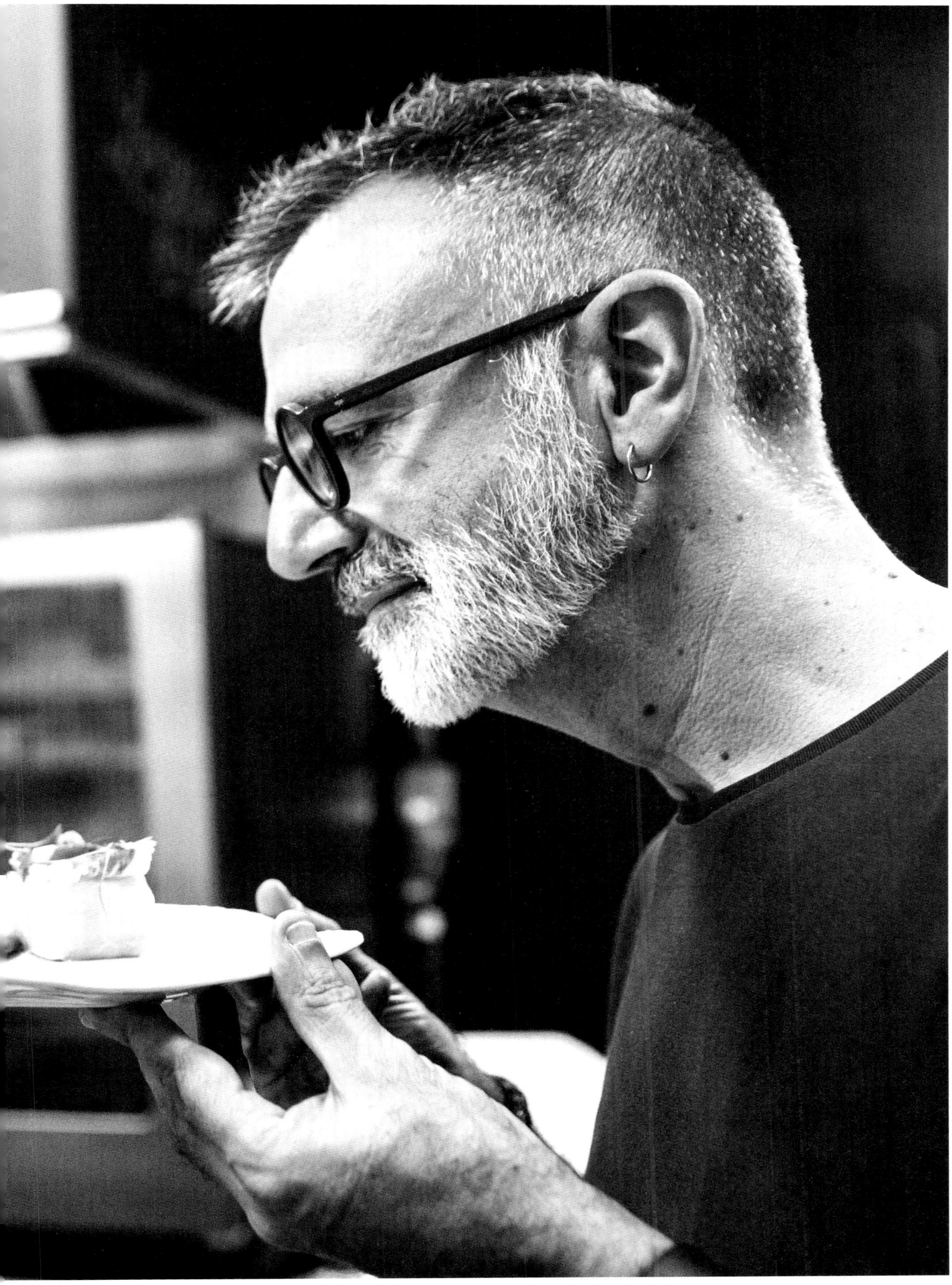

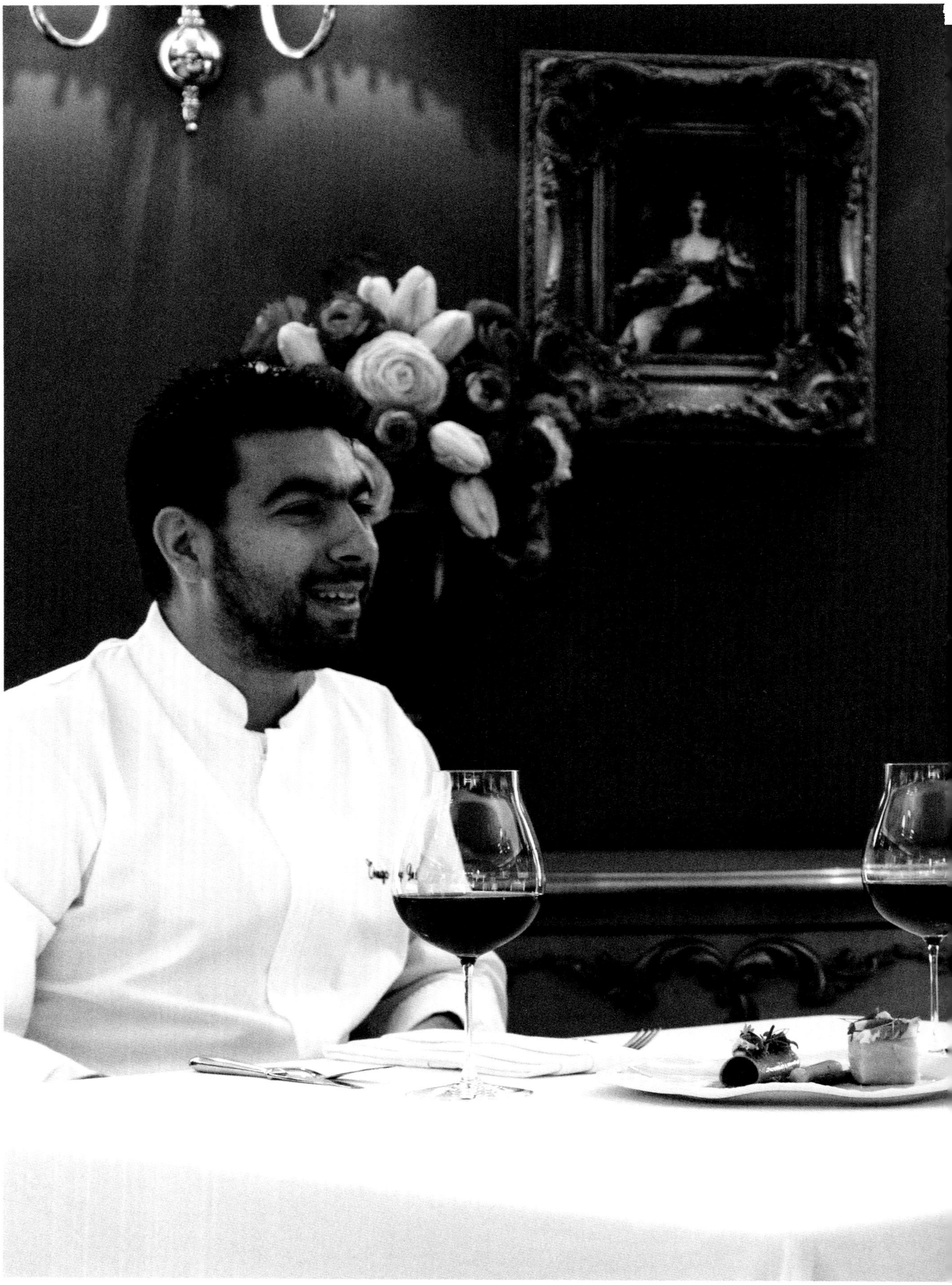

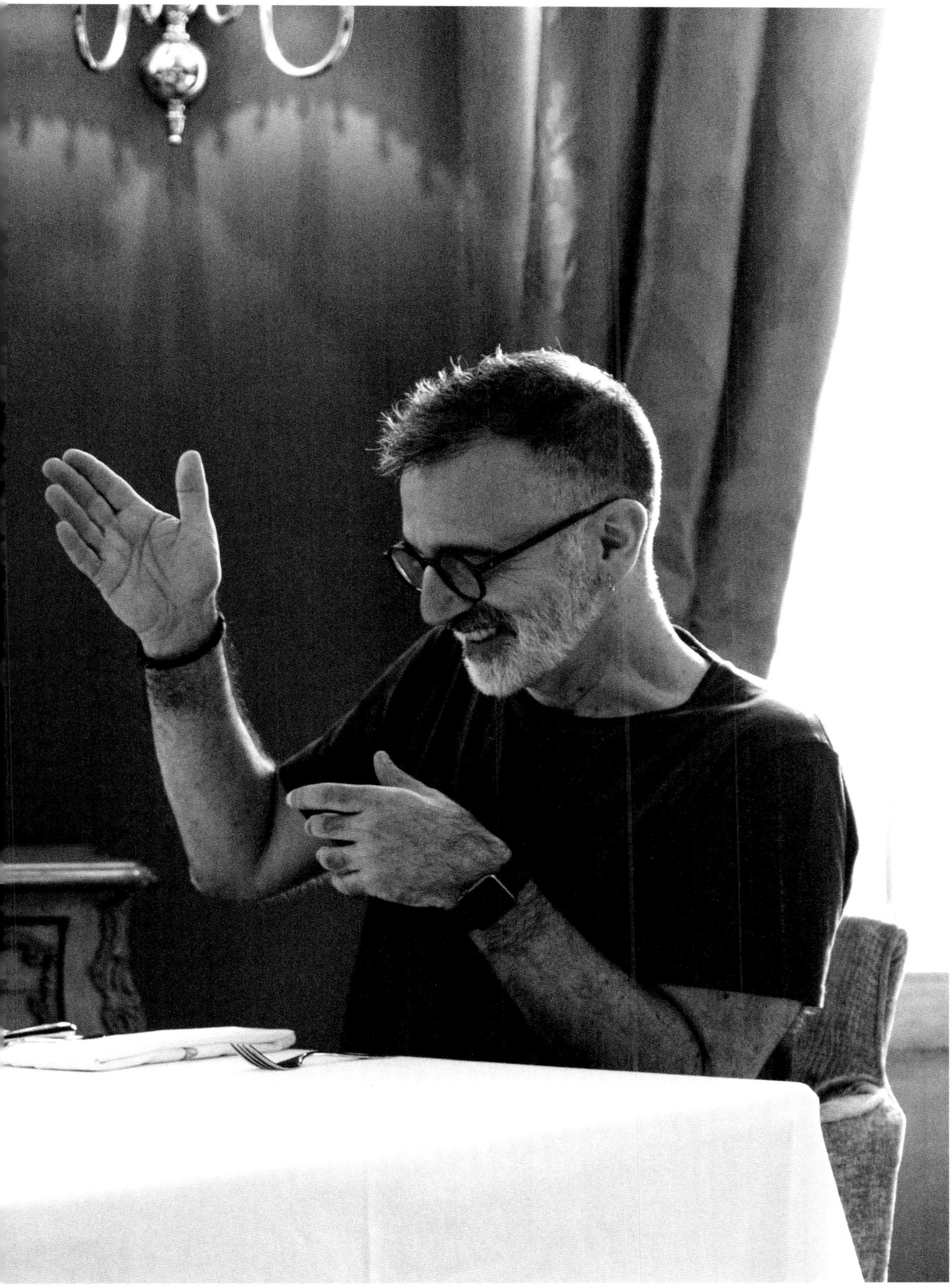

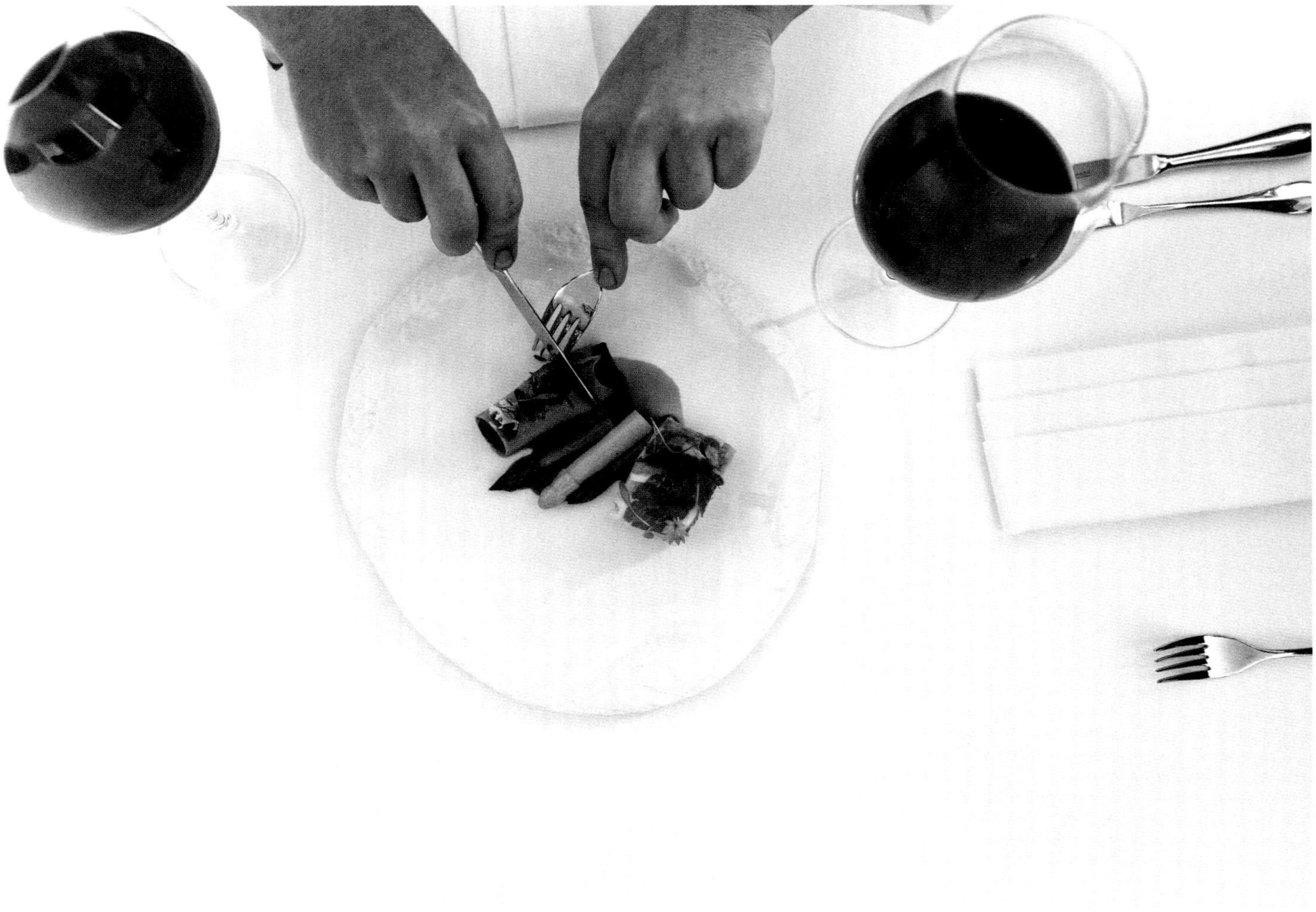

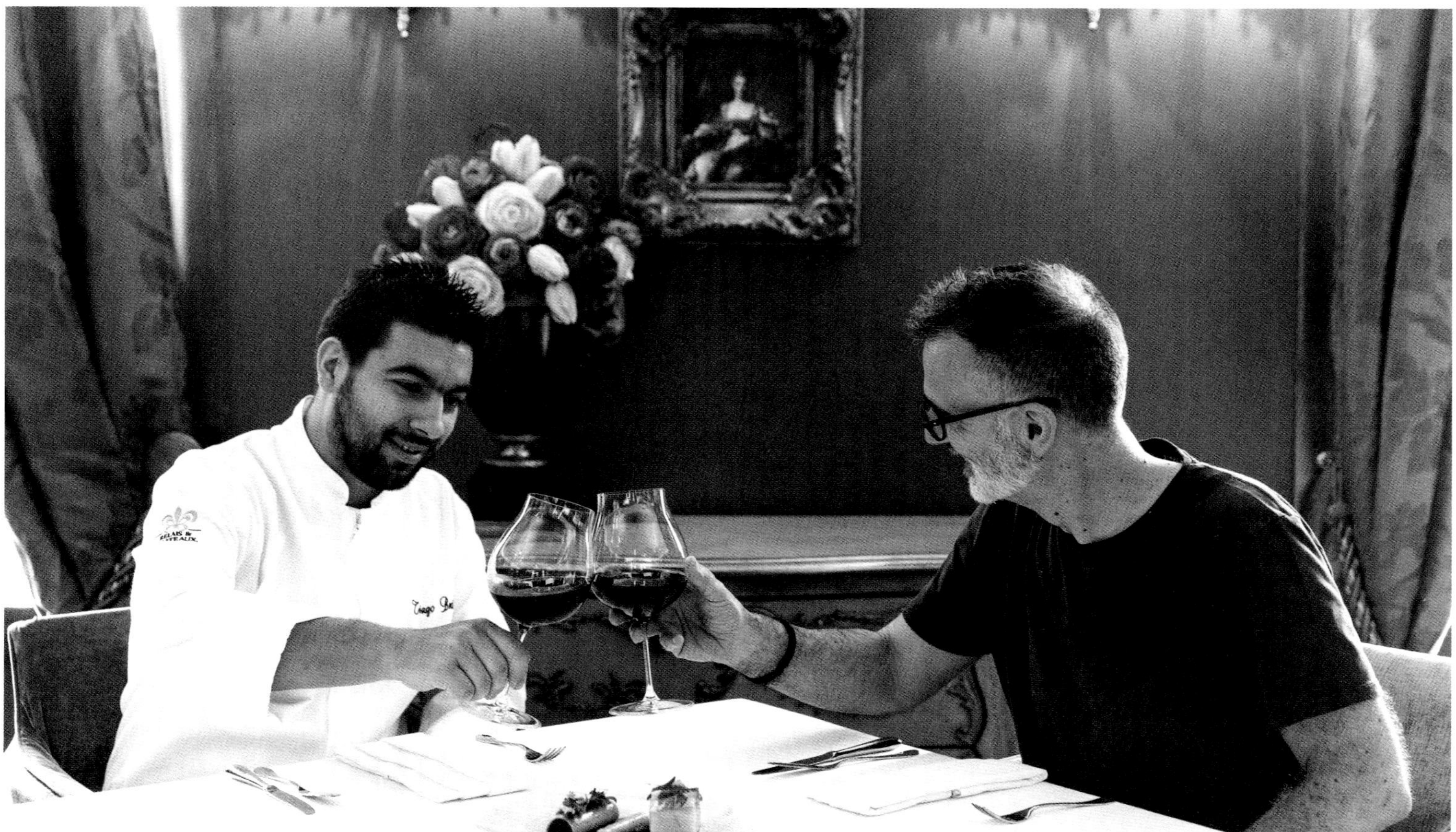

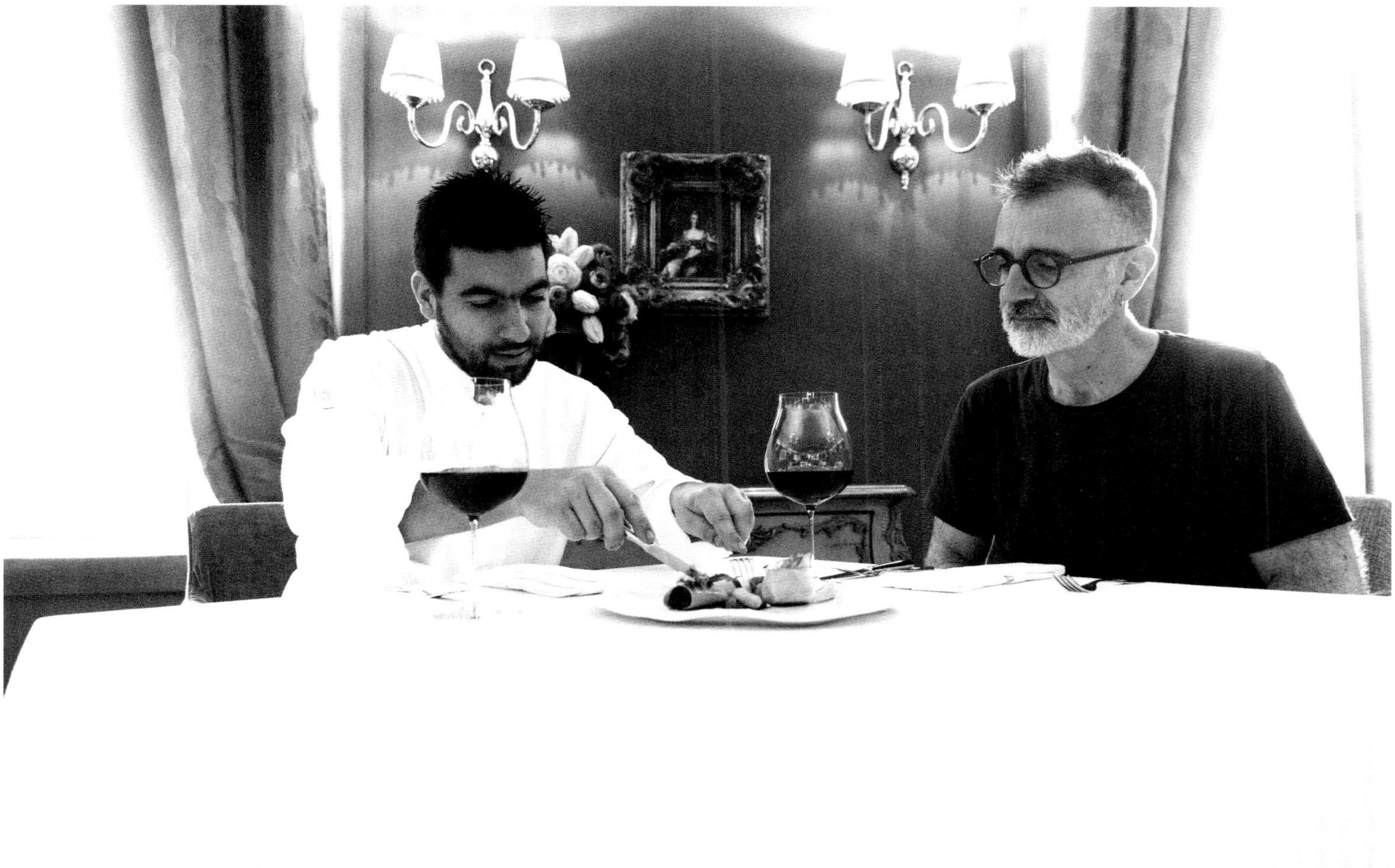

T I A G O

B O N I T O

SMOKED LAMPREY, COD, BÍSARO HAM AND FRAGATEIRA SAUCE

SMOKED LAMPREY LOINS
BRAND CÂNTARA

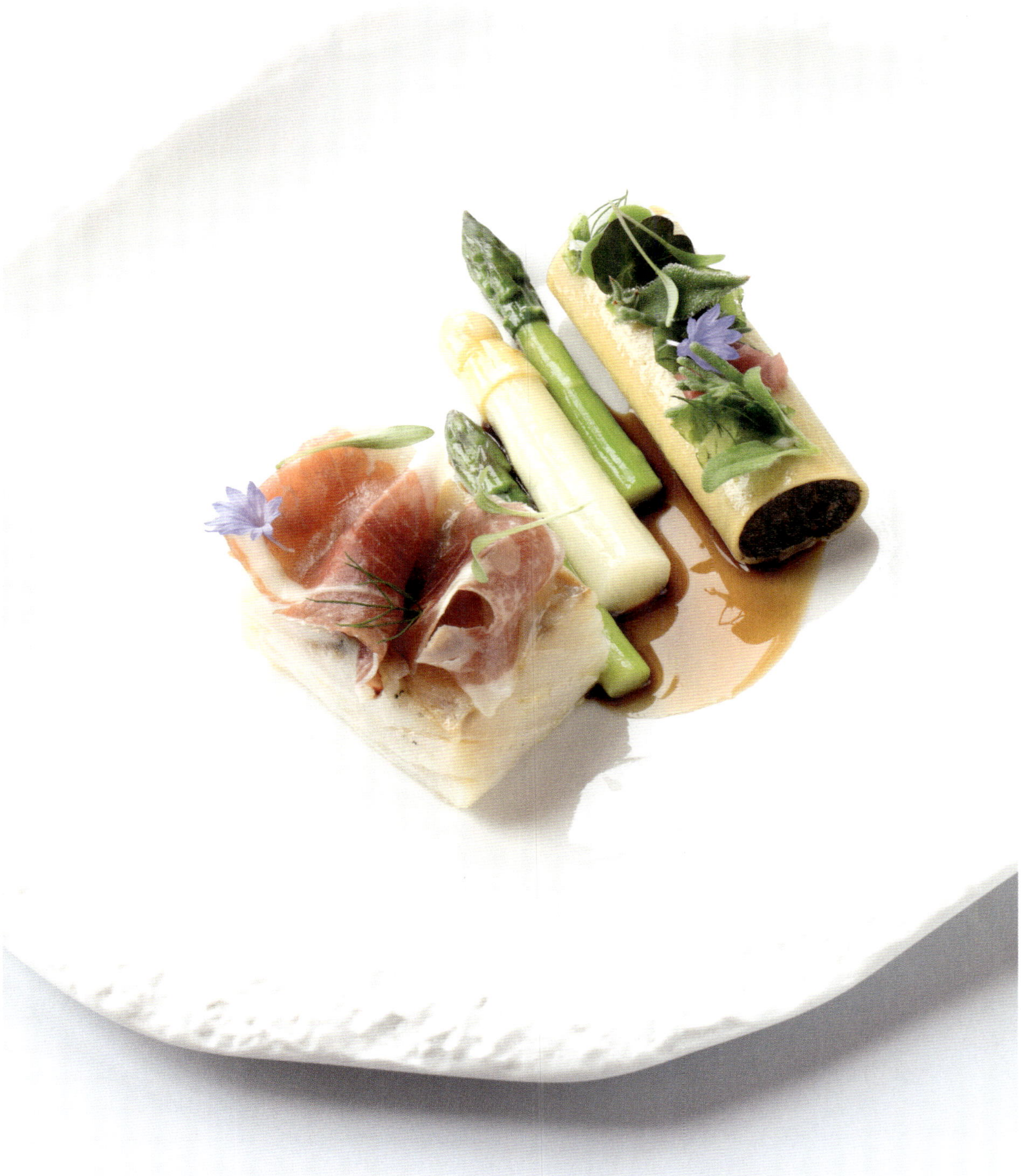

X-A-R-V-O-R-E
2017

PEDRO

IRON AND PLASTIC (OLD TIN CAN
OPENER KEYS AND PLASTIC CLAMP)

TUDELA

10 × 10 × 10 CM

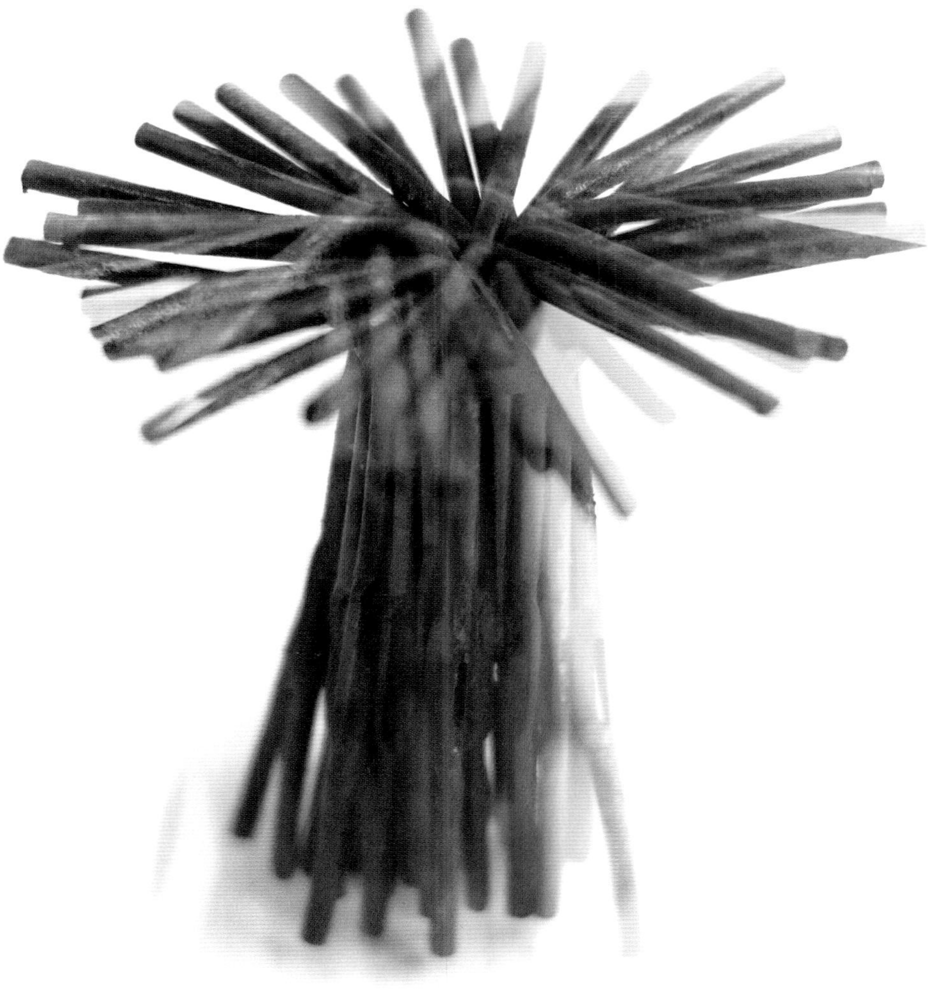

NOELIA

NUNO
NUNES
FERREIRA

NUNO
NUNES
FERREIRA

NOÉLIA

WELCOME TO THE ALGARVE

It's only 11.30am and the restaurant is already full of customers, talking in many languages, eating, asking for beers and being amazed by the fruits of the Ria Formosa. Welcome to the Algarve and to Noélia's restaurant.

It's April, but the sun streaming through the window and the constant swirl of customers and suppliers gives the illusion of a summer's day. Boxes open and eyes follow in astonishment: figs, anchovies, sea bream and other wonders. Noélia dashes about, commands, solves problems... and cooks. She's the soul of the place, providing not only its name but its energy.

I arrive with the artist Nuno Nunes Ferreira. While we wait, Nuno tastes some figs with almonds and bread with dried fig. "It's good, it's very good!" It has its secrets, says Noélia, smiling as she rushes to turn off some of the stoves and turn others on. He tries to master the plating: "This isn't easy, it's more complicated than it looks."

Nuno is from Silves, a different Algarve, but the language is the same. Memories, flavours and images are the components of their art – hers and his.

"I've been here for 32 years," says Noélia. "I fell in love with the people. This used to be a pastry shop, but the toasted sandwiches were a big success."

Many will confirm this success, while others will try to describe quite how good these creations were but they can't find the words: Noélia's toasted sandwiches are material for the dreams and memories of local people. "They were a big favourite with locals, but not just locals," says Noélia. "You should have seen the queues when people came back from the beach."

We move on to the questions. Where is it that ideas come from? Where are dishes and artworks born? Noélia talks of searching, of the eye always taking in what's going on. The Algarve is rich in imagination and flavours; it's about starting there and seeing what builds.

Nuno nods a yes: to the work; the seeking hands; to the experience that leads to ideas; and to the ideas which become real.

"You have to have real passion for things," says Noélia. "Without passion there's no point in doing anything."

Nuno agrees. After developing his eye in other geometries, he came to art through architecture. "It was easier for me back then. Later, I diversified."

We stay where we are, extending the afternoon. The wetland gleams with a light that illuminates as well as blinds. Wine is drunk and rich words are exchanged in between the guests eating the octopus and the sea bass rice. There are unique moments when the mystery becomes clear – how art became cuisine and how cuisine generates art.

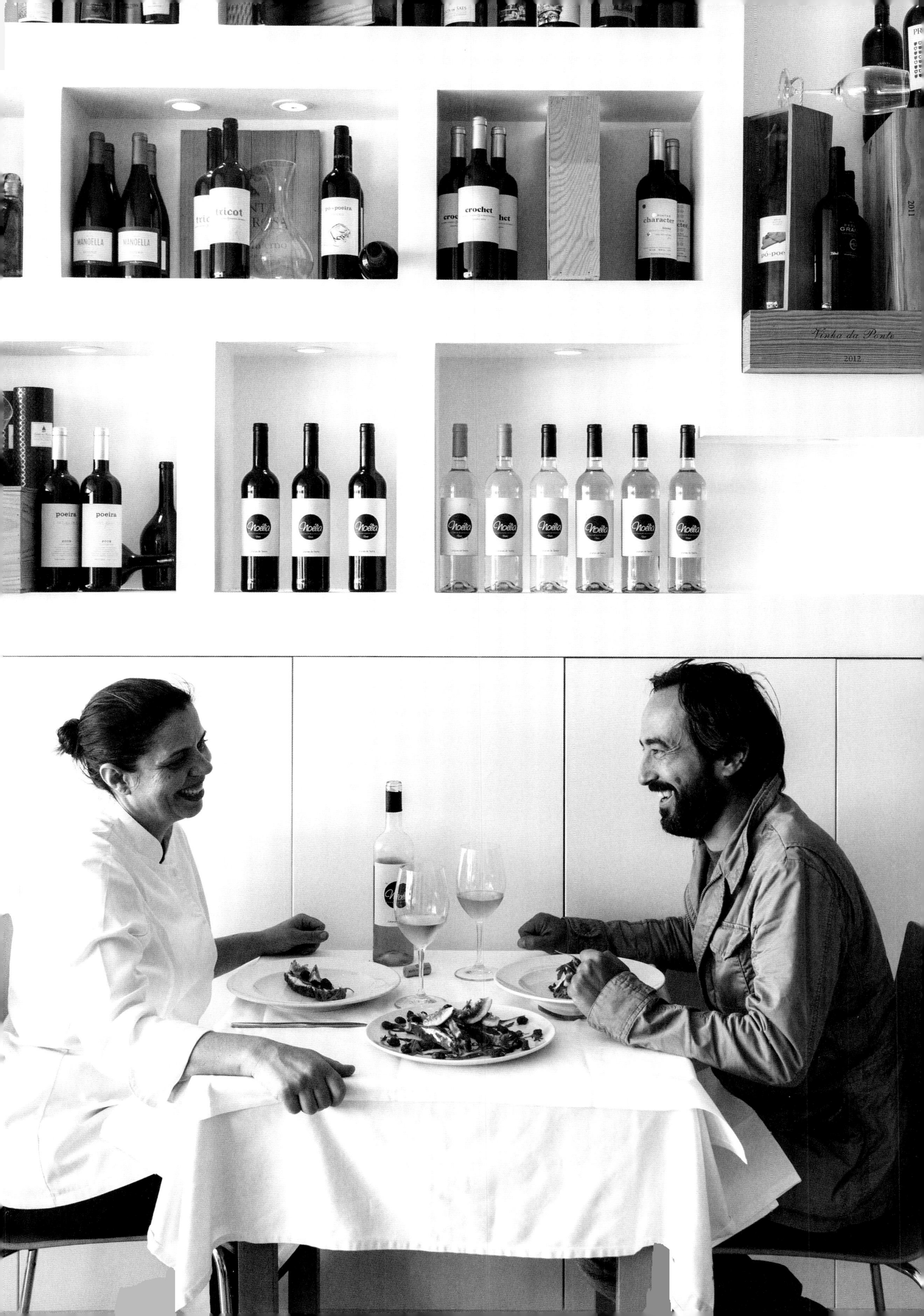
MANOELLA
MANOELLA
tricot
pó-poeira
crochet
character
pó-poe
poeira
poeira
Vinha da Ponte
2012
2011

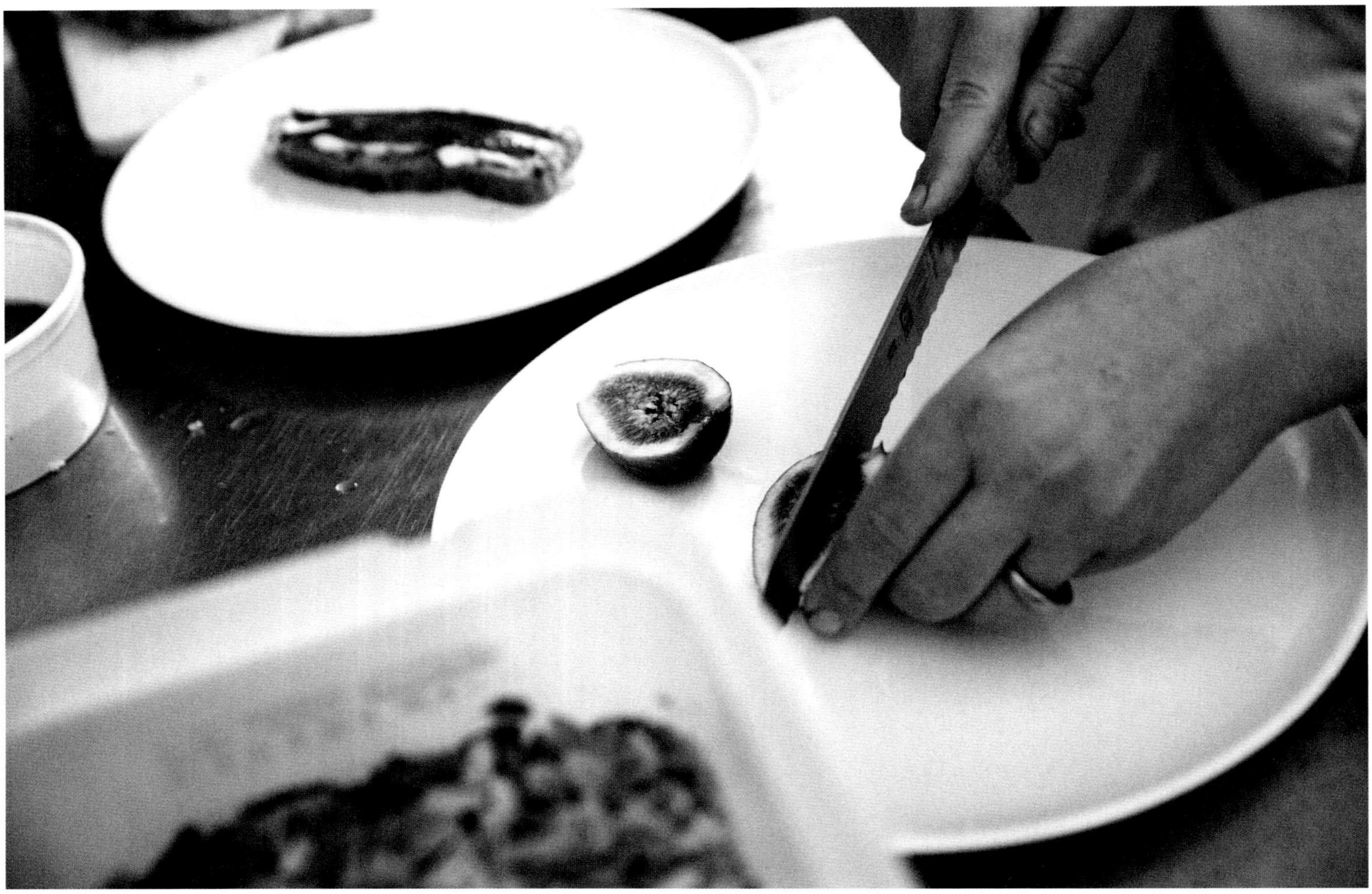

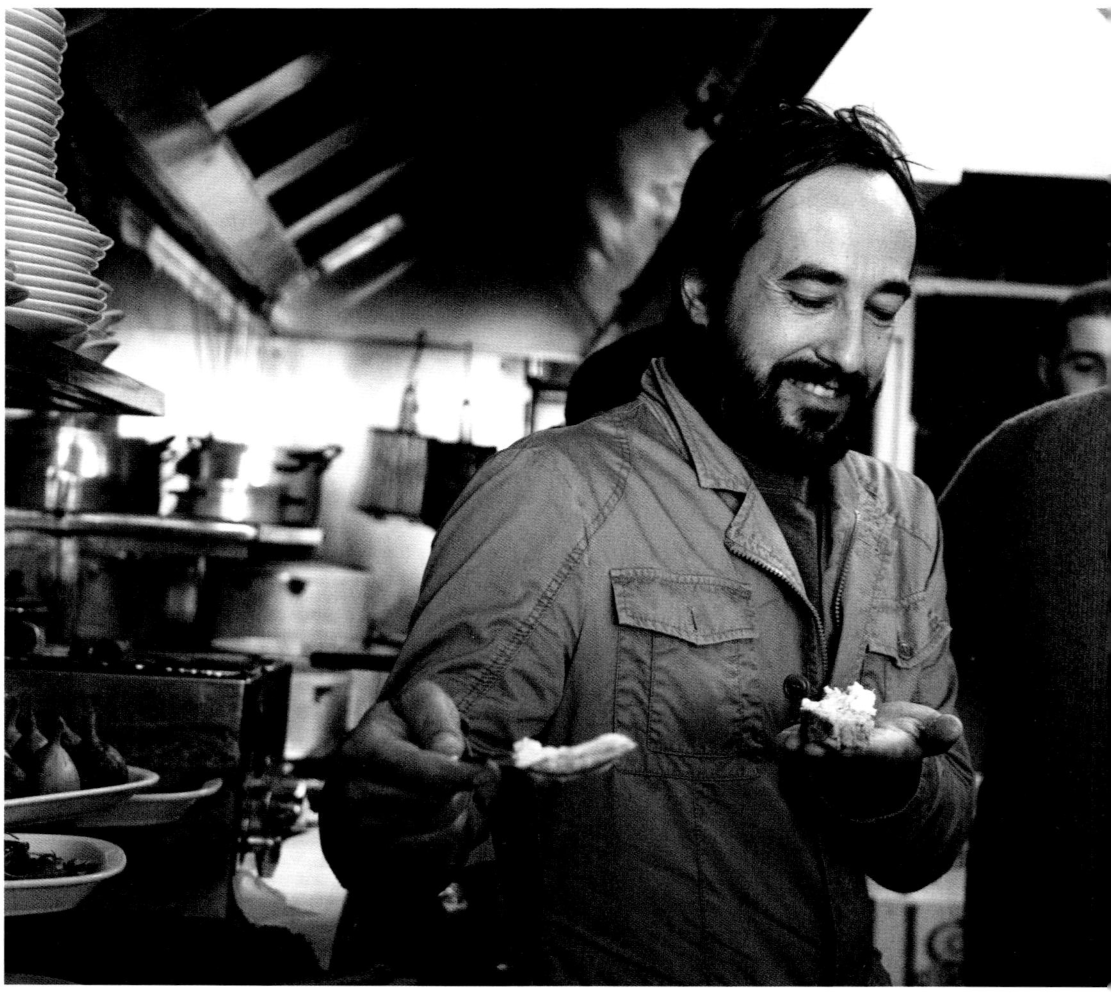

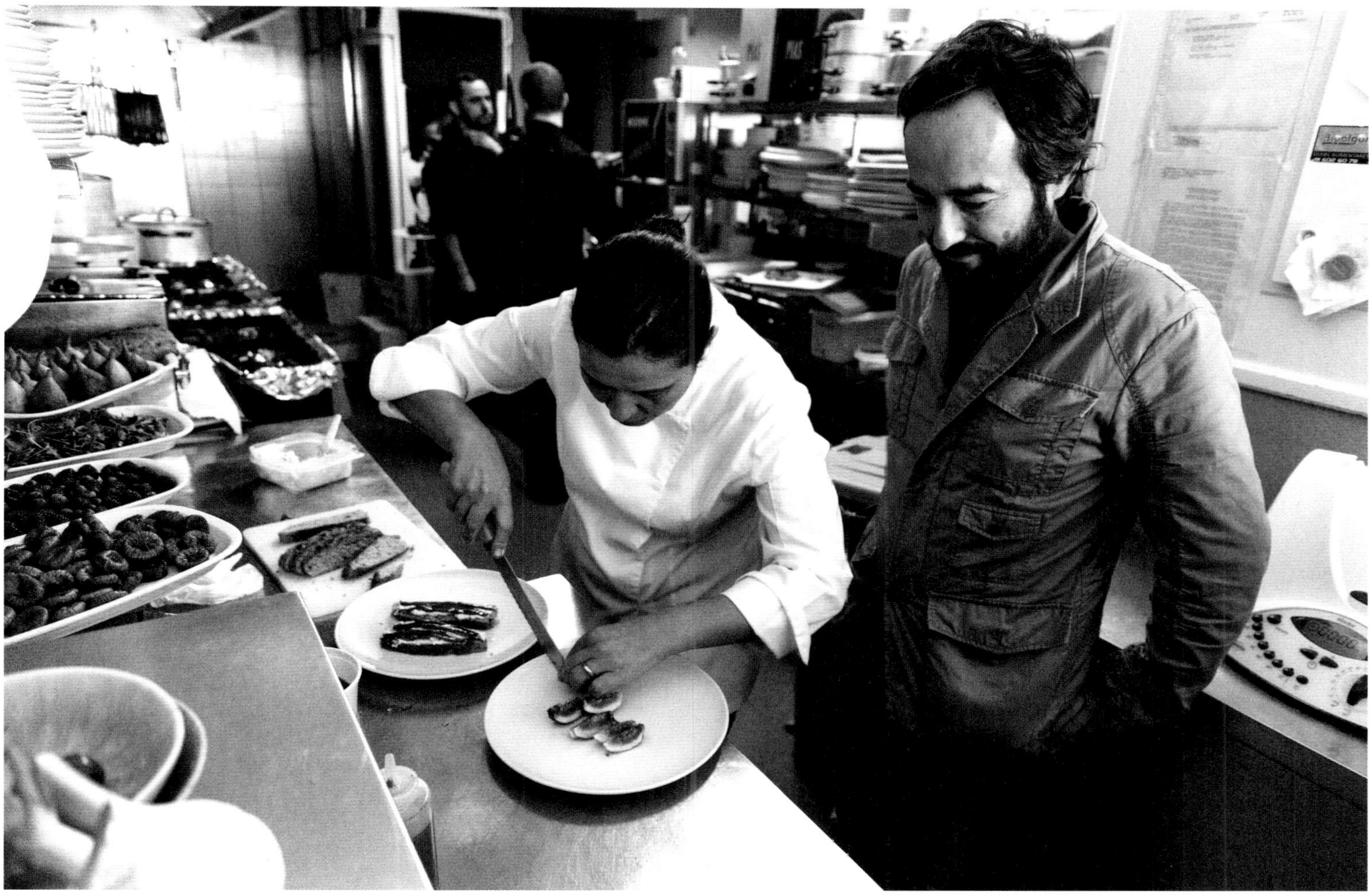

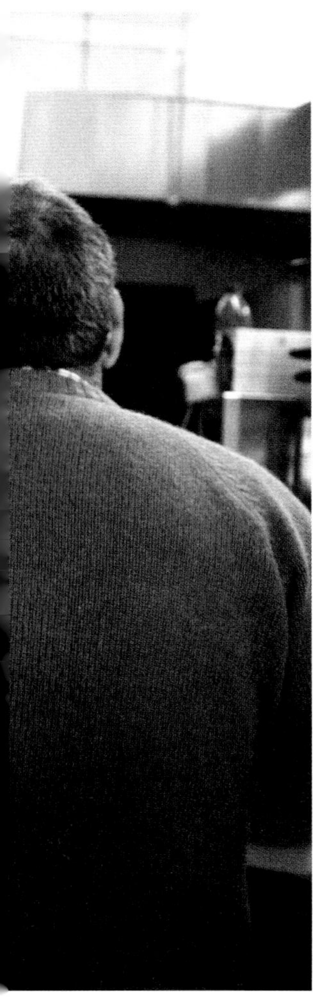

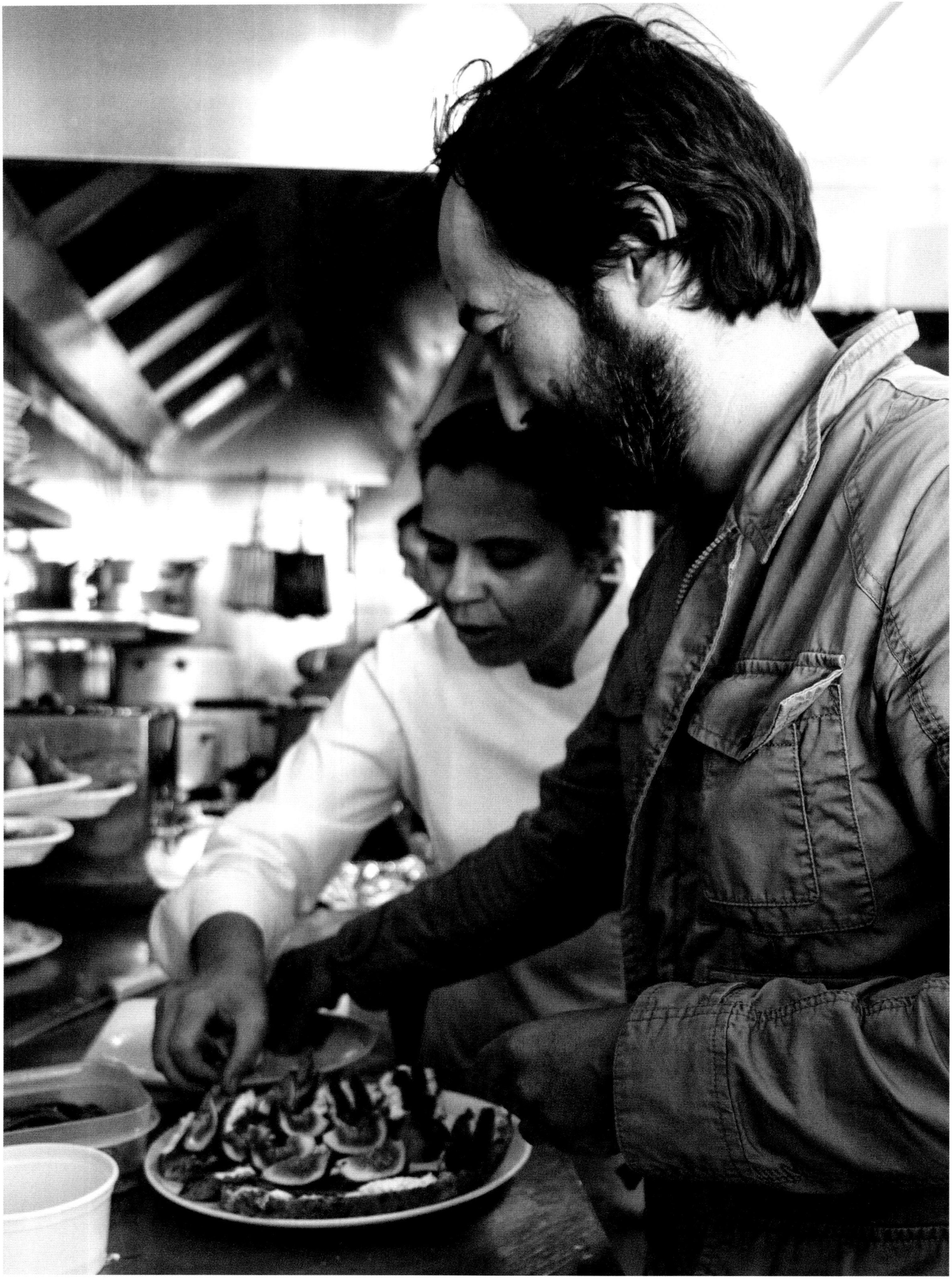

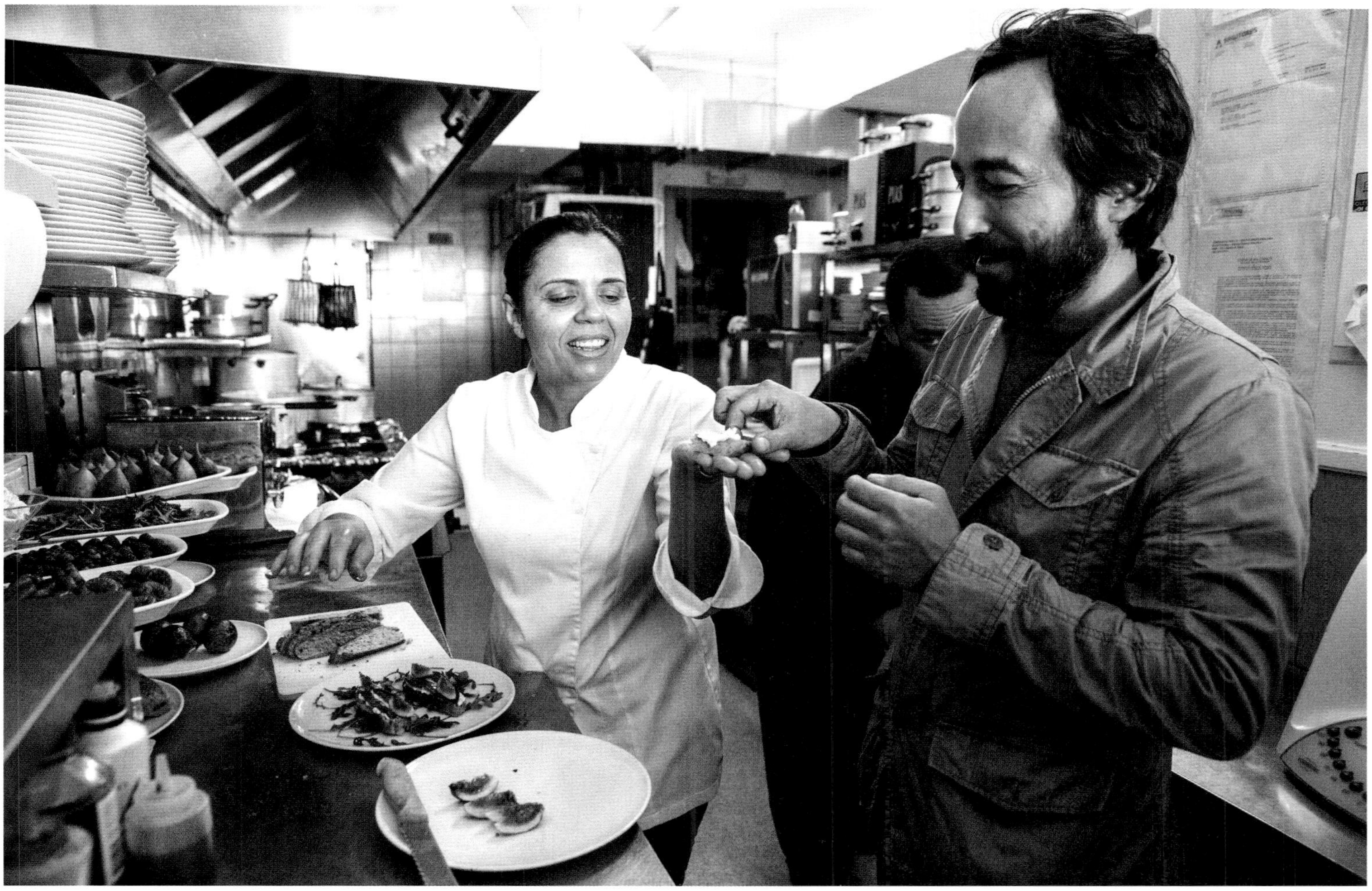

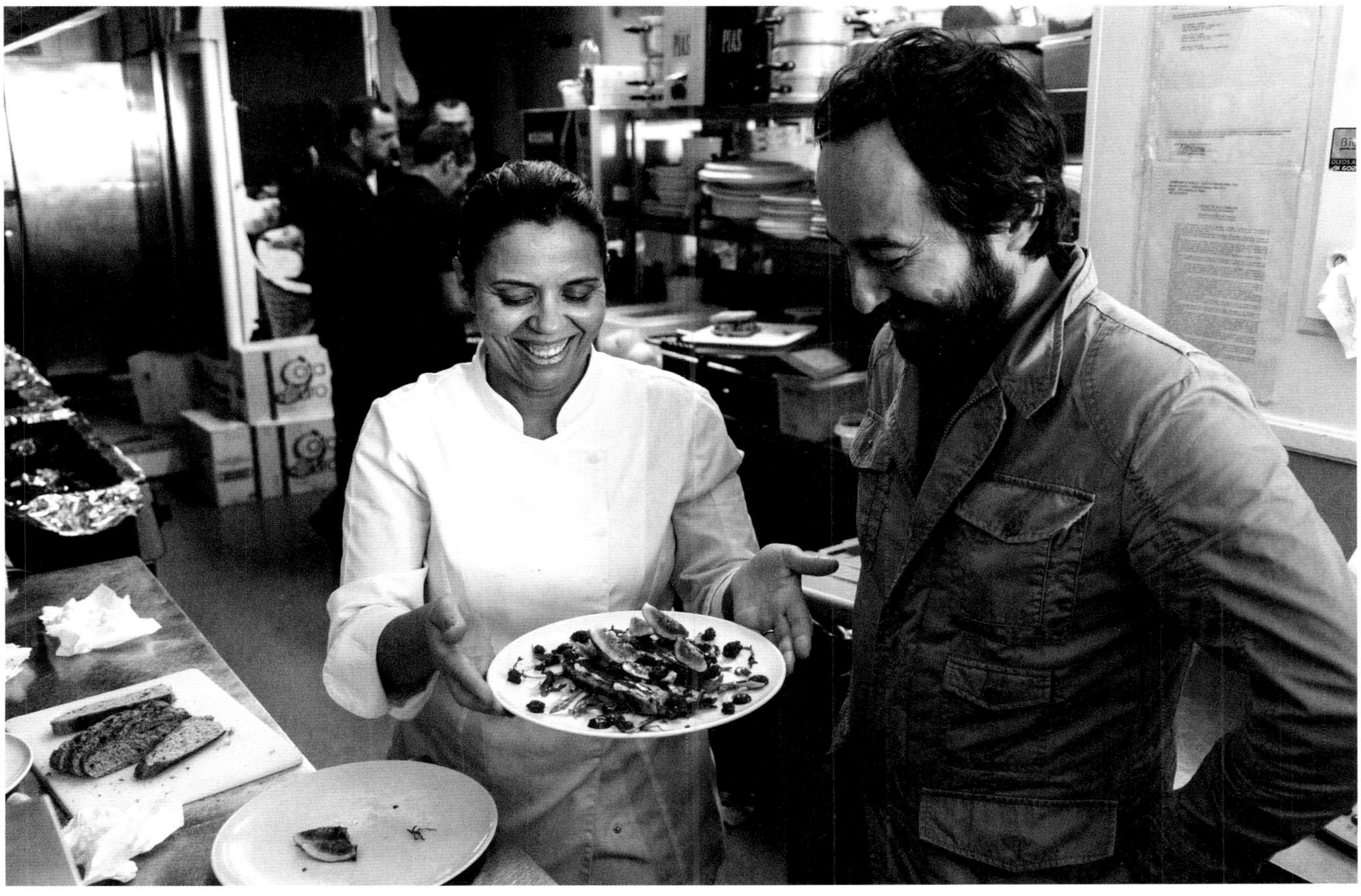

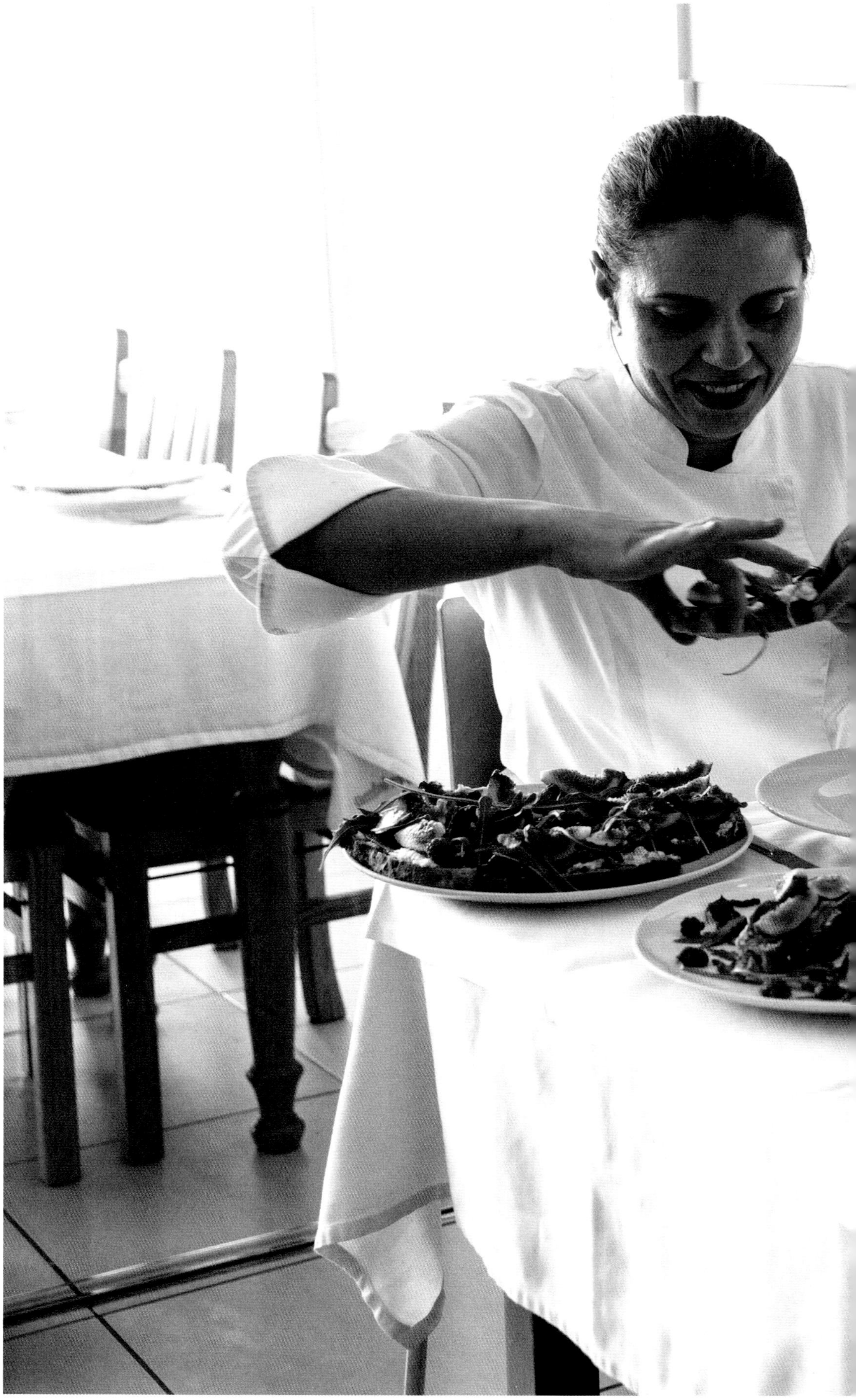

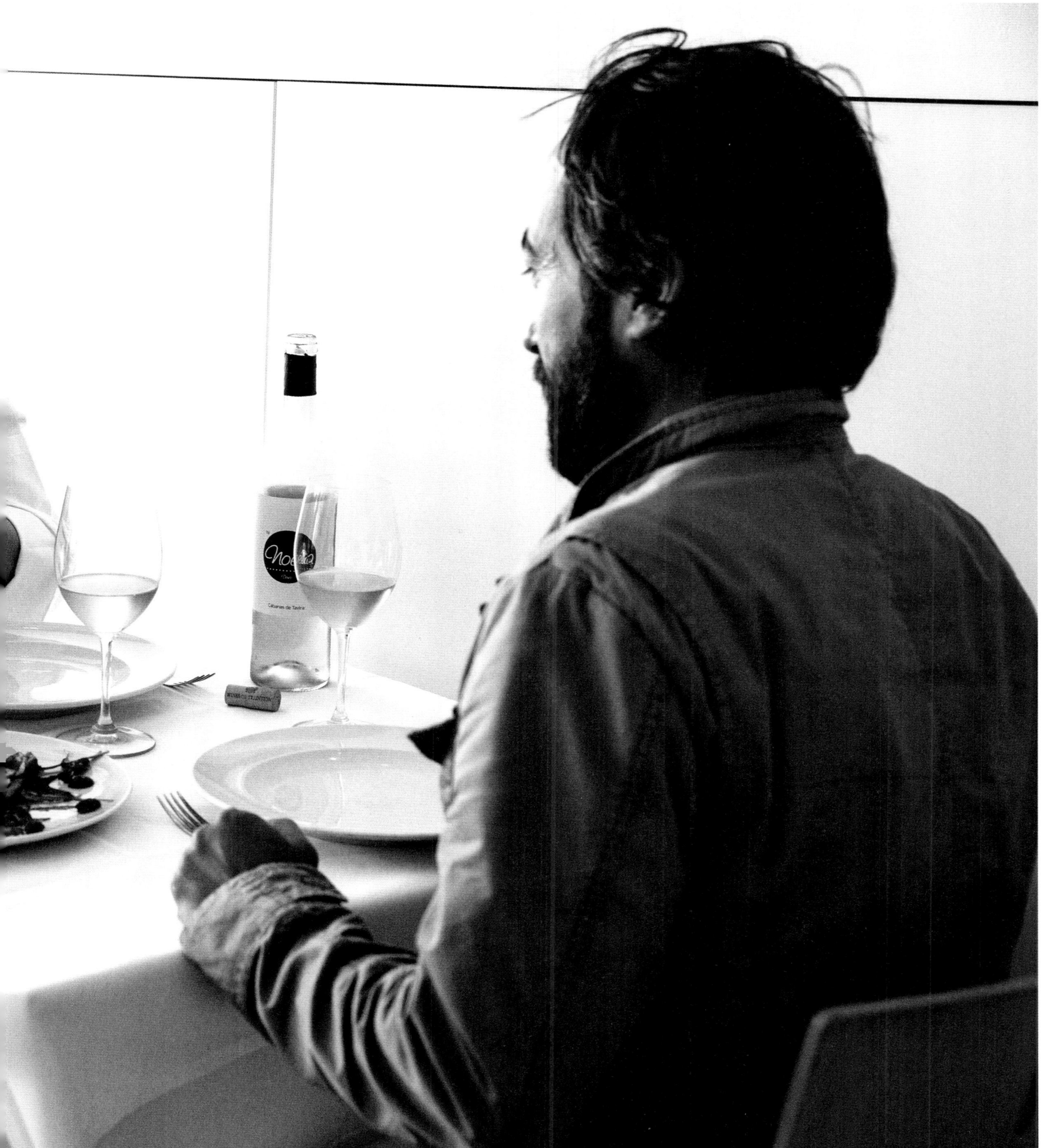

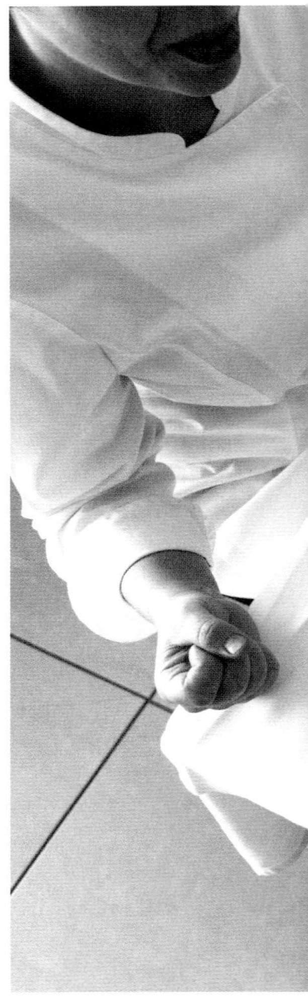

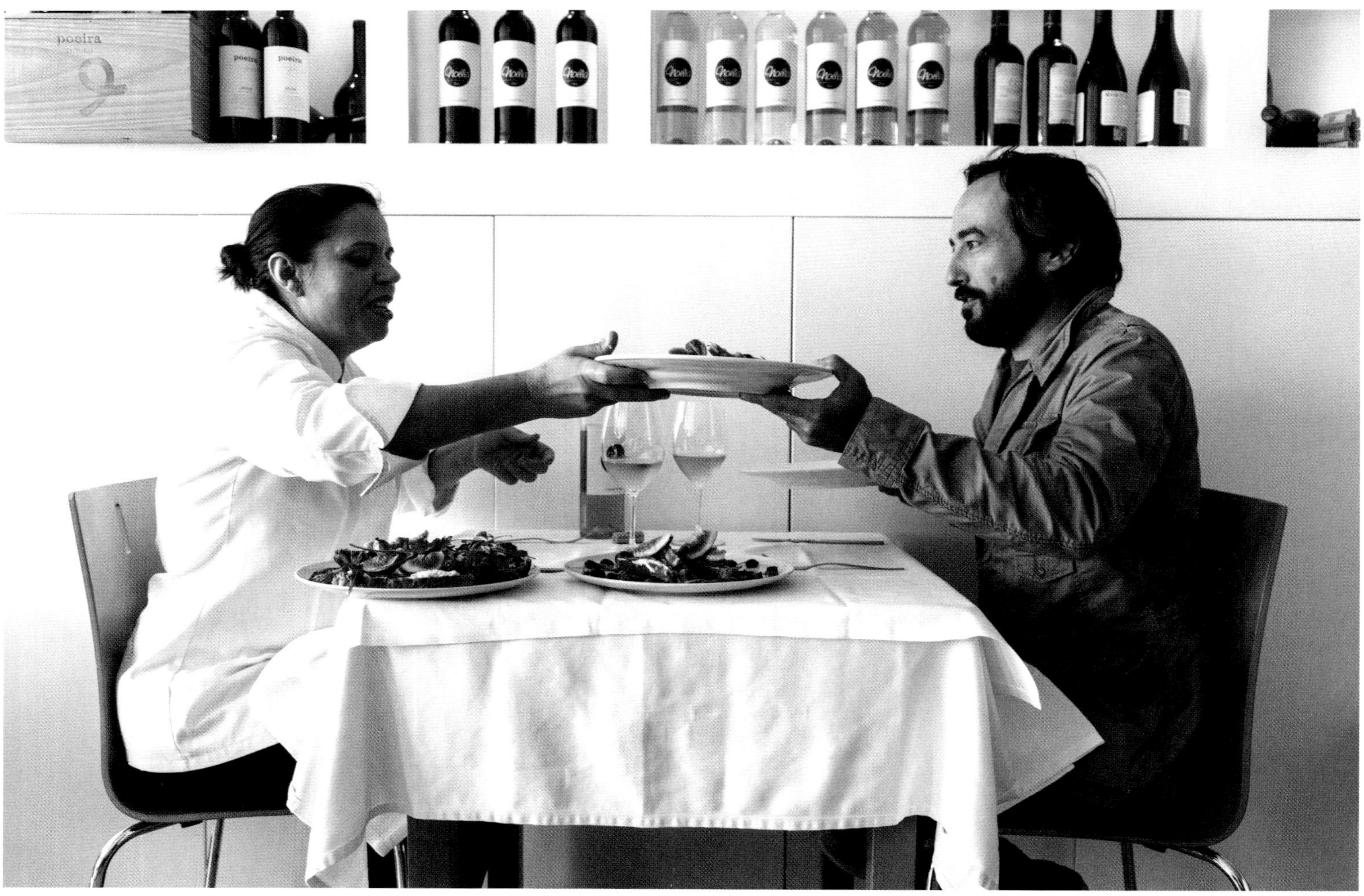

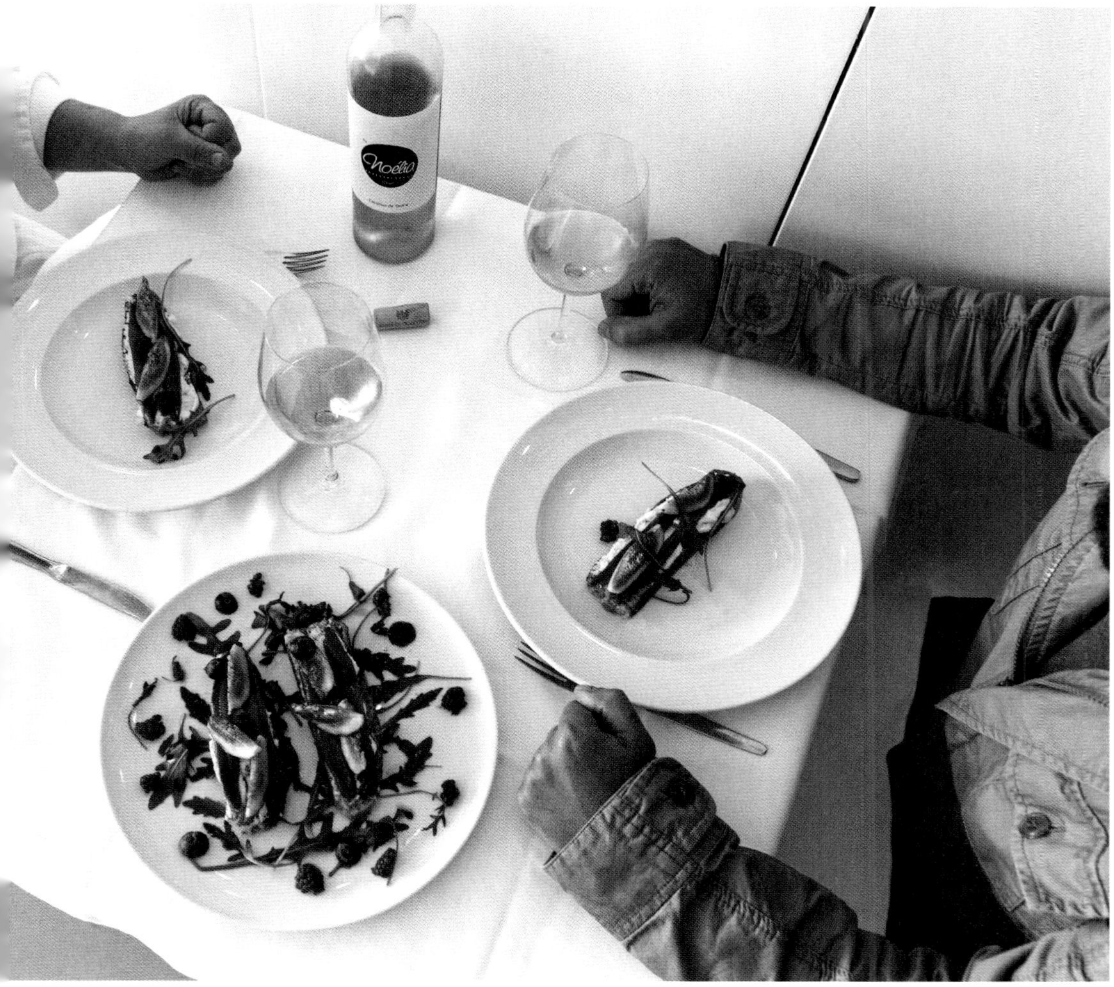
Noélia

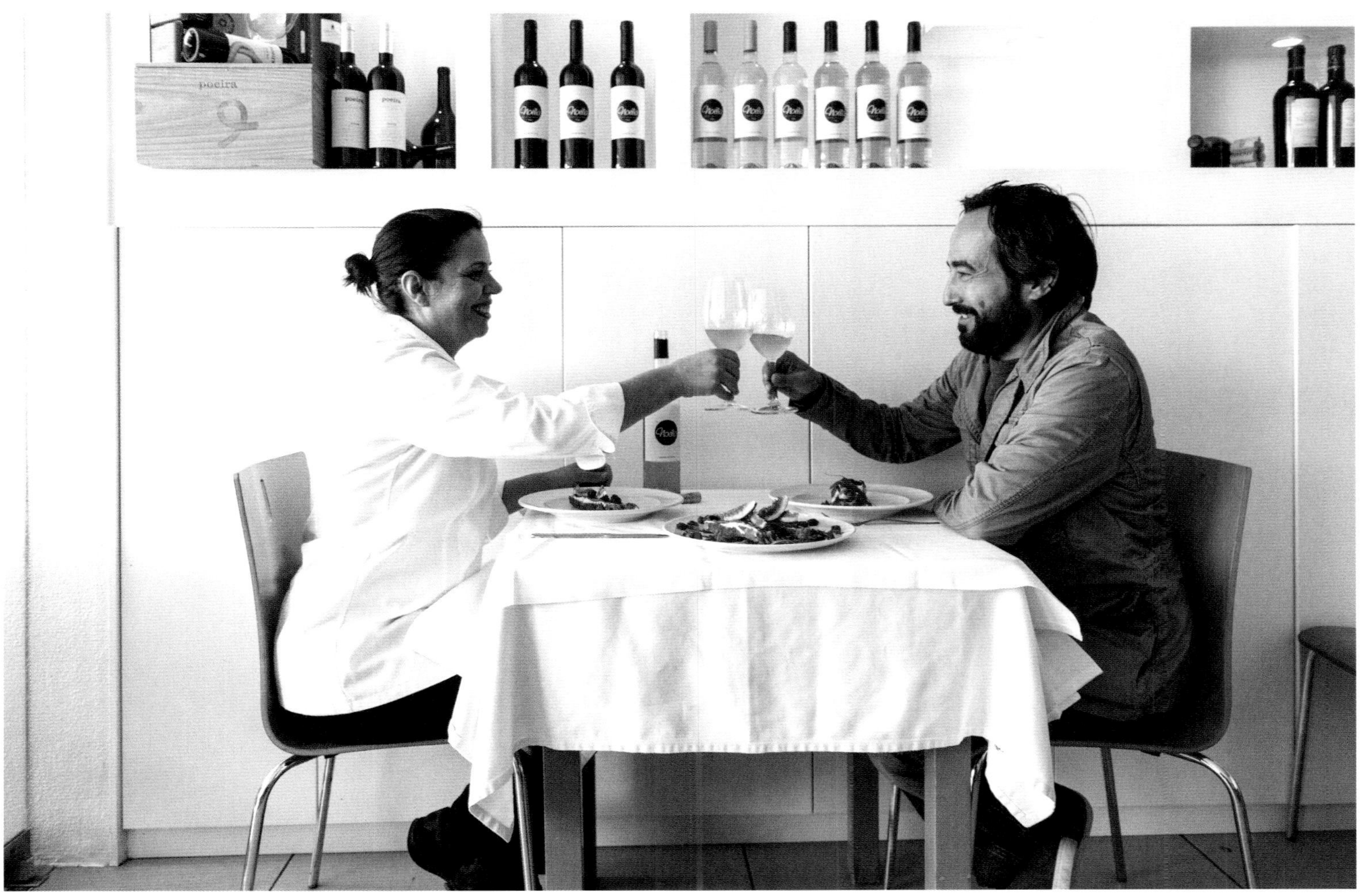
poeira

N O É L I A

BRUSCHETTAS WITH ANCHOVIES AND FIGS

ANCHOVY FILLETS IN OLIVE OIL

BRAND PITÉU

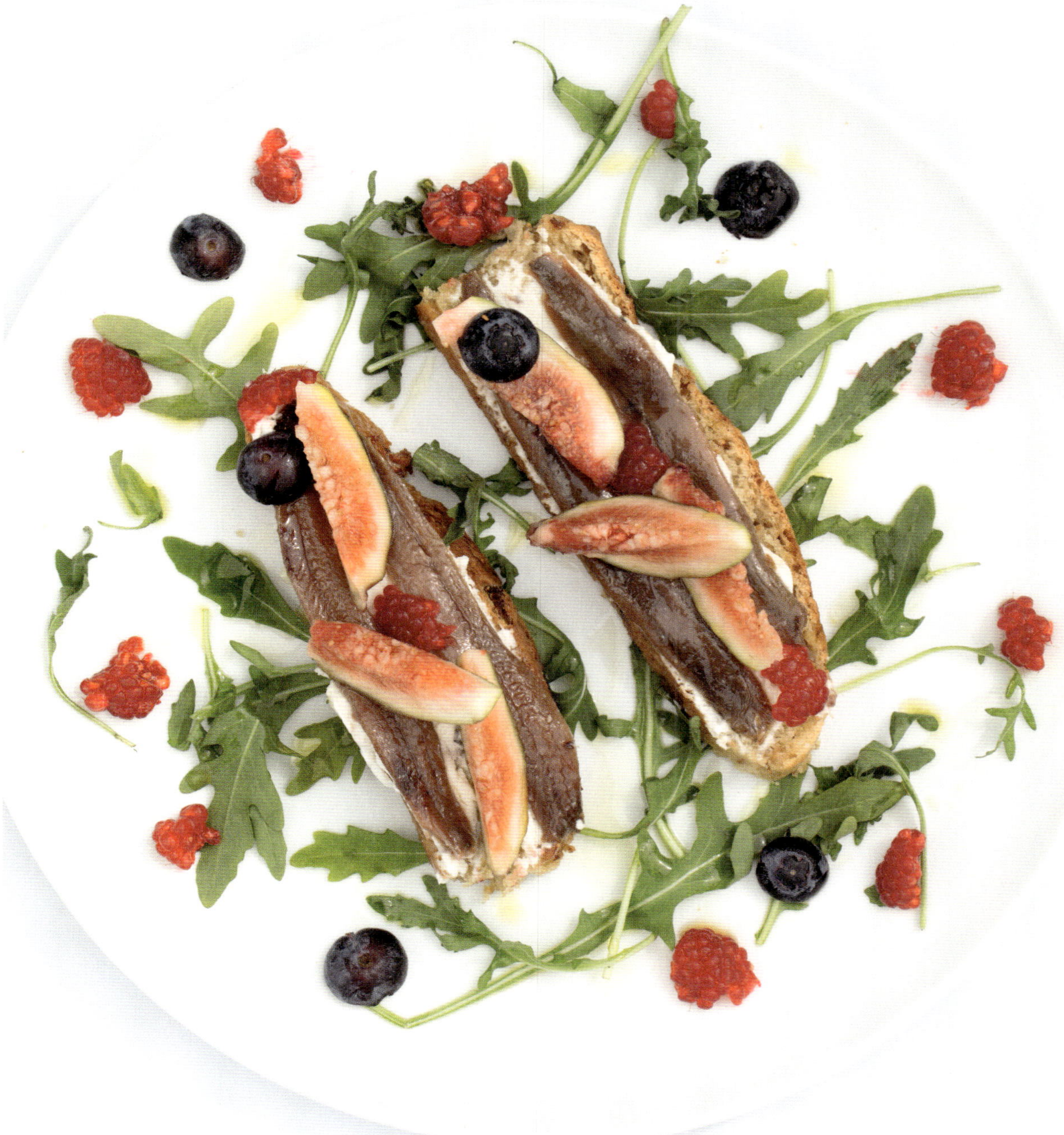

NUNO NUNES FERREIRA

SEVEN
FISHING
TRAWLERS
2017

PRINTED PAPER
COLLAGE

SEVEN ARTWORKS
18 × 24 CM

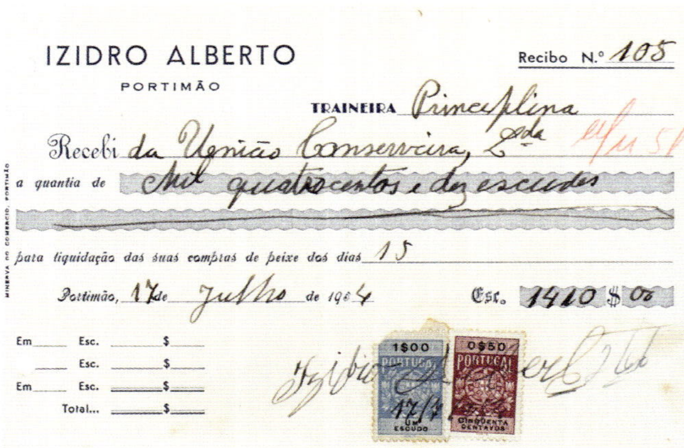

IZIDRO ALBERTO

PORTIMÃO

Recibo N.º 105

TRAINEIRA Princeplina

Recebi da União Conserveira, Lda

a quantia de Mil quatrocentos e dez escudos

para liquidação das suas compras de peixe dos dias 15

Portimão, 17 de Julho de 1954 Esc. 1410$00

Em ___ Esc. ___$___

___ Esc. ___$___

Em ___ Esc. ___$___

Total... ___$___

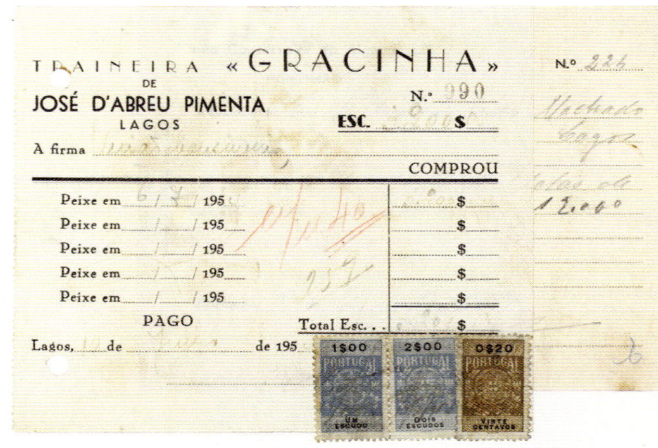

TRAINEIRA «GRACINHA»

DE

JOSÉ D'ABREU PIMENTA

LAGOS

N.º 990

ESC. $

A firma

COMPROU

Peixe em 6/7/195 $

Peixe em / /195 $

Peixe em / /195 $

Peixe em / /195 $

Peixe em / /195 $

PAGO

Total Esc. $

Lagos, de de 195

"PRINCEPLINA"

15 de Julho de 1954. A traineira de Portimão "PRINCEPLINA", pertencente a Izidro Alberto pesca peixe no valor de mil quatrocentos e dez escudos que o vende dois dias depois à União Conserveira.

14 ANOS ANTES

15 de Julho de 1940. Morre com 22 anos de idade Robert Wadlow, o homem mais alto de sempre, com uma altura de 2,72 metros. Wadlow ficou conhecido como o Gigante de Alton por ter nascido e crescido em Alton, Illinois. Foi detentor de dois outros recordes: o de maiores mãos (32,2 cm) e maiores pés (47 cm). Calçava o tamanho 70.

"GRACINHA"

6 de Julho de 1954. A traineira "GRACINHA" de Lagos, pertencente à casa José D'Abreu Pimenta, apanha peixe que vende quatro dias depois à União Conserveira pelo valor de três mil e duzentos escudos.

3 ANOS DEPOIS

6 de Julho de 1957. John Lennon e Paul McCartney encontram-se pela primeira vez como adolescentes numa festa em St Peter's Church, Woolton, Liverpool. Este encontro aconteceu três anos antes de formarem os Beatles.

'PRINCEPLINA'

15 July 1954. The trawler 'PRINCEPLINA' from Portimão, owned by Izidro Alberto, catches fish worth 1.410 escudos and sells it two days later to the União Conserveira.

14 YEARS EARLIER

15 July 1940. Robert Wadlow, the tallest man ever at 2.72 metres, dies at the age of 22. Wadlow became known as the Giant of Alton, the city in Illinois where he was born and raised. He held two more records: the biggest hands (32.2 cm) and biggest feet (47 cm). The size of his shoes was 70.

'GRACINHA'

6 July 1954. The trawler 'GRACINHA' of Lagos, belonging to the company José d'Abreu Pimenta, catches fish and sells it four days later to the União Conserveira for 3.200 escudos.

3 YEARS LATER

6 July 1957. John Lennon and Paul McCartney meet for the first time as teenagers in a party at St Peter's Church in Woolton, Liverpool. This meeting happened three years before the creation of The Beatles.

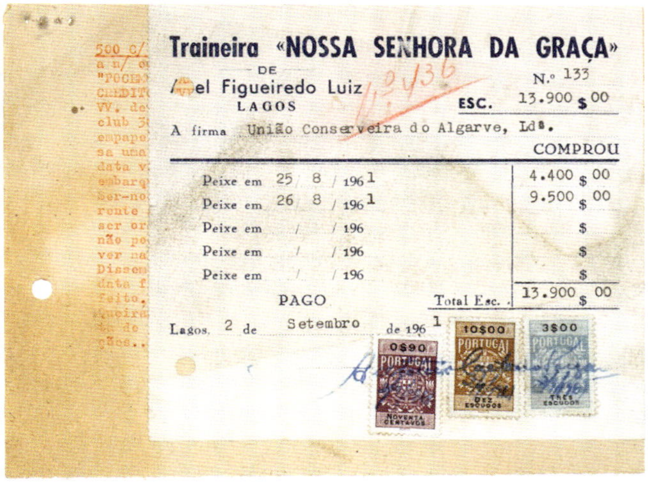
Traineira «NOSSA SENHORA DA GRAÇA»
DE
Abel Figueiredo Luiz
LAGOS
N.º 133
ESC. 13.900 $ 00
A firma União Conserveira do Algarve, Ldª.
COMPROU
Peixe em 25 / 8 / 1961 — 4.400 $ 00
Peixe em 26 / 8 / 1961 — 9.500 $ 00
Peixe em / / 196 — $
Peixe em / / 196 — $
Peixe em / / 196 — $
PAGO — Total Esc. 13.900 $ 00
Lagos, 2 de Setembro de 1961

"NOSSA SENHORA DA GRAÇA"

2 de Setembro de 1961. A traineira de Lagos "NOSSA SENHORA DA GRAÇA", da casa Abel Figueiredo Luiz vende peixe que pescou nos dias 25 e 26 de Agosto à União Conserveira do Algarve pela quantia de treze mil e novecentos escudos.

26 ANOS DEPOIS

2 de Setembro de 1987. Começa em Moscovo o julgamento do piloto amador alemão Mathias Rust de 19 anos de idade, que a 28 de Maio de 1987 voando desde Hamburgo num Cessna 172B atravessou a supostamente impenetrável defesa aérea soviética e conseguiu aterrar na Praça Vermelha, perto do Kremlin. Rust foi condenado a quatro anos de prisão mas foi libertado ao fim de 14 meses.
Mathias Rust disse que queria criar uma "ponte imaginária" para o Oriente e que o seu vôo tinha como objetivo reduzir a tensão entre os dois lados da Guerra Fria.

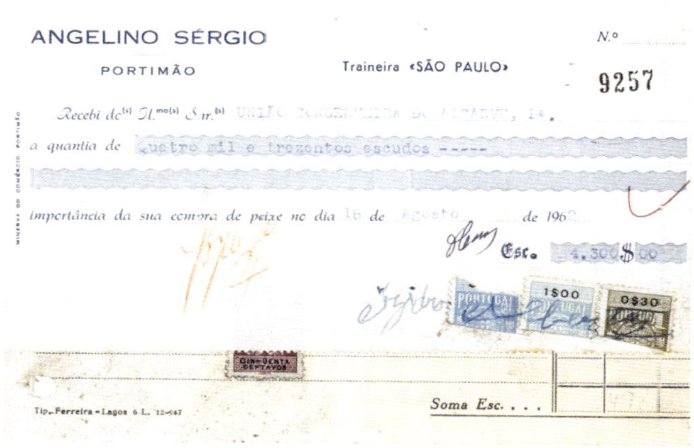
ANGELINO SÉRGIO
PORTIMÃO
Traineira «SÃO PAULO»
N.º 9257
Recebi de Ex.mo(s) Sr.(s) União Conserveira do Algarve, Ld.
a quantia de quatro mil e trezentos escudos -----
importância da sua compra de peixe no dia 18 de Agosto de 1962
Esc. 4.300$00
Tip. Ferreira - Lagos 6 L. 12-947
Soma Esc. . . .

"SÃO PAULO"

18 de Agosto de 1962. A traineira "SÃO PAULO" de Portimão, pertencente a Angelino Sérgio vende peixe à União Conserveira do Algarve pela quantia de quatro mil e trezentos escudos.

4 ANOS ANTES

18 de Agosto de 1958. É publicado nos Estados Unidos o controverso livro Lolita, escrito pelo romancista Vladimir Nabokov. Lolita rapidamente alcançou o estatuto de clássico é um dos principais livros da literatura do século XX e também um dos mais controversos, é frequentemente descrito como um romance erótico, a sua assimilação na cultura popular é tal que o nome "Lolita" tem sido usado para sugerir que uma menina é sexualmente precoce.

'NOSSA SENHORA DA GRAÇA'

2 September 1961. The trawler 'NOSSA SENHORA DA GRAÇA' from the house of Abel Figueiredo Luiz in Lagos, on 25 and 26 August, sells fish to the União Conserveira do Algarve for the amount of 13.900 escudos.

26 YEARS LATER

2 September 1987. The judgment of the 19-year-old German amateur pilot Mathias Rust begins in Moscow. On 28 May 1987, flying from Hamburg in a Cessna 172B, he crossed the supposedly impenetrable Soviet air defence and managed to land on Red Square, close to the Kremlin. Rust was condemned to four years in prison but was released after 14 months.
Mathias Rust said he wanted to create an "imaginary bridge" to the East and that the goal of his flight was to reduce the tension between the two sides of the Cold War.

'SÃO PAULO'

18 August 1962. The trawler 'SÃO PAULO' from Portimão, belonging to Angelino Sérgio, sells fish to the União Conserveira do Algarve for the amount of 4.300 escudos.

4 YEARS EARLIER

18 August 1958. The controversial book 'Lolita', written by the novelist Vladimir Nabokov, is published in the United States. 'Lolita' quickly achieved the status of a classic and is one of the most important and controversial literary books of the 20th century. It is frequently described as an erotic romance and its absorption into popular culture is such that the name 'Lolita' has become synonymous with a sexually precocious girl.

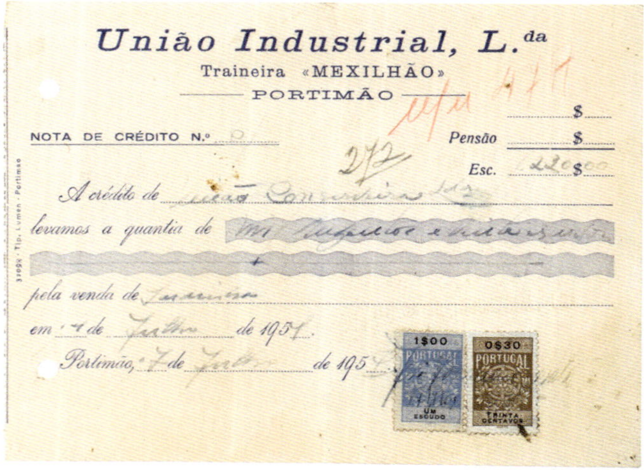

União Industrial, L.da
Traineira «MEXILHÃO»
PORTIMÃO

NOTA DE CRÉDITO N.º
Pensão $
Esc. 220$00

A crédito de
levamos a quantia de
pela venda de
em 7 de Julho de 1954
Portimão, 7 de Julho de 1954

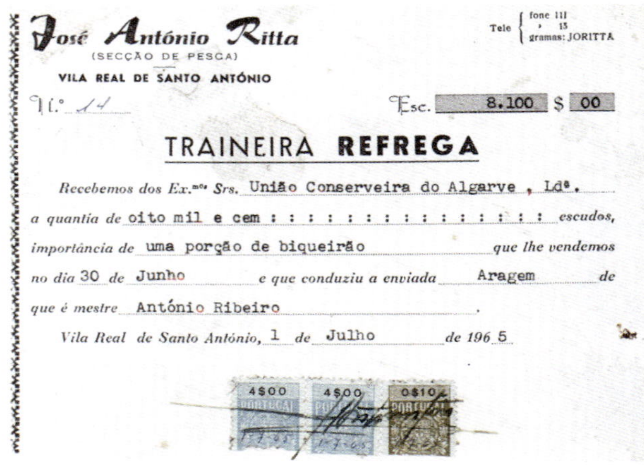

José António Ritta
(SECÇÃO DE PESCA)
VILA REAL DE SANTO ANTÓNIO
Tele fone 111 / 15 / gramas: JORITTA

N.º 11 Esc. 8.100 $ 00

TRAINEIRA REFREGA

Recebemos dos Ex.mos Srs. União Conserveira do Algarve , Ldª. a quantia de oito mil e cem : : : : : : : : : : : : : : : : escudos, importância de uma porção de biqueirão que lhe vendemos no dia 30 de Junho e que conduziu a enviada Aragem de que é mestre António Ribeiro.

Vila Real de Santo António, 1 de Julho de 1965.

"REFREGA"

30 de Junho de 1965. A traineira "REFREGA" pertencente a José António Ritta de Vila Real de Santo António e conduzida pelo mestre António Ribeiro, pesca uma porção de biqueirão que vende à União Conserveira do Algarve no dia seguinte pelo valor oito mil e cem escudos.

57 ANOS ANTES

30 de Junho de 1908. Em Tunguska na Sibéria, uma explosão provavelmente causada pela queda de um meteorito devasta uma área de milhares de quilómetros quadrados, derruba cerca de 80 milhões de árvores e provoca um terremoto de 5 graus na escala Richter . A ausência de uma cratera e de evidências diretas do objeto que teria causado a explosão levou a uma grande quantidade de teorias especulatórias sobre a causa do evento. Estima-se que a energia da explosão tenha sido aproximadamente mil vezes mais forte que a bomba lançada sobre Hiroshima.

"MEXILHÃO"

14 de Julho de 1954. A traineira "MEXILHÃO" da União Industrial Lda de Portimão pesca sardinha que vende à União Conserveira três dias depois por mil duzentos e vinte escudos.

73 ANOS ANTES

14 de Julho de 1881. "Billy the Kid", o famoso pistoleiro fora da lei e ladrão de gado e cavalos, é morto por Pat Garrett em Fort Sumner. Segundo a lenda, Billy terá morto 21 homens, exatamente o mesmo número de anos que terá vivido. No entanto registos históricos contabilizam apenas quatro mortes.

'REFREGA'

30 June 1965. The trawler 'REFREGA', owned by José António Ritta from Vila Real de Santo António and driven by the master António Ribeiro, fishes a for anchovies and sells them to União Conserveira do Algarve the day after for the amount of 8.100 escudos.

57 YEARS EARLIER

30 June 1908. In the Siberian city of Tunguska, one explosion, probably caused by the fall of a meteorite, devastated an area of thousands of square kilometres, felled 80 million trees and caused an earthquake measuring 5 on the Richter Scale. The absence of a crater and direct evidence of the object responsible for the explosion led to a lot of speculative theories about the cause of the occurrence. It is estimated that the energy of the explosion was approximately one thousand times stronger than the bomb dropped on Hiroshima.

'MEXILHÃO'

14 July 1954. The trawler 'MEXILHÃO' from the União Industrial Lda de Portimão fishes for sardines and sells them three days later to the União Conserveira for 1.220 escudos.

73 YEARS EARLIER

14 July 1881. 'Billy the Kid', the famous outlaw gunman and cattle-and-horse thief, is killed by Pat Garrett in Fort Sumner. According to legend, Billy killed 21 men, exactly the same number of years he supposedly lived. However, the historical records only counted four deaths.

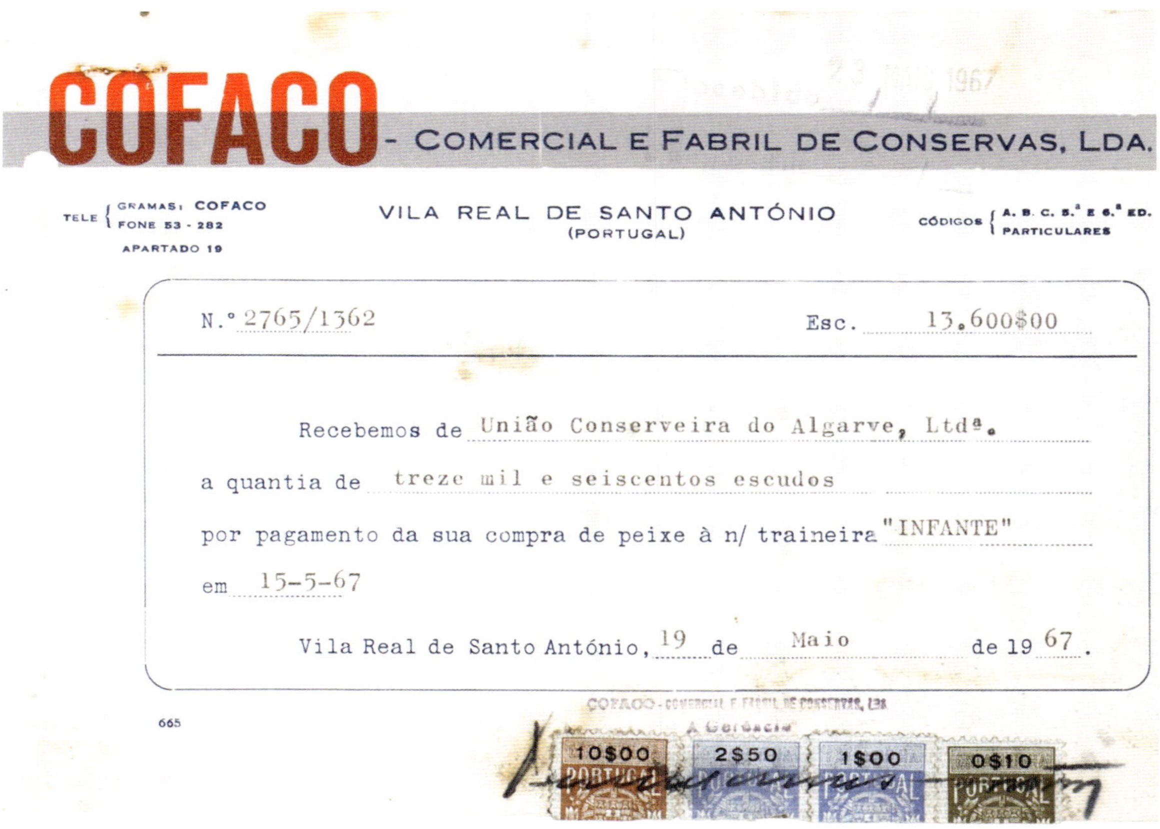

COFACO - COMERCIAL E FABRIL DE CONSERVAS, LDA.

TELE { GRAMAS: COFACO / FONE 53 - 282
APARTADO 19

VILA REAL DE SANTO ANTÓNIO
(PORTUGAL)

CÓDIGOS { A. B. C. 5.ª E 6.ª ED. / PARTICULARES

N.º 2765/1362 Esc. 13.600$00

Recebemos de União Conserveira do Algarve, Ltdª.
a quantia de treze mil e seiscentos escudos
por pagamento da sua compra de peixe à n/ traineira "INFANTE"
em 15-5-67

Vila Real de Santo António, 19 de Maio de 1967.

665

COFACO - COMERCIAL E FABRIL DE CONSERVAS, LDA
A Gerência

10$00 2$50 1$00 0$10

"INFANTE"

15 de Maio de 1967. A traineira "INFANTE" pertencente à COFACO de Vila Real de Santo António recebe quatro dias depois a quantia de treze mil e seiscentos escudos pela venda de peixe à União Conserveira do Algarve.

39 ANOS ANTES

15 de Maio de 1928. Mickey Mouse, o personagem criado por Walt Disney tem a sua estreia como desenho animado na curta-metragem "Plane Crazy". Este filme mudo foi exibido neste dia como teste para uma audiência de um teatro mas não consegue arranjar nenhum distribuidor. Só mais tarde quando é lançado "Steamboat Willie", o primeiro desenho animado com som, é que o personagem Mickey Mouse se torna no sucesso que conhecemos hoje.

'INFANTE'

15 May 1967. The trawler 'INFANTE', owned by COFACO from Vila Real de Santo António, earns the amount of 13 600 escudos four days after for selling the fish to União Conserveira do Algarve.

39 YEARS EARLIER

15 May 1928. Mickey Mouse, the Walt Disney character, has his premiere as a cartoon in the short movie 'Plane Crazy'. This silent film was screened that day as a test for the audience of a theatre but couldn't find any distributor. It took a little longer, when 'Steamboat Willie', the first movie with sound, was launched, for Mickey Mouse to become the success he is today.

PEDRO
LEMOS

ALBUQUERQUE
MENDES

ALBUQUERQUE MENDES

PEDRO LEMOS

PEDRO LEMOS
ALBUQUERQUE MENDES

"THE WORLD IS SO CONTEMPORARY NOW"

Pedro Lemos's eponymous restaurant is located in the old Porto neighbourhood of Foz, in the midst of bleak, multi-coloured houses (just as Pedro Lemos likes it) and close to the intriguing Central Alley. The interior is dim, kind of intimate, the walls painted a greyish blue and decorated with pottery pieces by Bordalo Pinheiro, Portugal's greatest ceramicist. Everything is elegant, simple and refined. And we have to surrender. The artist Albuquerque Mendes shoots immediately. "This reminds me of something my son once said to me: 'Dad, the world is so contemporary now.' And it's true, isn't it?"

We go to the kitchen to shoot the pictures, where Albuquerque dresses up and maybe even lifts up his heels to look taller. "Am I beautiful?" he asks. "I should have brought my clown's nose."

Pedro laughs. But his face grows serious as he talks about his kitchen.

"Our strength is our stocks. They are important, and difficult, too. But we have to show people how we use our time. Stocks give depth to the dishes."

We discover that both Pedro and Albuquerque were meant to study civil engineering. Pedro stayed on the course until the pots and pans got in the way and led him to other forms of engineering. But the story starts at the beginning...

"I had a magical childhood," says Pedro. "My father was an engineer and my mother was a nurse. There was a very traditional culture of great care. The table was always a special occasion. I learned how to cook and, later, when I invited friends to come over, they enjoyed my cooking. I came to the conclusion that in order to eat properly either I would need to learn how to cook or become a great engineer. In the end it was all very natural."

In matters of childhood and skewed paths, Albuquerque is second to none. "As a child, I was a bit of a sissy," he says. "I used to read, paint and cook. I lived in a house full of women and I loved that. At the age of ten, I moved from Trancoso to Coimbra and wanted to become a priest. My father, who was a communist, thought that a nonsense. But I felt it was about more than me and my body, so I was religious (and I still am). I loved colours, which, at the time, was complicated. When I was six, I went to buy my first suit and chose the fabric – it was an orange, brown and black tartan and I looked like a gangster. At the age of ten, I was using bright pink and lettuce green.

"In Coimbra, I started going to concerts at the age of 14 – seeing the likes of Vinícius Moraes and Nara Leão, operas in Lisbon, and so on. In 1969 I saw an exhibition in Coimbra organised by the CAPC (Coimbra Plastic Arts Circle) and I signed up on the spot. It was a new world. I met Paula Rego and Helena Almeida, and my horizons expanded."

And ideas, where do they come from? Pedro takes things up.

"At the start, I sought the work of those who were emerging. I began emulating and, little by little, I found my path. Our cuisine is wonderful, but monotonous. I admire it but I want to do new things. The ideas come from memories or from travels. They might come from a chip that we have missing, or an extra chip in our minds."

Albuquerque talks of how ideas come to him, and quotes a verse from José Jiménez: "Artists are angels who fall from heaven to their mother's womb." "I'm always giving ideas to everyone," he says. "Even if I tried, I could not keep them."

Pedro also likes to share, as long as it's here in his restaurant.

"I don't show anything on the internet or on social media," he says. "People must come and see. I'm here, away from the world, with my elderly neighbours whom I love. I used to be very aggressive, even impolite. Nowadays I'm more calm and I just want to be happy with what I have around me. I tell my 92-year-old neighbour that I want to grow old like her, but she tells me the secret is becoming a widow early."

We smile one to another, notebooks are closed and the camera lens is covered. "Did it go well?" asks Albuquerque. Everyone seems to think it went well, really well.

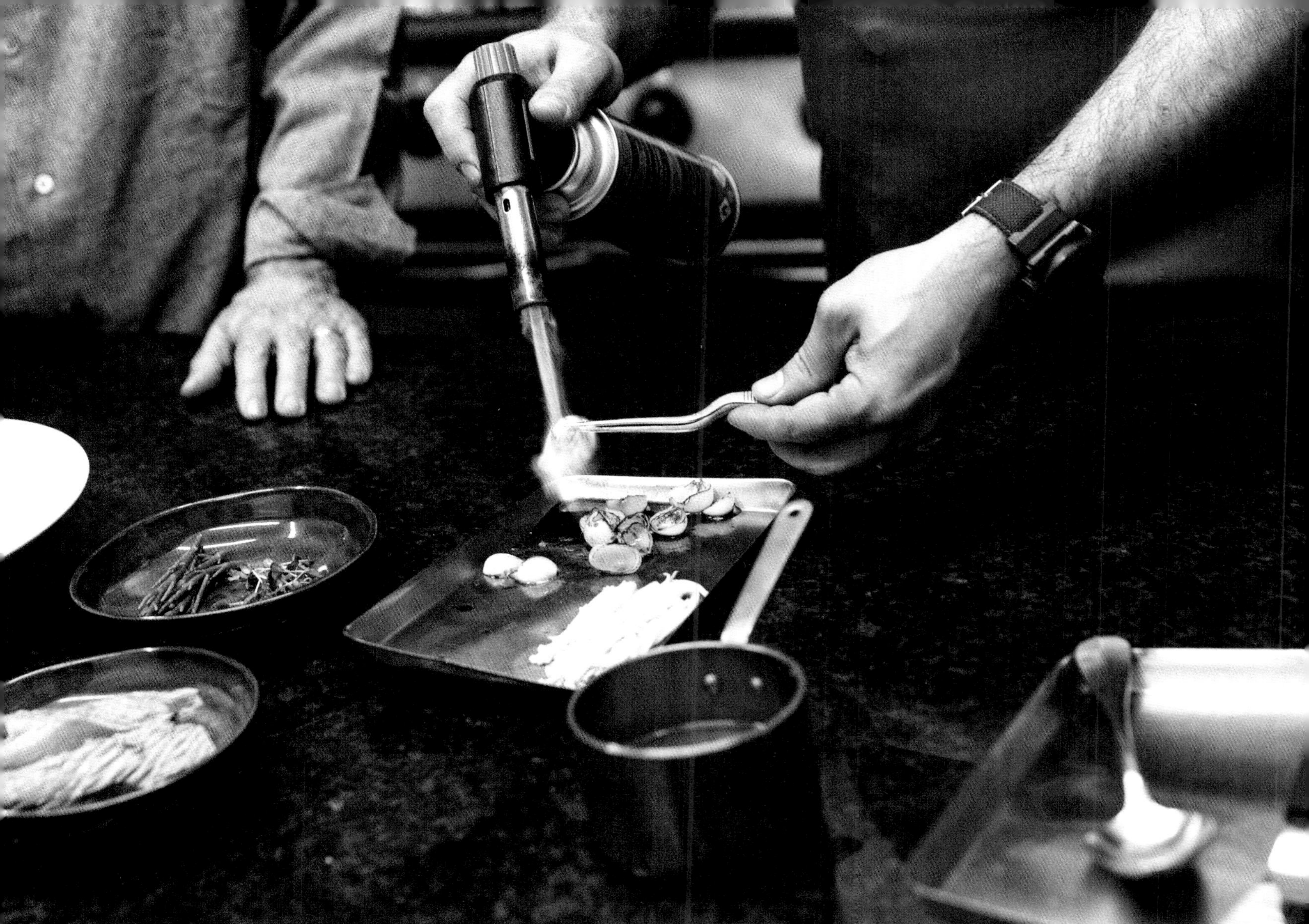

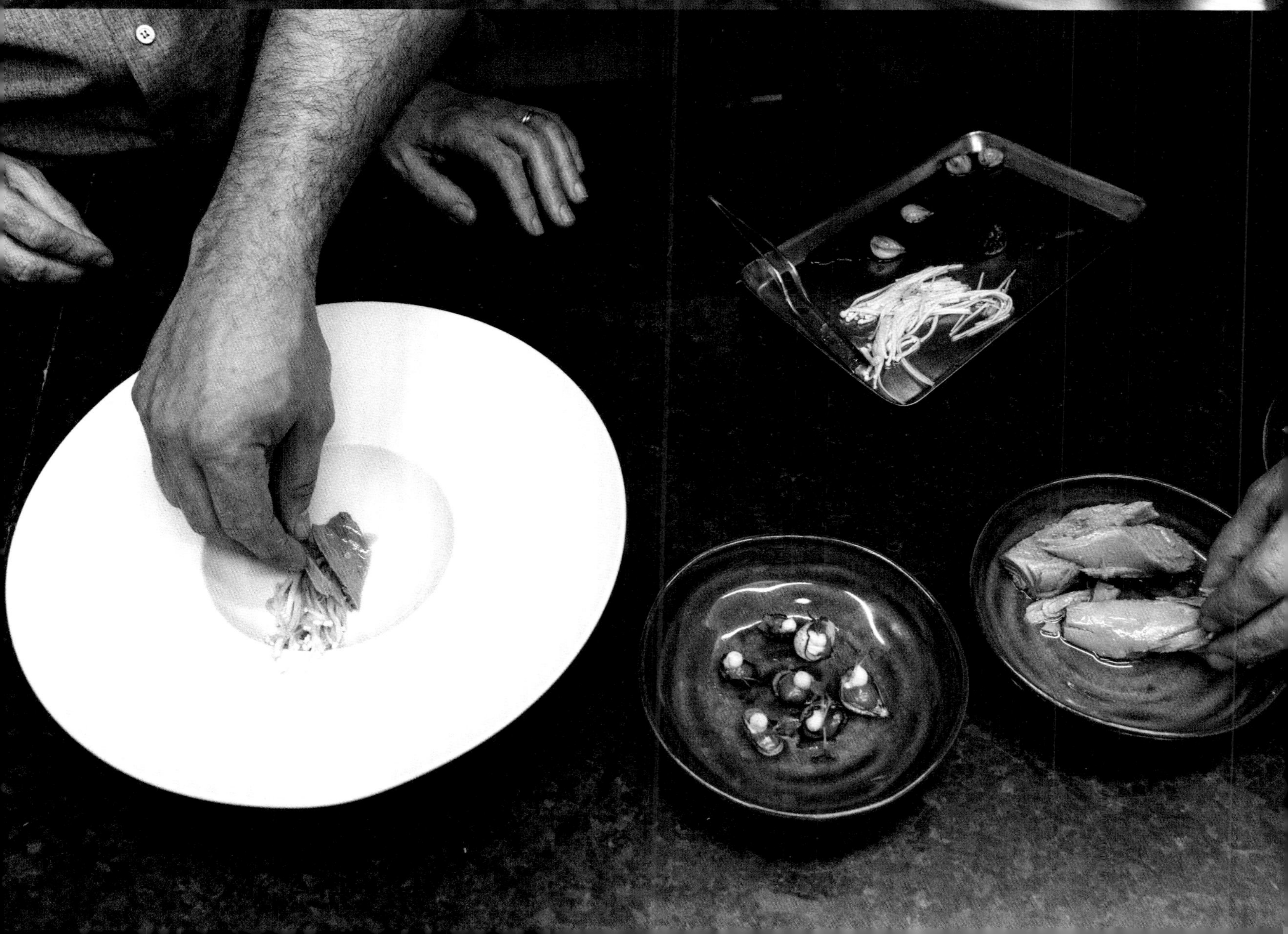

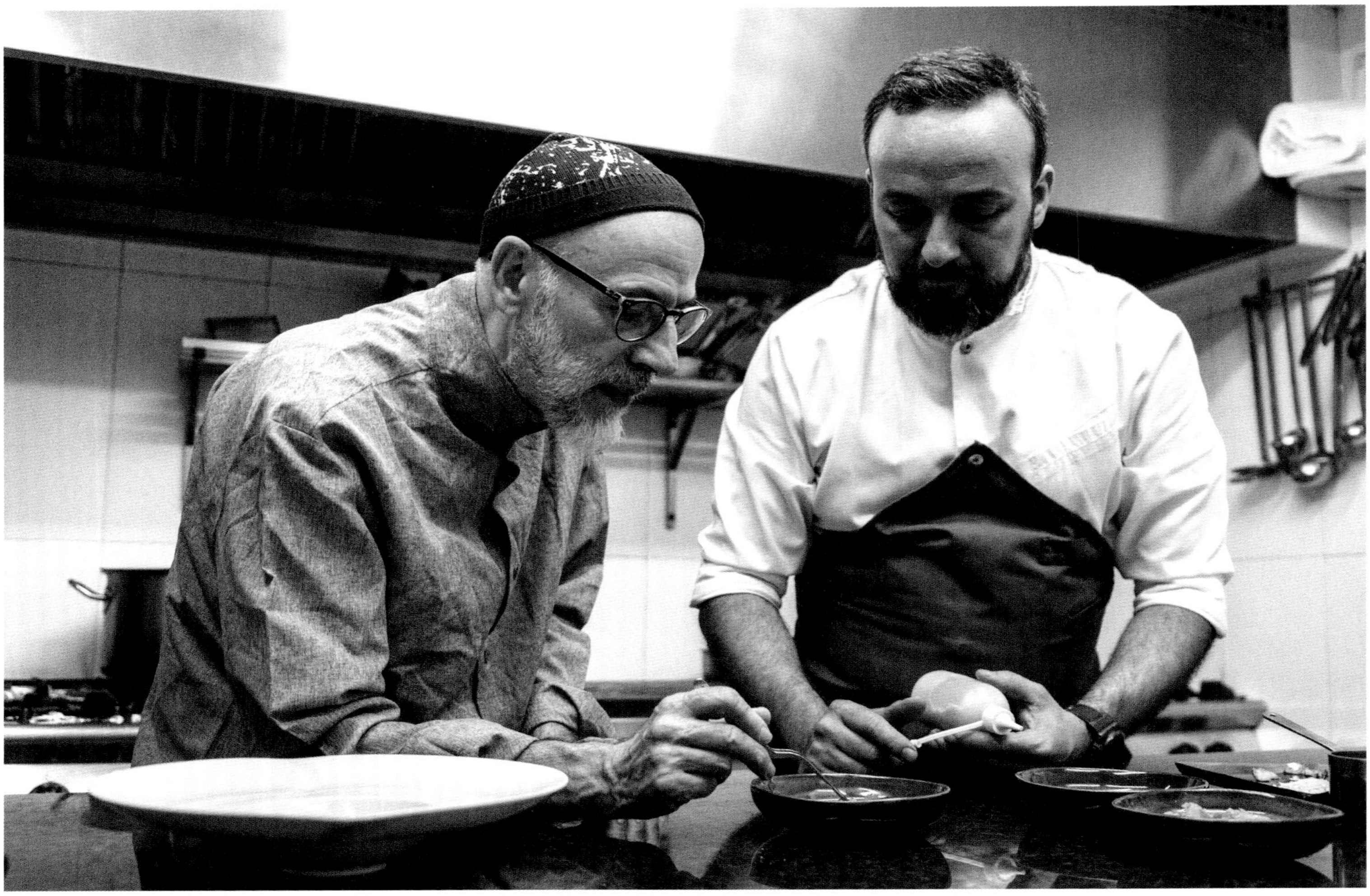

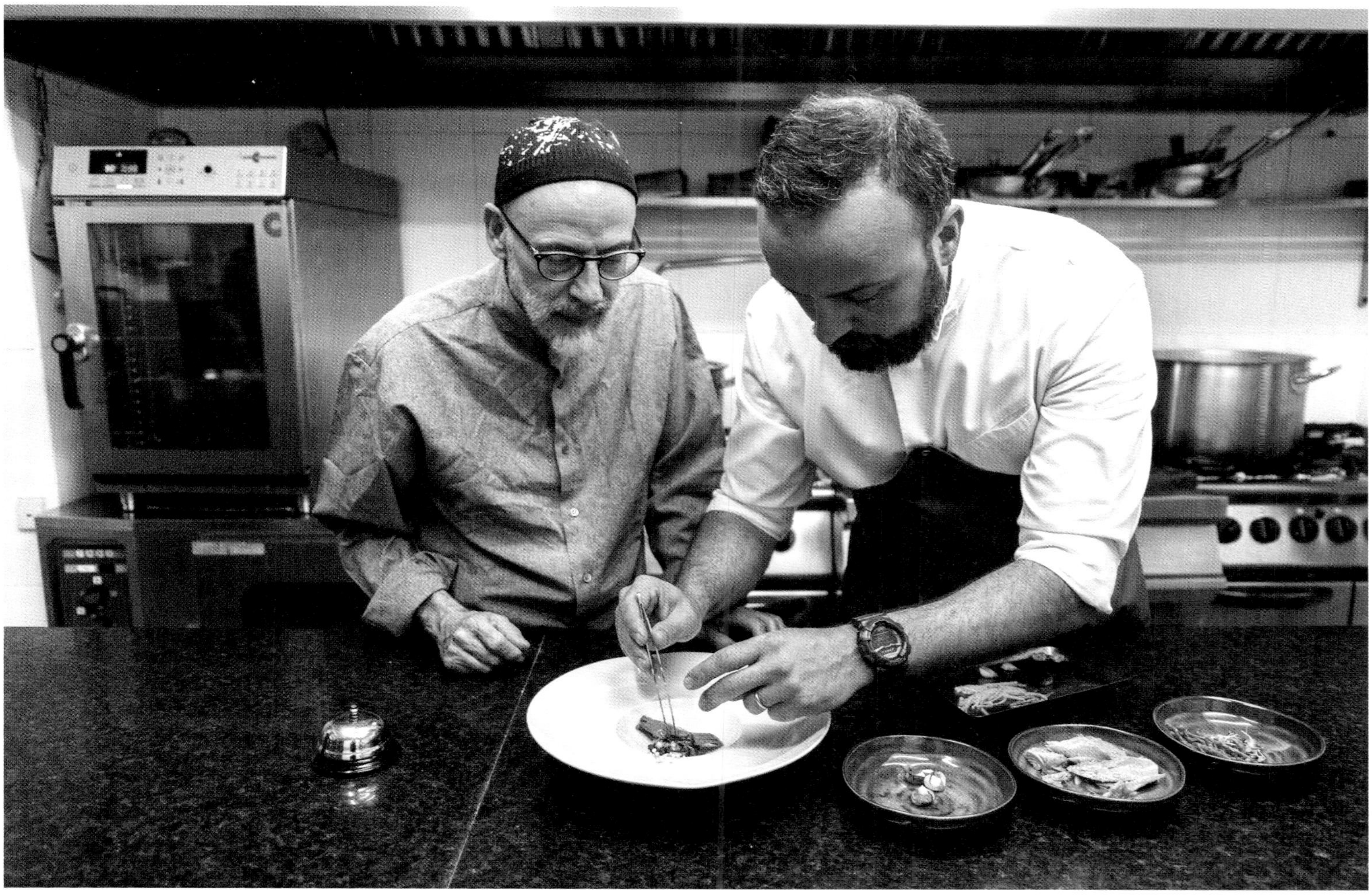

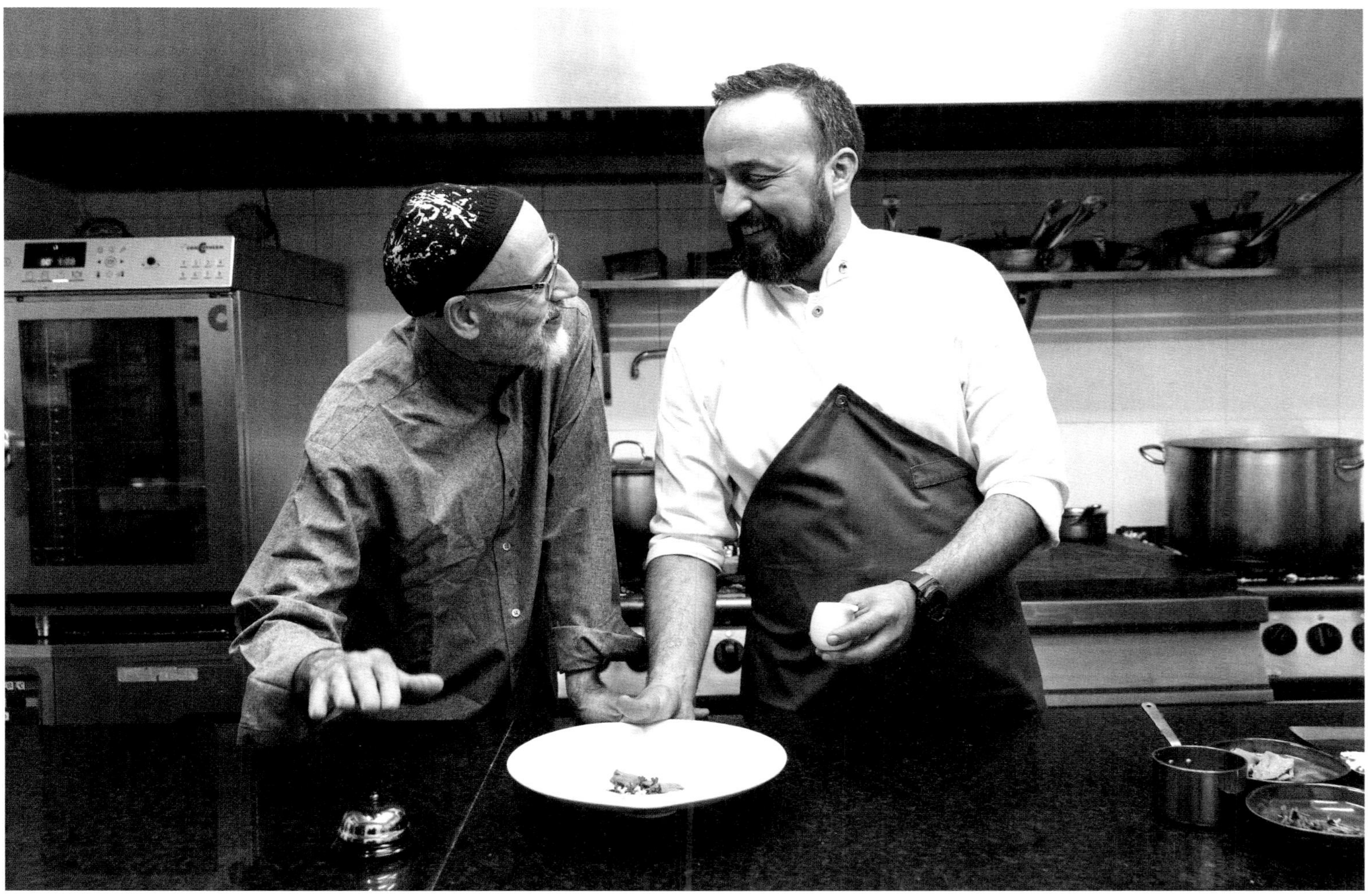

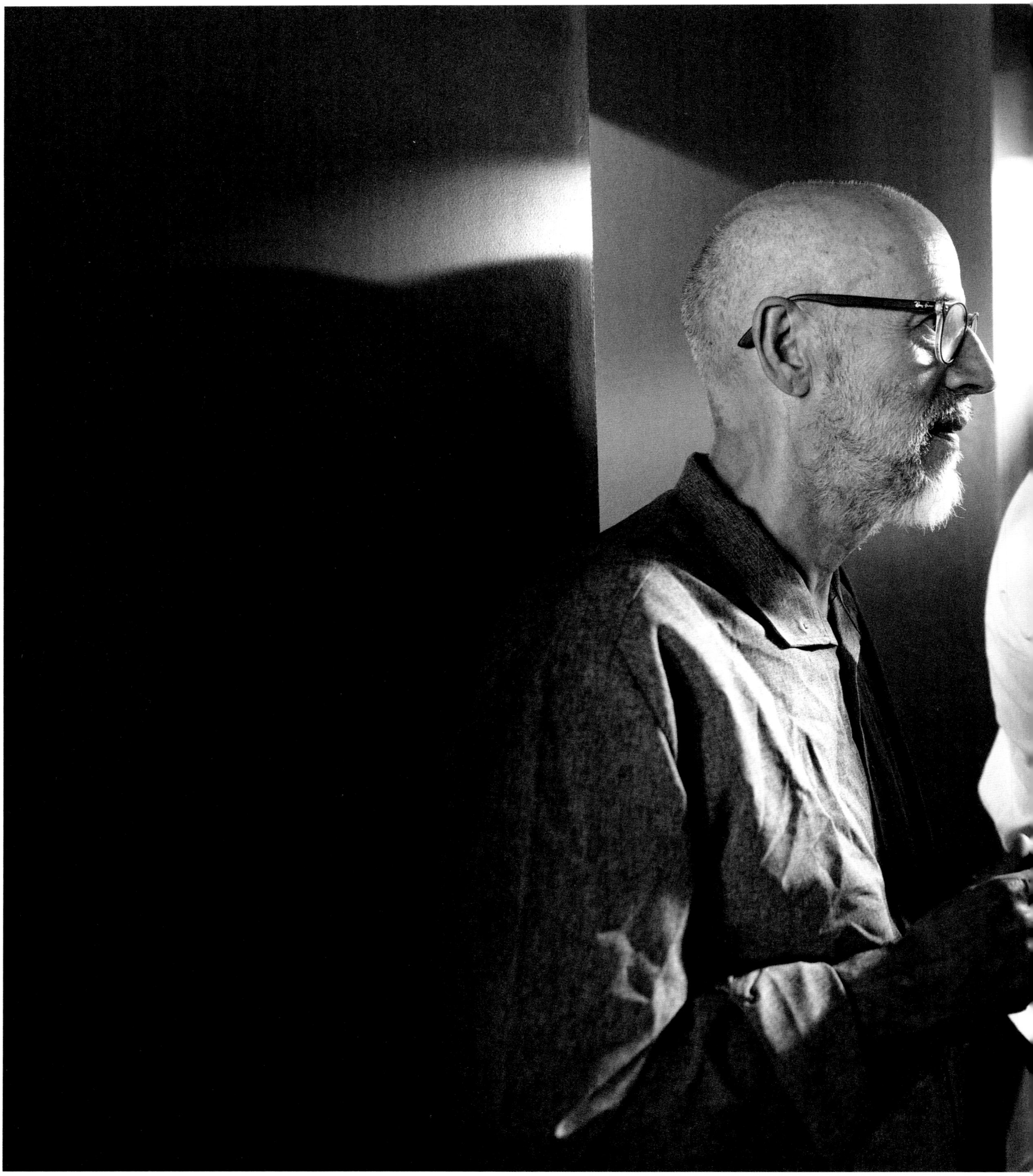

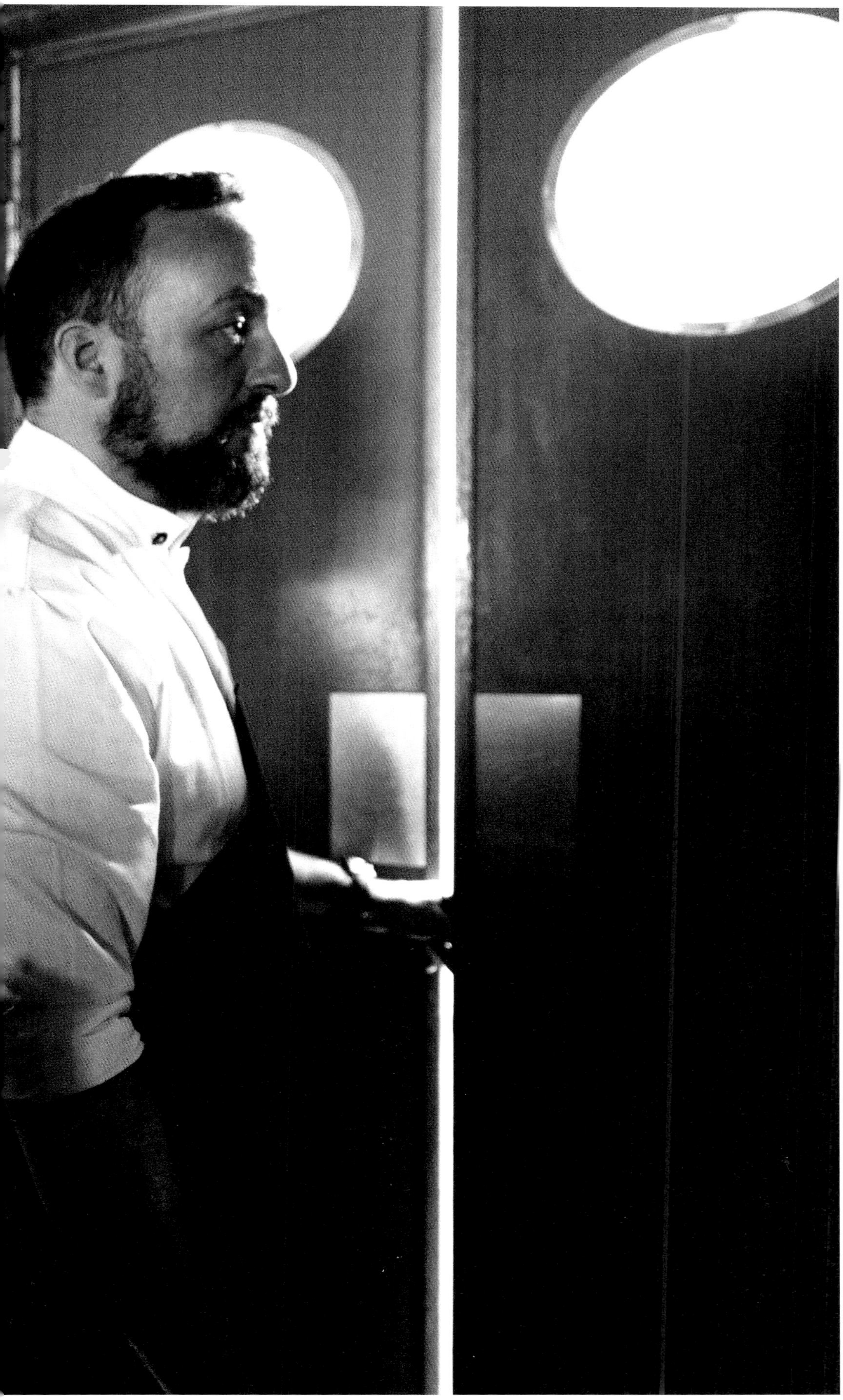

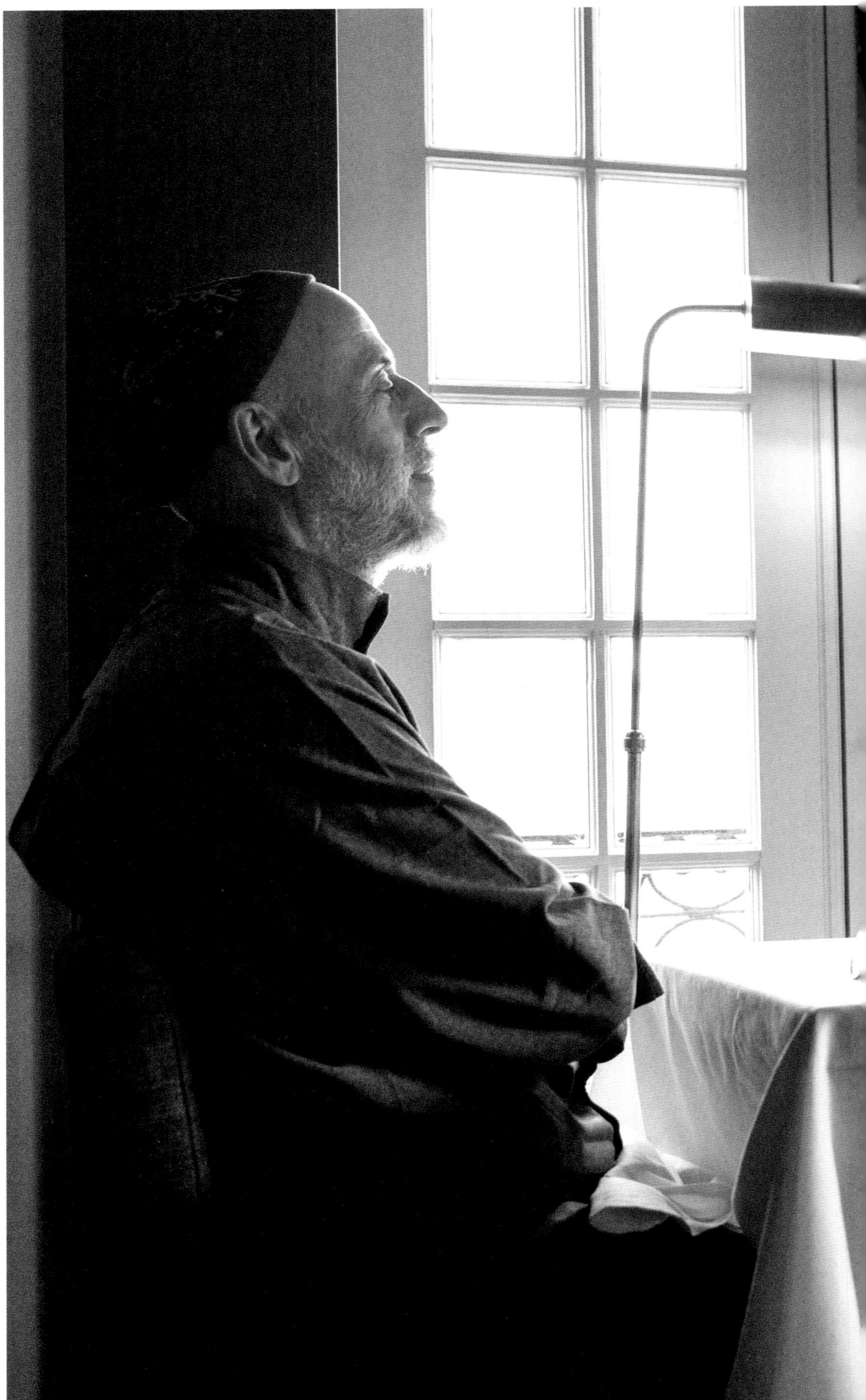

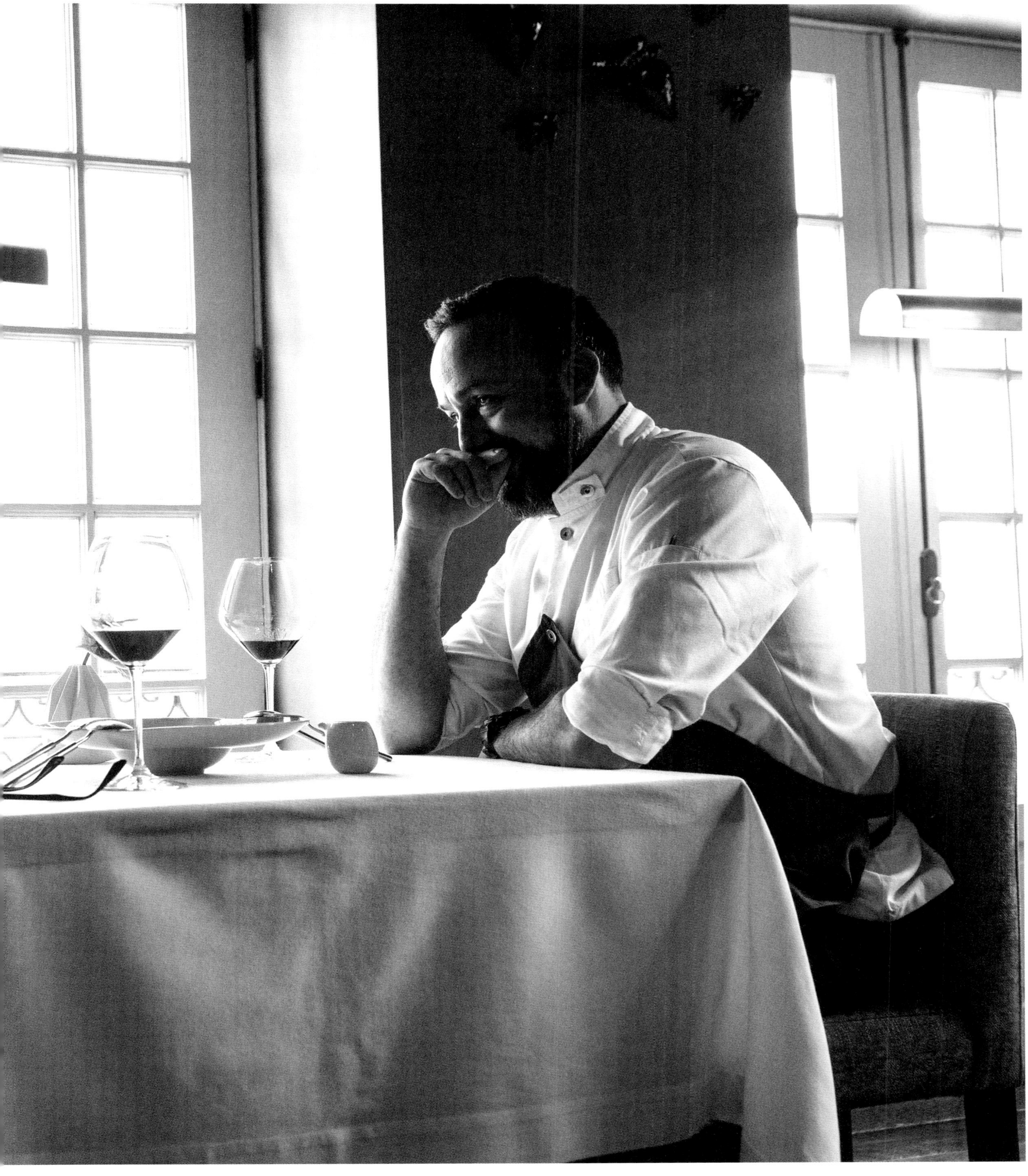

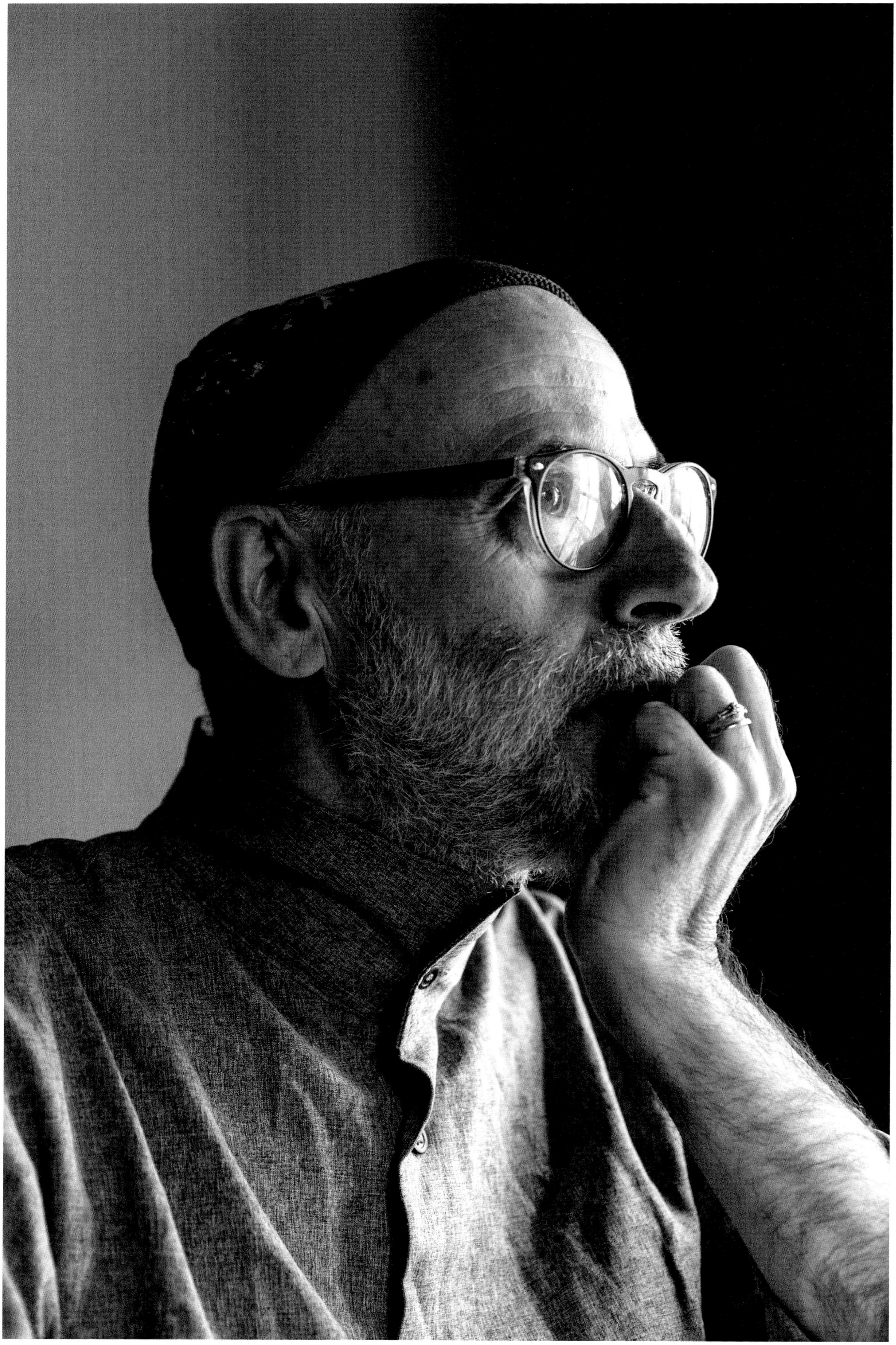

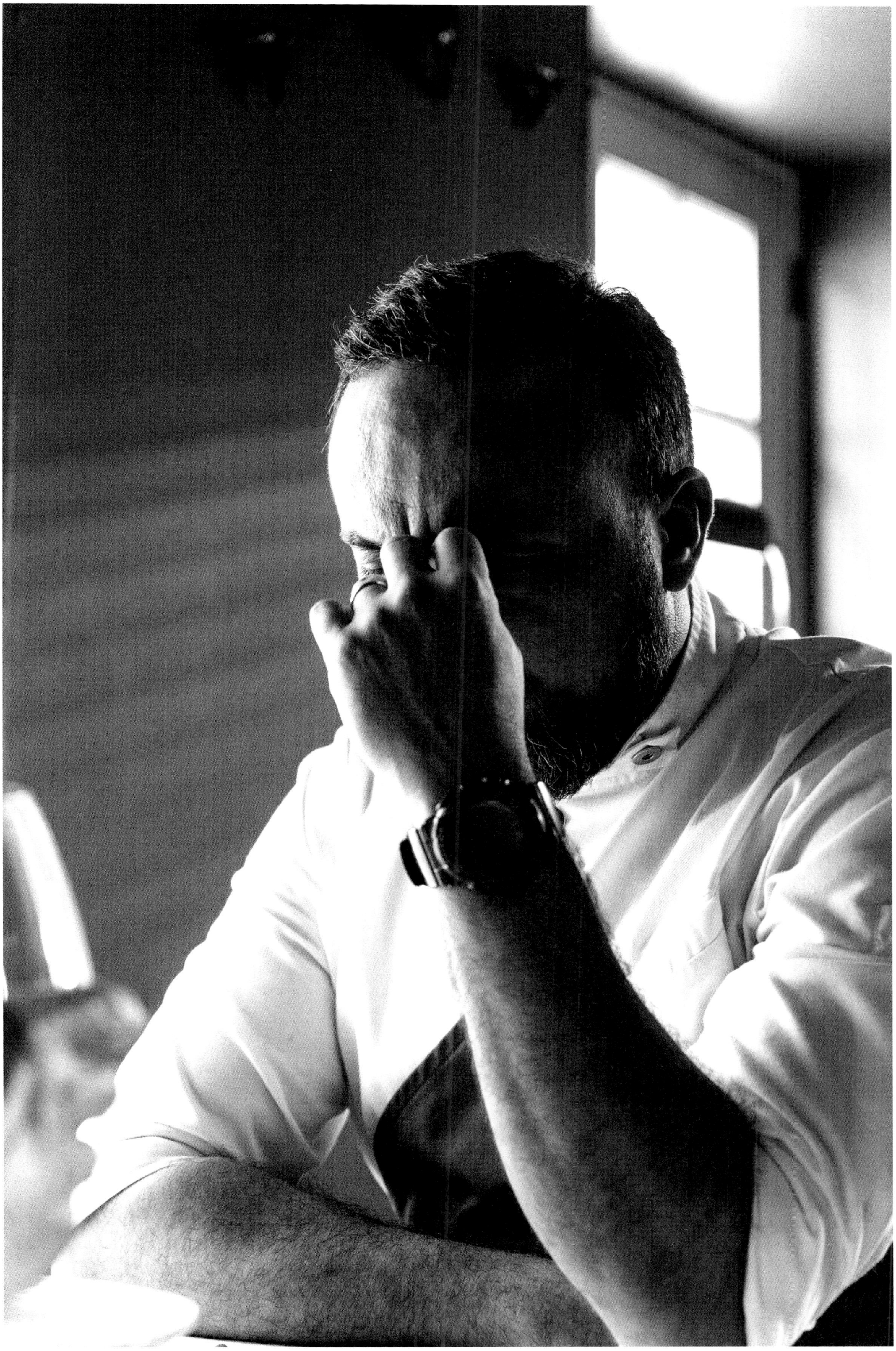

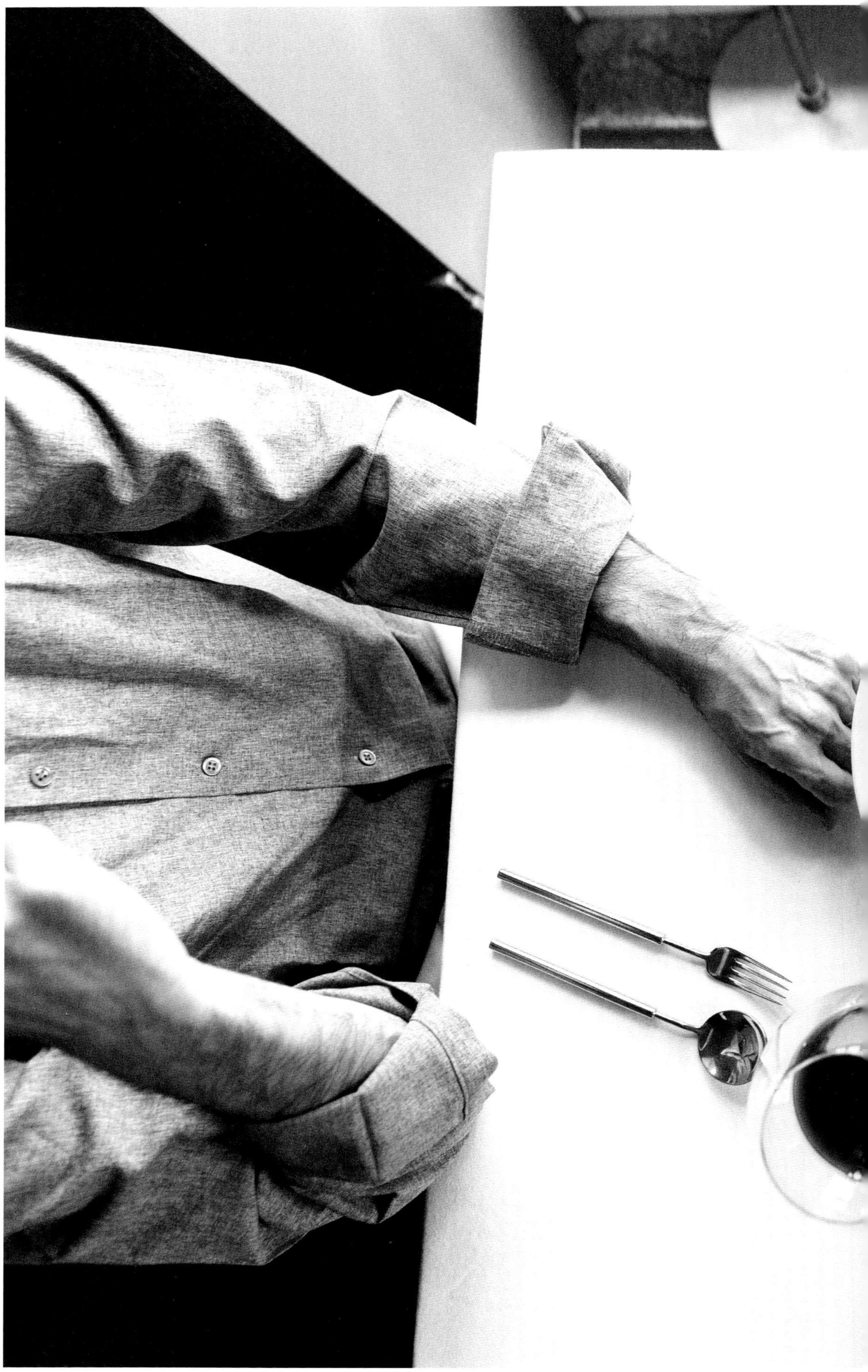

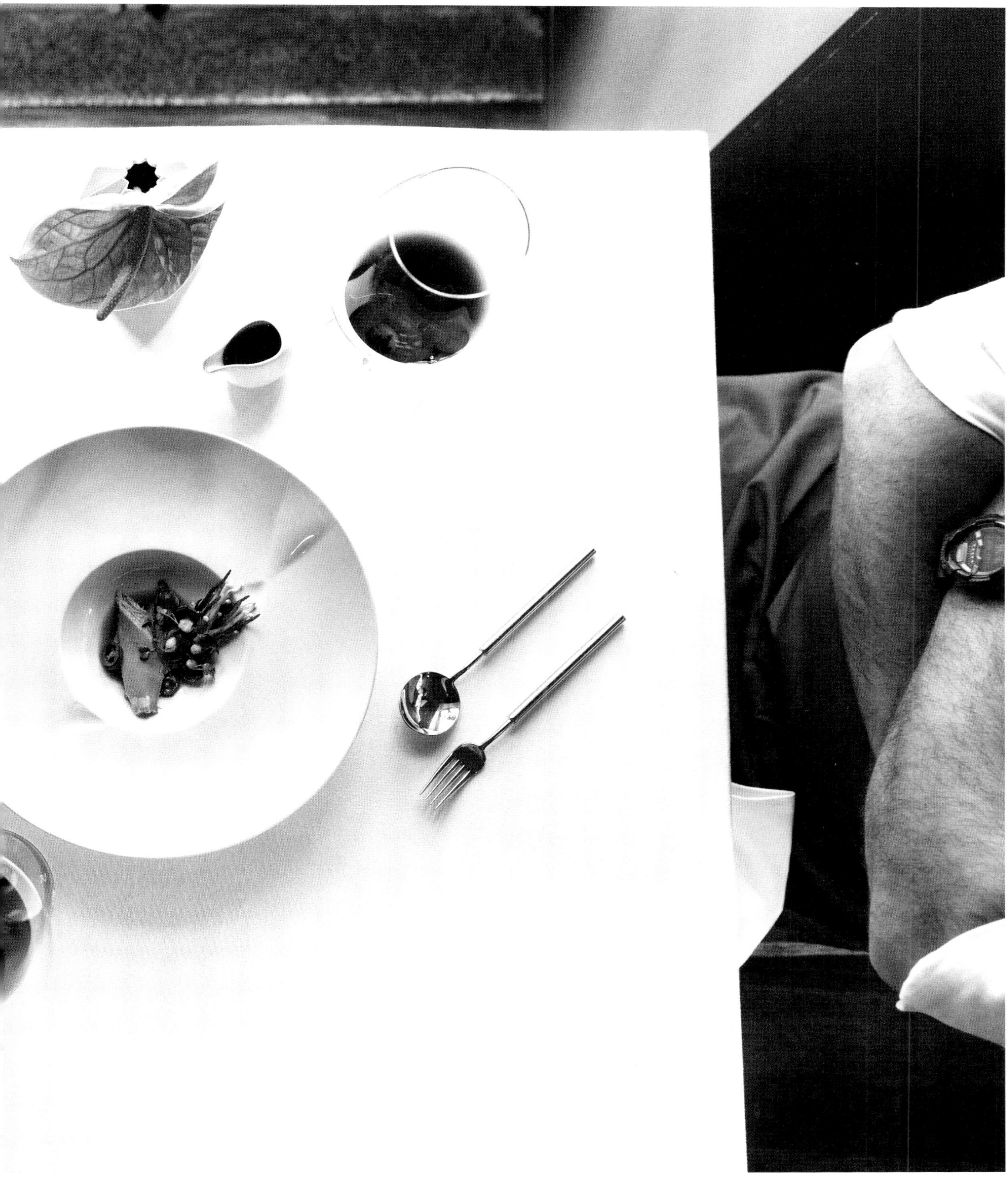

PEDRO

SPICY TUNA WITH FAVA BEAN AND SALICÓRIA

TUNA FILLETS IN
HOT VEGETABLE OIL
BRAND PORTHOS

LEMOS

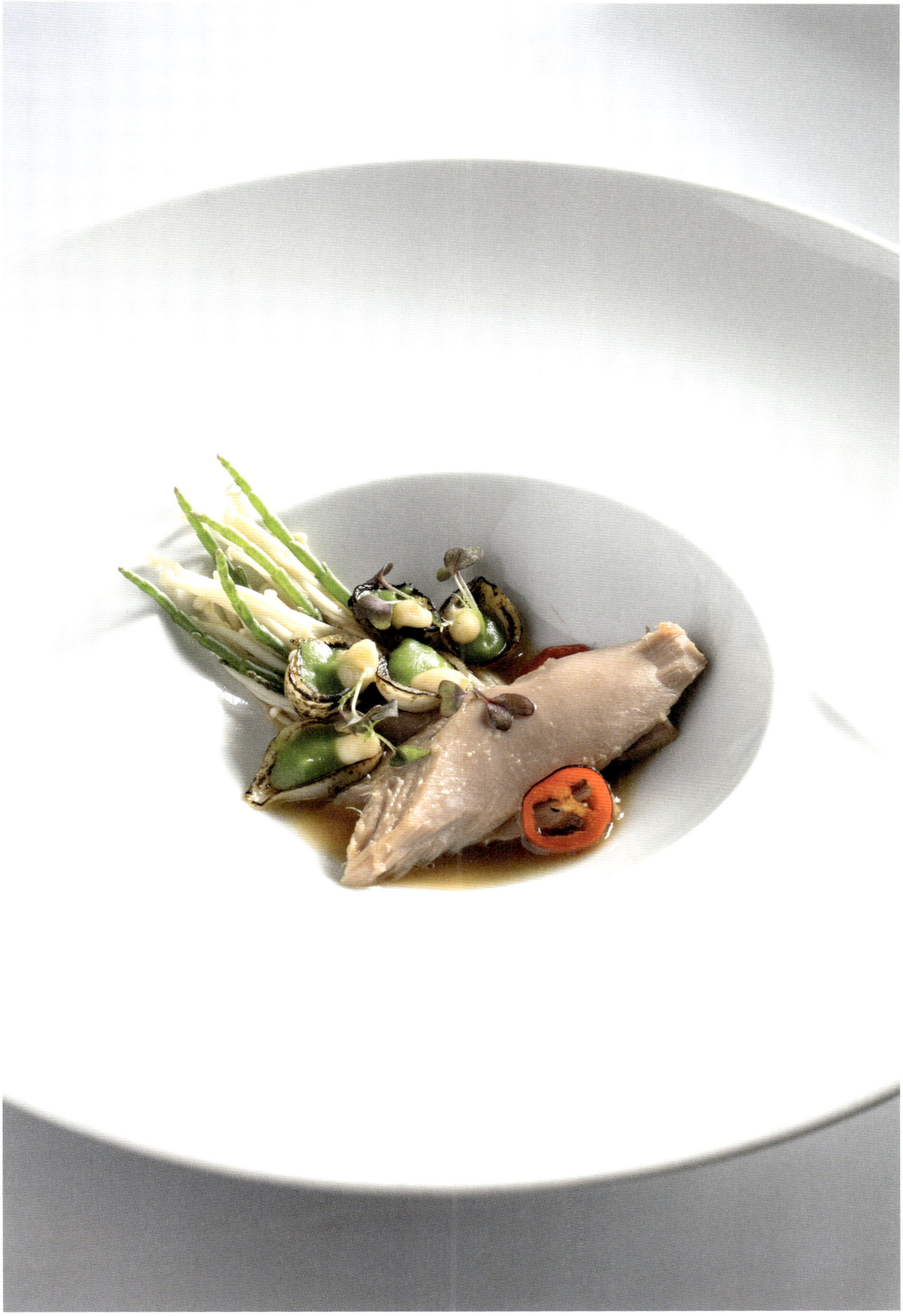

ALBU QUER QUE

THE FISHERMAN OF MEMORIES
2017

MEN DES

WATERCOLOUR AND ACRYLIC ON PAPER
41 × 29,5 CM

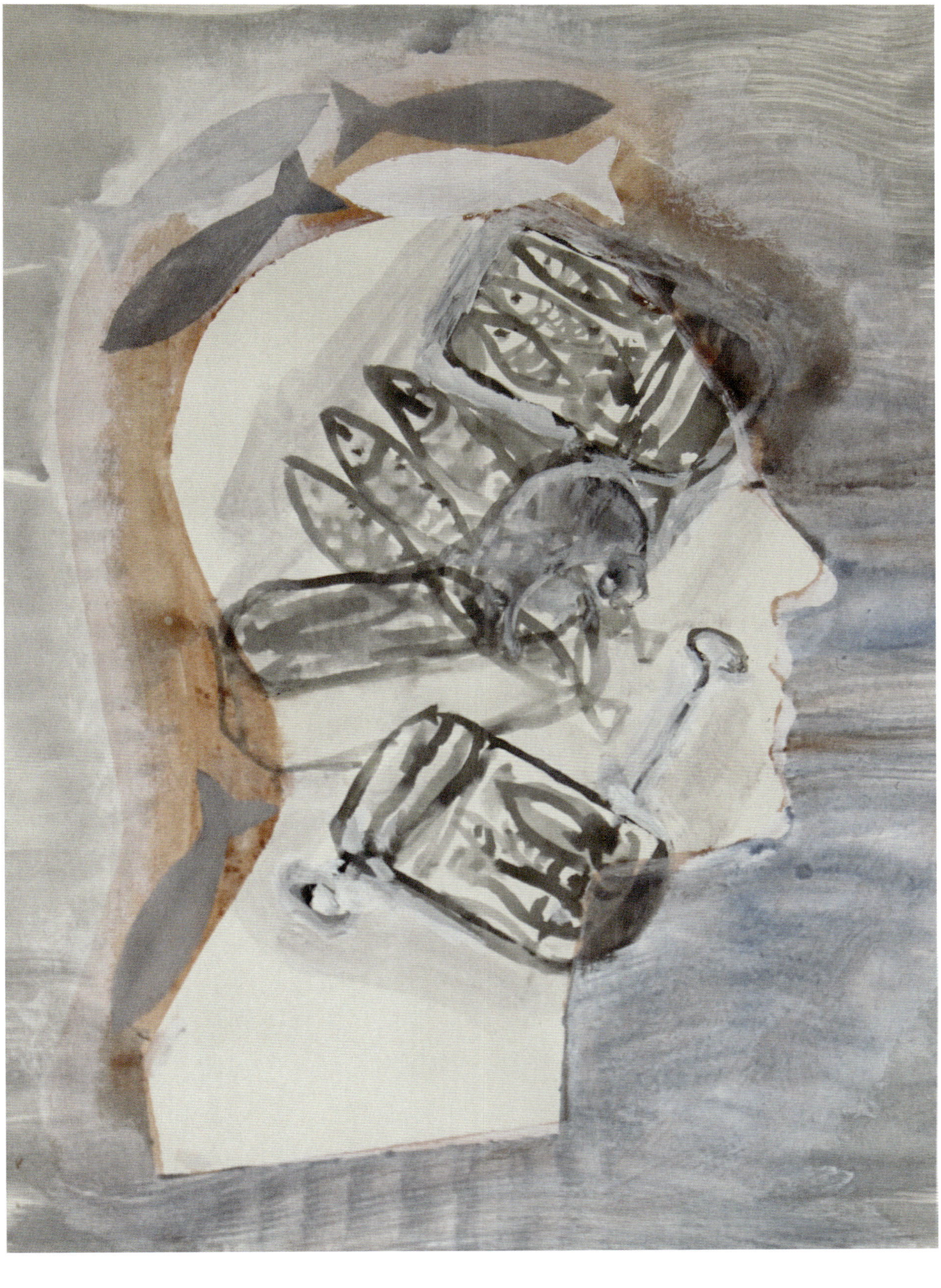

MARLENE
VIEIRA

HUGO
BRAZÃO

HUGO
BRAZÃO

MARLENE
VIEIRA

8 MARCH, WOMEN'S DAY

There aren't many women heading the best kitchens, and the few who are – like Marlene Vieira at the Panorâmico in Lisbon – must be celebrated. By chance, our meeting is on 8 March, Women's Day. A happy coincidence.

The restaurant's name does justice to the view and, while waiting for the artists, we praise the excellent taste in everything – the decoration, the room arrangement and the service. At the centre of the room, a table full of women are celebrating with good wine in the best way, and we join them.

It is a session of rich and sharp accents: Marlene is from Porto, the artist Hugo Brazão from Madeira. After introductions, we note immediately the personality traits. She is very resourceful and fast, he is more shy, just arrived from London and used to other rhythms.

The chosen can is the octopus. "It's good," says Marlene. "But it's overcooked. We need to work on it, give it some smoke. Smoke is a trend I've been working with."

Hugo gives us his little cans: abstract, colourful, seeming to smile like their author. "I've done a lot of things", he says. "I even worked in a deli. One has to fight for life, and it did me no harm."

Marlene says she likes to work with her hands, to touch things. Hugo nods: "Me too, me too."

We talk about many things and also about women in cooking. Marlene says it isn't easy, but she doesn't complain. She has a two-year-old son and that's that. Women learn to be tough. The arrangement of the dish is discussed. What does the artist say? Maybe like this, or like that – power to the octopus!

We move onto the creative processes and Marlene and Hugo agree:

"If the protein is good there's not a lot to do," says Marlene. "We have to hide the defects and praise the virtues."

"Manipulate the material, work it and learn from it," says Hugo.

"There's always a difference between the dish in our mind and the one we present," says Marlene.

"Or the artwork," says Hugo. "Or the artwork."

We go back in time and arrive at beginnings. Marlene remembers her first company, back in 2014. "The accountant said it would work." She realised that the kitchen would be her life when, around the age of twelve, she went with her father, who was a butcher, to a new restaurant. The cook was a nice girl with a certain aesthetic sense; she was serving French cuisine and the restaurant was called Costa Brava (Wild Coast). That stayed in her mind: "Perhaps I could do that." Perhaps... "I fell in love with professional cooking, not with home cooking."

Hugo used to go to the kitchen when he was home alone; he didn't know how to make anything, but he would amuse himself experimenting. "Art? I don't know, I was very young and someone took me to visit a museum. When I came home, I started playing with clay. I don't know why, but it was exactly what I wanted. I was six or seven years old, and I'm still here, in this artistic life."

The smoked octopus goes up in smoke and we feel obliged to say goodbye. We wish we could stay with Marlene and Hugo, playing with food and art, smiling with them and inventing new accents.

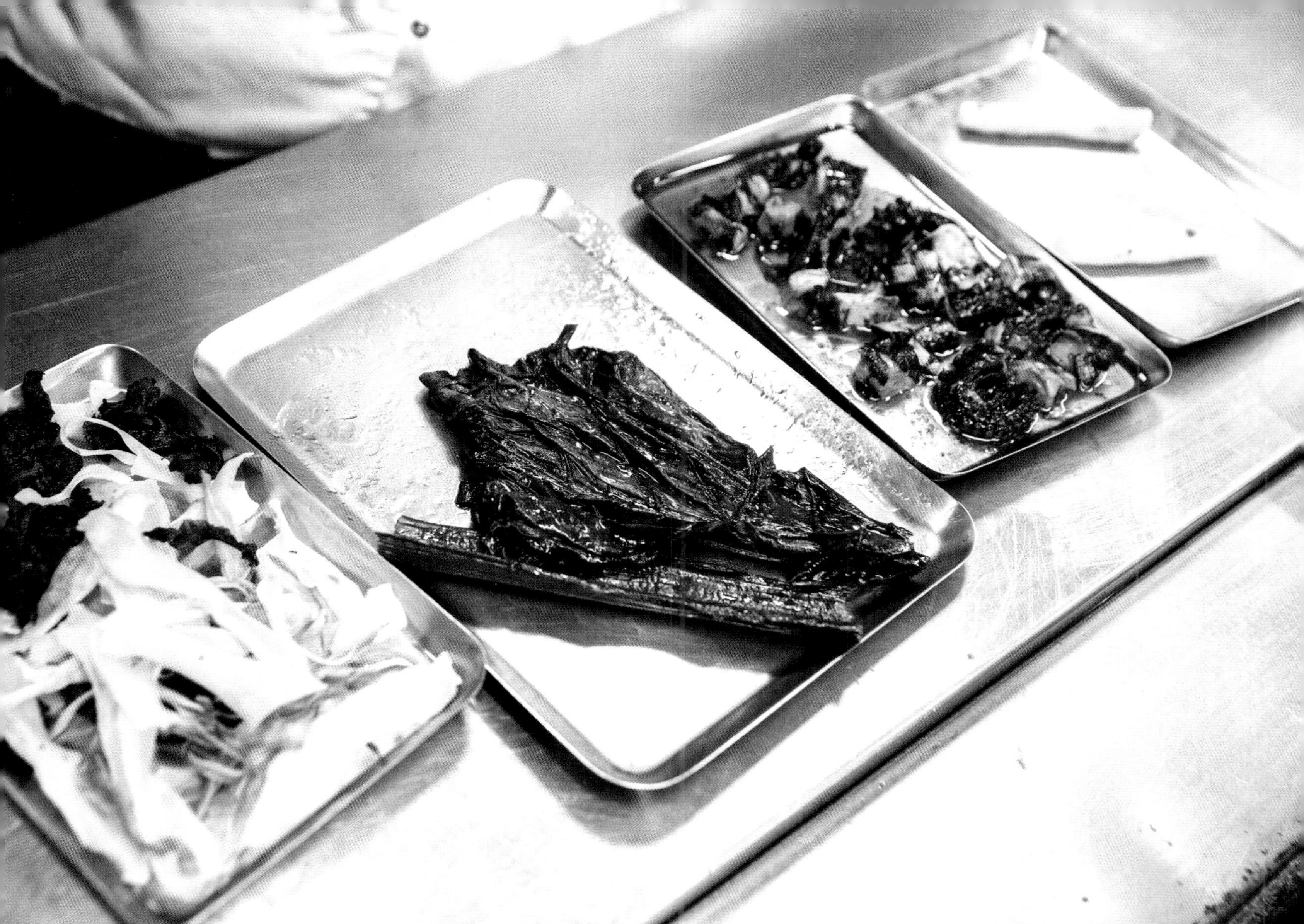

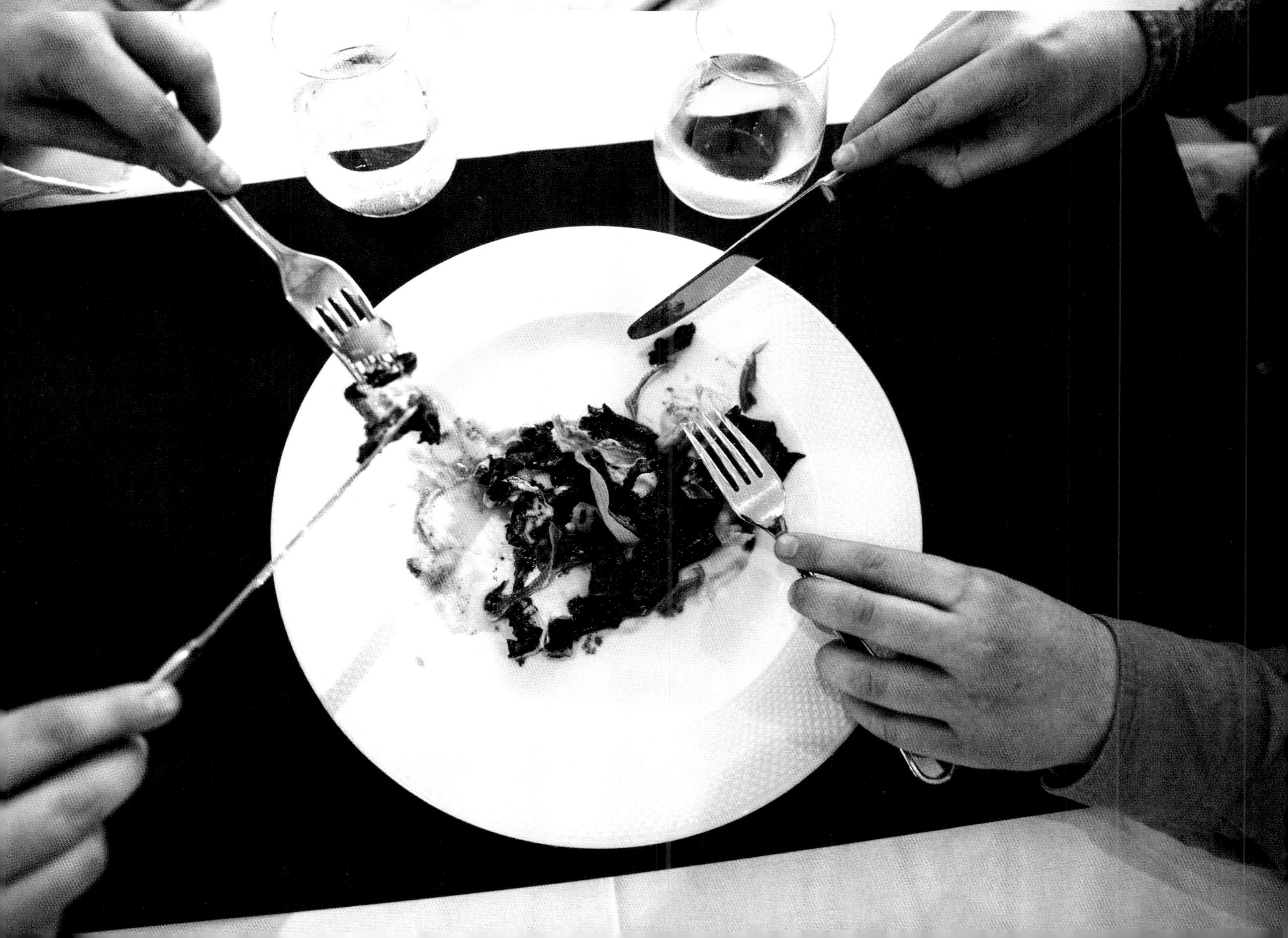

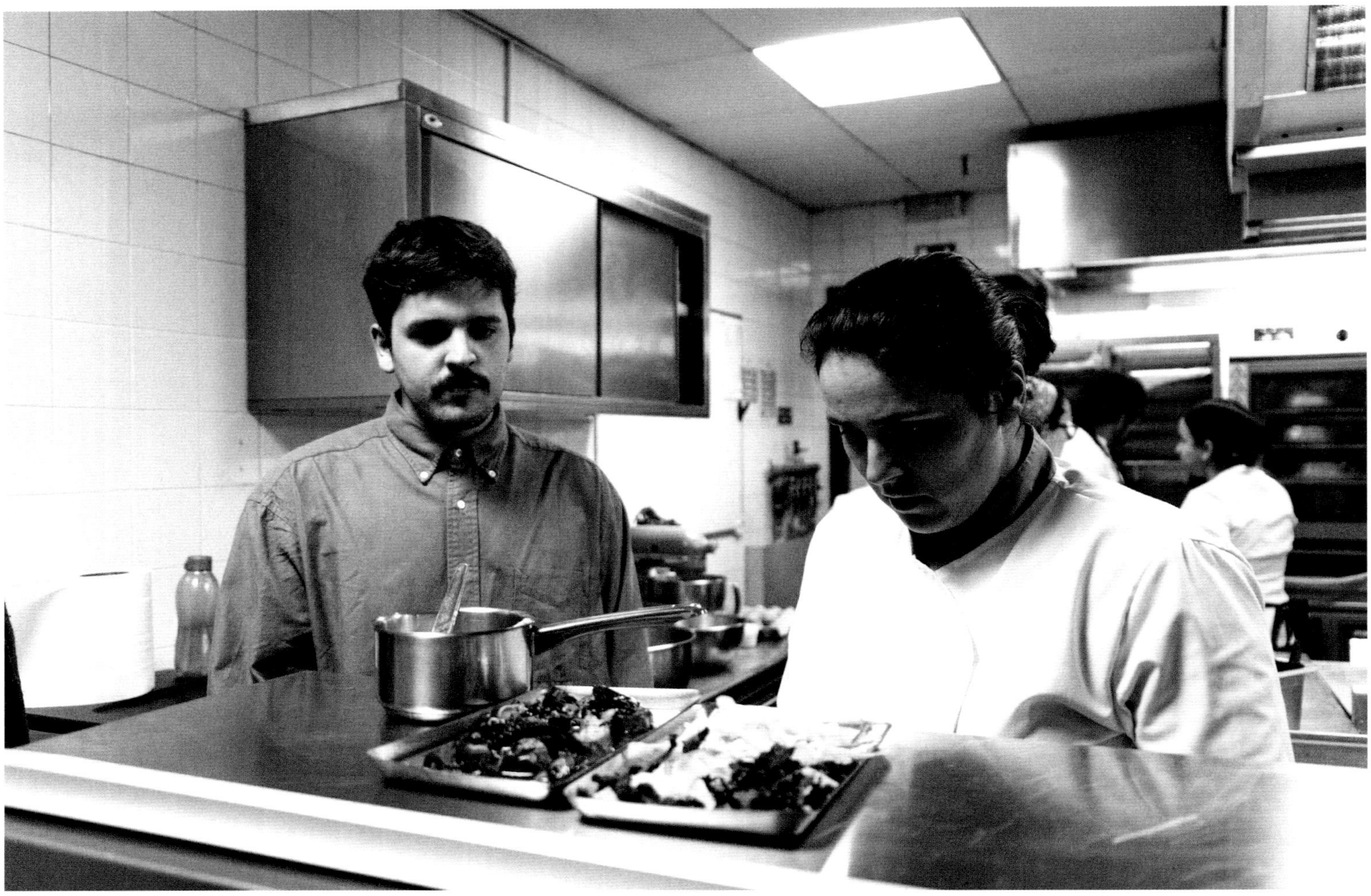

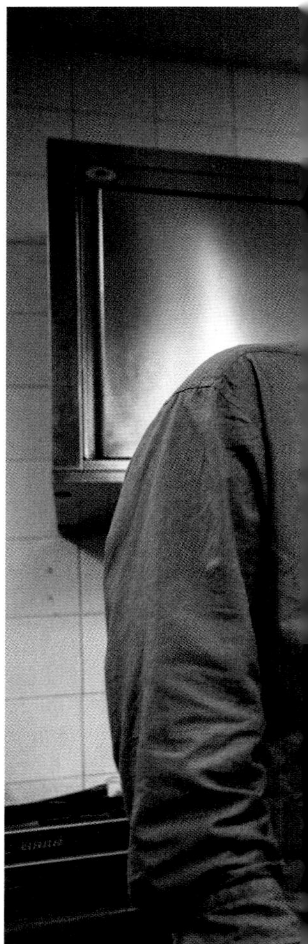

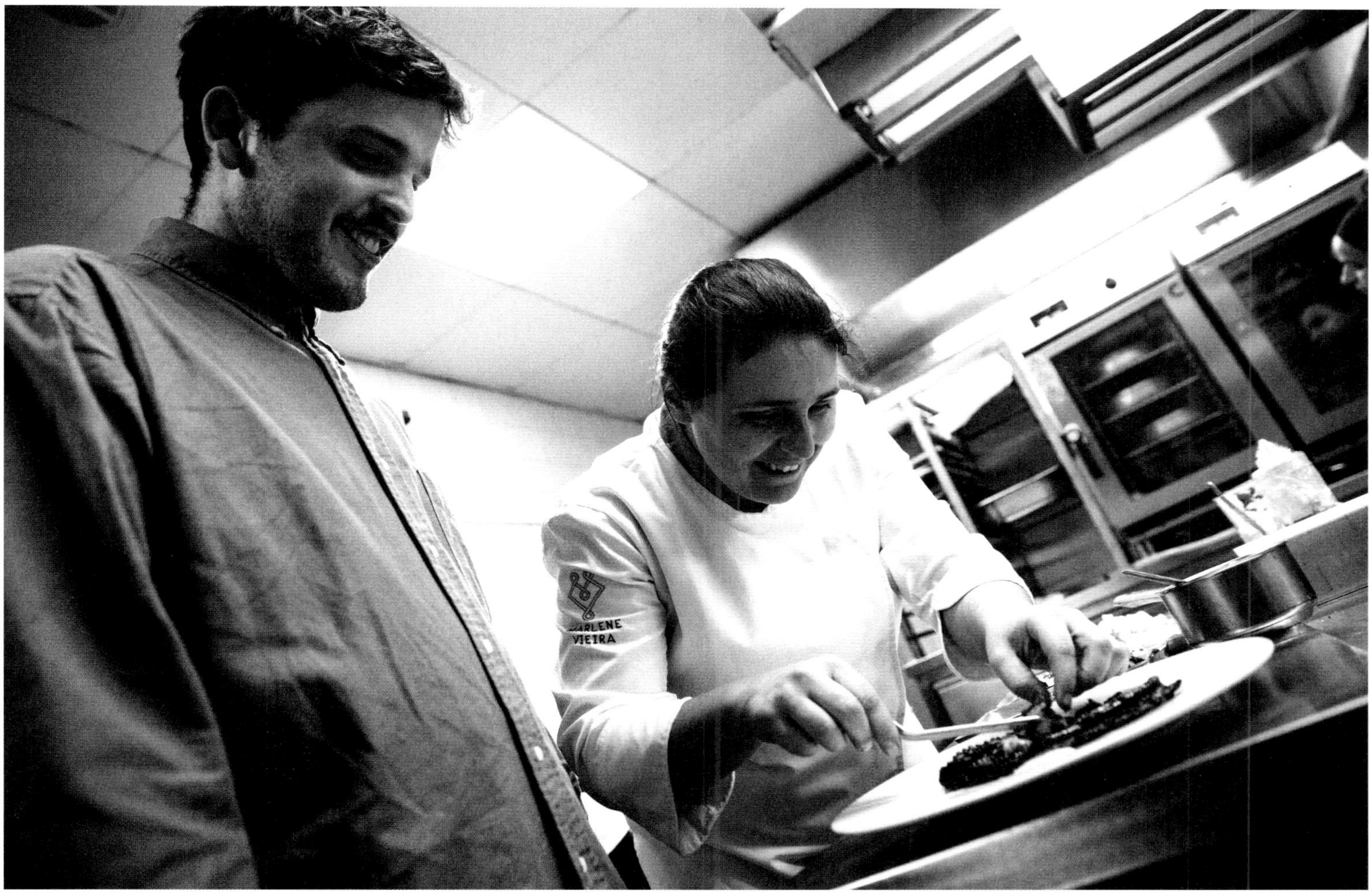
VIEIRA

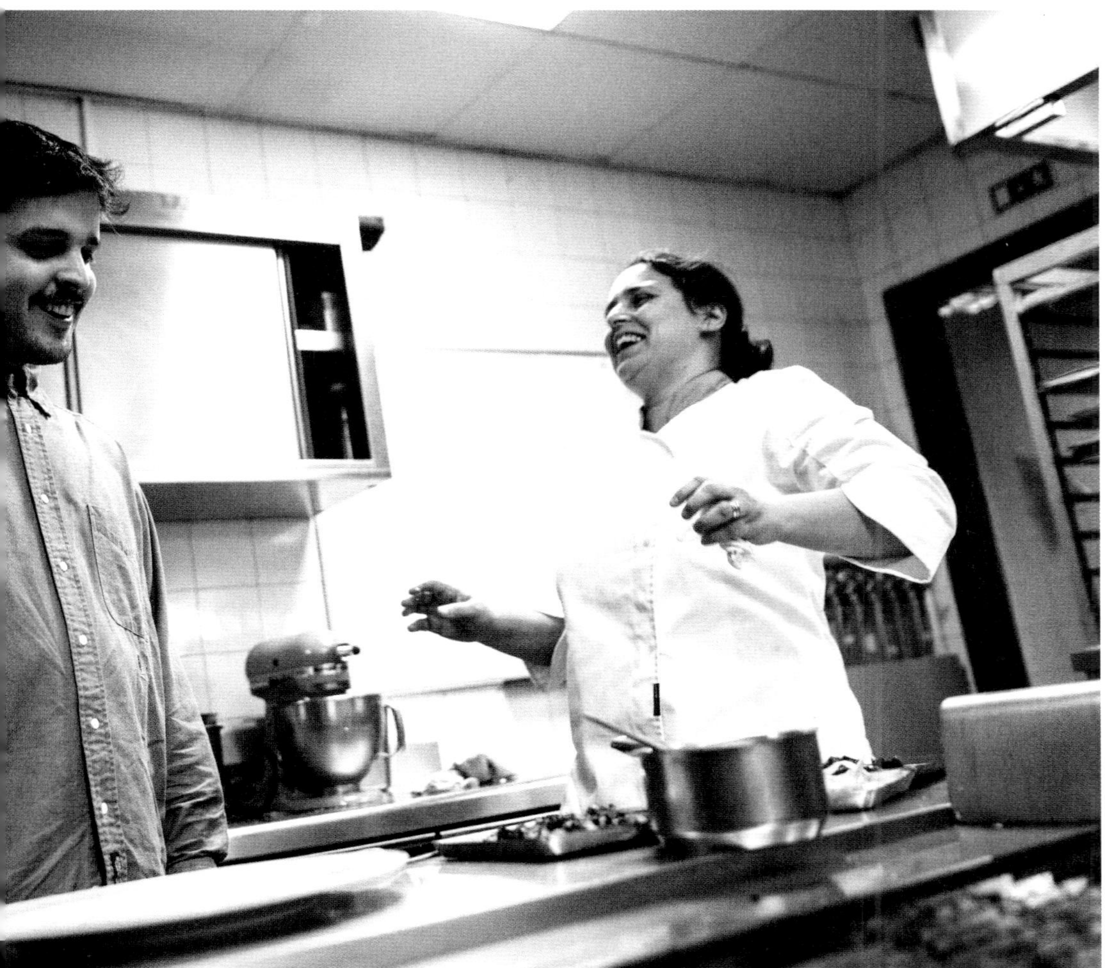

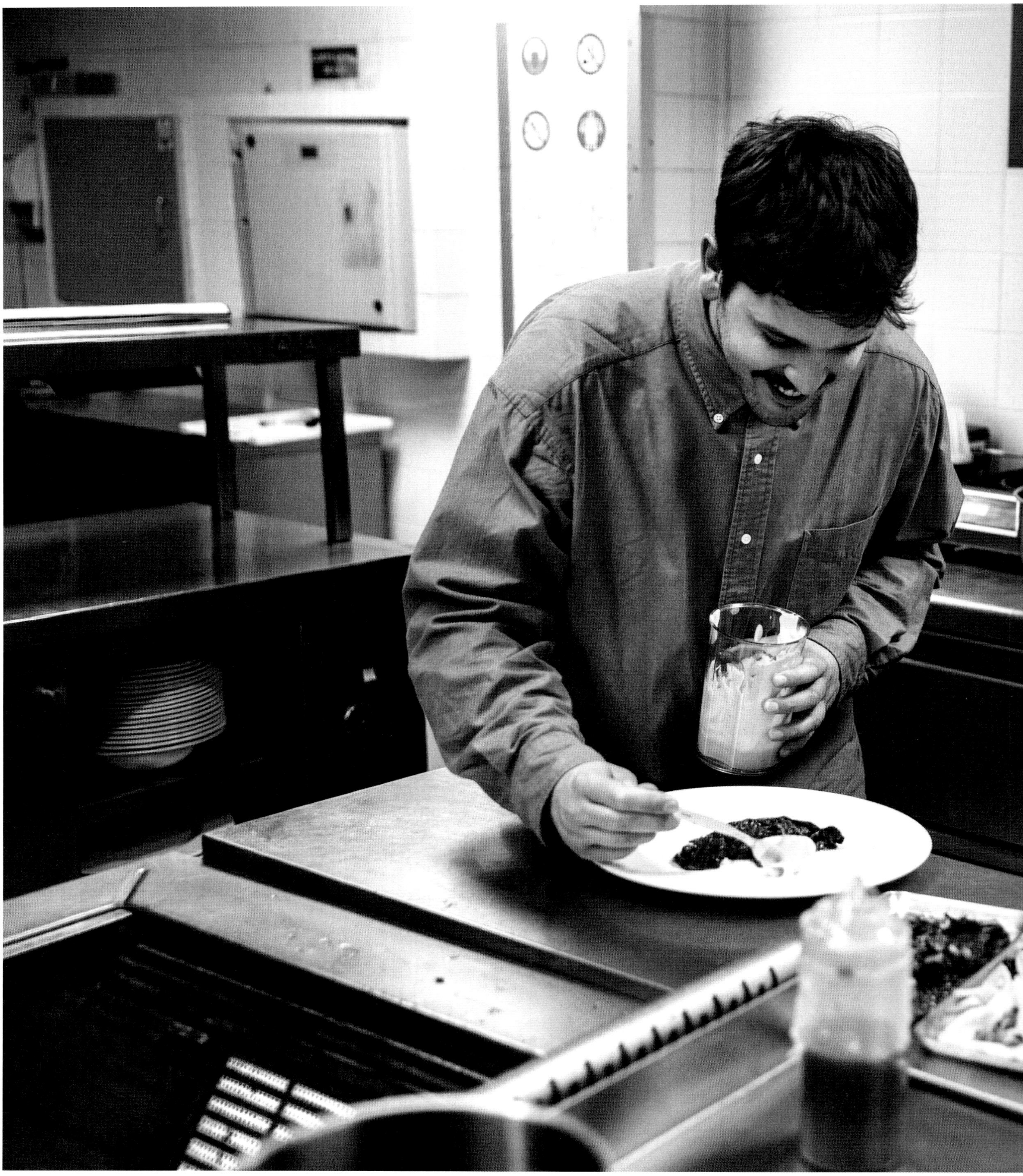

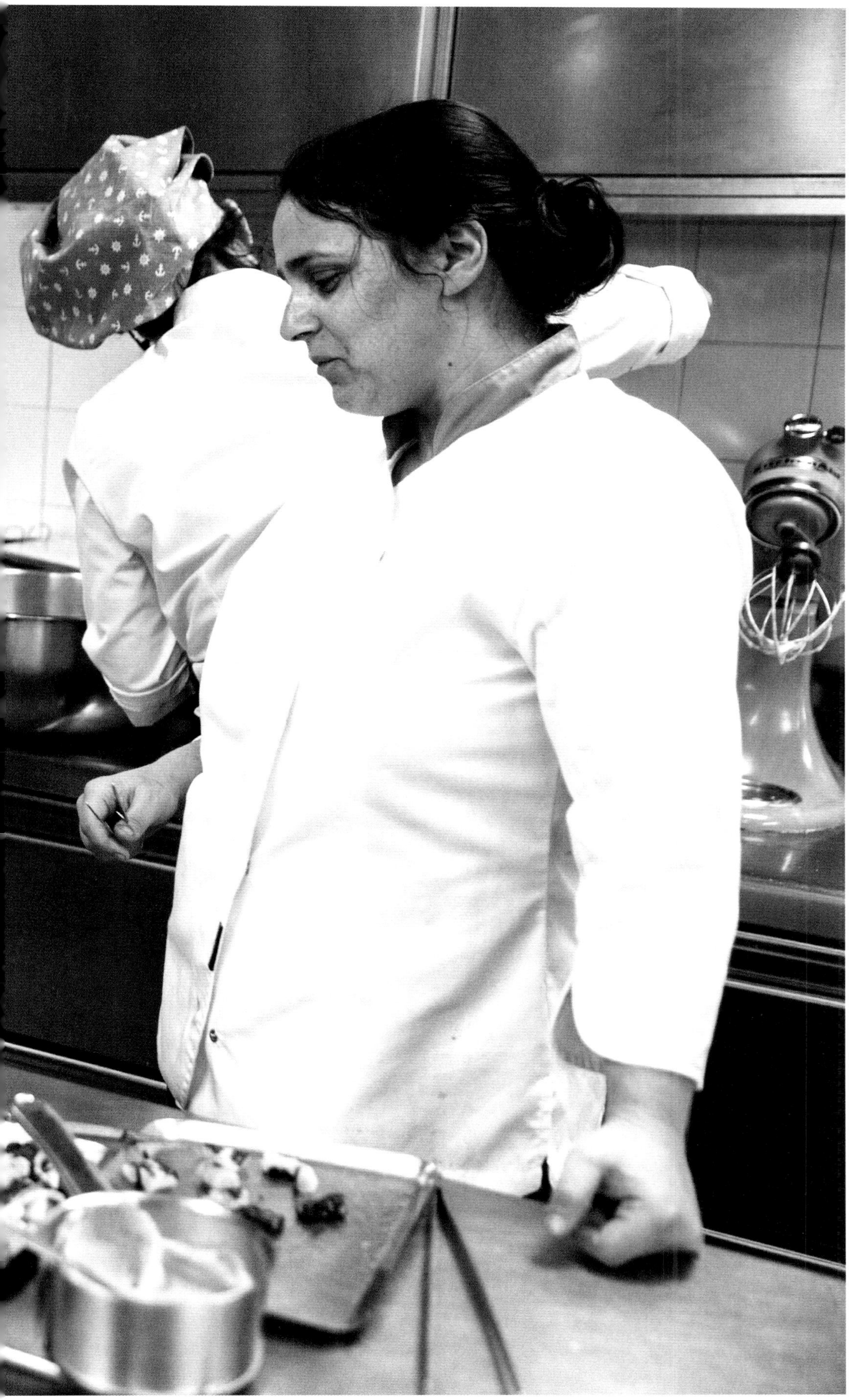

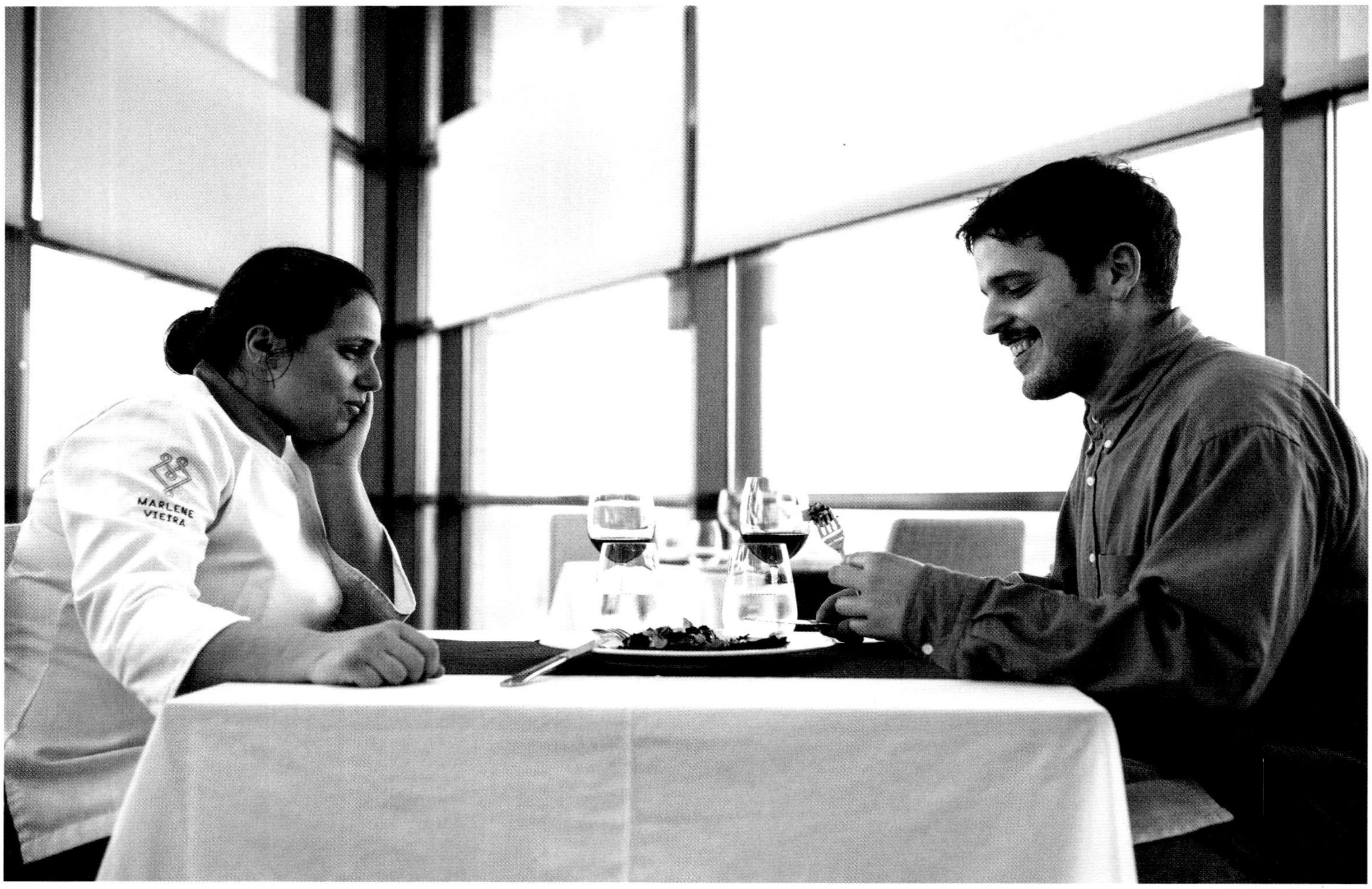
MARLENE
VIEIRA

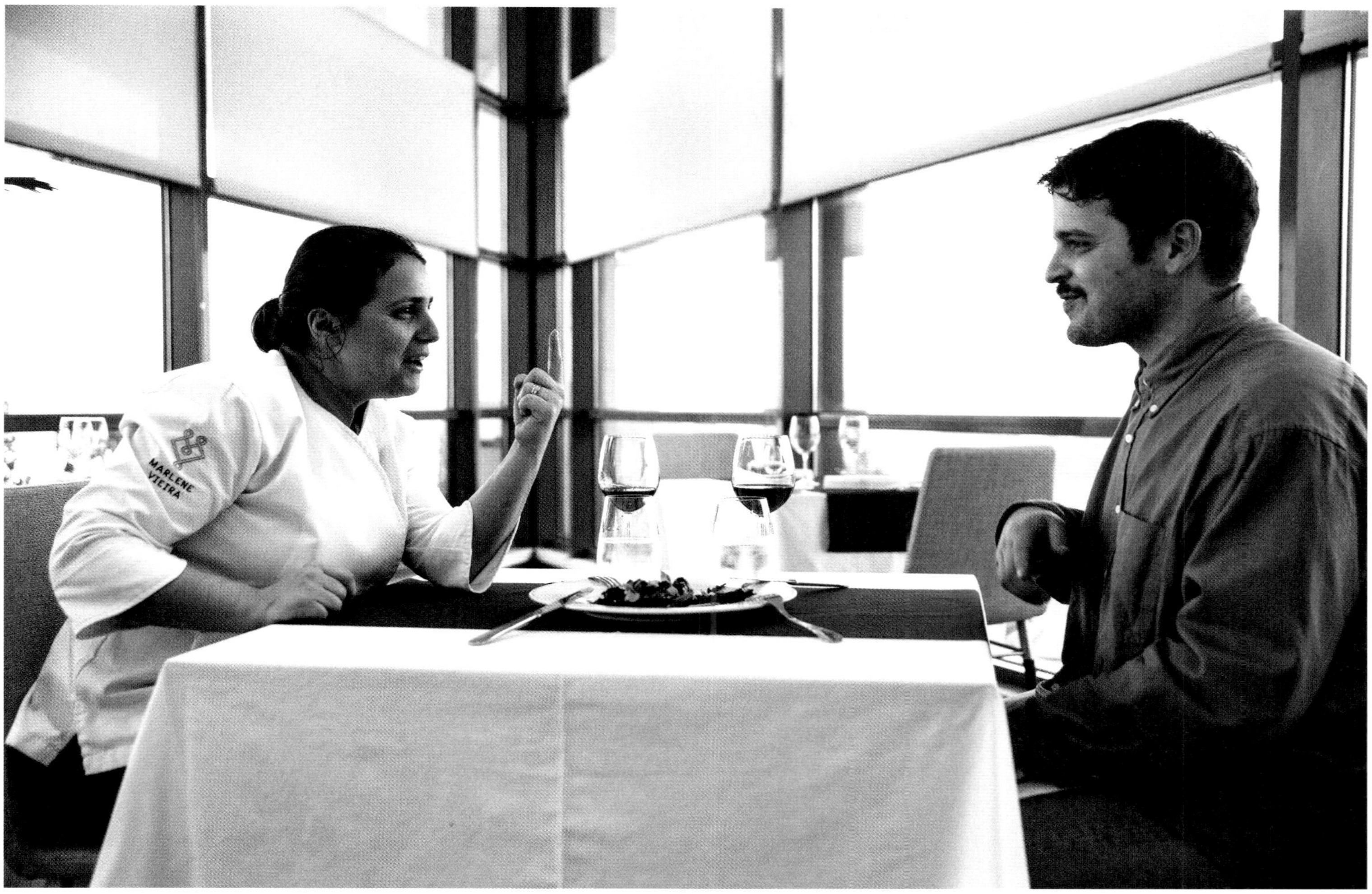
MARLENE
VIEIRA

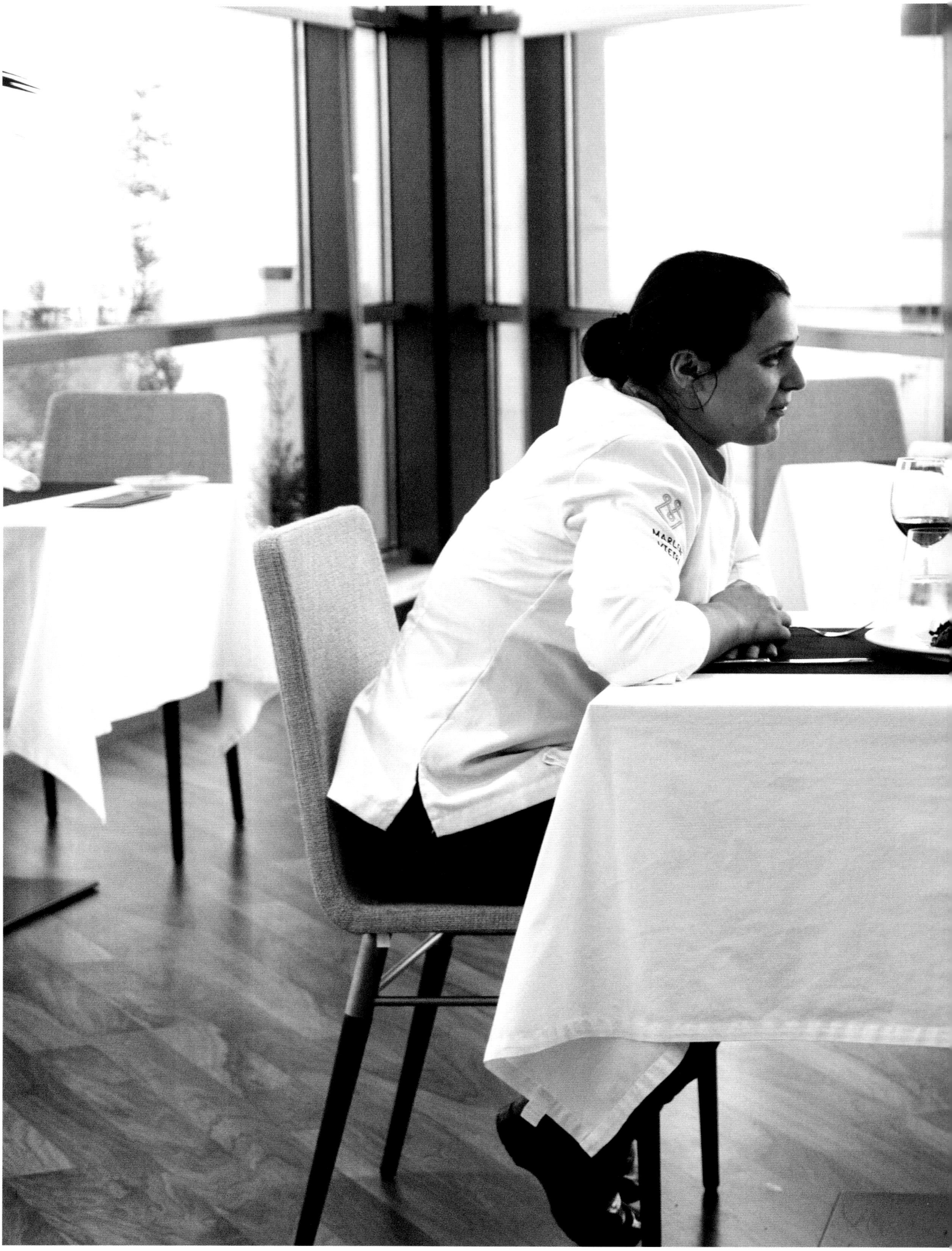

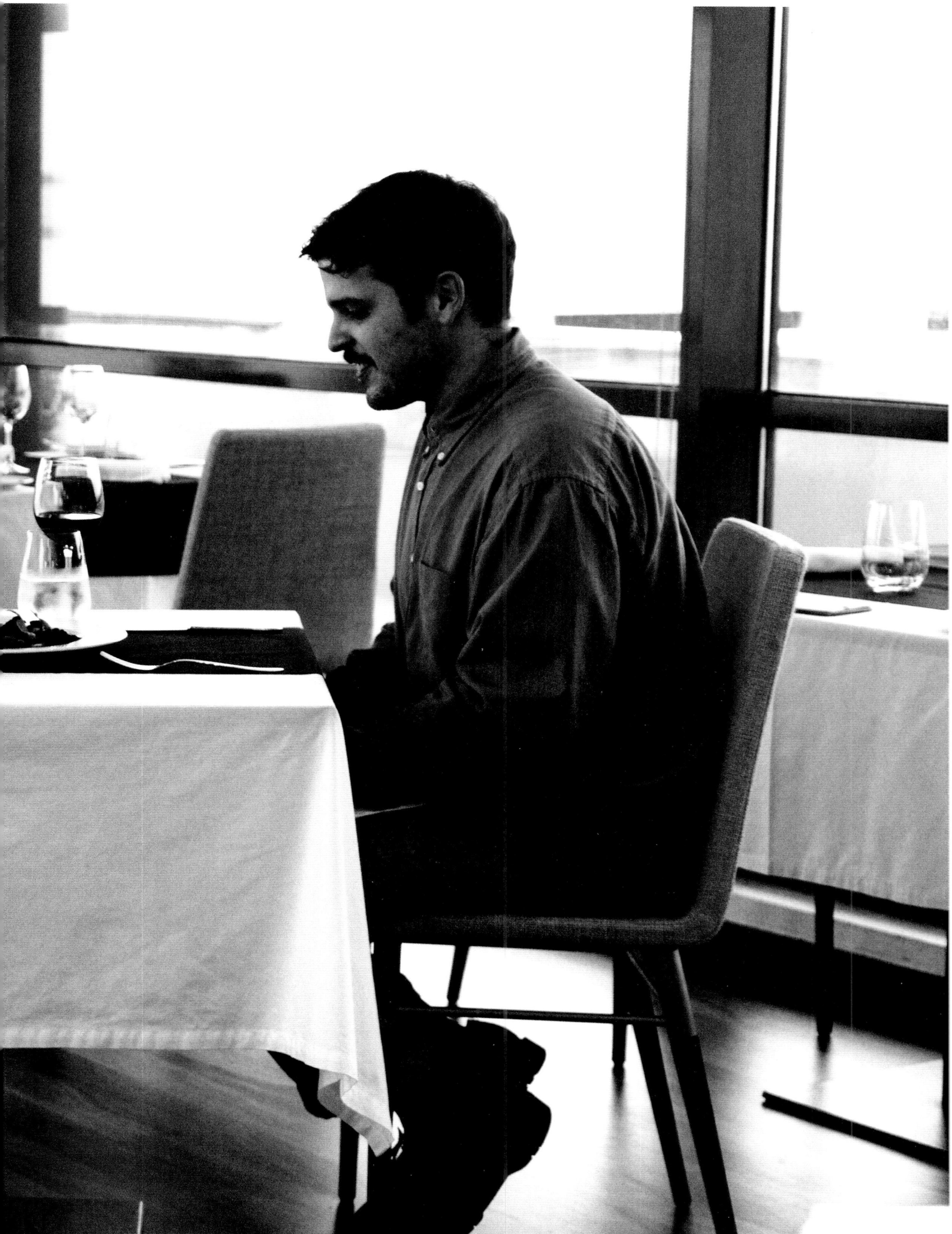

MARLENE VIEIRA

SMOKED OCTOPUS, SALSIFY AND CHARD

OCTOPUS IN OLIVE OIL

BRAND LA GONDOLA

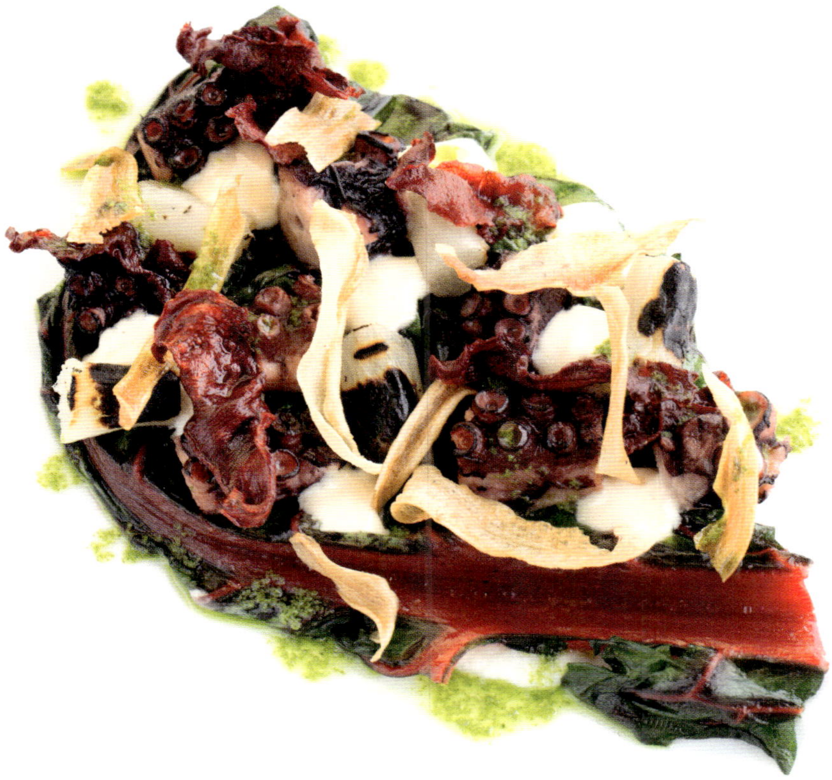

H U

LIKE SARDINES IN A CAN

2018

G O

B R

PLASTER, CLAY, IRON OXIDE, BAMBOO, ROPE AND ELECTRICAL INSULATION TAPE

47 × 30 CM

A Z

Ã O

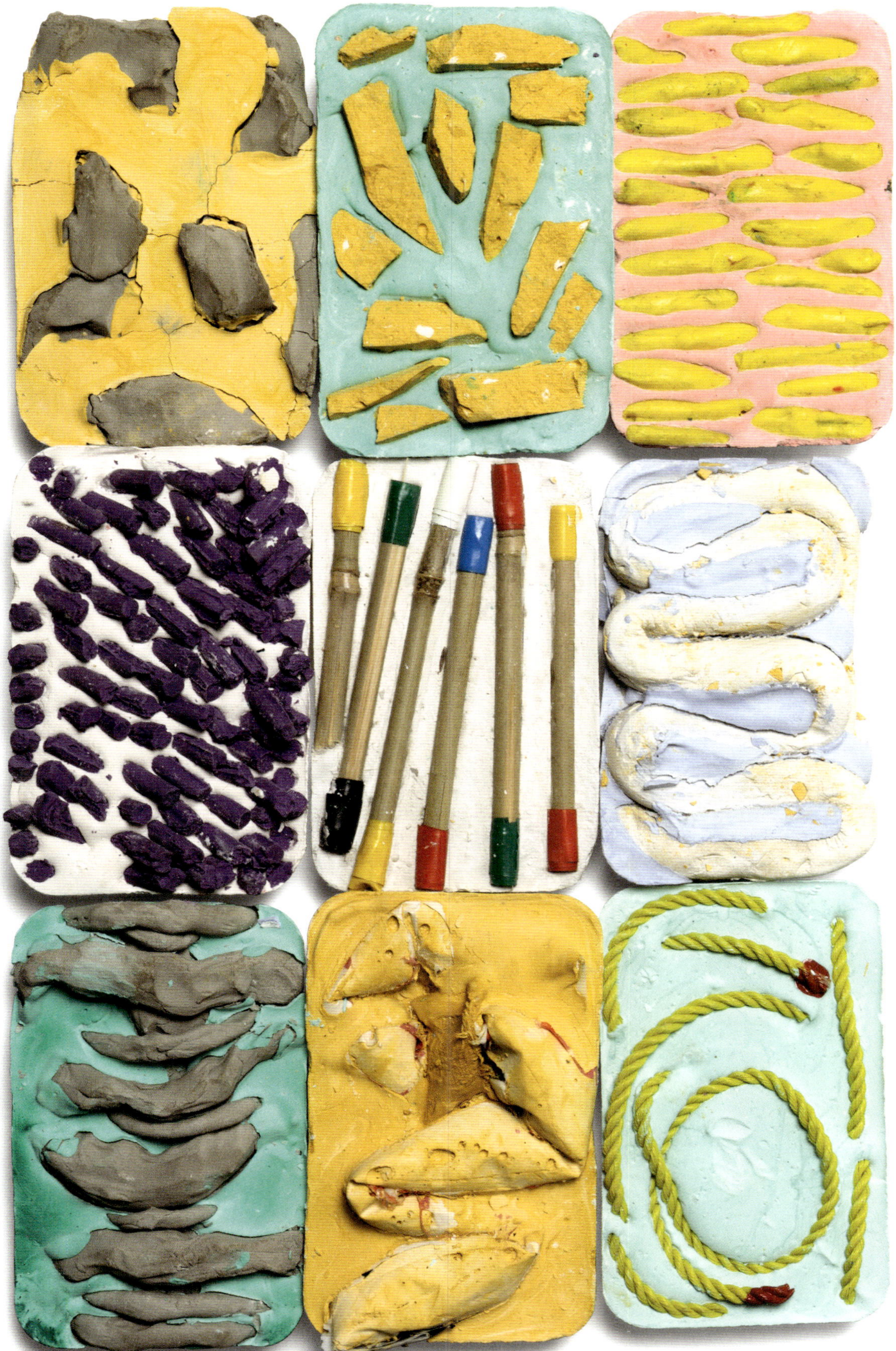

BERTÍLIO GOMES

FÁTIMA MENDONÇA

FÁTIMA
MENDONÇA

BERTÍLIO
GOMES

BERTÍLIO GOMES
FÁTIMA MENDONÇA

MAGNIFICENT TAGUS

Each chef has his or her own particular strength. For some, it's the technique. For others, the serving. And, for others still, the originality or boldness. Chef Bertílio Gomes has it all. But his smile is what first catches the eye of those who meet him. Bertílio cooks with a wide and truthful smile. And that's how he welcomes us to Chapitô, one of the most original spaces in Lisbon – a restaurant amalgamated with a circus arts school.

Smiling, Bertílio hugs the artist Fátima Mendonça and invites her into the kitchen.

The place is tiny, packed with nooks and crannies, stairs and surprises. One dish follows another in a capricious balance and the show goes on, thanks to the talent of those involved.

Fátima likes to cook. But simple things, she says, without any juggling. Bertílio shows us his tools: "This one is to dig vegetables, do you see? I'm a potato surgeon."

"How lovely, how lovely," says Fátima, inventing a description. "This is a kind of potato sushi!"

"Cooking is an interactive art, one that's always starting over," says Bertílio.

"The other art is the same," replies Fátima. "We make, we undo, we invent and we reinvent. It's a complex game."

The artists get along easily and ask for a white surface on which to play. But are we going to make art or cook? And is there any difference?

Potatoes, mackerel, *béarnaise* sauce... and this? It's a sauce. Do we eat the yellow part? The yellow, yes, and the green and the red, too. The chef has paintbrushes, Fátima paints with her fingers.

The work is finished and is photographed. We go up to the dining room to have lunch at the invitation of our chef and, suddenly, we stop, perplexed. Was that thunder? Everything trembled!

We watch two or three bolts of lightning as the magnificent Tagus remains unconcerned. "I'm scared," says Fátima. "But this is beautiful."

"Cuisine is an act of seduction," begins Bertílio as the octopus in coconut curry and lime juice blinks at us and embraces us with eight legs. "I started cooking when I was in the Scouts. At the end of the day, I would make a big pan of sweet rice. I never felt so satisfied..."

Fátima scribbles and shows us her drawings. The wine goes down drop by drop, like the rain on a parched Lisbon.

"I had to learn a lot about cooking," says Bertílio. "And me about art," says Fátima. "Now we must forget everything and write our own books."

It's warm and cold at the same time as, through the windows, the world drains like liquid. Friendship reveals itself on an afternoon in March with a river view.

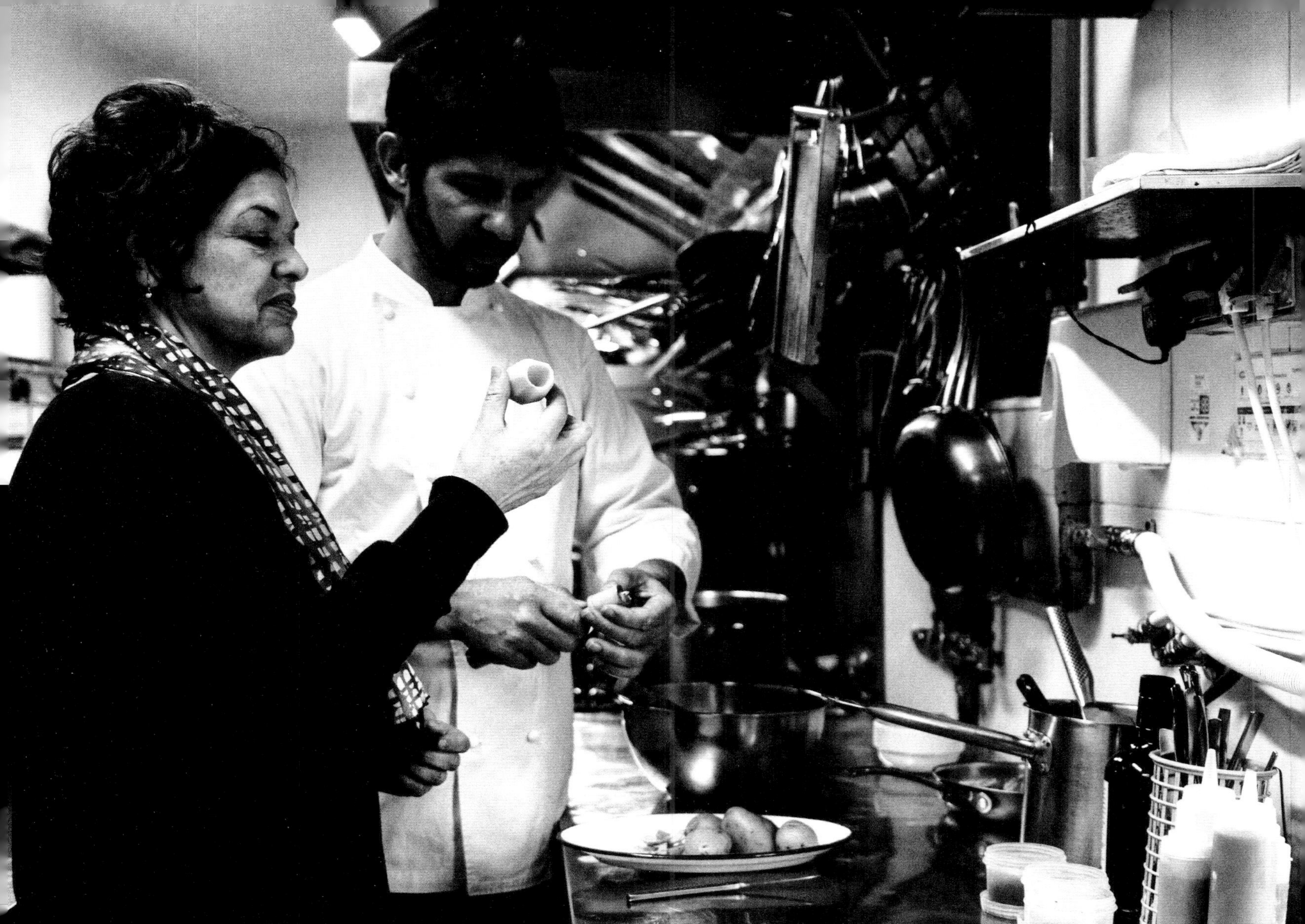

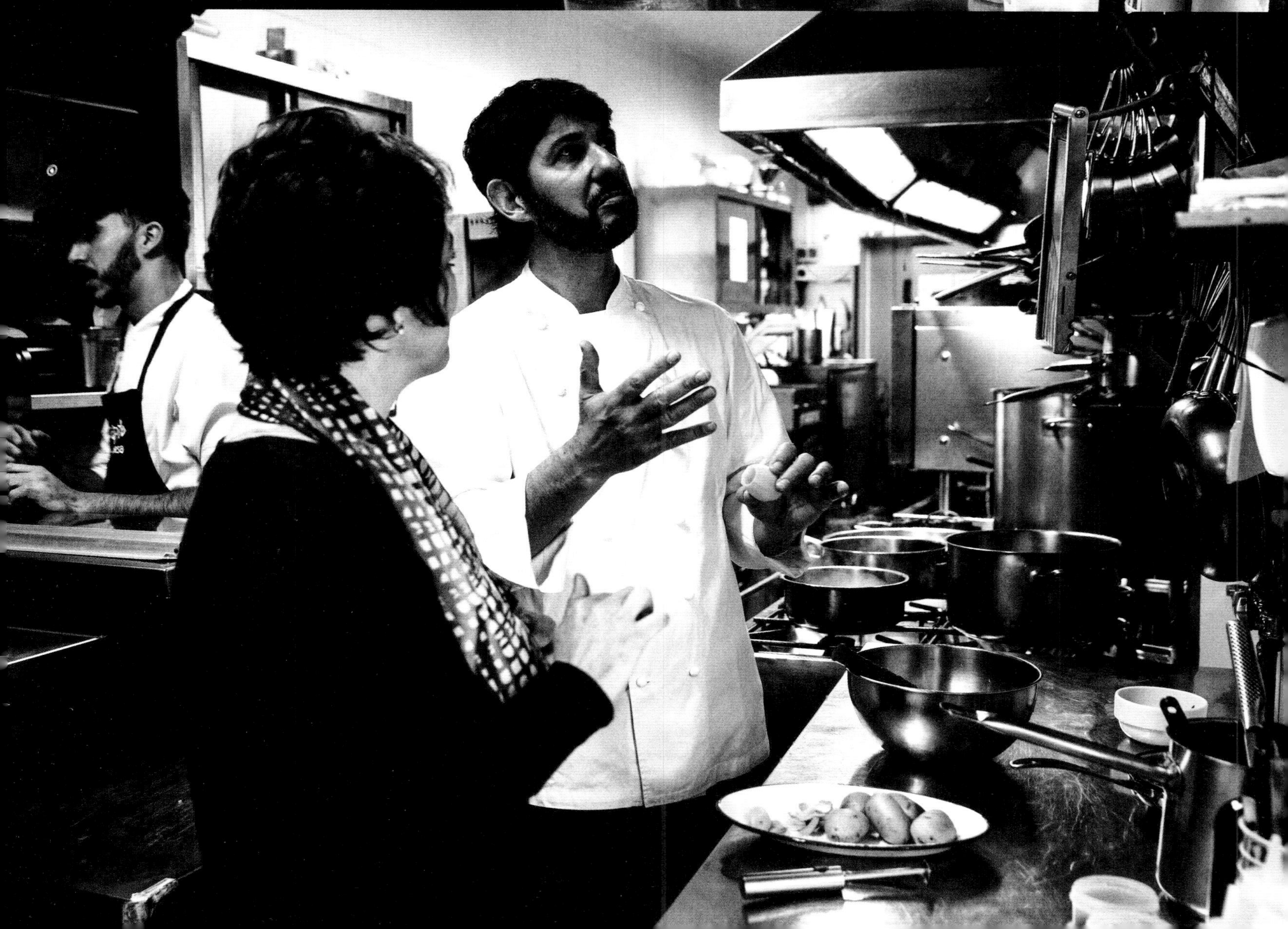

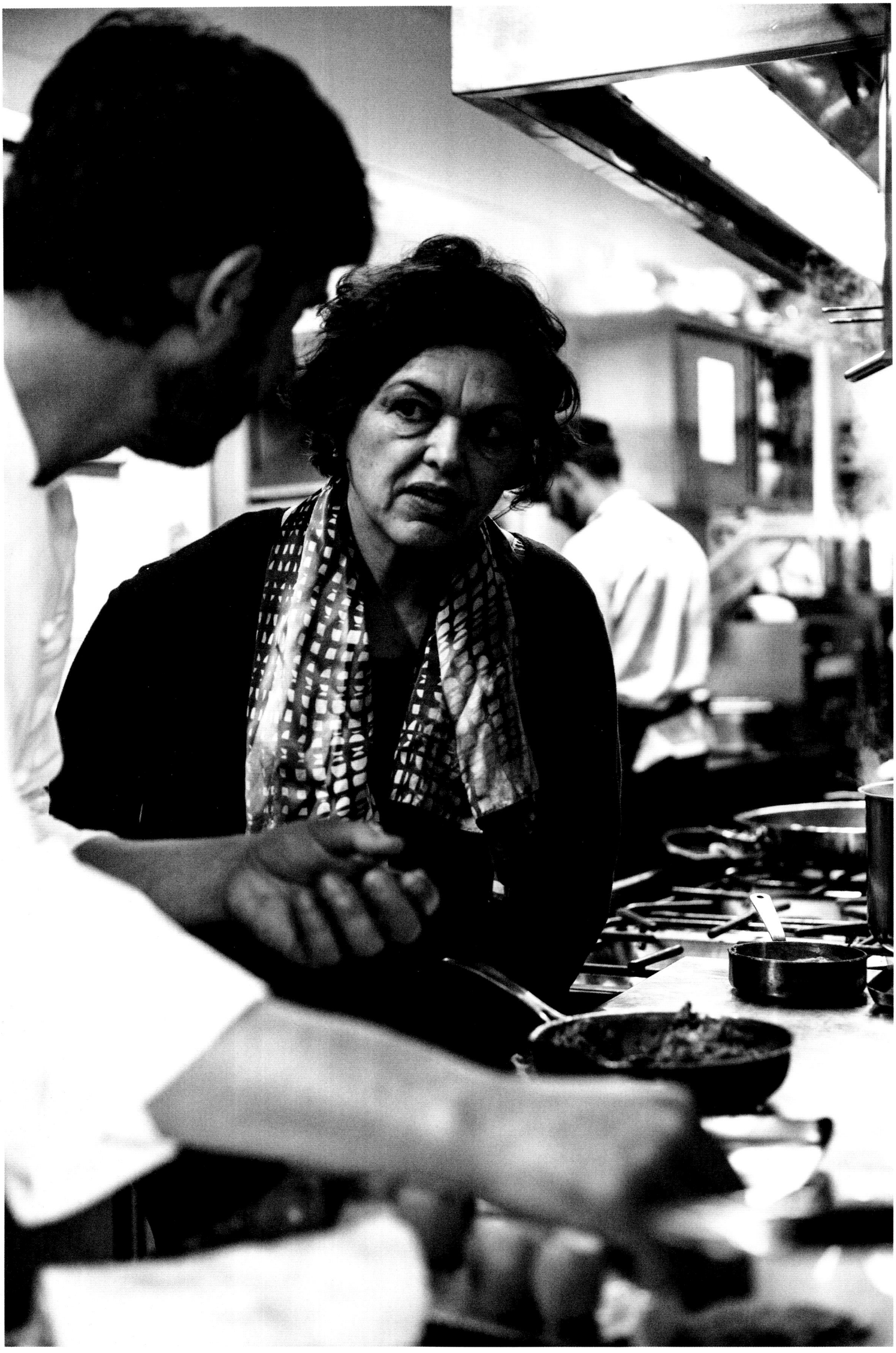

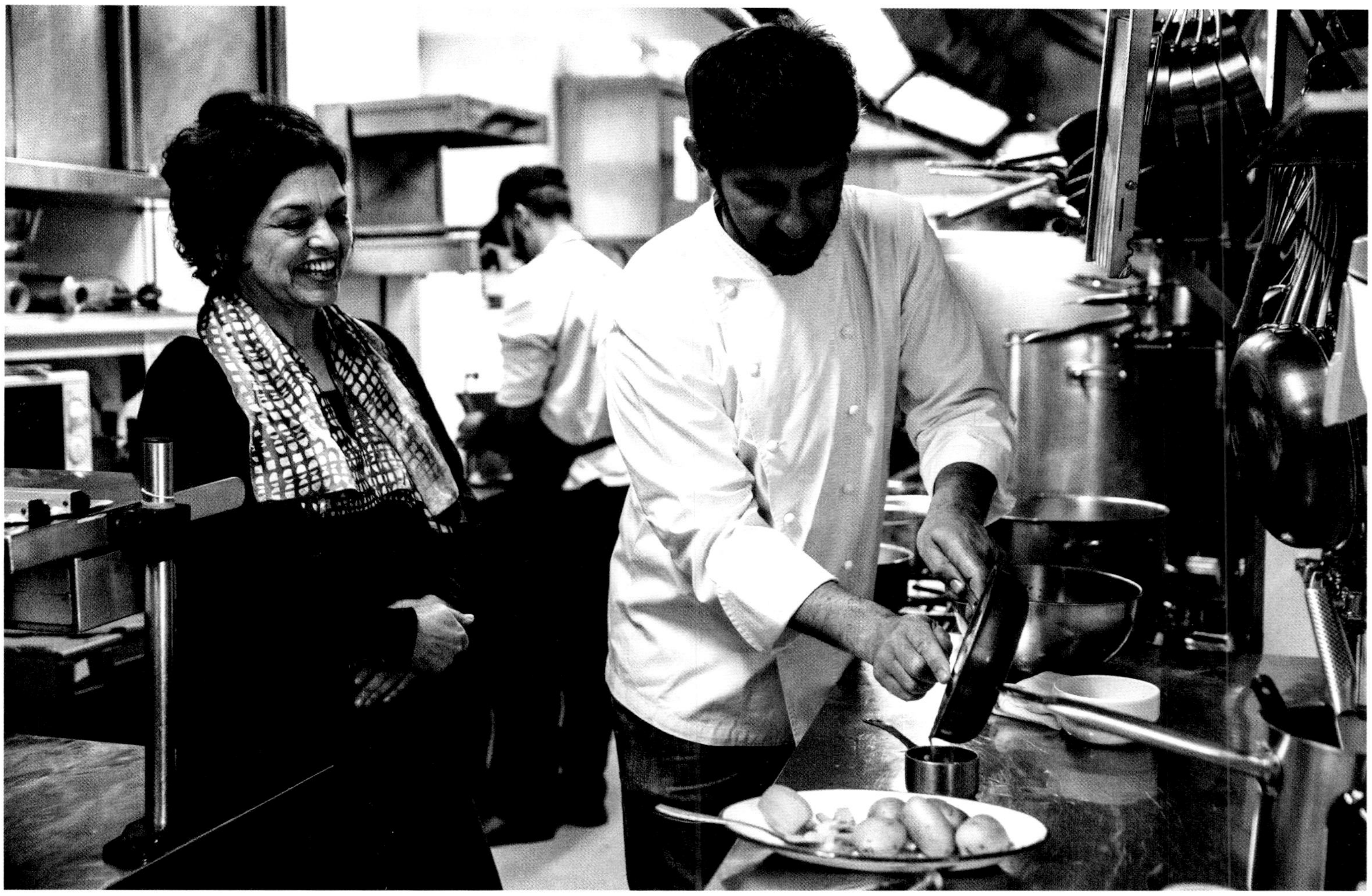

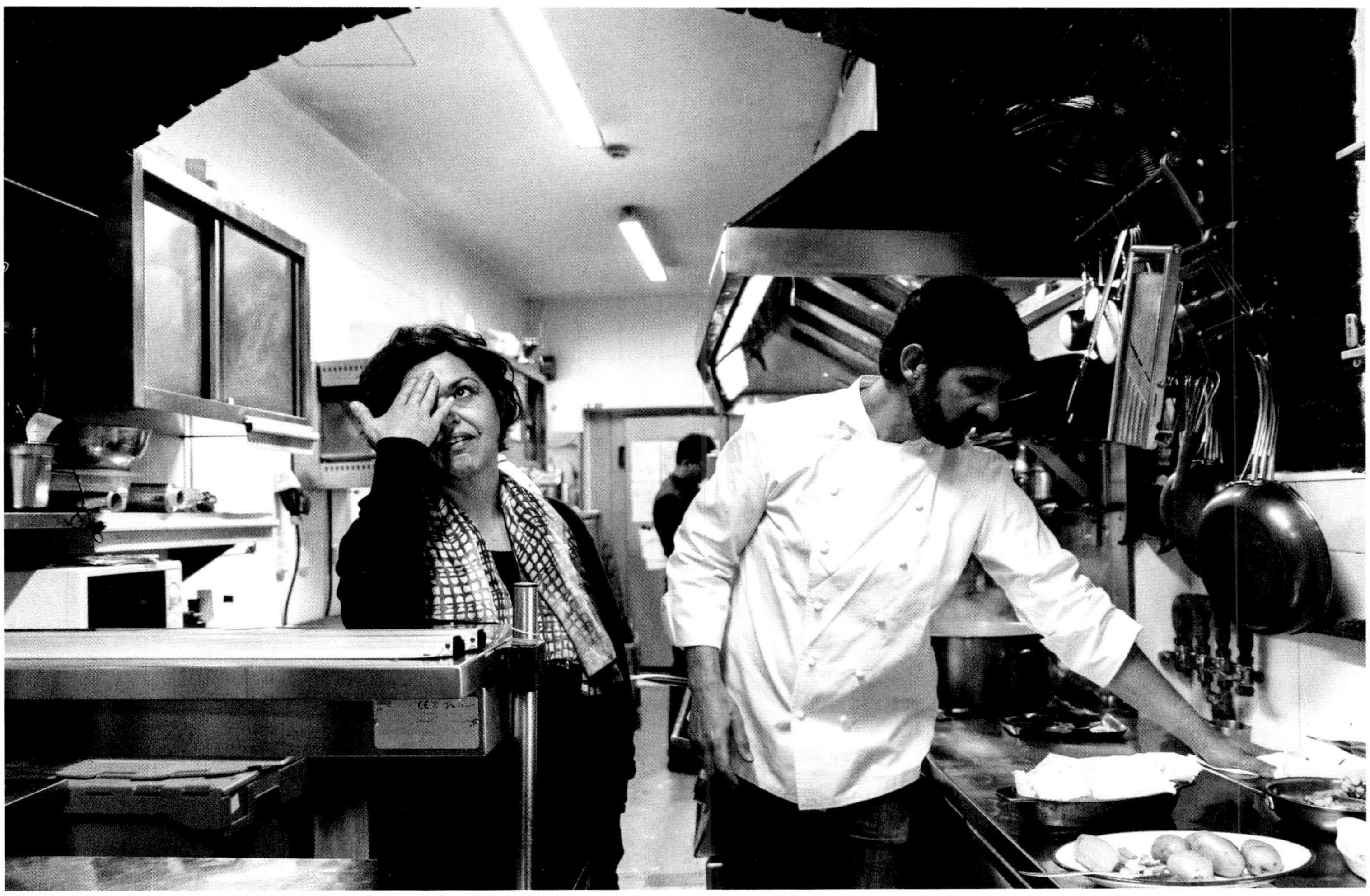

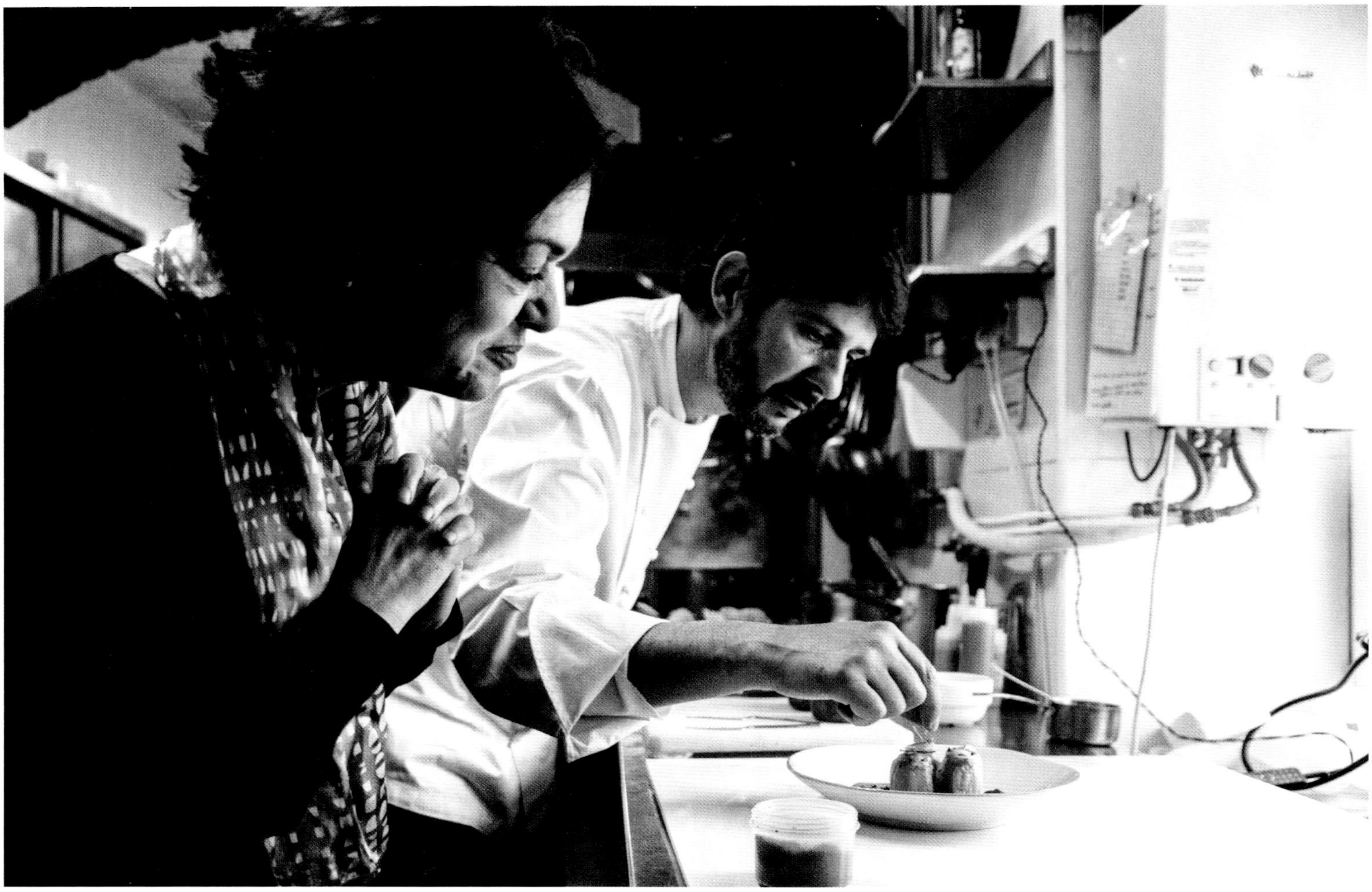

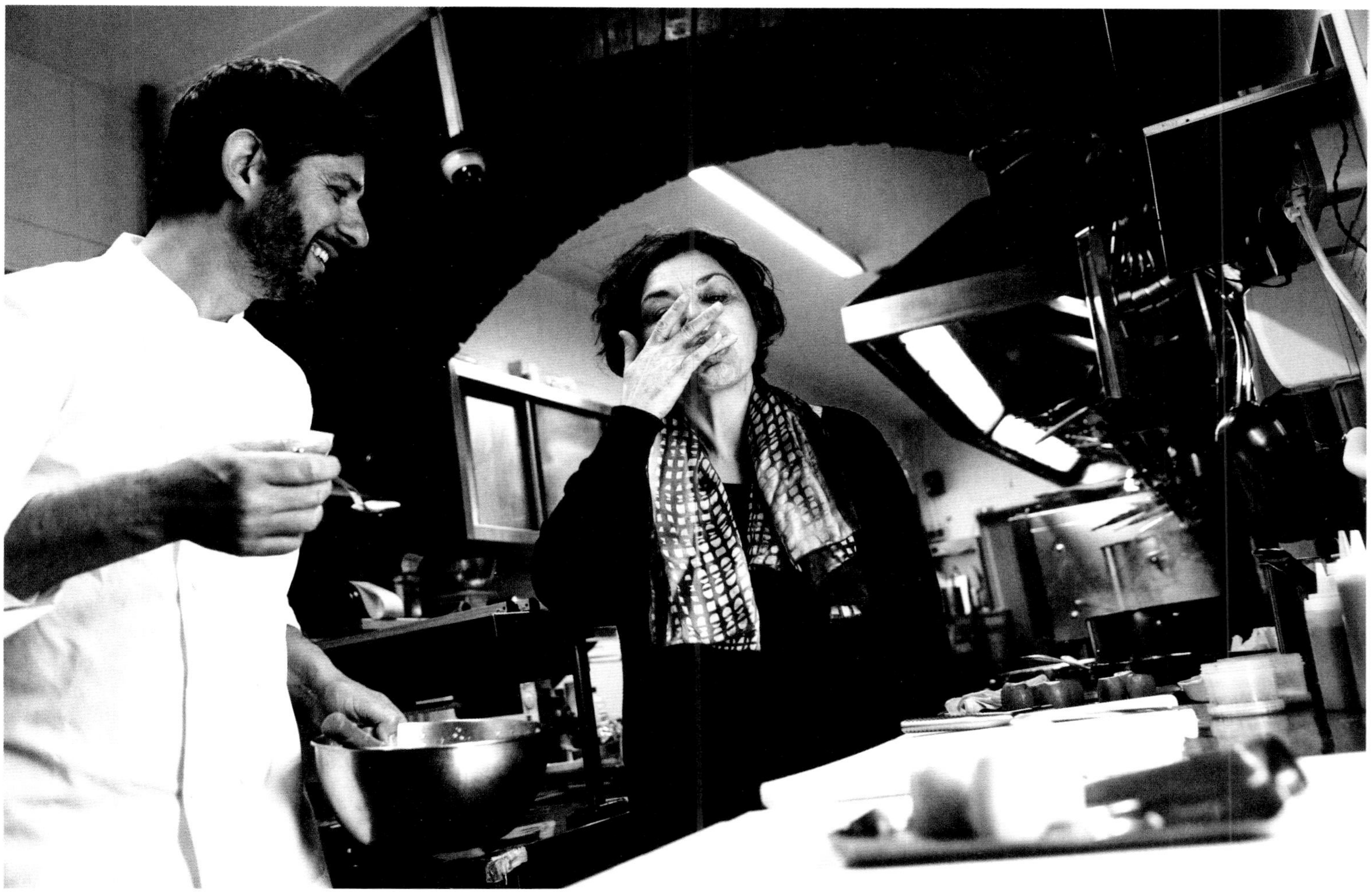

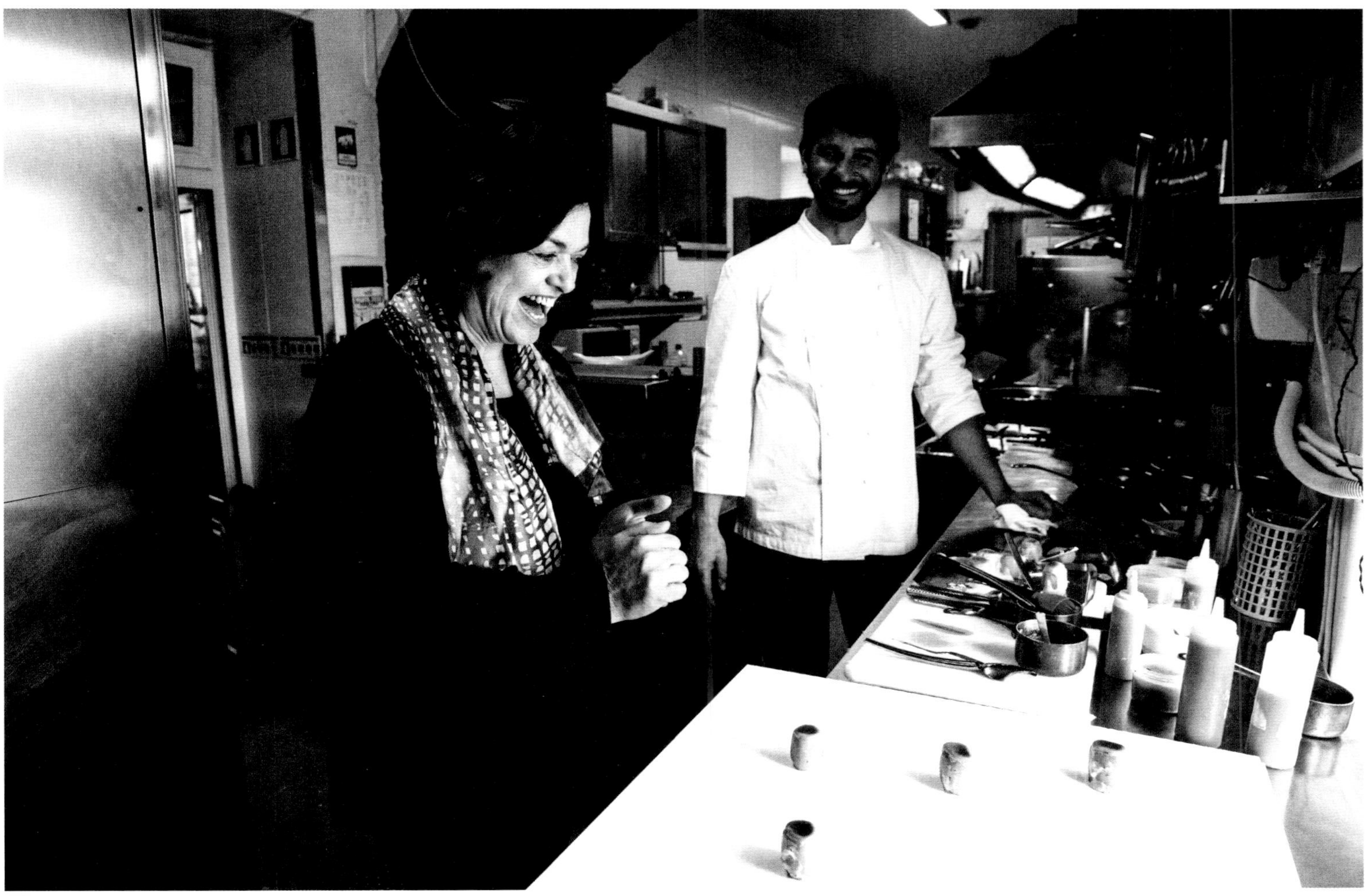

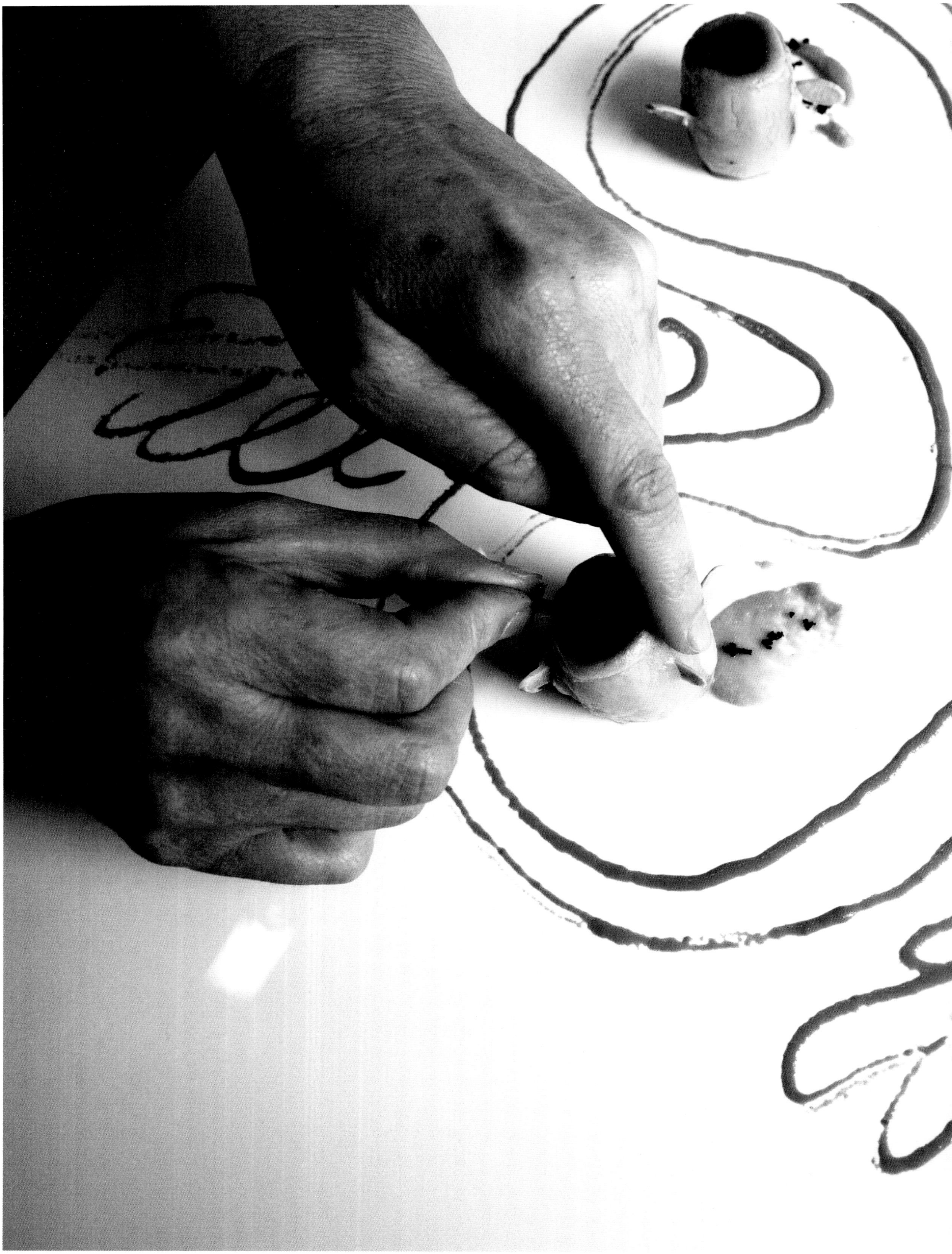

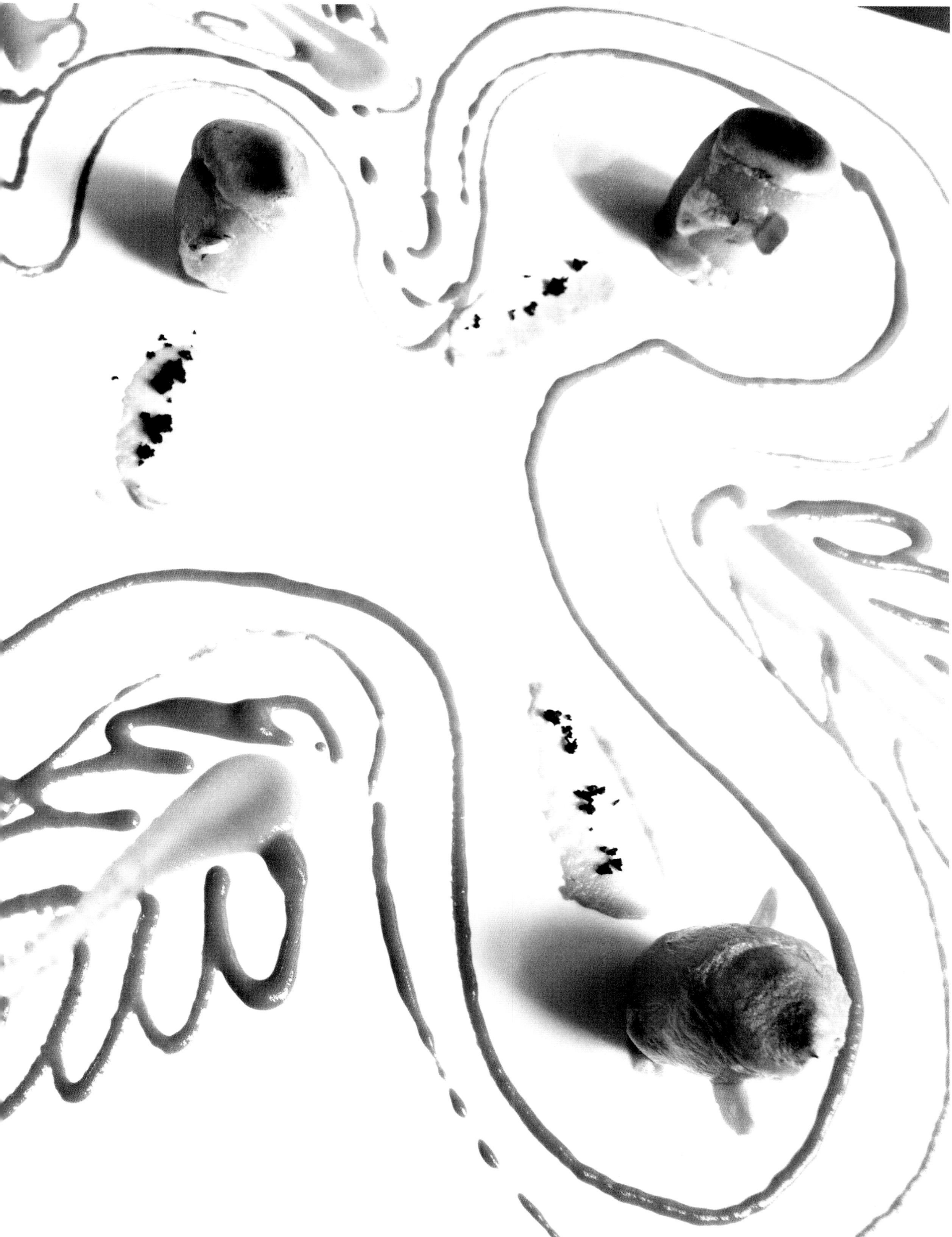

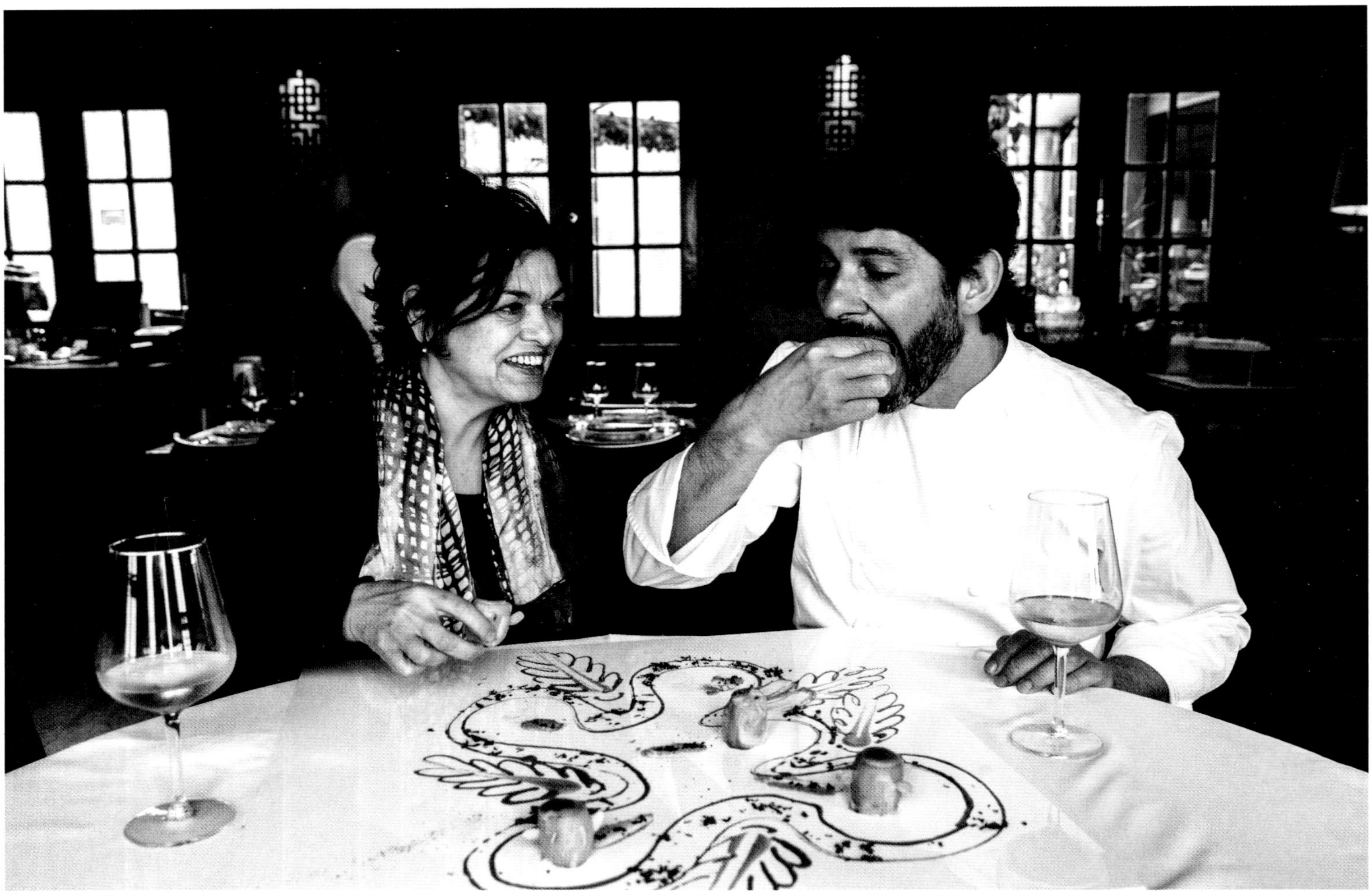

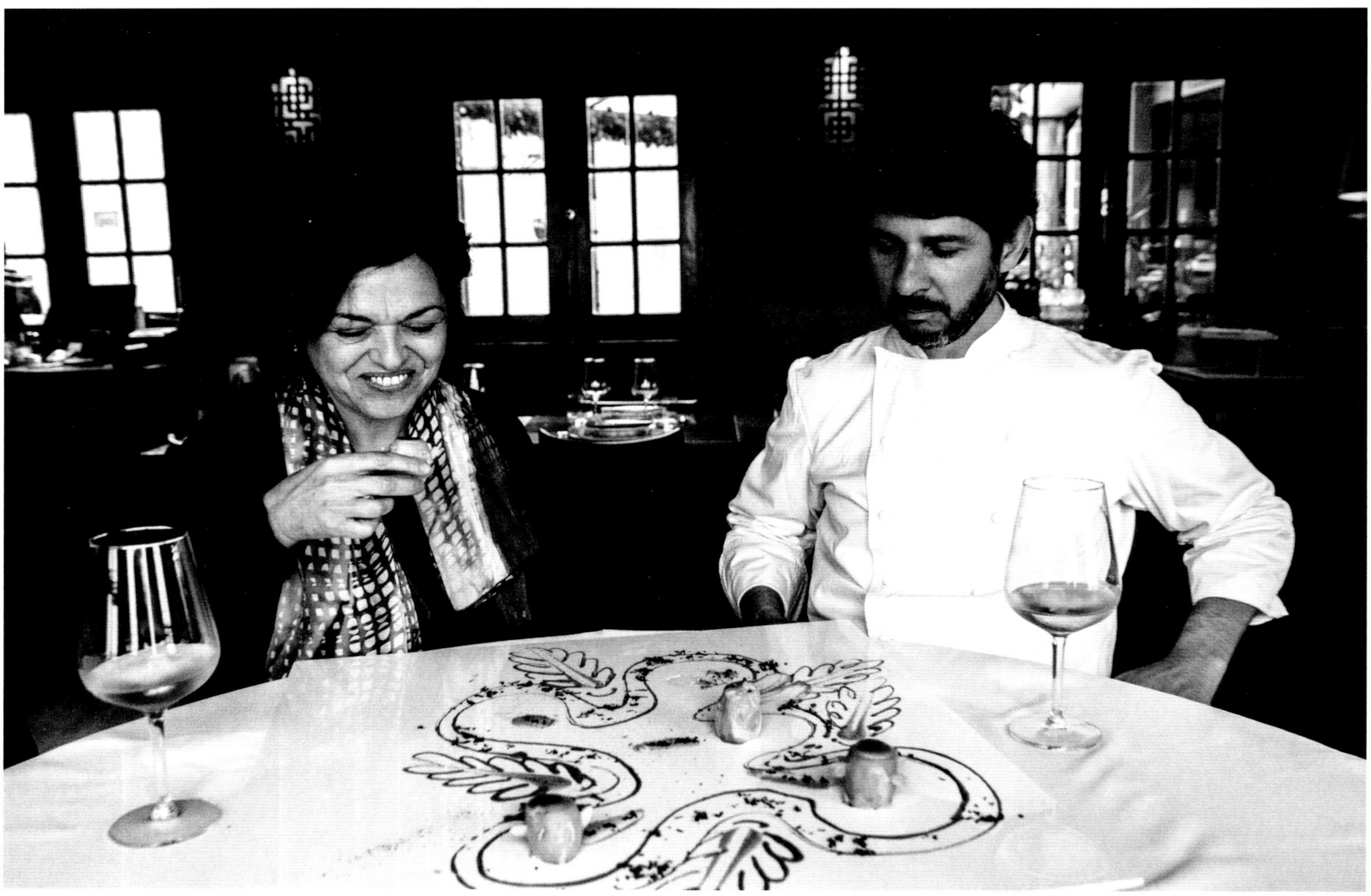

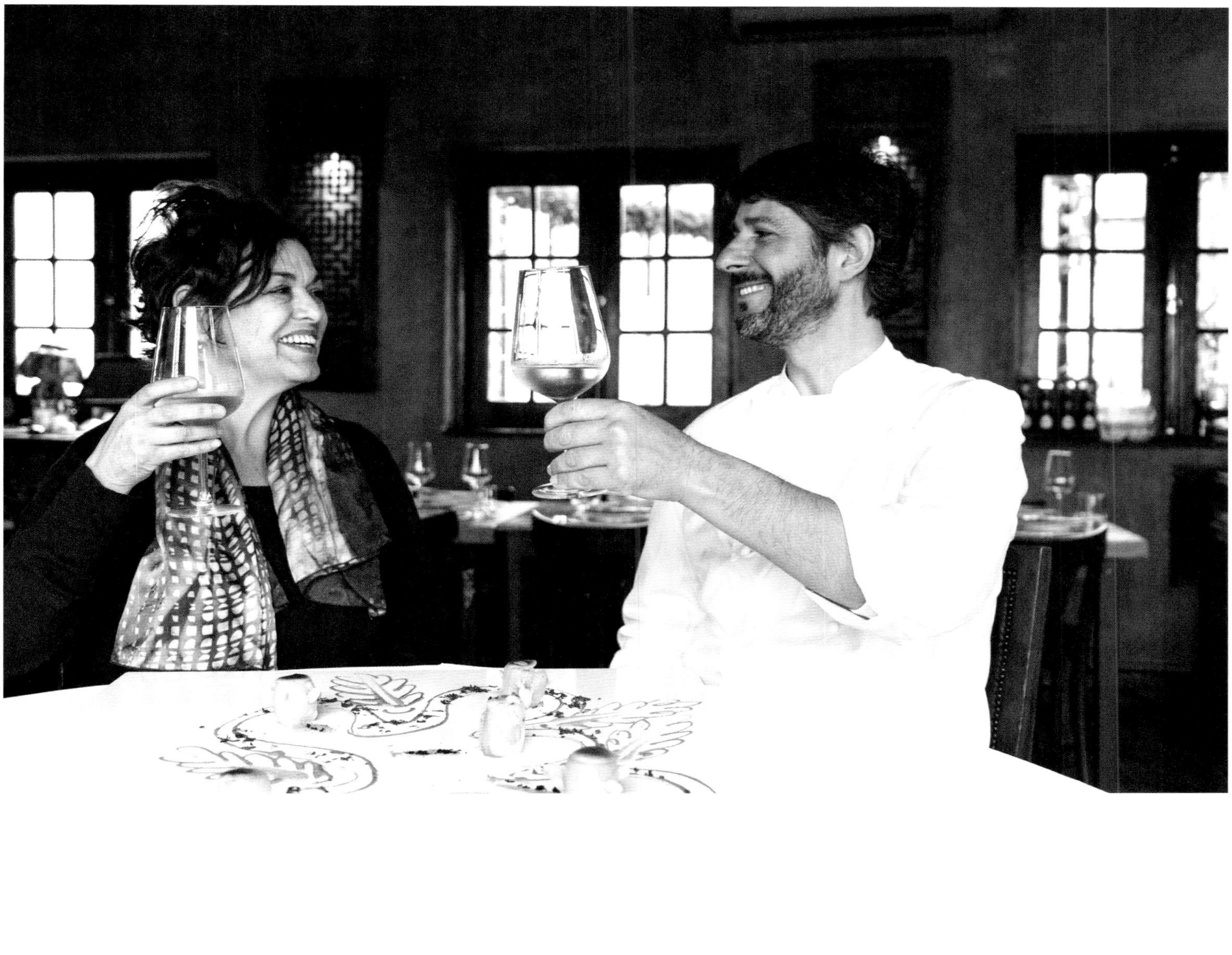

BERTÍLIO GOMES

MACKEREL WITH ONIONS, CANDIED POTATOES AND CREAM OF TOMATOES AND PEPPERS

MACKEREL FILLETS IN OLIVE OIL

BRAND VASCO DA GAMA

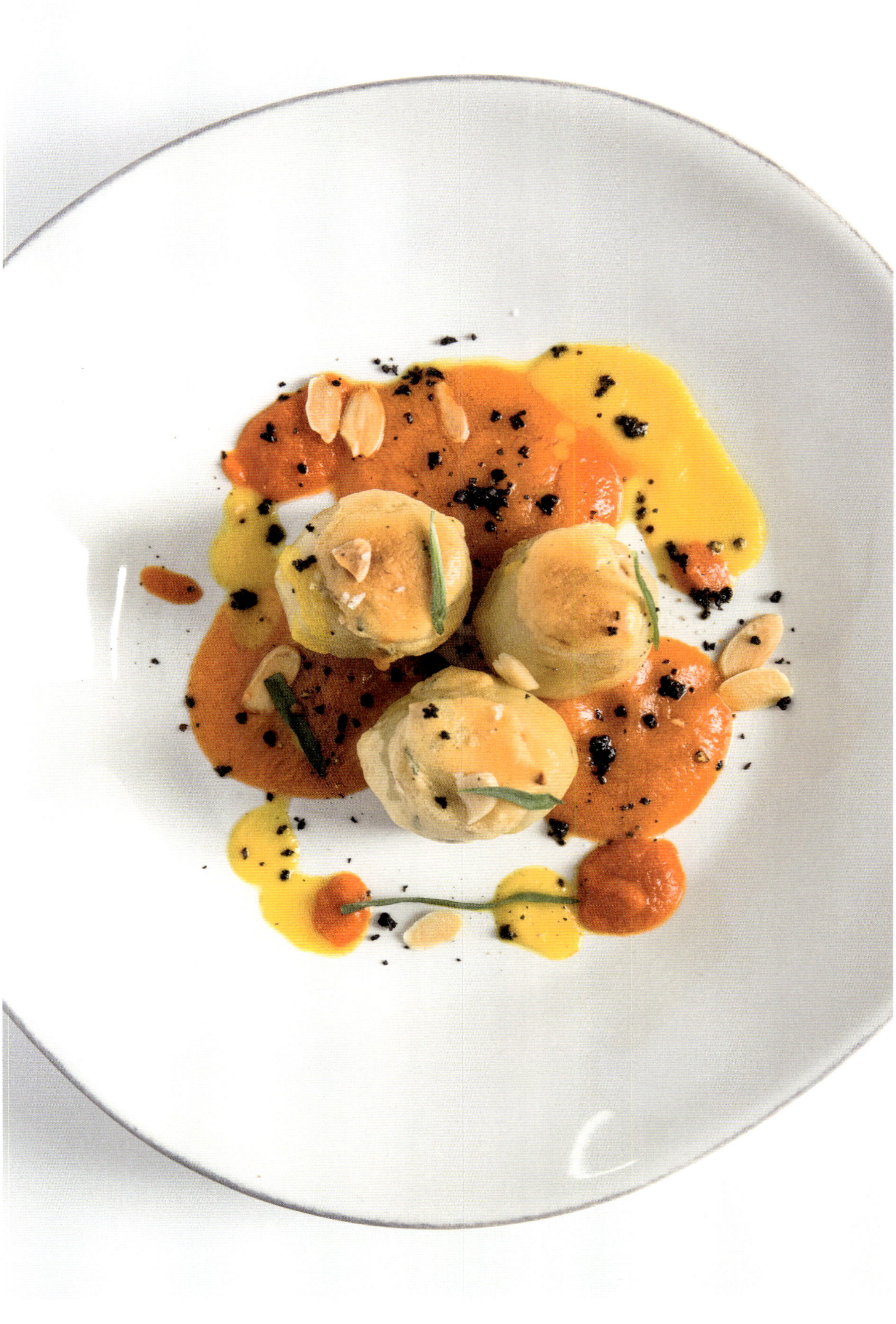

FÁT

GIFT IN A CAN

IMA

2018

MEN

MIXED TECHNIQUE ON PAPER

DON

42 × 29.7 CM

ÇA

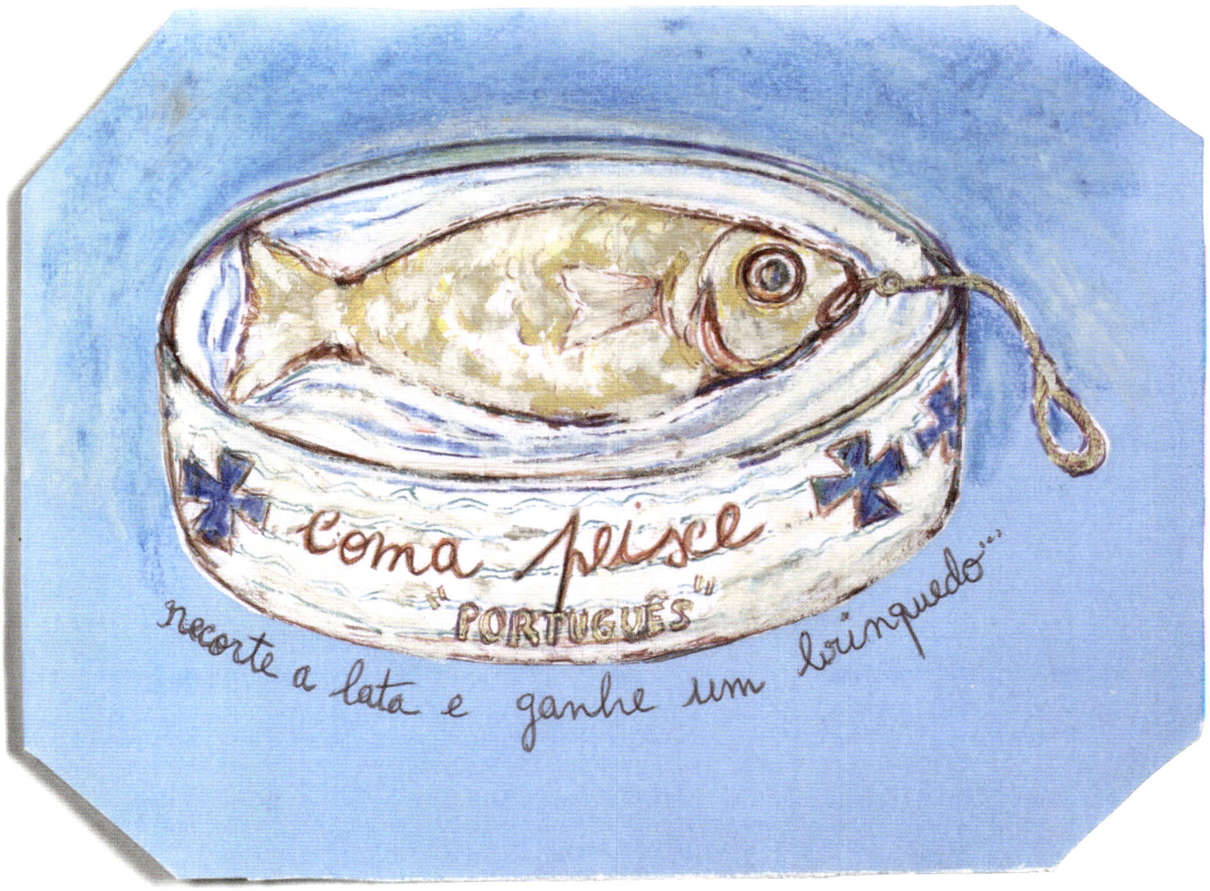
Coma peixe
"PORTUGUÊS"
recorte a lata e ganhe um brinquedo...

MIGUEL
CASTRO
E SILVA

ANA
VIDIGAL

ANA
VIDIGAL

MIGUEL
CASTRO
E SILVA

"I'M GOING TO PREPARE A STILL LIFE"

The dining room is a strange place to be – it's too late to have lunch and too early to think about dinner. Outside, Bairro Alto is waking up in a frenzy. This place is still the centre of Lisbon's nightlife, where the craziest, most innovative ideas are born and where, during the 1980s, (post)modern Lisbon was invented.

On the wall are portraits of models wearing sunglasses, the frames golden like the shafts of sun outside on the esplanade. Miguel Castro e Silva, a veteran chef and pioneer of auteur cuisine in Portugal, puts on his white jacket and prepares the herbs, a bulb of fennel and opens the cans. The artist Ana Vidigal laughs because she likes to laugh. She's slowly preparing herself to talk.

The dish grows in Miguel's hands with a little help from some tweezers. "It's not my thing," he says. "I'm going to prepare a still life." And he winks at Ana and the camera, before searching for the prettier side of the mackerel. He gives Ana radish sprouts to taste.

"They burn," she says.

"They do," says Miguel.

A rich marinade; the first confidences, dates, names and memories are exchanged. This city is so small. And so big.

Ana talks about her father, an architect, and about her grandmother, an artist. Neither encouraged her to follow in their footsteps, it just happened. It had to be.

Miguel mentions music. He played piano and guitar and was involved in the recording of António Variações' first album. Still, it was a different gift.

The arts intersect without a pattern; people don't respect boundaries.

They talk about the old country, Ana's Lisbon and Miguel's Porto. Old good times and bad times. A few dates. Ana remembers the first exhibition, in 1981, at the National Society of Fine Arts. Miguel remembers the first restaurant, in a country house in Maia. Misses, hits and the beginnings of new paths.

The chef brings Douro wine and we can see how proud he is. They toast. Ana pretends to drink and smiles at the scent. They both smile for the picture.

Cooking was no noble life... and art? Their paths cross. Miguel created dishes for artists in the cultural institution Serralves Foundation in Oporto and at the Gulbenkian art foundation in Lisbon. Ana reminds us that art is ephemeral, as fleeting as cuisine.

They talk about influences and journeys, about where ideas come from. Work, work and sometimes a little rip. Paths slowly dug, with a teaspoon or a chisel pointing at the chest. They both managed to find themselves.

We stay inside talking about everything, this book included. Ana tastes and approves the dish. Miguel calls us over, serves the wine and carries on playing with time.

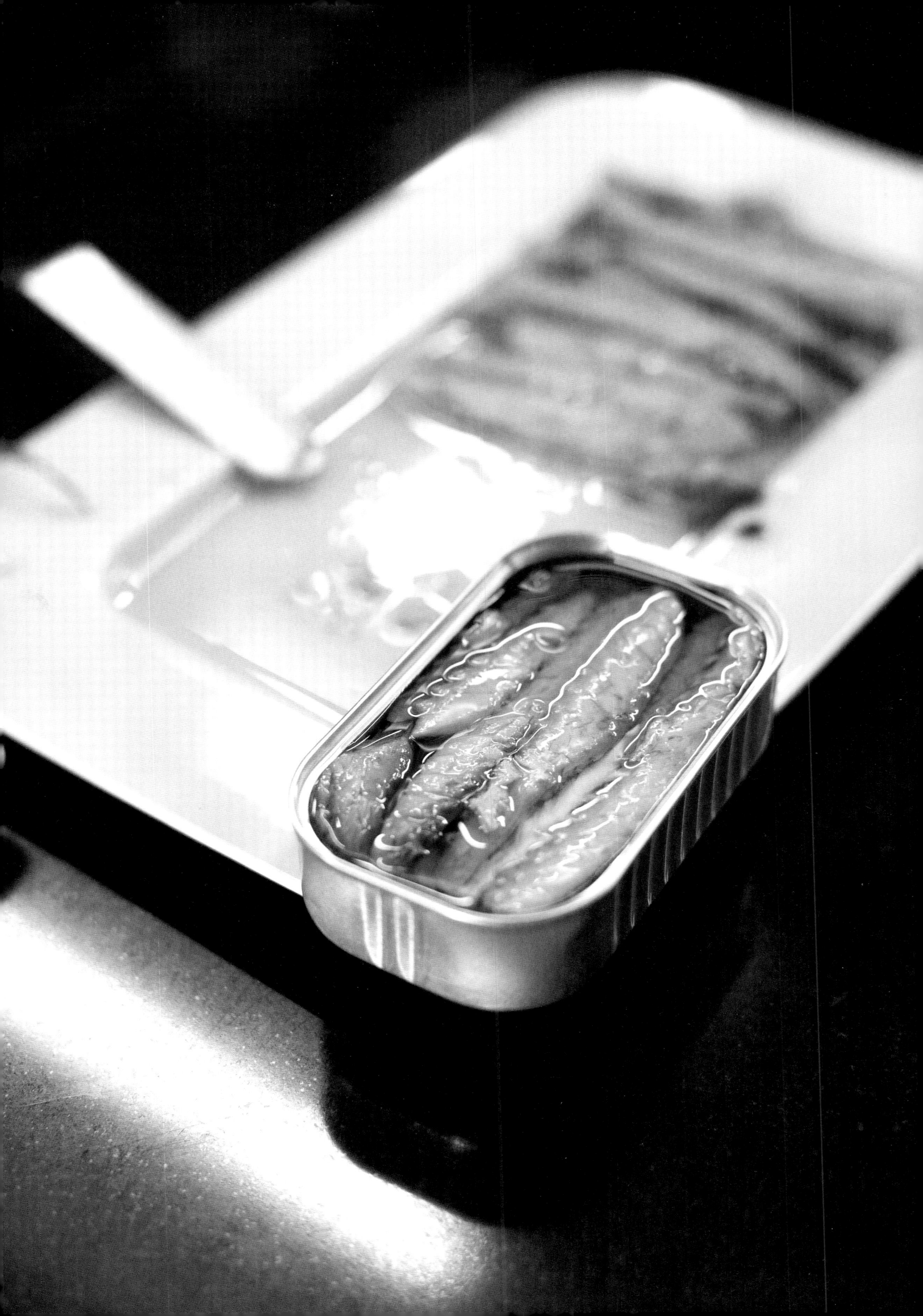

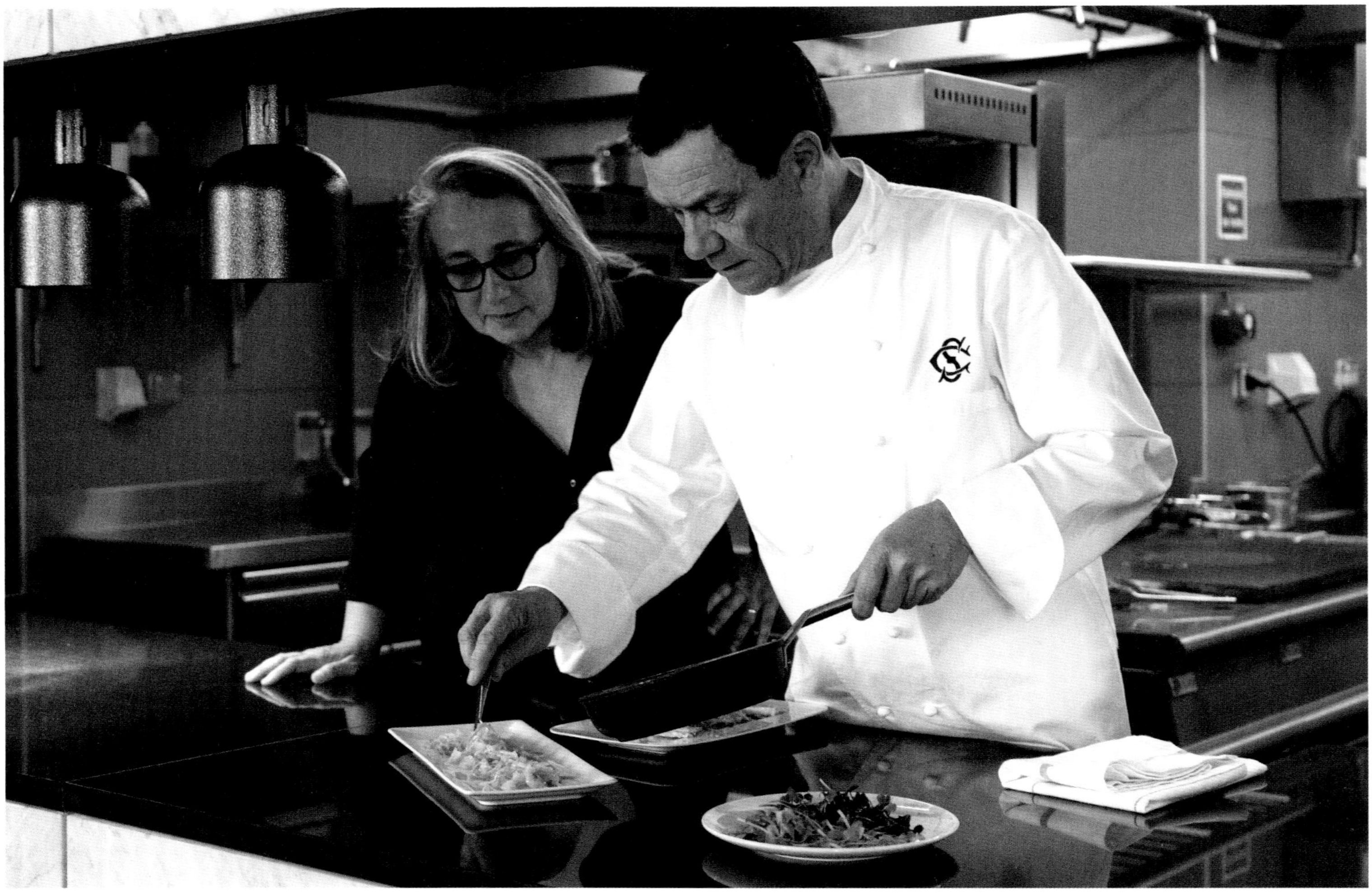

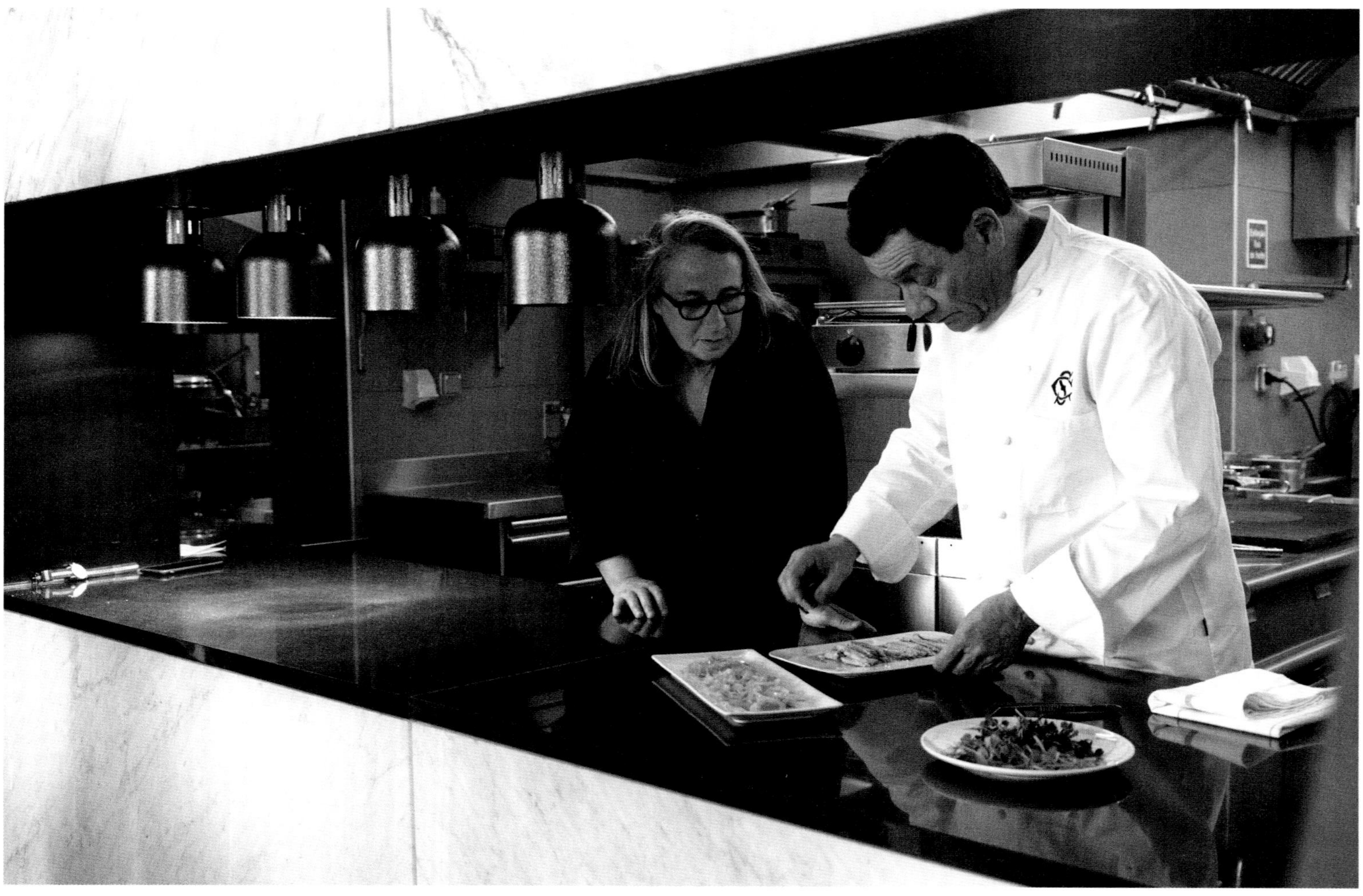

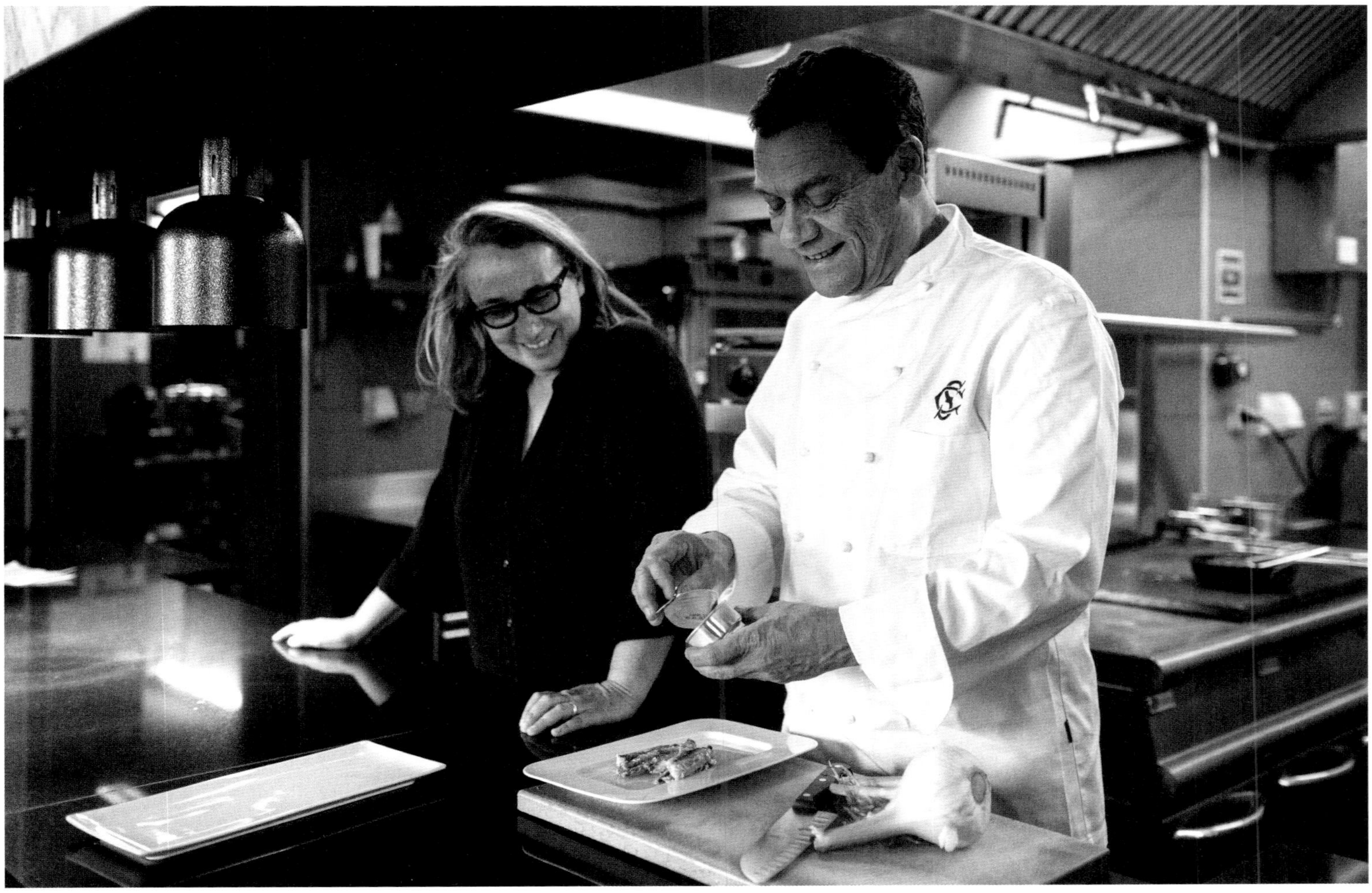

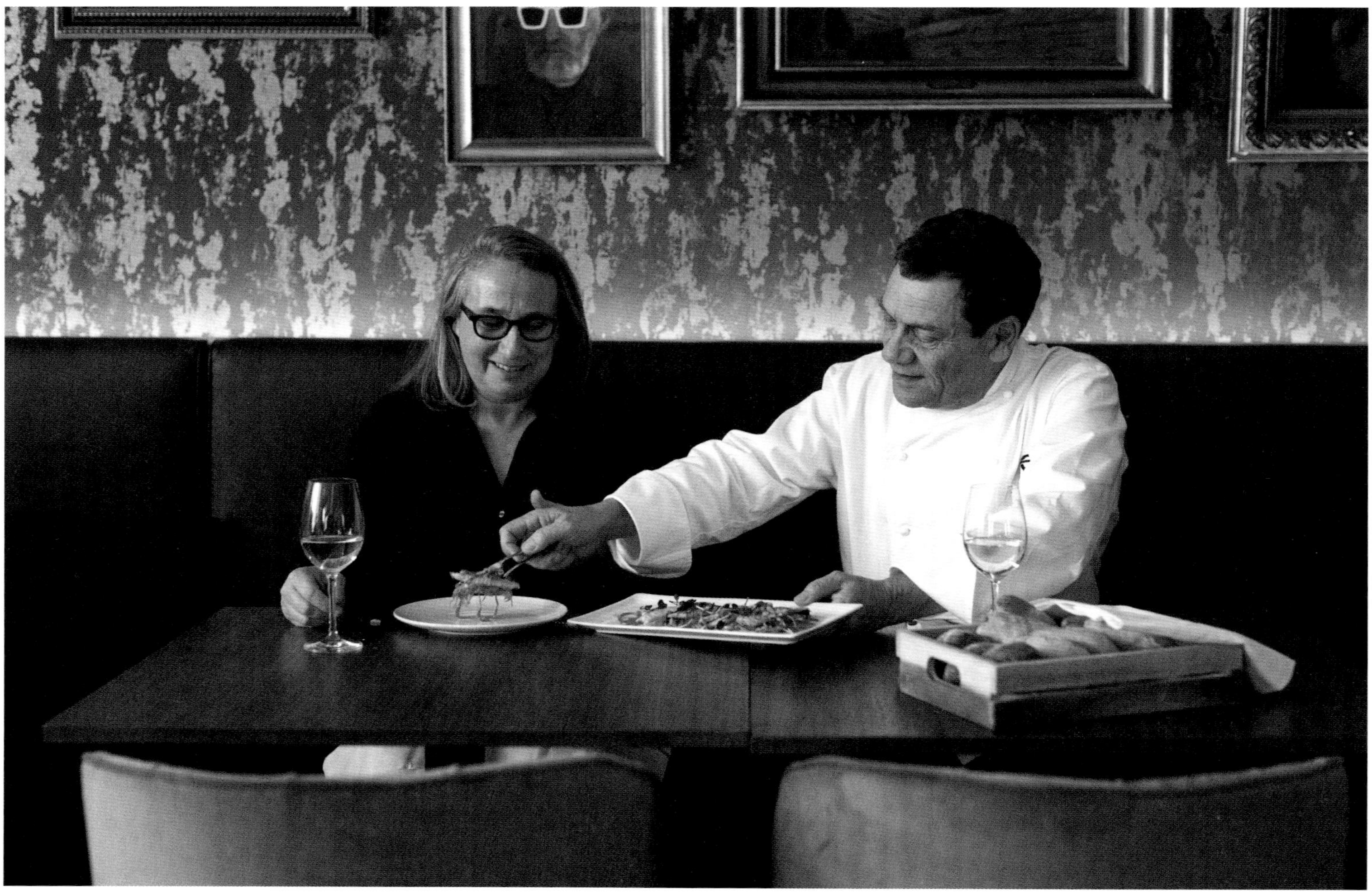

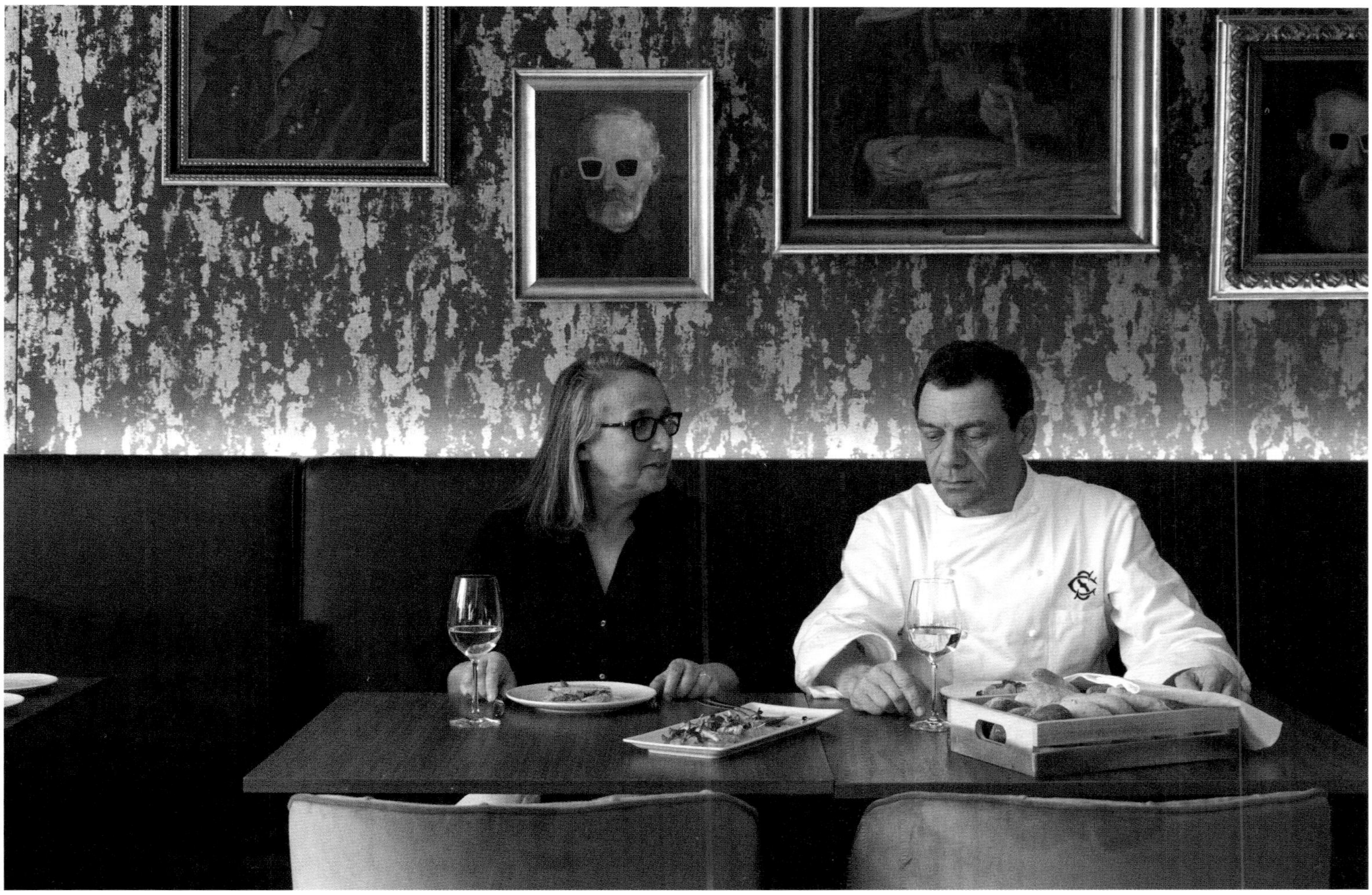

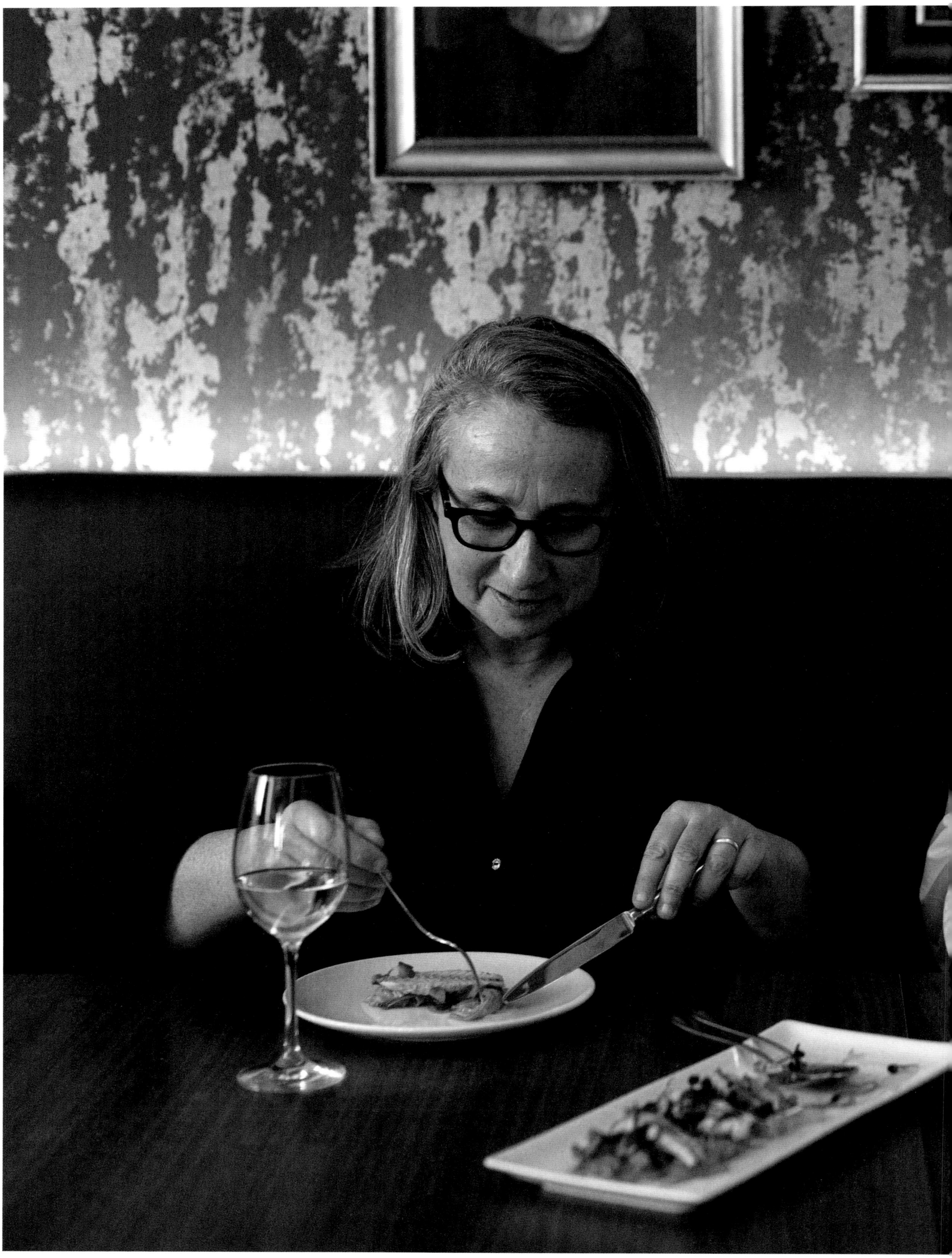

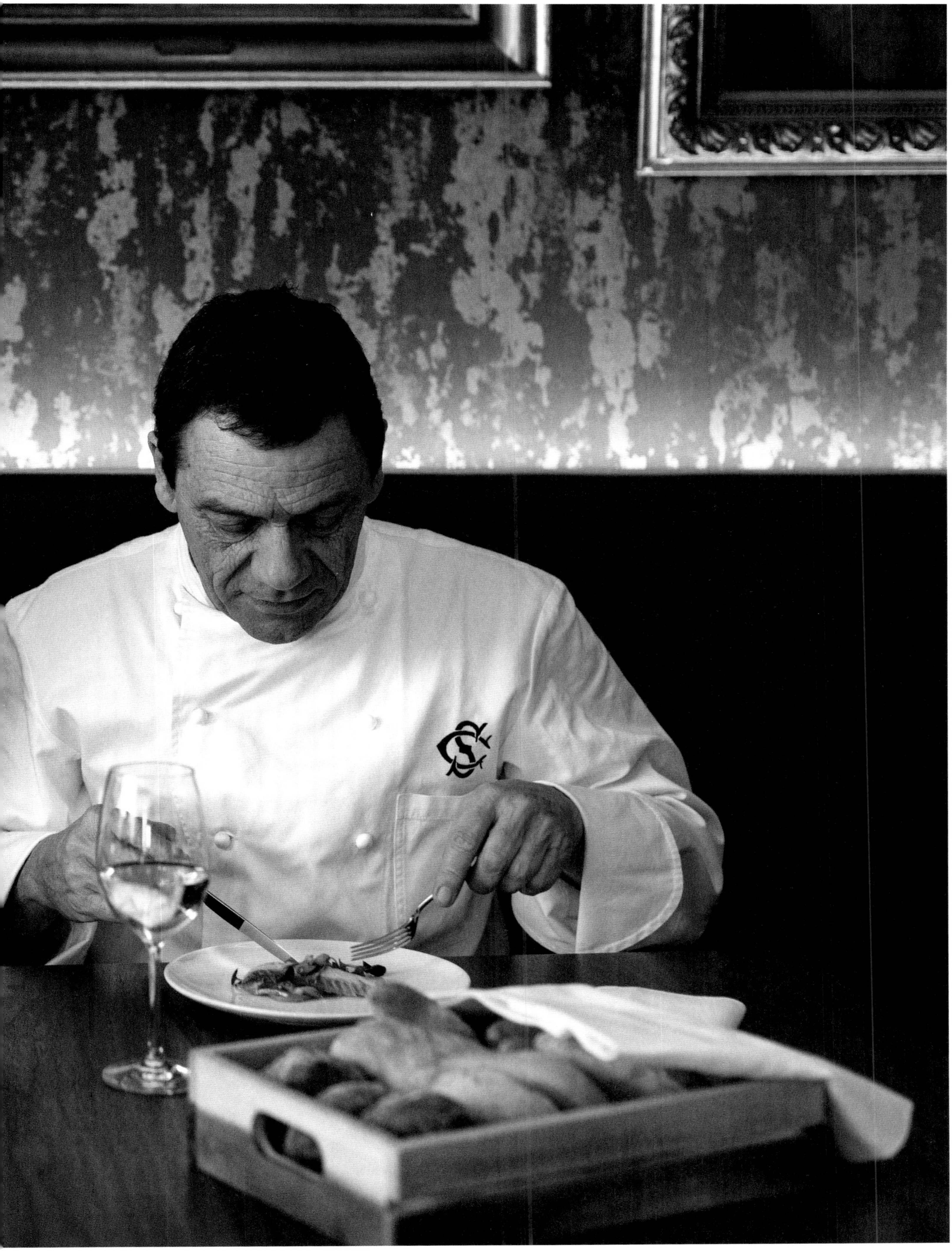

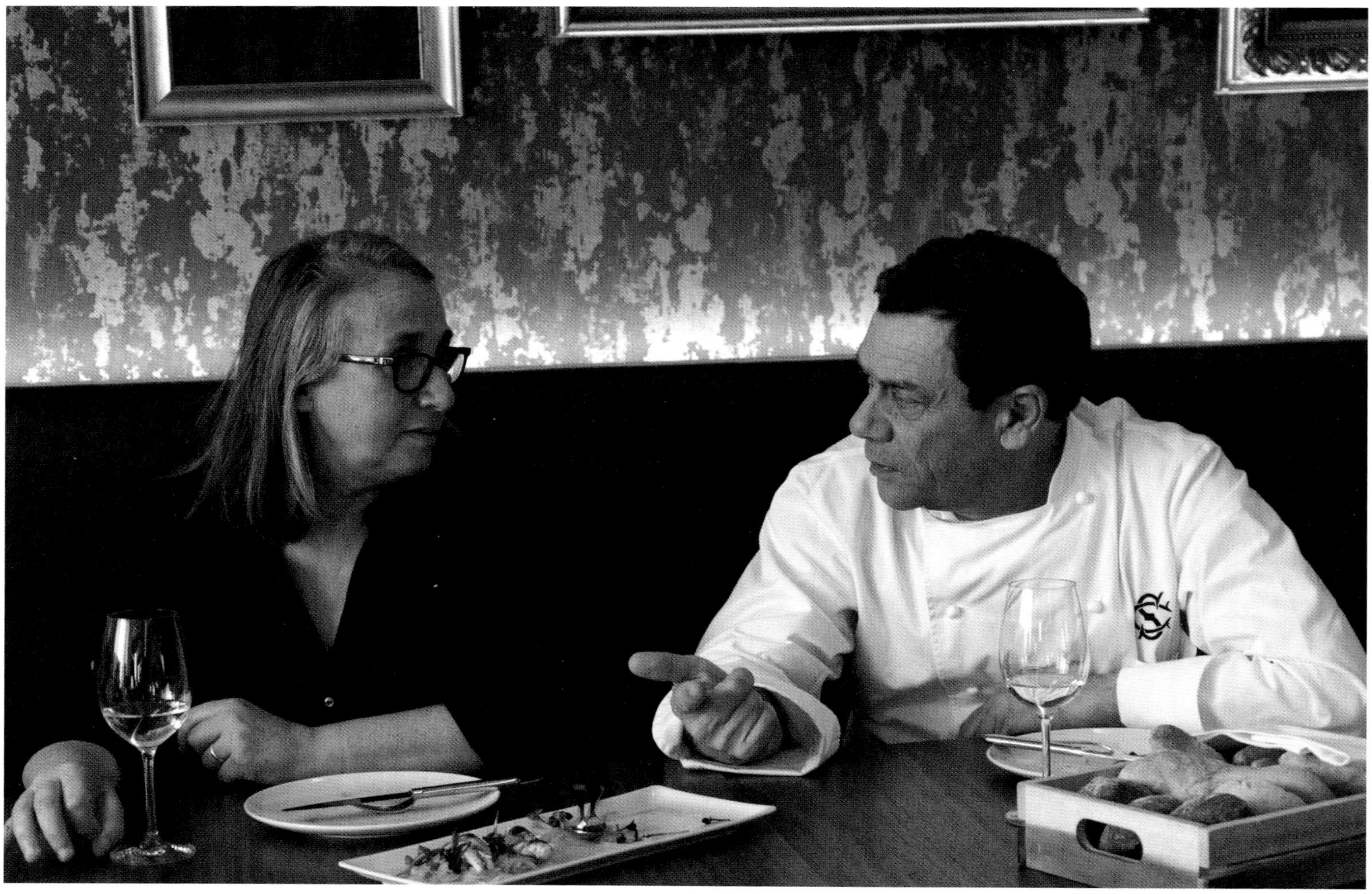

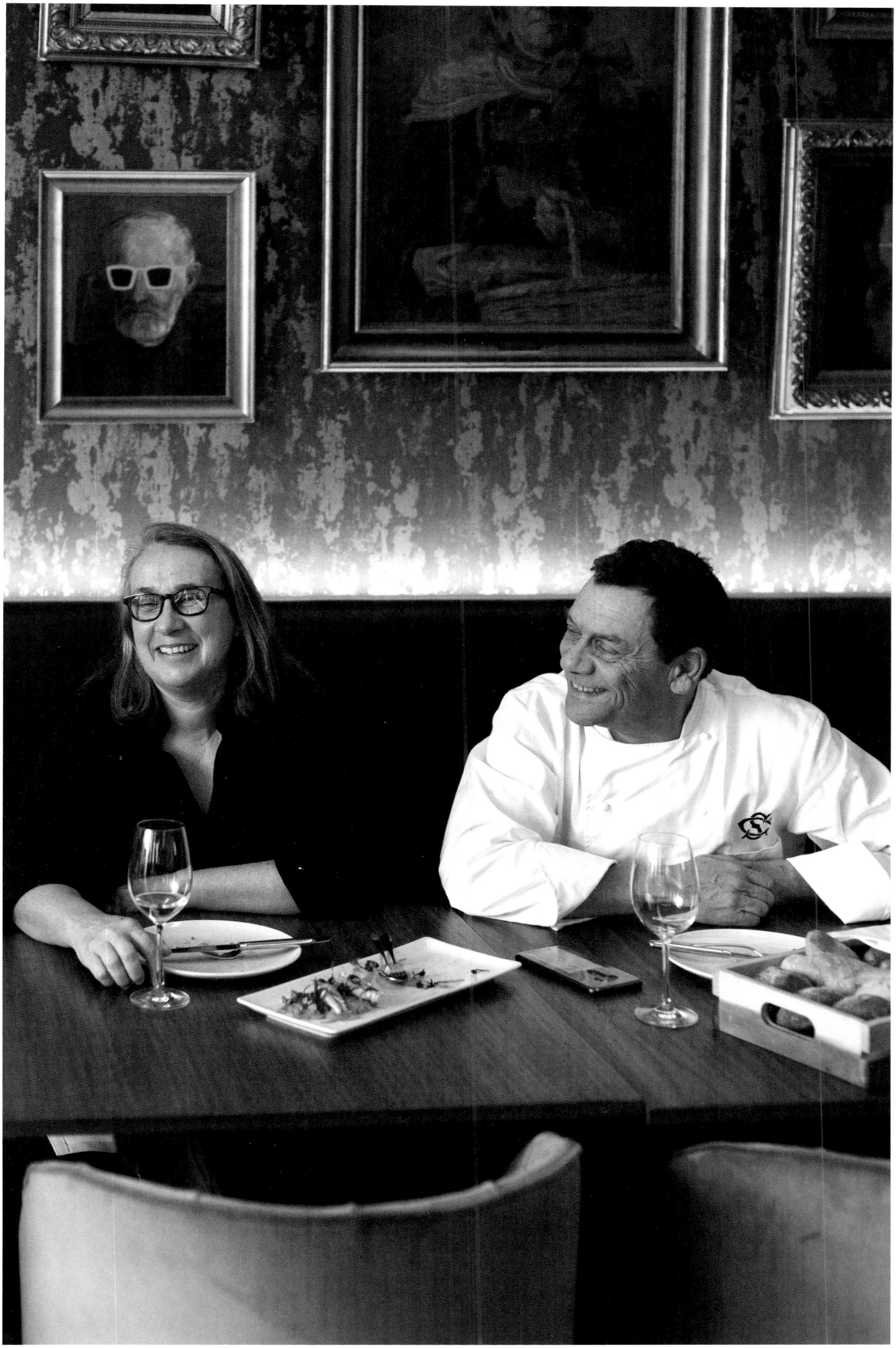

MIGUEL CASTRO E SILVA

MACKEREL
FILLETS IN
SMOKED
OLIVE OIL,
WITH FENNEL
MARINADE

MACKEREL FILLETS
IN SMOKED OLIVE OIL
BRAND VIANA PESCA

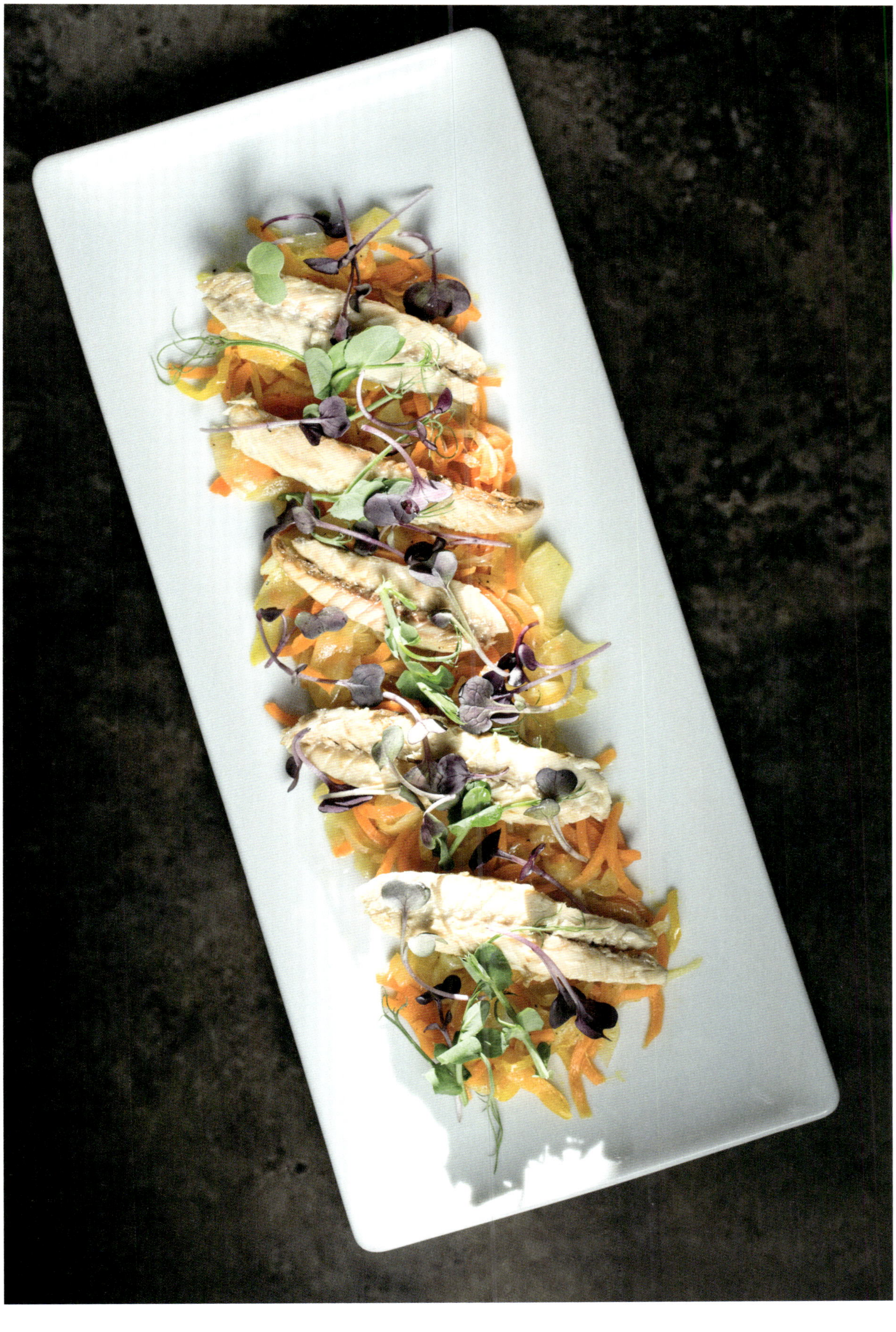

ANA VIDIGAL

HÁ SETE CÃES A UM
OSSO E SETE GATOS
A UMA SARDINHA, EU É
MAIS C(H)AVALINHAS
2018

MIXED TECHNIQUE
ON PAPER
49 × 39 CM

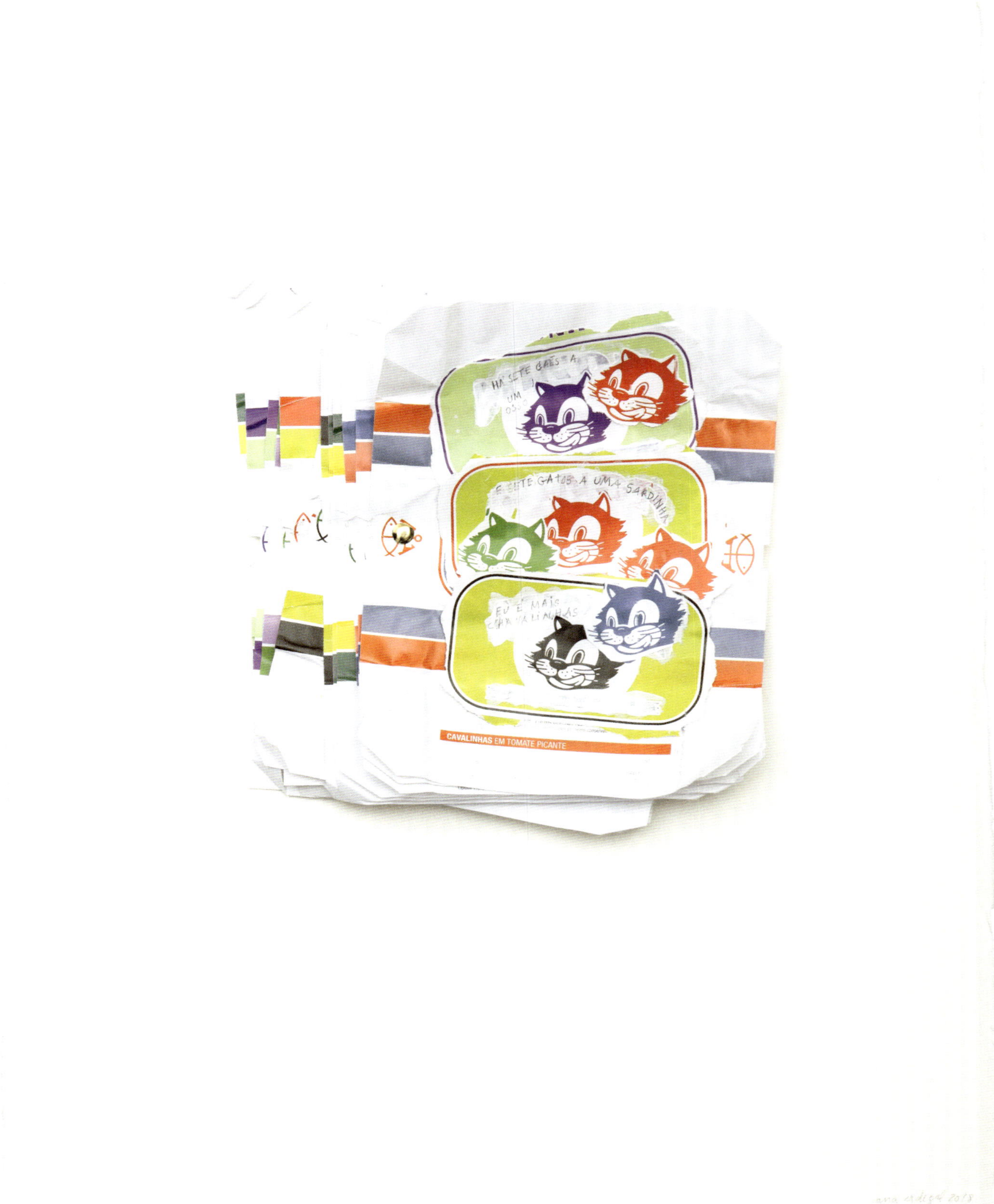
E SETE GATOS A UMA SARDINHA
CAVALINHAS EM TOMATE PICANTE

JOSÉ
AVILLEZ

JÚLIA
CÔTA

JULIA
CÔTA

JOSÉ
AVILLEZ

"PEOPLE ARE POOR, BUT THE MOUTH IS RICH"

"Oh child, I can't believe it – look, Avillez is right here with us..."

The craftswoman Júlia Côta tries to remain aloof, but José Avillez welcomes her at the iconic Belcanto restaurant in Lisbon with joy and a little curiosity all the same. "You're Júlia from Barcelos?" says the chef. "The rooster's granddaughter?"

Yes, it's her. And she begins to tell the story.

"It was my grandfather who made the first Barcelos roosters, then people liked it and now everyone is making them. But it's ours, Avillez, it is ours! Did you know someone offered one to Obama?"

Either the kitchen is too small or the cooks are too numerous. Either way, we squeeze into a corner and applaud the choreography of knives, spoons, dancing plates, coloured and exotic ingredients, smoke, foam and flashed smiles.

Júlia remains unflustered and takes the lead in the conversation. "My mother used to cook for weddings where my father would kill 50 chickens. It was my mother who would pluck them, scorch them and wash them with rose soap, believe me. Once they were well washed, she would cut them into portions."

The chef laughs and asks questions. It may seem a long way from strange machines to so much refinement, but tradition is at the root of all kitchens, and José Avillez knows it better than anyone.

"I have seven sons, 20 grandsons and ten great-grandsons who I managed to raise so that none of them died of hunger."

The chef presents the ingredients to Júlia, who receives them with surprise: sardine roes, tomato water, cuttlefish earth... "Ah, you son of a bitch!" she says, full of northern ways and a huge smile.

And what do you like to eat?

Júlia goes back to the chicken, the slaughtered pork, the soups. And they find a place in common.

"Do you know that when I travel I often ask to go to the hotel's kitchen to make a soup. It's just what I fancy," says Avillez. And Júlia nods, yes.

"What about the art?", we ask.

Clay is the first thing. "After the cars with the clay arrived, we would break it into pieces with a sickle and put it in a dunghill to be trampled by the oxen. We ended up loving it, and using our fingers to express our mind's ideas."

The chef smiles and repeats the word "matter". Doing the best with what we have, recreating the old, making customers think again – great cuisine is like theatre. One must use the emotions, the element of surprise, and tell a story.

And the imitators don't bother you?

"Don't even mention it! I have such a rage against those copying bastards..."

But Avillez seems calmer: "It doesn't bother me. In the end they are just paying us a tribute. The dish is never equal, because it's not me making it. And it forces me to think about new things... Those who copy will always follow."

It's time for tasting, and a sophisticated, modern dish is presented to Júlia.

She frowns, but takes courage. Her eyes widen, she smiles and says:

"This is good, you know, but it doesn't fill the stomach... Sorry, but I've been set up, Avillez! The thing is, people are poor but the mouth is rich."

Two absolute artists who are what they are and who owe no one an apology.

Júlia still wants a joint selfie for her daughter to put on Facebook. "Come on, let's go. Lisbon is beautiful, but the clay is waiting for us."

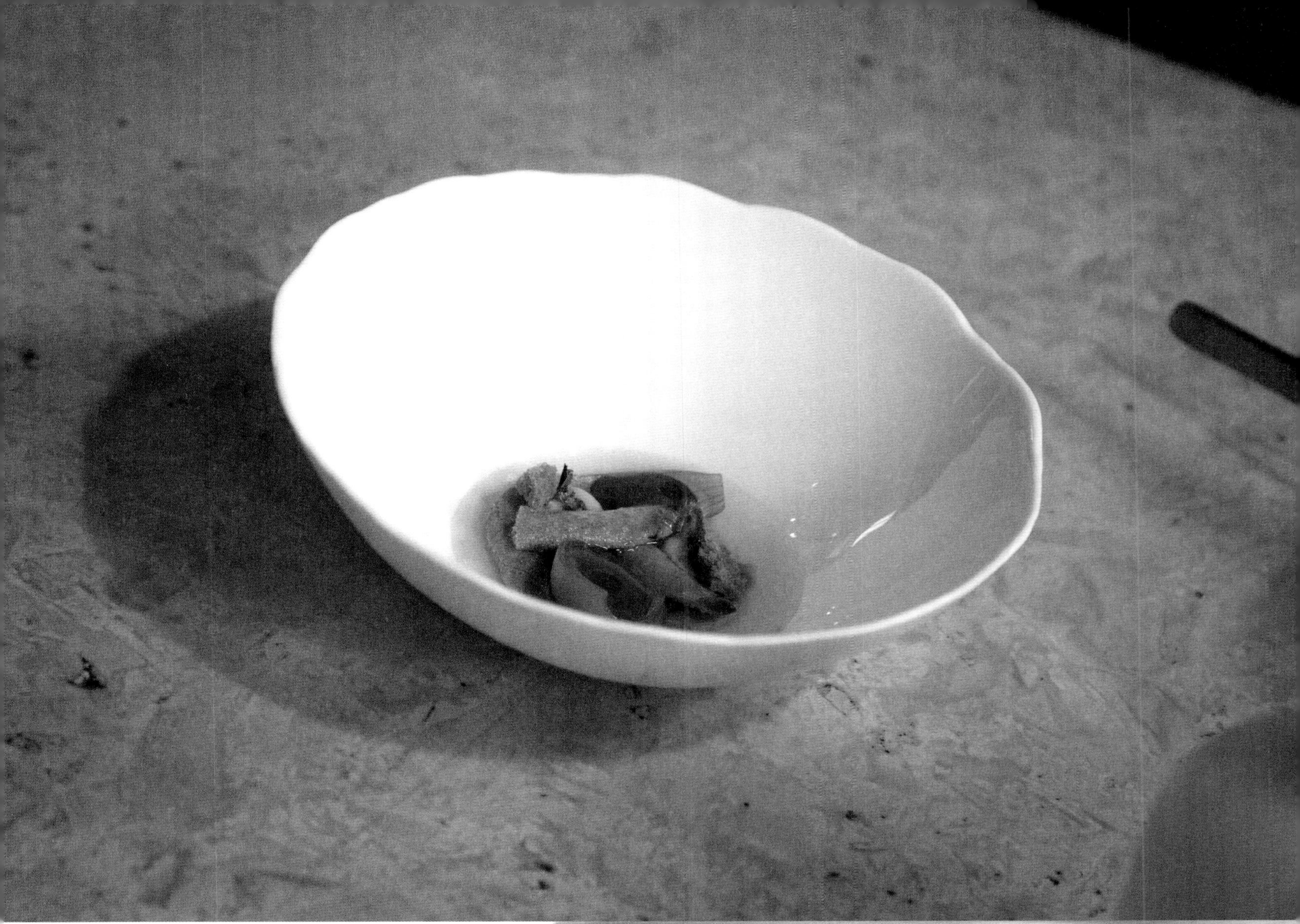

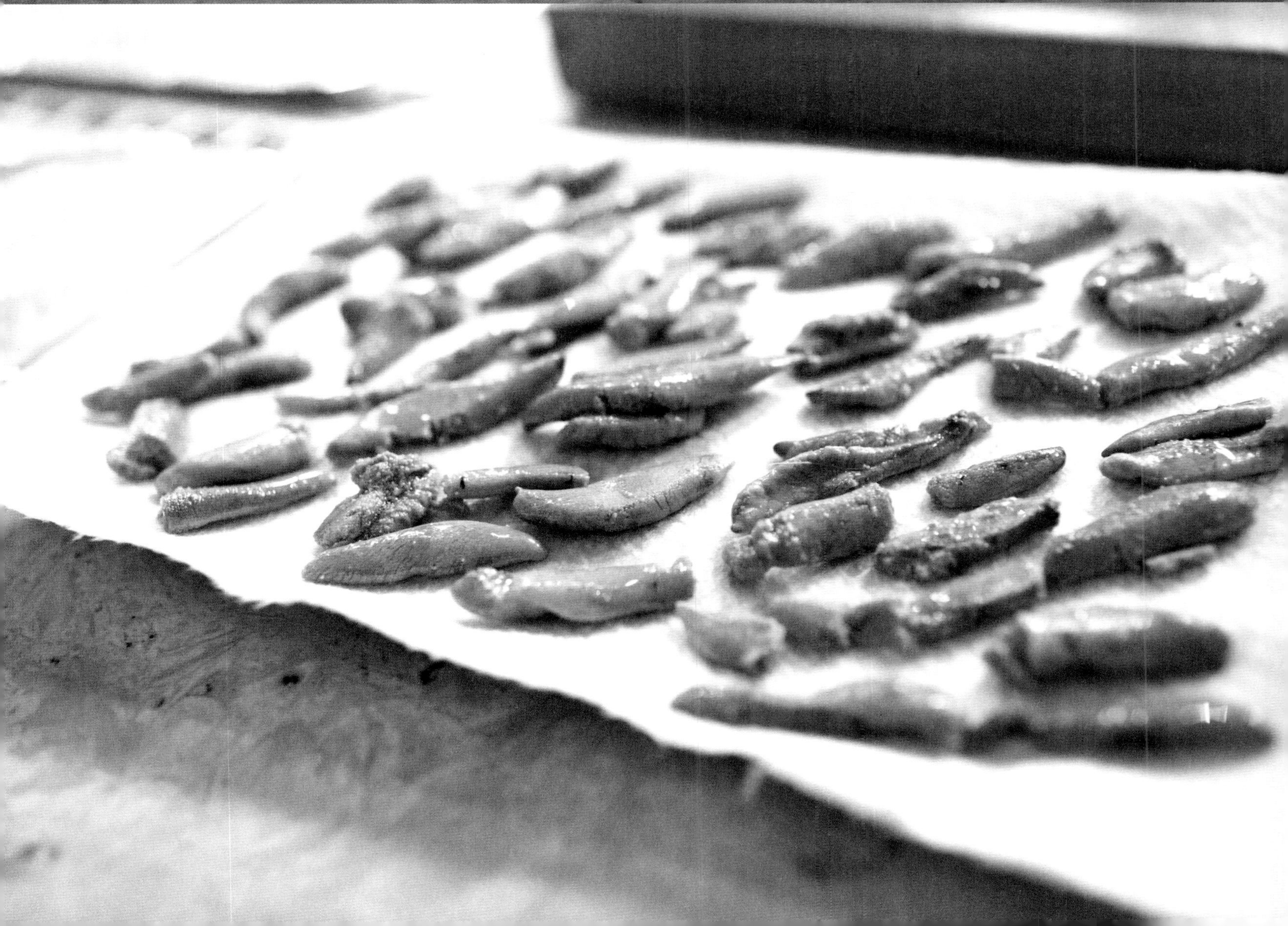

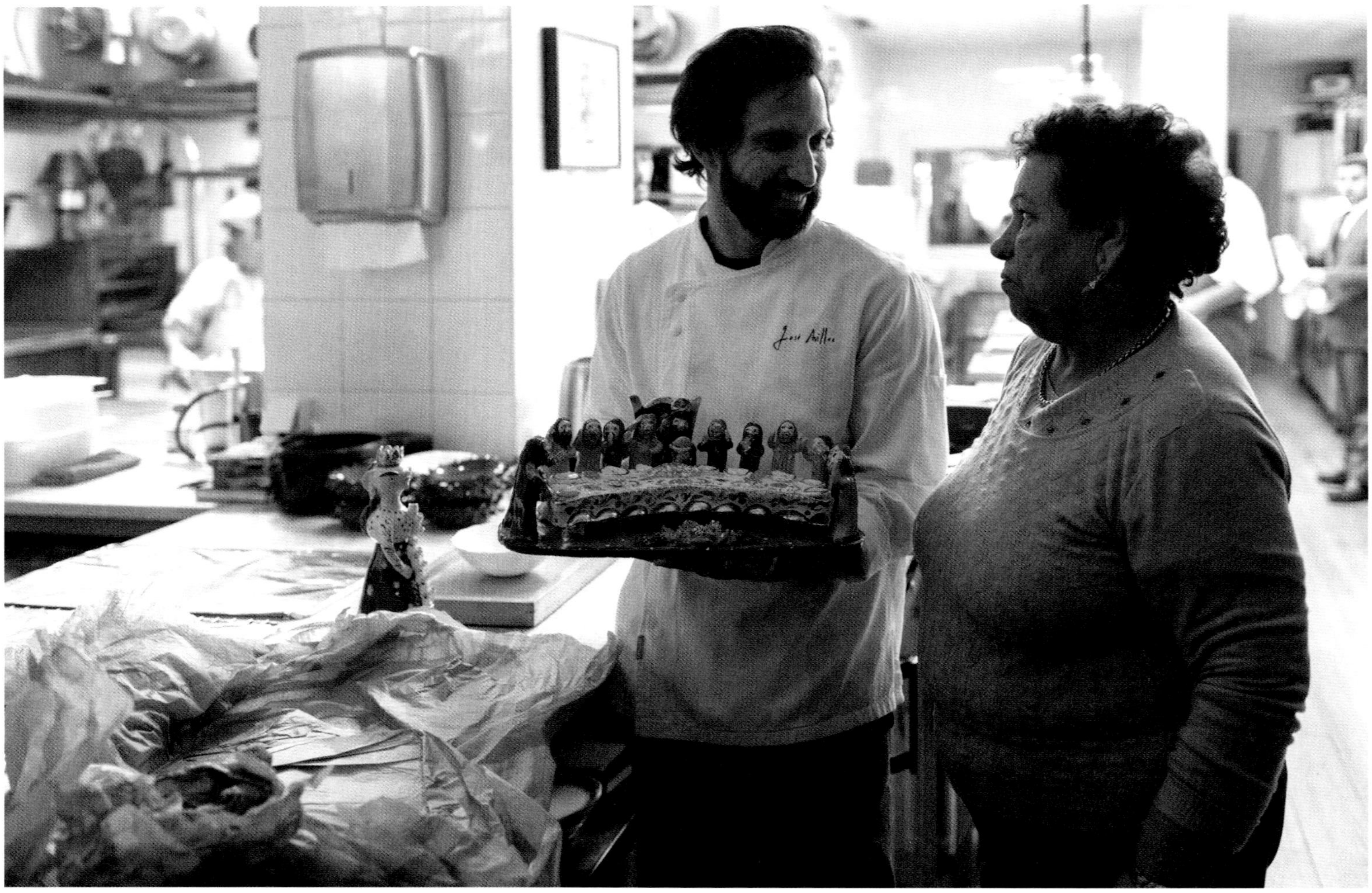

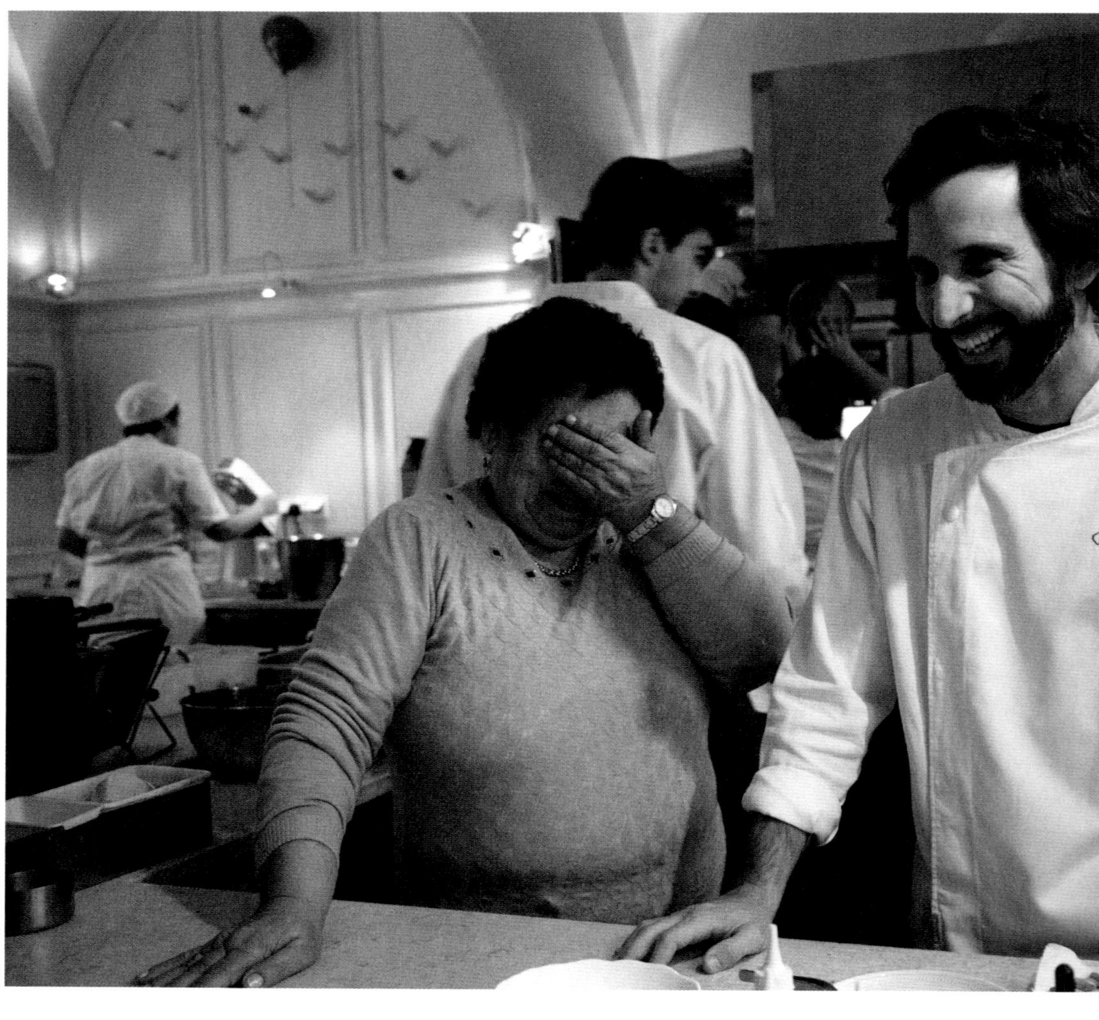

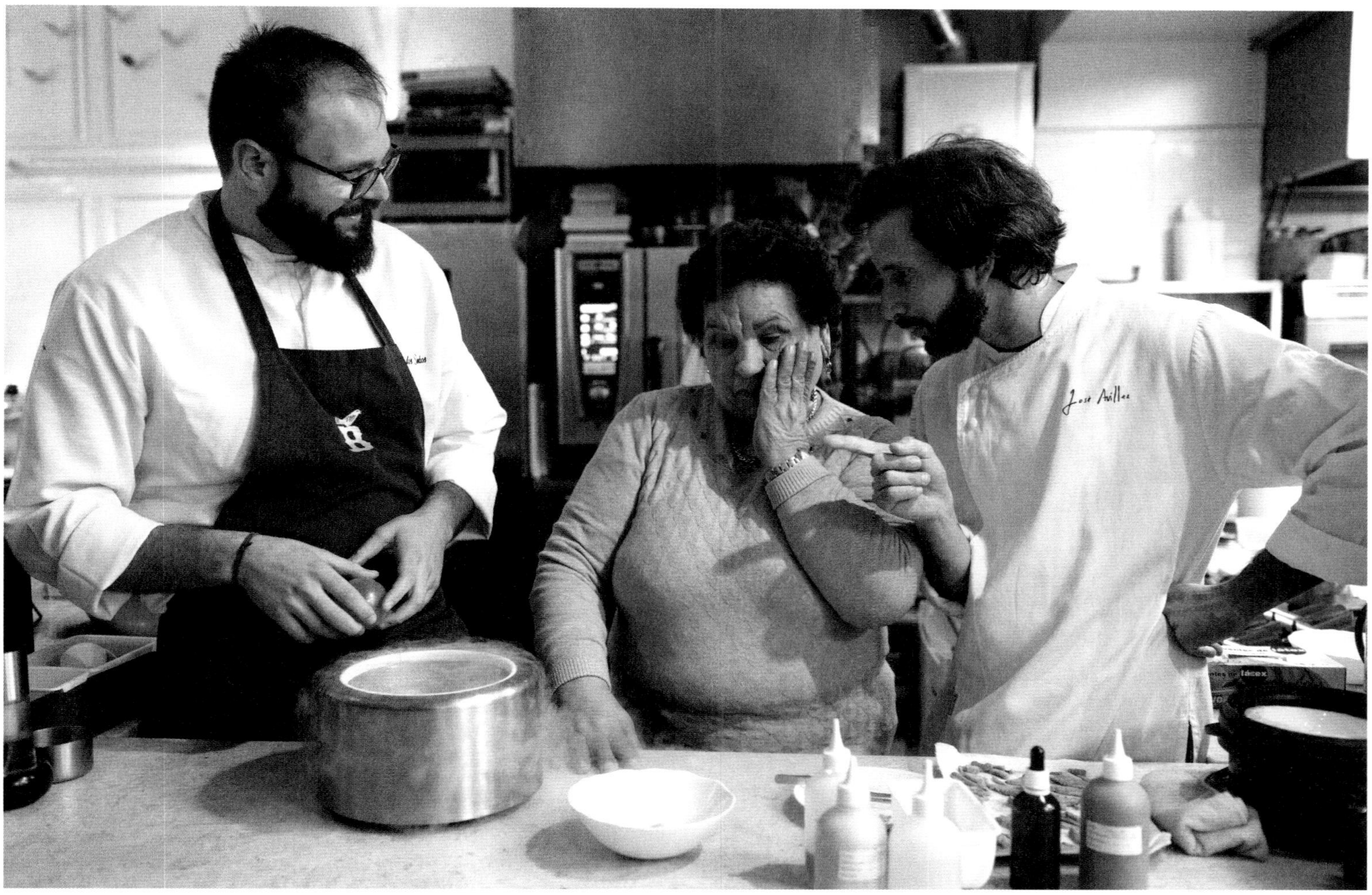

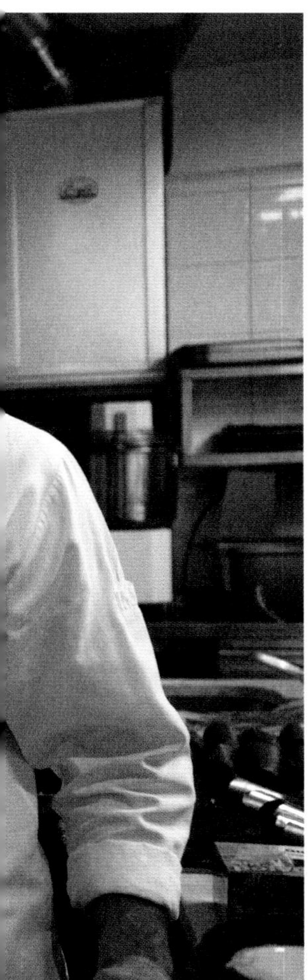

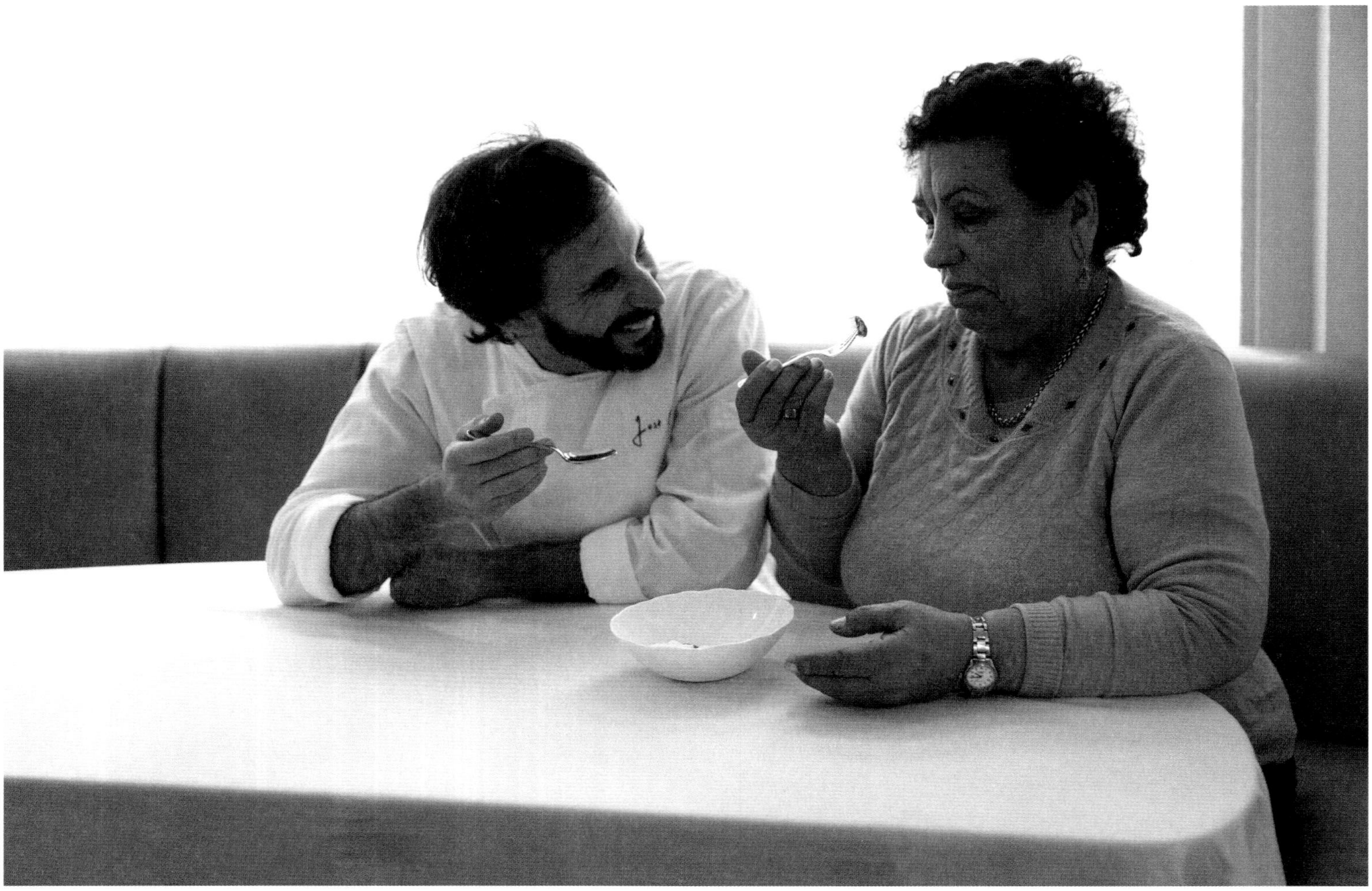

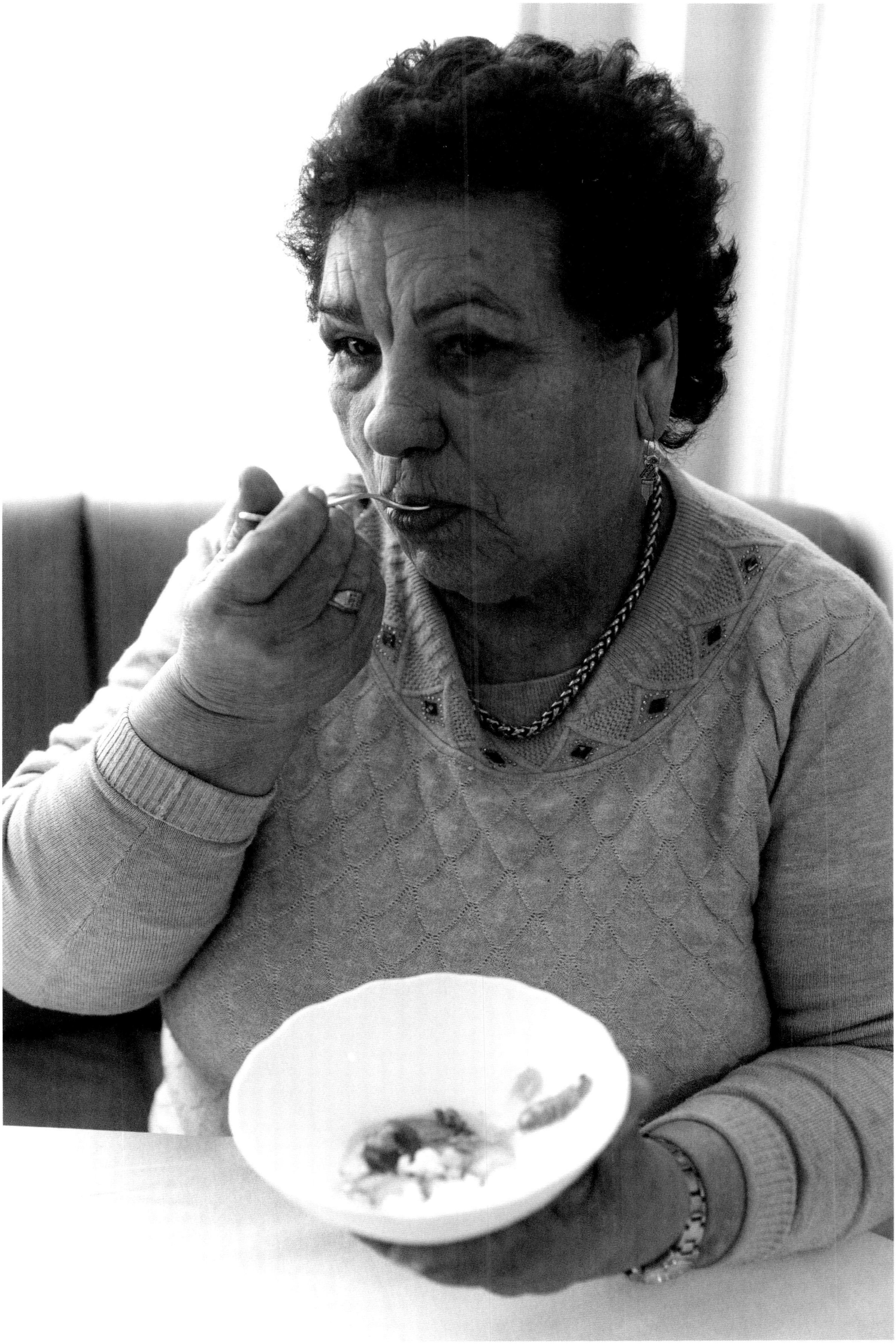

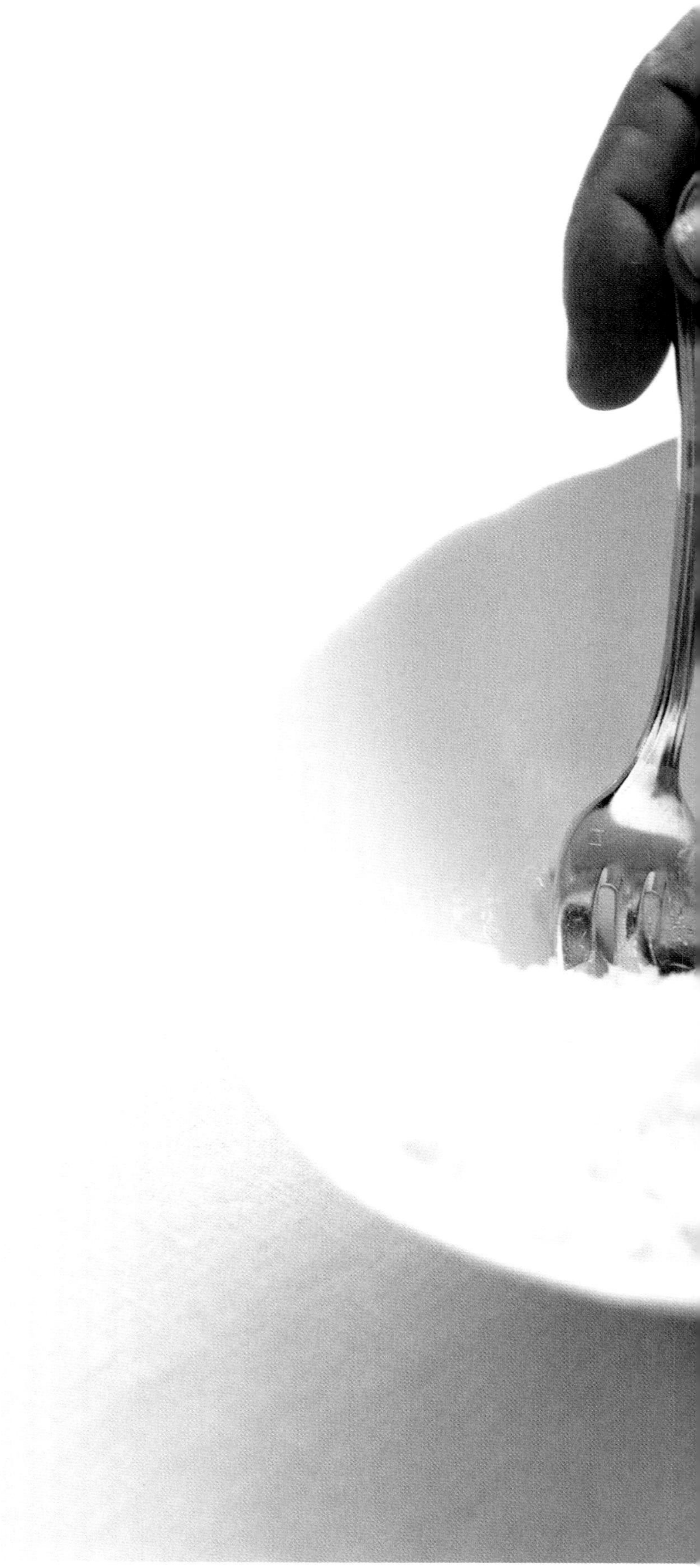

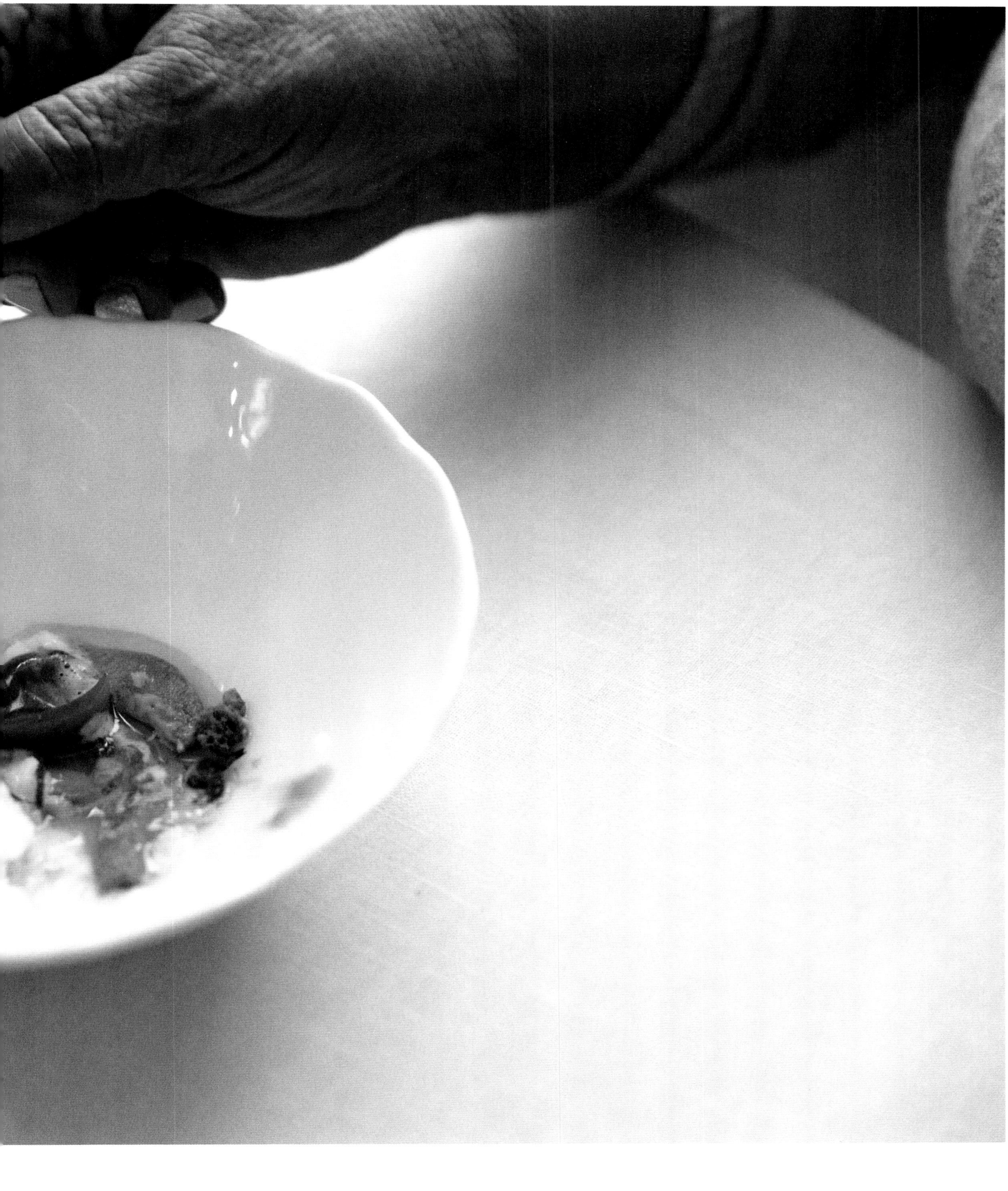

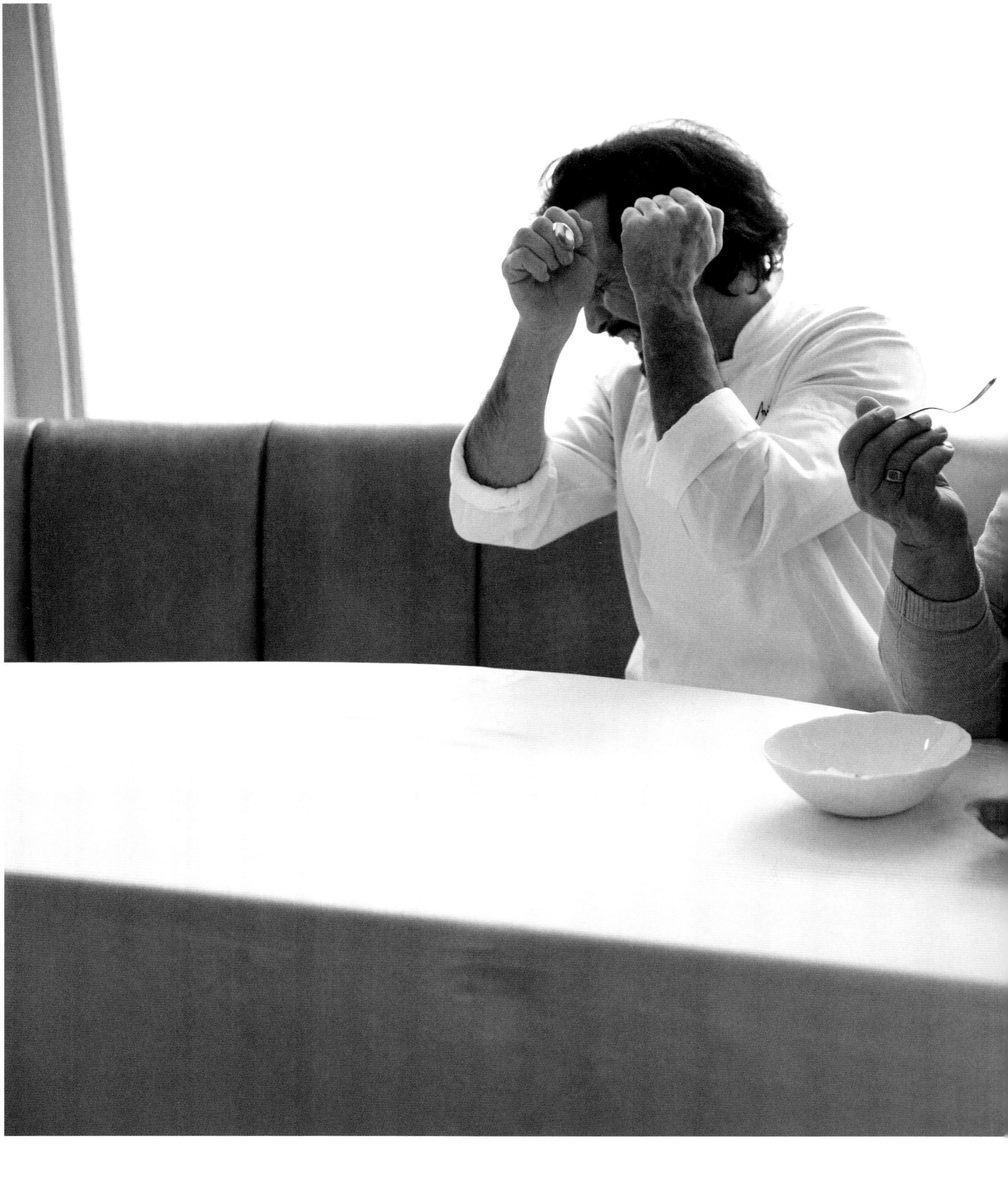

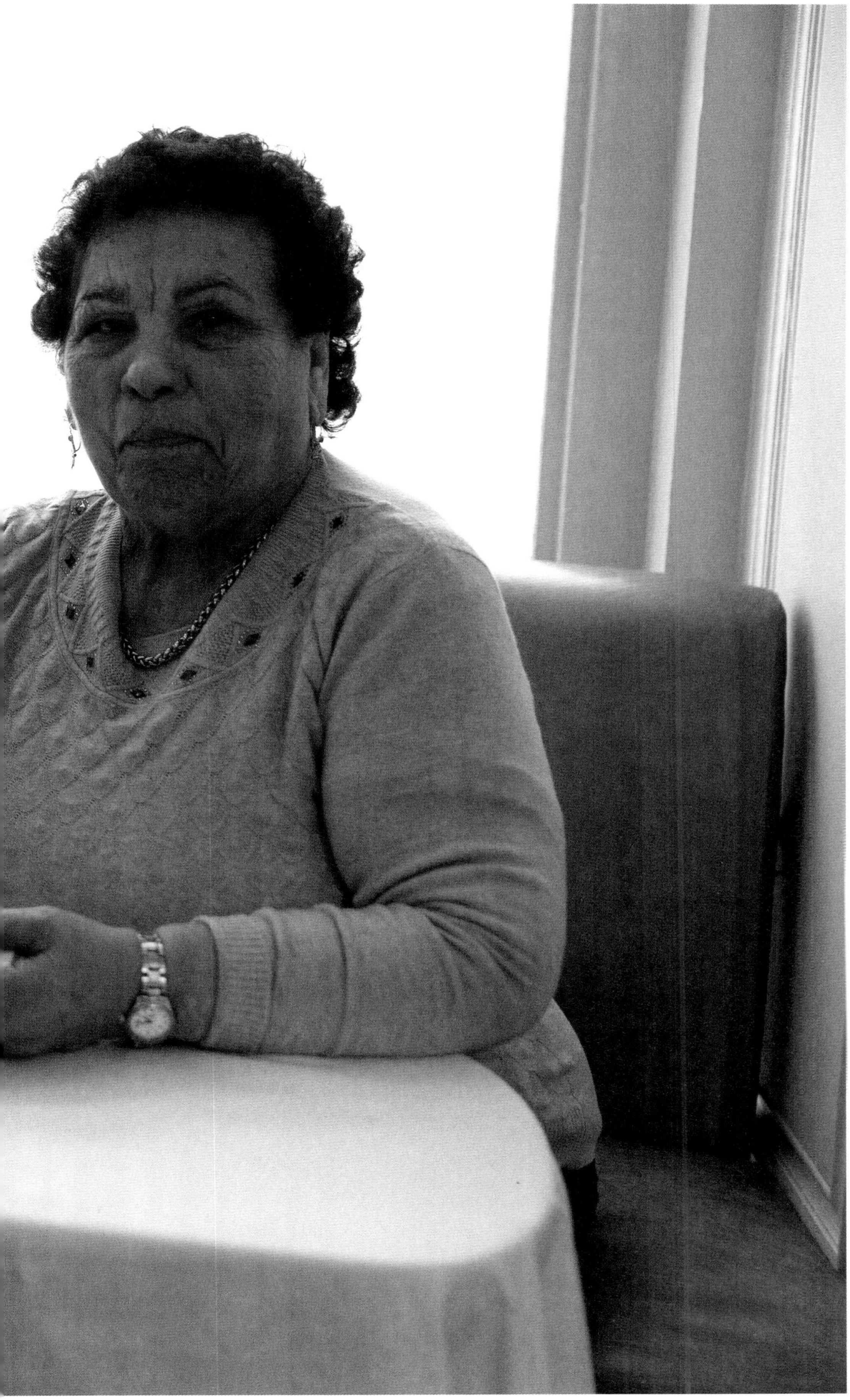

JOSÉ AVILLEZ

COLD TOMATO 'SOUP' WITH SARDINE ROES

SARDINE
ROES IN OLIVE OIL
BRAND MINERVA

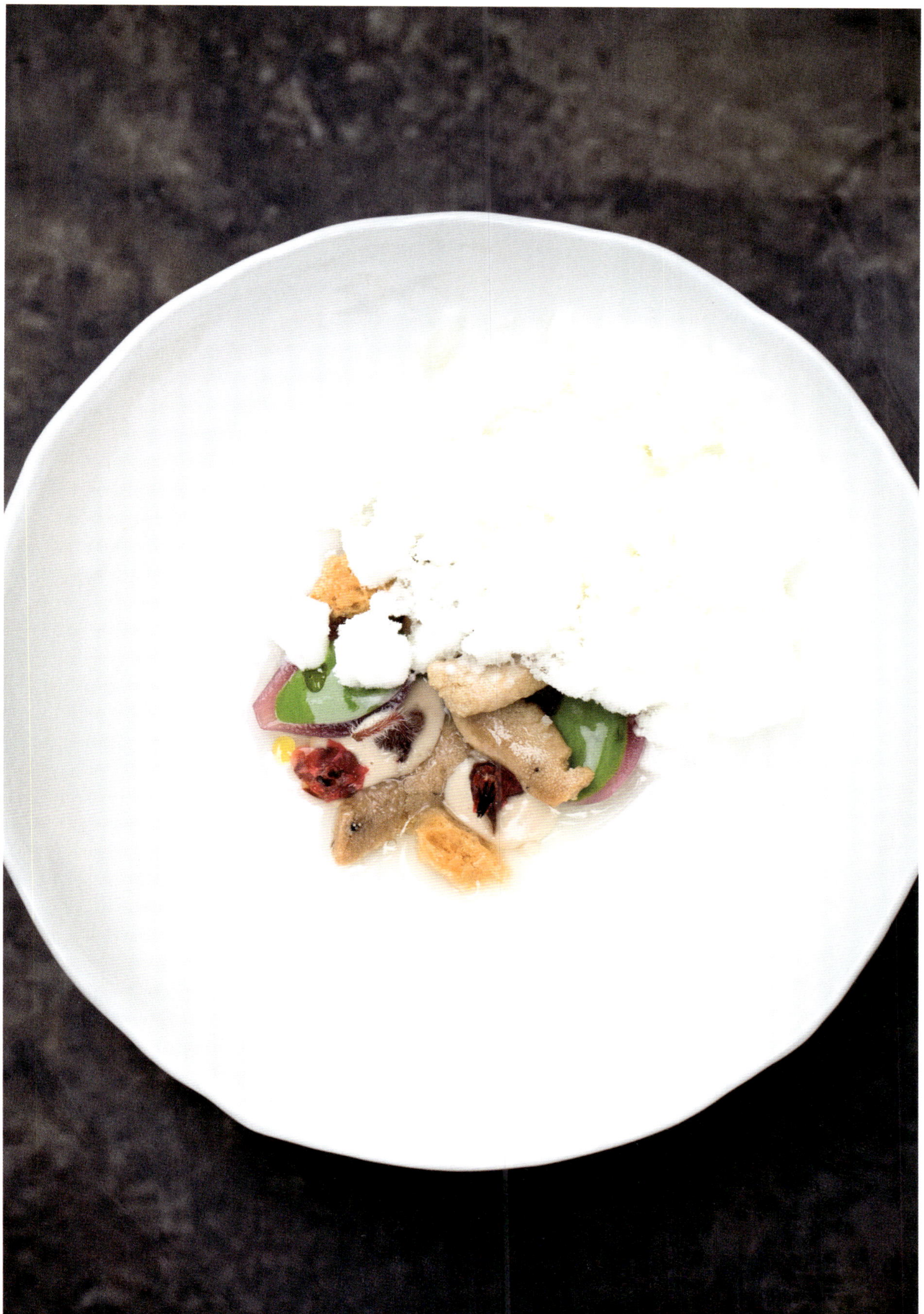

JÚLIA
JÚLIA

FISHMONGERS' DOLLS
2017

CÔTA
CÔTA

MIXED MEDIA CLAY SCULPTURE
70 CM HEIGHT

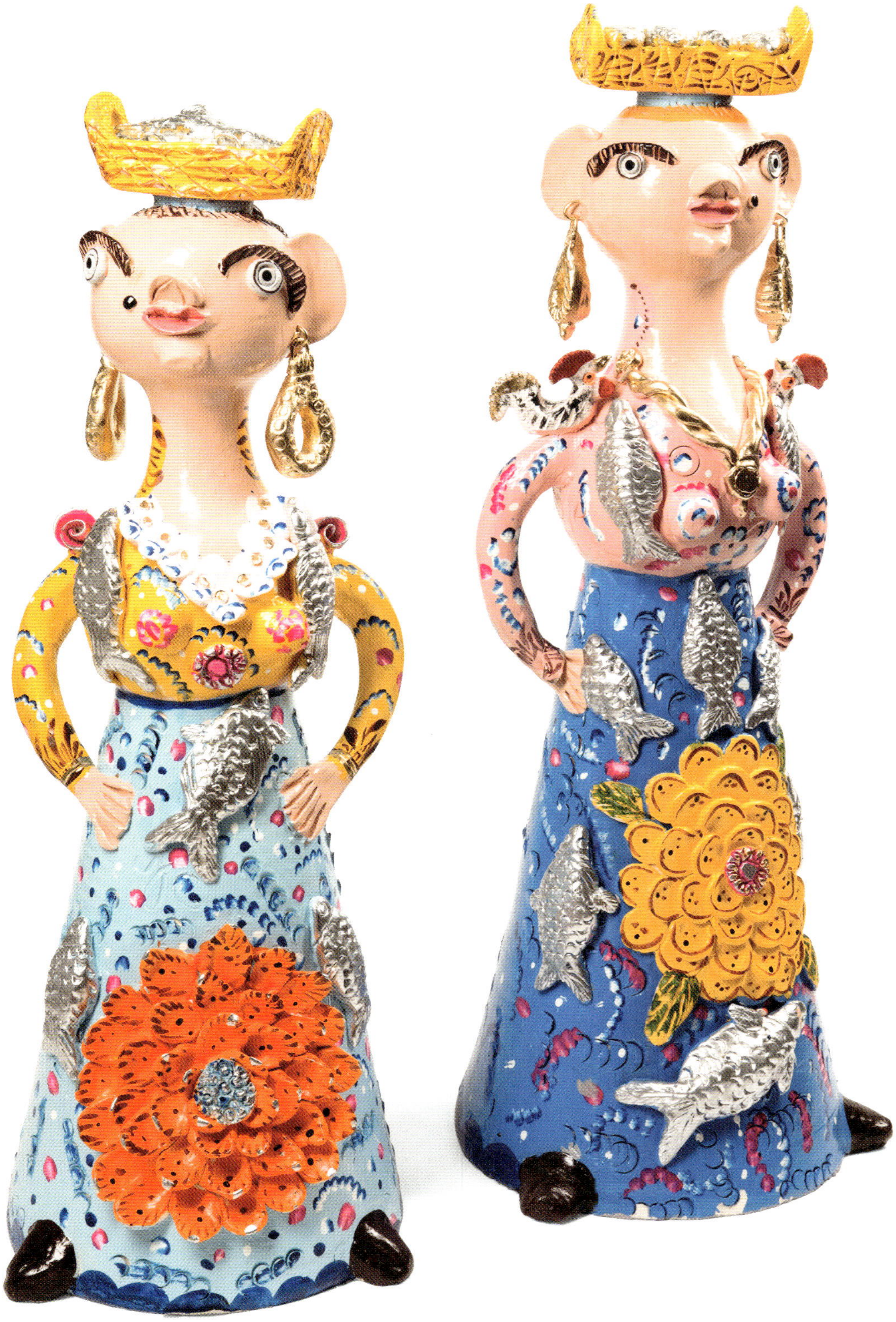

ALEXANDRE
SILVA

LILIANA
PORTER

LILIANA
PORTER

ALEXANDRE
SILVA

ART IS LIKE AN INDIVIDUAL LENS, THAT'S WHY THERE ARE SO MANY KINDS

Contemporary artist Liliana Porter was born in Buenos Aires but has lived in New York for more than 50 years. Chef Alexandre Silva was born in a village called Abrigada, close to Alenquer, but chose Lisbon a long time ago. We meet at his Lisbon restaurant, Loco, an ambitious and very personal project, which has become a gastronomic reference in the capital.

Reluctantly, Liliana tells us something of her professional life. Exhibitions in 40 countries and a constant pursuit of new forms: etching, painting, drawing, photography, video, installation, theatre and performance.

"My creative act spans the ideas to the technique," she says. "It's the ideas who choose the form, the materials, formats, scale and so on."

Alexandre nods in agreement. He's younger but has followed a similarly rich path. He went to the right schools, chose the right specialities and found everything a chef deserves. He tells us of some important restaurants and, above all, Bocca. We'll see why. Amidst it all, he's still had time to participate in TV's *Top Chef* in 2012. When we ask him to talk about the creative process, Alexandre talks about everything bar cooking.

"Ideas come from so many places – from the books I read and the travelling I do," he says. "But also from objects, artworks, things that don't necessarily belong to the world of gastronomy. Then there is studying and getting to know the product knowledge. I want first to know the story of a piglet, and only after to know what I should do with it."

Liliana improvises on the importance of the unexpected, of what we can't control. "Many years ago there was an exhibition of Latin American art at MoMA in New York," she says. "One of my works was included: a doodle and a dropped pencil, just like if someone had dropped it. A visitor picked up the pencil and added another sketch, stronger, more intense – as I should have done. So I ended up integrating that act into my piece."

There is no suspicion that a client ever leapt into to the kitchen to add ingredients to Alexandre's pans, but he tells us about the importance of boldness and irreverence. "At Bocca, we were known as the '*enfants terribles*'," he says. "We used to say whatever we wanted, without worrying. When you're young and you want to assert yourself, it's natural. It's the creativity blooming."

The meeting and the talking are nearing their end. But Liliana has still time to add another morsel.

"Art is like an individual lens, that's why there are so many kinds. Everyone's relation with reality is different: philosophy, politics, thought. It's a place that's special and very free. If you get there, it's down to no one else. It's an act of individual freedom."

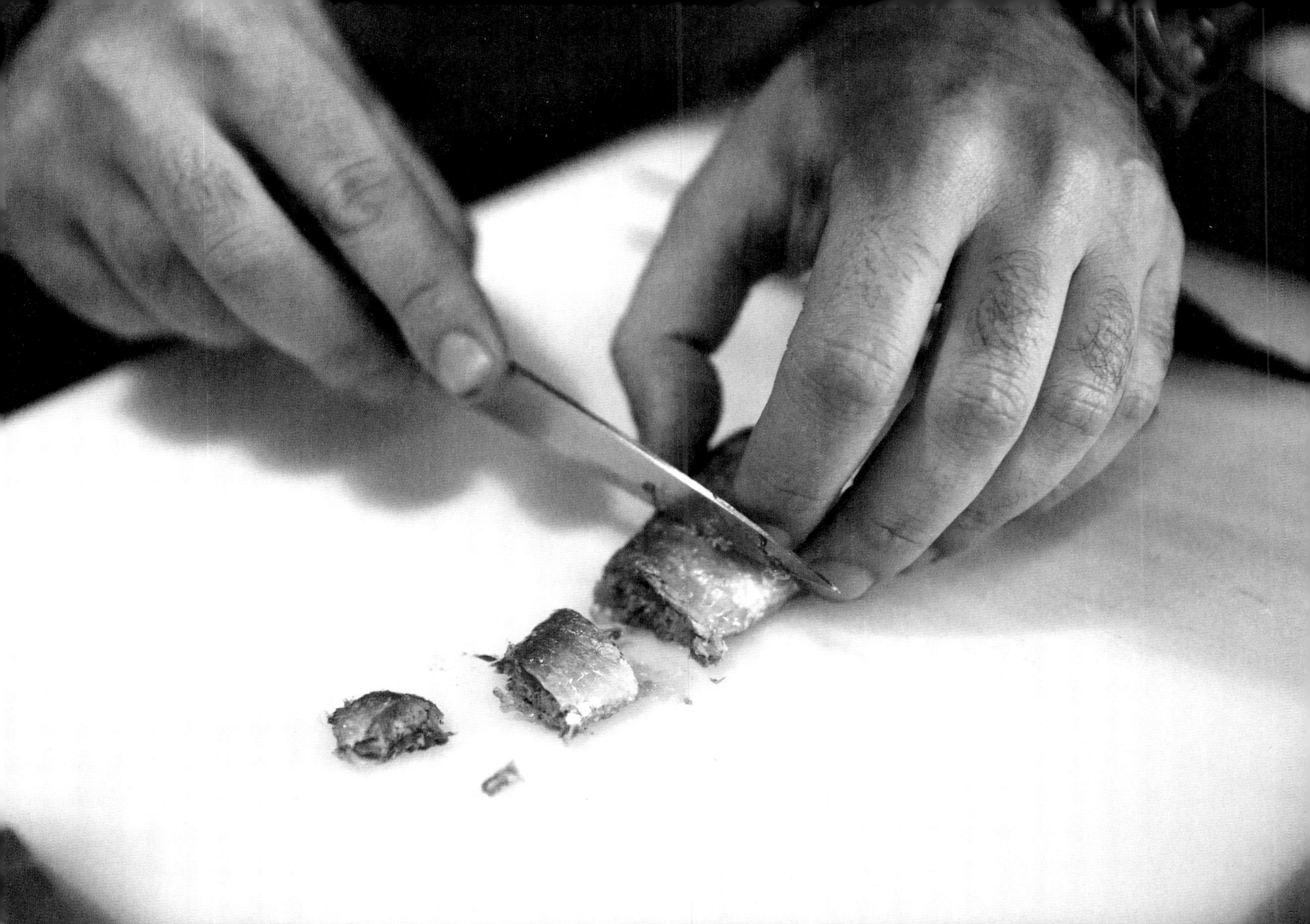

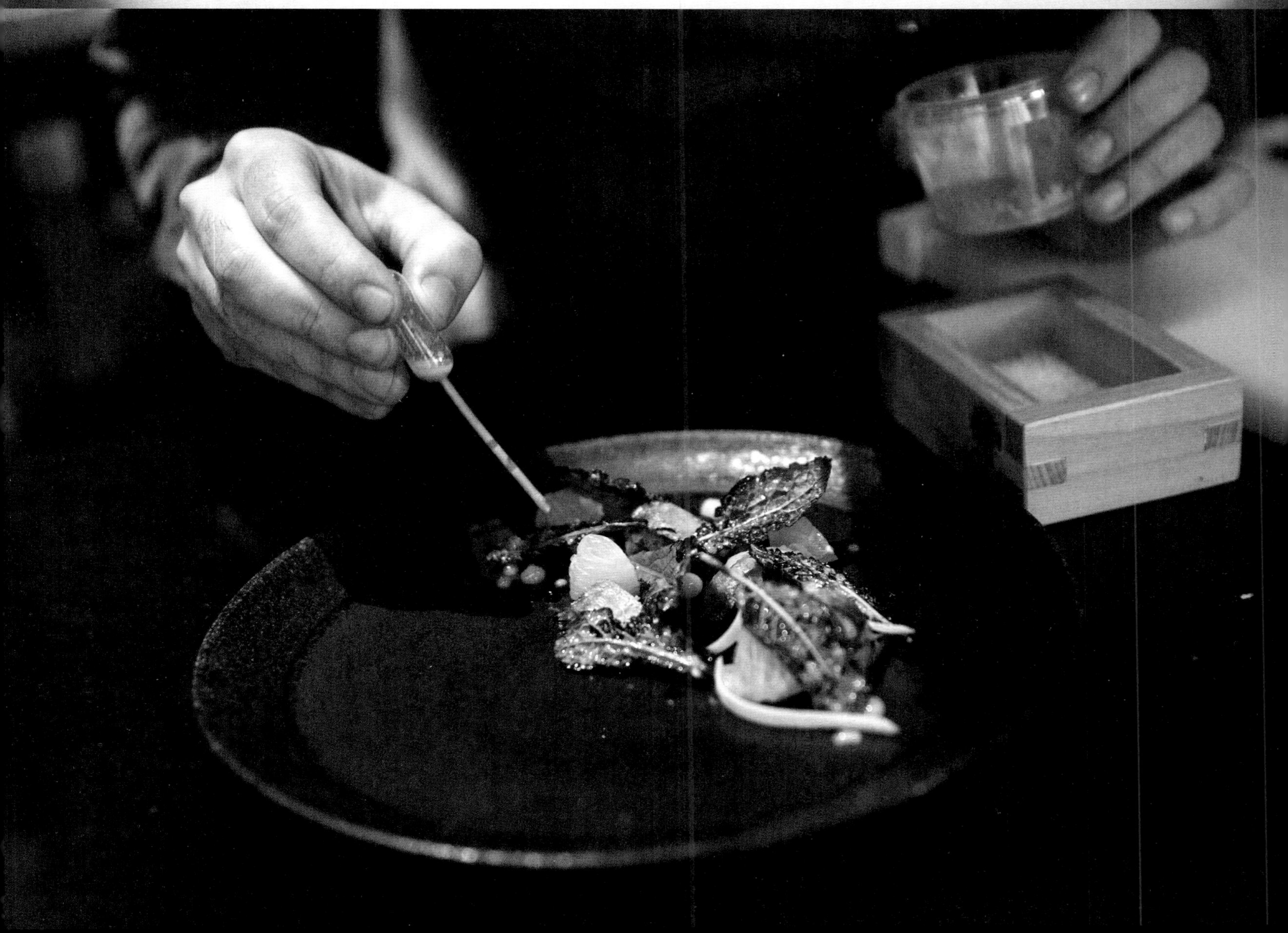

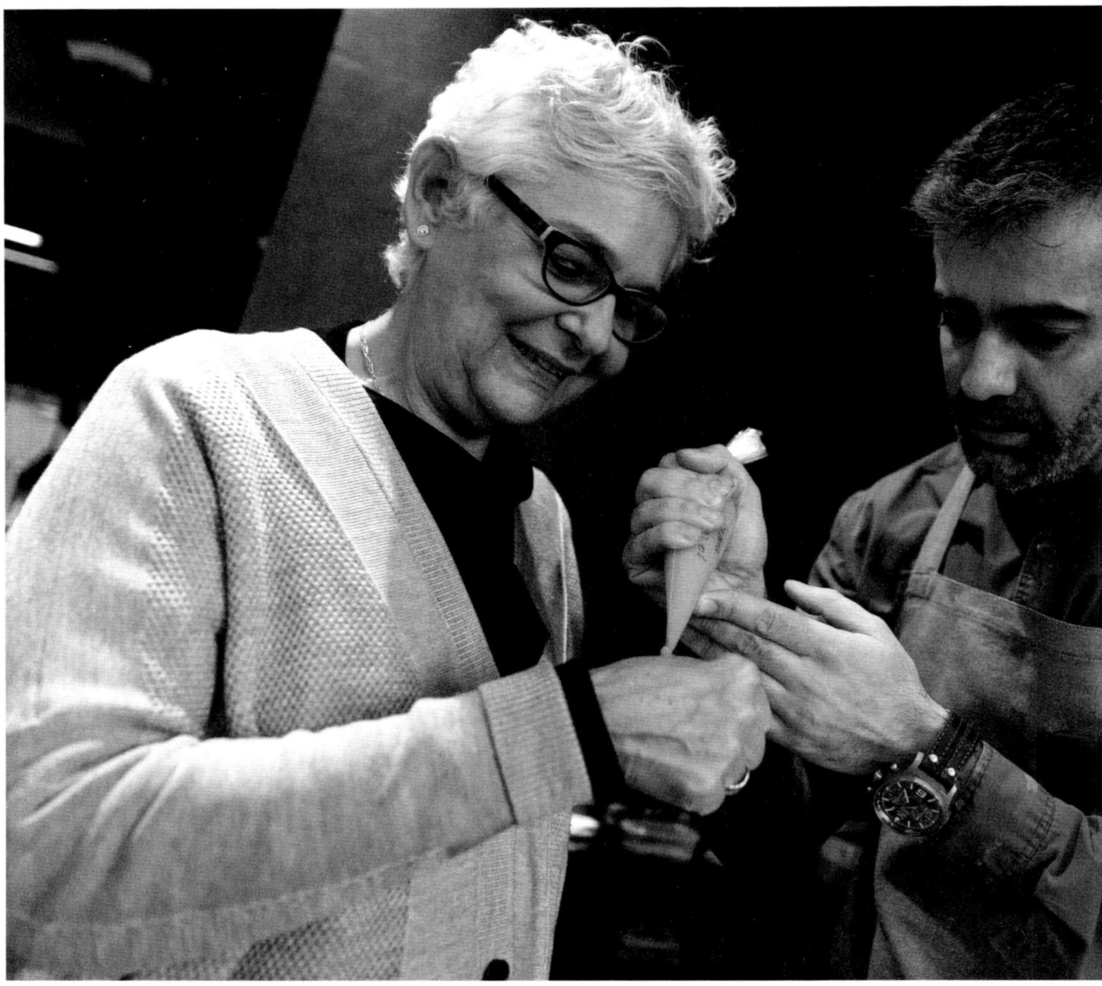

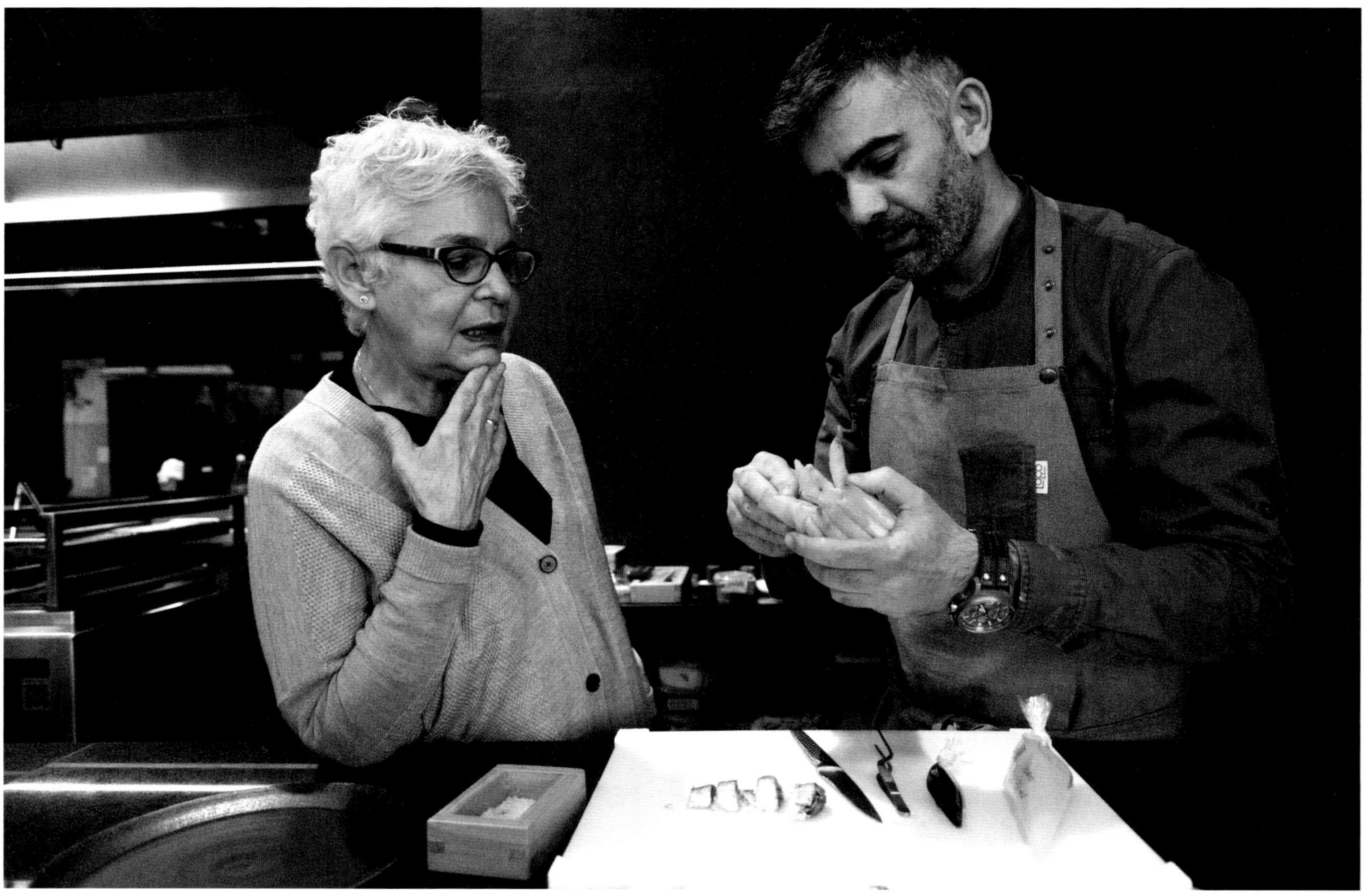

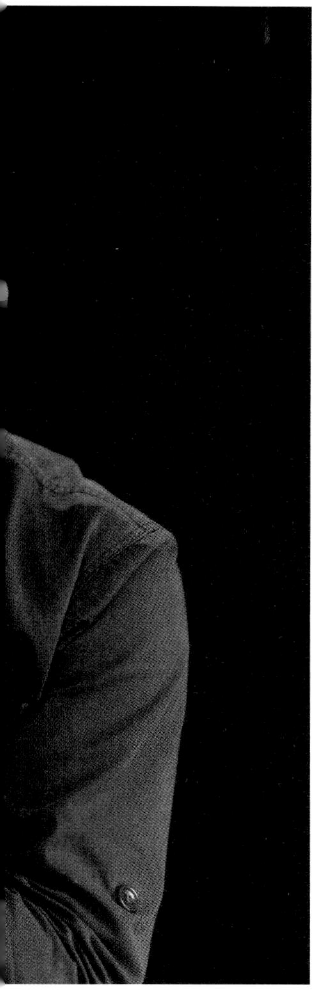

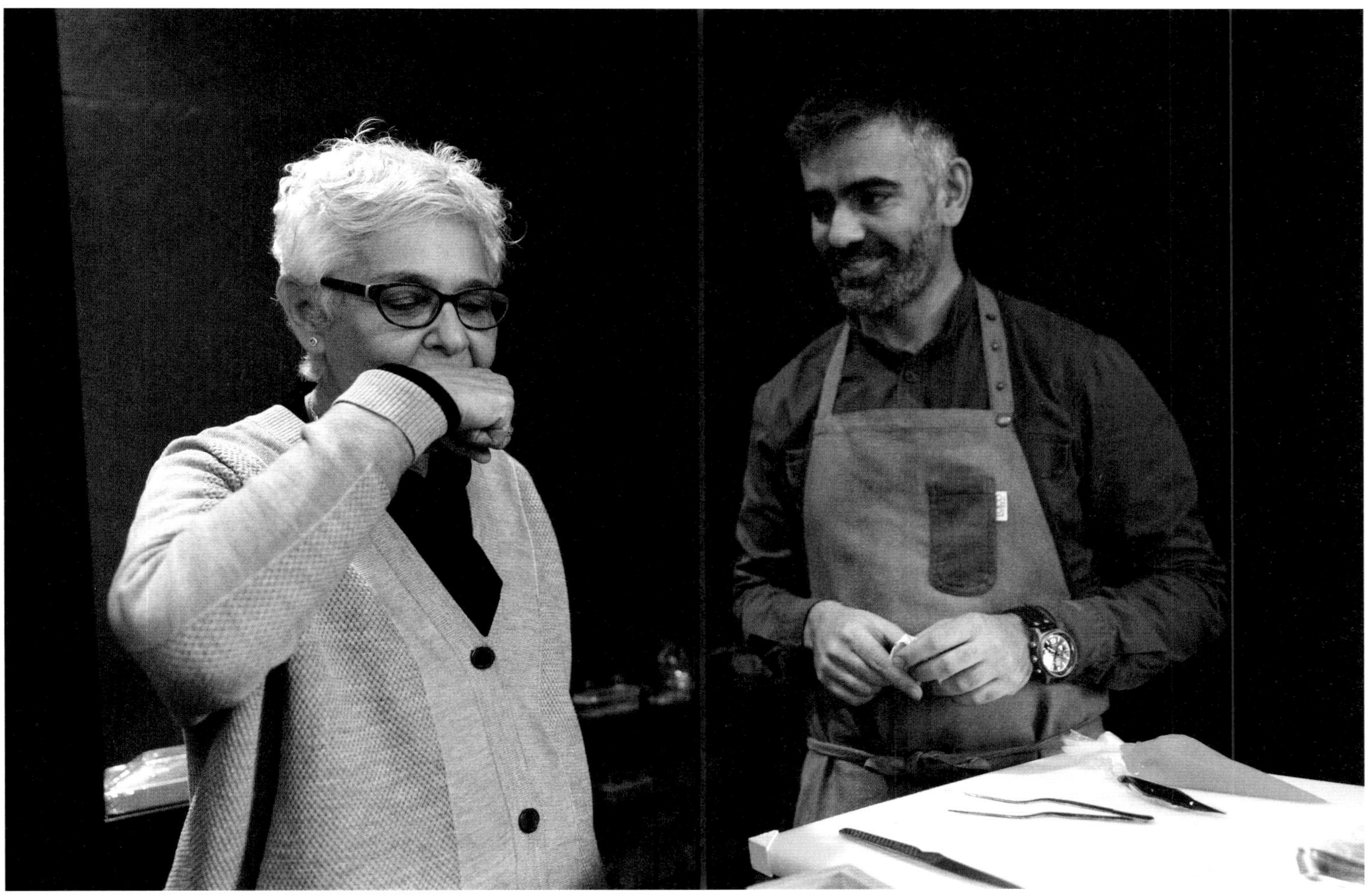

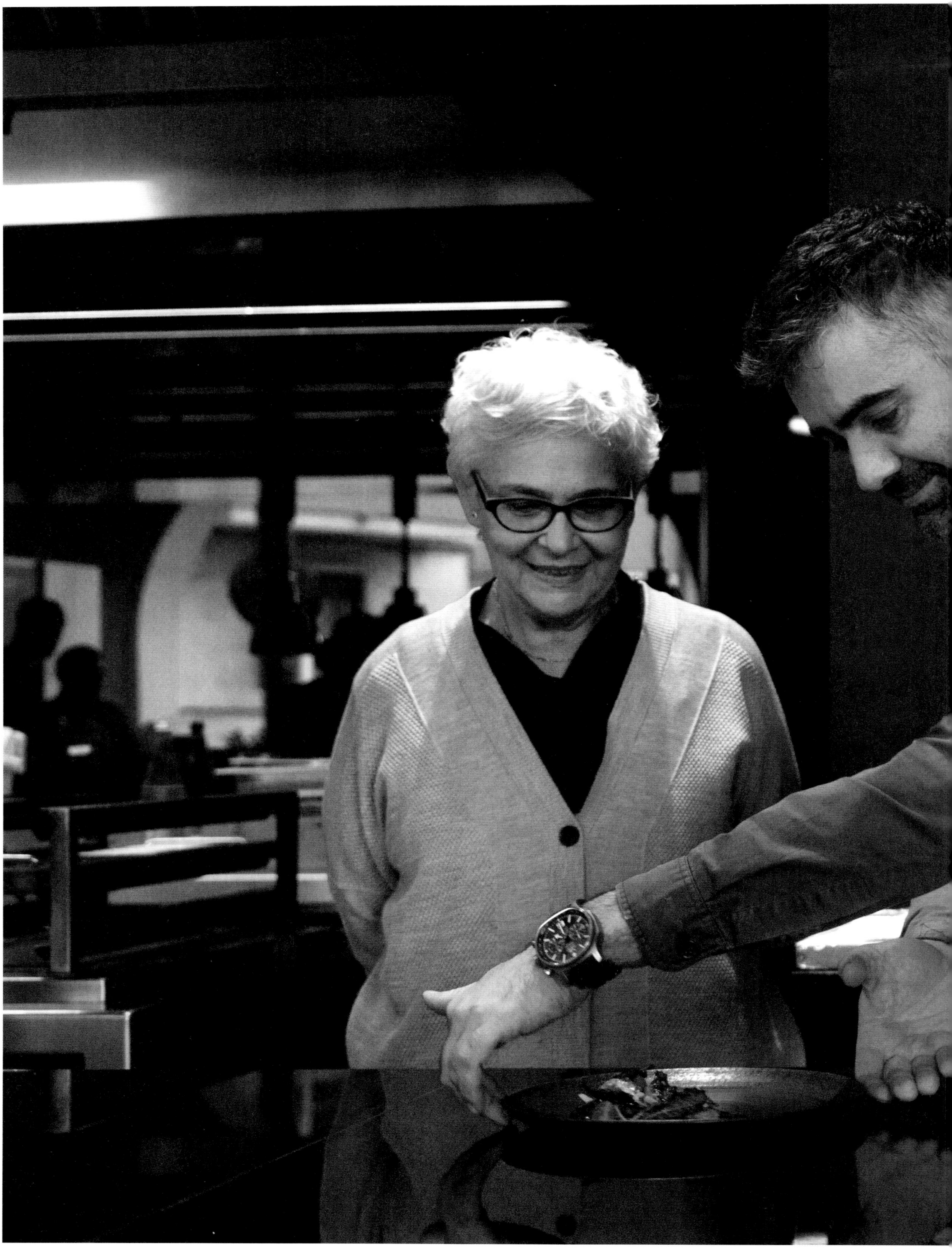

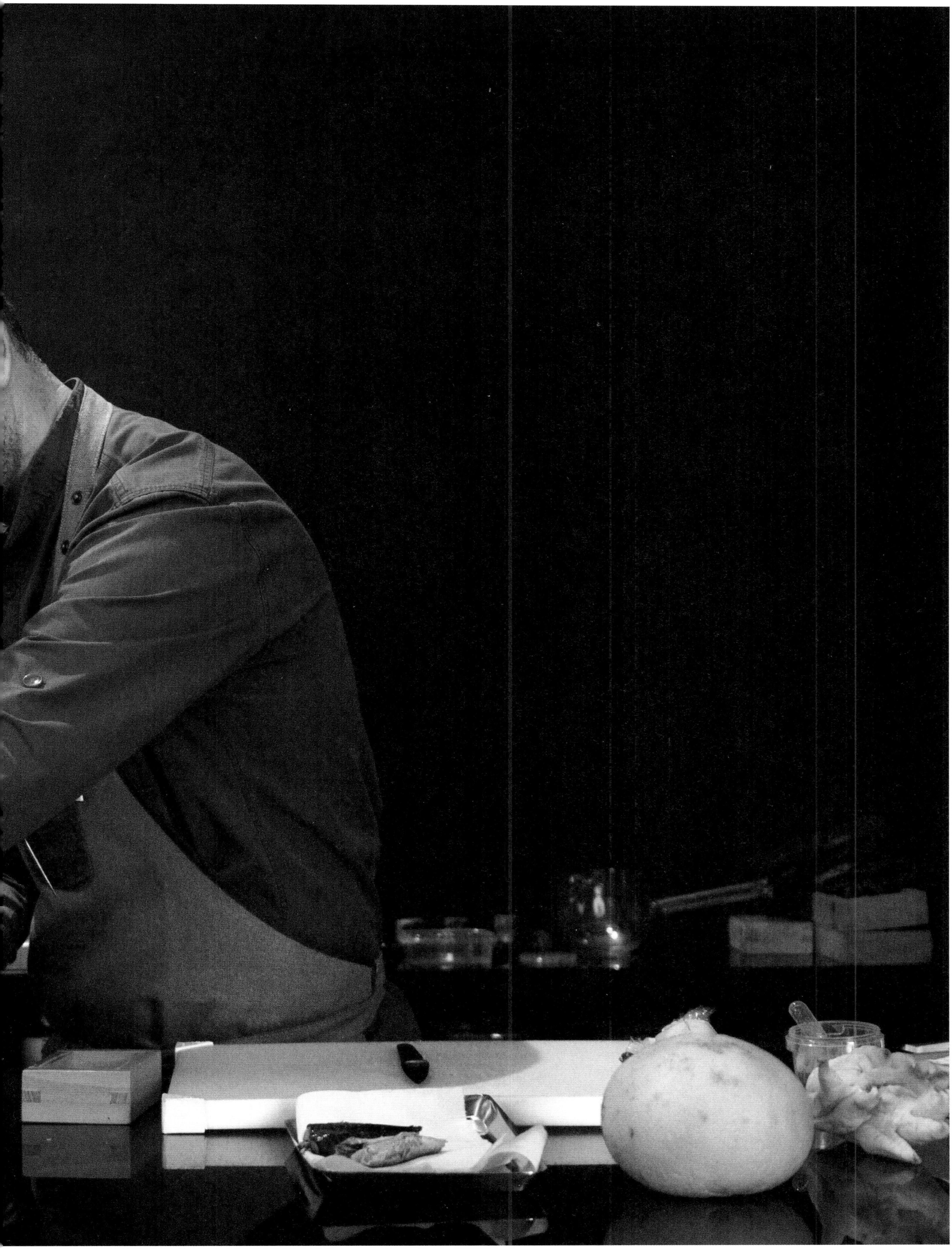

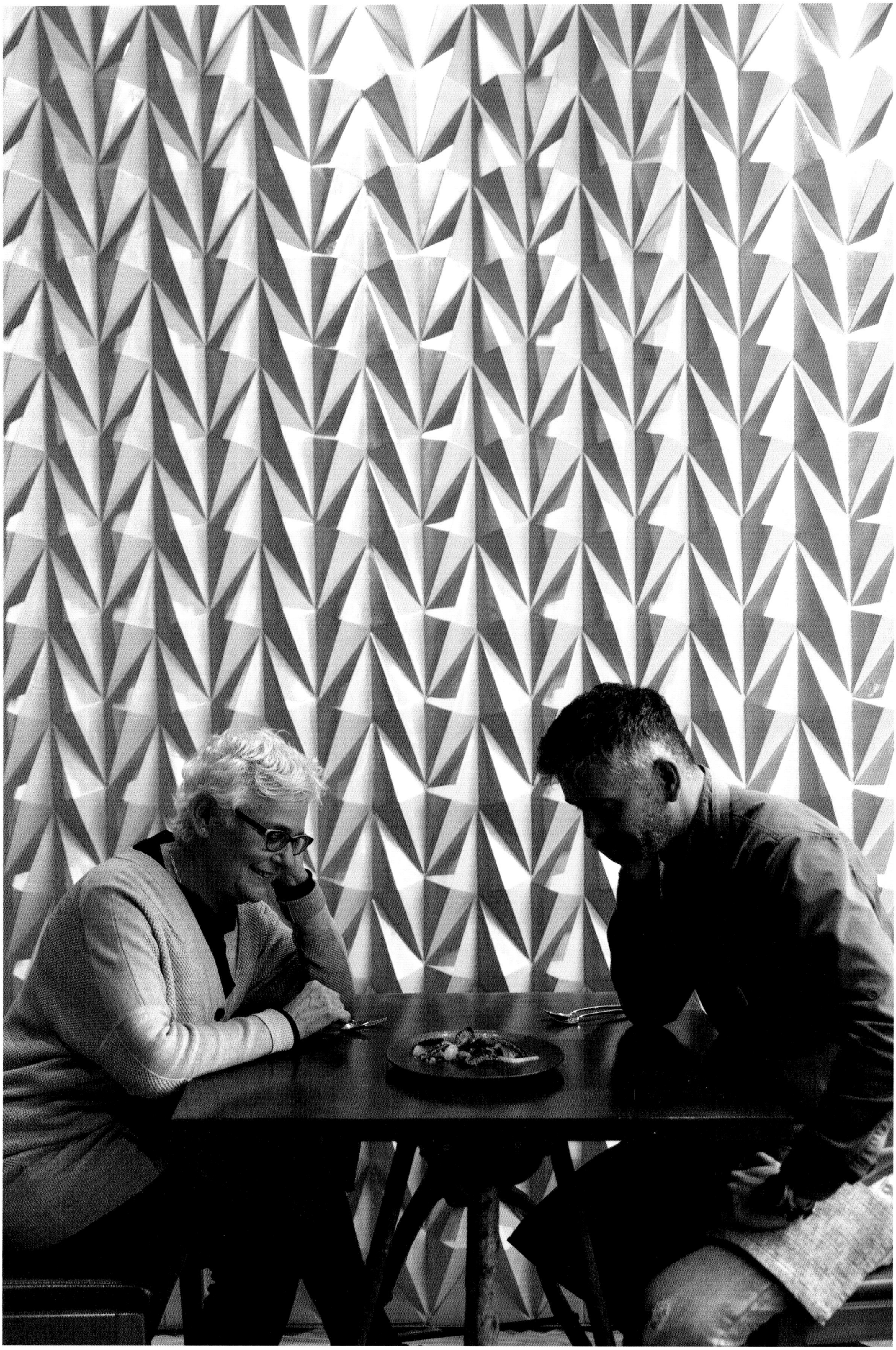

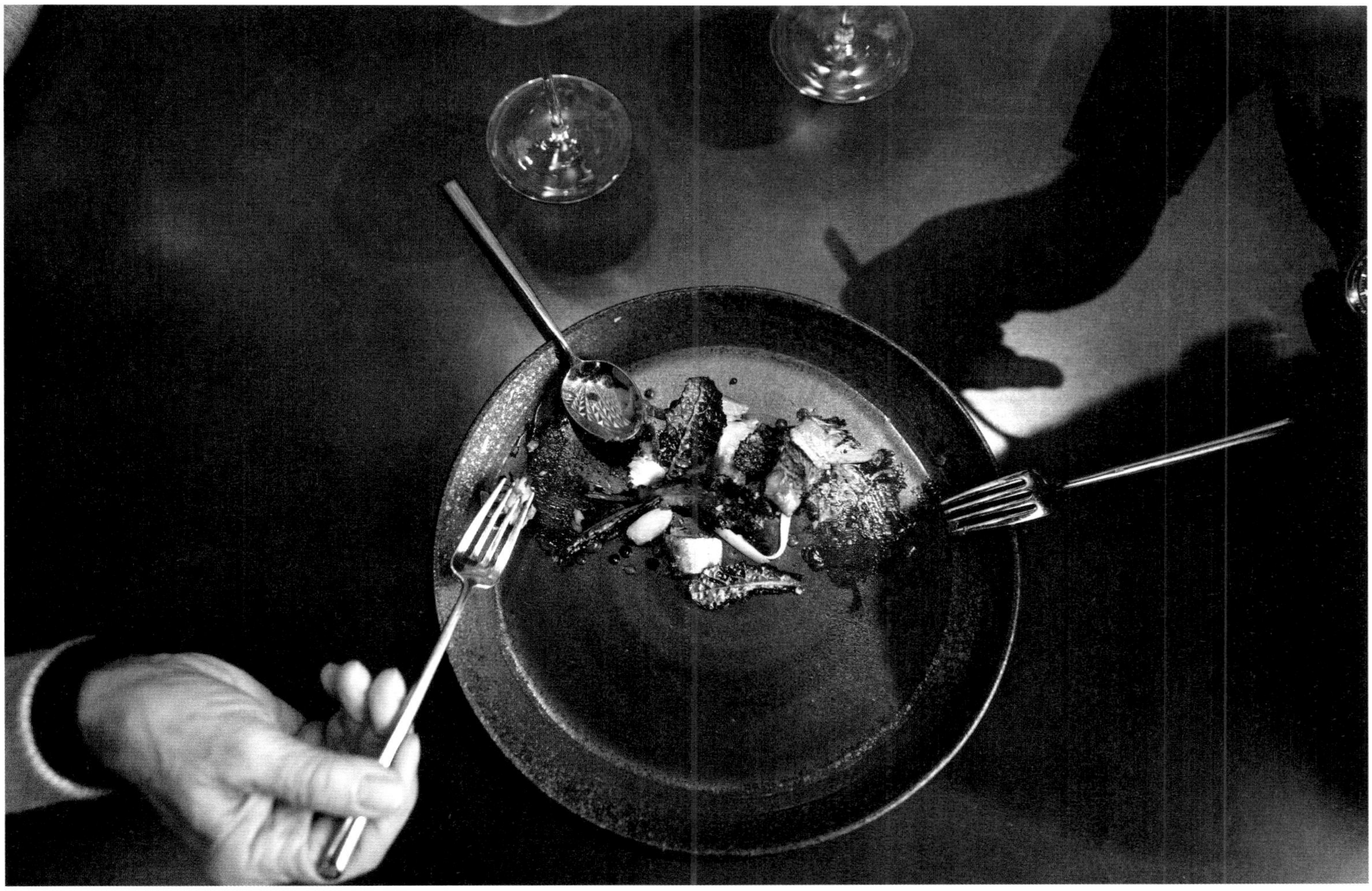

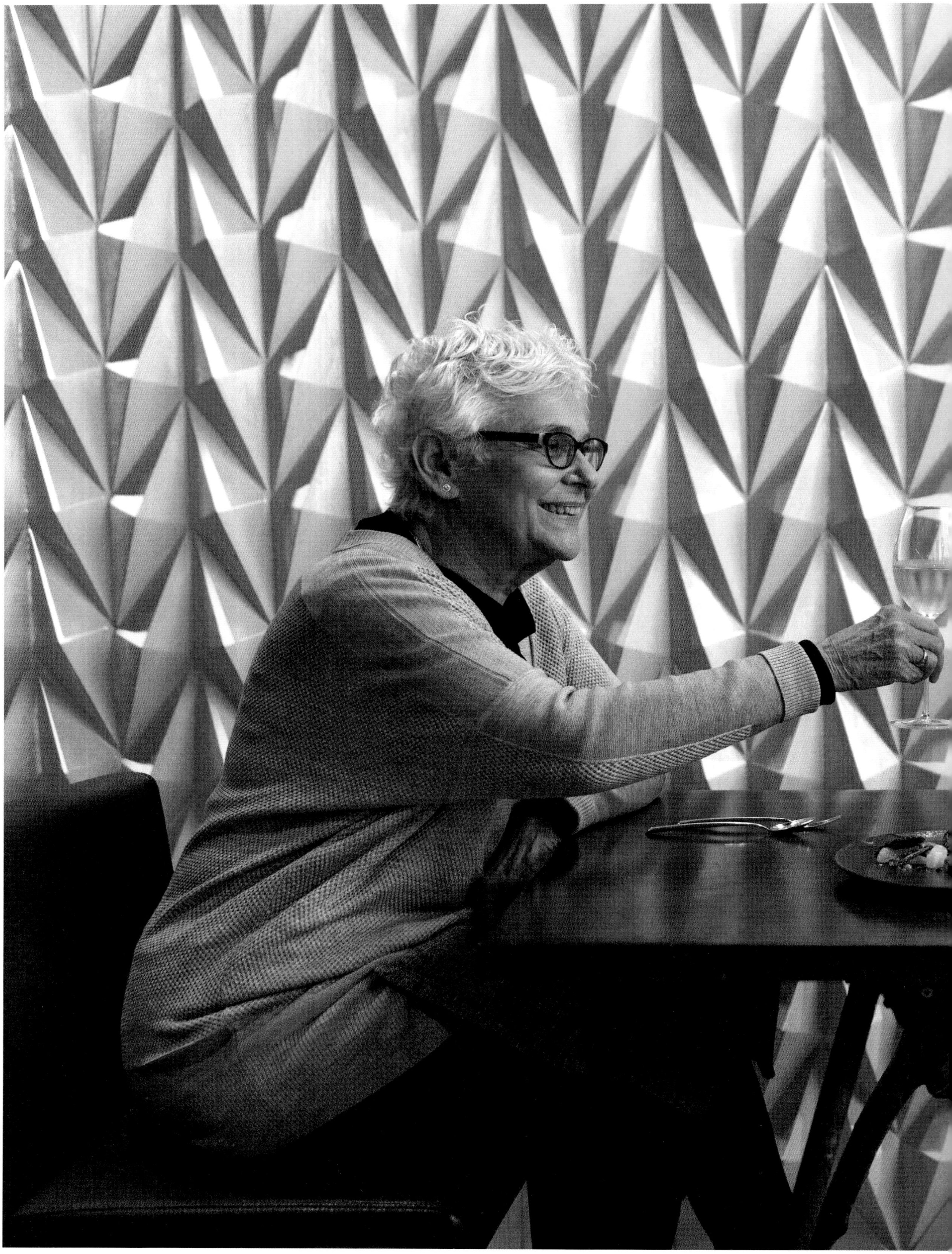

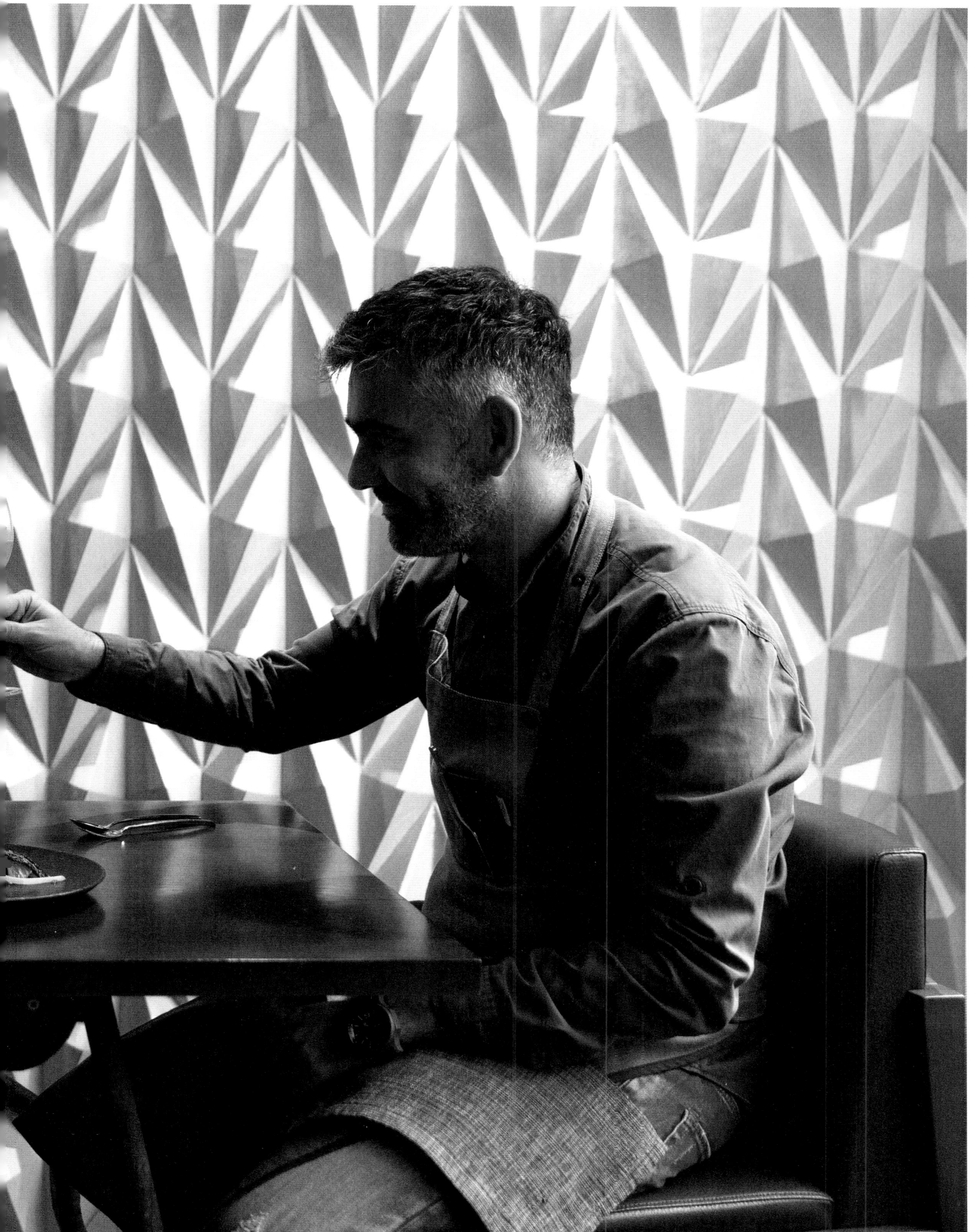

ALE XAN DRE

SARDINE, CITRUS FRUIT
AND GRILLED CABBAGE

SIL VA

SARDINES IN OLIVE
OIL WITH LEMON
BRAND MARINA

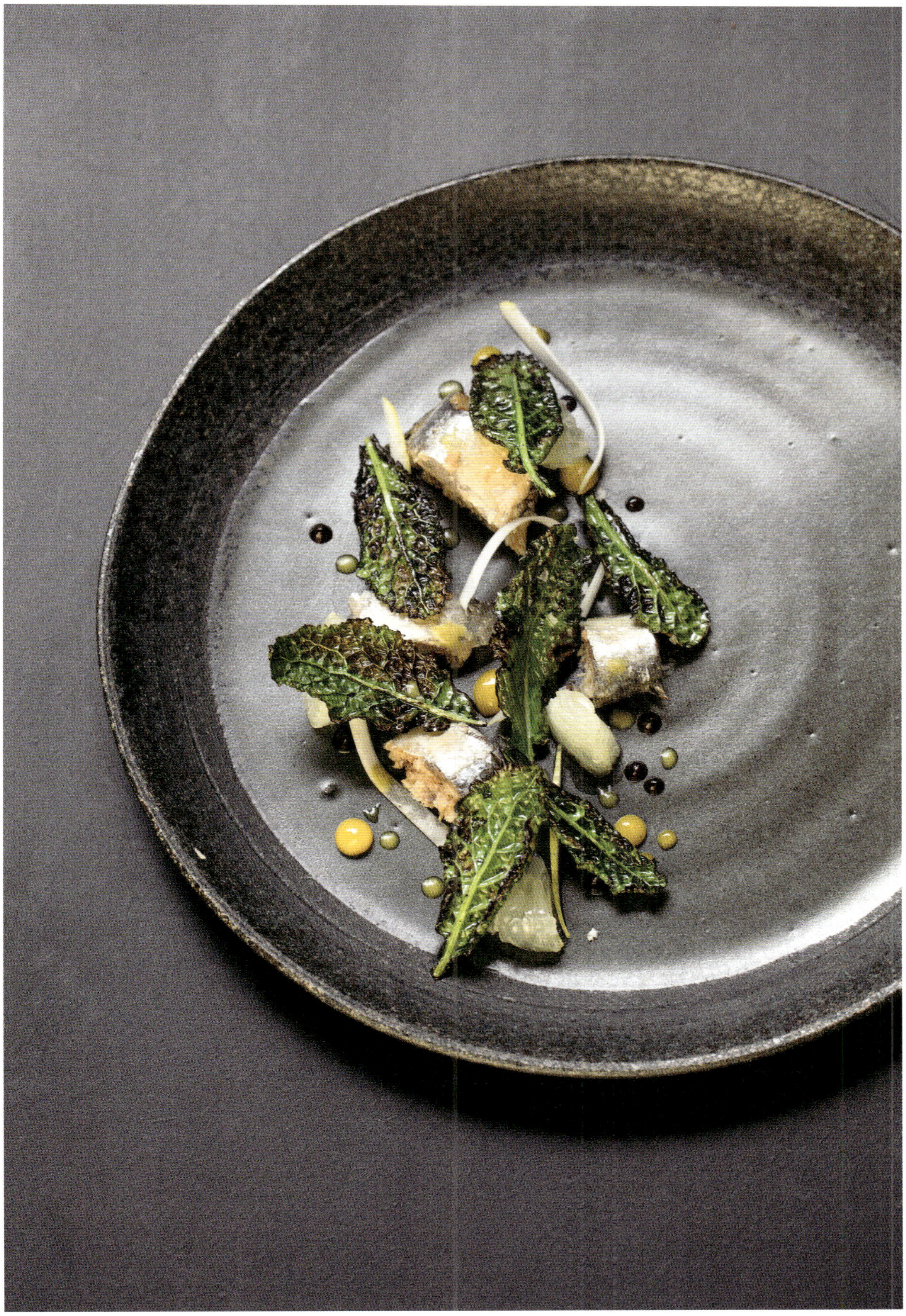

LILIANA PORTER

HÁ MAR
E MAR HÁ IR
E VOLTAR
2018

MIXED
TECHNIQUE
ON PAPER
56 × 77 CM

UNIÃO CONSERVEIRA DO ALGARVE, Lª
129
DOENTE

VITOR
SOBRAL

ANA
TISCÓRNIA

ANA
TISCÓRNIA

VÍTOR
SOBRAL

"THE MOST IMPORTANT THING IS TO KNOW HOW TO FORM TEAMS"

"I grew up watching people slaughter pigs, and I must have killed my first one at the age of sixteen." It's Vítor Sobral who says it, a chef who is as forthright as he is famous and respected in Portuguese gastronomy. "I started playing with pans when I was about seven, and haven't stopped since." He worked in some of the most iconic spaces in Lisbon and, in 2009, opened Tasca da Esquina, since replicated in São Paulo and João Pessoa in Brazil. We meet here, with the artist Ana Tiscórnia, in a restaurant dedicated to the best Portuguese gastronomic tradition.

"I was born in Montevideo, in Uruguay, but lived in New York for more than twenty-five years," says Ana. "My career has encompassed architecture, the arts, curating and editing, research and university teaching. It's a lot..."

Ana laughs at herself.

She is curious and attentive, you can see it in her eyes and in the questions she asks. There's a sentence she likes to repeat and that she incorporates into her life and work: "Art ends in the gaze of another."

We ask her if she still feels like an architect. "I studied architecture in Uruguay and it turned out to be a good mistake," she says. "I was an architect for eighteen years, but when I moved to New York I was in conflict with the discipline. I felt that, in some way, the most plastic part of it limited me, at the same time as interesting me most. During the first fifteen years in New York I untied myself as much as I could from architecture, but for the past decade I've been becoming reconciled. In my latest work there's something of a game with architectural language."

Meanwhile, Vítor Sobral is silently preparing the dish. His hands are safe and precise, in absolute concentration. Where does all this come from? How did he become a chef?

"I come from a middle-class family that, after the 25 April revolution, was able to send its children to study to become doctors, engineers, architects, things like that. And I decided to become a cook. With my parents it was easy, they always supported me. But the neighbours and relatives found it weird – a cook? But that's what I wanted. I think I always did."

We return to Ana and the multiplicity of techniques and materials she's used on her artistic path.

"After many years doing one thing, it's great to change and start to do something we don't know," she says. "When we're not film-makers and we decide to make cinema, something new comes out. Because we're not formatted. It might not be cinema, but it is what it is. And that interests me. I also had a big interest in photography because it would let me use the objects almost without touching them."

And you, Vítor, what did you learn in all these years of being a professional? What can you teach us? The chef becomes very serious, thinks for a while and answers.

"The most important thing is to know how to form teams. It's not about the chef, but about the whole work group. You can't do anything without a good team, especially when you have restaurants in different continents. Everything has to function, the group has to be more than the sum of its parts."

Ana and Vítor sit down at the table to taste the dish. They are people of few words, but their intense gaze communicates in silence. They are serious, competent professionals. Masters of their arts, but discreet. Their art speaks for them.

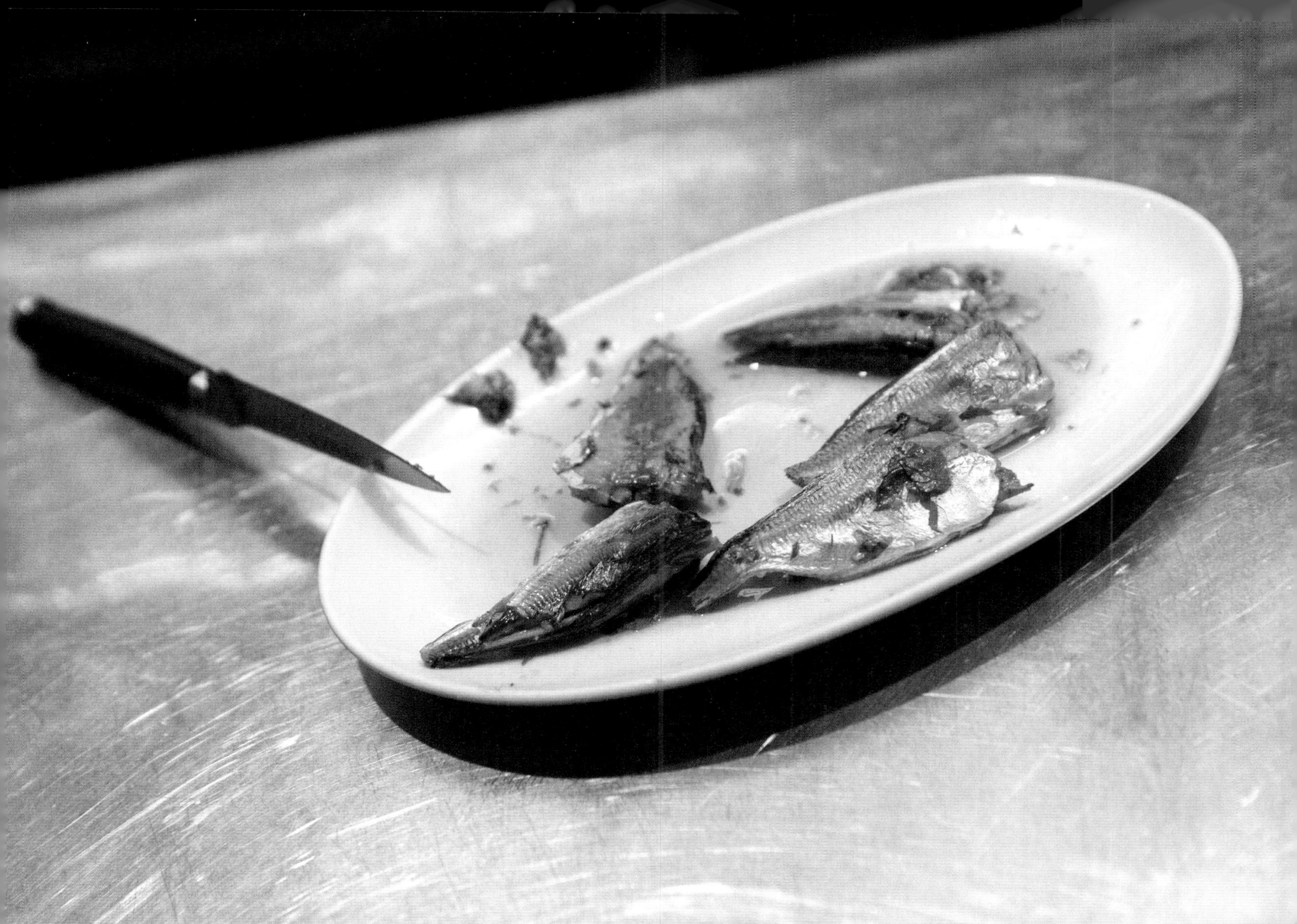

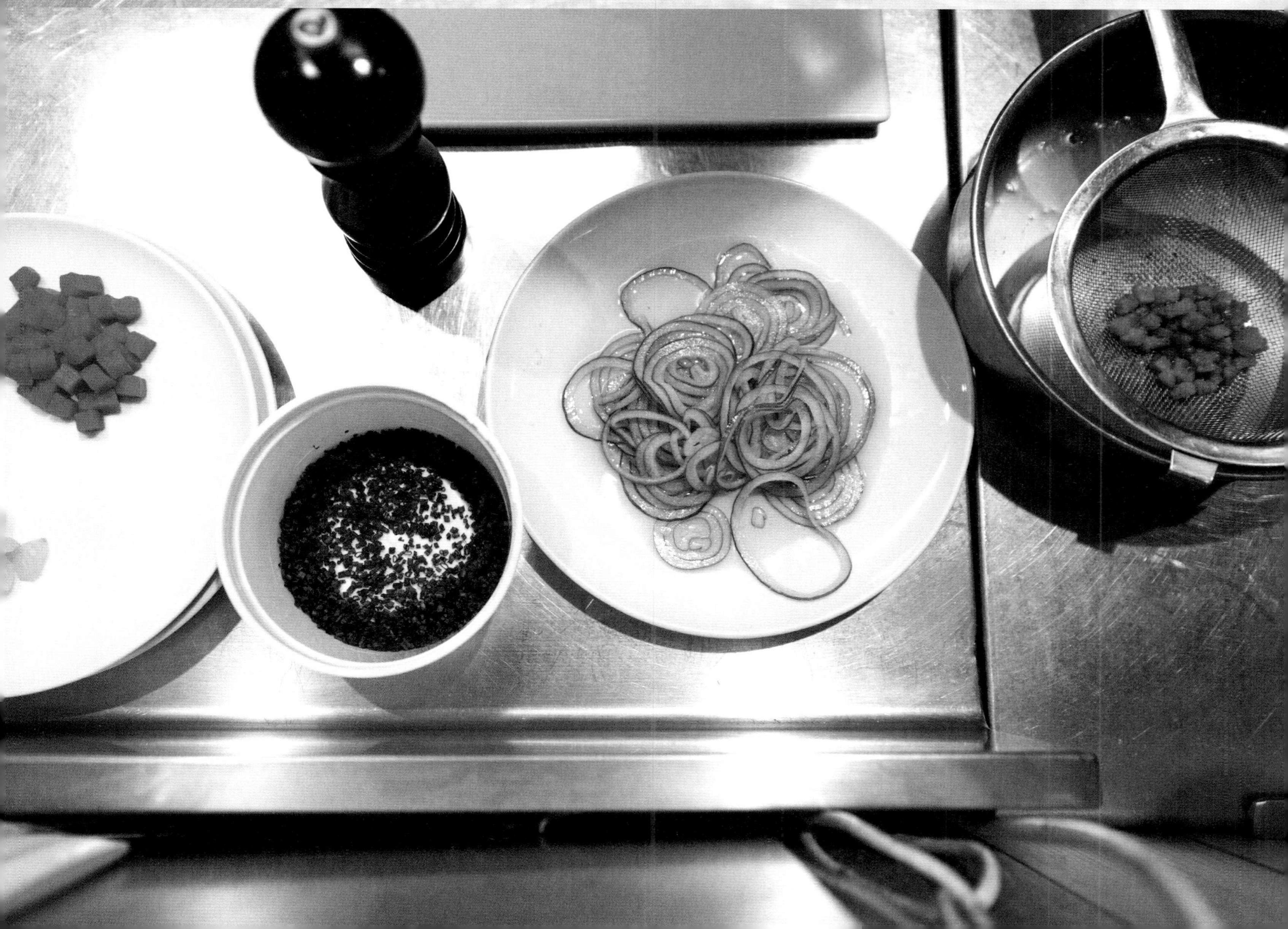

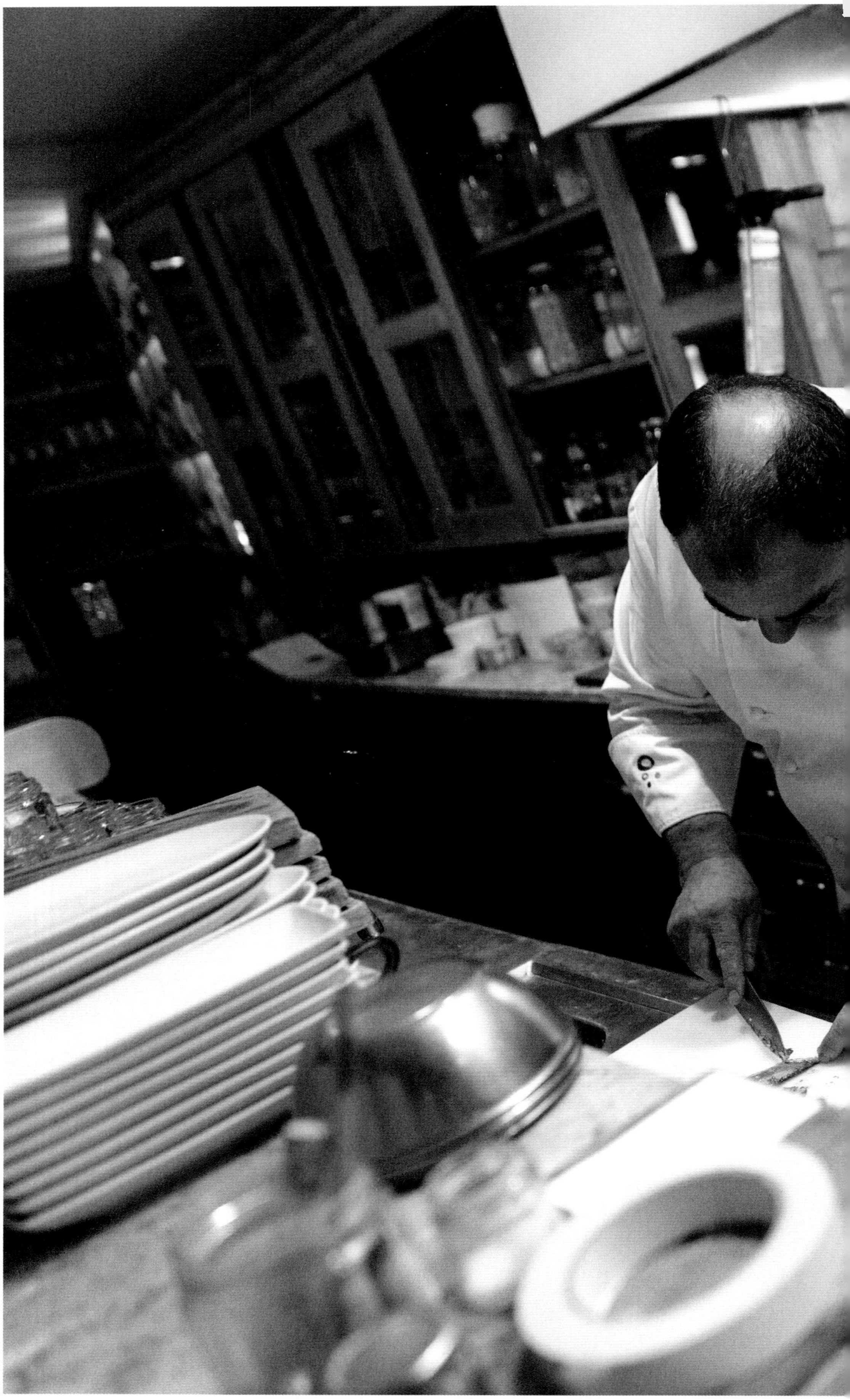

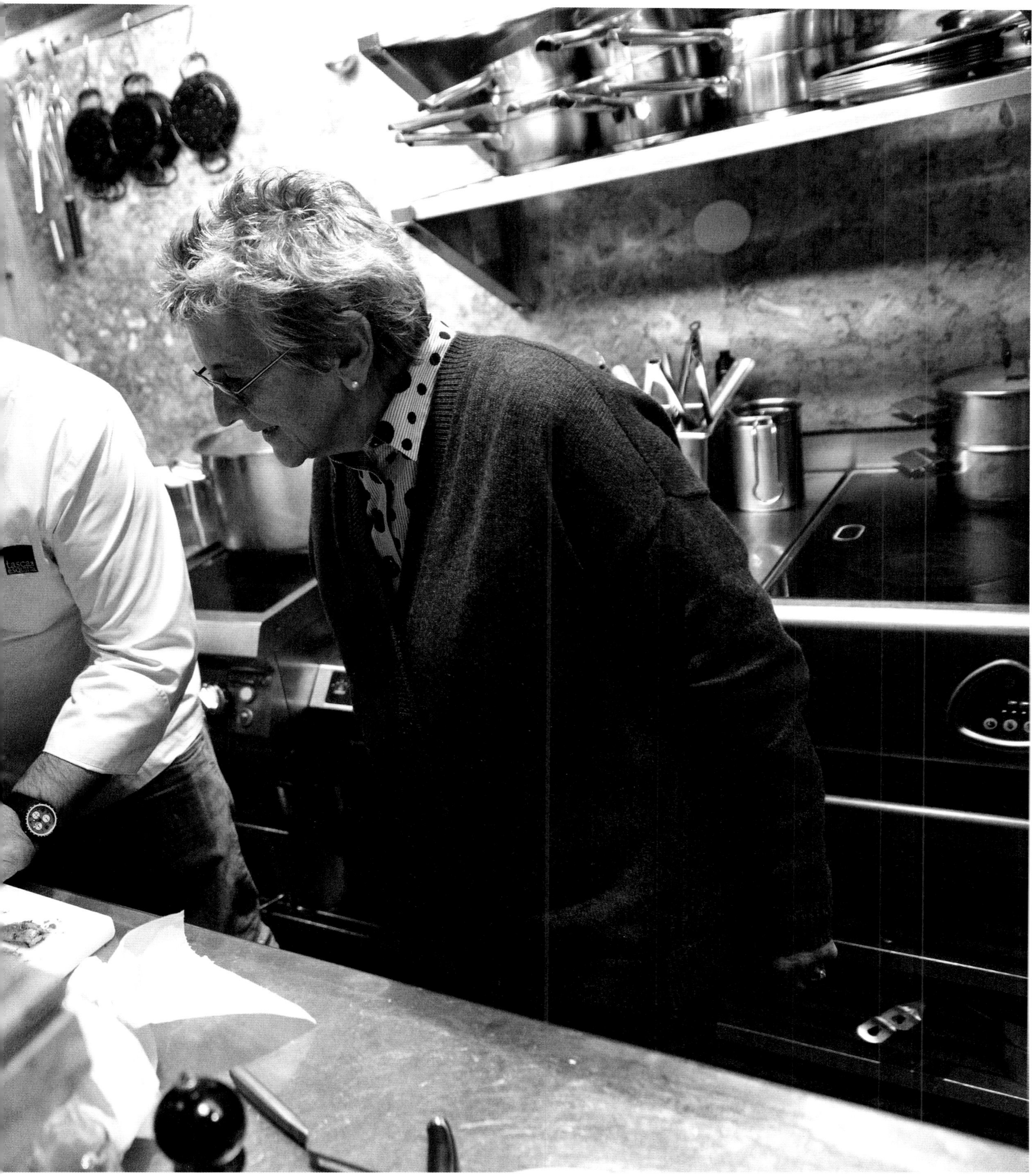

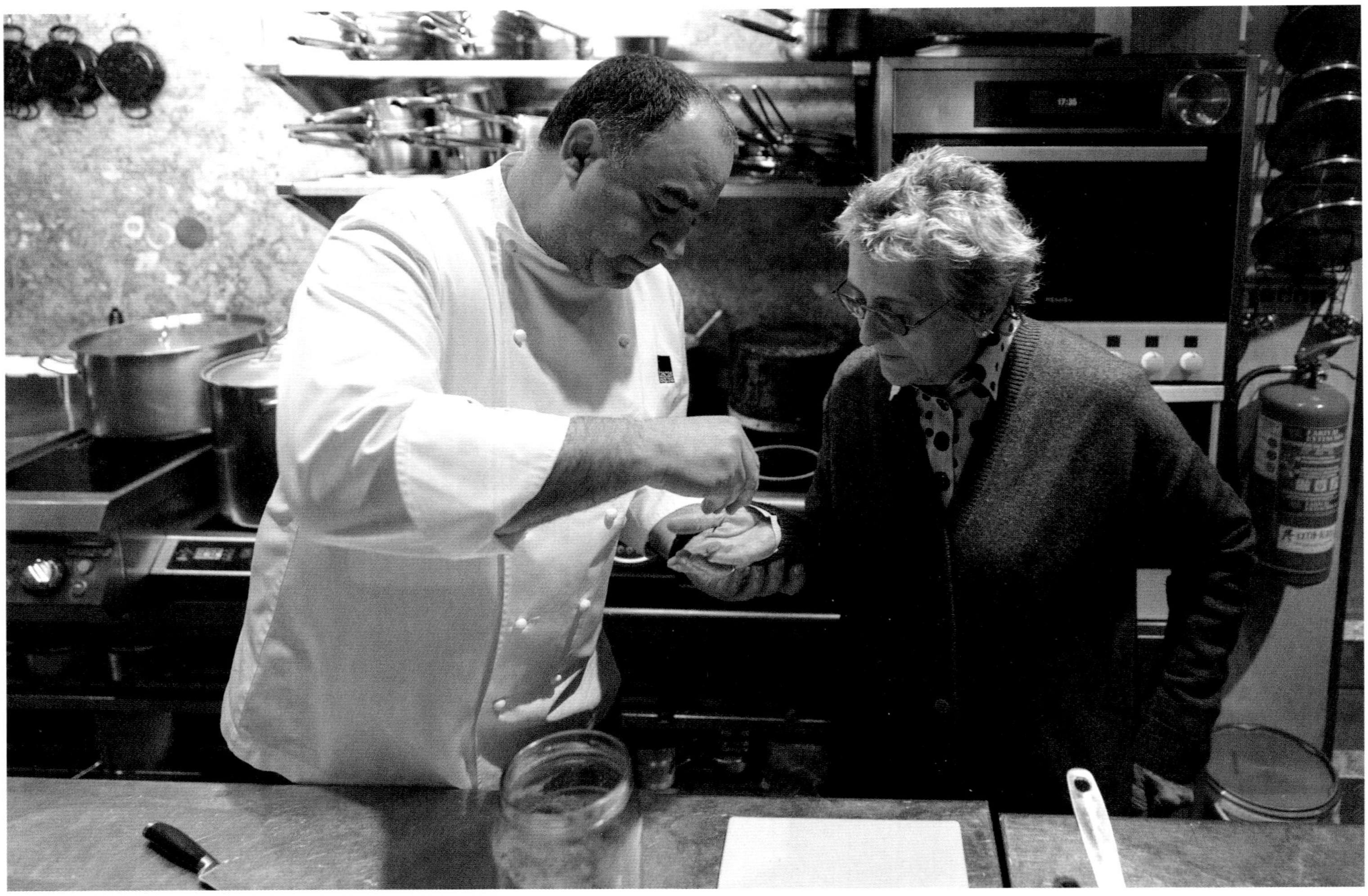

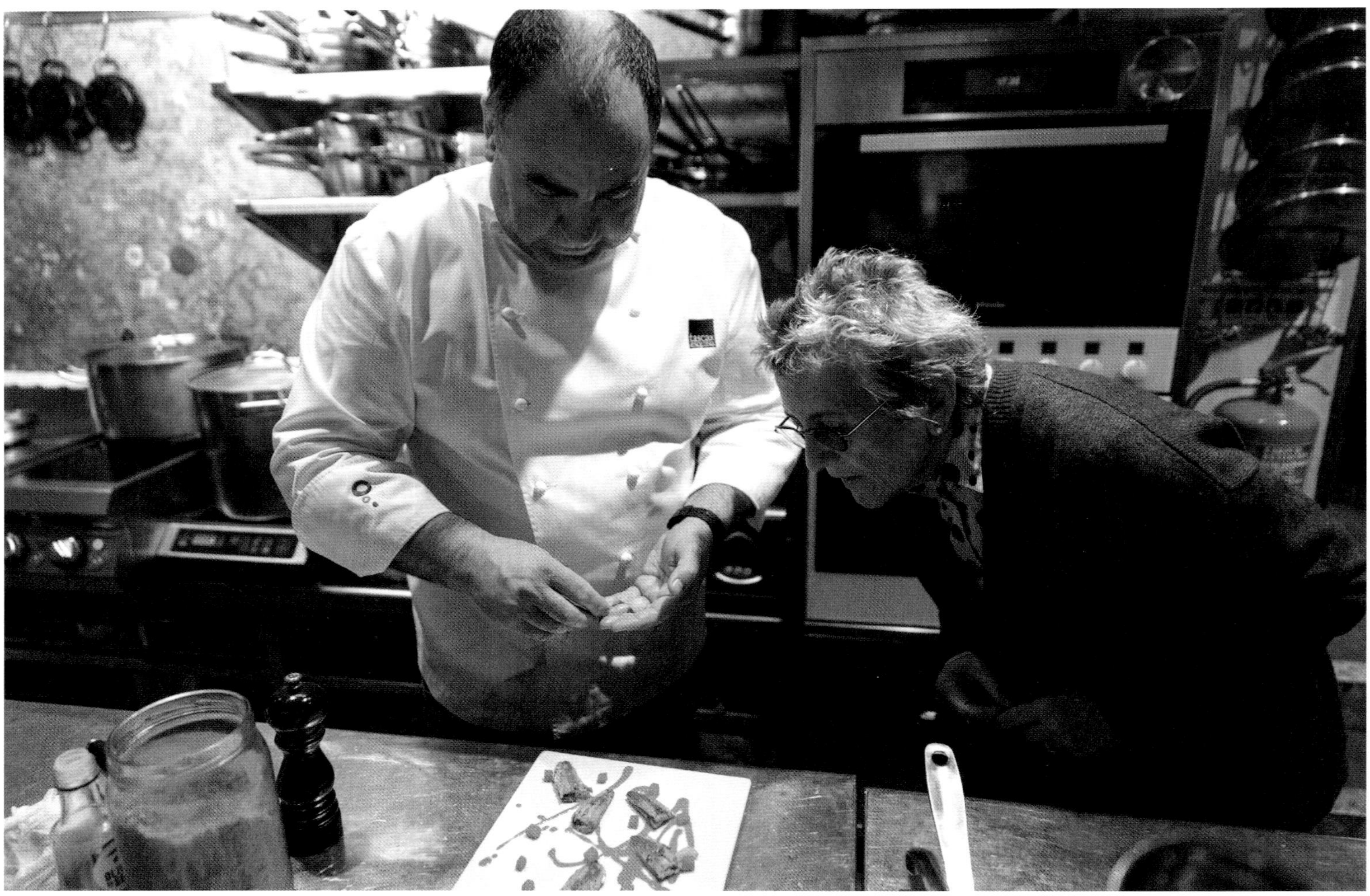

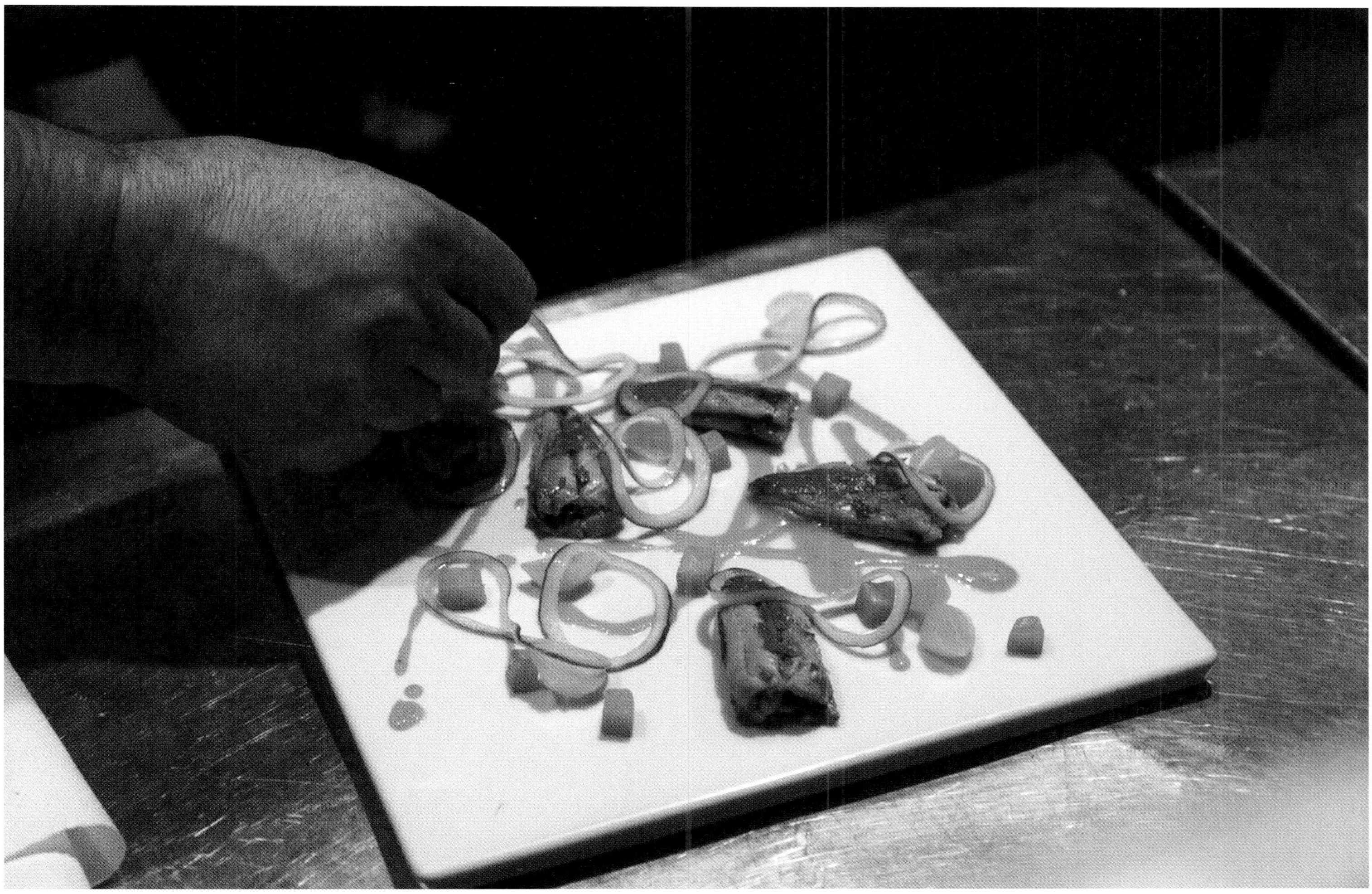

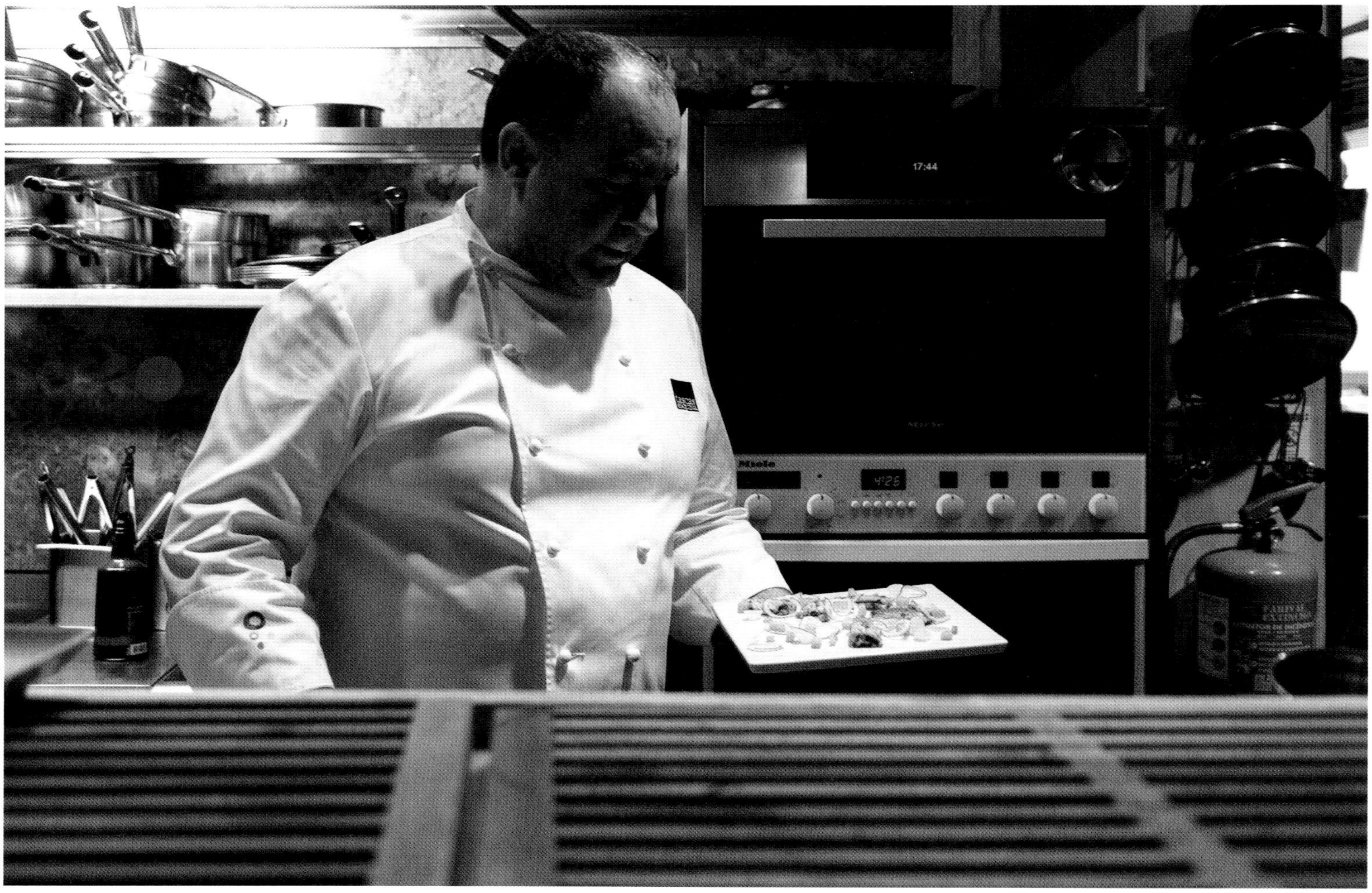

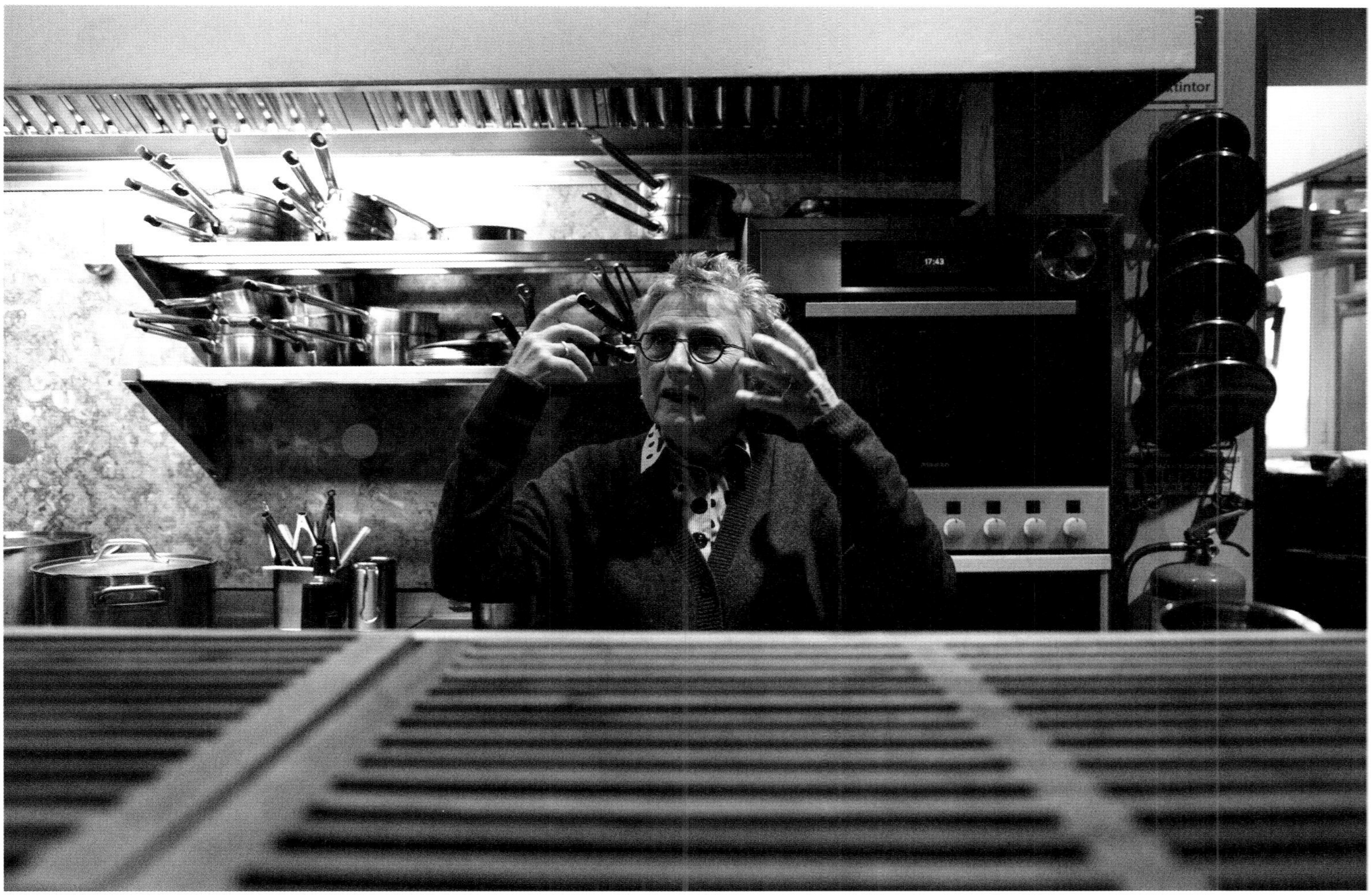

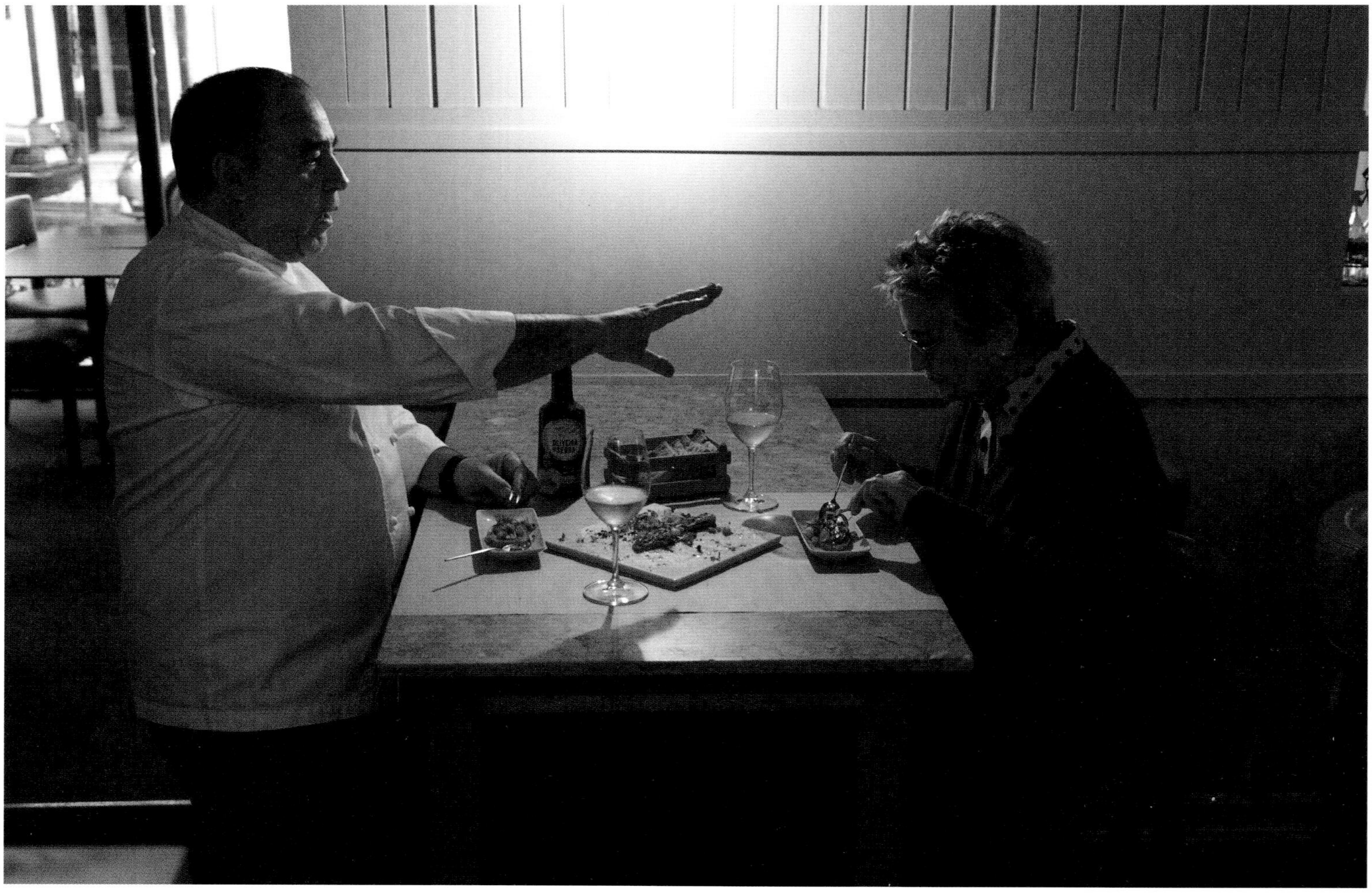

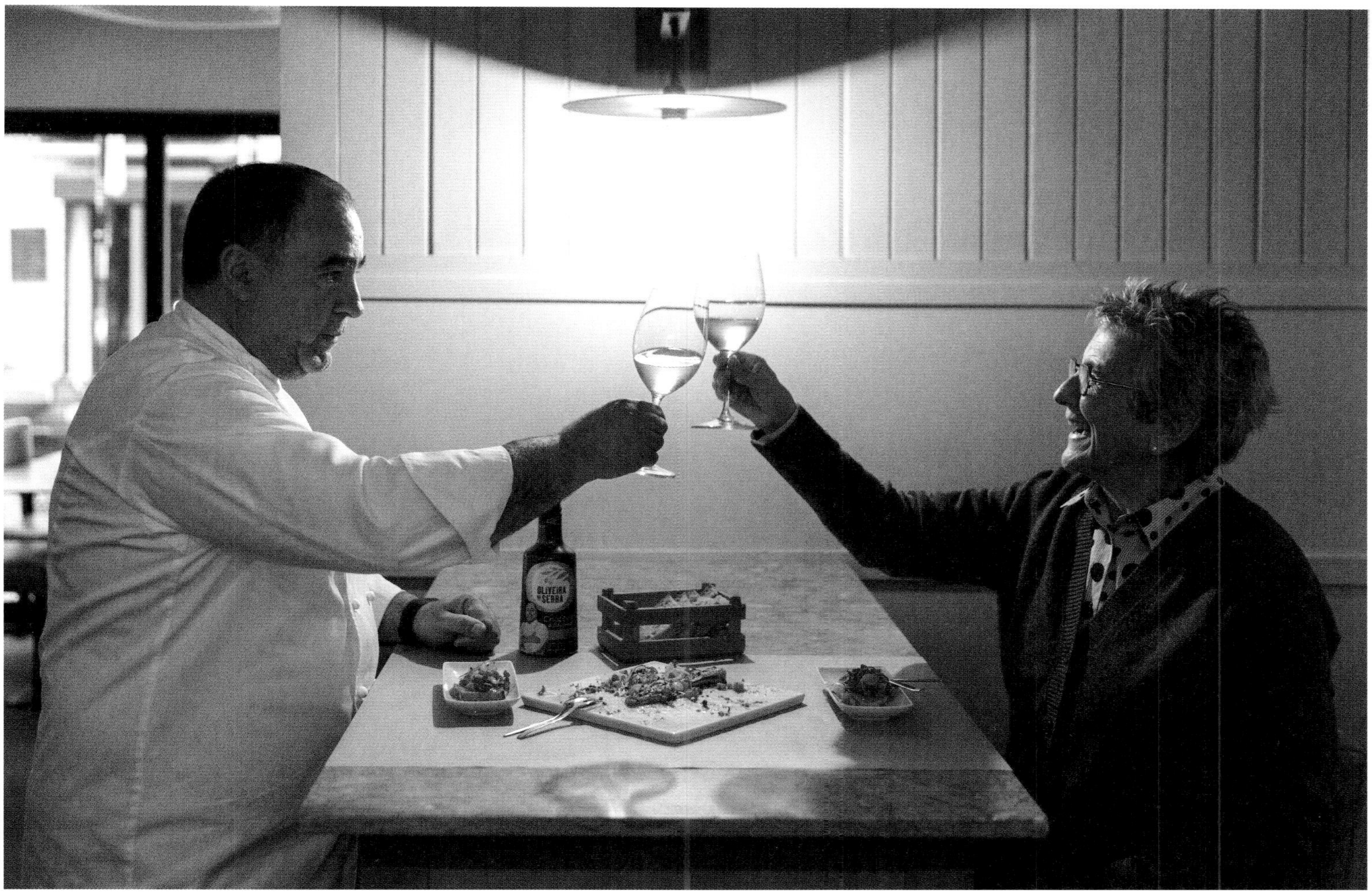
OLIVEIRA DA SERRA

VÍTOR

CANNED HORSE MACKEREL,
DRIED FRUITS, MARINATED
ONION AND PUMPKIN PICKLES

SOBRAL

HORSE MACKEREL
IN OLIVE OIL

BRAND PINHAIS

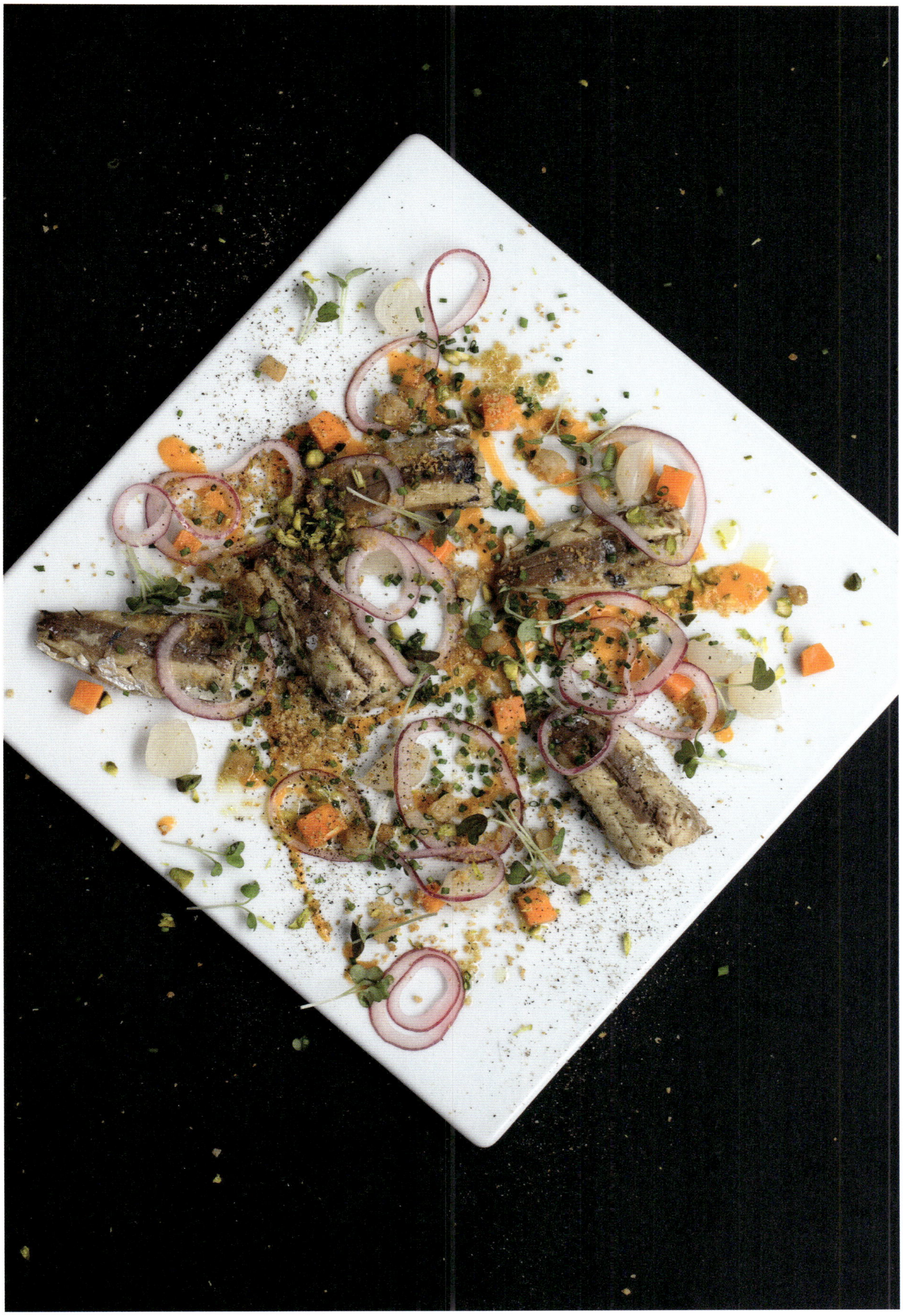

A N A

CONSERVEIRA
2018

T I S

C Ó R

N I A

MIXED TECHNIQUE ON PAPER
50 × 70 CM

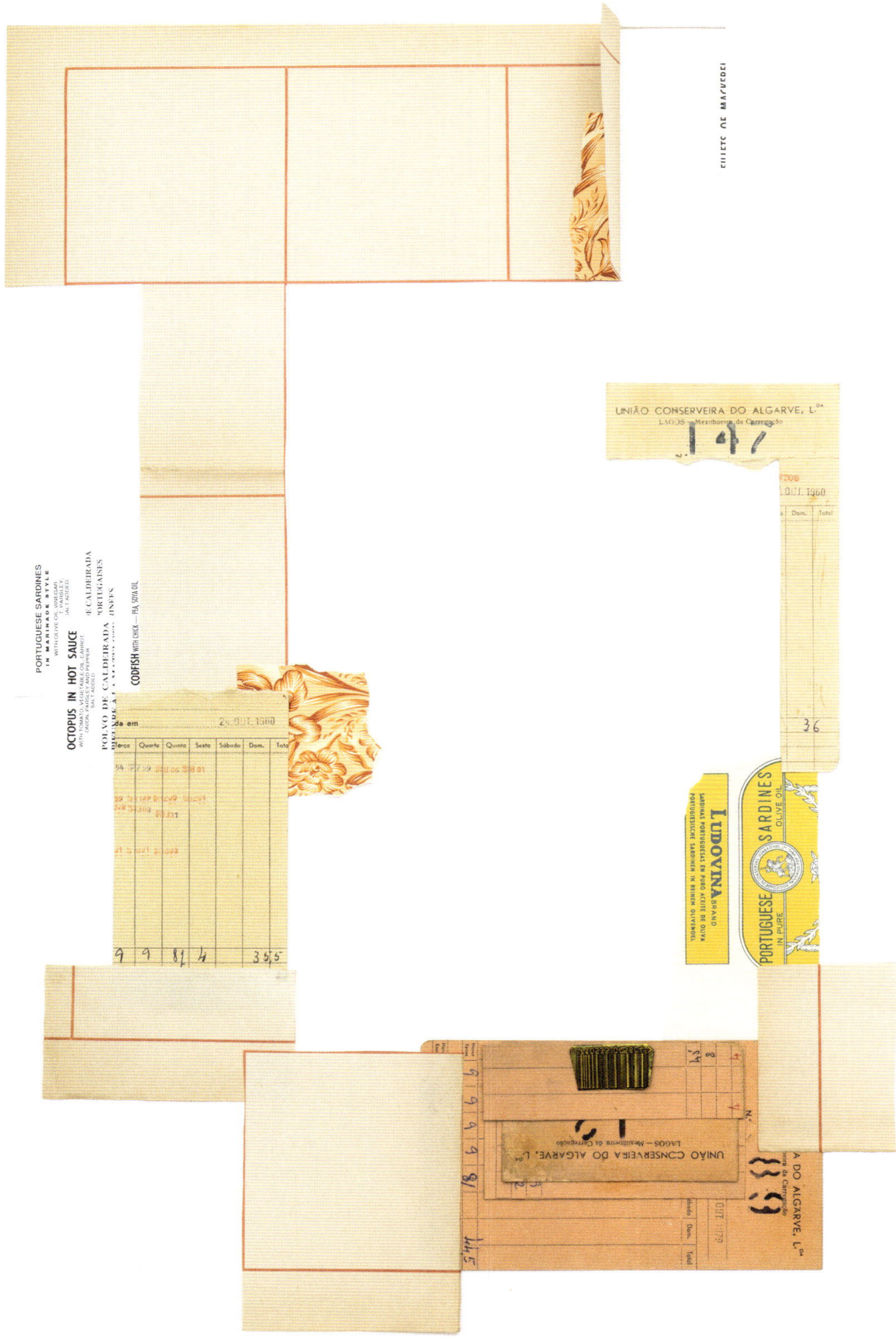
UNIÃO CONSERVEIRA DO ALGARVE, L.da
PORTUGUESE SARDINES IN MARINADE STYLE
OCTOPUS IN HOT SAUCE
POLVO DE CALDEIRADA
LUDOVINA BRAND
PORTUGUESE SARDINES IN PURE OLIVE OIL

MIGUE

LAFFAN

MAFALDA

SANTOS

MAFALDA
SANTOS

MIGUEL
LAFFAN

MIGUEL LAFFAN
MAFALDA SANTOS

"COOKING SAVED ME MANY TIMES"

"Cooking saved me many times," says chef Miguel Laffan. His voice comes out in a low, confessional tone. We all believe it and the artist Mafalda Santos nods. "Art can do that, yes."

Before we arrived at the restaurant where Miguel won the first Michelin star for Alentejo, we crossed the Tagus and the plains of this region, one of the most beautiful parts of Portugal.

The conversations flowed in the car, until the moment when the yellow and purple flowers and the immense sky called for some silence and solemnity.

The restaurant and hotel are part of the landscape and, as soon as we arrive, we are welcomed with smiles and handshakes. Chef and artist share a badly hidden shyness. Glasses in hand, we sit around a magnificent table, as twisted and capricious as the olive tree from which it was carved.

Miguel presents the ingredients to us with the joy of a child: bean purée, cooking foam, sea lettuce, smoked eels and various other colourful and defiant surprises.

Mafalda widens her eyes in astonishment and confesses to envy: "I enjoy cooking and experimenting with things, but this is another league." Miguel admits that he's not so adventurous at home. "I'm like the Formula One drivers who don't drive on their days off."

"Cooking is a gift, it chooses us more than we choose it," says the fortunate man. "About ideas I don't know, it's rough stuff that needs to be processed."

Mafalda agrees. She talks about fuzzy images that gain shapes, colours and intention. "Sometimes they arrive through the senses," she says. "It's not always intellectual."

To Miguel, the worst thing of all is the pressure to create. Mafalda disagrees – pressure leads her to the creative act, then the time comes to mature it.

"Like the wine and cheese," someone says. From the large sash window, Alentejo seems to agree.

"I've had many crises," says Miguel. "I became a father at the age of twenty-one and the kitchen was like a place of escape. It reached out its hand many times. It was where I reconnected with myself, even in the hardest times."

Another silence, full of fellowship.

"Art can save us a little from the world," says Mafalda, who may also save us through her work.

We make a toast, we taste the dish, we thank the artists.

"All my life, I never had a plan B."

So said one, or maybe the other.

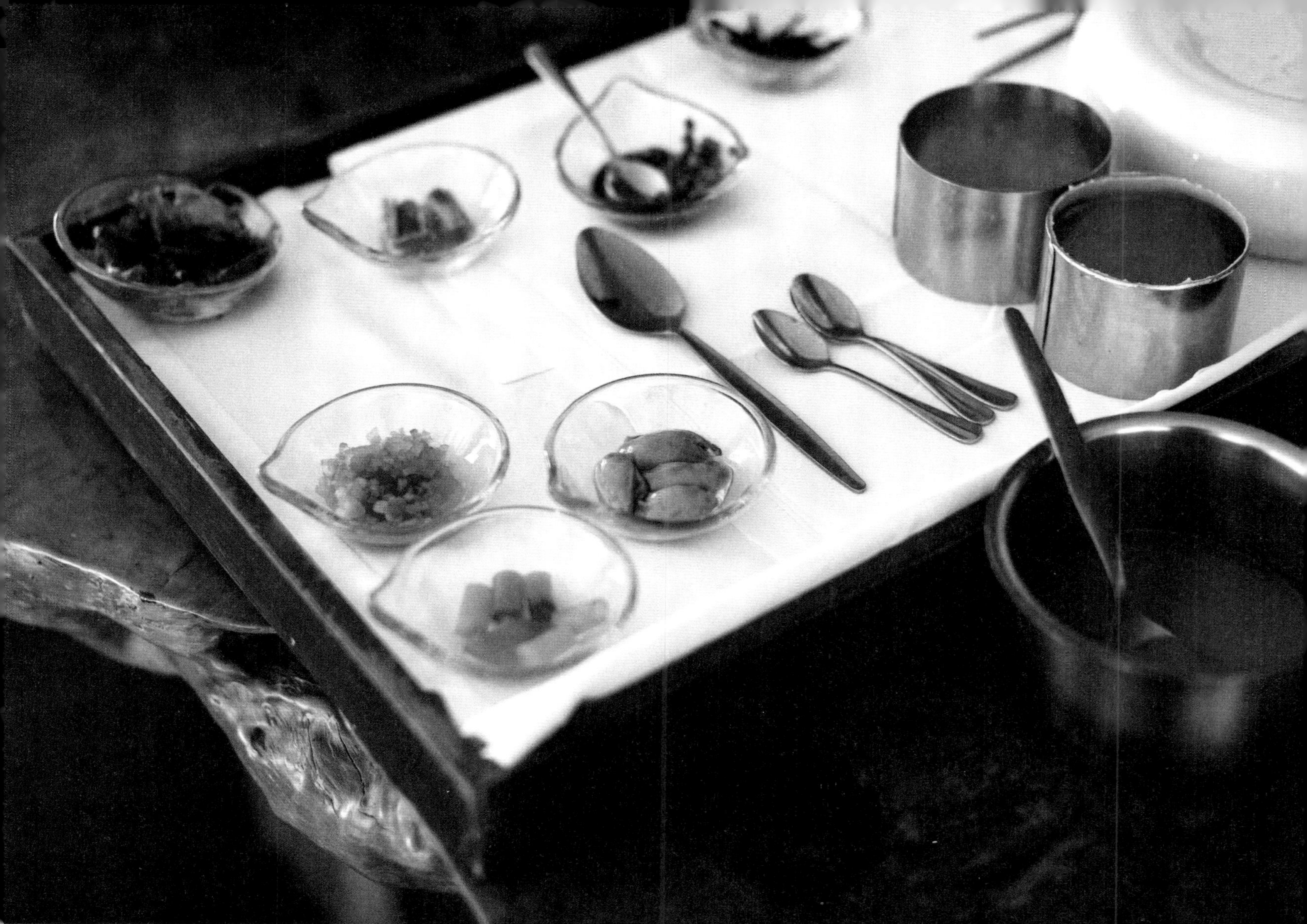

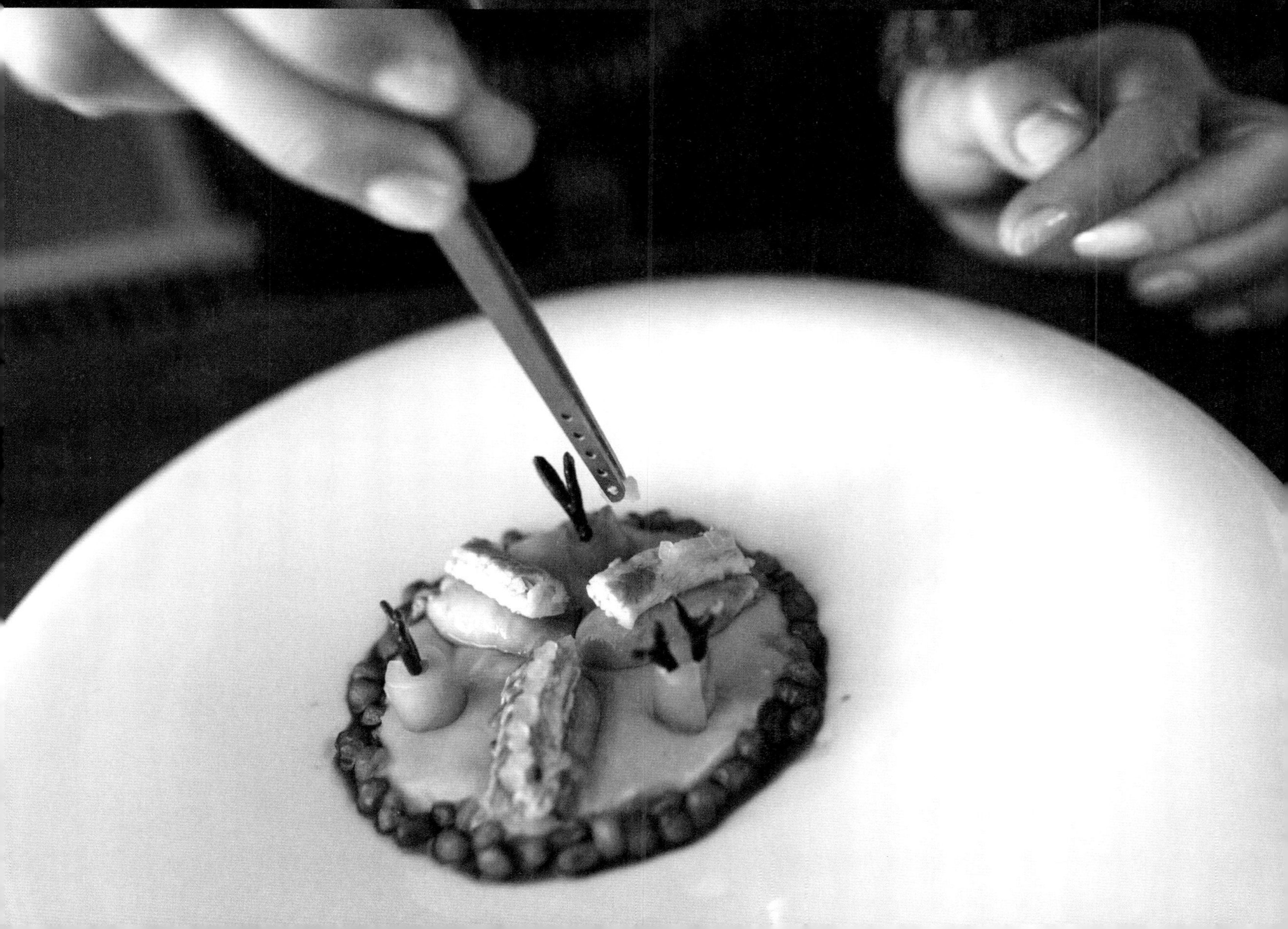

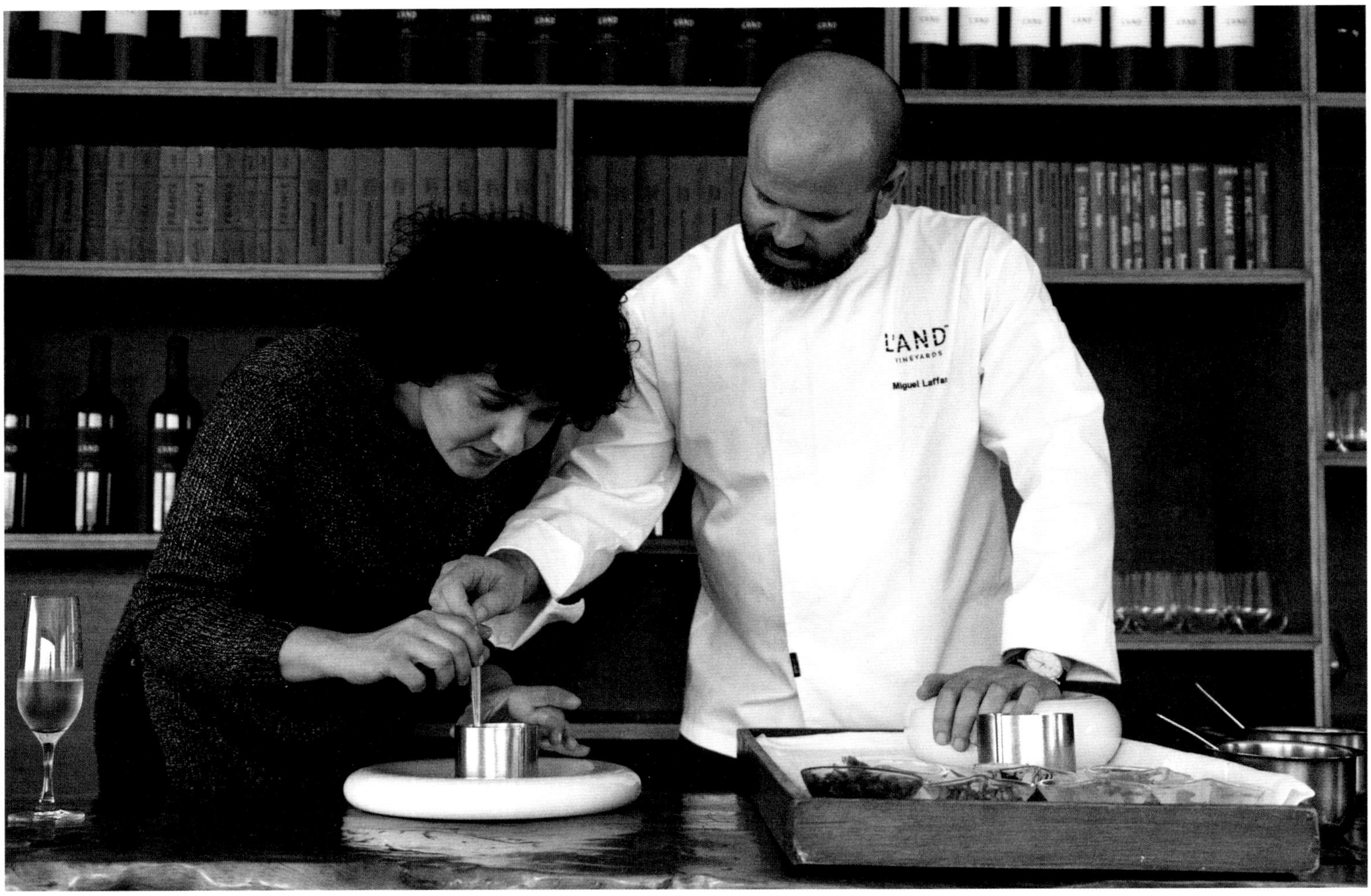
L'AND
VINEYARDS

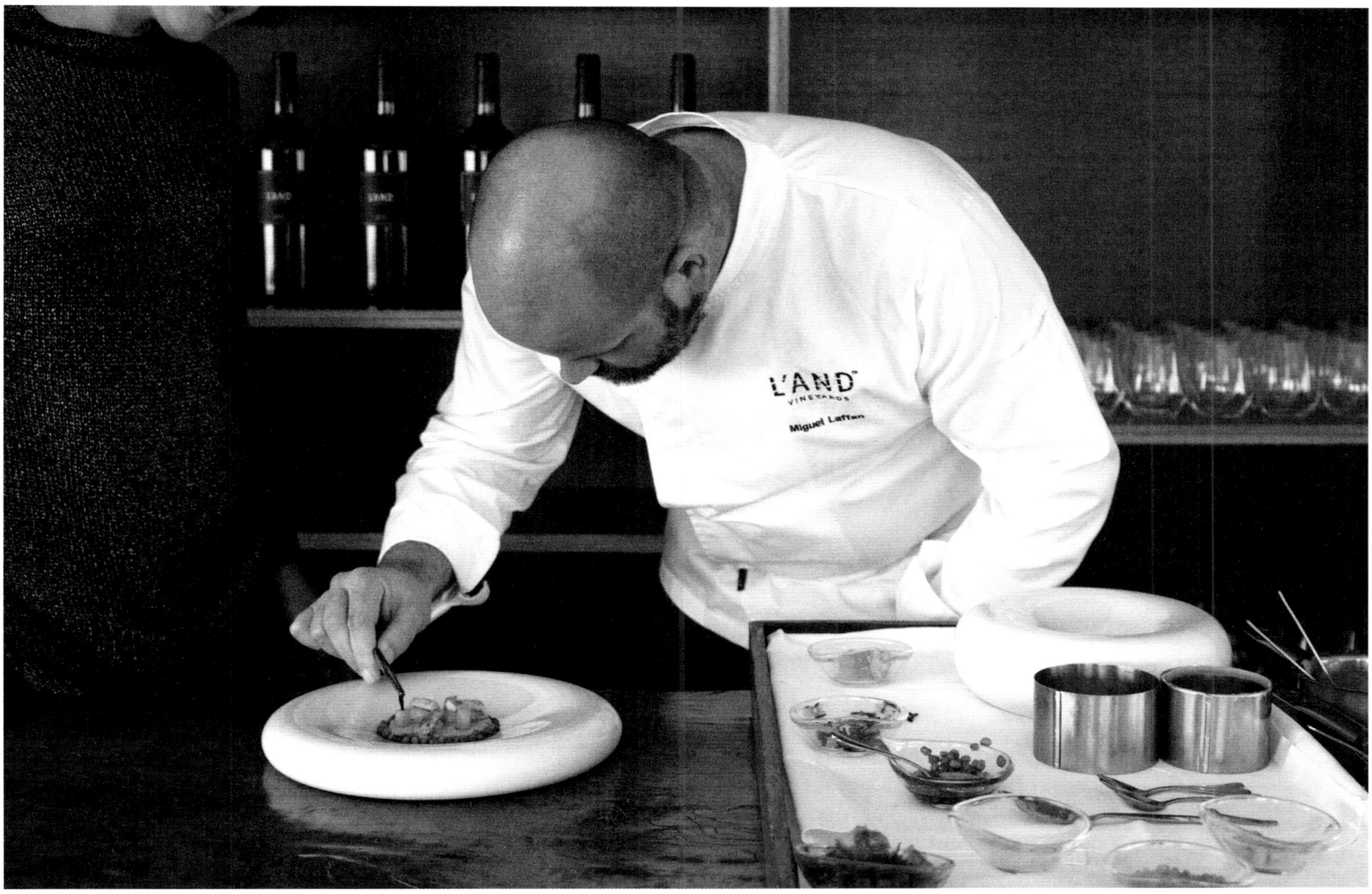
L'AND
VINEYARDS
Miguel Laffan

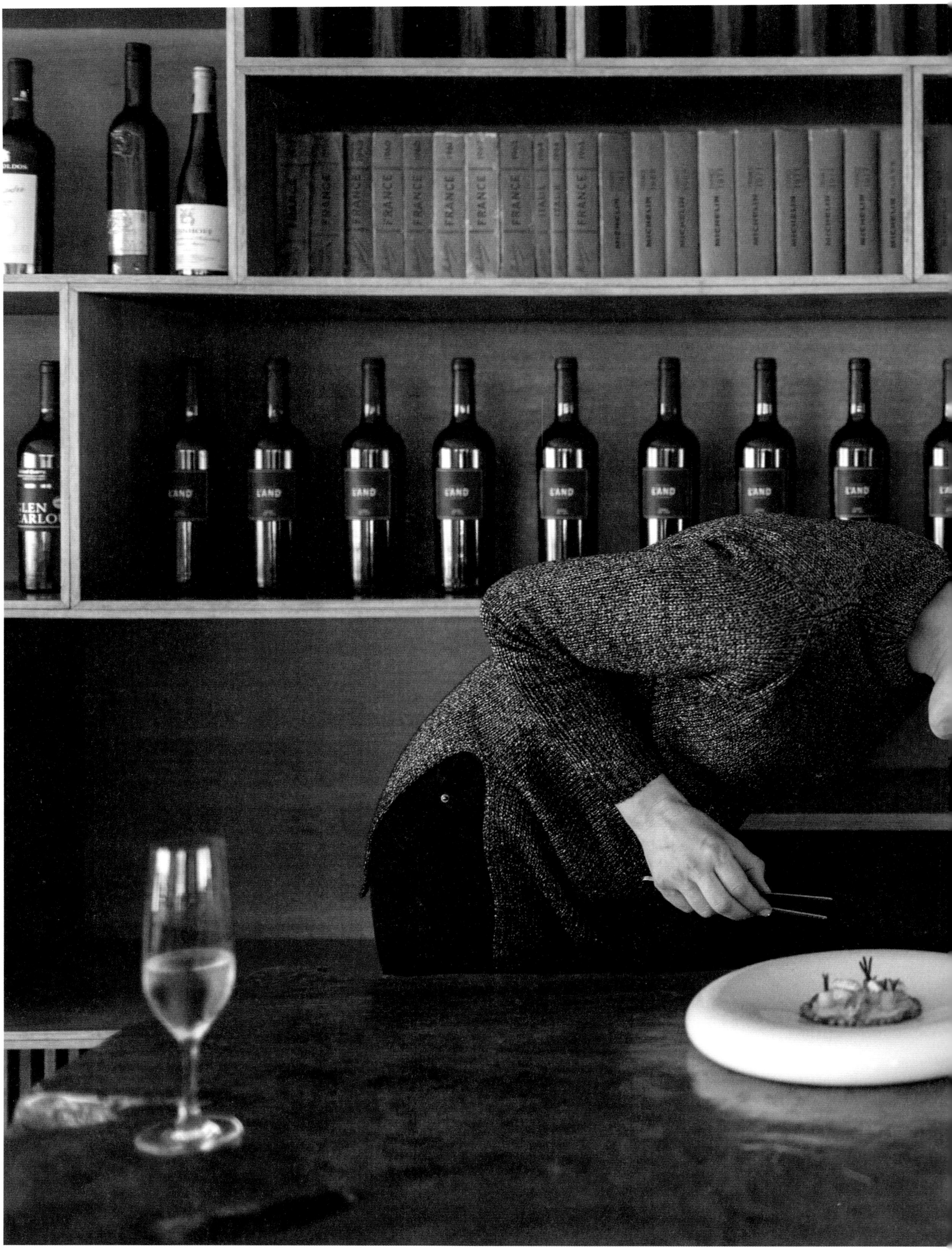
FRANCE
MICHELIN
L'AND

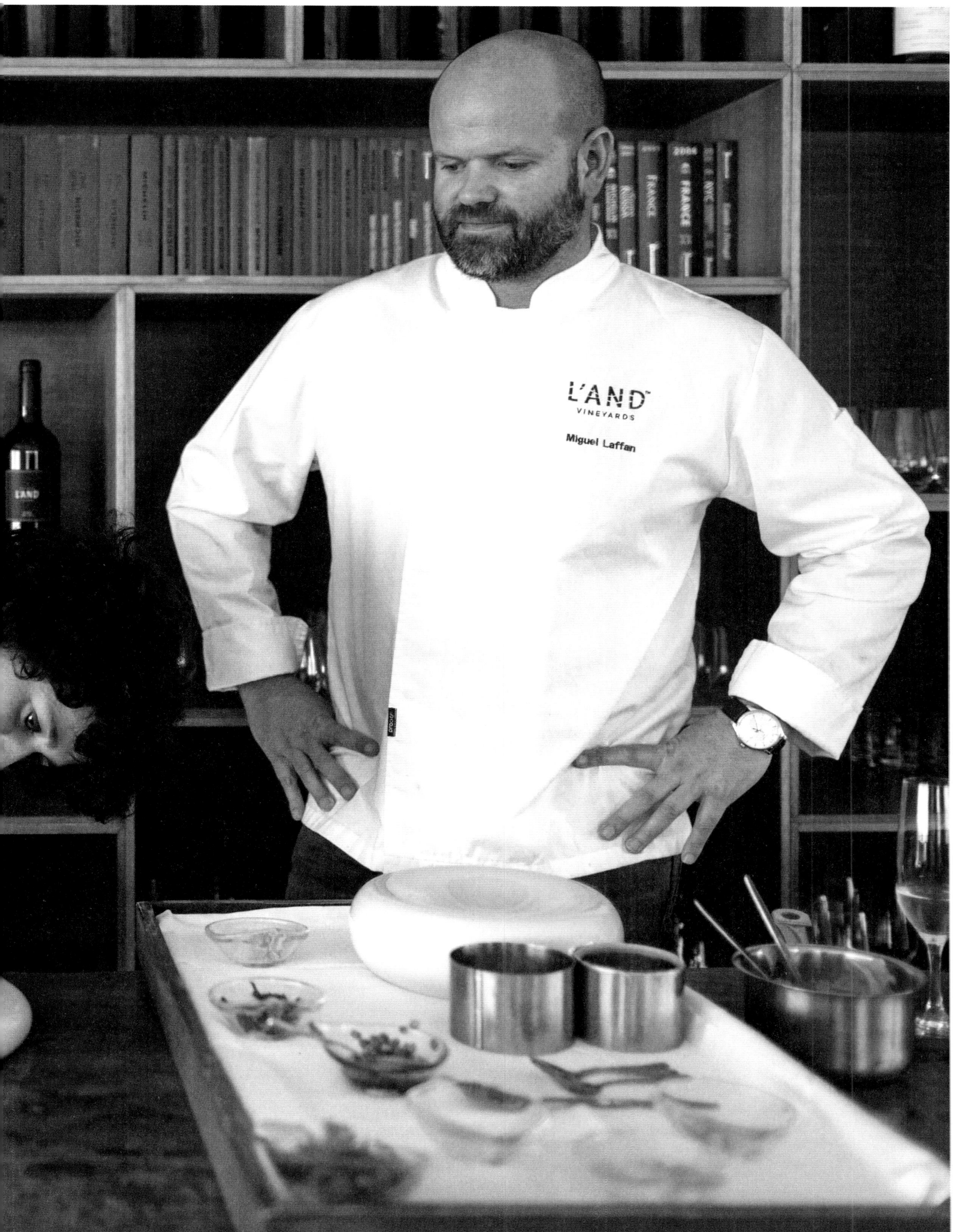
L'AND
VINEYARDS
Miguel Laffan

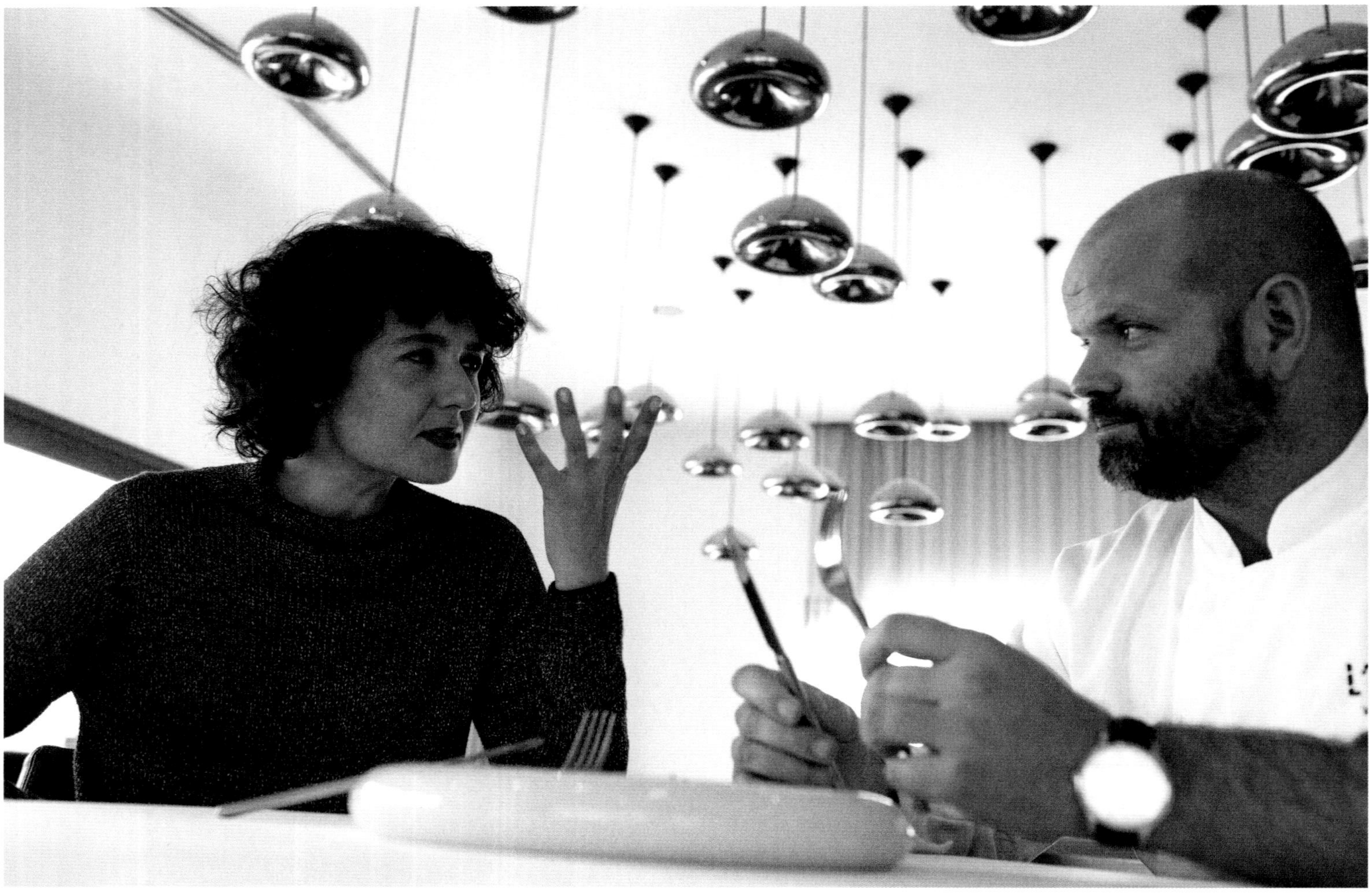

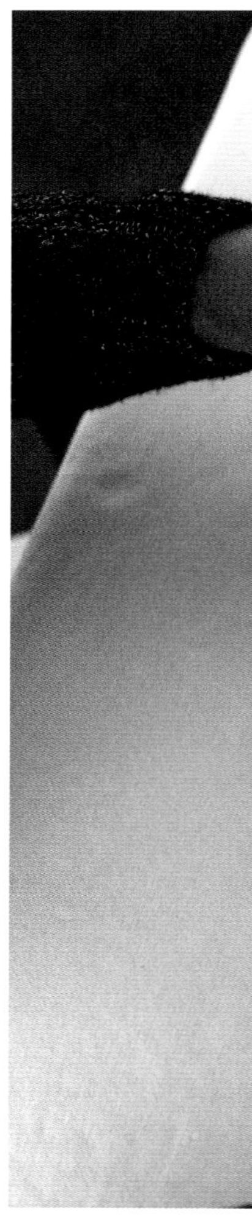

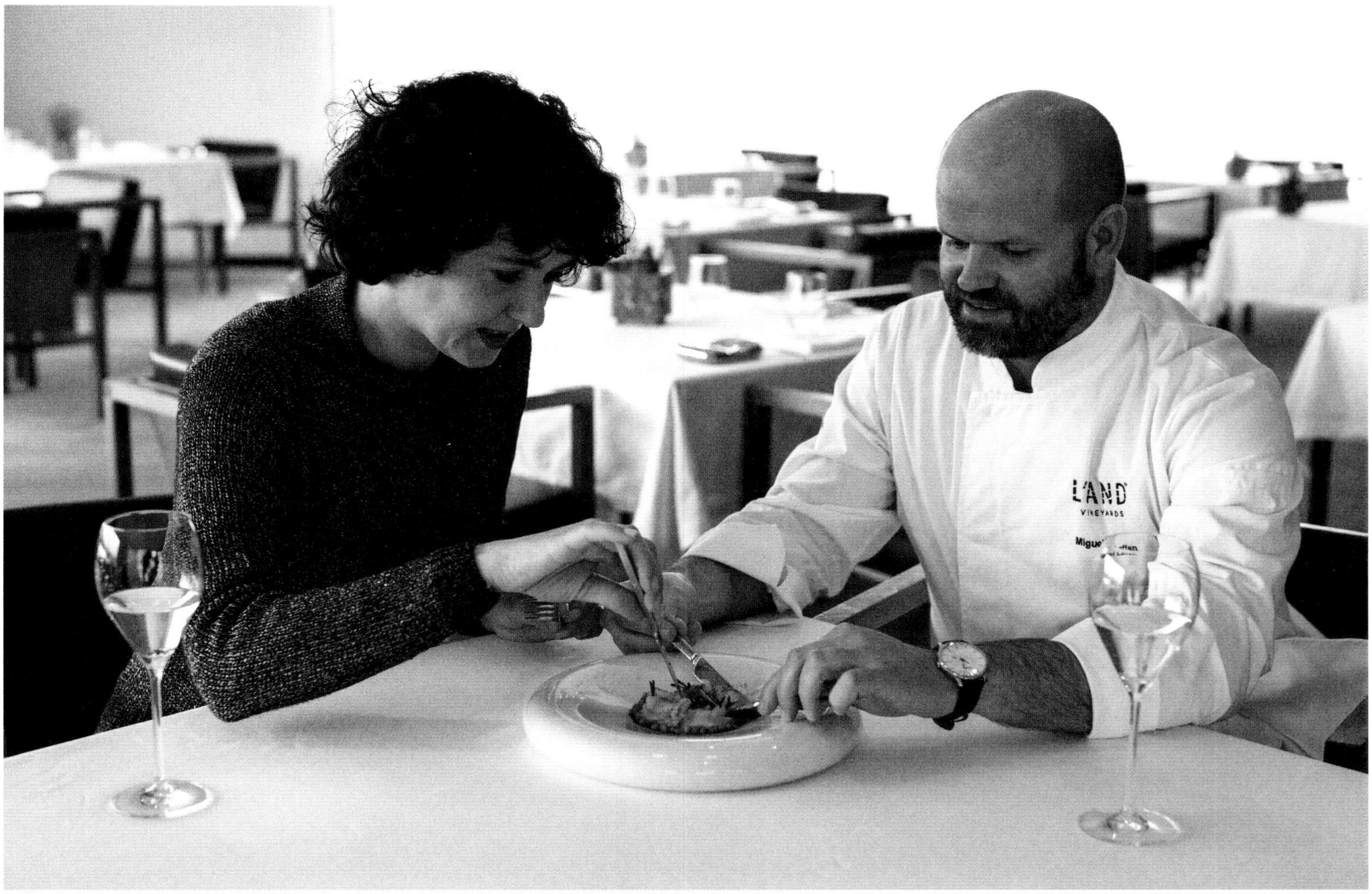
L'AND
VINEYARDS

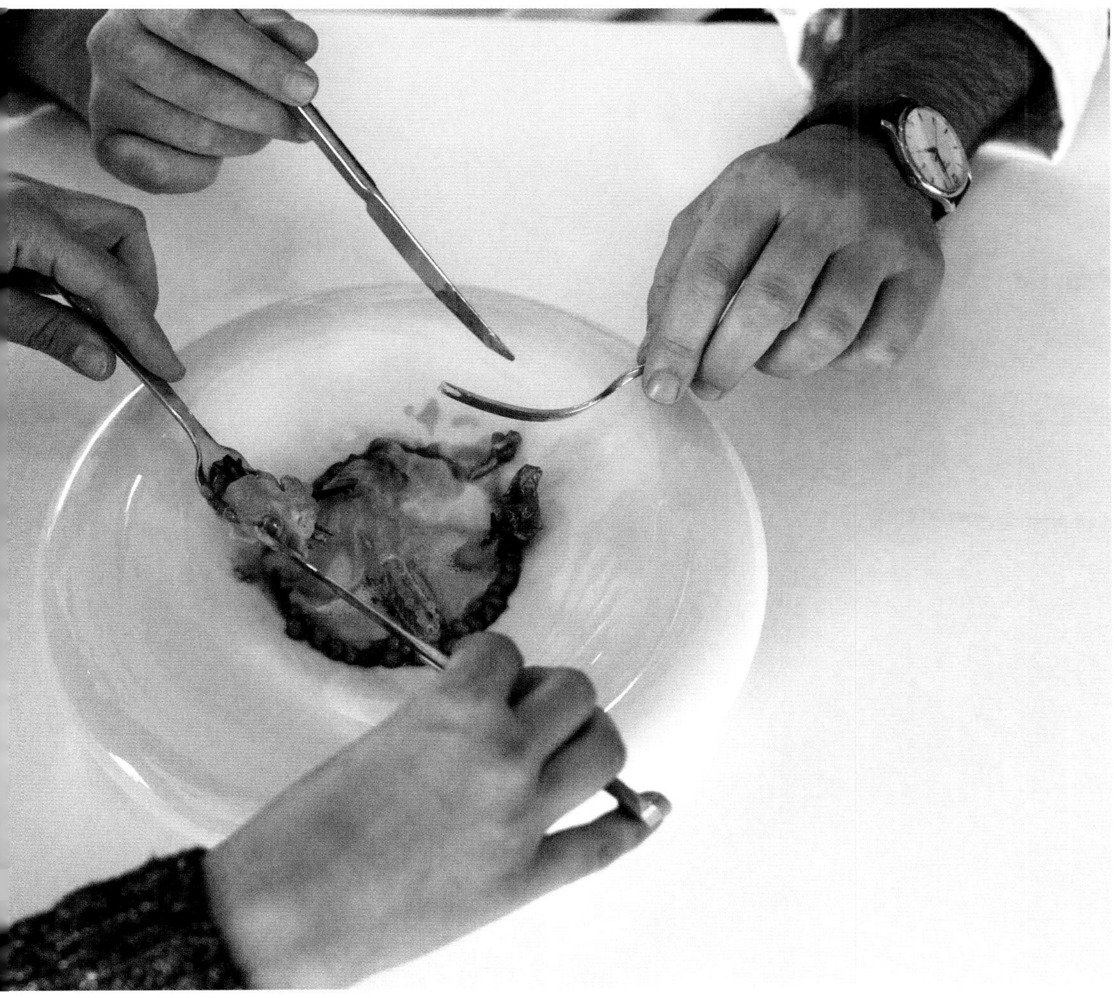

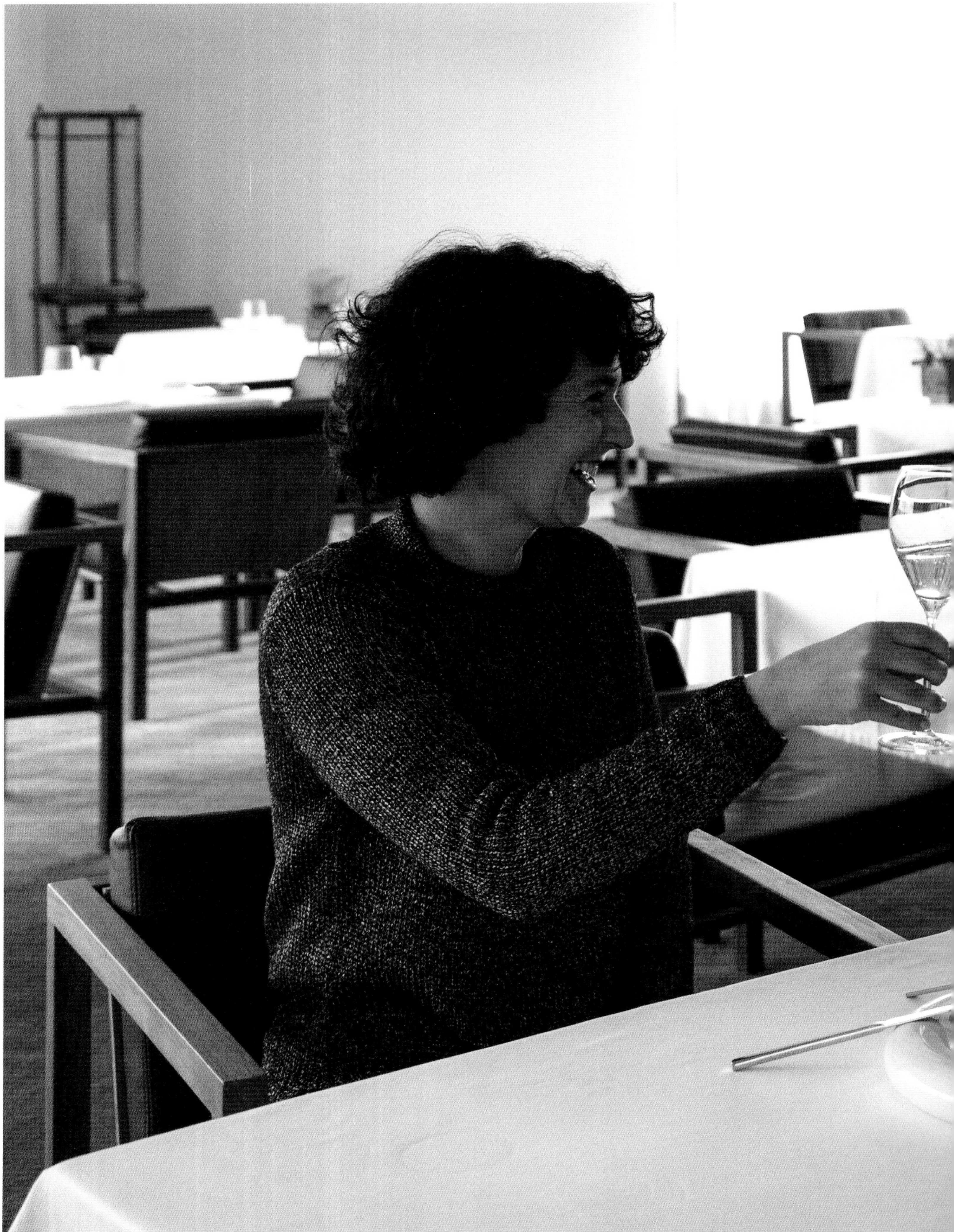

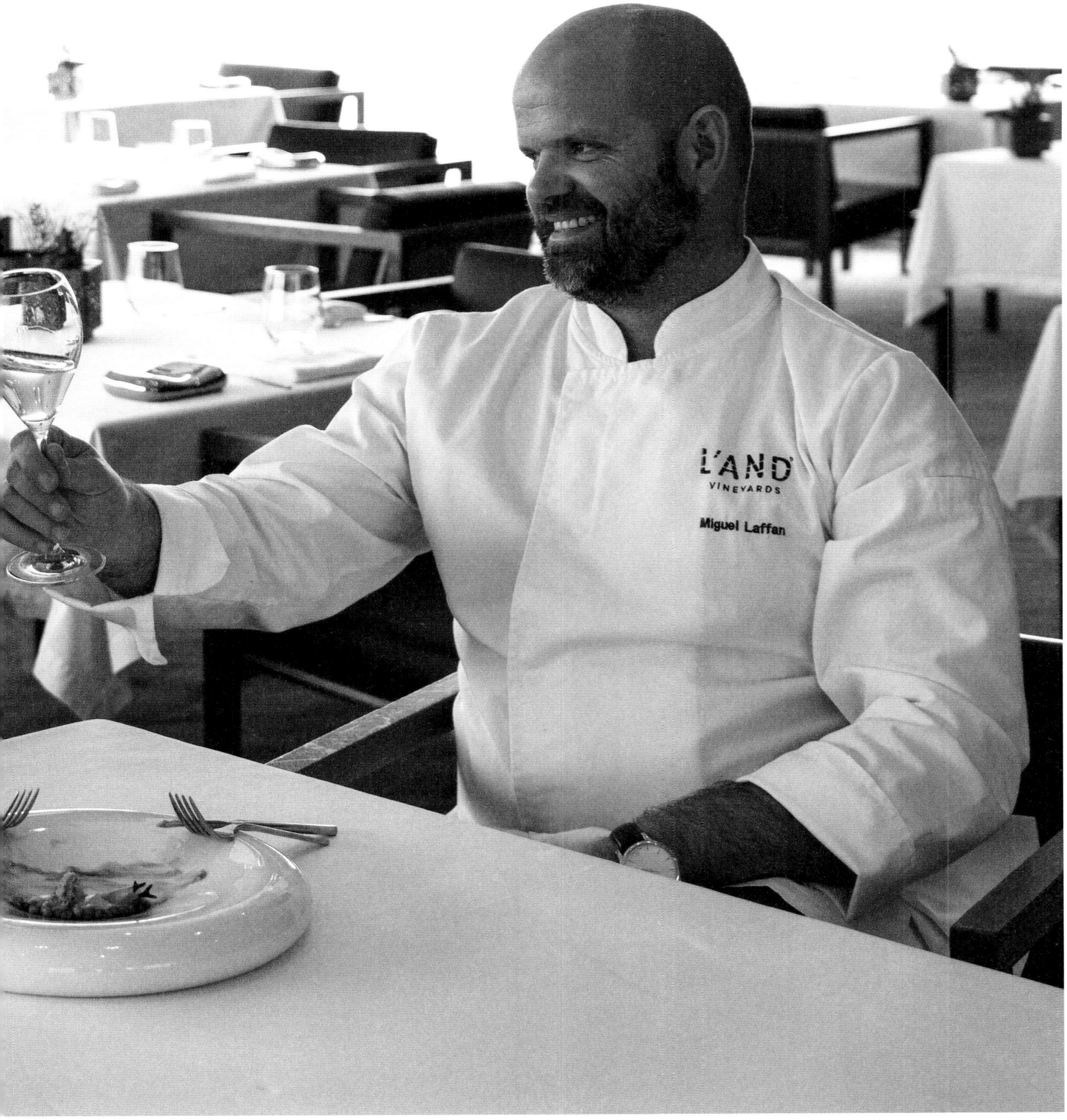
L'AND
VINEYARDS
Miguel Laffan

MIGUEL

LAFFAN

SMOKED EEL, FERMENTED WHITE BEAN CREAM WITH MIRIN, SOYBEAN AND MISO, SEAWEED AND SEA EMULSION, SANTARÉM BEANS IN PICKLE

SMOKED EELS
BRAND COMUR

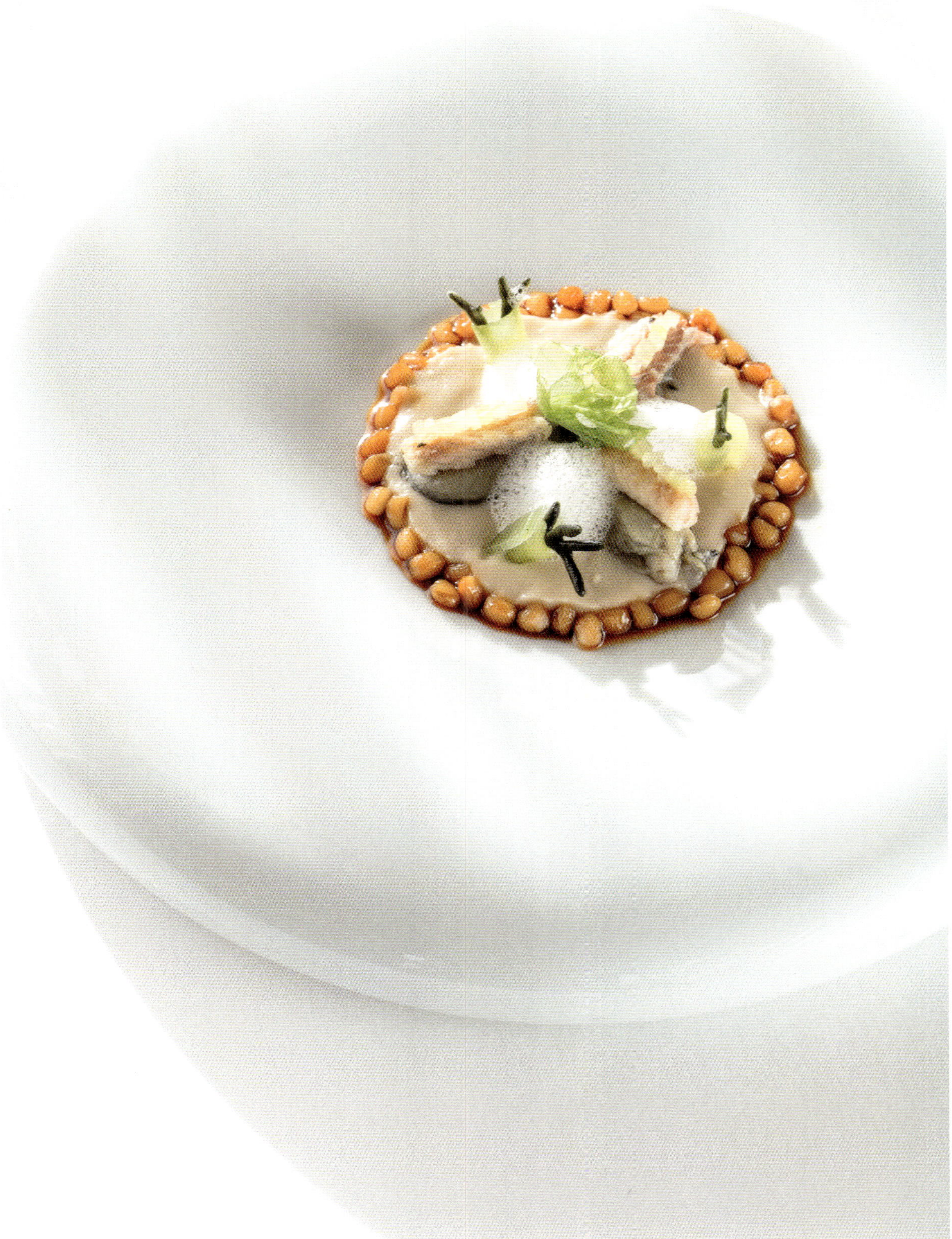

M A F
A L D A

SARDINE, COD,
TUNA, MACKEREL
2017

S A N
T O S

STAMP ON PAPER
4 DRAWINGS OF 65 × 50CM

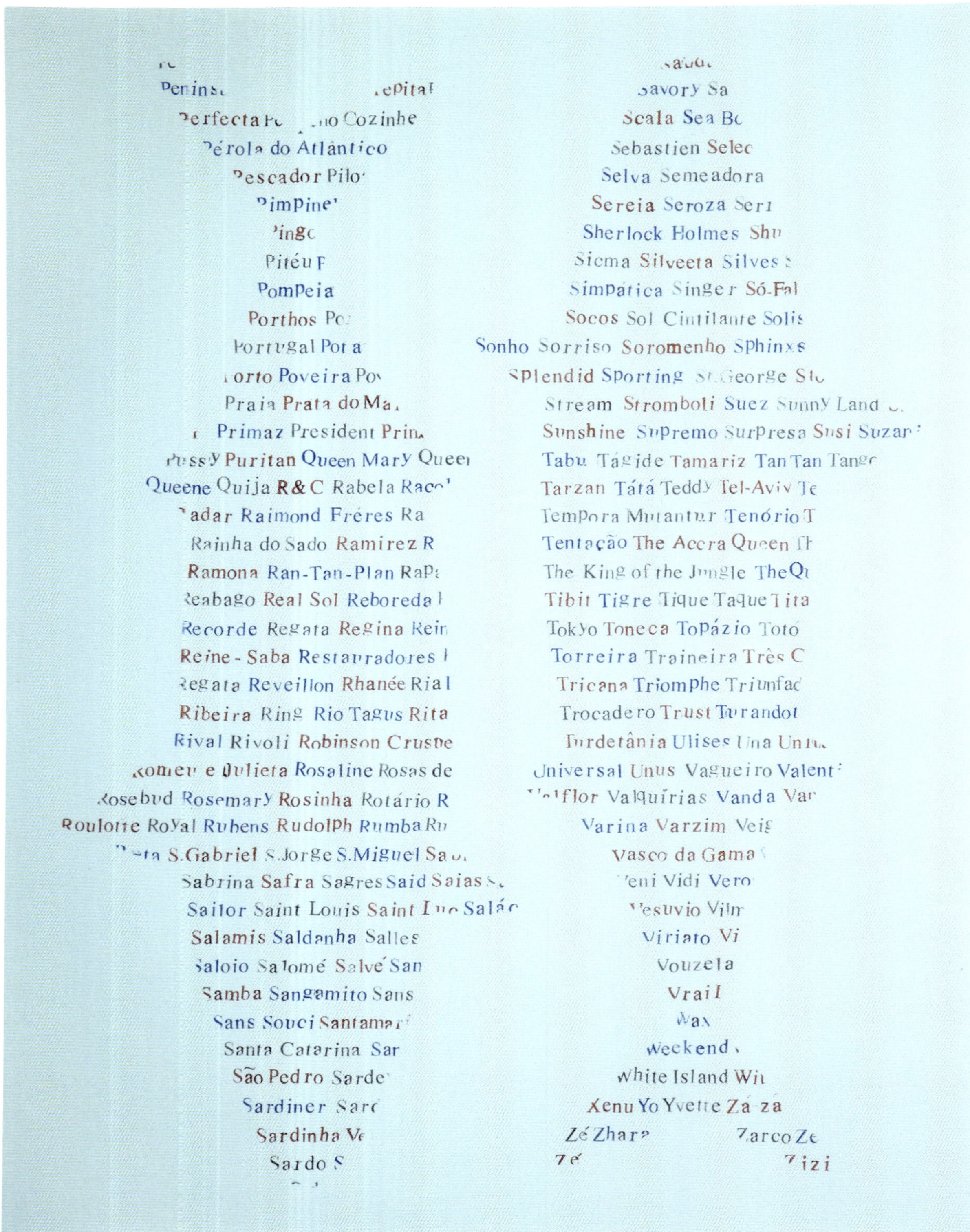
Perfecta Pe no Cozinhe
Pérola do Atlântico
Pescador Pilo
Pimpine
Pingo
Pitéu P
Pompeia
Porthos Po
Portugal Pot a
Porto Poveira Po
Praia Prata do Ma
Primaz President Prin
Pussy Puritan Queen Mary Queen
Queene Quija R&C Rabela Rac
Radar Raimond Fréres Ra
Rainha do Sado Ramirez R
Ramona Ran-Tan-Plan RaPa
Reabago Real Sol Reboreda
Recorde Regata Regina Reir
Reine-Saba Restauradores
Regata Reveillon Rhanée Rial
Ribeira Ring Rio Tagus Rita
Rival Rivoli Robinson Crusoe
Romeu e Julieta Rosaline Rosas de
Rosebud Rosemary Rosinha Rotário R
Roulotte Royal Rubens Rudolph Rumba Ru
S.Gabriel S.Jorge S.Miguel Sa
Sabrina Safra Sagres Said Saias
Sailor Saint Louis Saint Luc Salão
Salamis Saldanha Salles
Saloio Salomé Salvé San
Samba Sangamito Sans
Sans Souci Santamar
Santa Catarina Sar
São Pedro Sarde
Sardiner Sar
Sardinha Ve
Sardo S
Savory Sa
Scala Sea Bo
Sebastien Selec
Selva Semeadora
Sereia Seroza Ser
Sherlock Holmes Shu
Sicma Silveeta Silves
Simpática Singer Só-Fal
Socos Sol Cintilante Solis
Sonho Sorriso Soromenho Sphinxs
Splendid Sporting St.George St
Stream Stromboli Suez Sunny Land
Sunshine Supremo Surpresa Susi Suzan
Tabu Tágide Tamariz Tan Tan Tango
Tarzan Tátá Teddy Tel-Aviv Te
Tempora Mutantur Tenório T
Tentação The Accra Queen Th
The King of the Jungle The Q
Tibit Tigre Tique Taque Tita
Tokyo Toneca Topázio Totó
Torreira Traineira Três C
Tricana Triomphe Triunfad
Trocadero Trust Turandot
Turdetânia Ulises Una Uni
Universal Unus Vagueiro Valent
Valflor Valquírias Vanda Var
Varina Varzim Veig
Vasco da Gama
Veni Vidi Vero
Vesuvio Vilm
Viriato Vi
Vouzela
Vrail
Wax
Weekend
White Island Wi
Xenu Yo Yvette Za-za
Zé Zhara Zarco Ze
Zizi

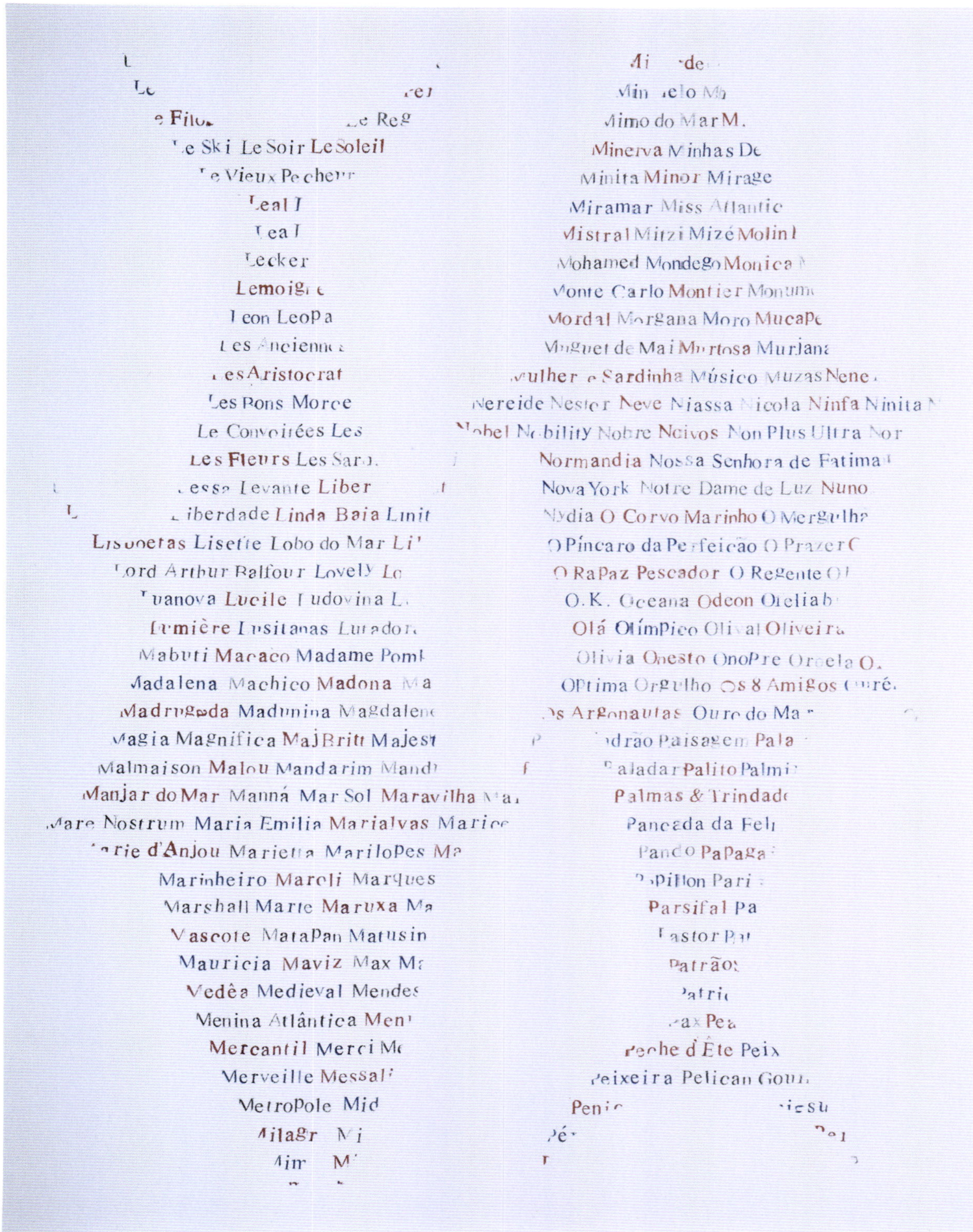

Mimo do Mar M.
Le Ski Le Soir Le Soleil
Minerva Minhas De
Le Vieux Pecheur
Minita Minor Mirage
Leal
Miramar Miss Atlantic
Mistral Mitzi Mizé Molin
Lecker
Mohamed Mondego Monica
Lemoigne
Monte Carlo Montier
Leon LeoPa
Mordal Morgana Moro MucaPe
Les Anciennes
Muguet de Mai Murtosa Murjana
Les Aristocrat
Mulher e Sardinha Músico Muzas Nene
Les Bons Morce
Nereide Nestor Neve Niassa Nicola Ninfa Ninita
Le Convoirées Les
Nobel Nobility Nobre Noivos Non Plus Ultra Nor
Les Fleurs Les Sar
Normandia Nossa Senhora de Fatima
Lessa Levante Liber
Nova York Notre Dame de Luz Nuno
Liberdade Linda Baia Linit
Nydia O Corvo Marinho O Mergulha
Lisboetas Lisette Lobo do Mar
O Píncaro da Perfeição O Prazer
Lord Arthur Balfour Lovely
O RaPaz Pescador O Regente
Luanova Lucile Ludovina
O.K. Oceana Odeon Ofelia
Lumière Lusitanas Lutador
Olá OlímPico Olival Oliveira
Mabuti Macaco Madame Pom
Olivia Onesto OnoPre
Madalena Machico Madona
OPtima Orgulho Os 8 Amigos
Madrugada Madunina Magdalene
Os Argonautas Ouro do Ma
Magia Magnifica Maj Britt Majest
Padrao Paisagem Pala
Malmaison Malou Mandarim
Paladar Palito Palmi
Manjar do Mar Manná Mar Sol Maravilha
Palmas & Trindade
Mare Nostrum Maria Emilia Marialvas
Paneada da Feli
Marie d'Anjou Marietta MariloPes
Pando PaPaga
Marinheiro Maroli Marques
PaPillon Pari
Marshall Marte Maruxa
Parsifal Pa
Mascote MataPan Matusin
Pastor
Mauricia Maviz Max
Patrão
Medêa Medieval Mendes
Menina Atlântica
Pax Pe
Mercantil Merci
Peche d'Ete Peix
Merveille Messal
Peixeira Pelican
MetroPole Mid
Peni
Milagr

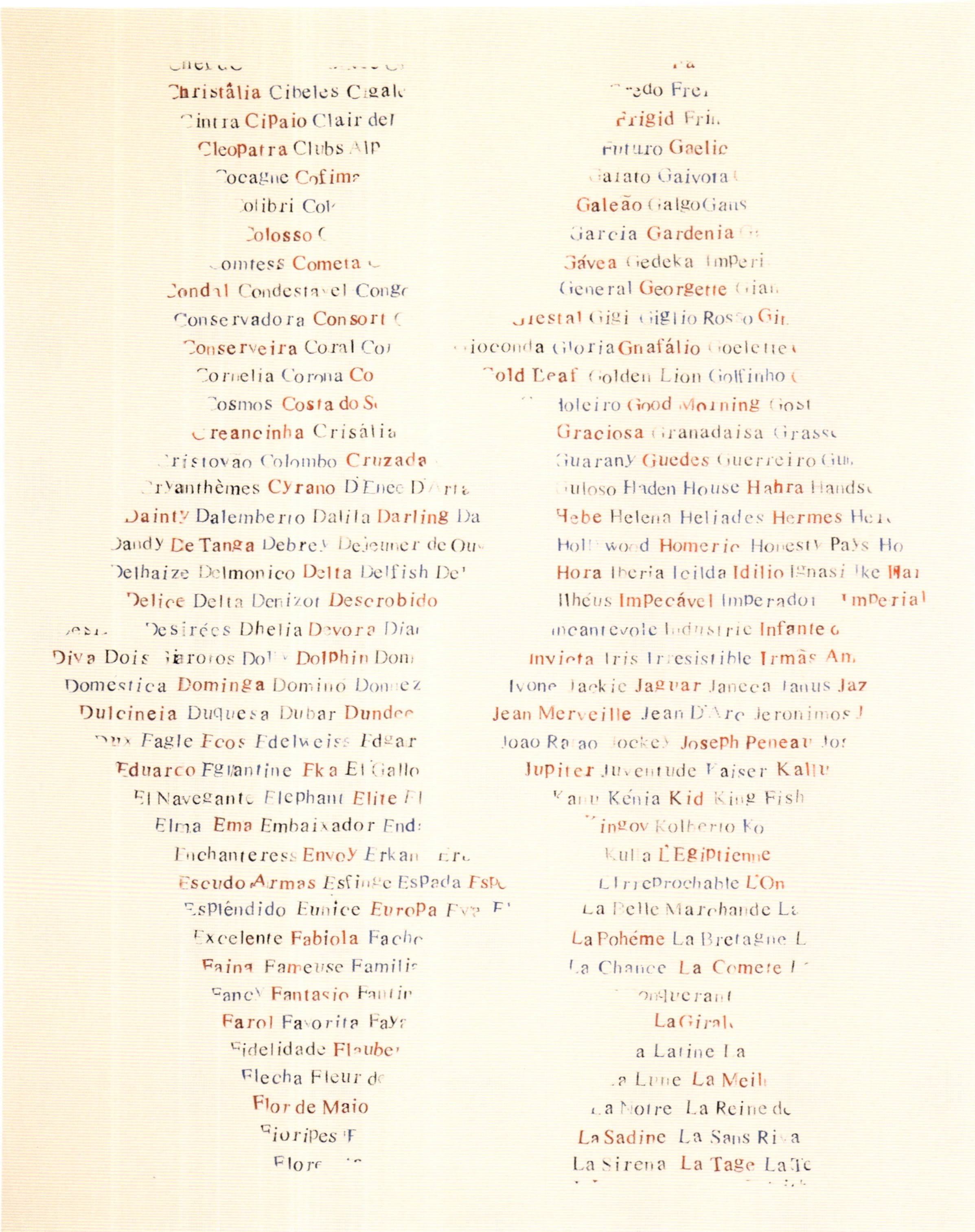

Christália Cibeles Cigale
Cintra Cipaio Clair de
Cleopatra Clubs Alp
Cocagne Cofima
Colibri
Colosso
Comtess Cometa
Condal Condestavel Congo
Conservadora Consort
Conserveira Coral
Cornelia Corona Co
Cosmos Costa do S
Creancinha Crisália
Cristovão Colombo Cruzada
Crysanthèmes Cyrano
Dainty Dalemberto Dalila Darling Da
Dandy De Tanga Debrey Dejeuner de Ou
Delhaize Delmonico Delta Delfish
Delice Delta Denizot Desorobido
Desirées Dhelia Devora
Diva Dois Garotos Dolly Dolphin Dom
Domestica Dominga Dominó
Dulcineia Duquesa Dubar Dundee
Dux Eagle Ecos Edelweiss Edgar
Eduardo Eglantine Eka El Gallo
El Navegante Elephant Elite
Elma Ema Embaixador
Enchanteress Envoy Erkan
Escudo Armas Esfinge Espada
Espléndido Eunice Europa
Excelente Fabiola
Faina Fameuse
Fancy Fantasio
Farol Favorita
Fidelidade Flaube
Flecha Fleur de
Flor de Maio
Floripes
Fredo
Frigid
Futuro Gaelic
Gaiato Gaivota
Galeão Galgo Gans
Garcia Gardenia
Gávea Gedeka Imperi
General Georgette
Giestal Gigi Giglio Rosso
Gioconda Gloria Gnafálio Goelette
Gold Leaf Golden Lion Golfinho
Goleiro Good Morning
Graciosa Granadaisa
Guarany Guedes Guerreiro
Guloso Haden House Hahra
Hebe Helena Heliades Hermes
Hollywood Homeric Honesty Pays
Hora Iberia Ieilda Idilio Ignasi Ike Ha
Ilhéus Impecável Imperador Imperial
Incantevole Industrie Infante
Invicta Iris Irresistible Irmãs
Ivone Jackie Jaguar Janeca Janus Jaz
Jean Merveille Jean D'Arc Jeronimos
Joao Ratao Jockey Joseph Peneau
Jupiter Juventude Kaiser Kalu
Kanu Kénia Kid King Fish
Kingov Kolberto
Kulla L'Egiptienne
L'Irreprochable L'On
La Belle Marchande
La Bohéme La Bretagne
La Chance La Comete
La Giralda
a Latine
La Lune La Meil
La Notre La Reine de
La Sadine La Sans Riva
La Sirena La Tage

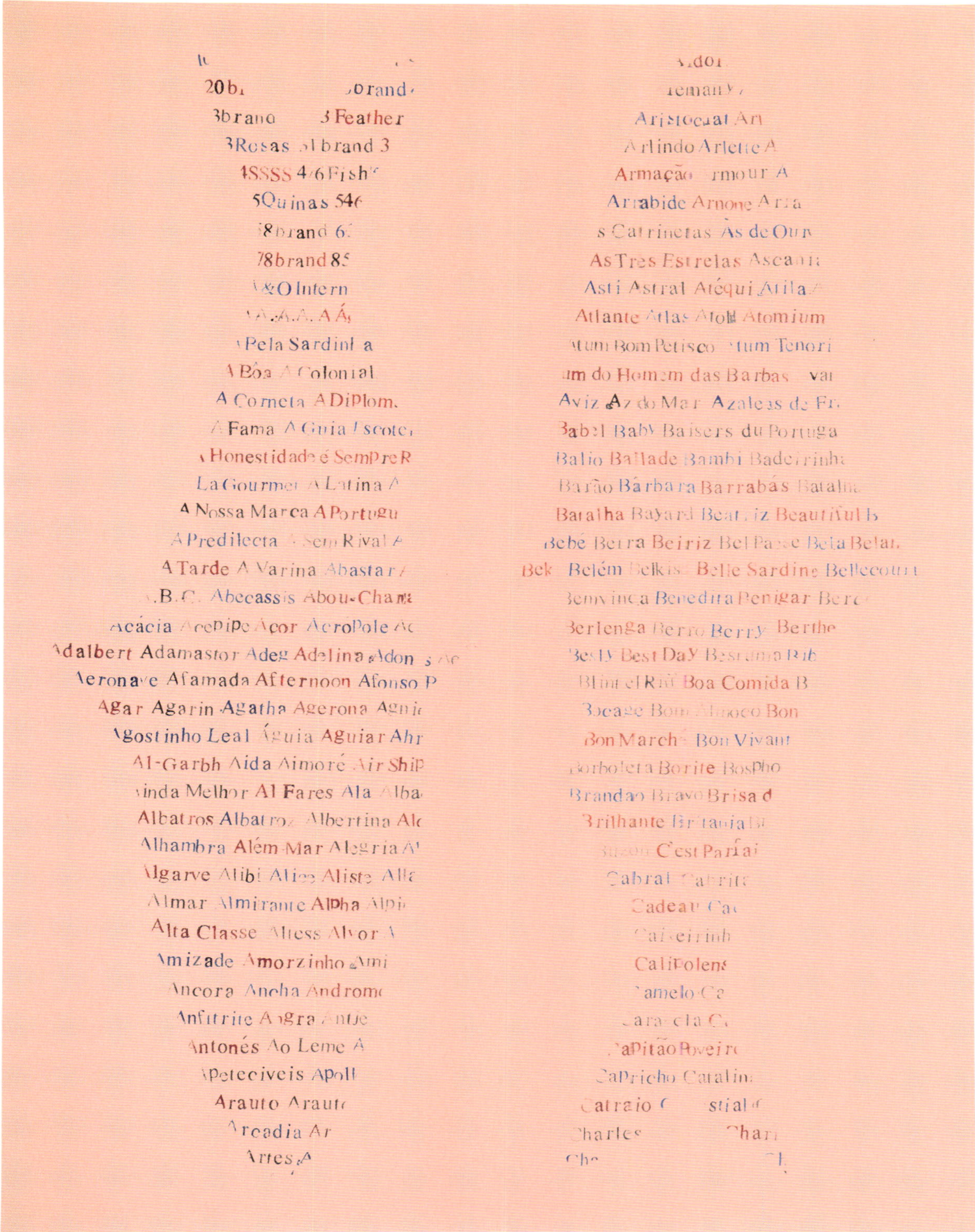
20b brand
3brand 3 Feather
3Rosas brand 3
4SSSS 4/6 Fish
5Quinas 546
78brand 85
A Pela Sardinha
A Boa A Colonial
A Corneta A Diplom
A Fama A Guia Escote
A Honestidade é Sempre R
La Gourmet A Latina A
A Nossa Marca A Portugu
A Predilecta A Sem Rival A
A Tarde A Varina Abastar
A.B.C. Abecassis Abou-Chama
Acácia Acepipe Açor AcroPole Ac
Adalbert Adamastor Adeg Adelina Adon
Aeronave Afamada Afternoon Afonso P
Agar Agarin Agatha Agerona
Agostinho Leal Águia Aguiar Ahr
Al-Garbh Aida Aimoré Air Ship
Ainda Melhor Al Fares Ala Alba
Albatros Albatroz Albertina Al
Alhambra Além-Mar Alegria A
Algarve Alibi Alice Aliste Alla
Almar Almirante Alpha Alpi
Alta Classe Altess Alvor A
Amizade Amorzinho Ami
Ancora Ancha Androme
Anfitrite Angra Antje
Antonés Ao Leme A
Apeteciveis Apoll
Arauto Araut
Arcadia Ar
Artes
Aristocrat Ari
Arlindo Arlette A
Armação Armour A
Arrabide Arnone Arra
As Catrinetas Ás de Ouro
As Tres Estrelas Ascan
Asti Astral Atéqui Atila
Atlante Atlas Atoll Atomium
Atum Bom Petisco Atum Tenori
Atum do Homem das Barbas Ava
Aviz Az do Mar Azaleas de Fr
Babel Baby Baisers du Portuga
Balio Ballade Bambi Baderrinha
Barão Bárbara Barrabás Batalha
Batalha Bayard Beatriz Beautiful B
Bebé Beira Beiriz Bel Paese Bela Bela
Bek Belém Belkis Belle Sardine Bellecour
Benvinda Benedita Penigar Berc
Berlenga Berro Berry Berthe
Best Day Bestuma Bib
Blinet Ritz Boa Comida B
Bocage Bom Almoço Bon
Bon Marché Bon Vivant
Borboleta Borite Bospho
Brandão Bravo Brisa d
Brilhante Britania B
Buzon C'est Parfai
Cabral Cabrita
Cadeau Ca
Caixeirinh
Calipolens
Camelo Ca
Caravela C
Capitão Poveir
Capricho Catalin
Catraio Celestial
Charles Char

JOÃO
RODRIGUES

SUSANNE
S.D.
THEMLITZ

SUSANNE S.D. THEMLITZ

JOÃO RODRIGUES

JOÃO RODRIGUES
SUSANNE S.D. THEMLITZ

THE MARKED BODY

Our conversation takes almost no setting up. We meet at the sophisticated Altis Belém, by the Tagus, on a sunny, windy day. Outside, the myriad tourists flow, wielding cameras and phones to point at the Monument to The Discoveries, the Tower of Belém and the river, where once the ships departed in search of more world. The light dazzles, the city too.

Inside, the atmosphere is silent and serene. The staff circulate diligently and without noise. Chef João Rodrigues is already waiting for us with his team. We introduce him to the artist Susanne S.D. Themlitz and simply observe. It's they who do everything.

The dish (a reinvented ceviche with sardines and tiger almond milk) is ready to be put on the plates. Susanne quickly makes her mark.

"I'd like to try it!" she says. "I want to get my hands dirty! I talk better with hands than with words."

João demonstrates and invites Susanne to follow suit.

"I like this kind of packaging," says the artist. "I like the colours and I like the octopus, it's an interesting animal. That's why I decided to make the woman with the octopus head."

João asks what led Susanne to the arts. "I didn't know which way to go – to theatre or fine arts," she replies. "I chose the more reclusive artform, because I like silence and working with my hands. Then I grew up with my choice."

João recalls a theatre class he attended at Camões College. "Such a shame," he says, and smiles. Susanne returns to the hands. Always the hands.

"I believe they work faster than the head," she says.

João asks: "Do you think the body can change itself?"

"Yes, the body is marked," says Susanne. "But it wins over the will, it gets used to the material."

"It's true," says João. "In the beginning we need to think a lot."

"And imitate," says Susanne.

Interviewers are always obsessed by ideas and inspiration, but João is ready and answers before the question is asked.

"My cuisine is me, it's simple," he says. "It's my travels and the conversations I have. It's the music, the surf, everything. It's impulsive."

Susanne finishes, as if they were a duo.

"The ideas and questions come from all directions, without hierarchies of anything that seems to make sense to me."

"Ideas are just the beginning," says João,

"Landscapes, a book, whatever touches me," says Susanne.

They smile at one another, they understand and agree in silence.

It's done, what was meant to be said has been said. But we persist with a last question. What, for each of you, is the most important date?

Neither finds much sense in the question.

"A date?" says Susanne. "I can't remember any."

"Nor me, except today," says João.

"Yes," echoes Susanne. "Maybe today."

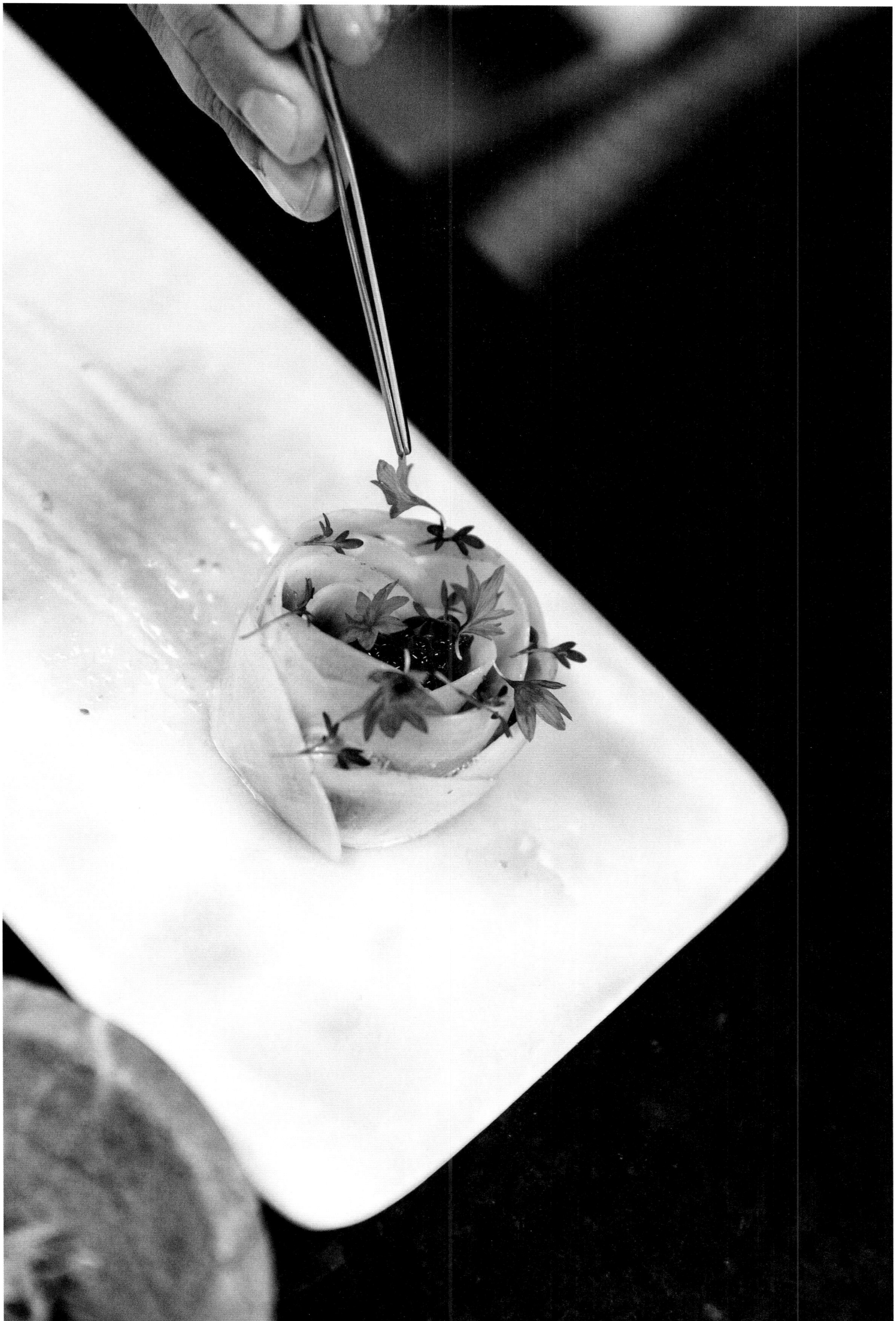

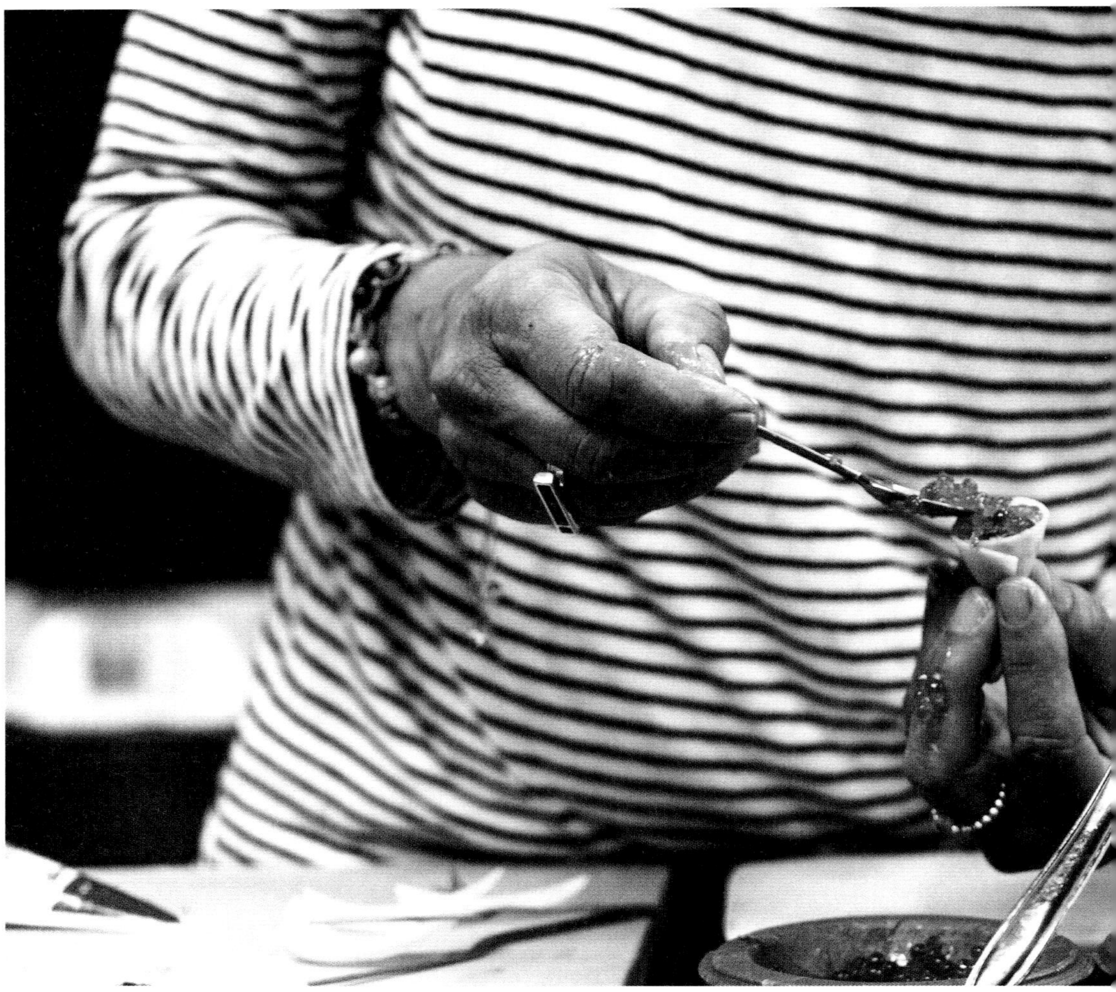

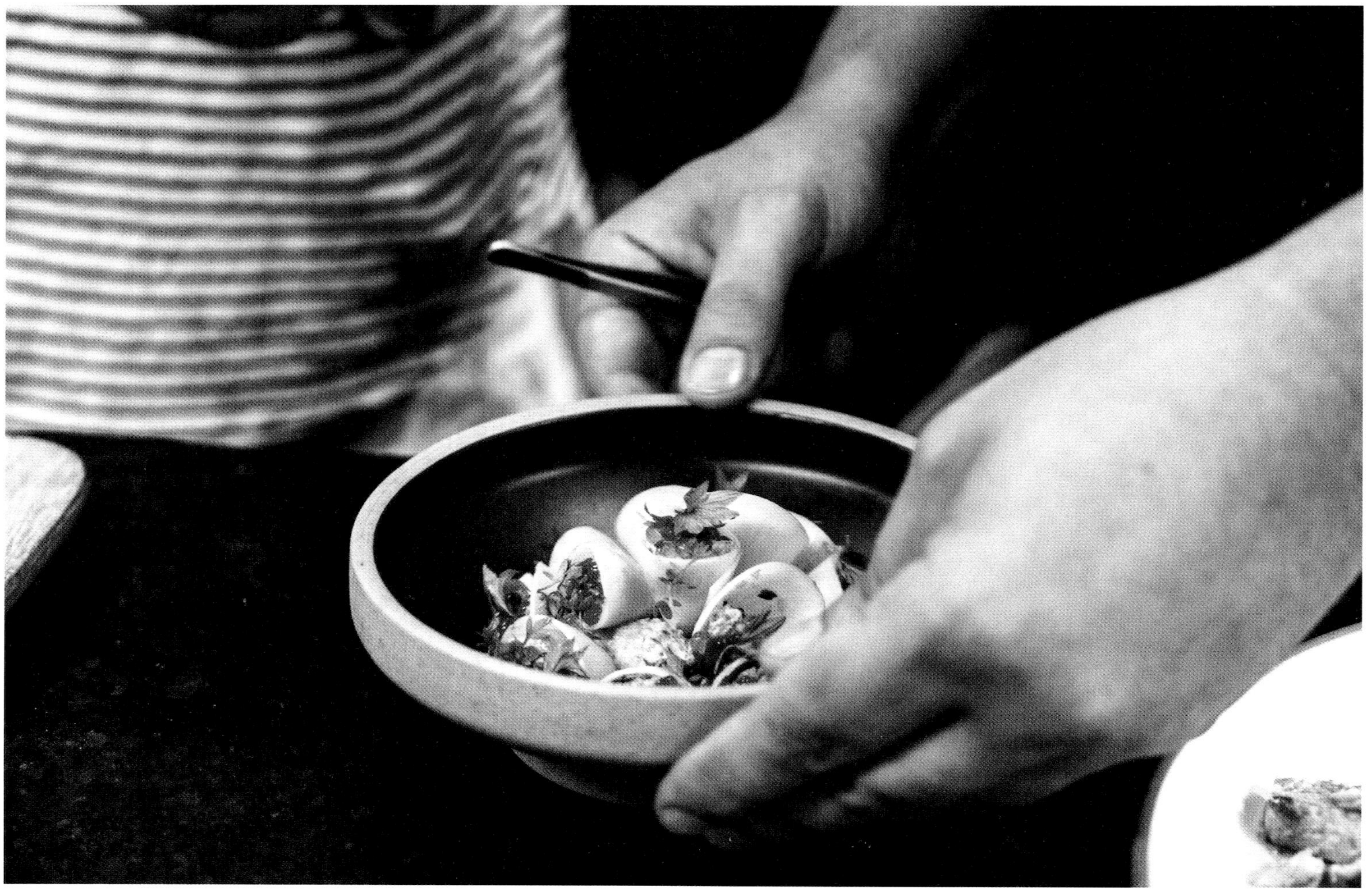

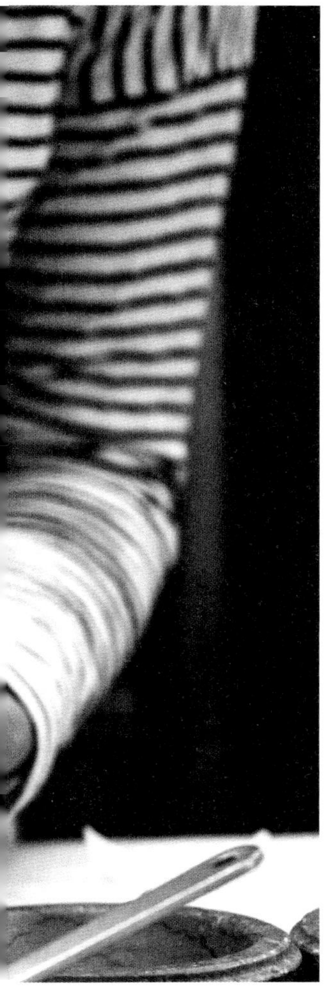

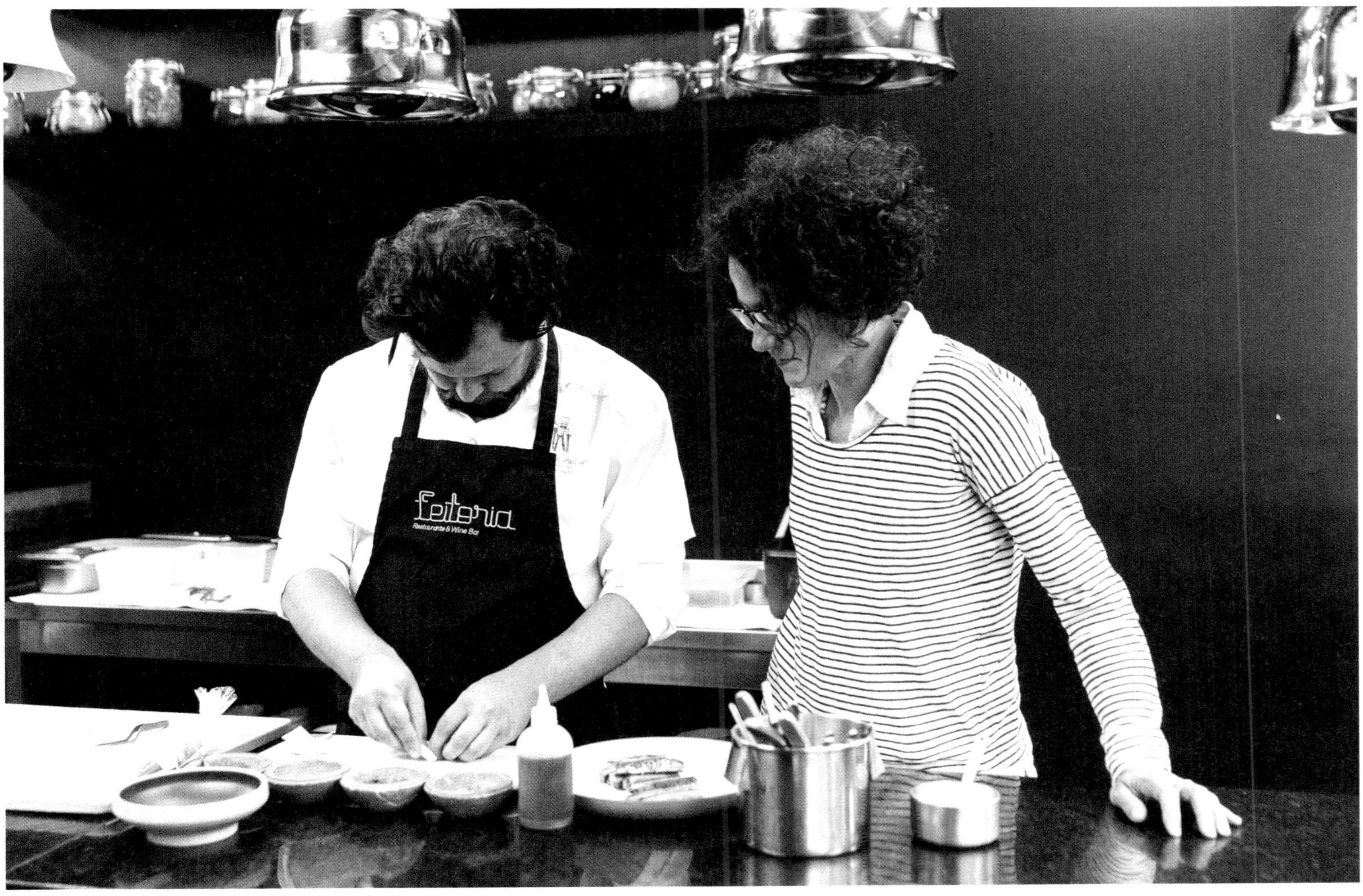
Feitoria

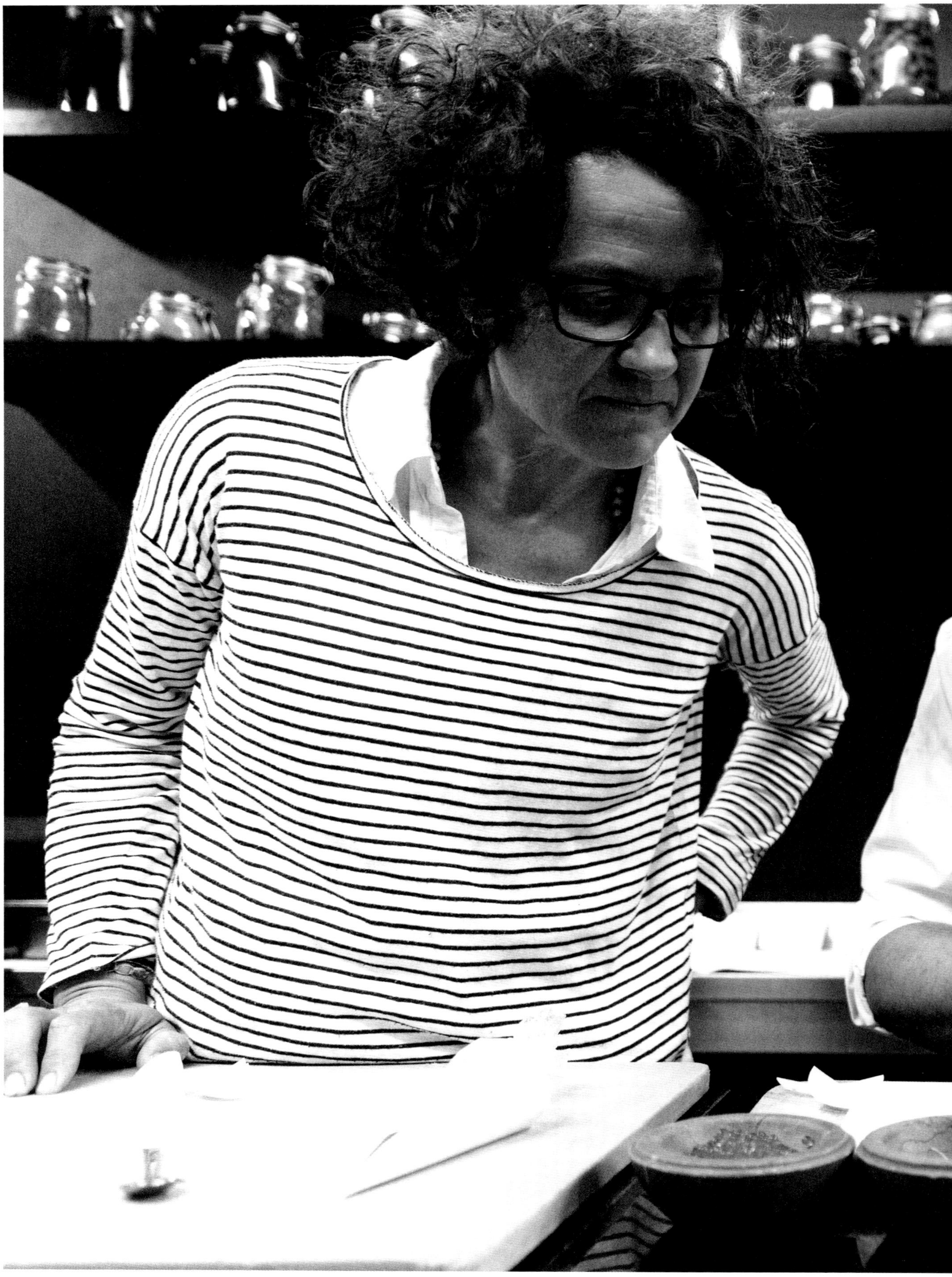

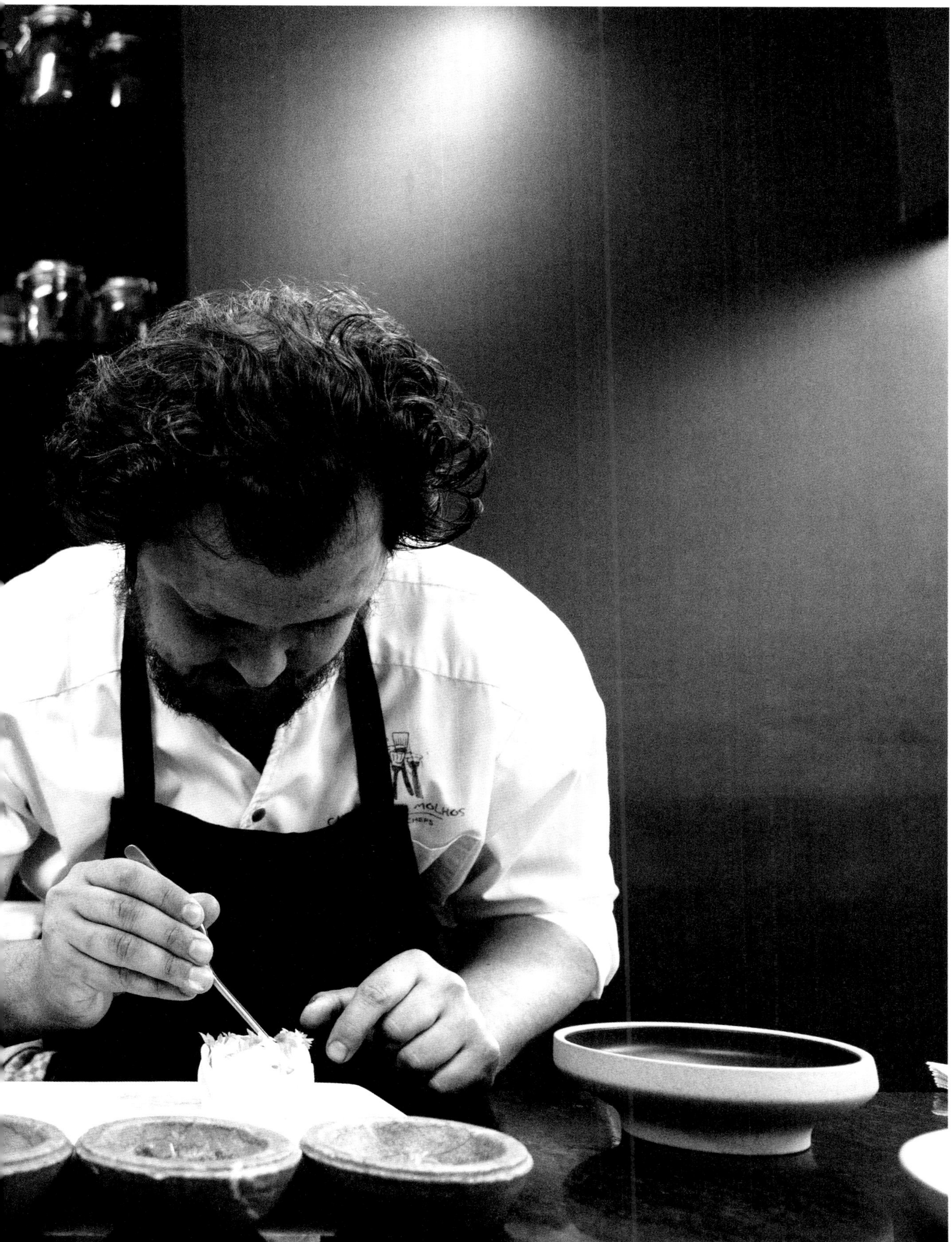

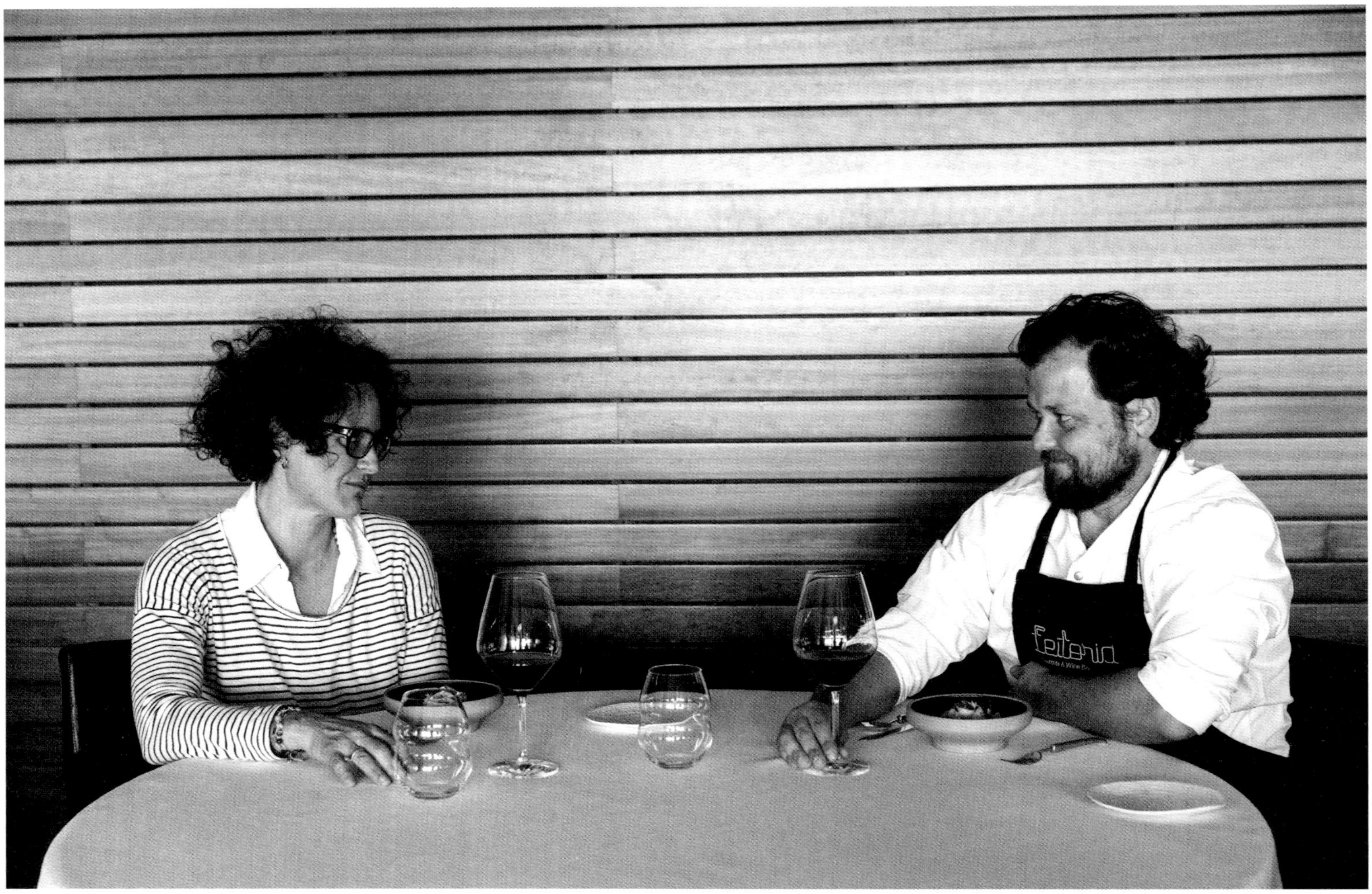
Feitoria

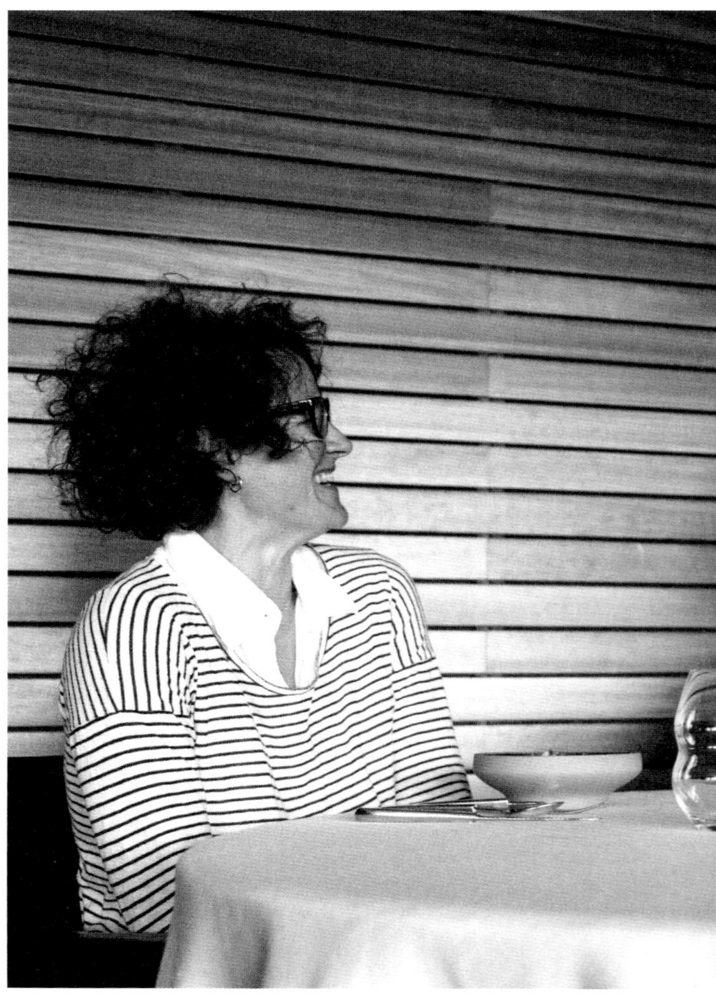

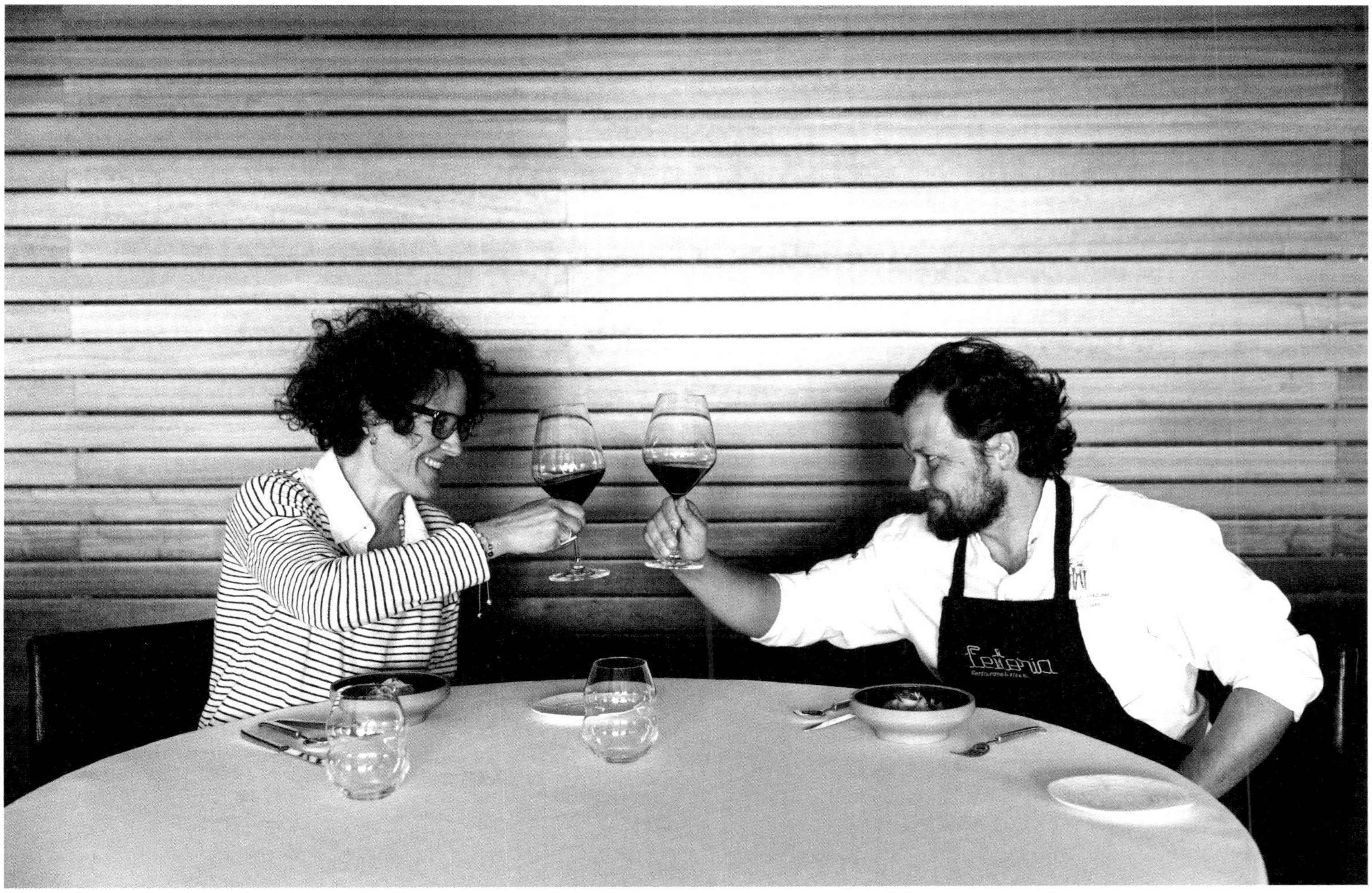

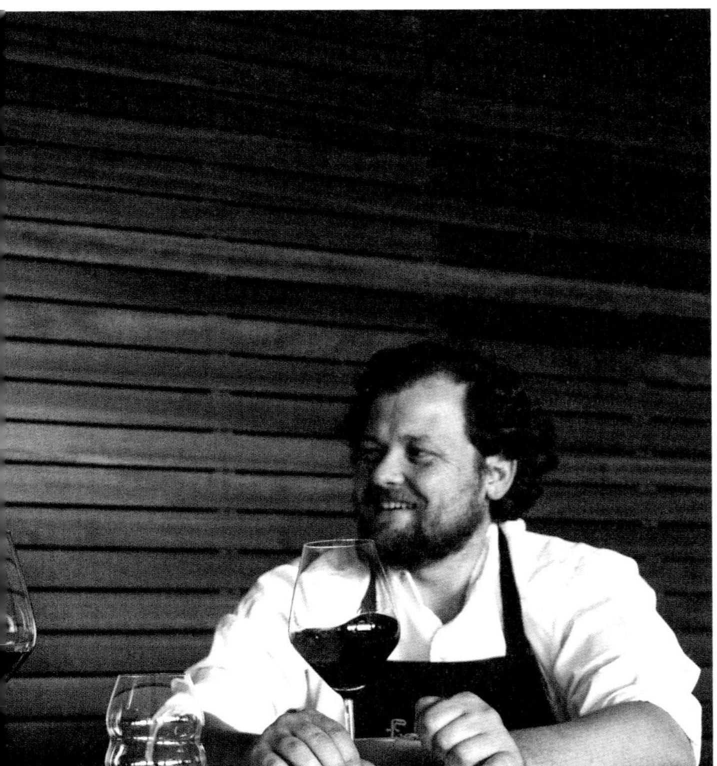

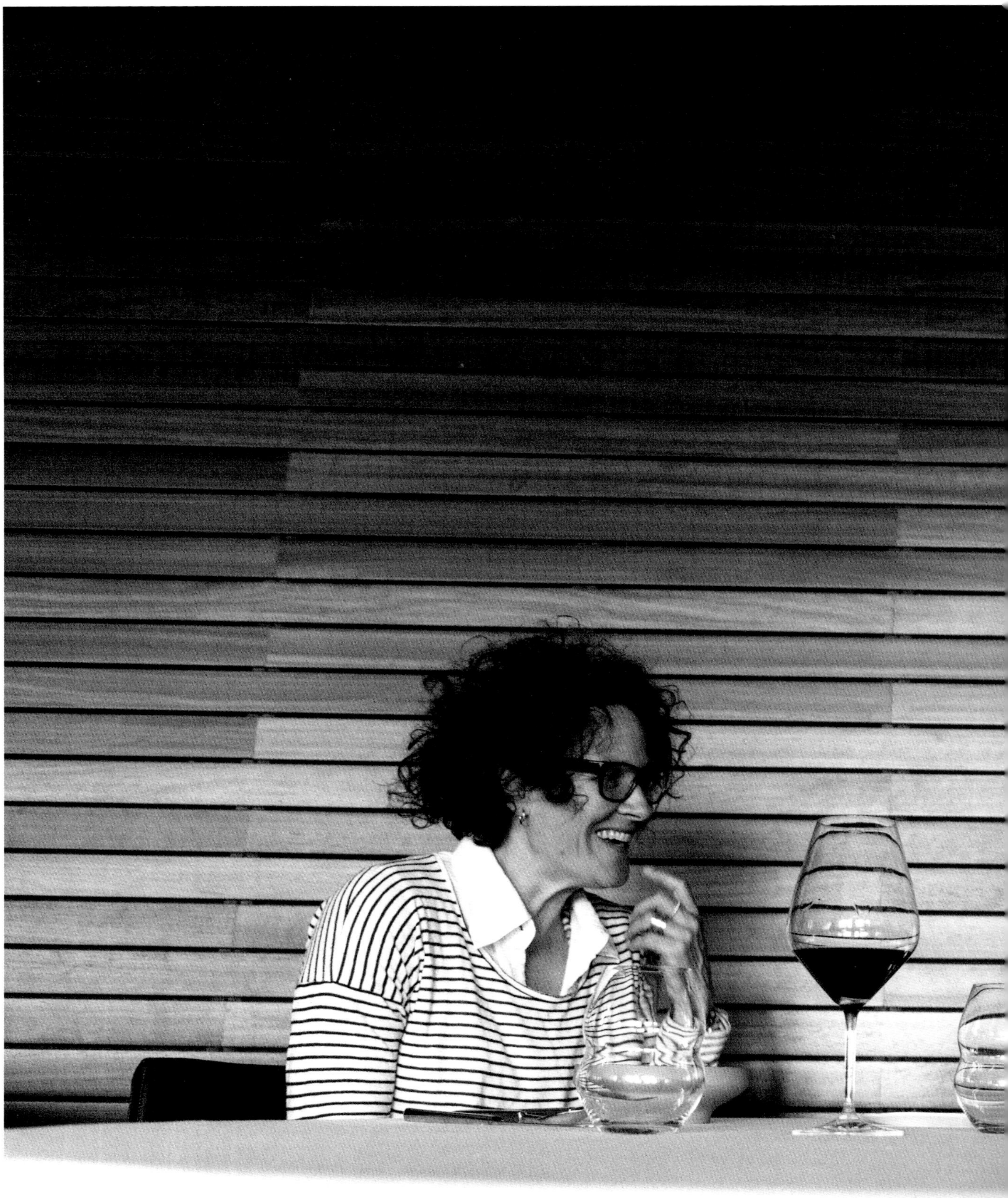

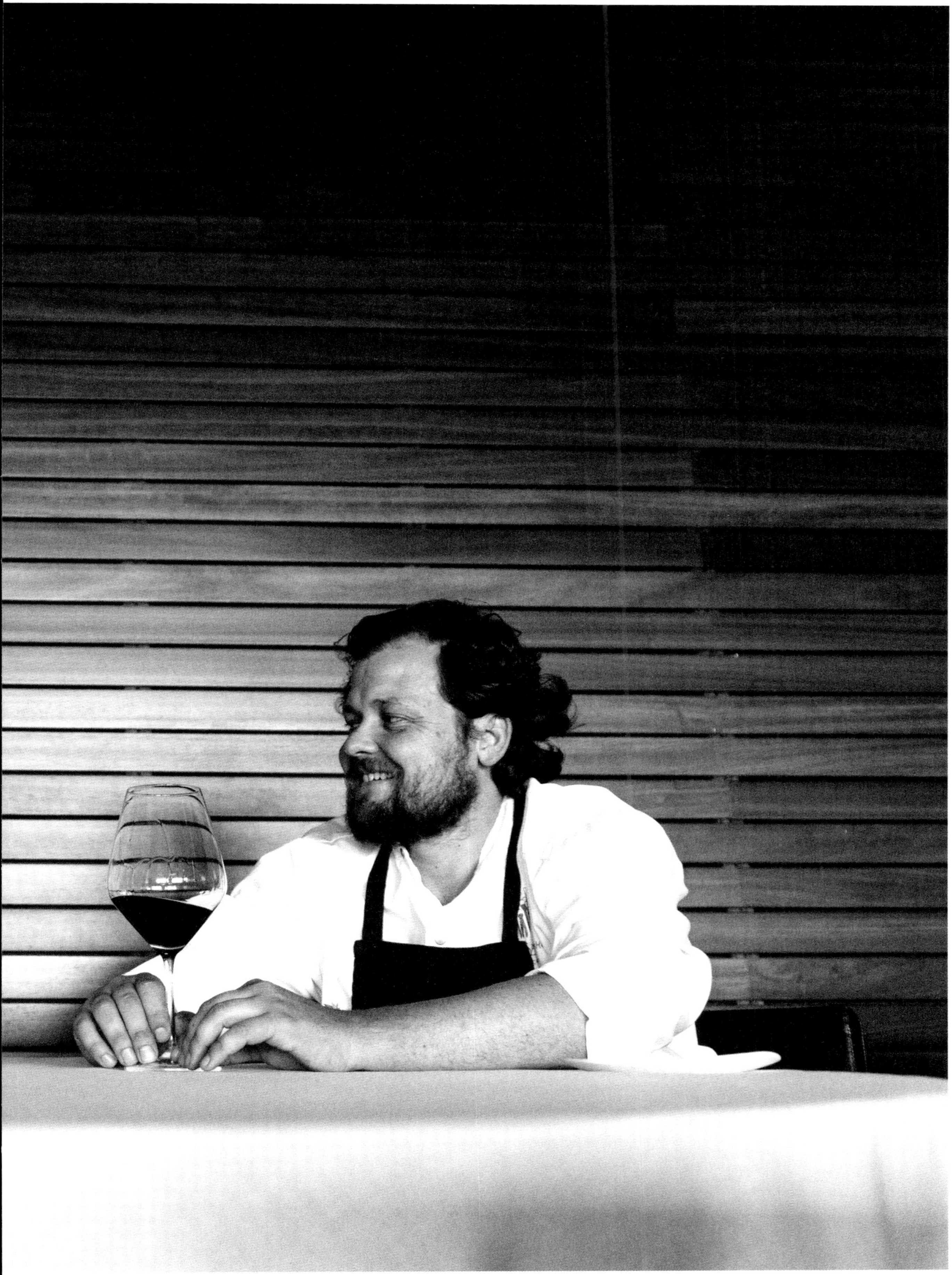

JOÃO RODRIGUES

SARDINES, ALMOND TIGER MILK AND DAIKON

SARDINES IN OLIVE OIL

BRAND MARIE ELISABETH

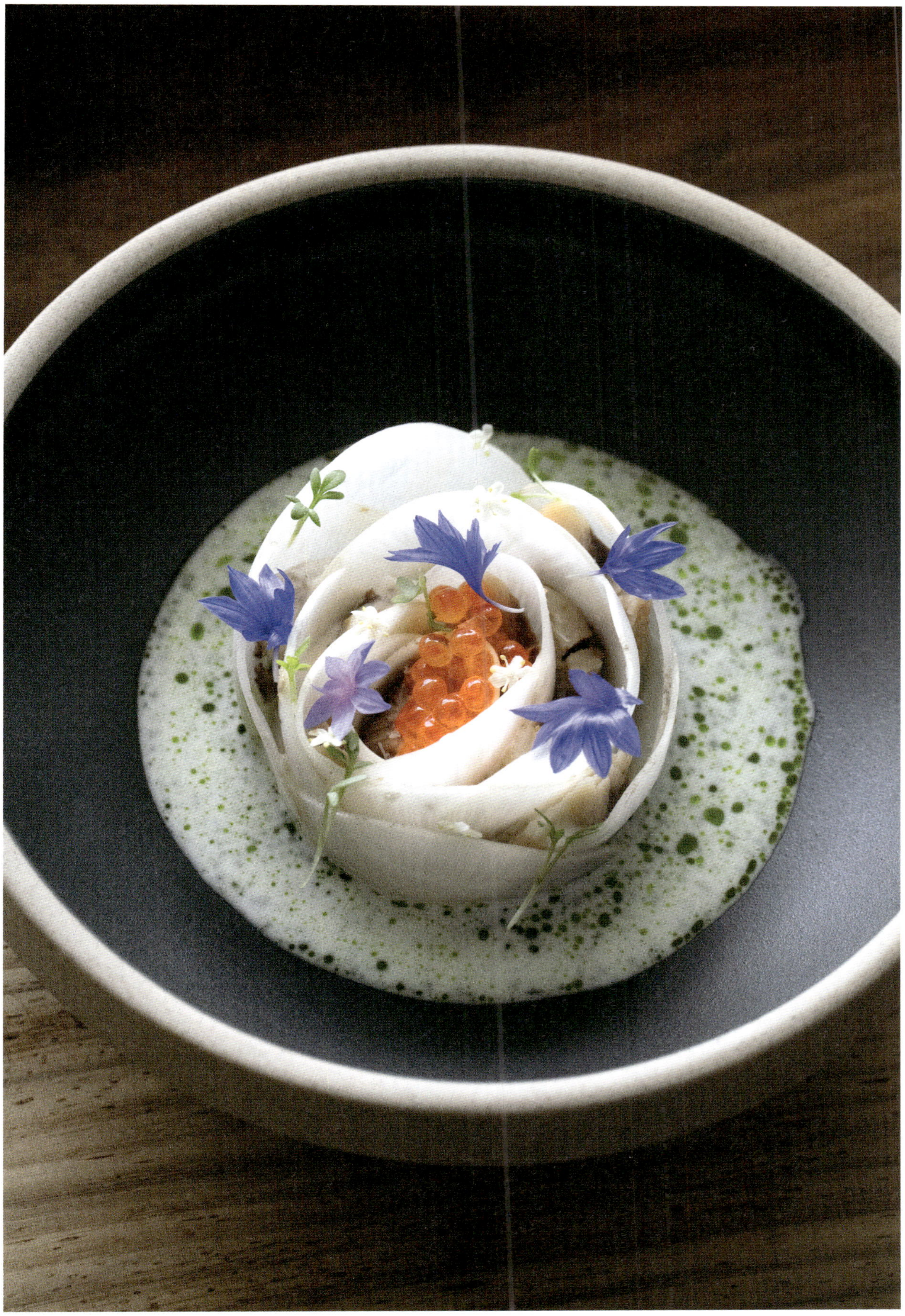

SUSAN

TIN (ESTHER)
2018

NE S.D.

FINE ART PRINT ON
HAHNEMÜHLE

THEM

12 × 7 CM

LITZ

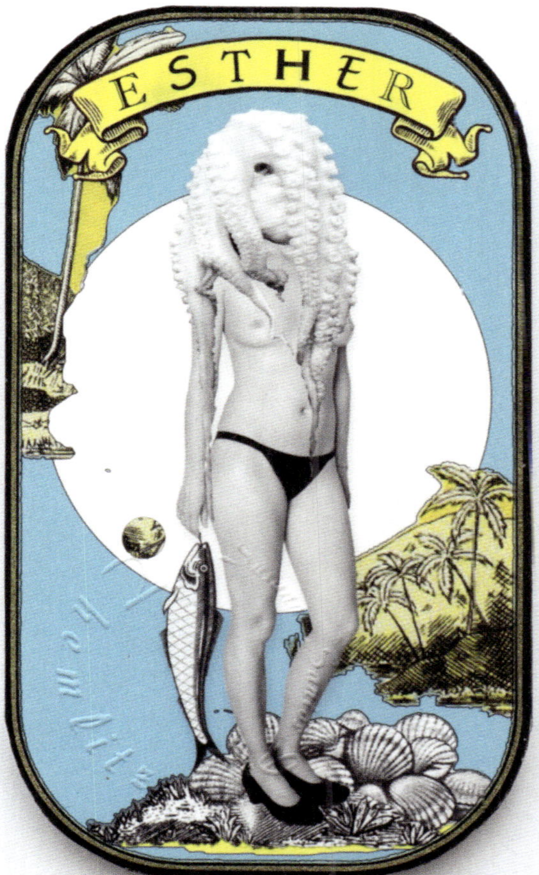
ESTHER

MIGUEL
ROCHA
VIEIRA

GRAÇA
PEREIRA
COUTINHO

GRAÇA PEREIRA COUTINHO

MIGUEL ROCHA VIEIRA

MIGUEL ROCHA VIEIRA
GRAÇA PEREIRA COUTINHO

MEDICINE BOXES

The London-based artist Graça Pereira Coutinho and the Michelin-starred chef Miguel Rocha Vieira get along right away. A passion shines in their eyes and that's the subject they choose without choosing.

"There are people who go the wrong way and then have no courage to change," says Miguel. "I don't understand. You need to like what you do, even if it means you have to change."

"If I wasn't passionate, I couldn't do it," says Graça.

"Me neither," says Miguel.

It's agreed by both and both leave to look for what they want, as if they were hunting. Maybe fishing would be a more appropriate analogy. "Ninety per cent of our menu comes from the sea," explains Miguel. "We only have one meat dish. Fish, crustaceans, algae, herbs and flowers, that's what we like."

"Fantastic," says Graça, and we all agree.

"Ideas come from everywhere", says Miguel. "From what we see and eat, from the days and sometimes in bed, before sleeping. We think a lot about food."

Graça nods in agreement. "We're a tunnel that ideas flow through, like the poets who receive a poem without knowing where it's come from." She reflects and thinks of an example. "When my husband fell ill, I used to see all these medicine boxes and I started to collect them. I love to pick up rubbish and I thought of using them as sculptures. I wanted the drawings to come out of the picture, and I started tying the boxes with cloths and swab. Later I understood that in wrapping the boxes I was healing him again. It helped me a lot."

Miguel ponders it all, our triggers and our availability to be creative.

"After I opened a restaurant in Budapest in 1998, I had no day off for two years," he says. "My life was only that and, at the end, I wasn't able to create any more. Everything was very forced. I was moody, always tired, without patience. I couldn't stand myself any more."

"Are you someone who screams?" asks Graça.

"I used to, a lot," says Miguel. "I was a massive idiot."

We take a break from the past and a make a toast to the future. It's time to taste the dish and the chef does the honours.

"This is the black swordfish fillet you sent," he says. "We cut it to make it look nicer and we burnt it to give the taste of a summer barbecue. With the oil from the can, we made a mayonnaise, then a purée of melon and cantaloupe, using the skins for a juice. Here we are like Graça, we like to make the most of everything."

Blessed rubbish that has triggered so many smiles from the diners.

The conversation nears its end, but still we head back to the beginning. Where does it all come from? How did it happen, Graça?

"I was about three or four years old," she says. "My mother sent me to a very avant-garde school and, when I first touched clay, I felt so happy that I thought, 'That's what I want to do.' To create forms, concepts and objects that people could take home. Around the age of fourteen or fifteen, my mother tried to convince me to study architecture, as it was a more serious course than fine art. But it was too late, I already knew what I wanted and I chose sculpture."

What about you, Miguel? We give him the honour of closing proceedings and the chef doesn't waste the opportunity.

"I was in university and thought, 'I'm not going to finish college – I'm taking a cooking course.' I called my grandmother to tell her about it and she begged me not to abandon my course, and especially not to become a cook: 'What a disaster!' So, I thought, 'Okay, I won't tell her to avoid upsetting her.' She only found out I was a cook when the news broke that I had won a Michelin star in Budapest."

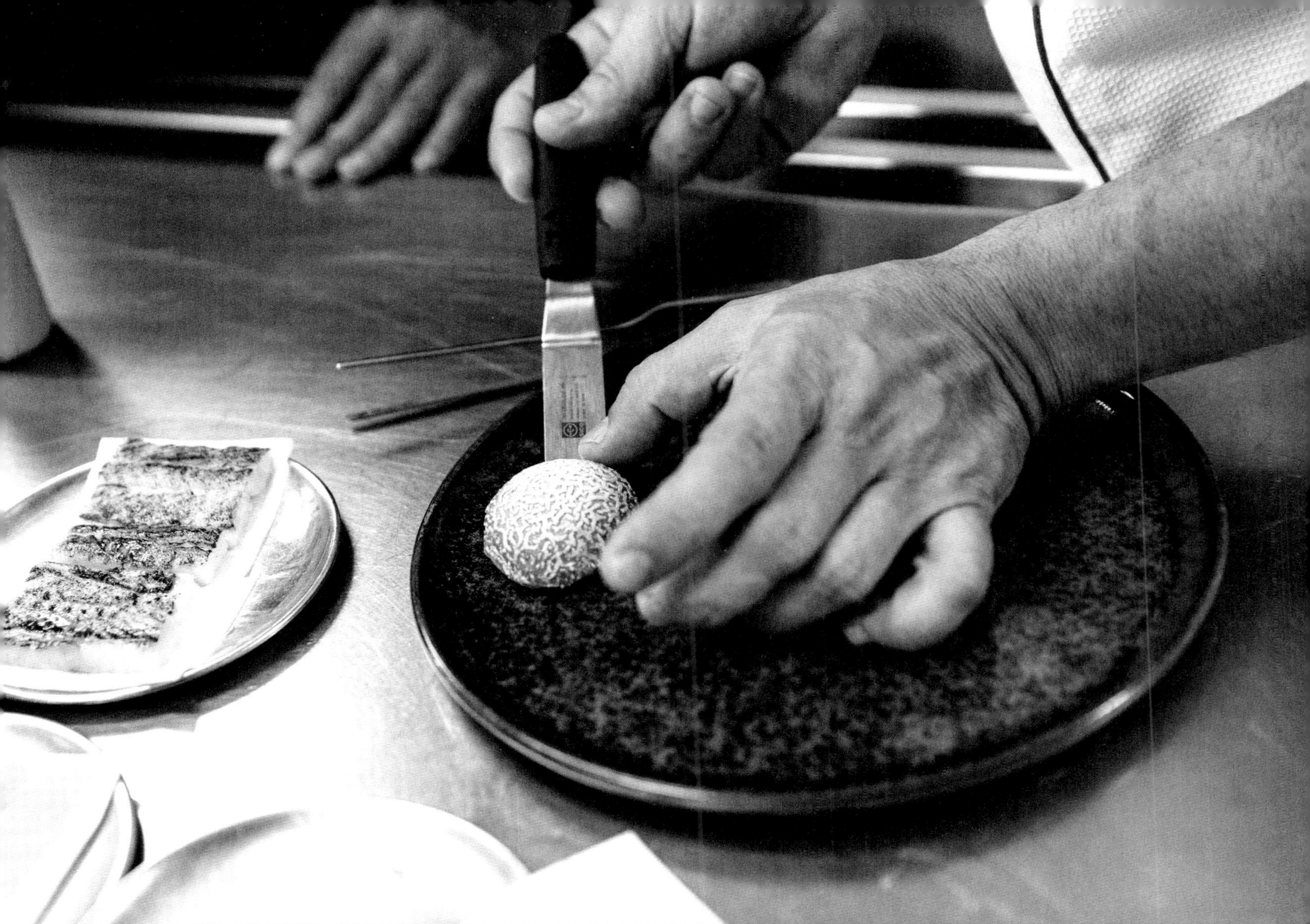
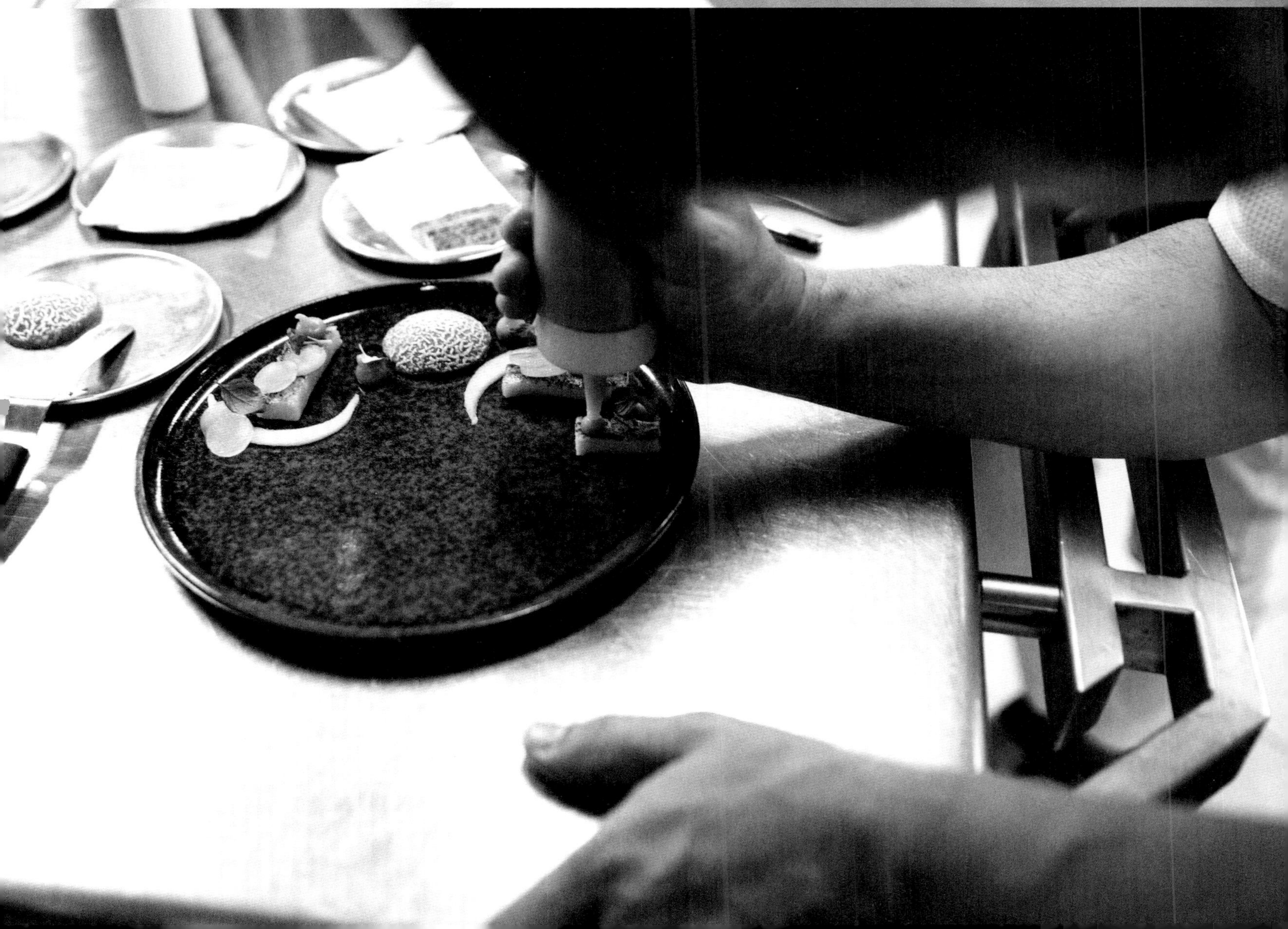

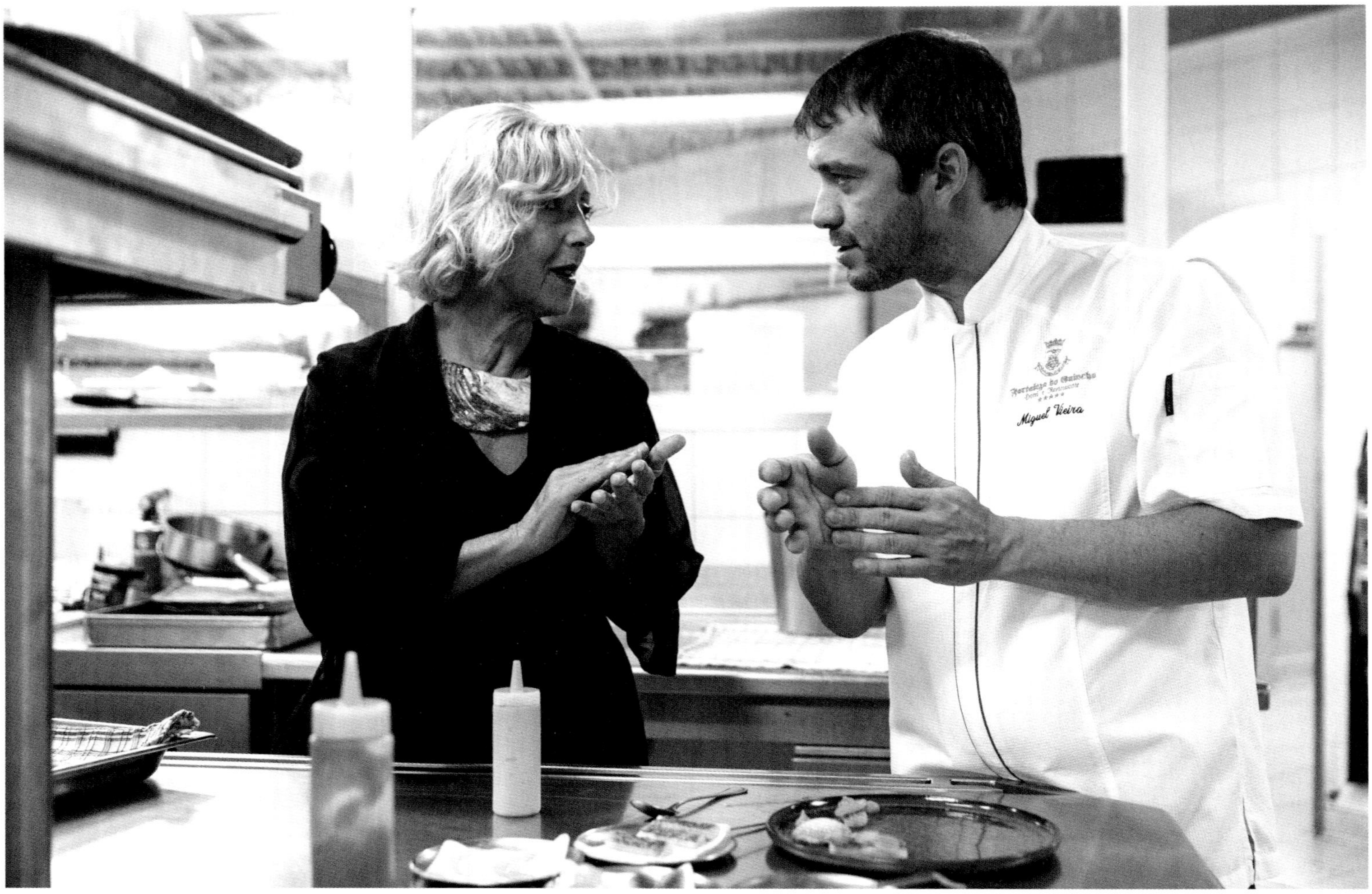
Miguel Vieira

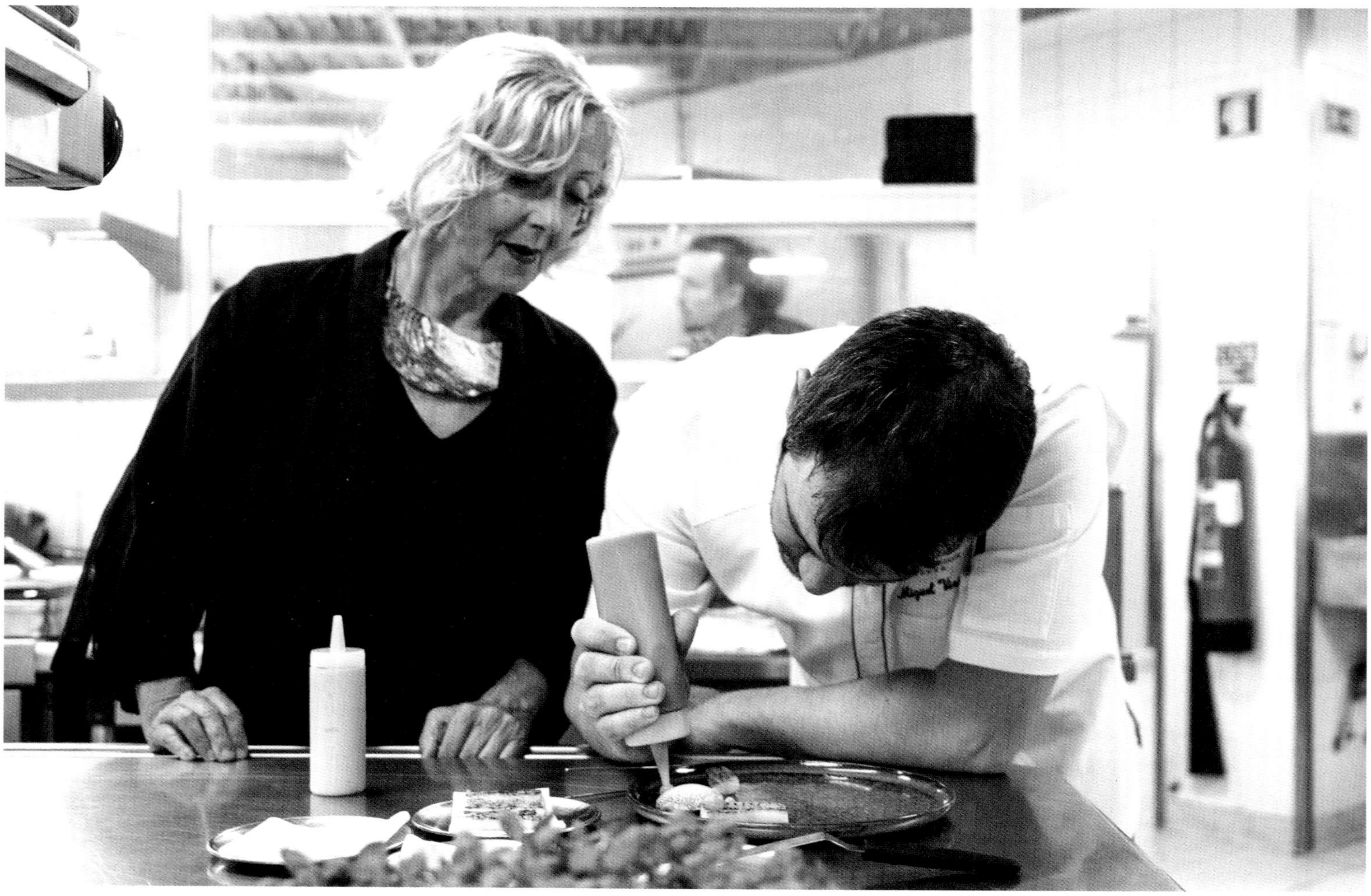

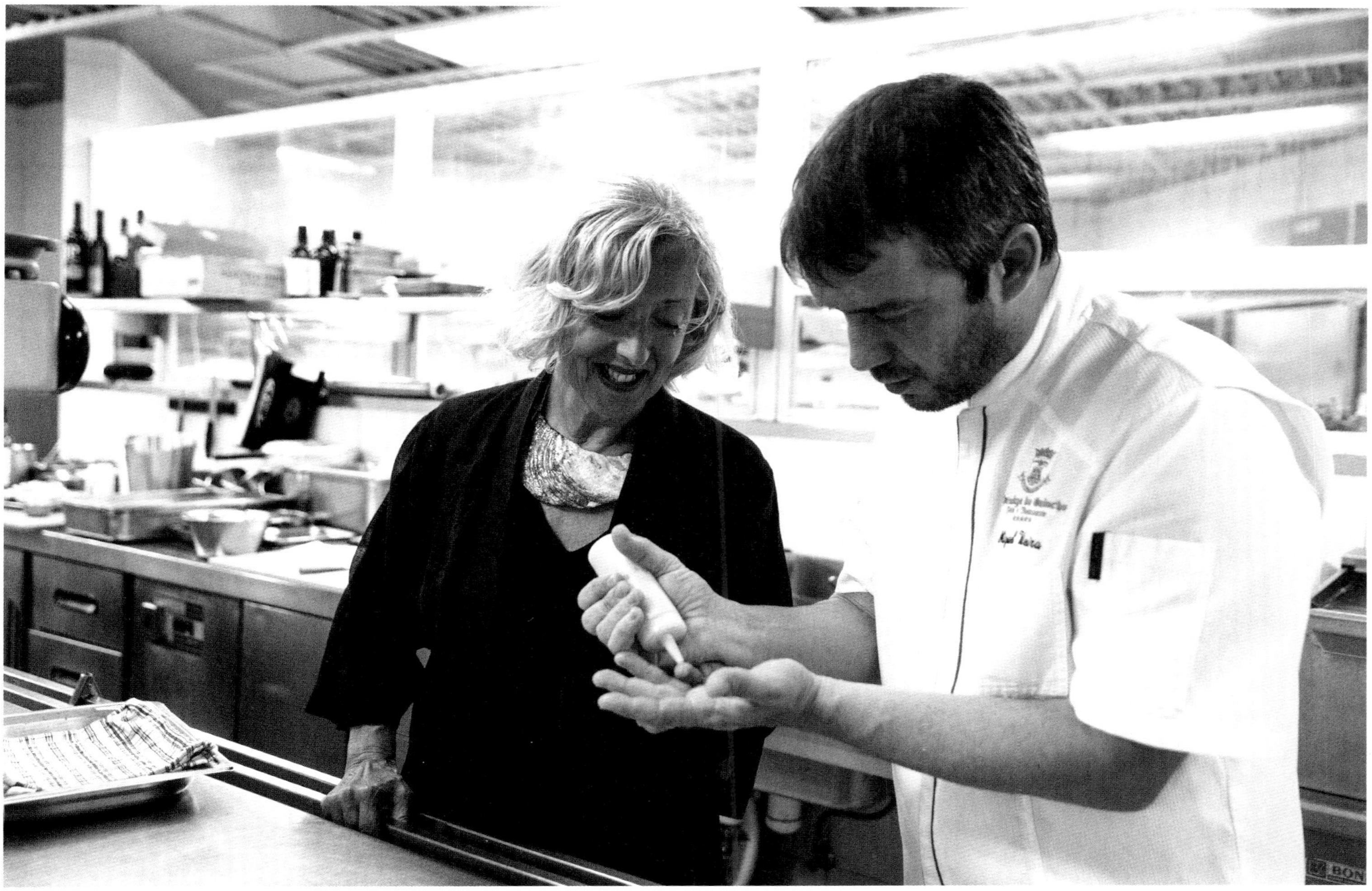

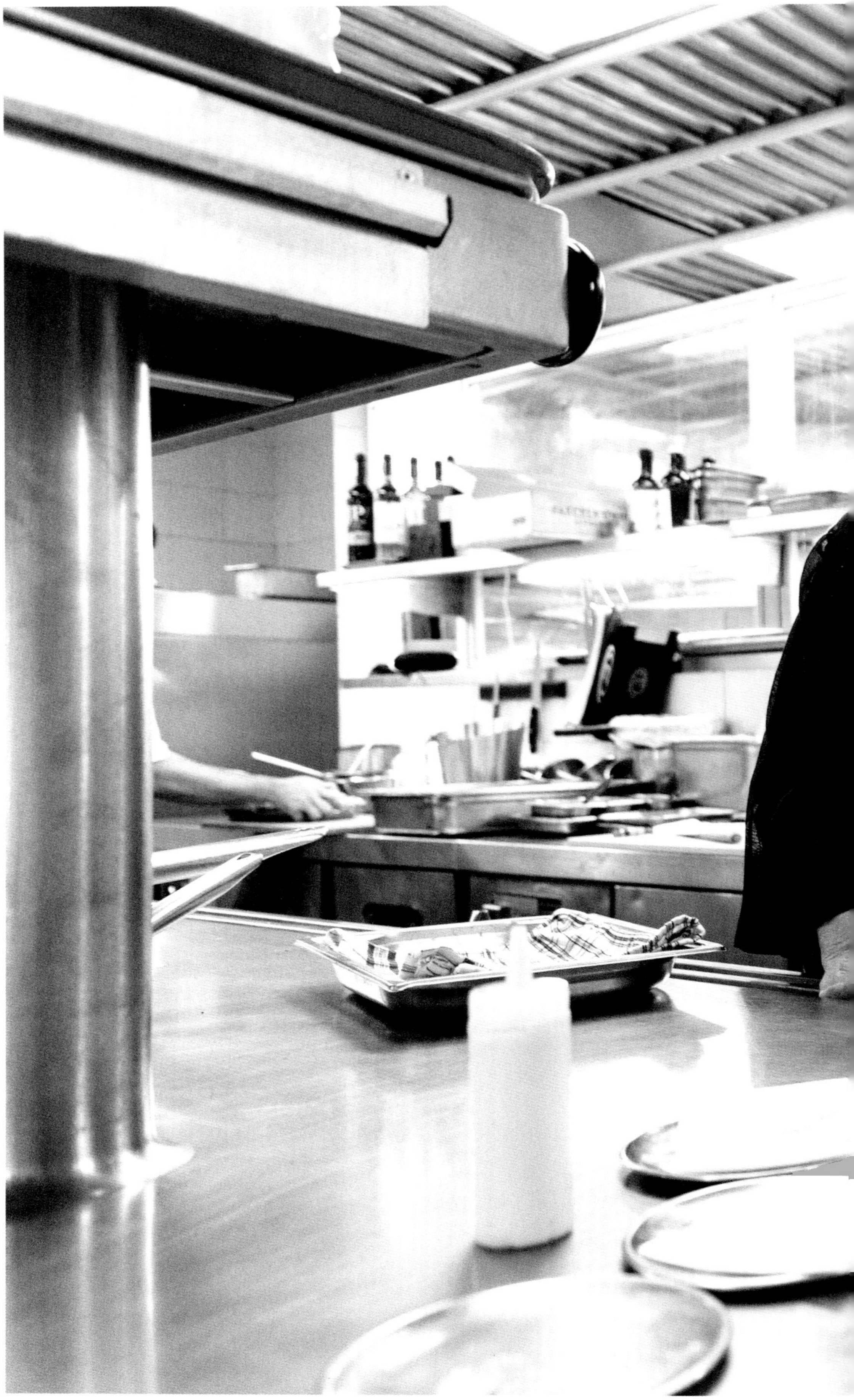

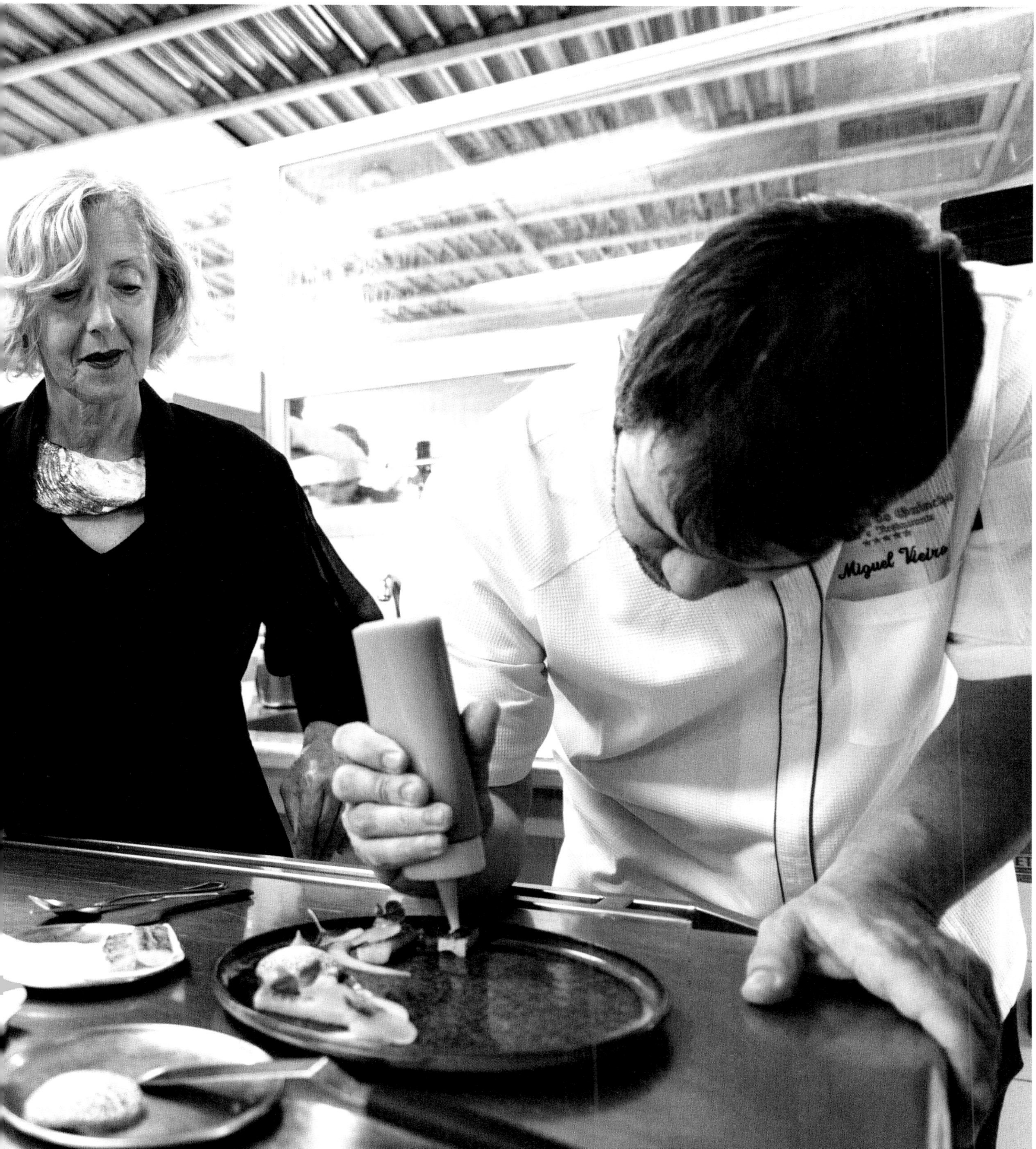
Miguel Vieira

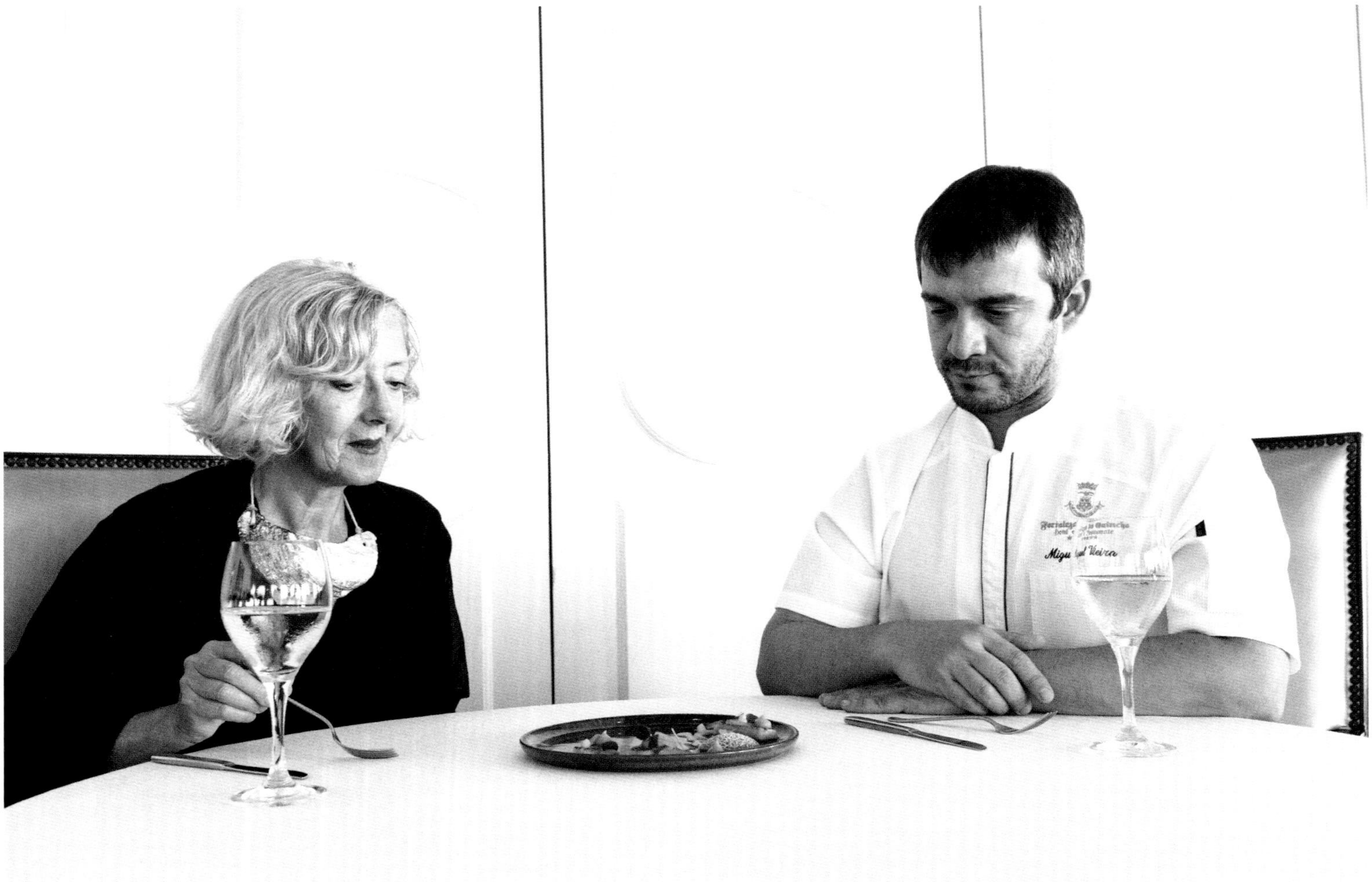

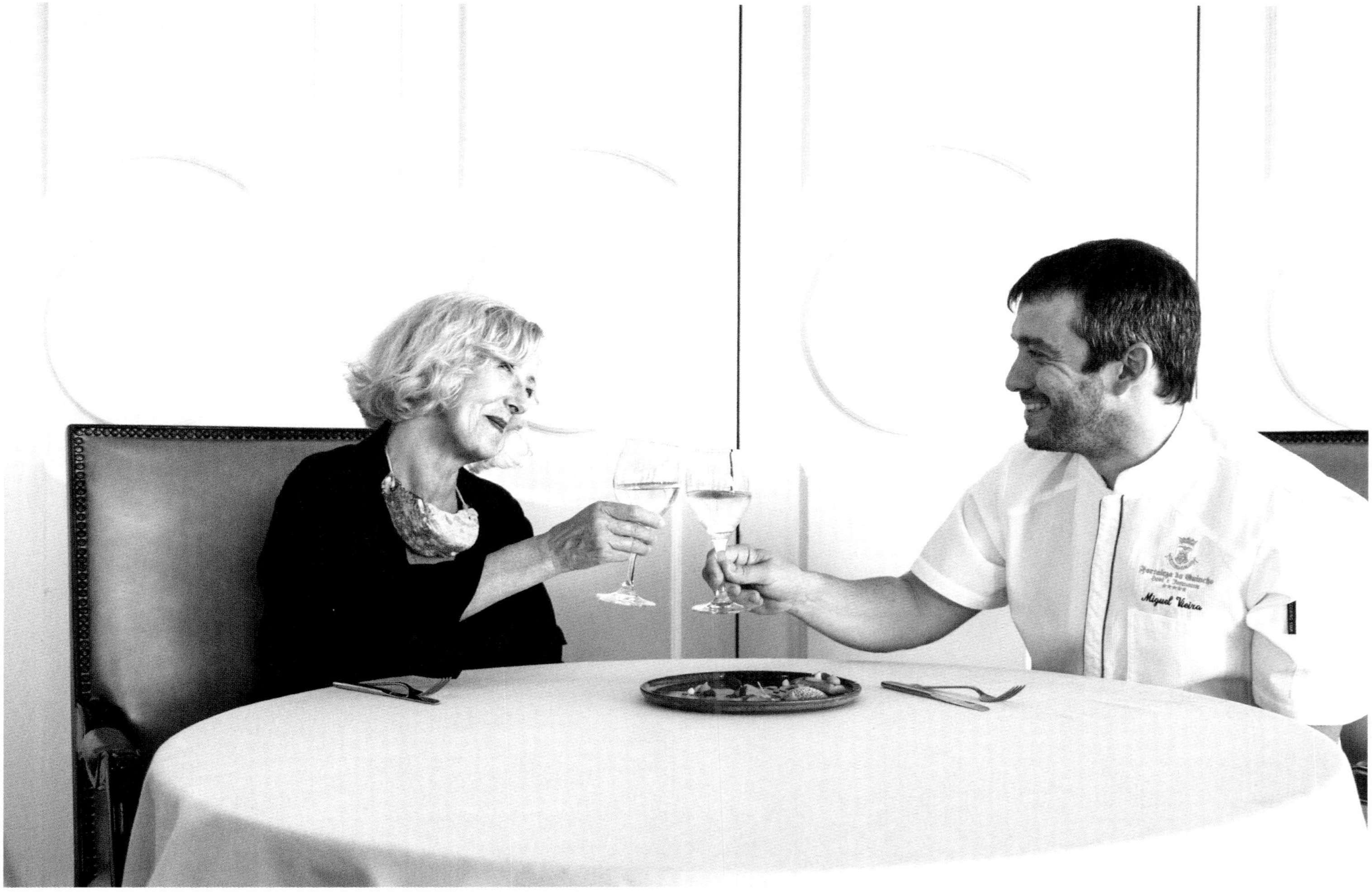
Miguel Vieira

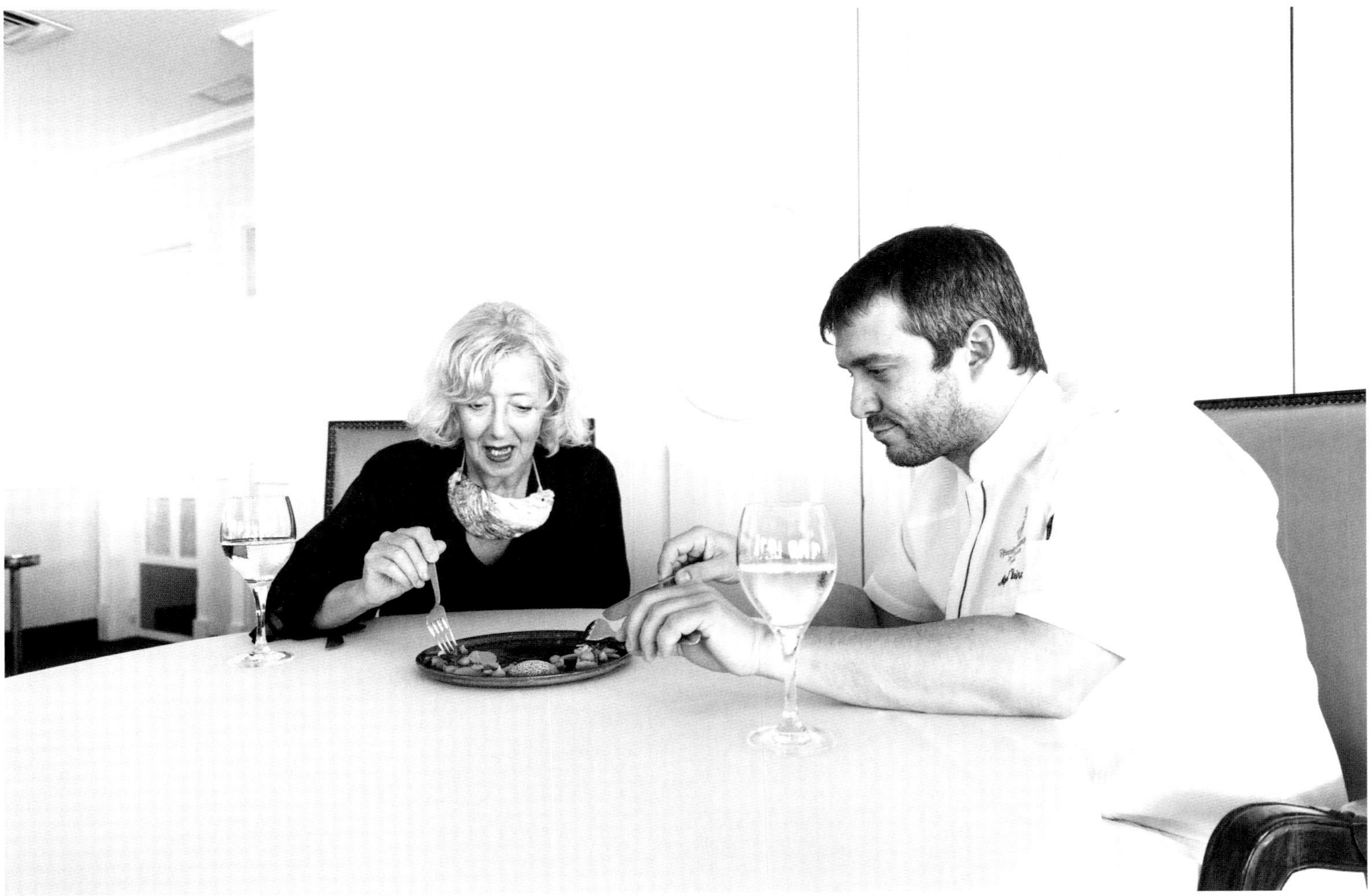

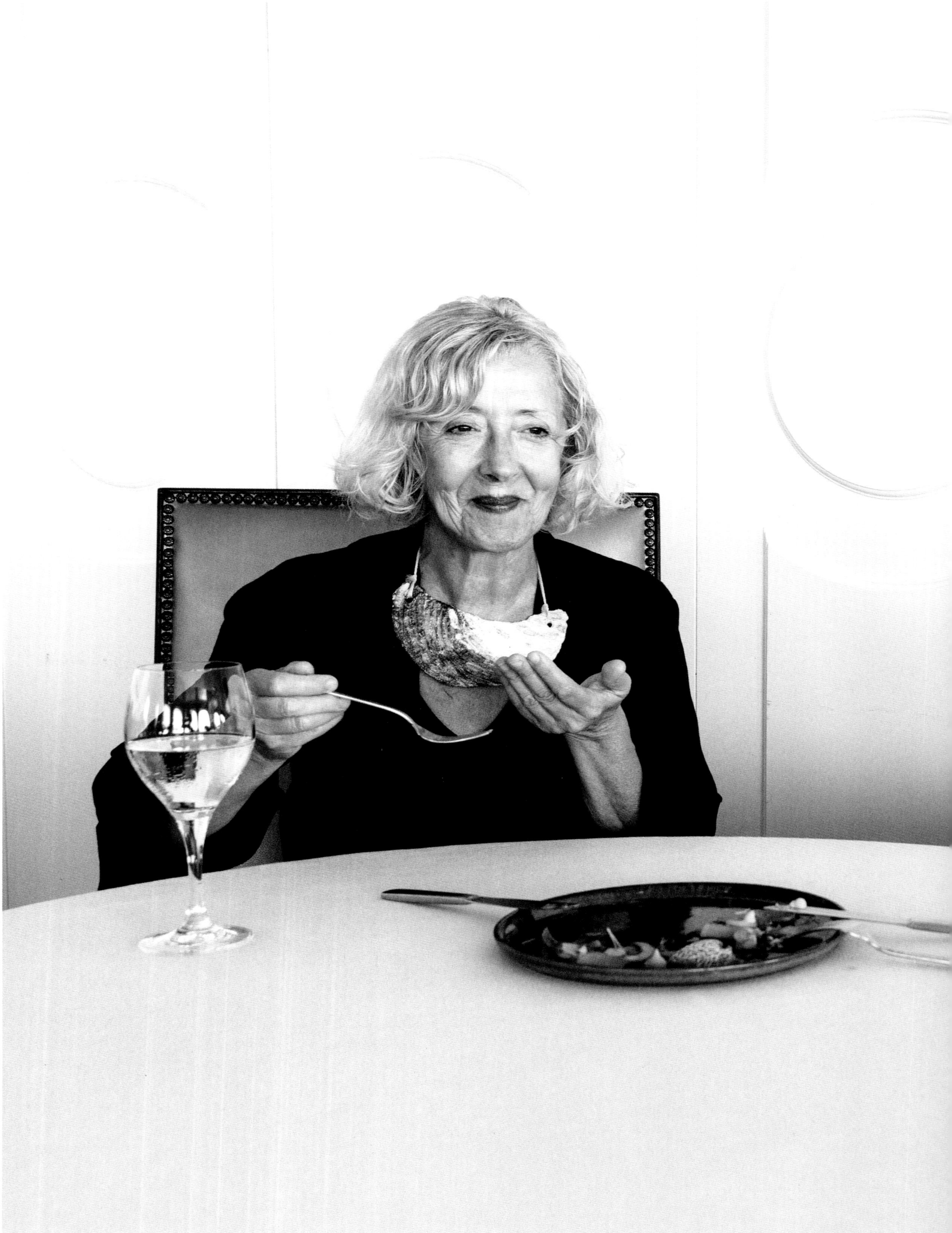

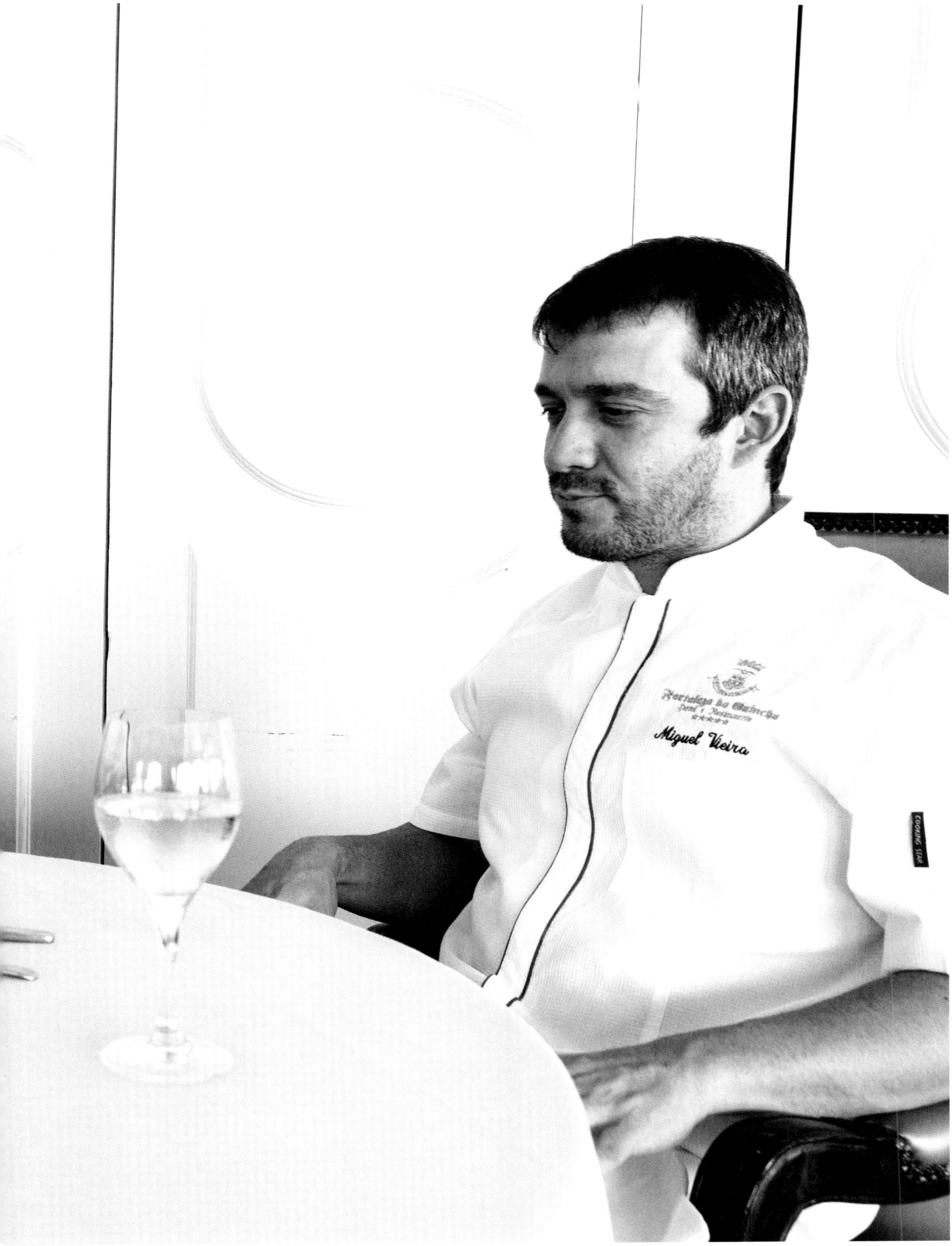
Miguel Vieira

MIGUEL ROCHA VIEIRA

BLACK SWORDFISH FILLETS
BRAND LUÇAS

SWORDFISH FILLETS, SLIGHTLY BRAISED, MELON AND CANTALOUPE

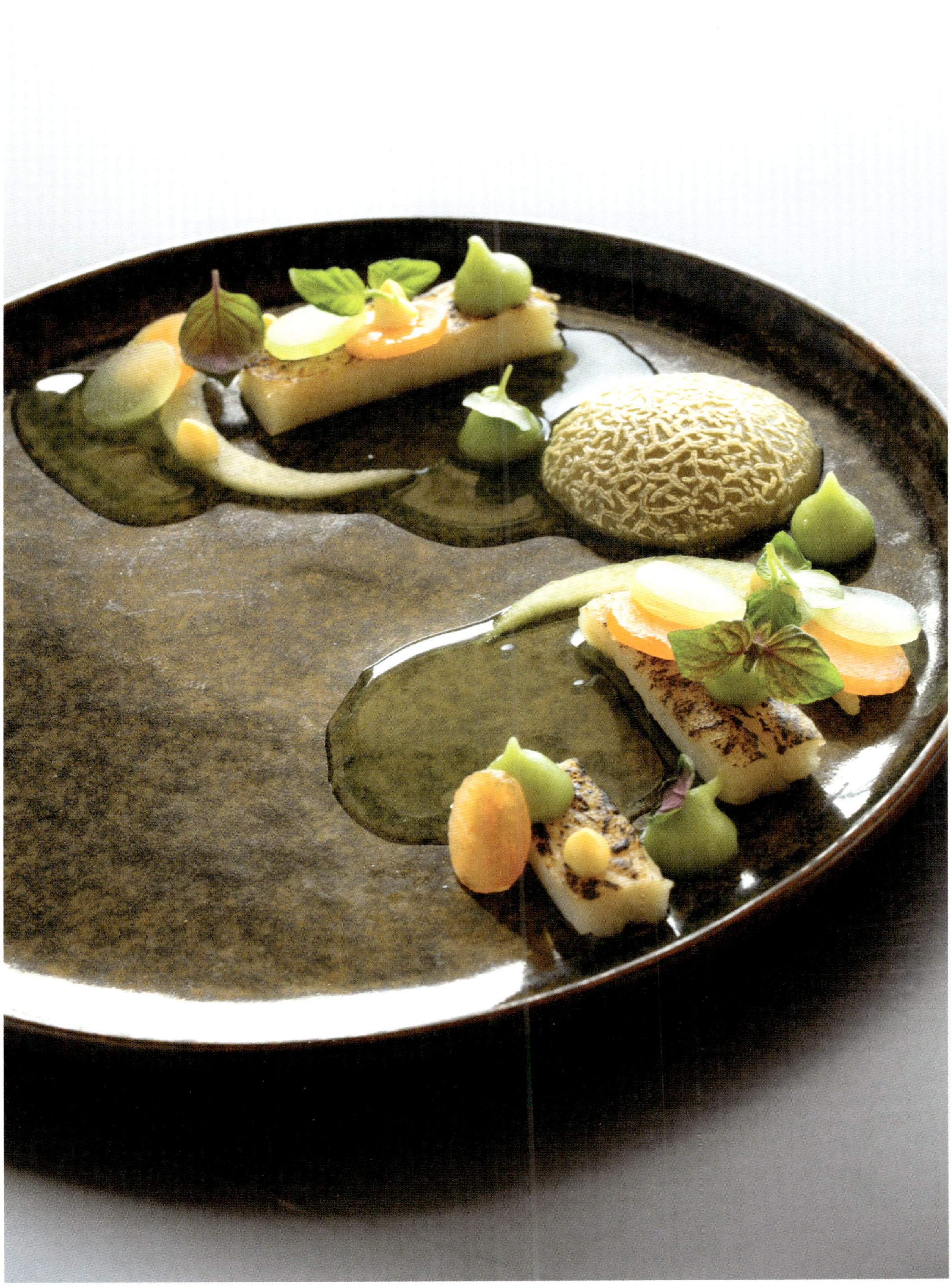

GRAÇA PEREIRA COUTINHO

THE SEA
IN A TIN
2017

MIXED
TECHNIQUE
ON PAPER
24 × 32 CM

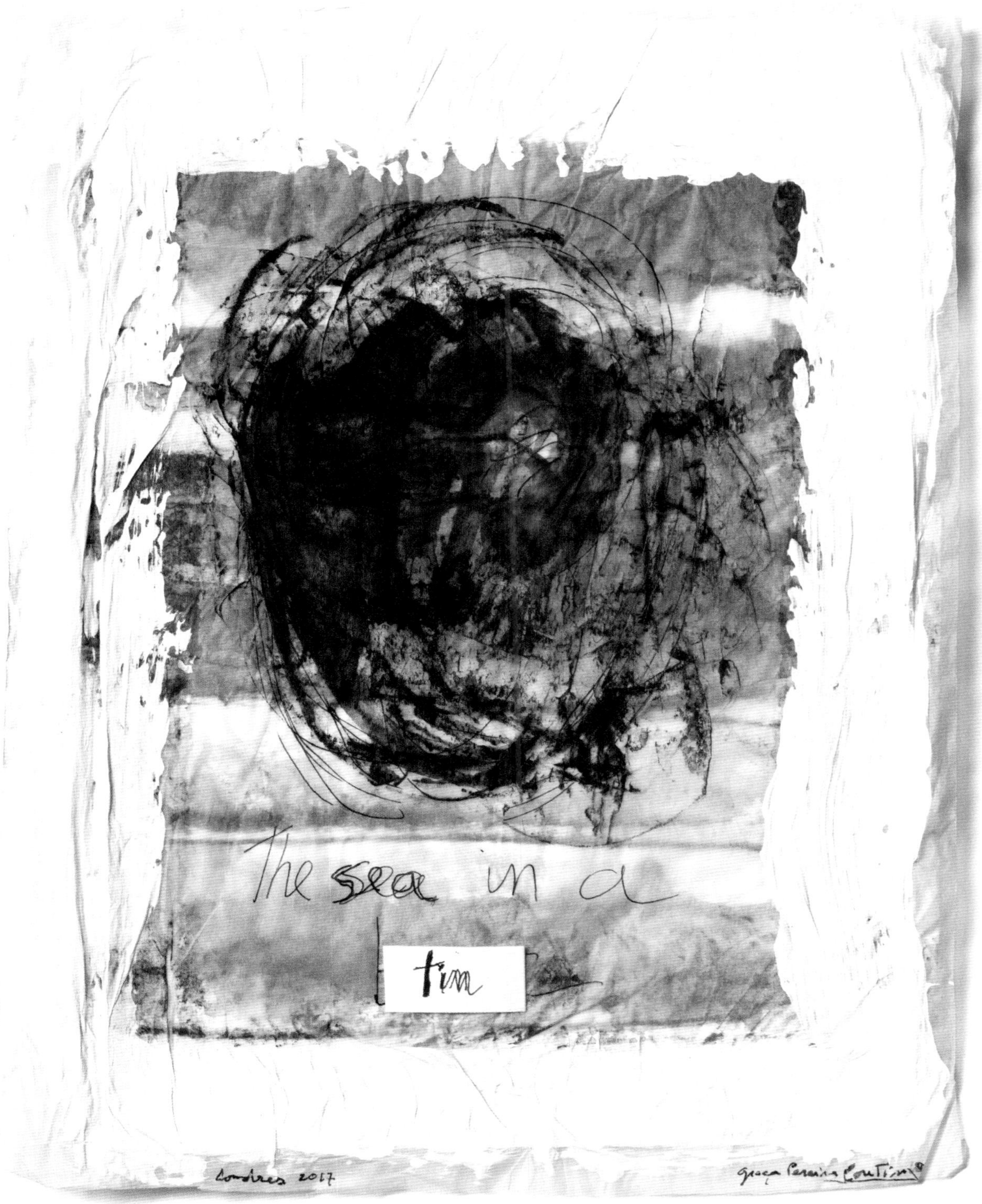
The sea in a
tin
Londres 2017

PEDRO
PENA
BASTOS

ALICE
GEIRINHAS

ALICE
GEIRINHAS

PEDRO
PENA
BASTOS

PEDRO PENA BASTOS
ALICE GEIRINHAS

FEIRA DA LADRA

There's something dramatic about the space – one could almost describe it as a set for a play performed around a table. The walls are white, the furniture is elegant but minimal, there are no noises or distractions. The effort to emphasise the essential is evident. Ceia is located in the hotel Santa Clara 1728, in the 'Feira da Ladra' next to Campo Santa Clara in Lisbon, where every Tuesday and Saturday people come to buy and sell the most wonderful objects (antiques, records, mannequins, second-hand toys, clothes and more).

Here we are, at the start of a sunny afternoon, with the artist Alice Geirinhas and the chef Pedro Pena Bastos. Alice, this is Pedro. Pedro, this is Alice. Shy smiles, a shaking of hands.

The chef gives us a tour of a kitchen that seems more like a laboratory or an operating room – nothing out of place, nothing that doesn't belong. Prepared ingredients sparkle on the counter: garfish, lime, caviar, fried broccoli and ogonori seaweed. Next to these, the chef's knives. Japanese and more than simple instruments, they are symbols of a philosophy, simplicity and expertise – essential concepts for someone who takes cuisine seriously.

Alice can't hide her joy. She loves to cook and, above all, to eat and drink. She's a fan of *MasterChef* and would love to take part.

So, about the dish, how was it born?

Pedro shrugs and answers with a smile: "I had nothing prepared. I looked at the fridge in the morning and it took shape."

"And the serving?" asks Alice.

"The most important thing is to know that, once we've placed it, we can't move it again," explains Pedro. And he shows us what he means.

"So, how do we eat it?" she asks.

"First, with the eyes," says Pedro. "Then all together, in one bite."

We taste it and rate it highly. We make a toast to the artists. But who are they and how did they become artists? It's Alice who starts.

"There was no epiphany that I remember," she says. "I come from Viseu, but my family was from the south and they were very open-minded. I revealed myself early. I liked to be alone, drawing..."

Now, Pedro.

"The first time I remember cooking was around the age of six. I did a mayonnaise for a tuna sandwich to take to the beach. I was always surrounded by people who cooked, but I was also self-taught. Later, I did a course in food production, as I needed a diploma anyway. My real wish was to be an aeronautical engineer."

The words take flight...

Alice: "I like to avoid competition and follow my own path. Competition puts me off. I also seek solitude. I'm very restless and I still need to learn how to deal with pressure."

Pedro tells us of his journey: "Herdade do Esporão restaurant had a huge team and it was hard to manage everything. This involves fewer people, and I enjoy that. I'm sure this isn't the best job in the world, but I like it and I know how to cook."

They exchange a few ideas about creation and the processes it comprises. Maintain the freshness while refining the result, they say. Mix the old with the new, they say.

Pedro talks about a class he gave, in which he divided the creative process into three factors: creativity, the social and cultural context (the *terroir*), and the aesthetic. He believes the cultural context is the most important. "I'm not going to serve coastal shrimps in Alentejo, nor lamb in Lisbon."

Laughing, Alice says she understands about the shrimp, if not the lamb. "I'm more chaotic, I like the Dadaists, I like fusion. It's kind of my line."

And so we get lost while finding so much. Creation and art have their mysteries, their unique non-transferable paths linking the author to the piece of work.

We make a few more toasts and think a little more about all that.

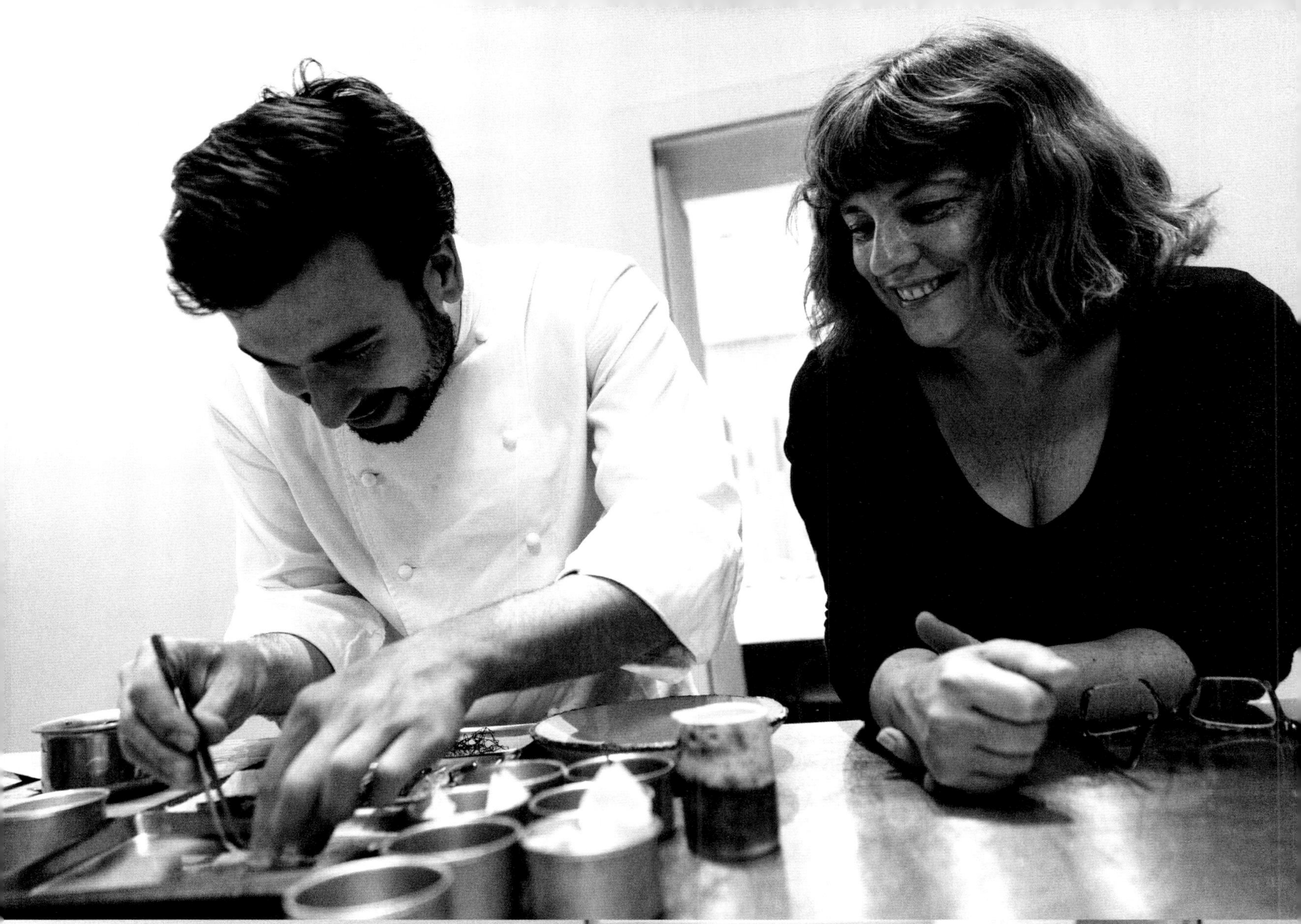

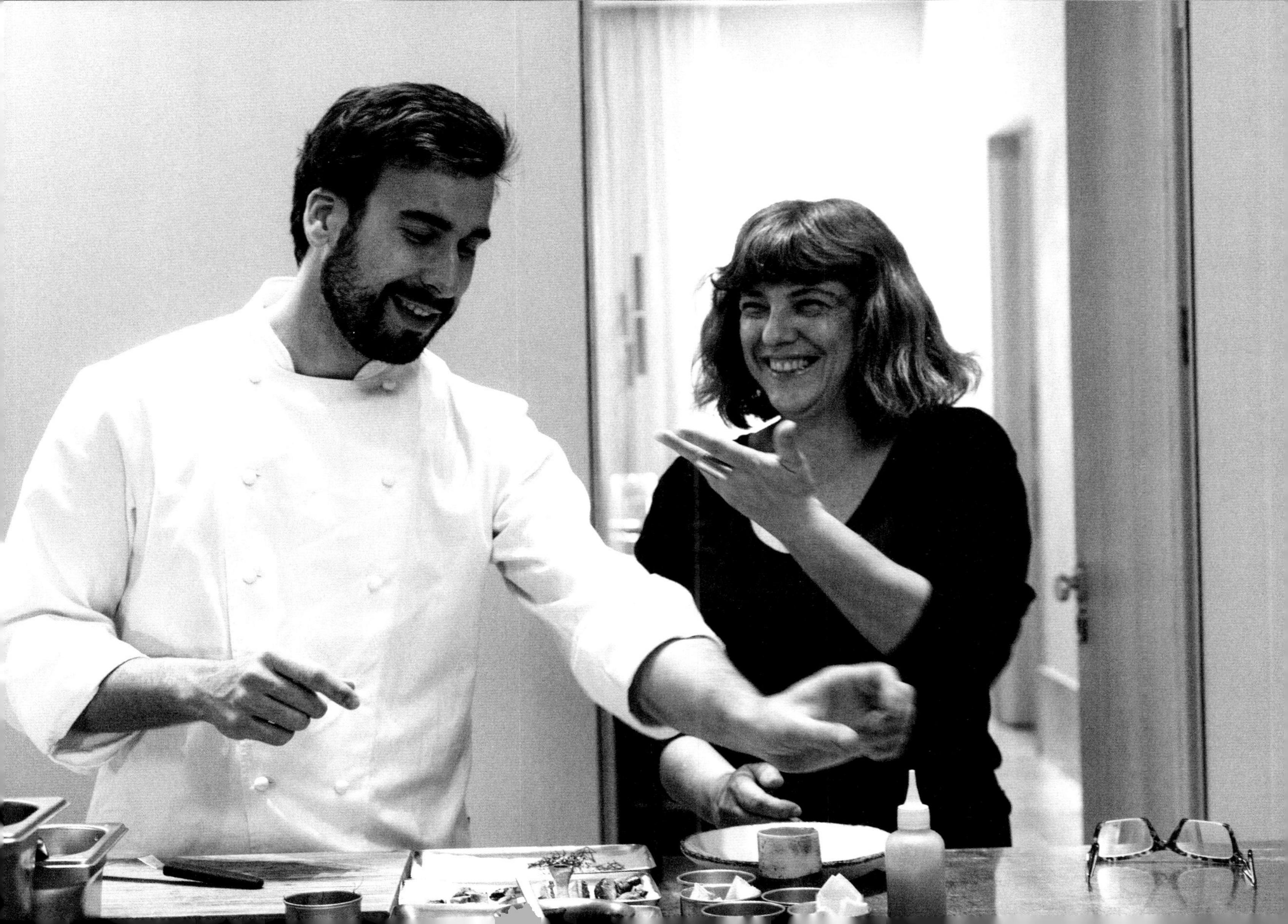

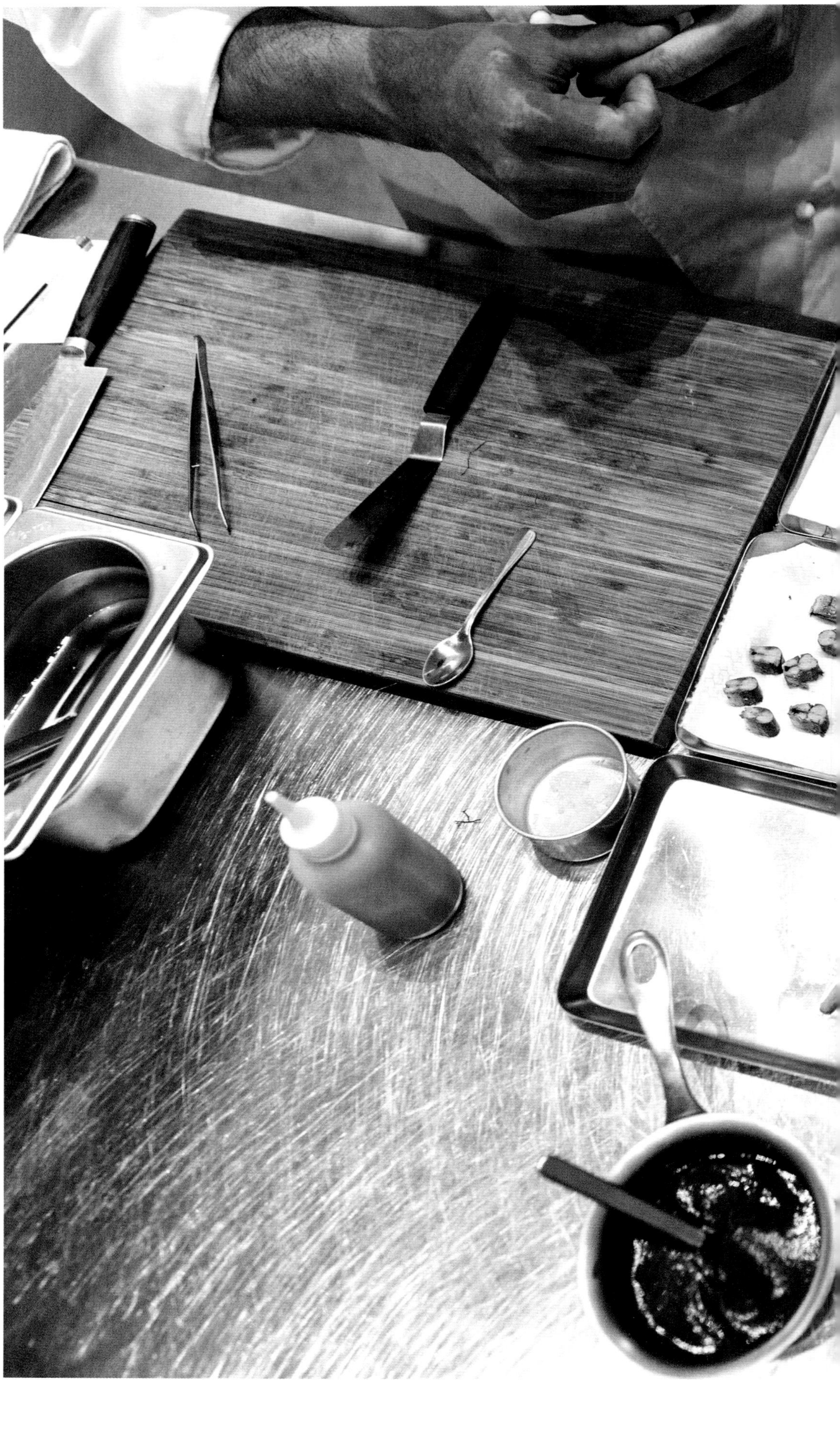

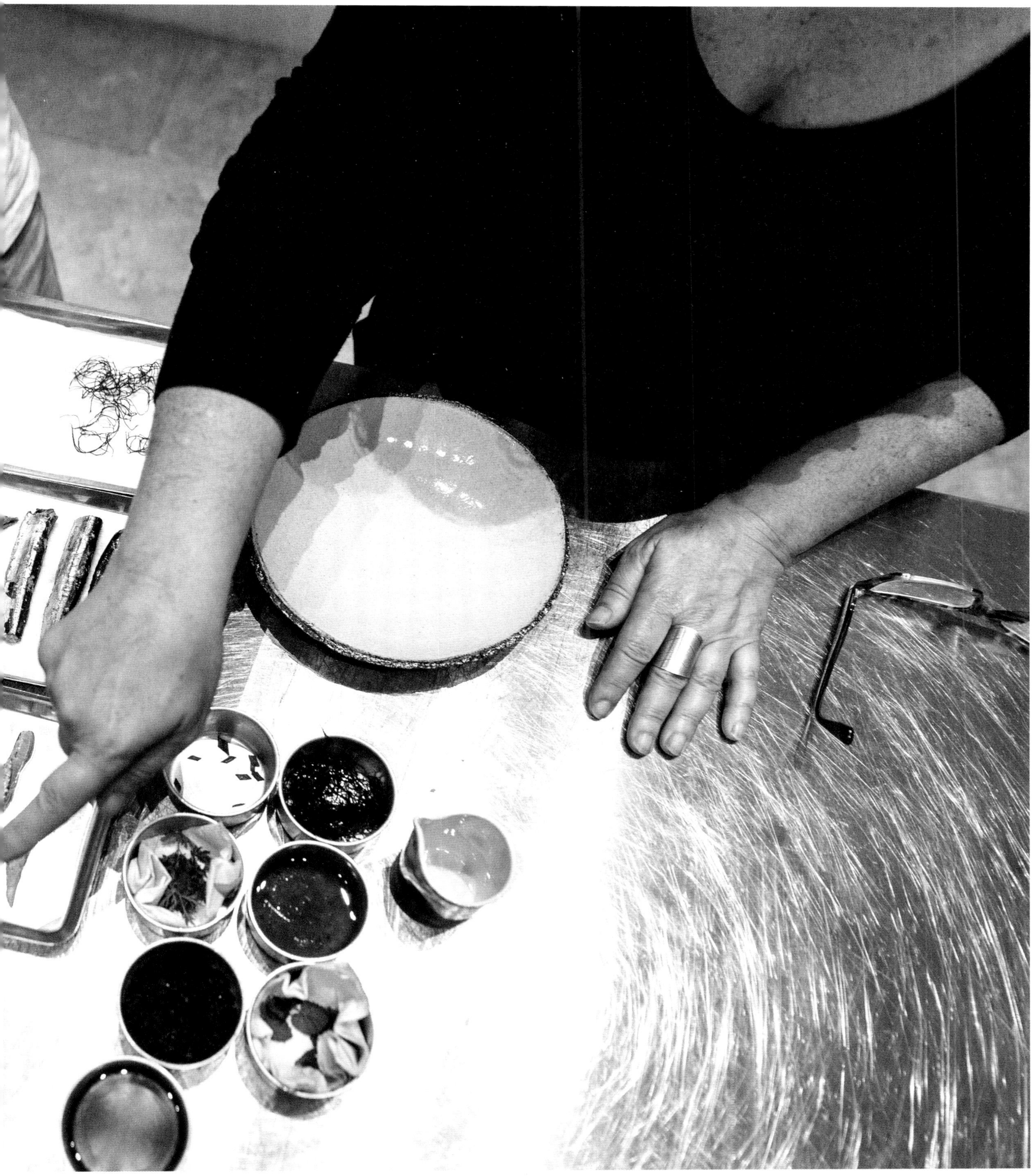

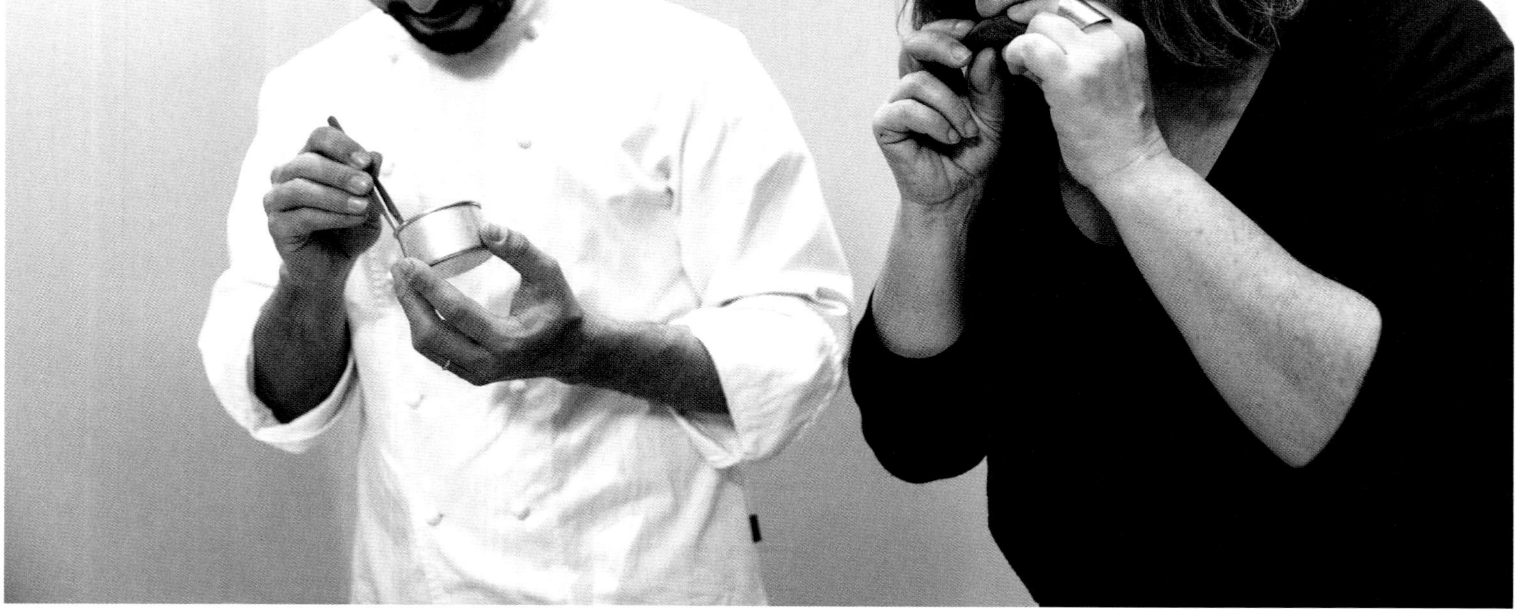

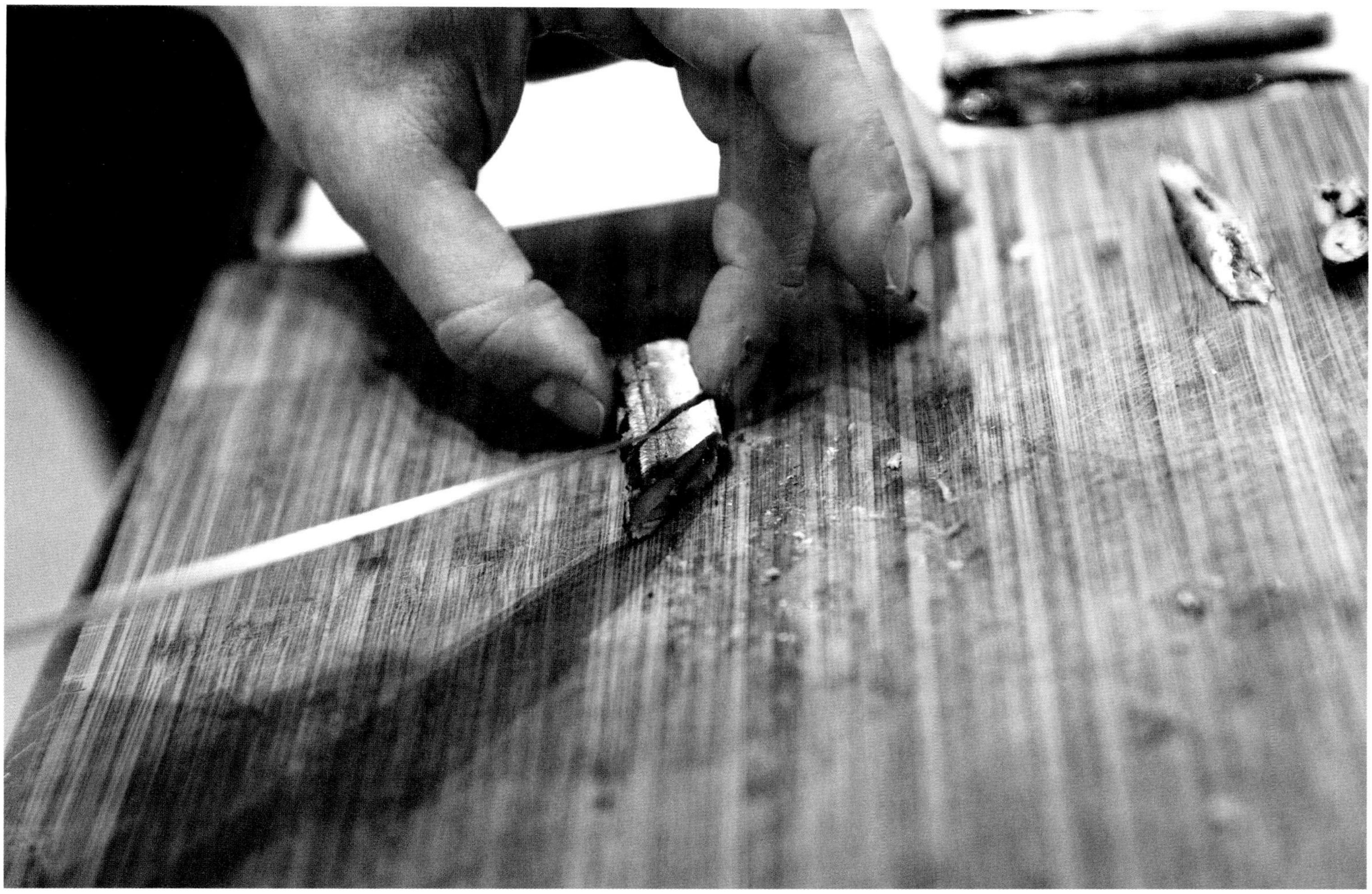

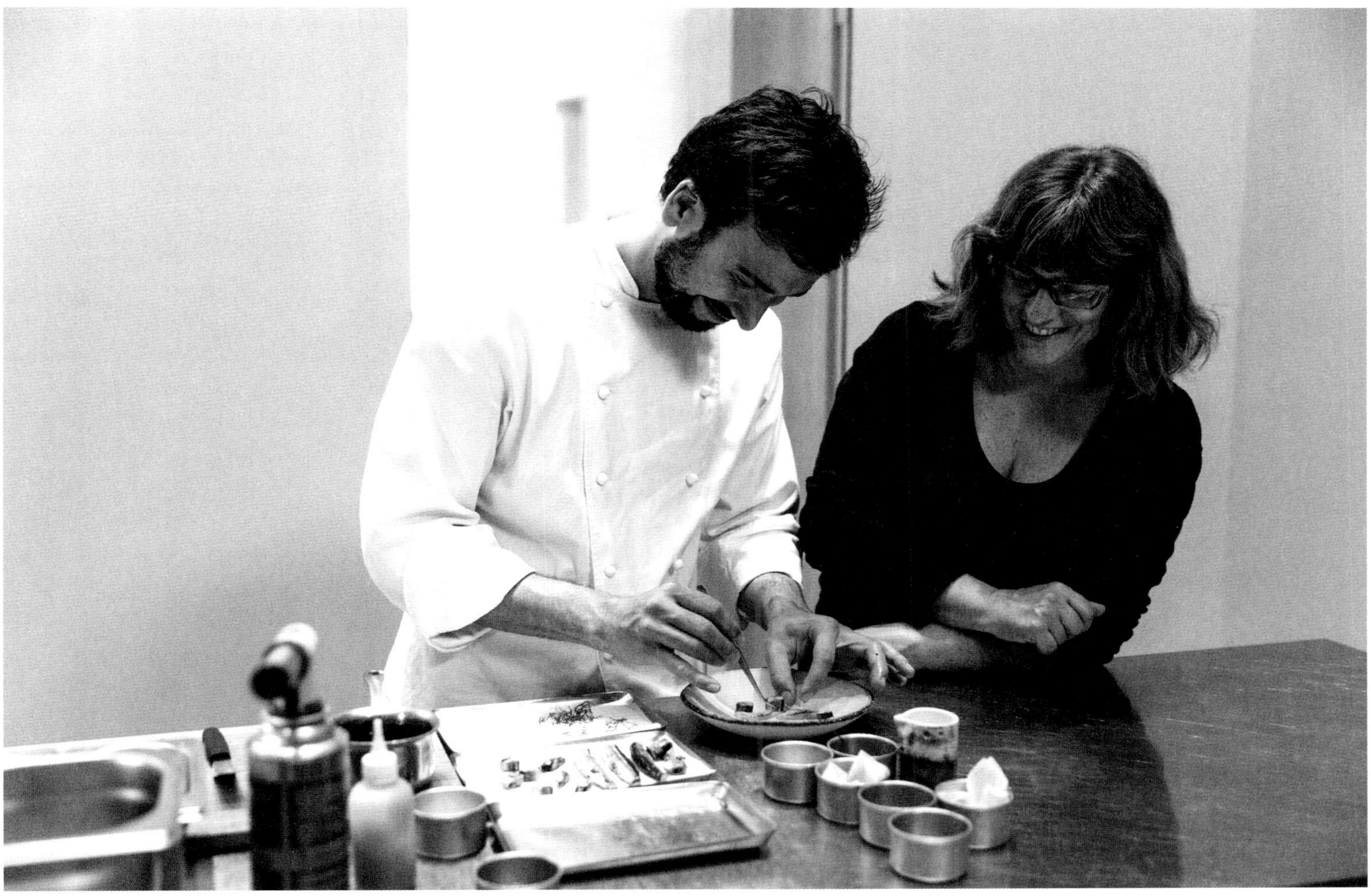

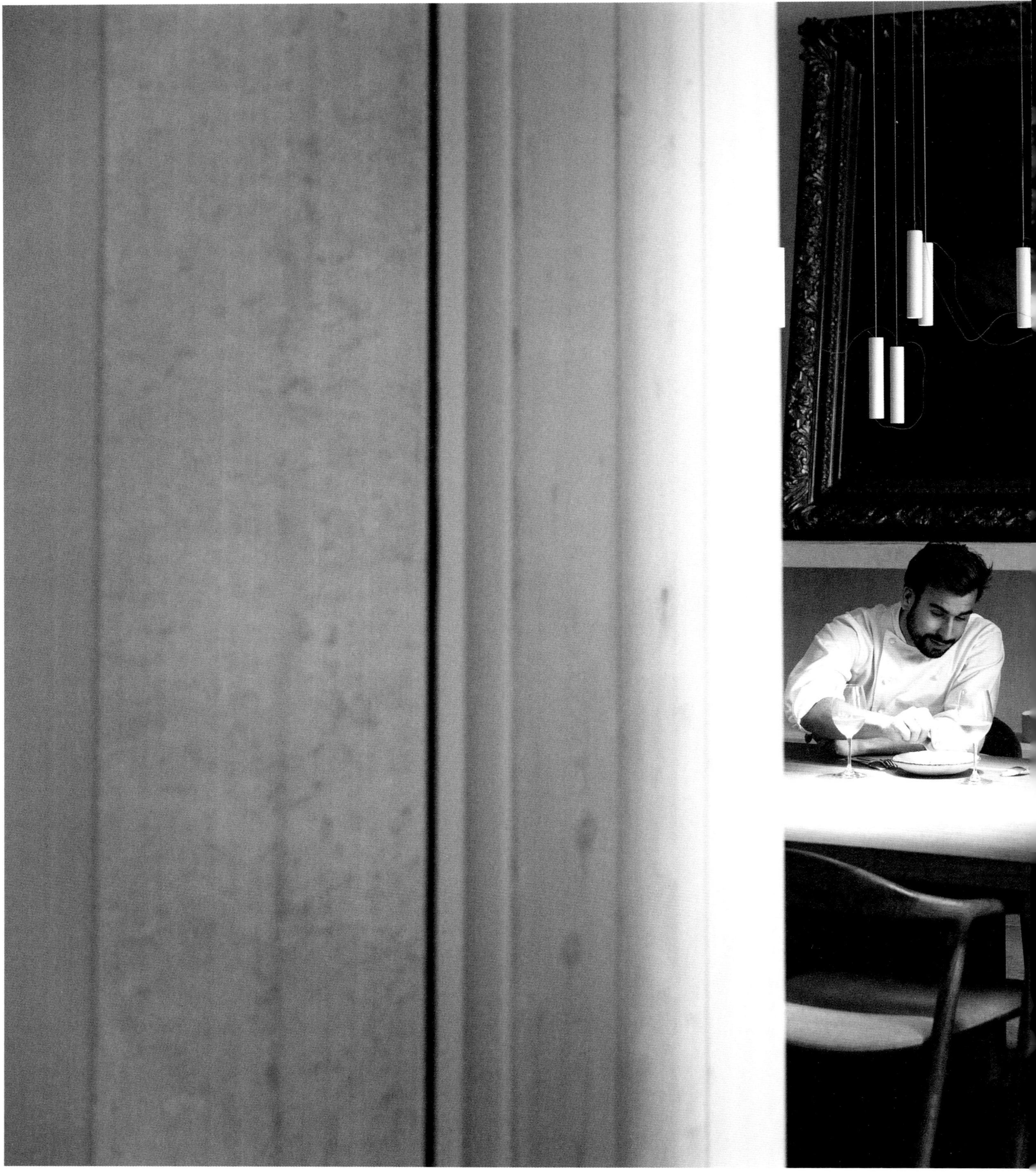

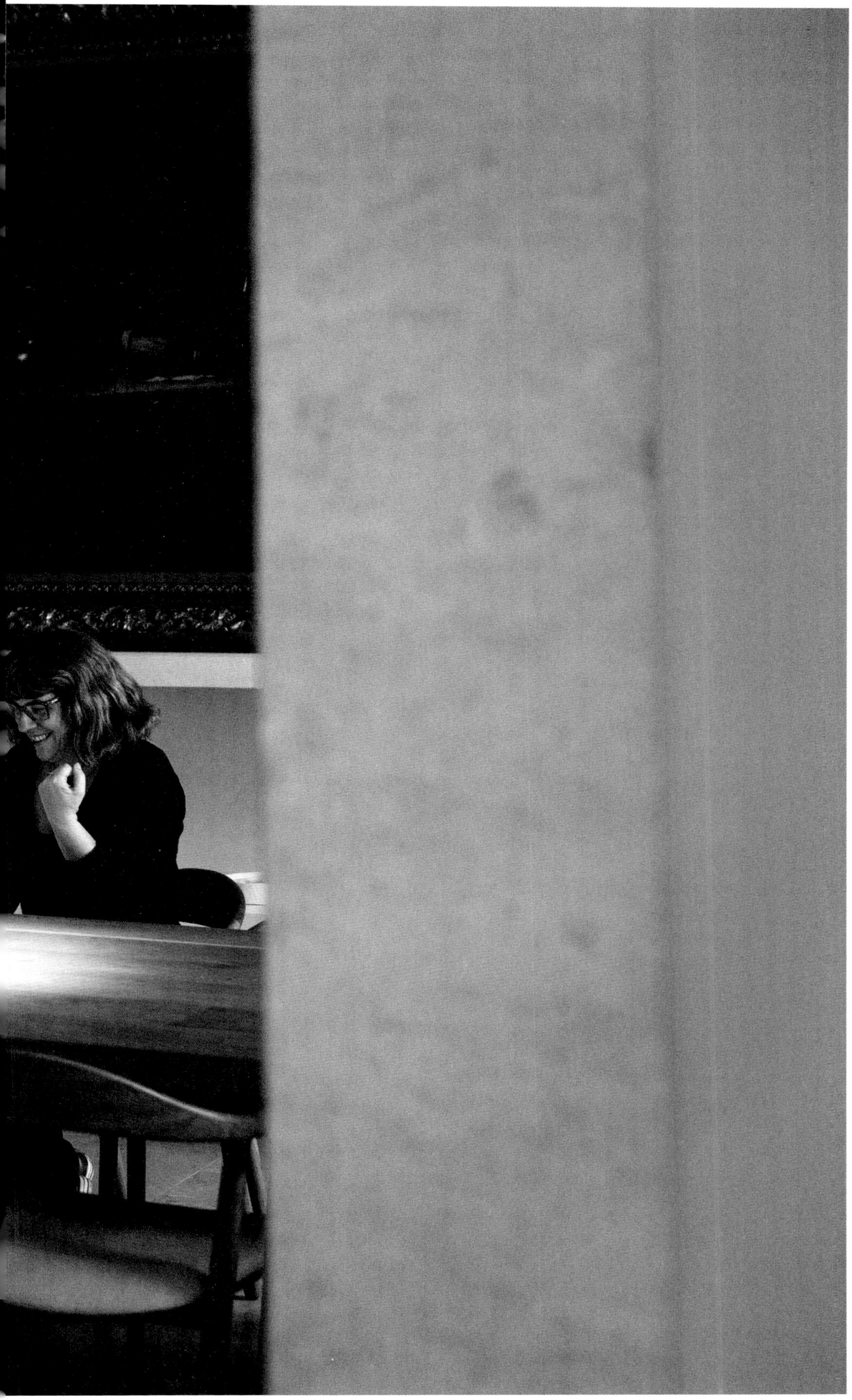

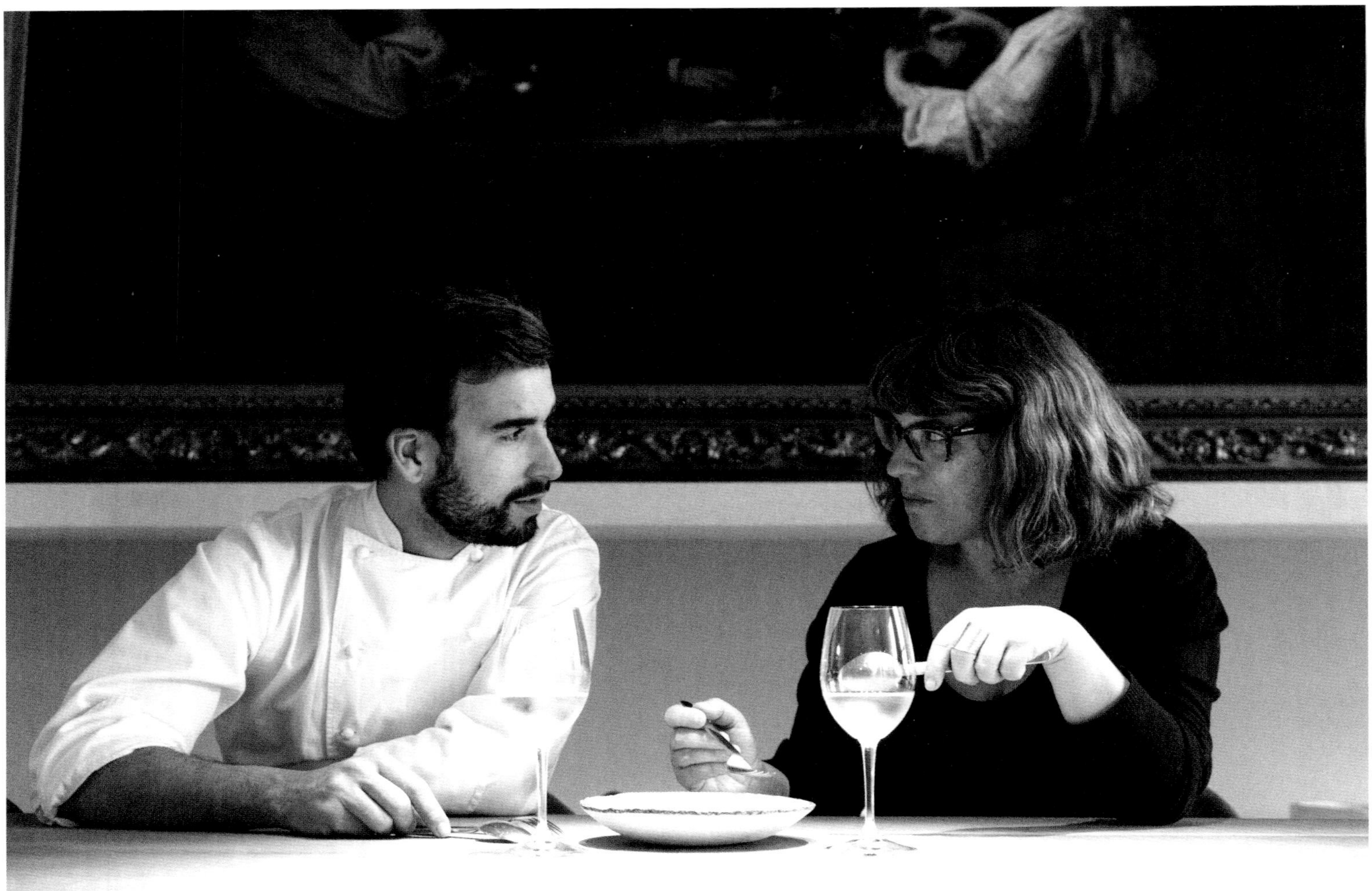

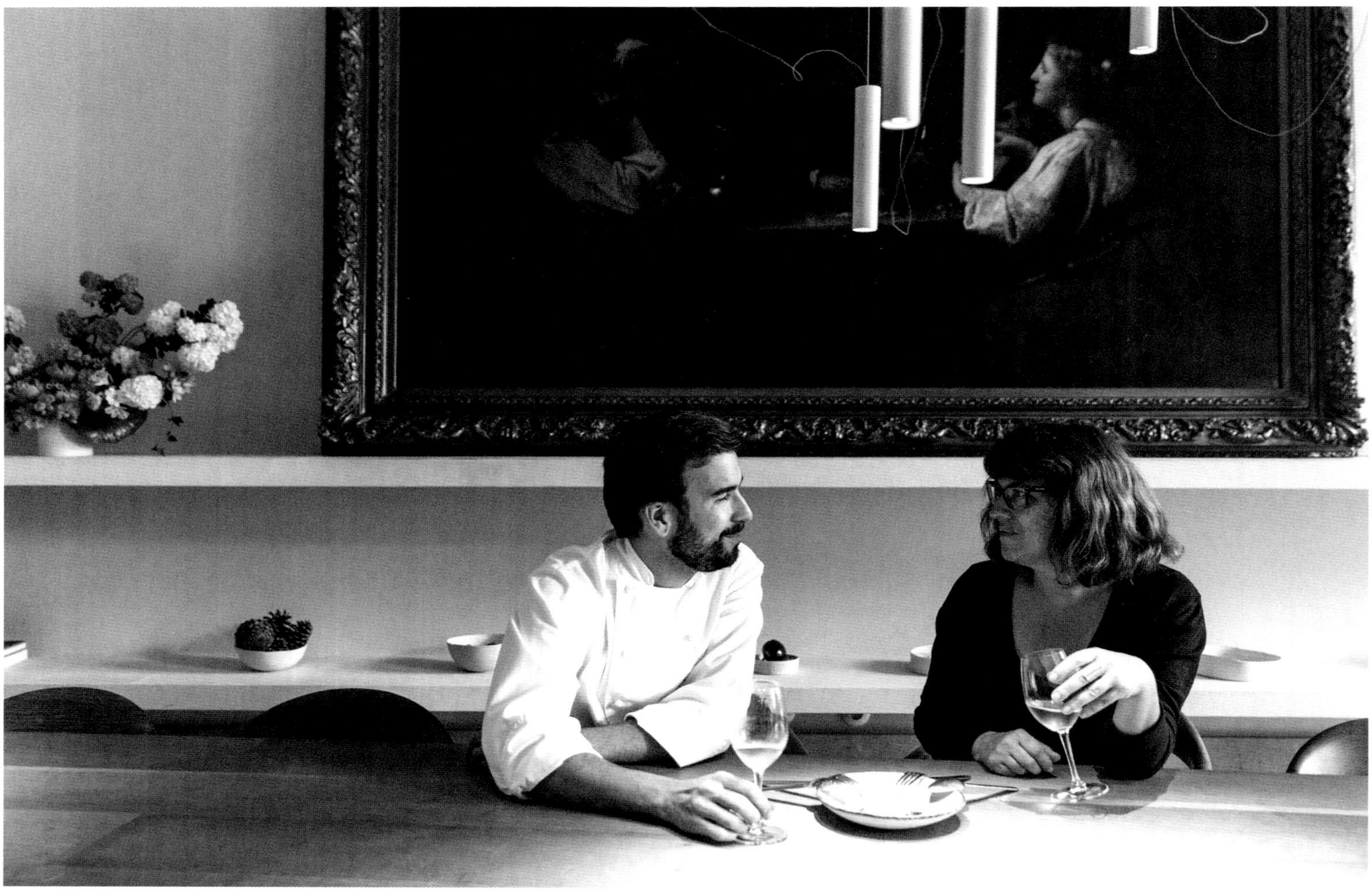

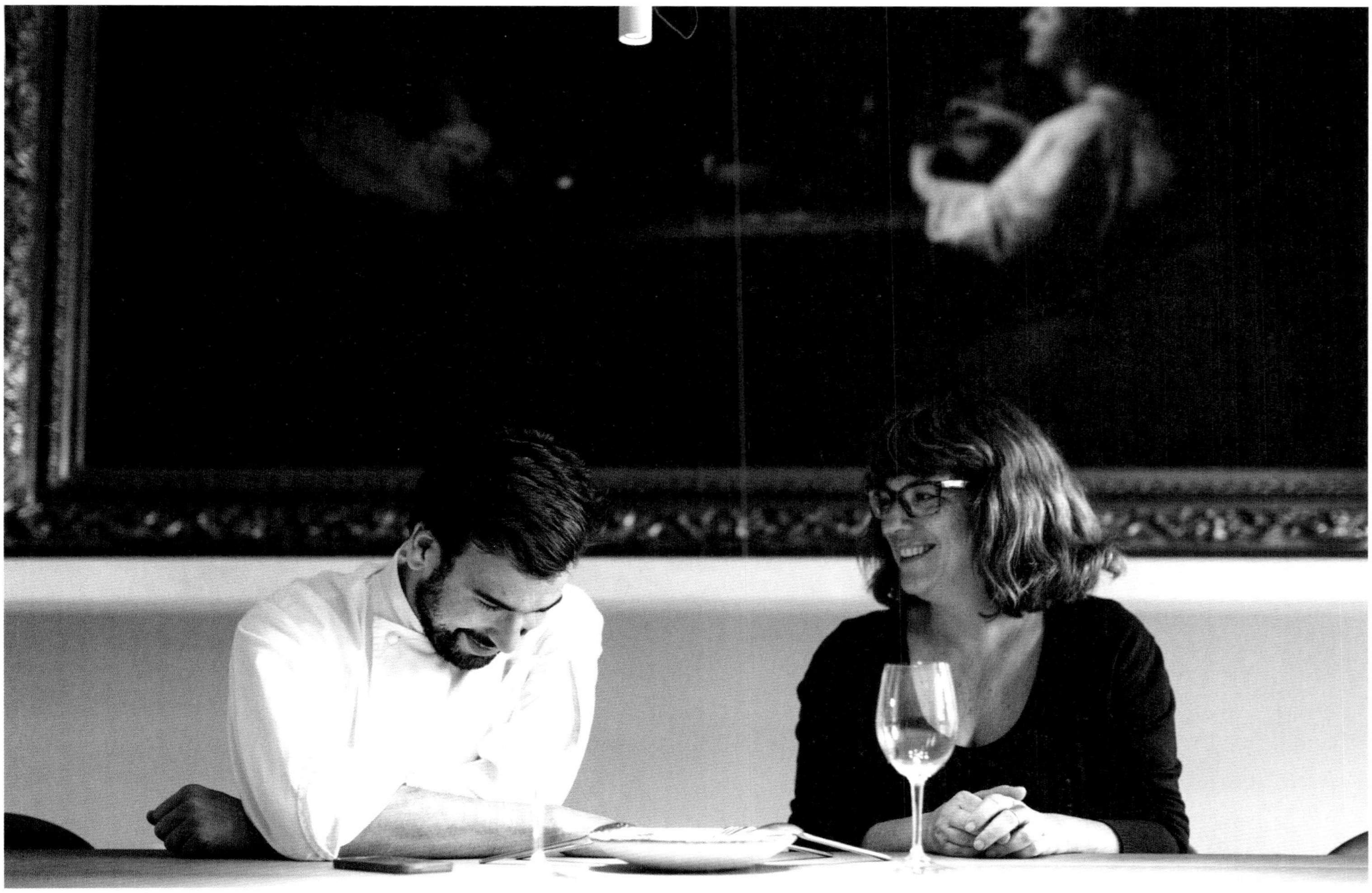

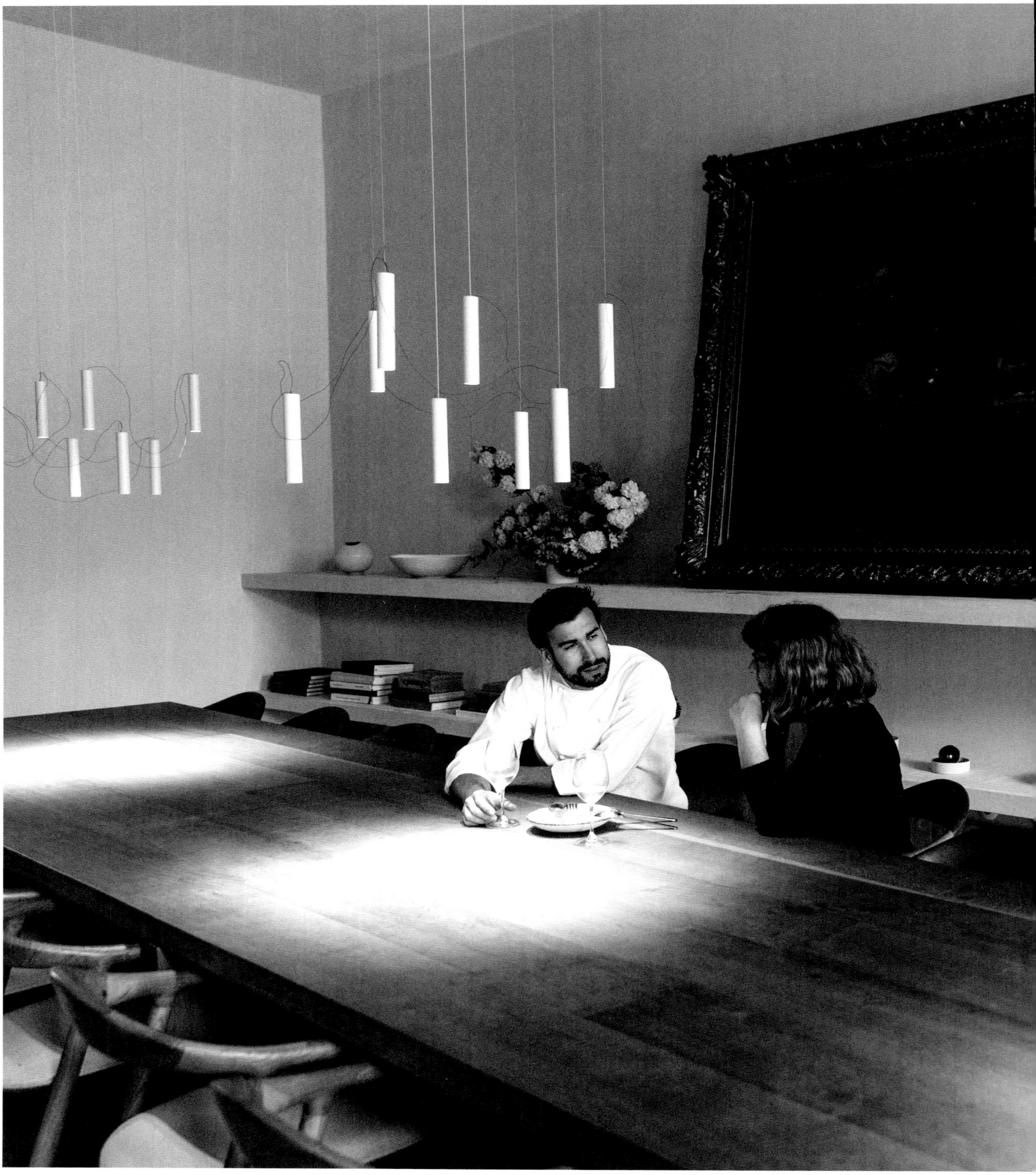

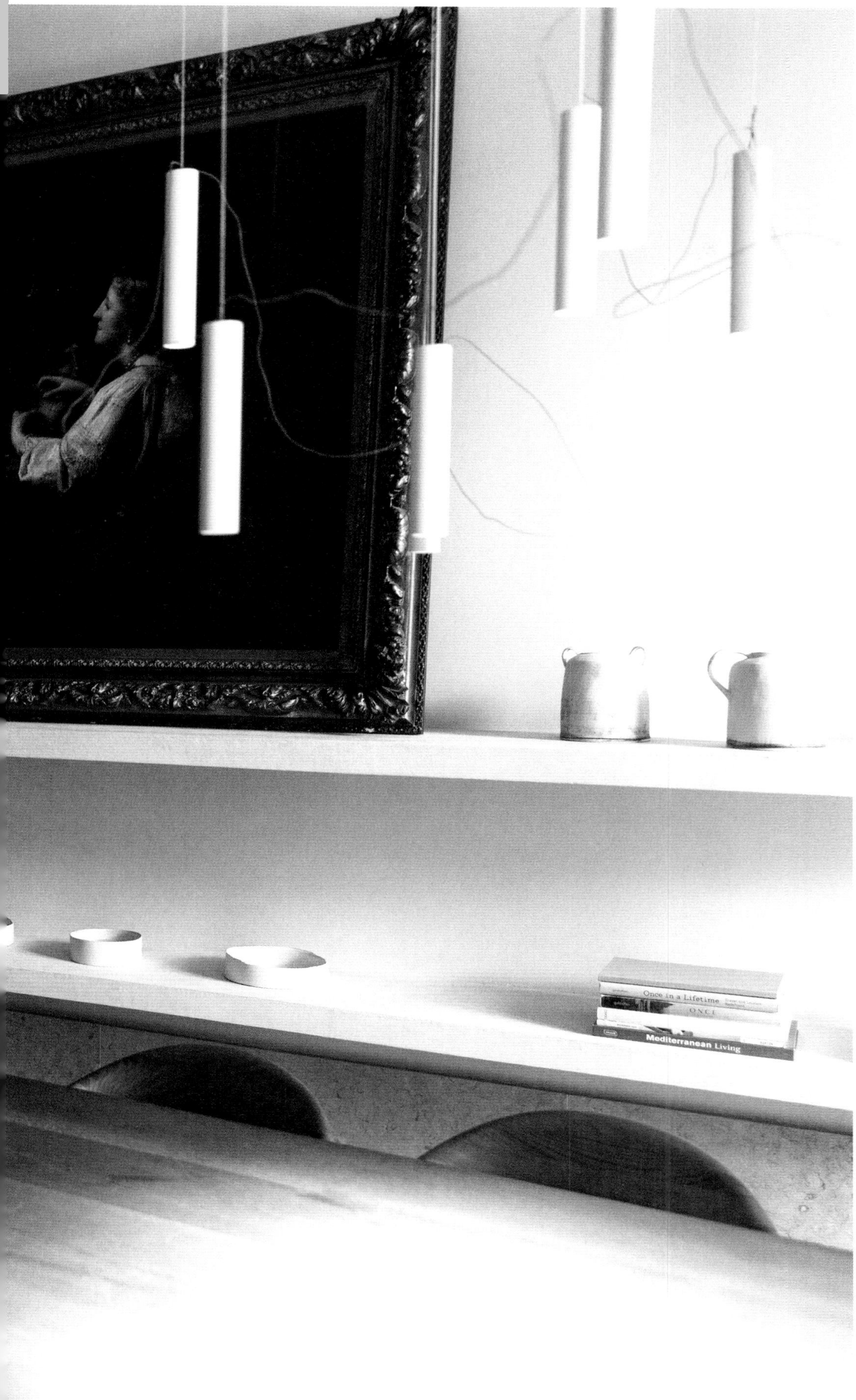
Once in a Lifetime
Mediterranean Living

GARFISH, CAVIAR
LIMES, FENNEL

PEDRO PENA BASTOS

GARFISH IN SPICY
OLIVE OIL

BRAND BRIOSA

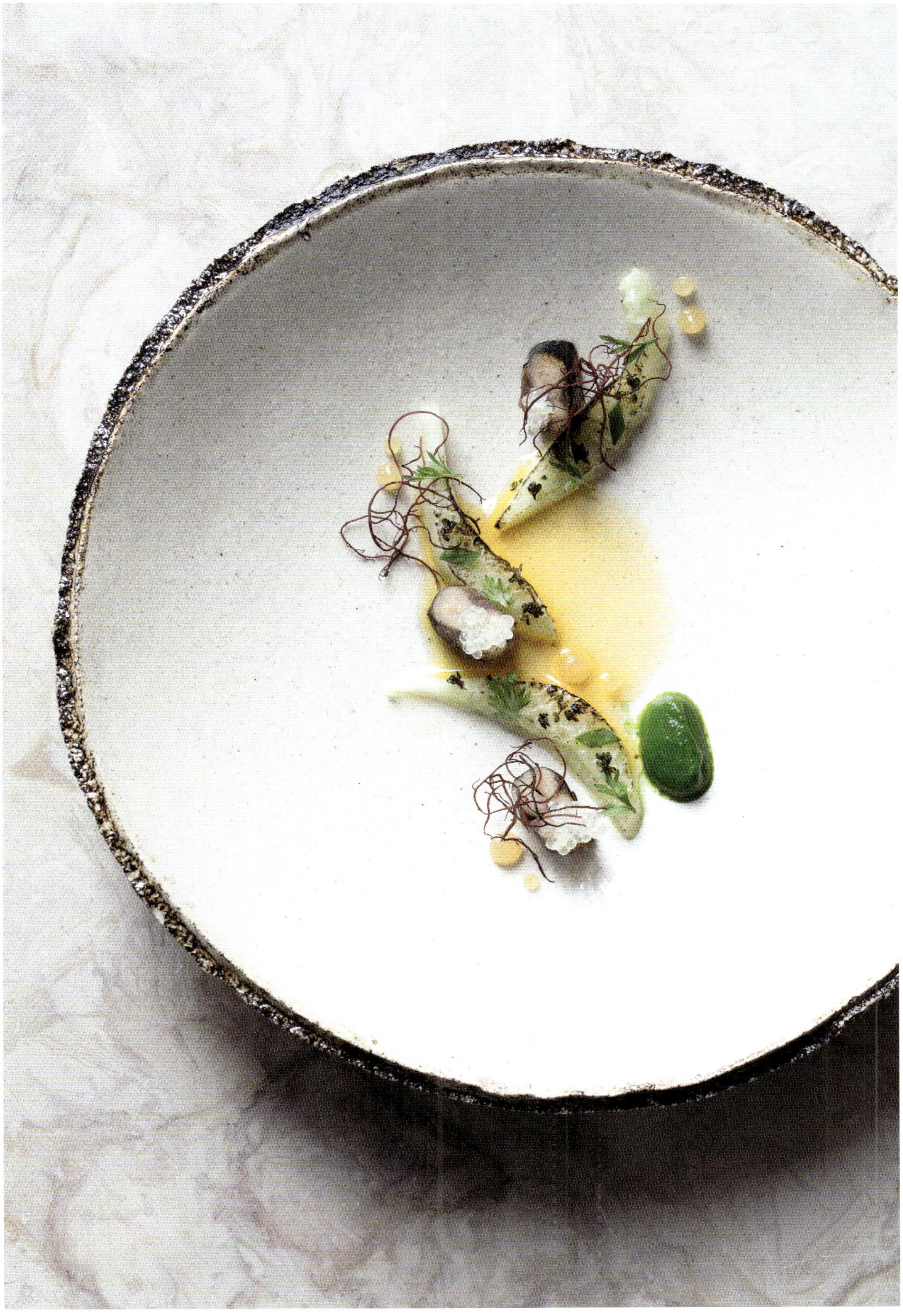

ALICE GEIRINHAS

LITTLE
MERMAIDS
2017

INDIAN INK
AND ECOLINE
ON PAPER
100 × 70 CM

g) Women and child labour

Clause 49 — All the services which aren't strictly forbidden by this contract, are the fish worker's responsibility.

Clause 50 — The following tasks are strictly forbidden to the workers, wherefore the boss or the clerk cannot order or allow their execution.

1) Individually carry weights over 21 kg;
2) Place and remove carts in the autoclave or carry more than one rack with fish at a time during the cooking process;
3) Nail or carry fish can boxes;
4) Wash sterilisation tanks, vaults, autoclaves or pre-cookers, insert or remove racks from the tanks where they're washed with hot water, except on the automatic machines to wash racks or cans;
5) Work as operators on the following machineries:
   — Can making machinery, except the rubber gasket fixing machine, the welding guns, flanging and sheet metalworking machines and tinning machines
   — Canning machines
   — Steam or gas generating machines or driving and electrical energy stations

§ 1 — The women who, at the date of entry of this contract, appear as machine operators among the staff establishment plan of the companies can continue to provide these services, but can't be replaced by other women, except those working with the rubber gasket fixing machine.

§ 2 — Pregnant women and minors under 16 years old, of both genders, cannot work, in all circumstances, more than 23 hours or with machines which generate or use gas.

In Contrato Colectivo de Trabalho 1957. Celebrated between the Grémio dos Industriais de Conservas de Peixe de Setúbal and the Sindicato Nacional dos Operários da Indústria de Conservas do Distrito de Setúbal

g) Trabalho das mulheres e dos menores

Cláusula 49.ª — Às operárias manipuladoras de peixe competem todos os serviços que não sejam expressamente proibidos por este contrato.

Cláusula 50.ª — Às operárias são proibidos os trabalhos seguintes, pelo que os patrões ou encarregados não poderão permitir ou mandar que se executem:

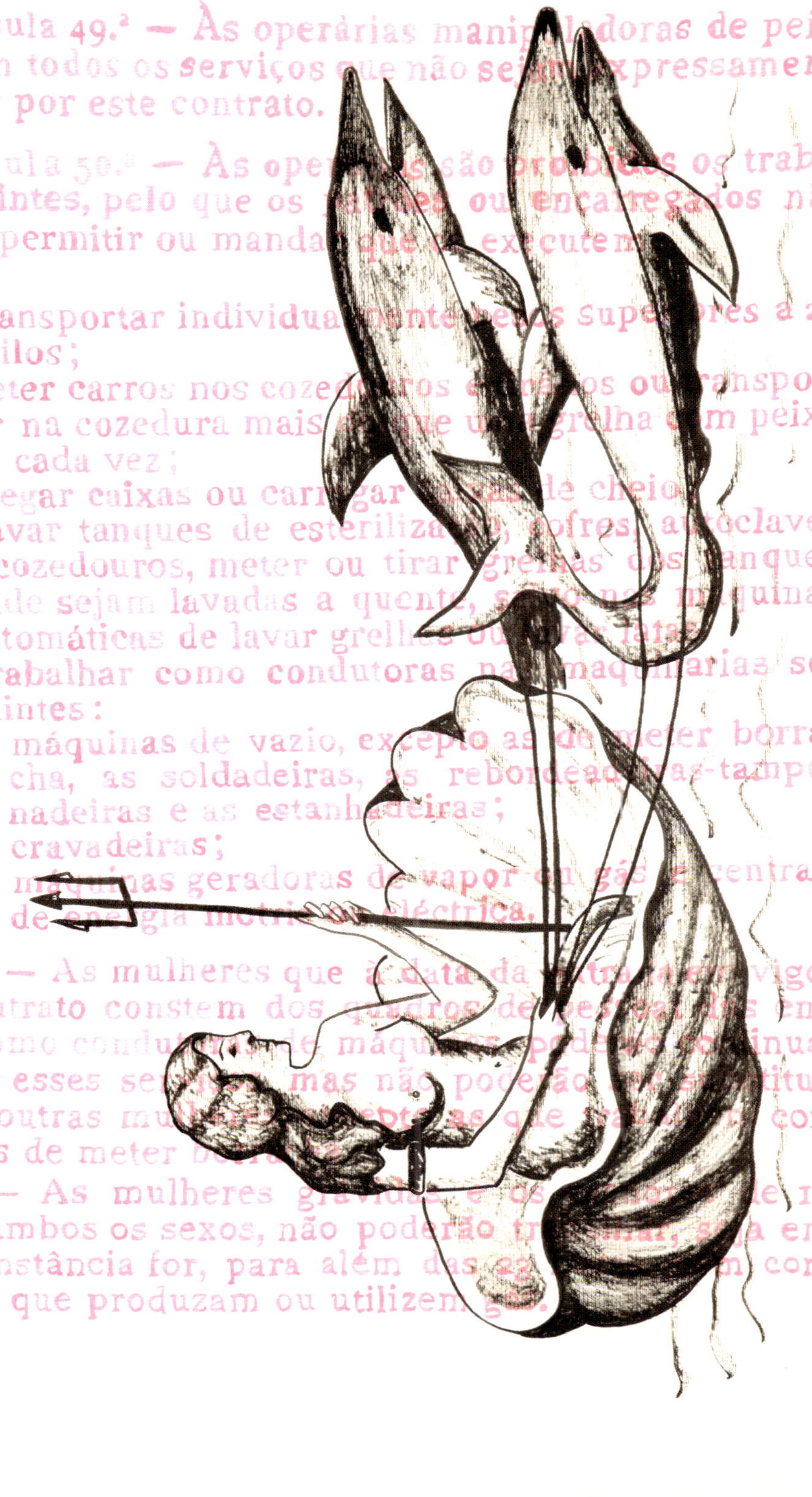

1) Transportar individualmente pesos superiores a 21 quilos;
2) Meter carros nos cozedouros e grelhas ou transportar na cozedura mais do que uma grelha com peixe de cada vez;
3) Pregar caixas ou carregar latas de cheio;
4) Lavar tanques de esterilização, cofres, autoclaves e cozedouros, meter ou tirar grelhas dos tanques onde sejam lavadas a quente, salvo nas máquinas automáticas de lavar grelhas ou lavar latas;
5) Trabalhar como condutoras nas maquinarias seguintes:
   — máquinas de vazio, excepto as de meter borracha, as soldadeiras, as rebordeadeiras-tamponadeiras e as estanhadeiras;
   — cravadeiras;
   — máquinas geradoras de vapor ou gás e centrais de energia motriz ou eléctrica.

§ 1.º — As mulheres que à data da entrada em vigor deste contrato constem dos quadros de pessoal das empresas como condutoras de máquinas poderão continuar a prestar esses serviços, mas não poderão ser substituídas por outras mulheres, excepto as que trabalhem com máquinas de meter borracha.

§ 2.º — As mulheres grávidas e os menores de 16 anos, de ambos os sexos, não poderão trabalhar, seja em que circunstância for, para além das 22 horas, em máquinas que produzam ou utilizem gás.

JOÃO
OLIVEIRA

RODRIGO
OLIVEIRA

RODRIGO
OLIVEIRA

JOÃO
OLIVEIRA

JOÃO OLIVEIRA
RODRIGO OLIVEIRA

ORCHIDS

There's no way of mistaking it. Look for the most beautiful building in Praia da Rocha, the oldest and best-preserved one, and you will find the Hotel Bela Vista, where the Vista Restaurant is located, work and pride of the chef João Oliveira.

From Lisbon we brought the artist Rodrigo Oliveira, and together we entered the hotel, both feeling delighted. The view is breathtaking, except for the wretched eucalyptus that no one can cut down. "They won't let us do it, there's a law about it," says João. "Maybe one day lightning will strike here..."

We go down to the kitchen guided by João, and the temperature increases 10 degrees. But it's not hell. And if it were, with such a punishment I wouldn't mind being a sinner.

The space is minimal and very organised. On a counter illuminated by infrareds (10 or 20 degrees more) we can see the food lined up, with the star dish in the middle: mackerel cured with sugar and salt. The chef pulls out tweezers and offers another pair to Rodrigo: "Want to try?"

Rodrigo says yes, but his hands tremble with the responsibility. It's normal, says João. "Each dish has a logic of serving, an algorithm," he explains. "We have to follow the rules and do it many times. The beauty is born of the logic and repetition of the gesture."

The proceedings continue and the plate appears, to be photographed by Jorge. It is beautiful. Perfect. If it weren't for the mackerel and the river seaweed scent, we could frame it. It's art and we feel like hanging it.

We sit around the table, chat and listen to the conversation. Two lives full of adventures and twists. João starts.

"I miss Porto, I miss Valongo. The Algarve is beautiful, but different. It was really hard when I arrived here, it's a different rhythm." He smiles. "When I was a child, 11 or 12 years old, my grandparents got sick and I had to start cooking for everyone."

His voice has a mix of love and regret. No one interrupts him. It's as if we are seized by some fragile purity.

"I come from a rural environment and I wanted to be a vet, to take care of the hens, pigs and birds," says João. "I was crazy about birds and my mother about orchids, but she didn't have the time, so I would take care of them... and I did, for many years."

Now Rodrigo becomes nostalgic, remembering school days and the first drawings he made on the wet ground or on kitchen rolls. "It was a film," he recalls. "I used to draw stories on the rolls just as if it was a movie. I started using my hands through art; the need to touch things for them to be born. I learned it and liked it."

João continues to surprise. He used to be a football referee, he studied public relations, all while doing a cooking internship. Always in a rush, crossing Porto by bus before the sun rose. Hard days, but important. It's him who says so.

Rodrigo studied corporate communication, was seeking and managed to find himself. He sips from his glass while he tastes the dish. "It's excellent," he says. "The alcohol helps me communicate."

The visitors surrender themselves to the view and the place, as do we, even if we're trying to hide it.

We ask a last question of the chef: Why all this effort? What are you trying to reach?

João pauses before answering. "I shouldn't be talking about this, but I will. One day, while my mother was still among us, I made her a promise. I promised that one day I would be the chef of a Relais & Châteaux. And I was. That I would have a Michelin star. And I did. That one day I would give her grandchildren... and I'm working on it."

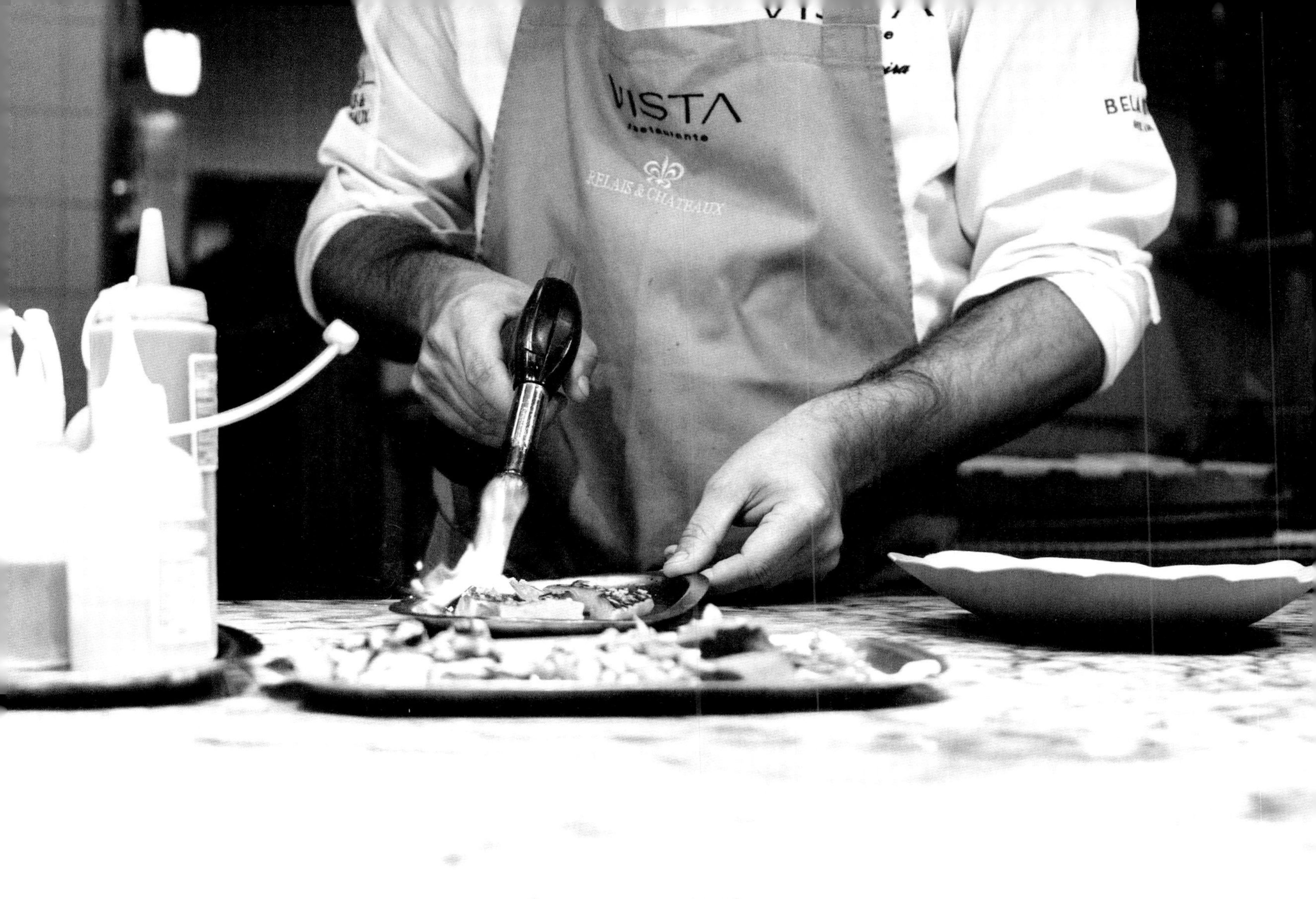
VISTA
RELAIS & CHATEAUX

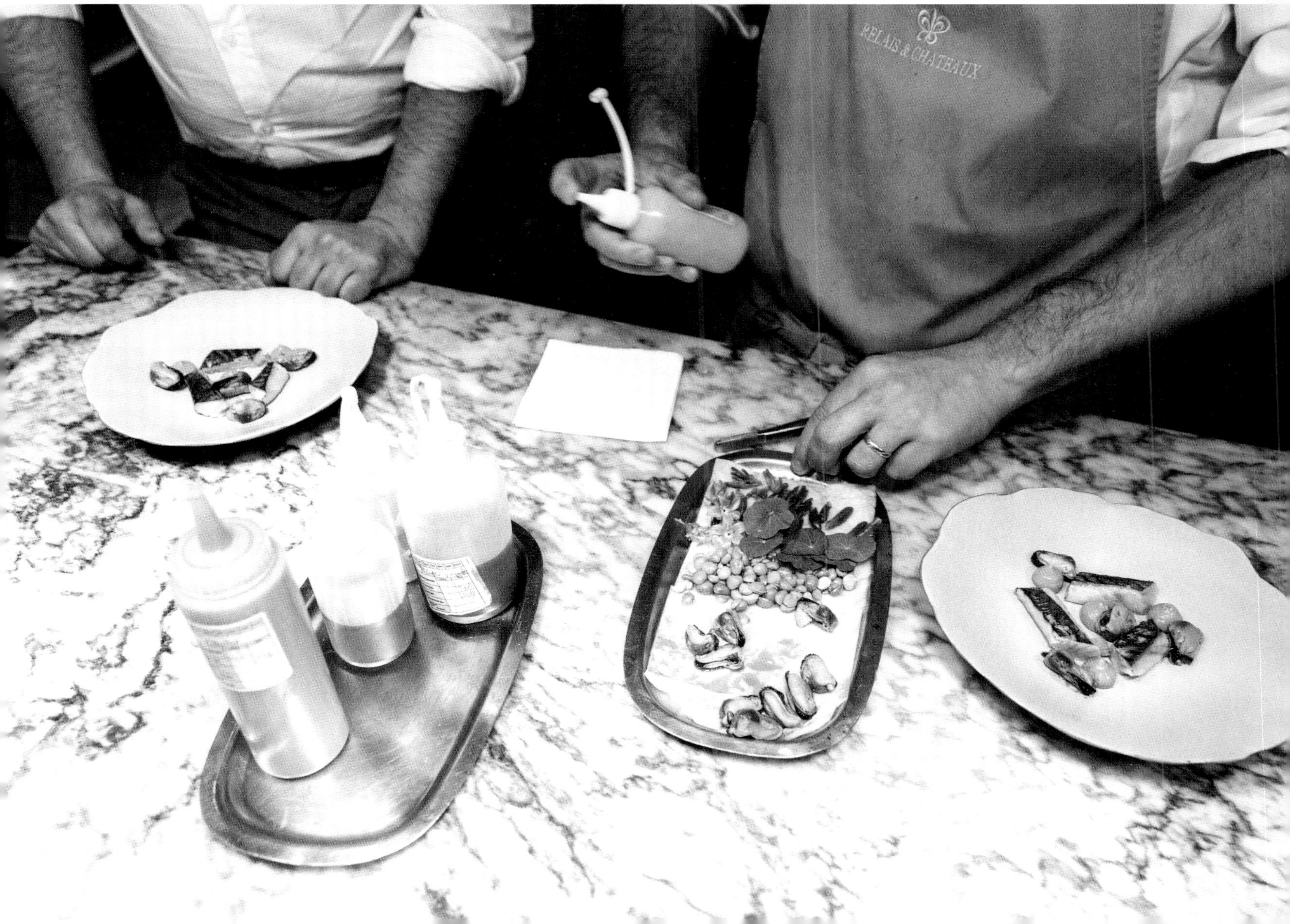
RELAIS & CHATEAUX

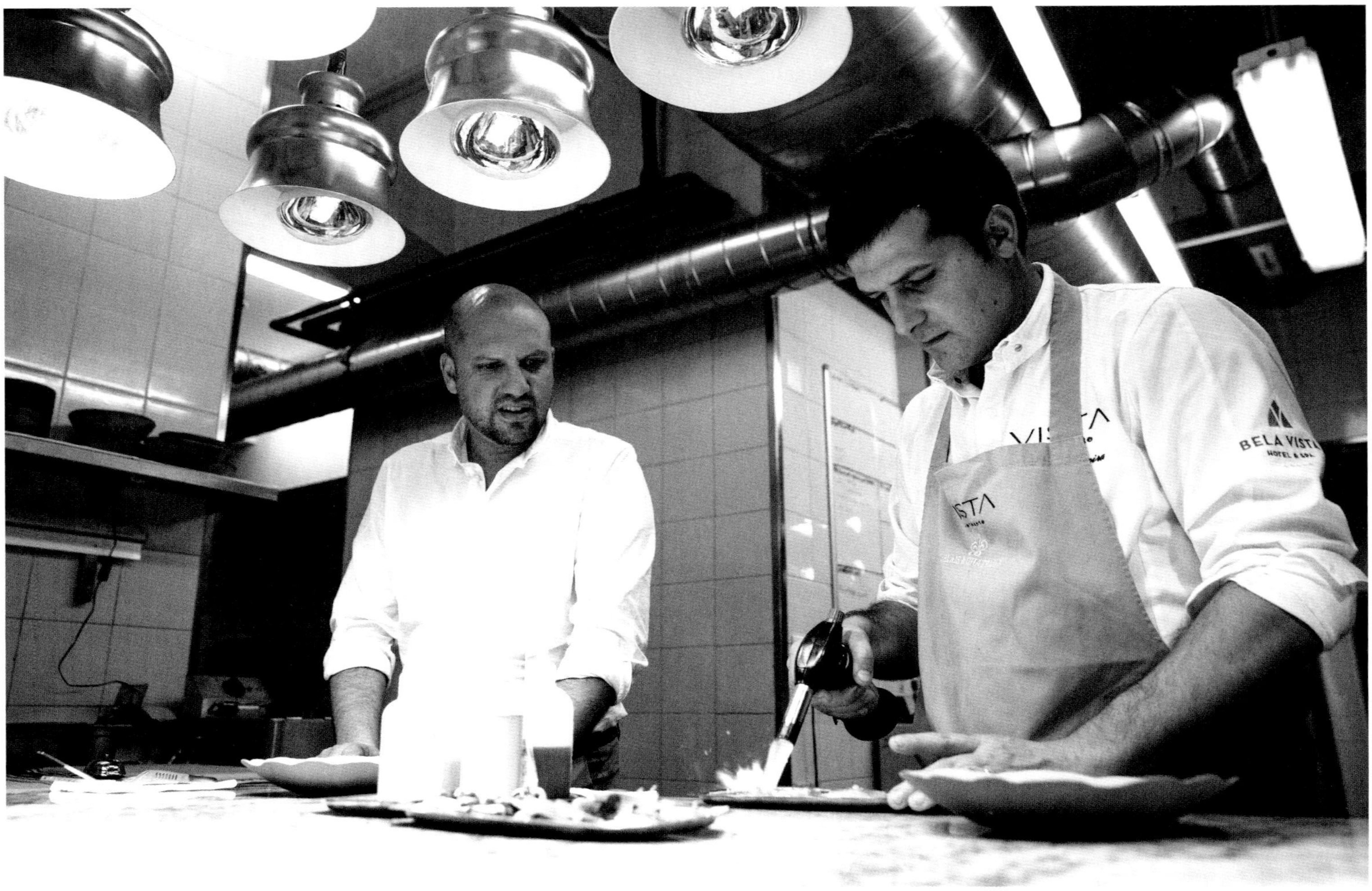
BELA VISTA

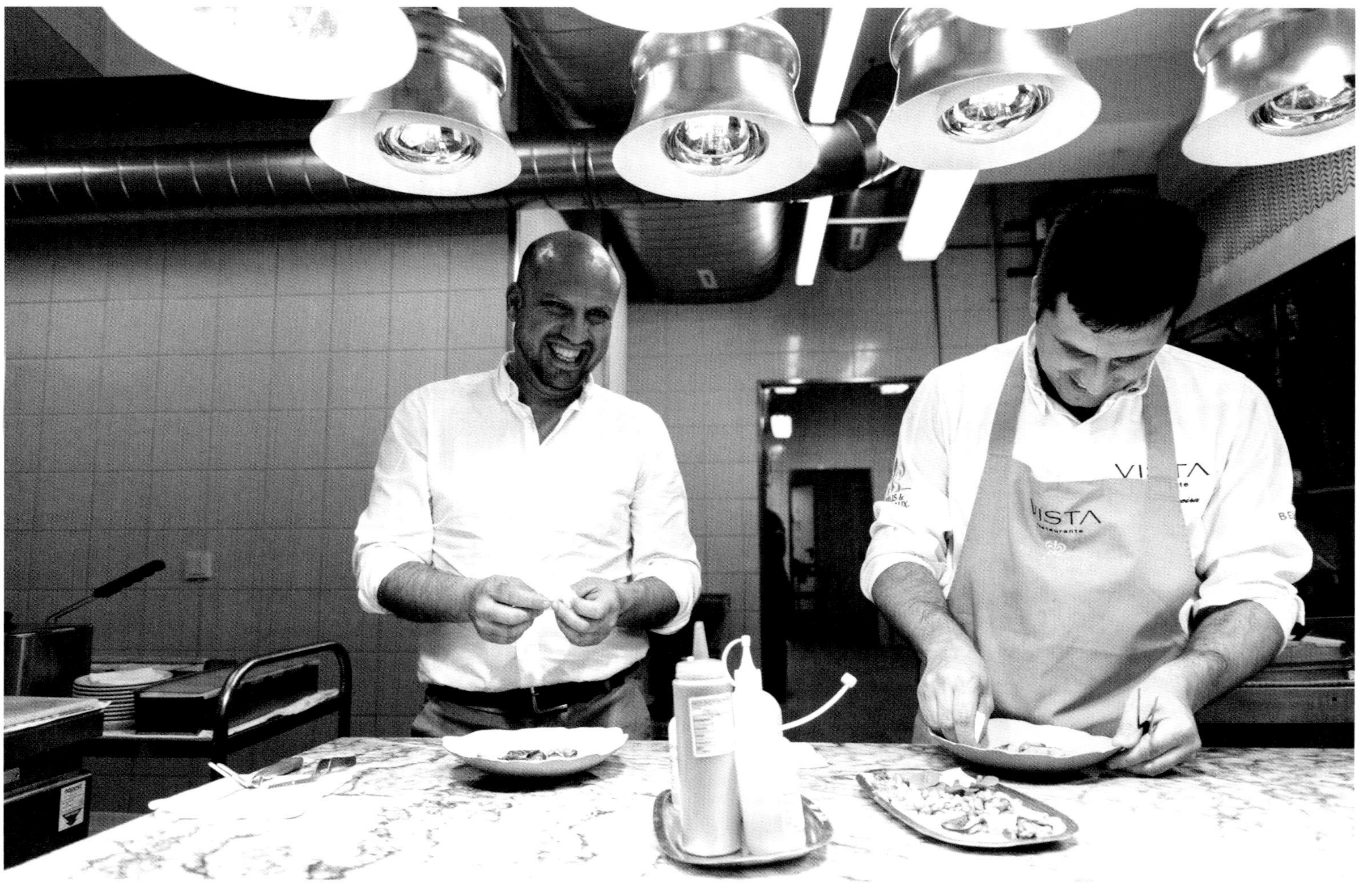
VISTA

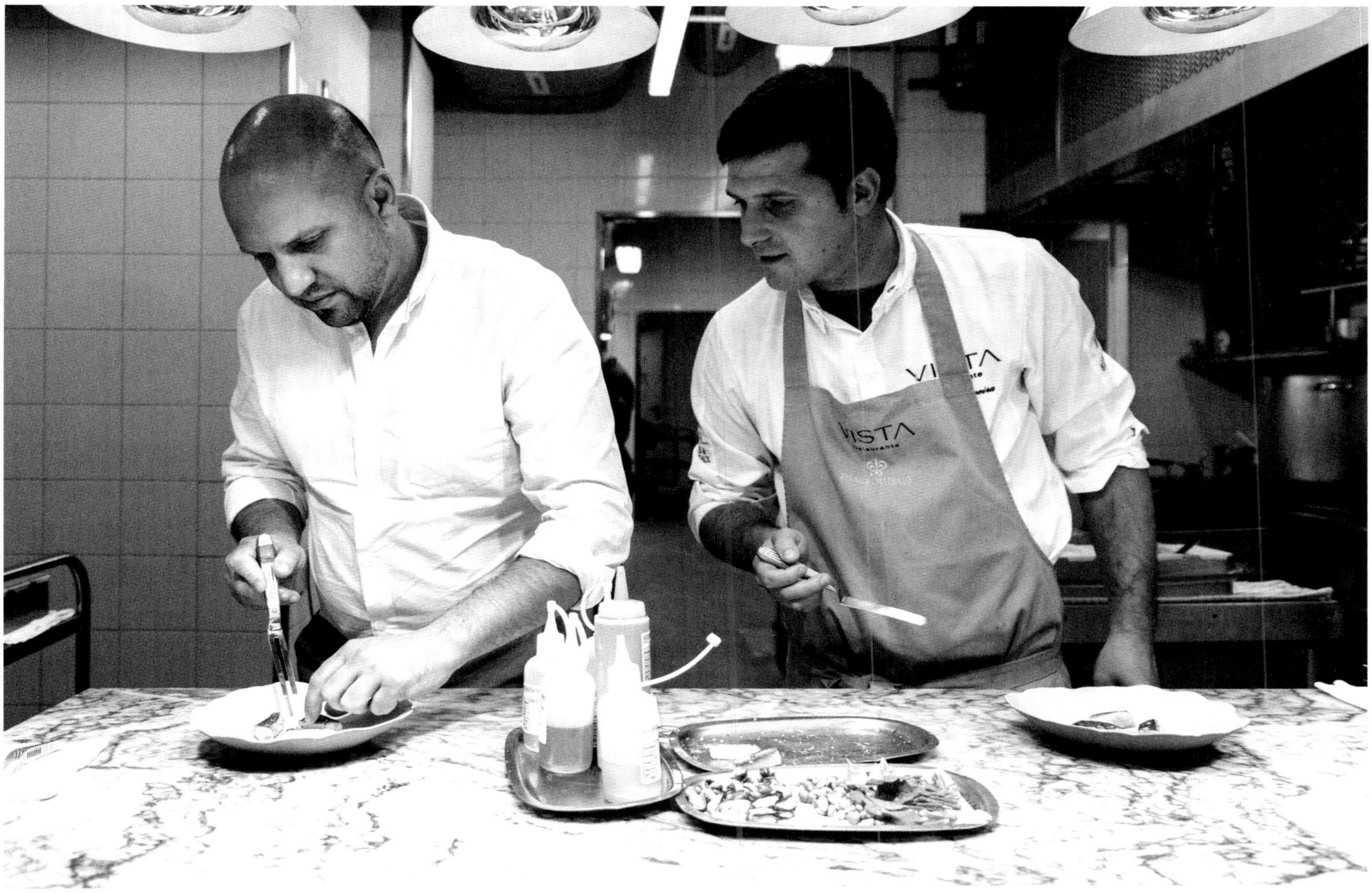
VISTA

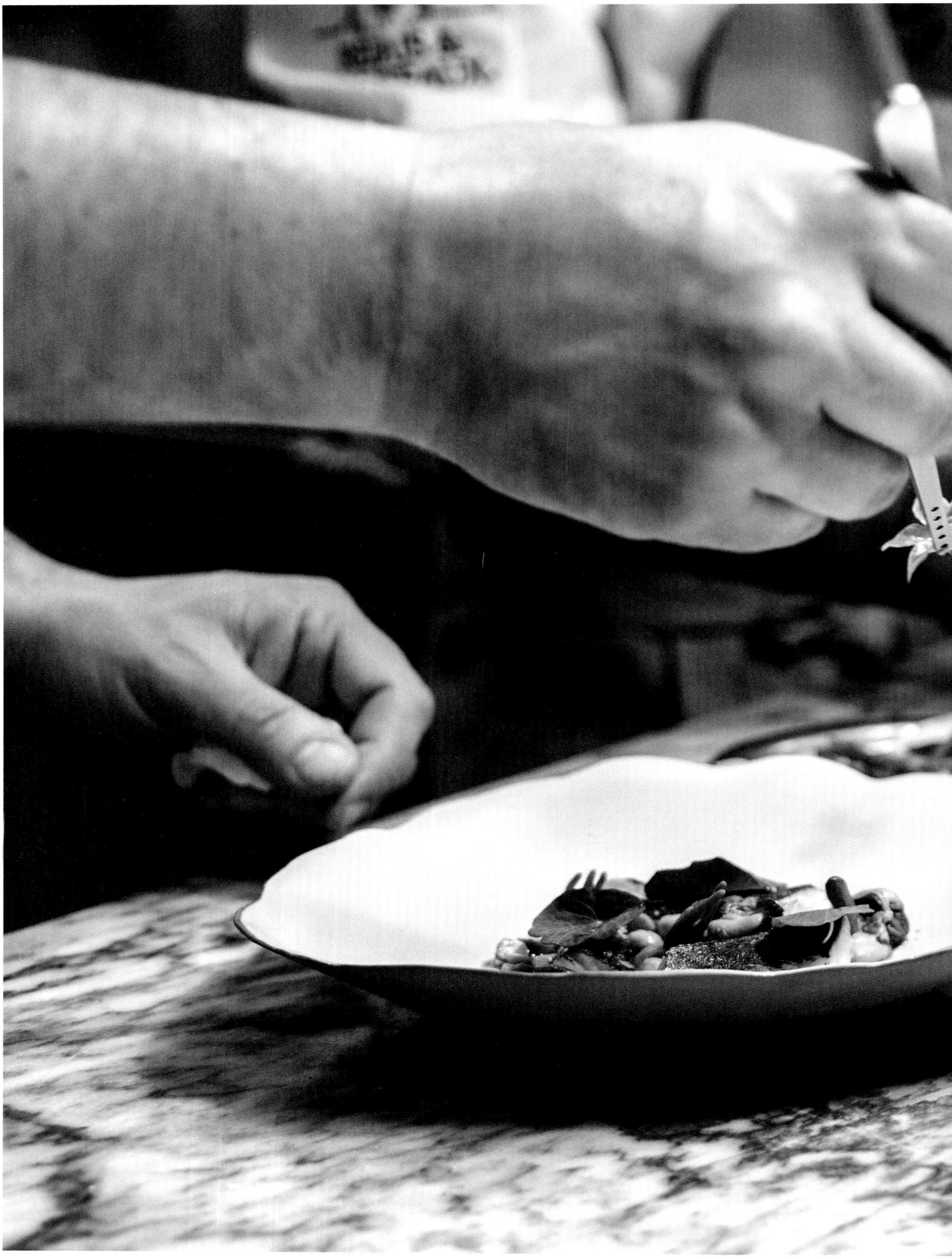

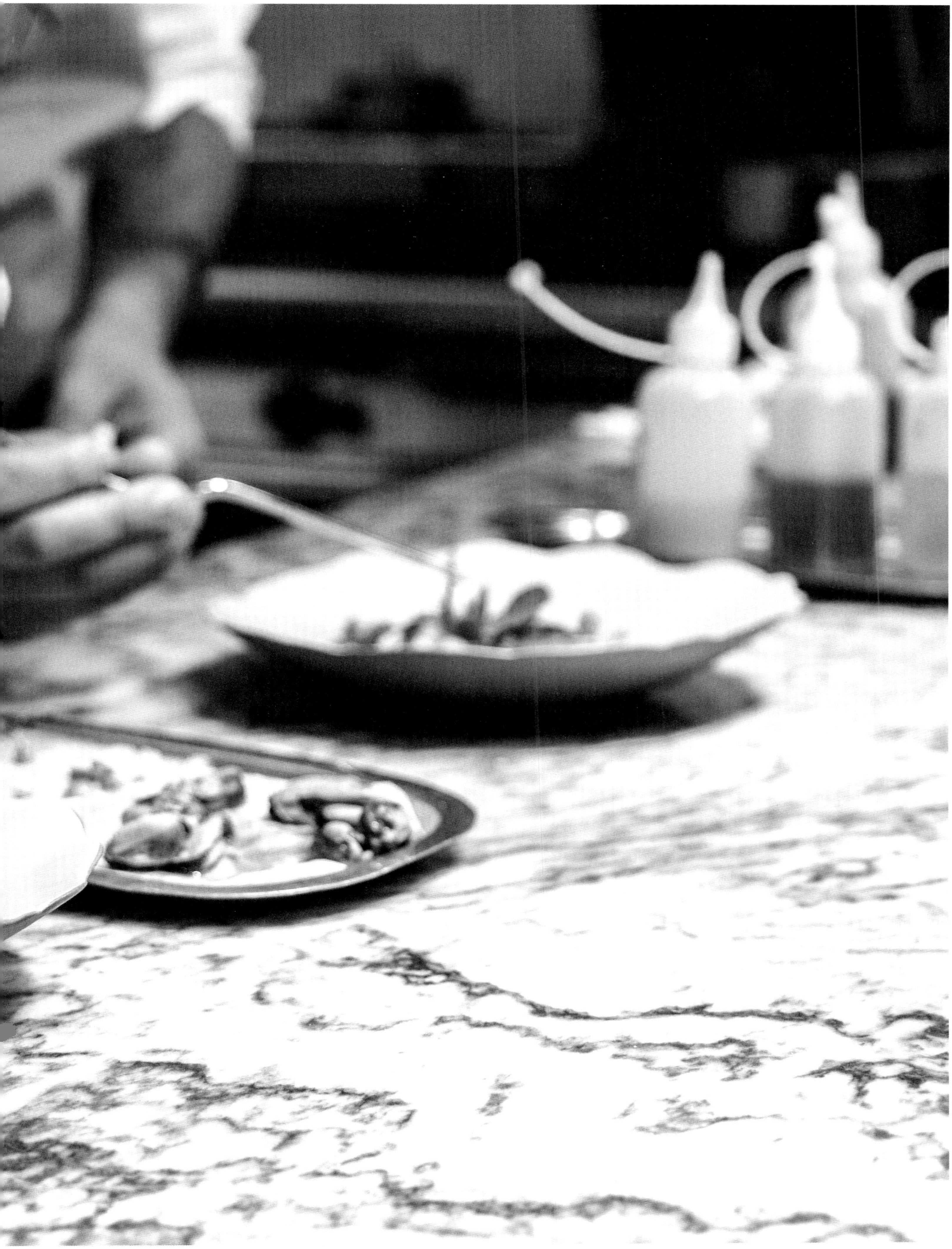

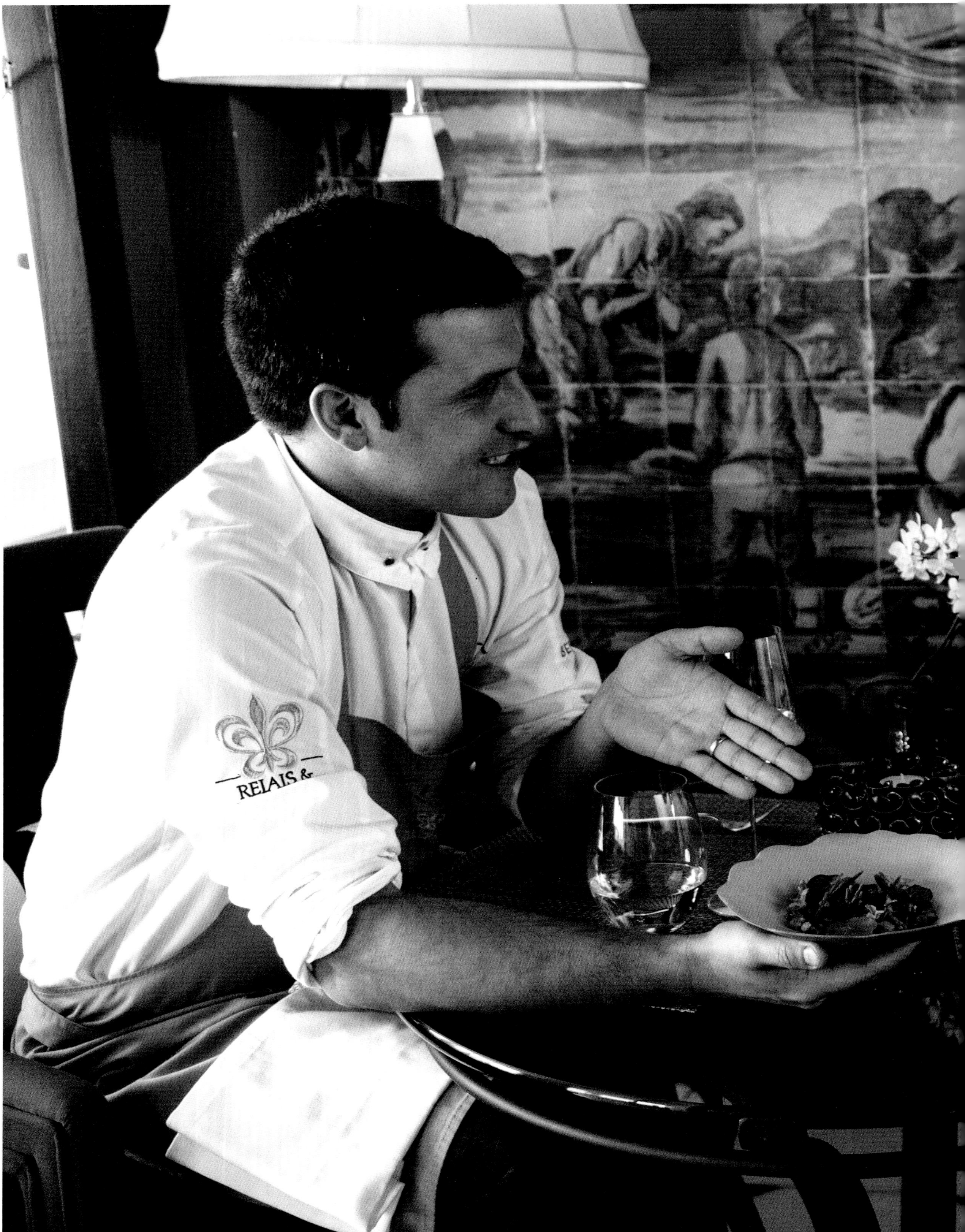
RELAIS &

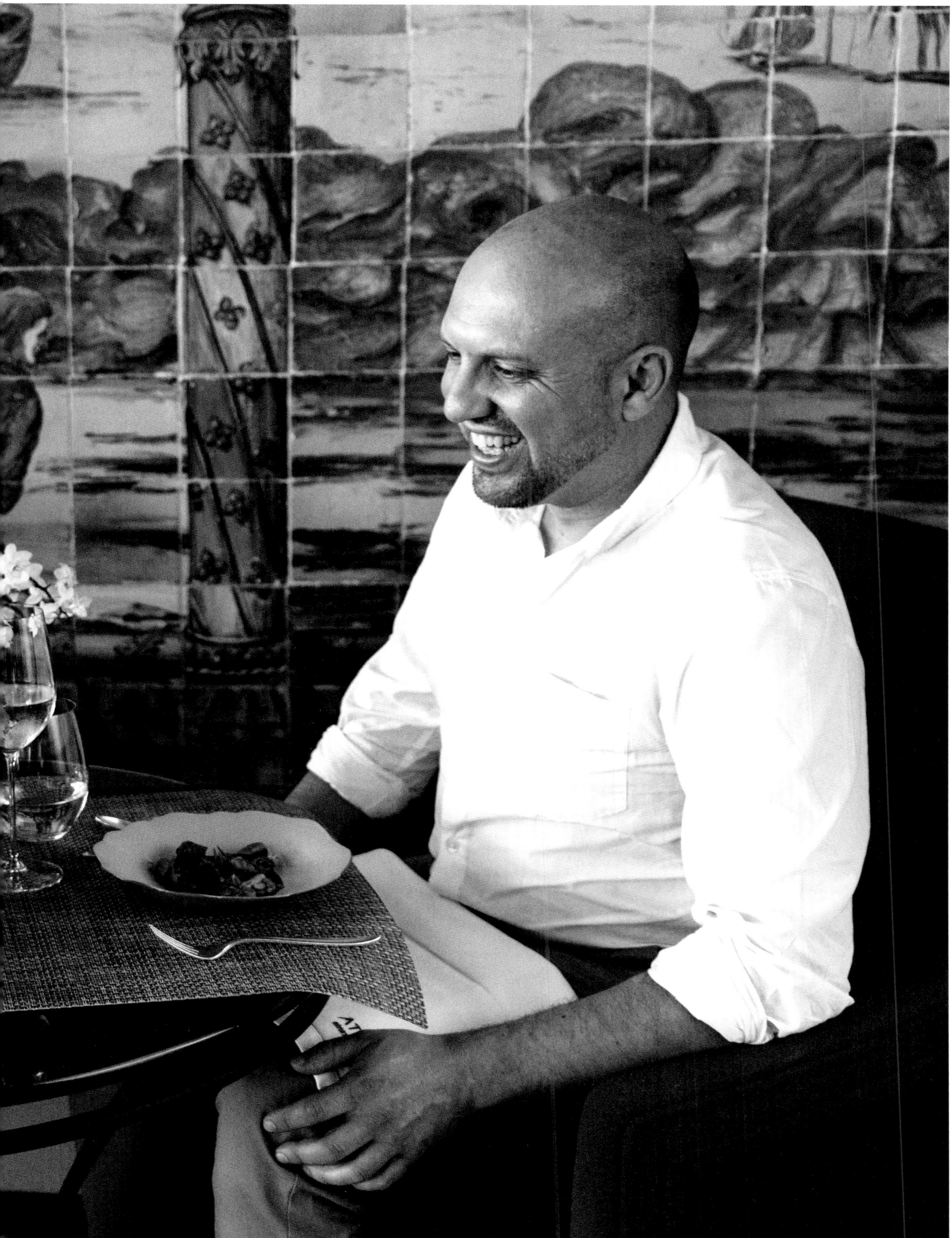

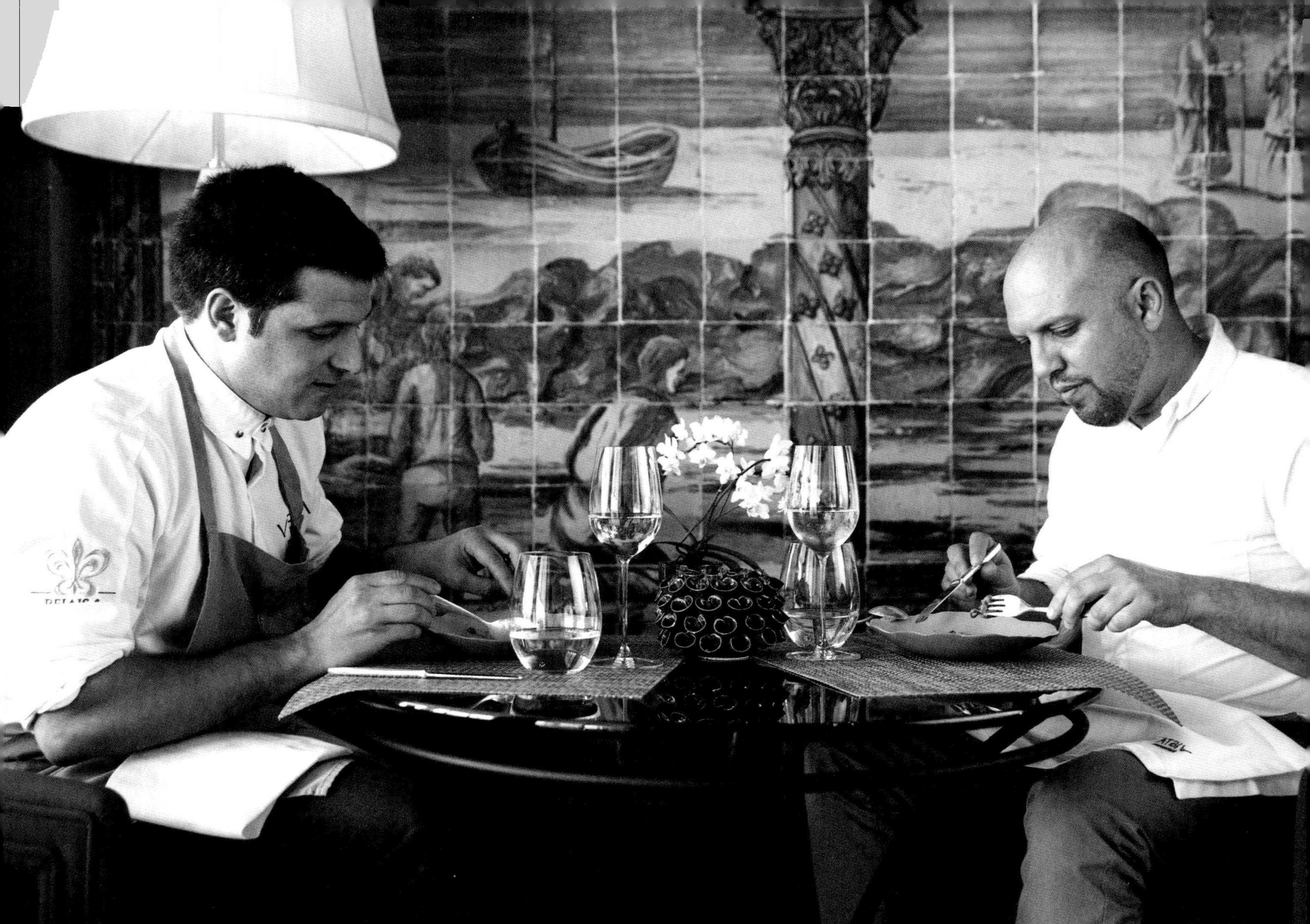

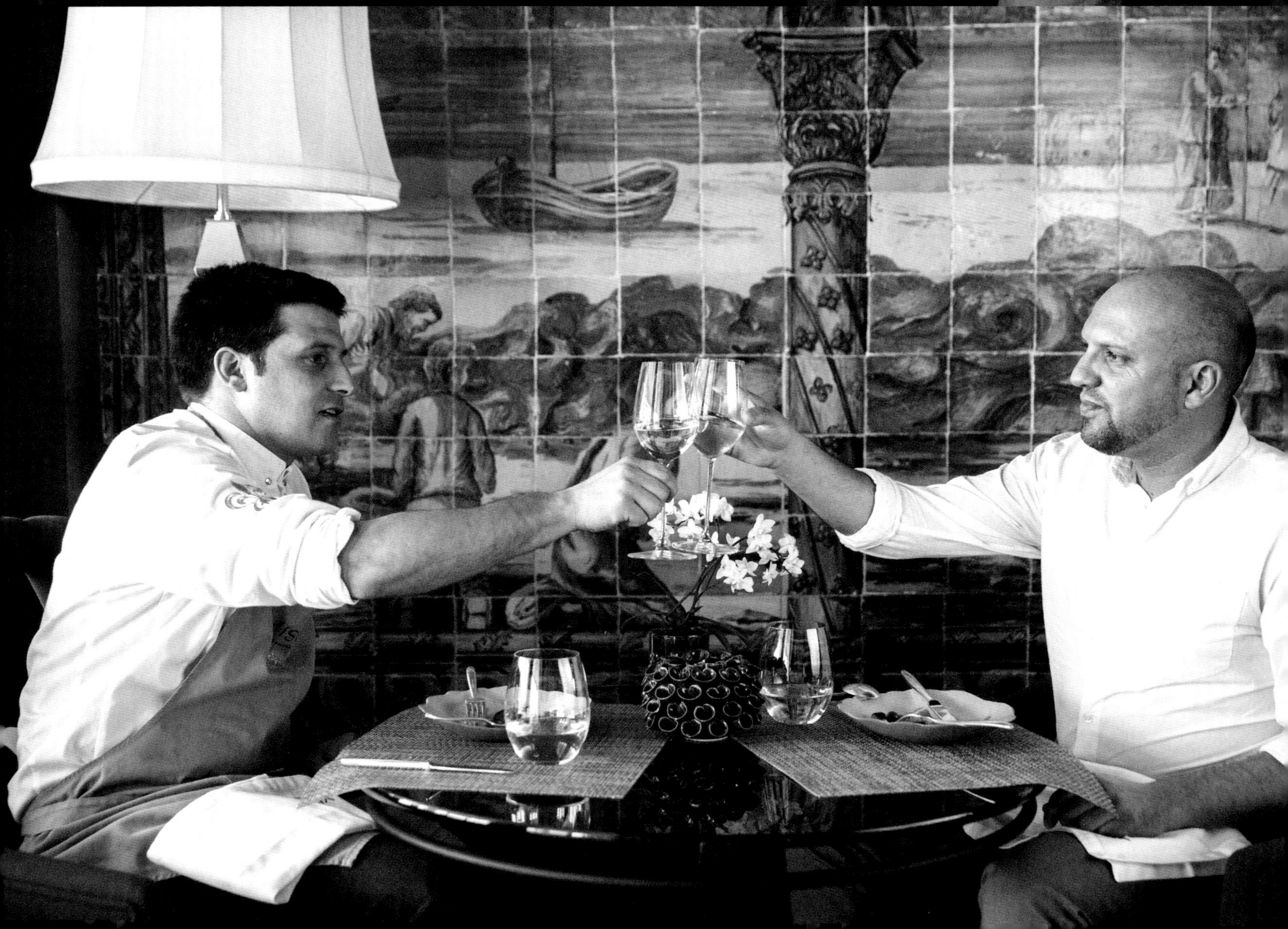

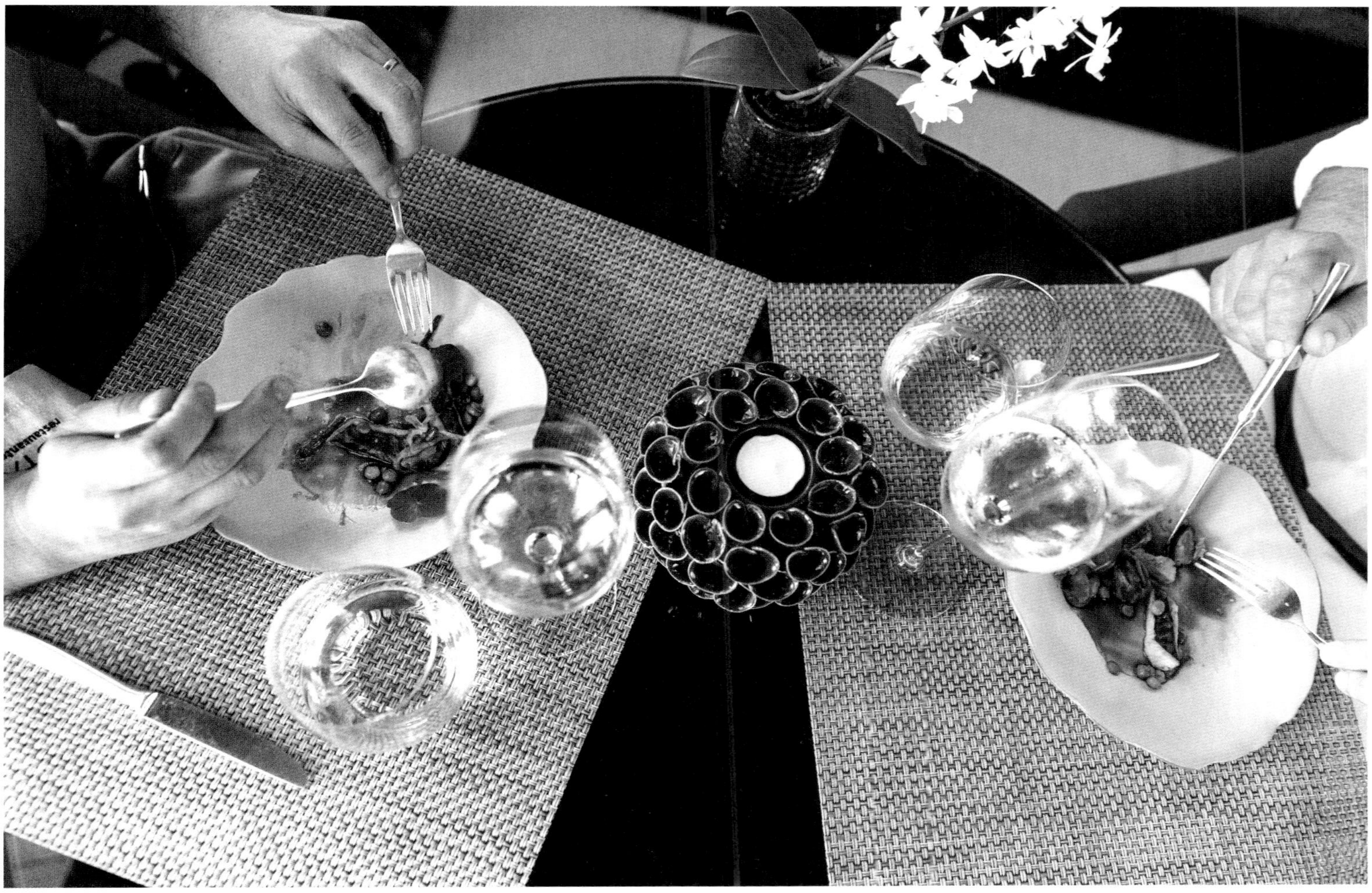

JOÃO OLIVEIRA

CANNED MUSSELS, MACKEREL AND SWEET PEAS

MUSSELS
IN MARINADE
BRAND RAMIREZ

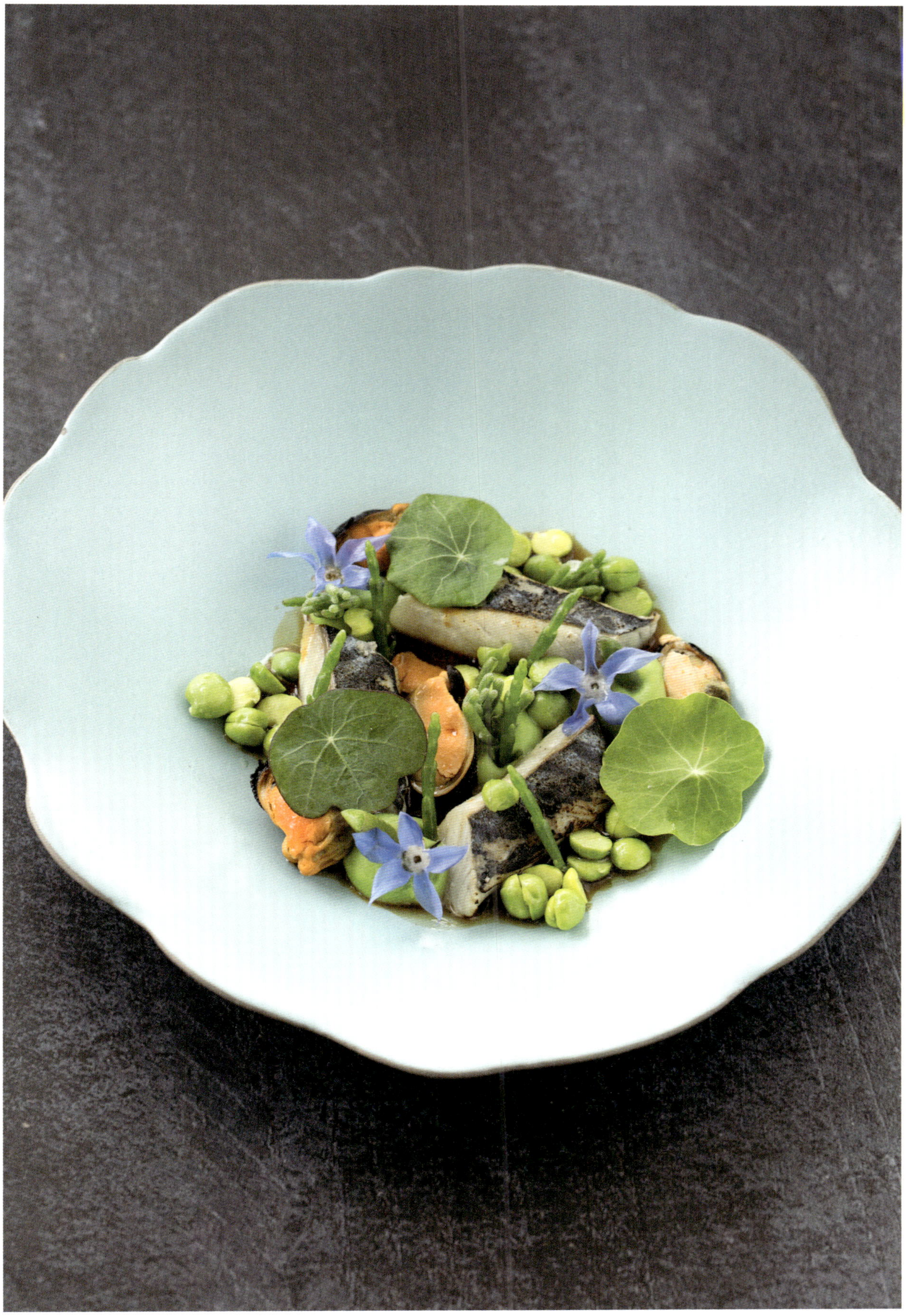

R O D

COMPLEX
2018

R I G O

CANS PAINTED
WITH ACRYLIC, CARDBOARD,
WOOD AND CEMENT

O L I V

80 × 60 × 15 CM

E I R A

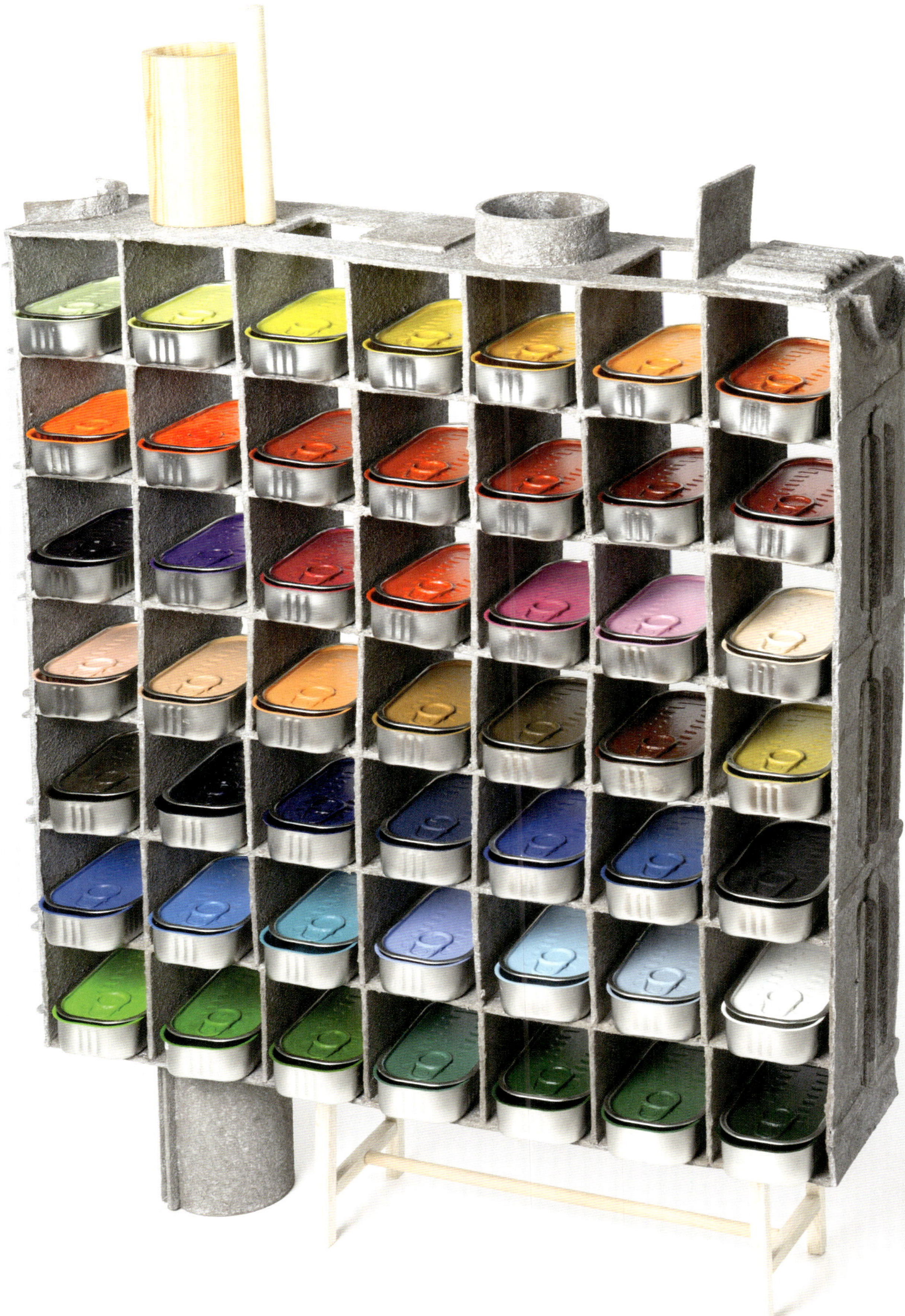

RICARDO
COSTA

CRISTINA
ATAÍDE

CRISTINA
ATAÍDE

RICARDO
COSTA

RICARDO COSTA
CRISTINA ATAÍDE

THE BRAIN IS ALWAYS EATING

If this five-star hotel and two-Michelin-starred restaurant weren't here, it would still be one of the most beautiful places in Portugal. On the top of a hill in Vila Nova de Gaia, close to the wineries, Yeatman is proud of having the most stunning view over the city of Porto.

While waiting for the chef, we take a coffee and get to know the artist Cristina Ataíde. She tells us about her travels with the passion of a little girl. India, Brazil, Africa... her eyes shine and the places transform themselves into works, memories and experiences poured into matter through the eyes and the hands, sometimes with the help of the angle grinder.

We are invited to enter the restaurant and we dally a little, admiring the space. The contrast between the sumptuous lounge and the panorama outside the windows creates a sense of dizziness – which shouldn't surprise us, as we are in one of the most famous restaurants in the land.

The chef Ricardo Costa does the honours and describes the project. "In this restaurant, I invite customers on board on the condition that they accept my proposals. They give themselves to me and I do my best to deserve their trust."

Then he introduces the ingredients. "I like tuna, but I also included some cuttlefish. This is veal tendon, boiled, laminated, dried and fried until we have a biscuit."

The chef starts assembling and Cristina asks if she can try the same. Of course. He does like this and she does like that, trade black for white, concave for convex. "Can I work here?" she asks. Ricardo says yes, he can always use another pair of hands.

In the lounge, the tables are being set using a tape measure. On the terrace in front, a formally dressed Sikh takes photographs of Ribeira, Porto's historic and picturesque seafront neighbourhood.

"Here we work at the level of the millimetre and the gram," says Ricardo. "Everything with the utmost rigour and detail."

So how did you get here? From where does your vocation come?

"In my case, it all started early," says Ricardo. "I was required to cook from a young age, around seven years old. Later, during the school holidays, I used to work because I was restless. In my last year, I worked at a restaurant and the chefs suggested that I study cuisine. And so it was: I went to Coimbra and I evolved more and more. At the time it wasn't really anything prestigious – no one was thinking of becoming famous."

Cristina tells her story. "For me, I used to make beautiful sculptures in soap – I was 10, 11, 12 years old," she says. "And I ended up deciding to study fine arts. But you are not an artist because you study fine art – those who work with art are artists. I love nature and looking around, and then came the marble..."

The marble?

"Yes. I used to work with clay, but it never satisfied me, it was too temporary. I wanted a definitive material. In the 1980s I attended a seminary with João Cutileiro in which we worked the stone directly with tools, and I fell in love with marble. It is a crystalline stone that gives good energy. I also make large dimension drawings, but that's because I'm small..."

And the ideas?

In Ricardo's case they come from technique, from travelling, from people he meets and also from the ingredients. "There's a concept, an idea that we want to pass to the restaurant."

"It's always an idea as a whole, right?" Cristina asks. From one we step to the other...

Ricardo nods. "Yes, there are always common threads and methods we repeat without noticing," he says. "I try to think as a whole but sometimes there are important dishes that I seek out."

The sun is going down outside as the tourists on the terrace surrender themselves to the city. They are on the other side of the curtain, where the spectacle appears without sight of the backstage, the hands working, the heads thinking. It's Ricardo who sums up everything in a few words.

"Everything here is slow, all this process," he says. "But the brain is always eating."

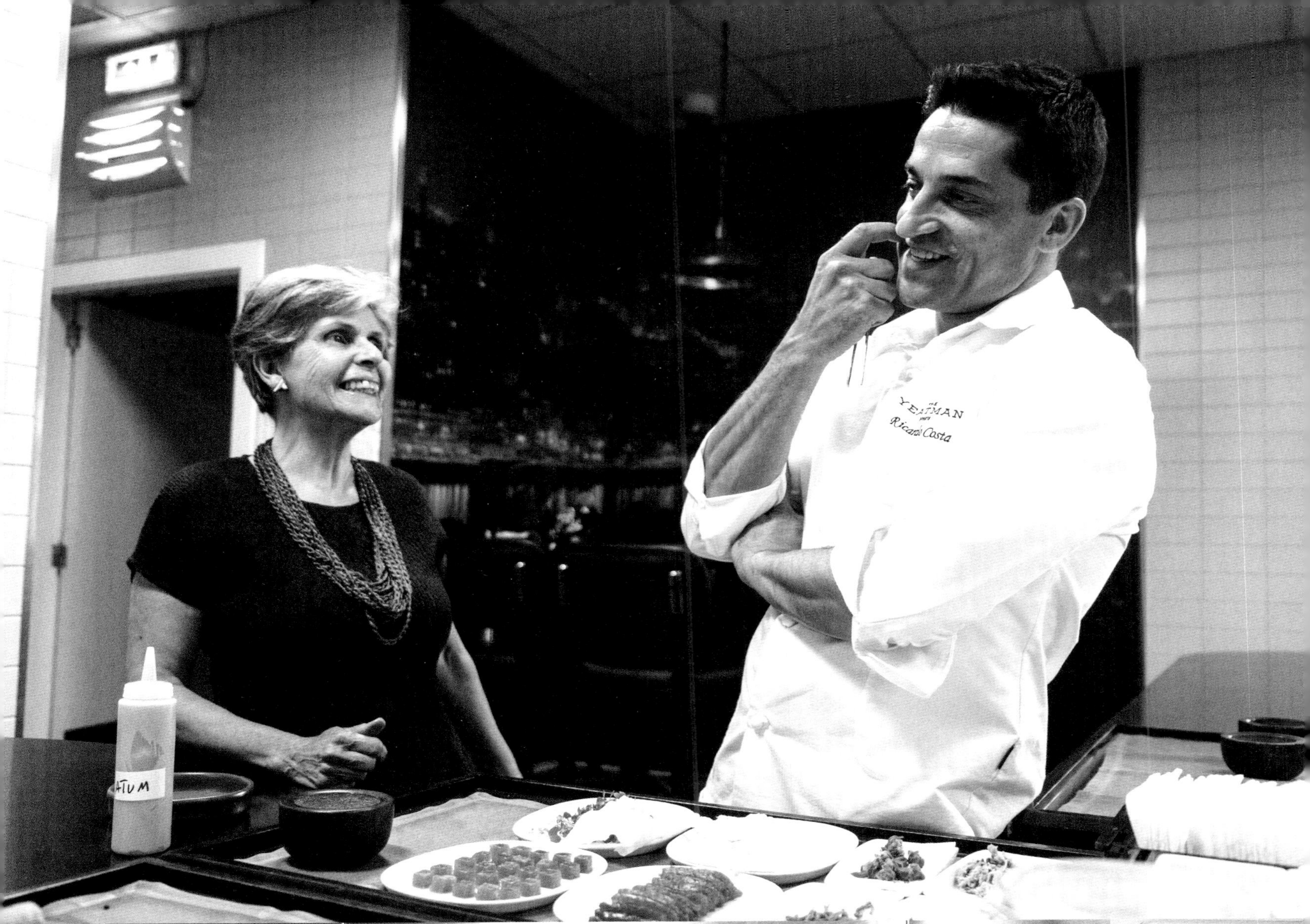
YEATMAN
Ricardo Costa
ATUM

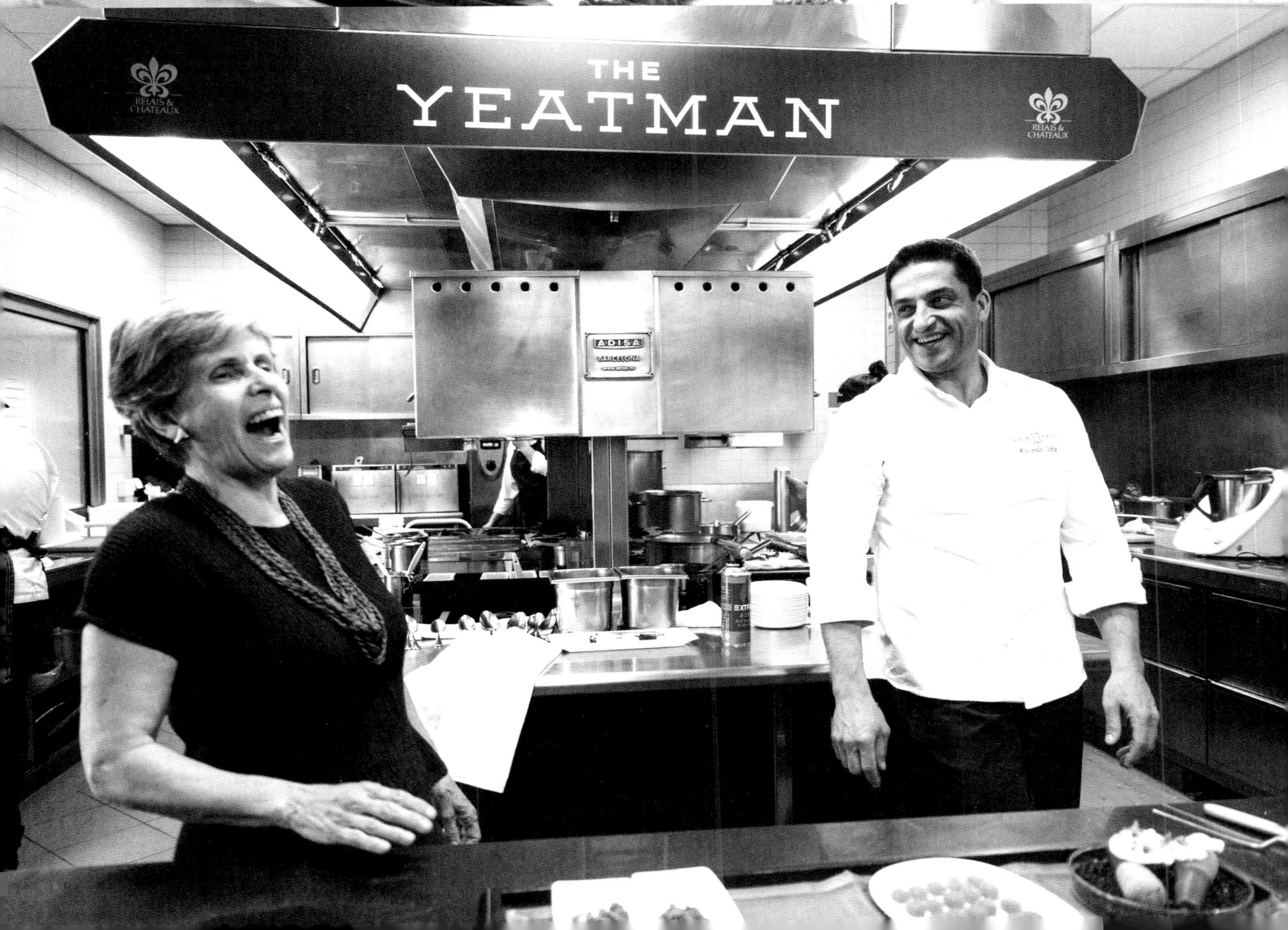
THE
YEATMAN
RELAIS & CHATEAUX
RELAIS & CHATEAUX
ADISA
BARCELONA

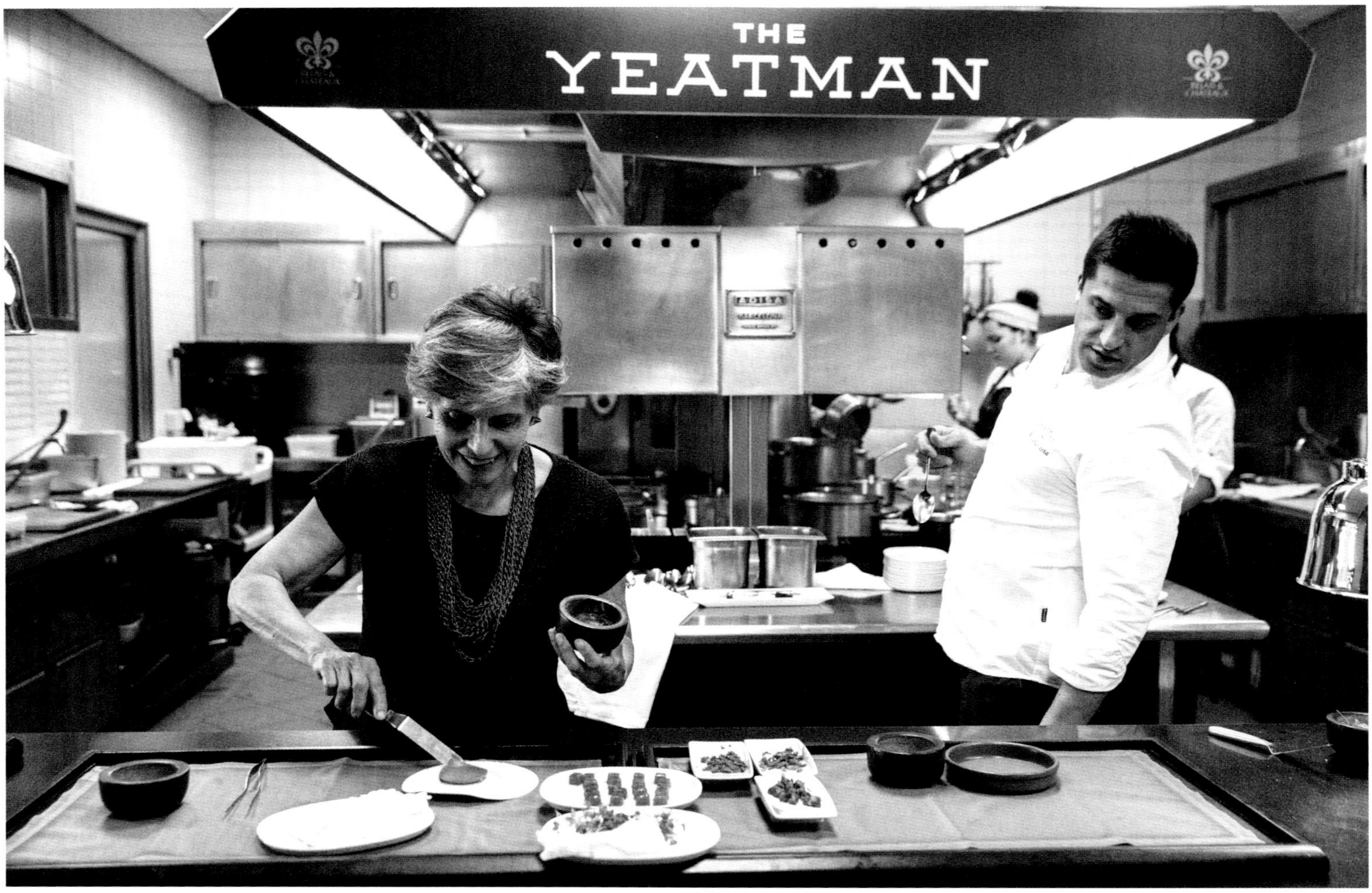
THE
YEATMAN

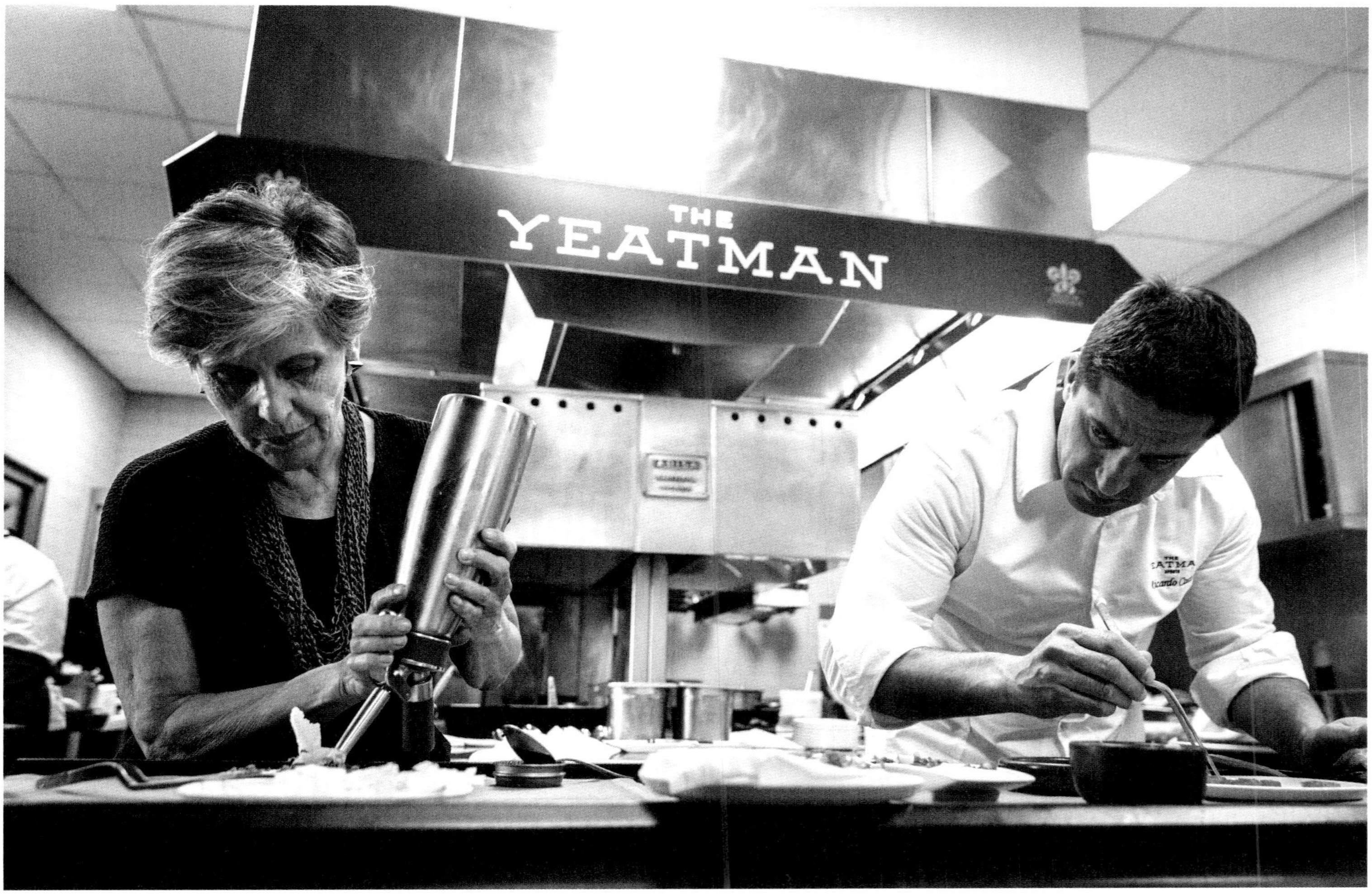
THE
YEATMAN

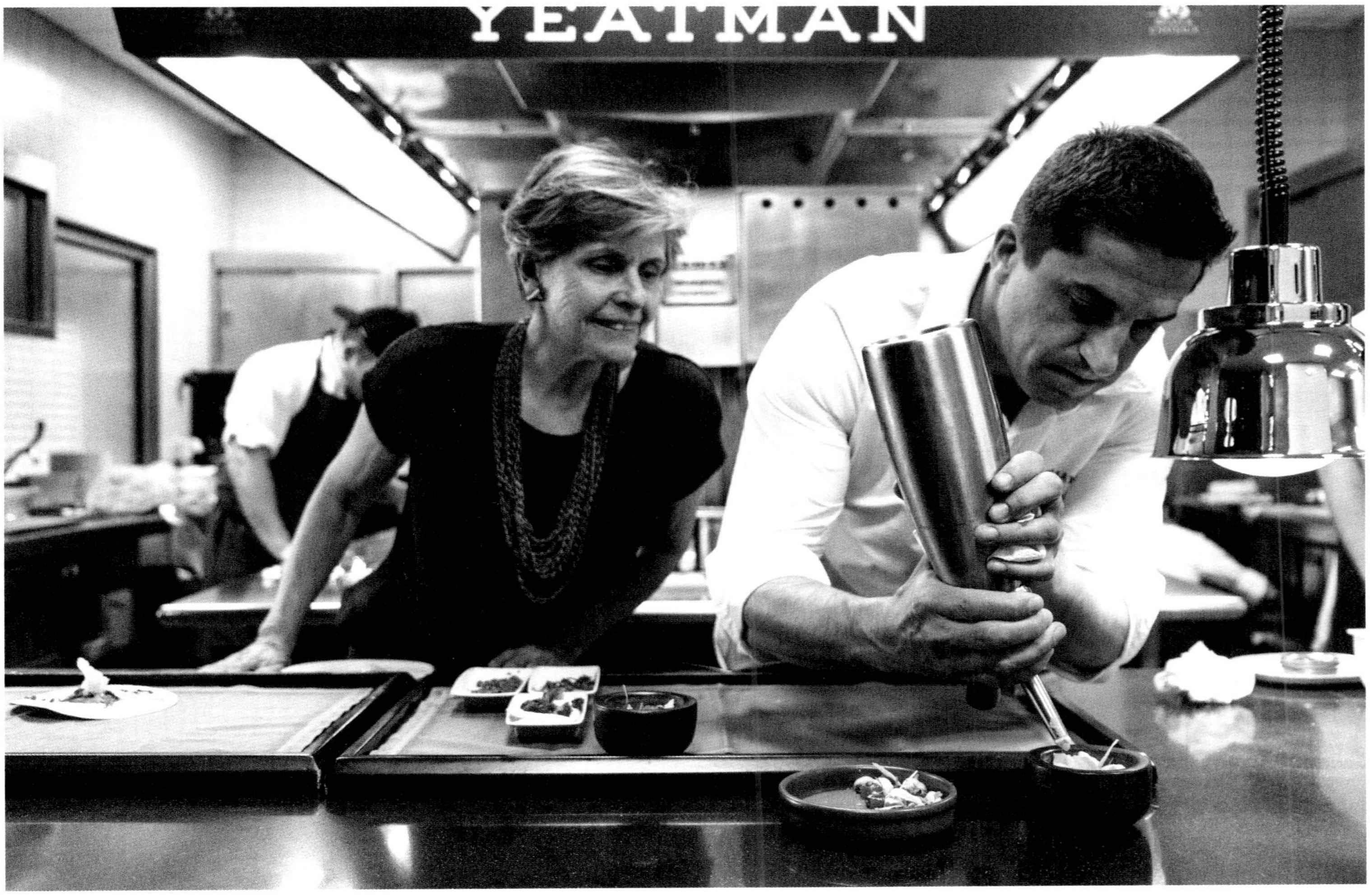
YEATMAN

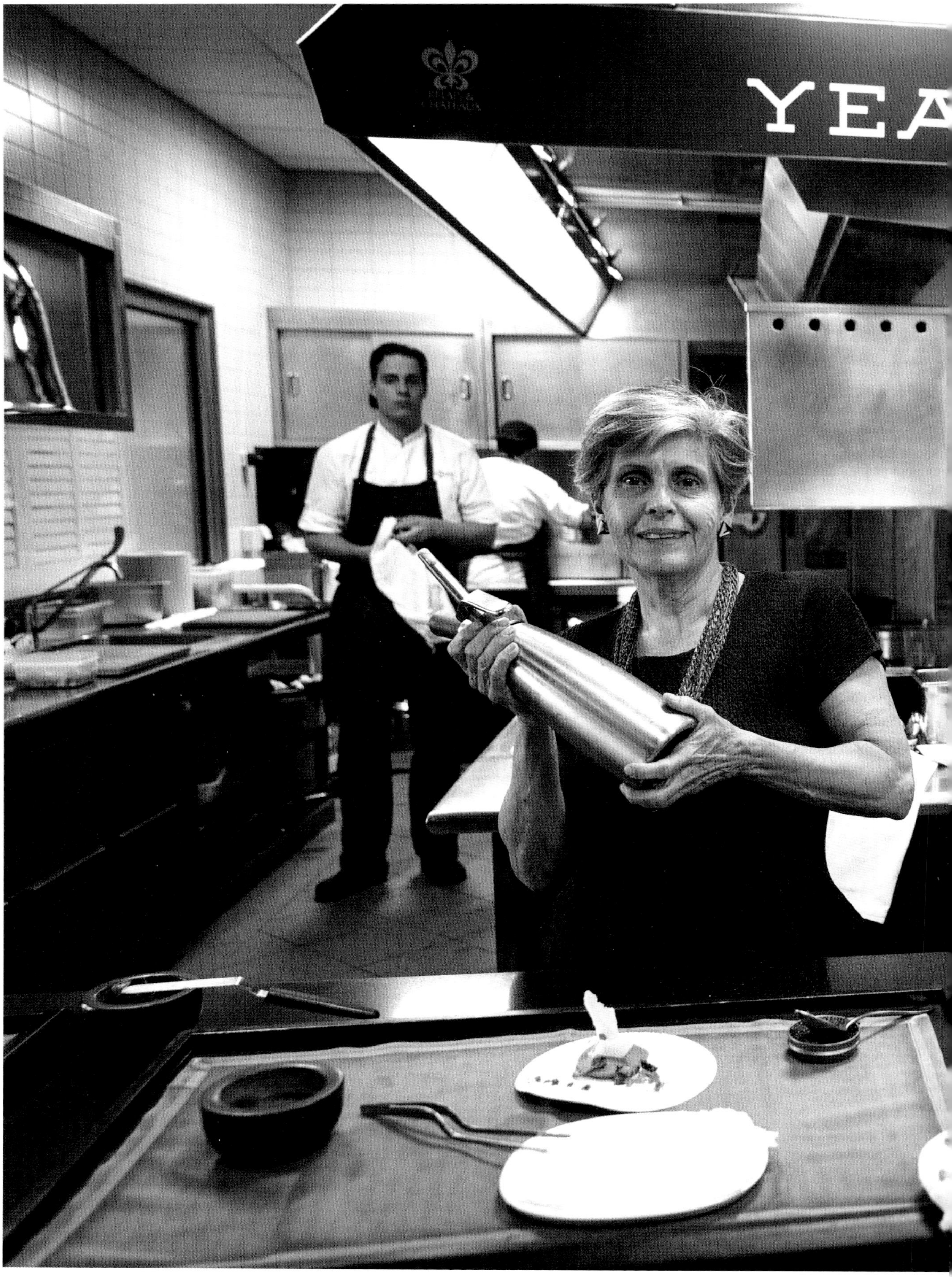

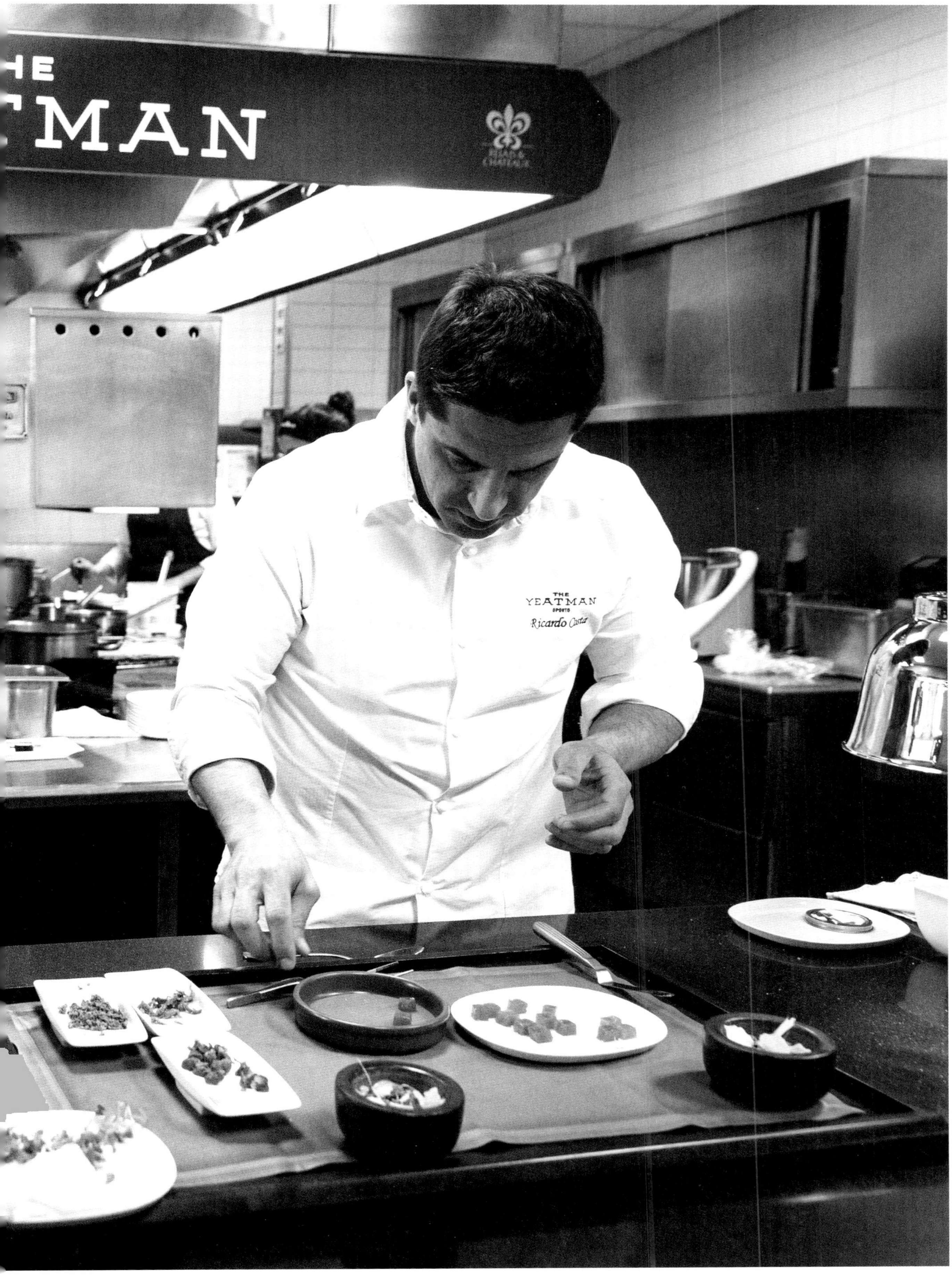
THE
YEATMAN
THE
YEATMAN
Ricardo Costa

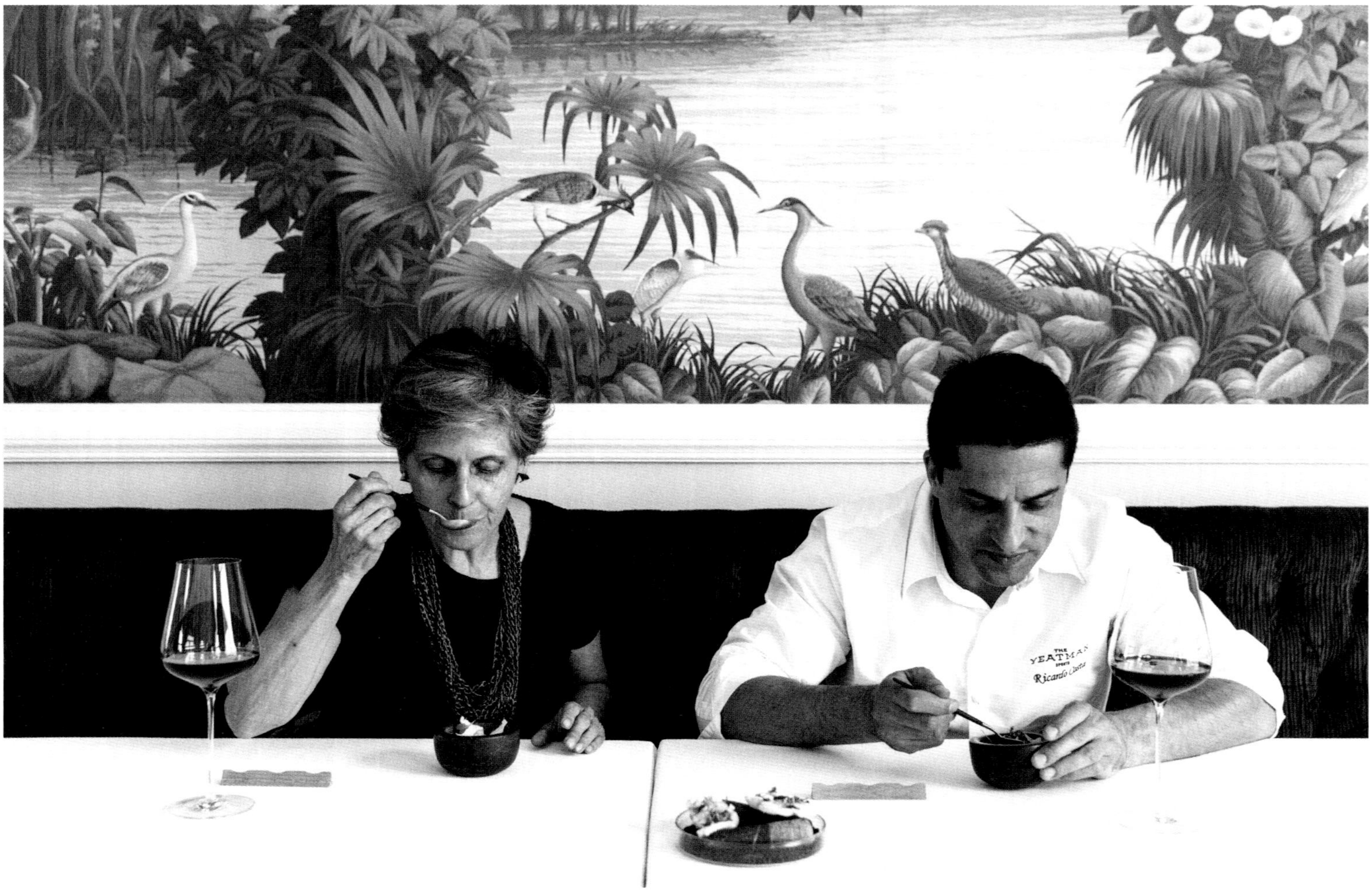

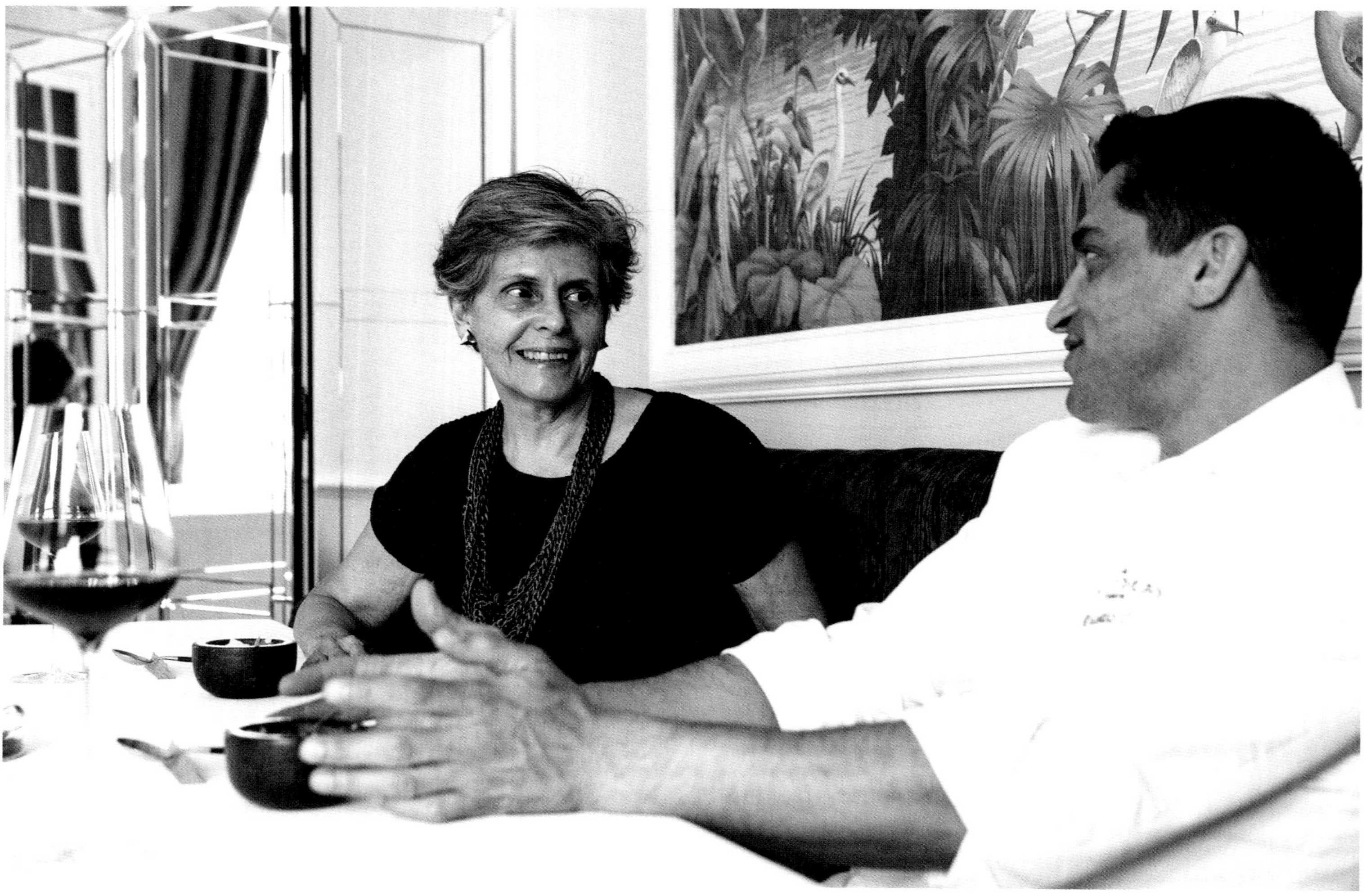

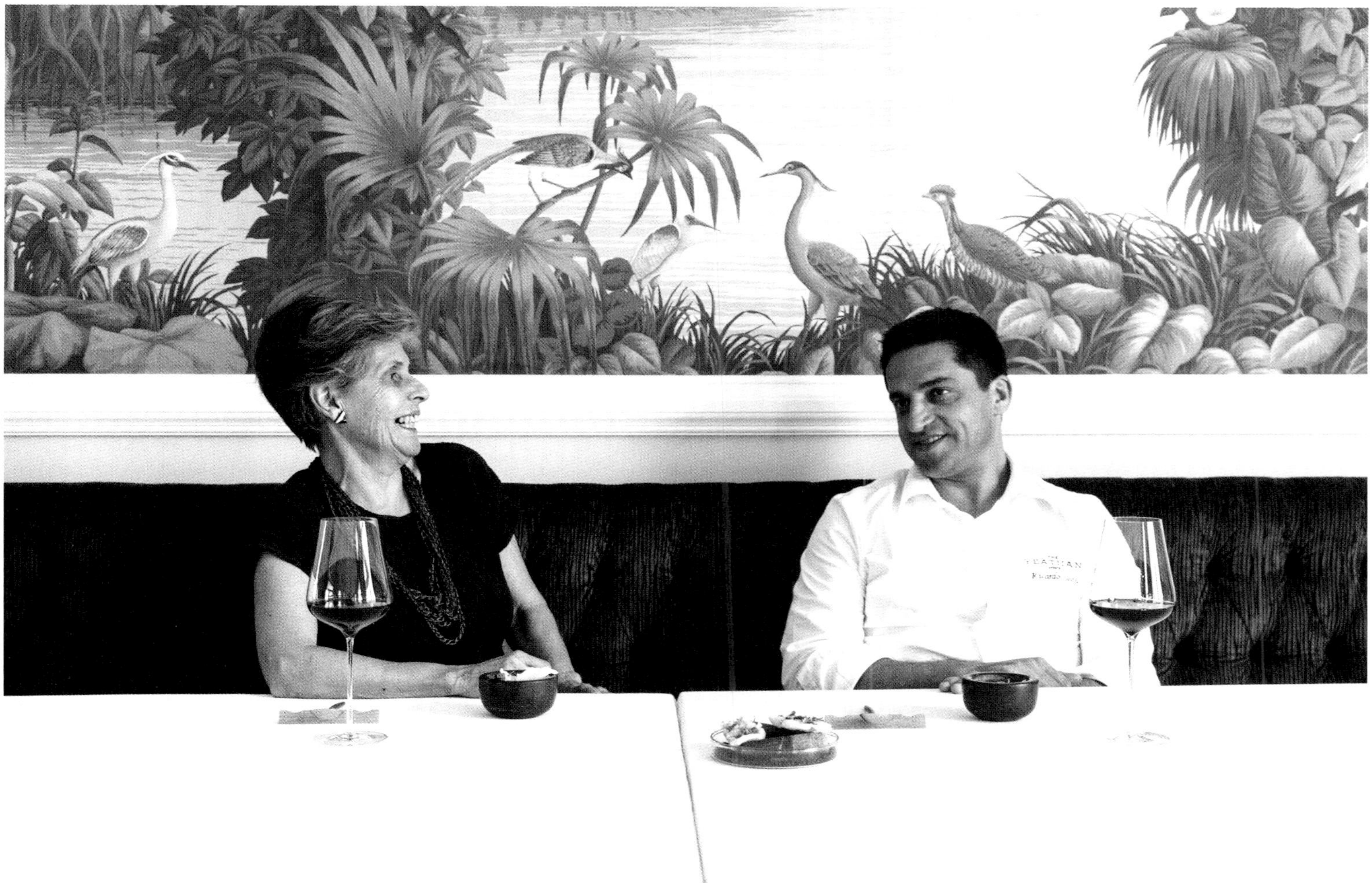

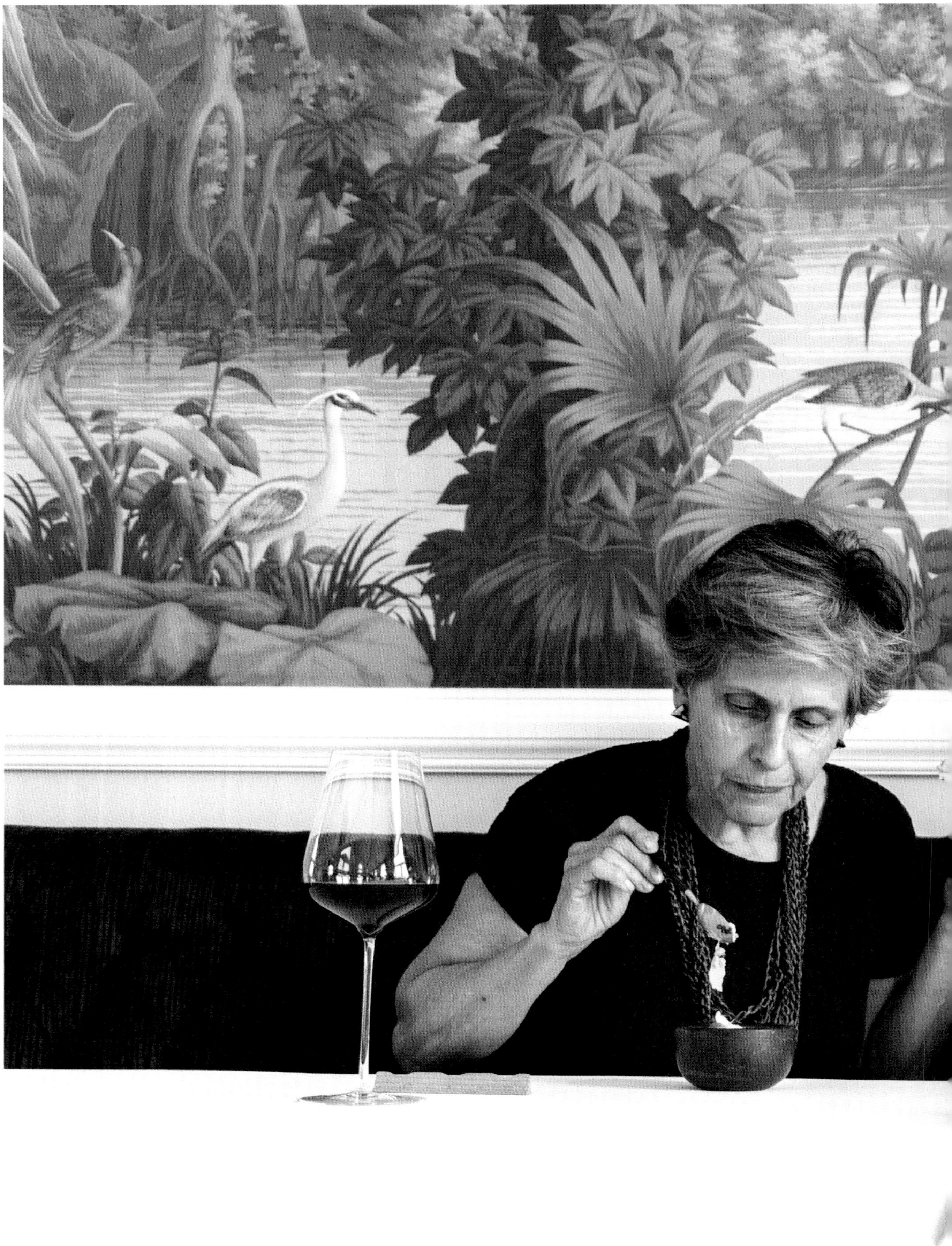

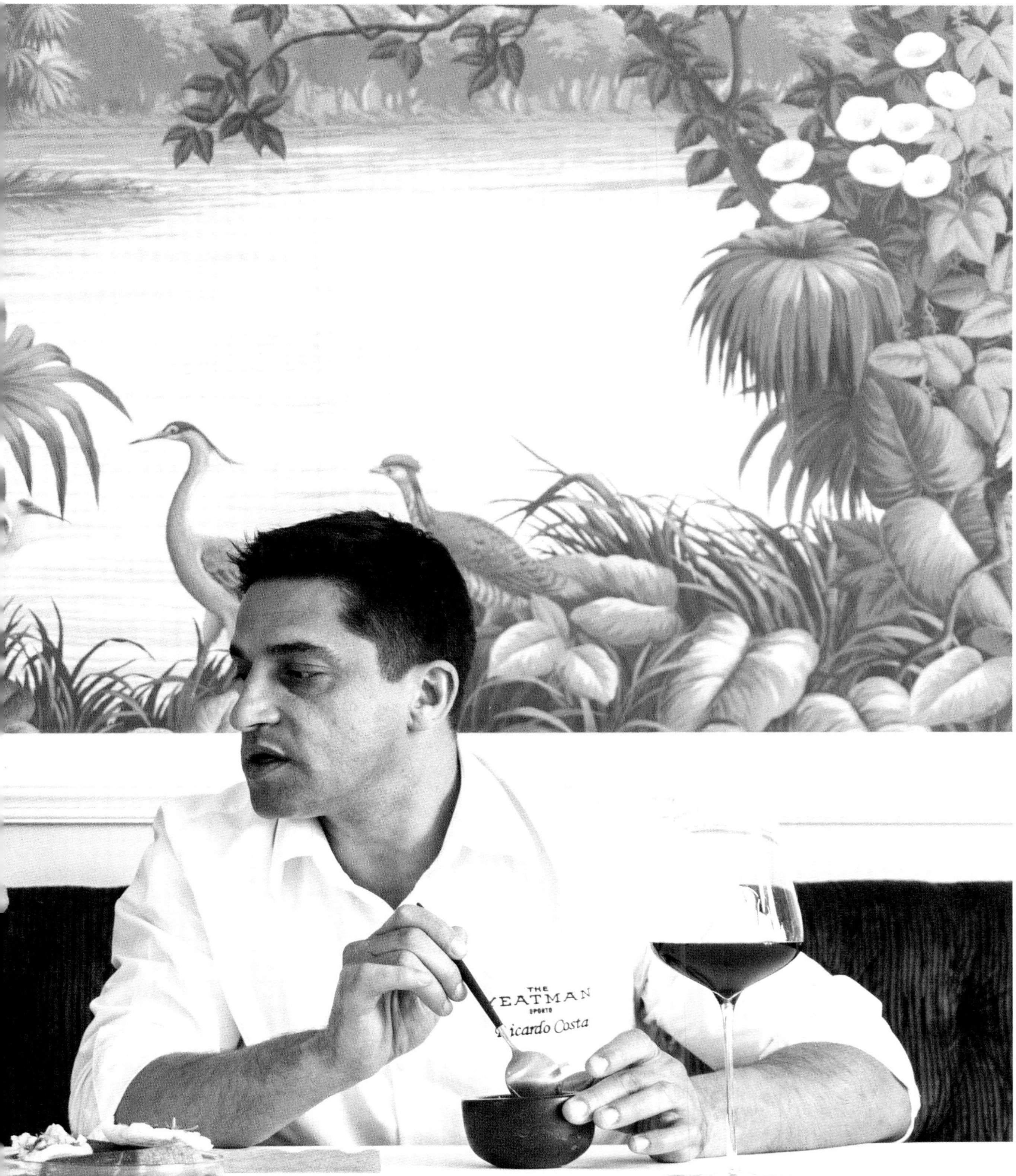
THE
YEATMAN
OPORTO
Ricardo Costa

RICARDO COSTA

VITELLO TONNATO WITH CAPERS, ANCHOVIES AND TUNA

TUNA VENTRESCA
BRAND MANNÁ

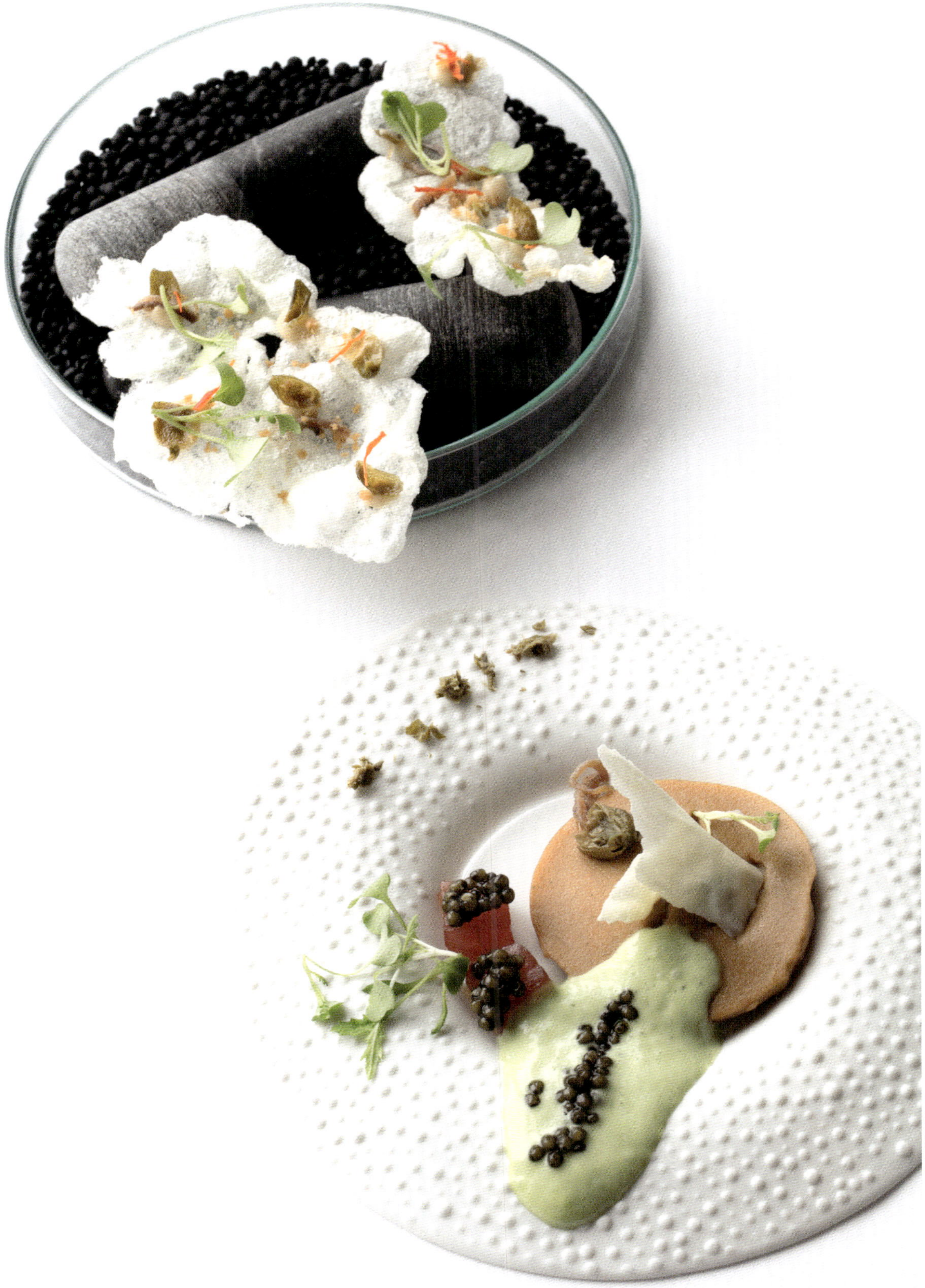

CRISTINA ATAÍDE

STANDING WATER
2018

ESTREMOZ
MARBLE SCULPTURE
45 × 30 × 3 CM

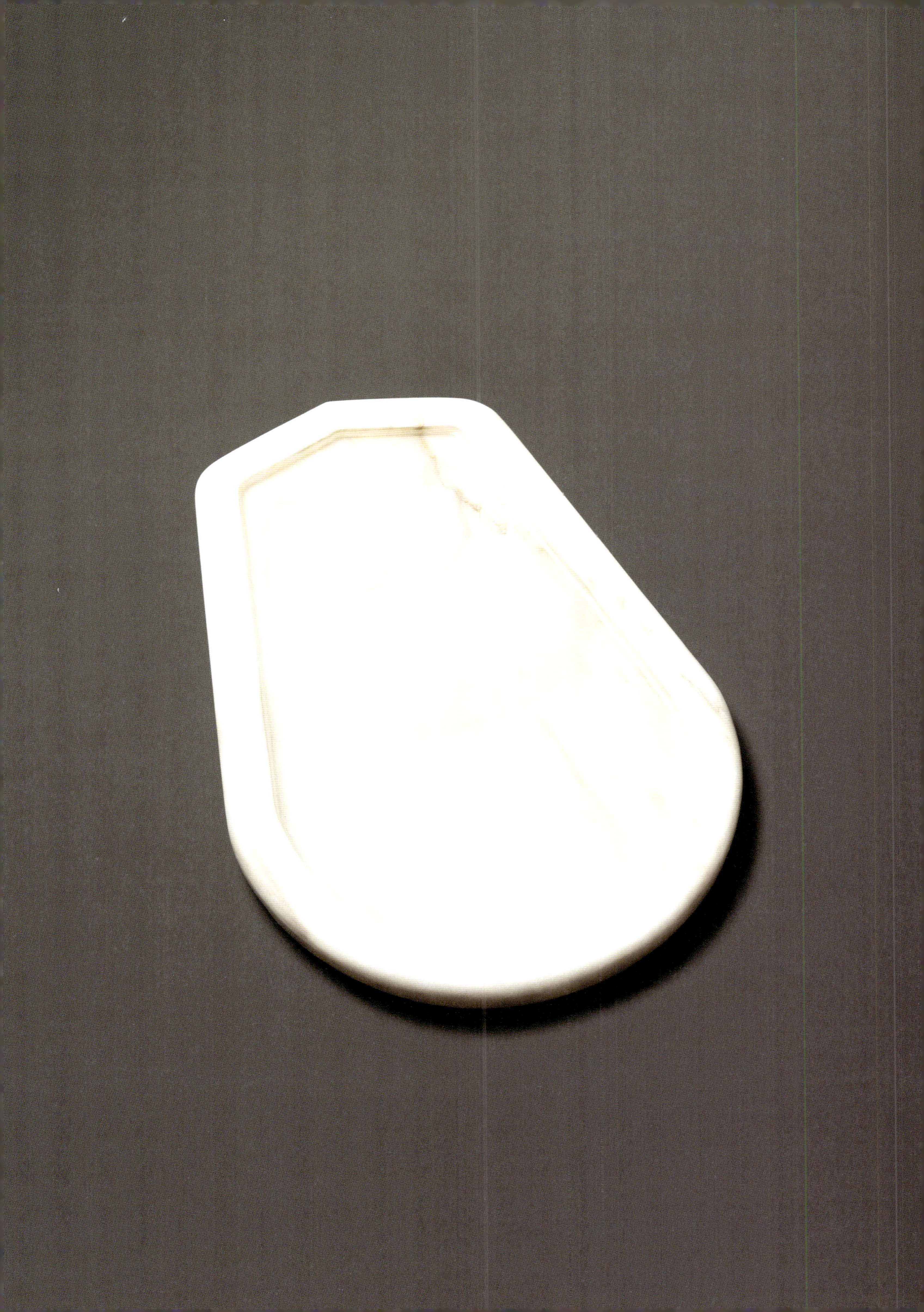

HENRIQUE
SÁ PESSOA

MIGUEL
PALMA

MIGUEL
PALMA

HENRIQUE
SÁ PESSOA

HENRIQUE SÁ PESSOA
MIGUEL PALMA

THE CRISIS THAT SAVED US

It's not really a kitchen. Nor is it a laboratory or restaurant. But it's all of them. As well as being an art gallery and a living room for friends. This is the Atelier Henrique Sá Pessoa in Lisbon.

The chef Henrique Sá Pessoa and the artist Miguel Palma have never met. No one would know it, as here they are now, side by side, holding tweezers and dissecting ingredients as if they were objects worthy of serious study. They are brothers in arts, the products of twin careers based on delicacy.

"In London they used to call me 'fairy hands', and ask me to place the food on the plates, because of my delicate hands," says Henrique. "I was the 'fairy hands' guy."

Miguel chips in. "Well, I'm also hand-skilful, that's why I'm an artist. At one time, when someone was skilled with their hands, they would go into the arts.

Henrique shows how to cut the tomatoes and then the beans. These are surgical arts. "Like this, you see? In this way, and in a single blow." Miguel learns quickly.

We return to Henrique. "Many times, the hardest thing is to make a proper classic in the kitchen. The quality of the protein is fundamental."

"Don't you think that taste is constantly evolving?" asks Miguel. "As we get older, there are flavours we seek, from childhood..."

"Yes, and it's becoming increasingly difficult – you can't always find the best products," replies Henrique. "But we must search for them..."

We give the floor to Miguel to take us back to the start.

"In 1974, I went to a state school in Alvalade, and that's where everything happened... When I arrived home after a gym class, I took some watercolours and painted an explosion with my fingers on a piece of cardboard. Then I thought, 'Wow, I'm an artist! I'm streets ahead!' The sort of thing I like is to bury toys as summer ends, so as to see how they are the following year – the wear of the materials..."

The coincidences mount.

"I buried odder things. When I was a kid, my dog died from rat poison, and I hid the tissue with my tears beneath the floor tiles."

A sensitivity, a delicacy of soul.

"To be a chef, you need to have a certain level of sensitivity when you cook," says Henrique. "Even if many of us are beasts."

"I'm listening and agreeing with everything," says Miguel. "You have to be conscious of suffering."

"You have to suffer," says Henrique.

"You have to know how to suffer," says Miguel.

We move on to the financial crisis and its advantages. "During the crisis," says Henrique, "people who had never had a creative career would tell me, 'I always wanted to be a cook – and you know, as things stand, it's worth taking the risk.' The crisis was the seed for many a success."

Miguel nods in agreement. "I learned a lot from the crisis," he says.

The conversation continues at the table, around and among the plates and wine glasses. Both recall the highlights of their careers, the discoveries and the surprises. Henrique's mother had guessed her son's future before he went to the US to study at one of the world's best cookery schools.

"My mother used to say that I didn't eat well, but I was peculiar, with a refined palate," he says. "She wasn't at all surprised when I became a cook."

We make a toast to art, to fairy hands everywhere, and to sensitivity. We don't toast the crisis because it was an ugly thing, even if it saved us...

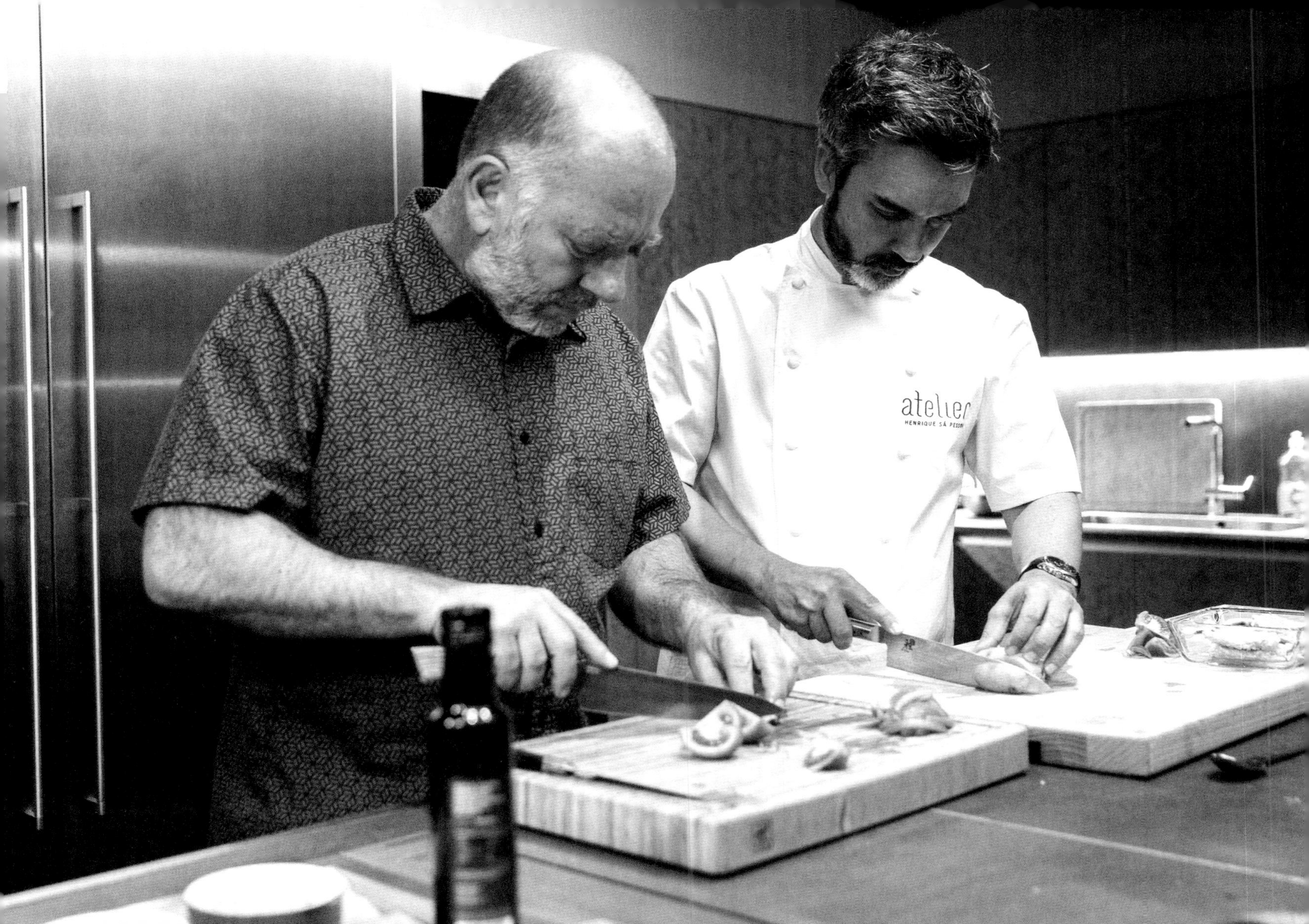

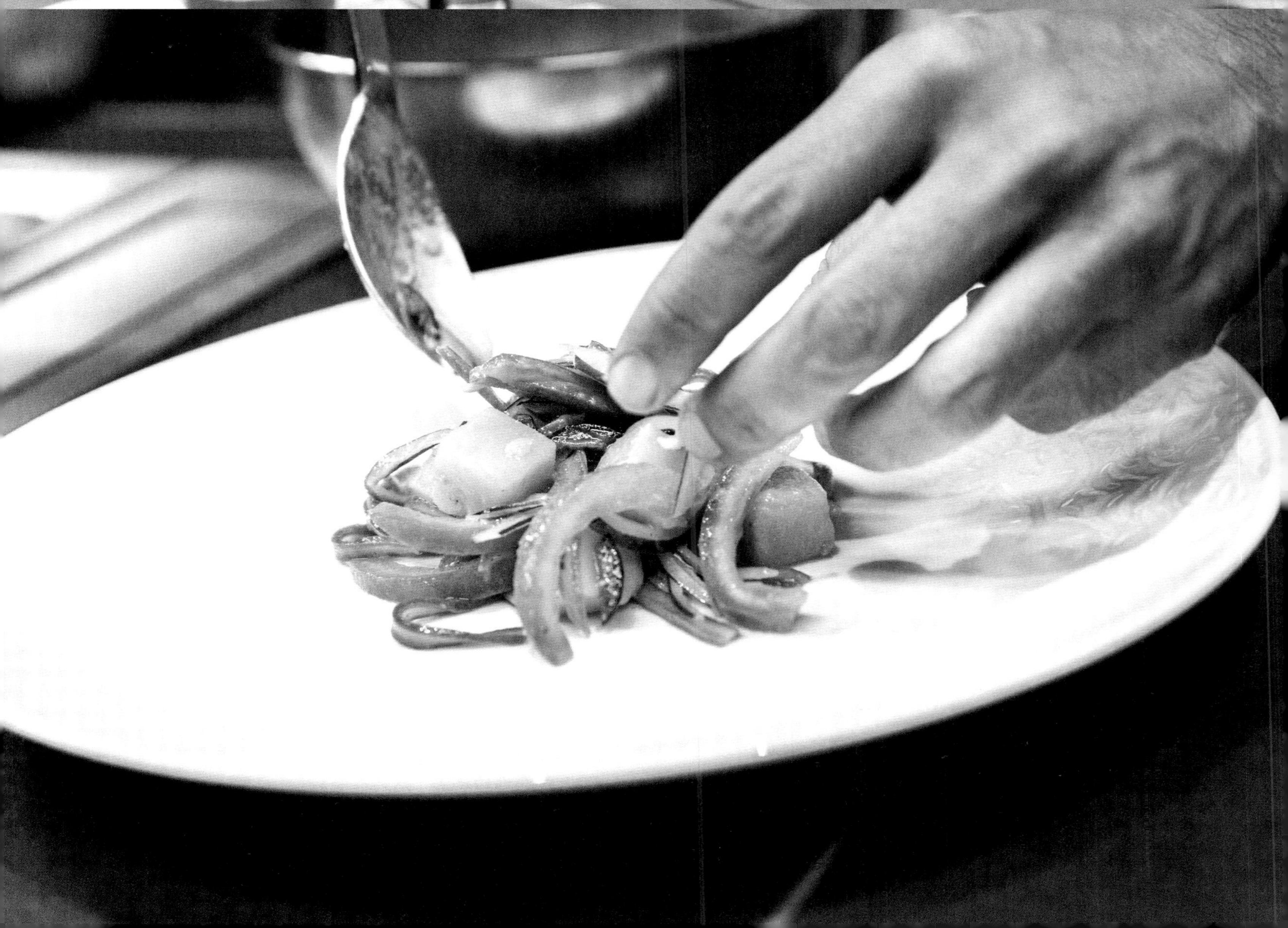

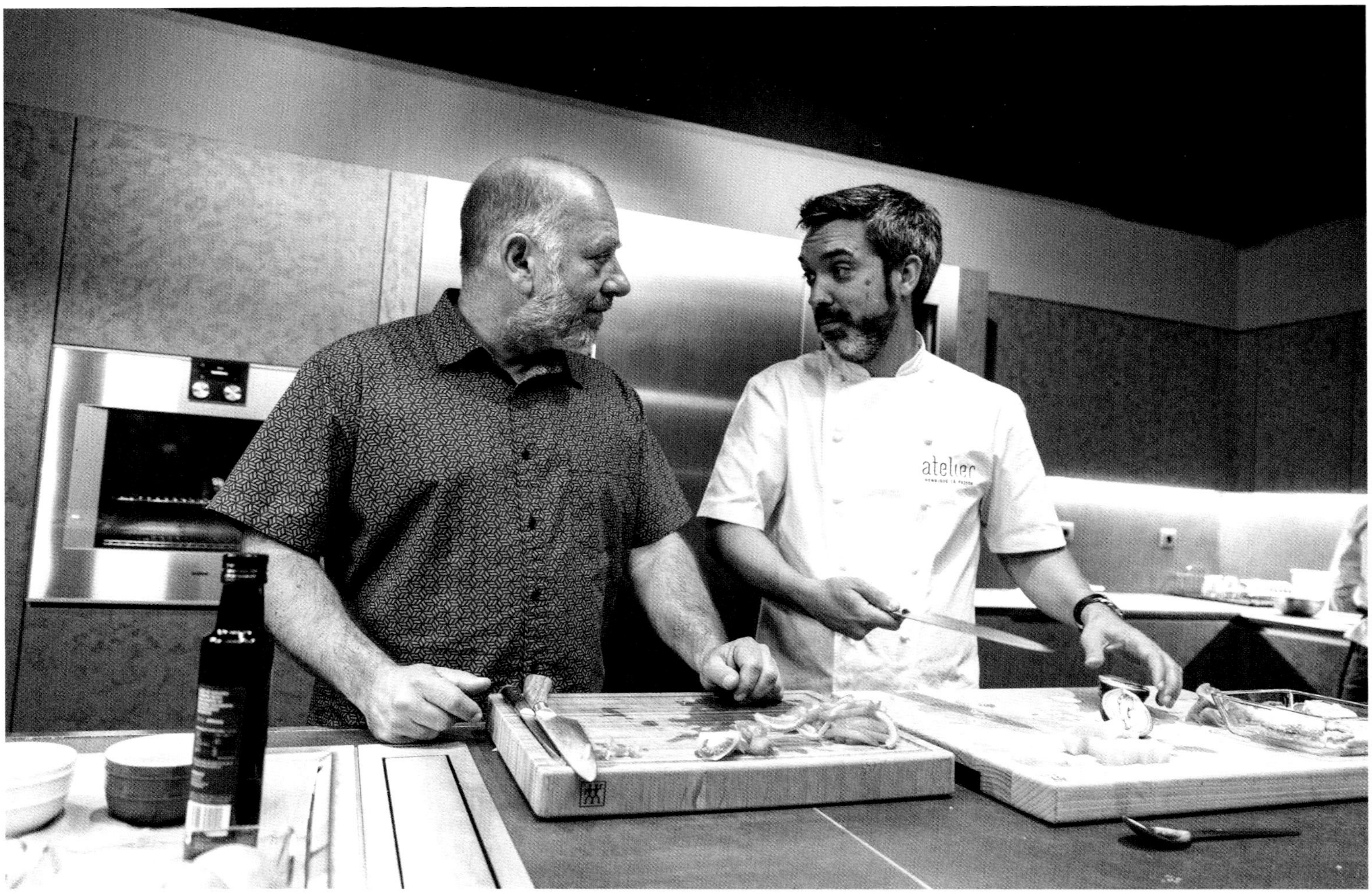
atelier

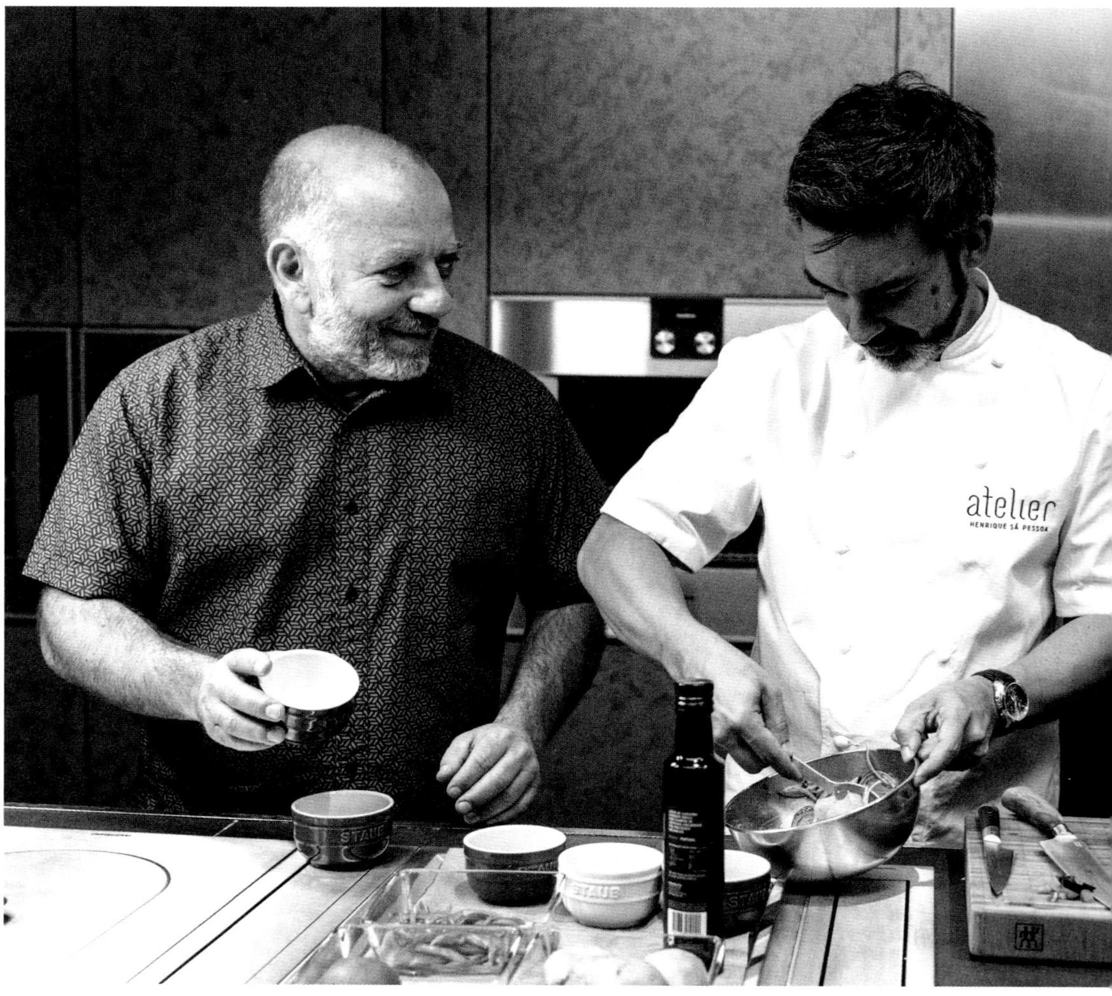
atelier
HENRIQUE SÁ PESSOA
STAUB

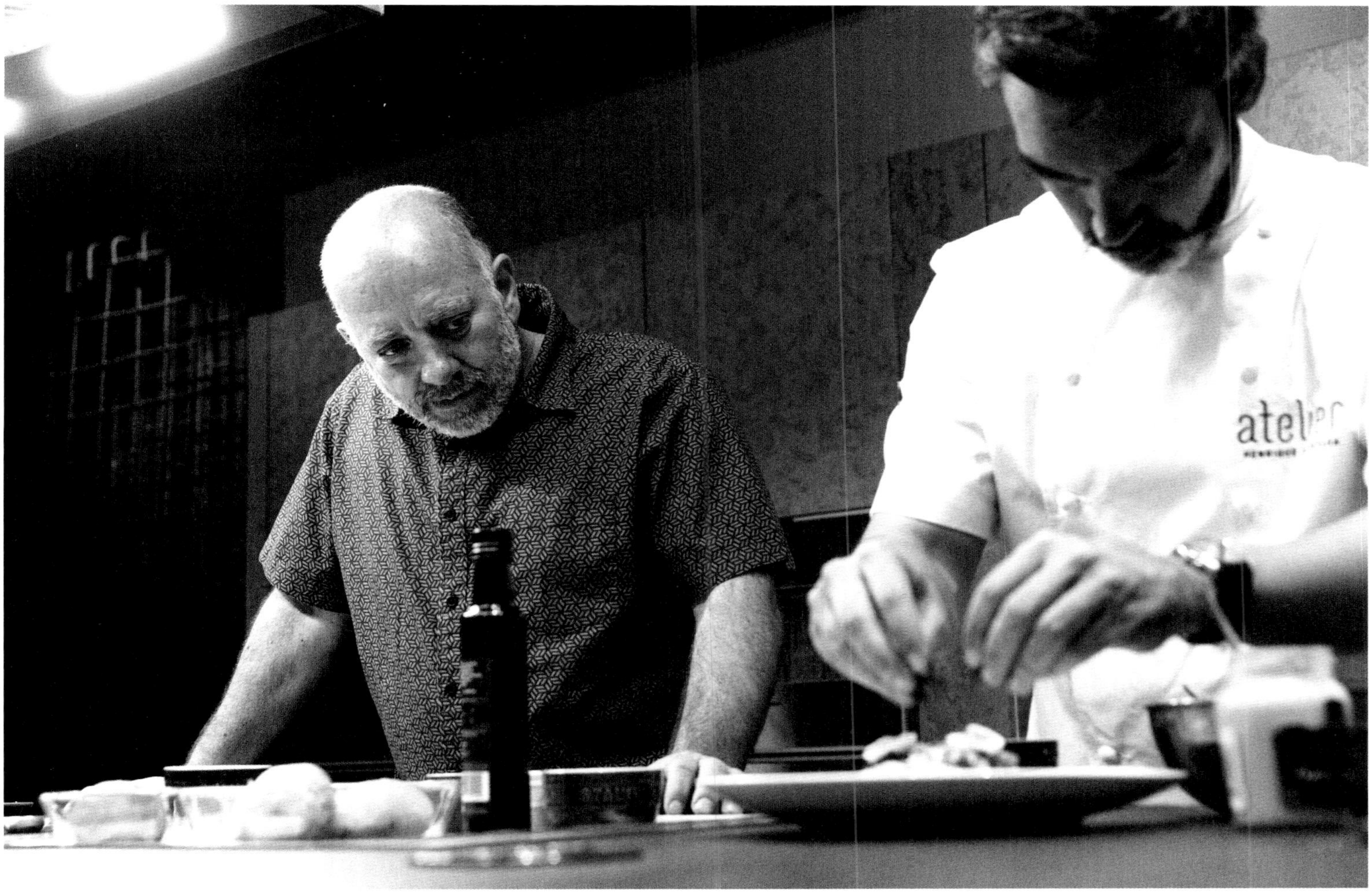

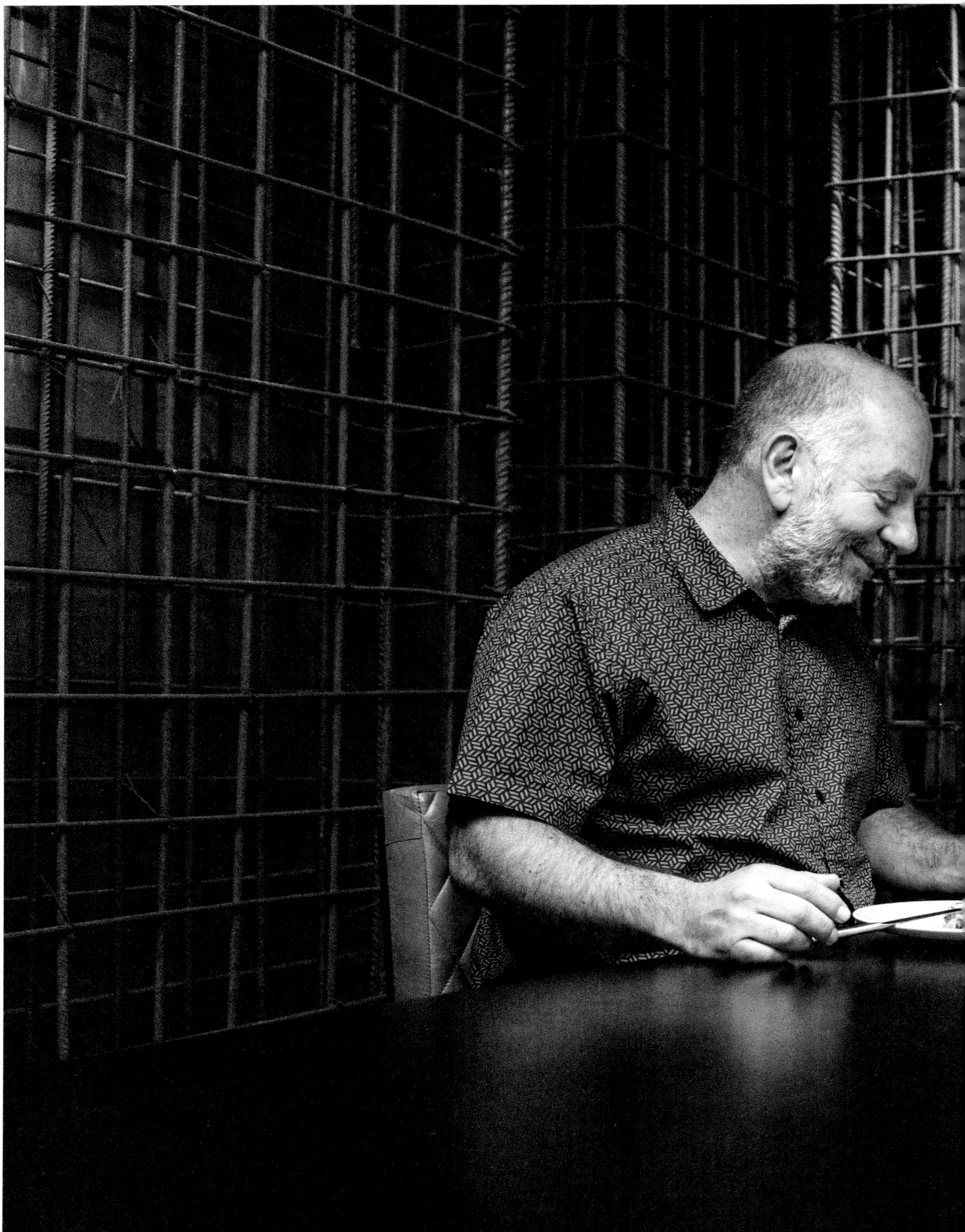

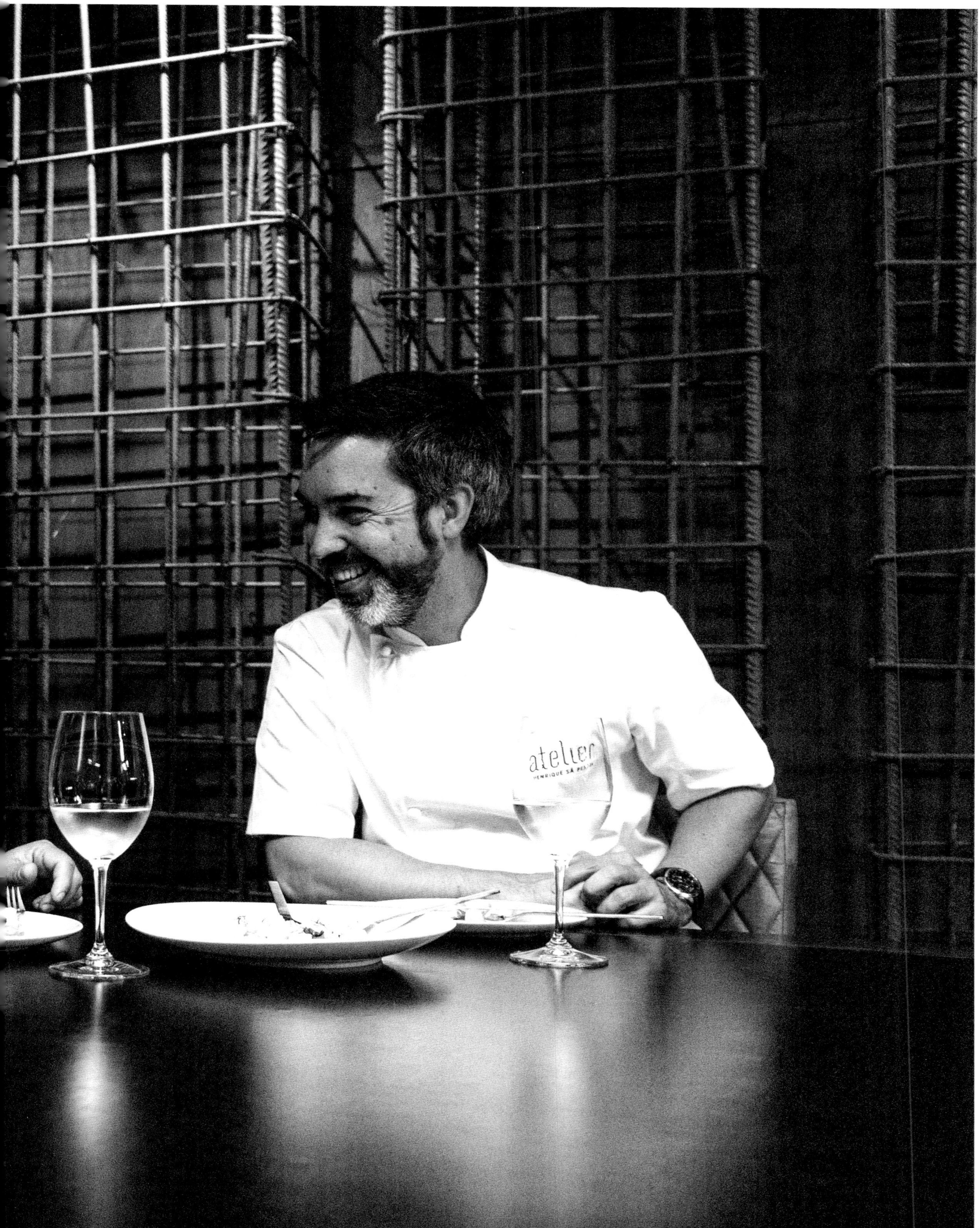
atelier

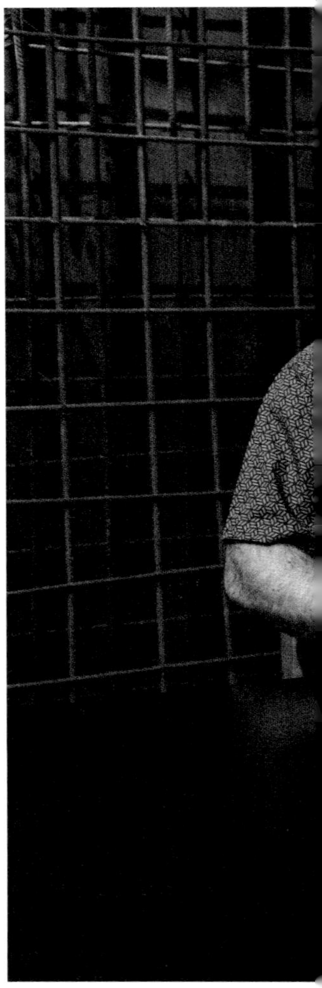

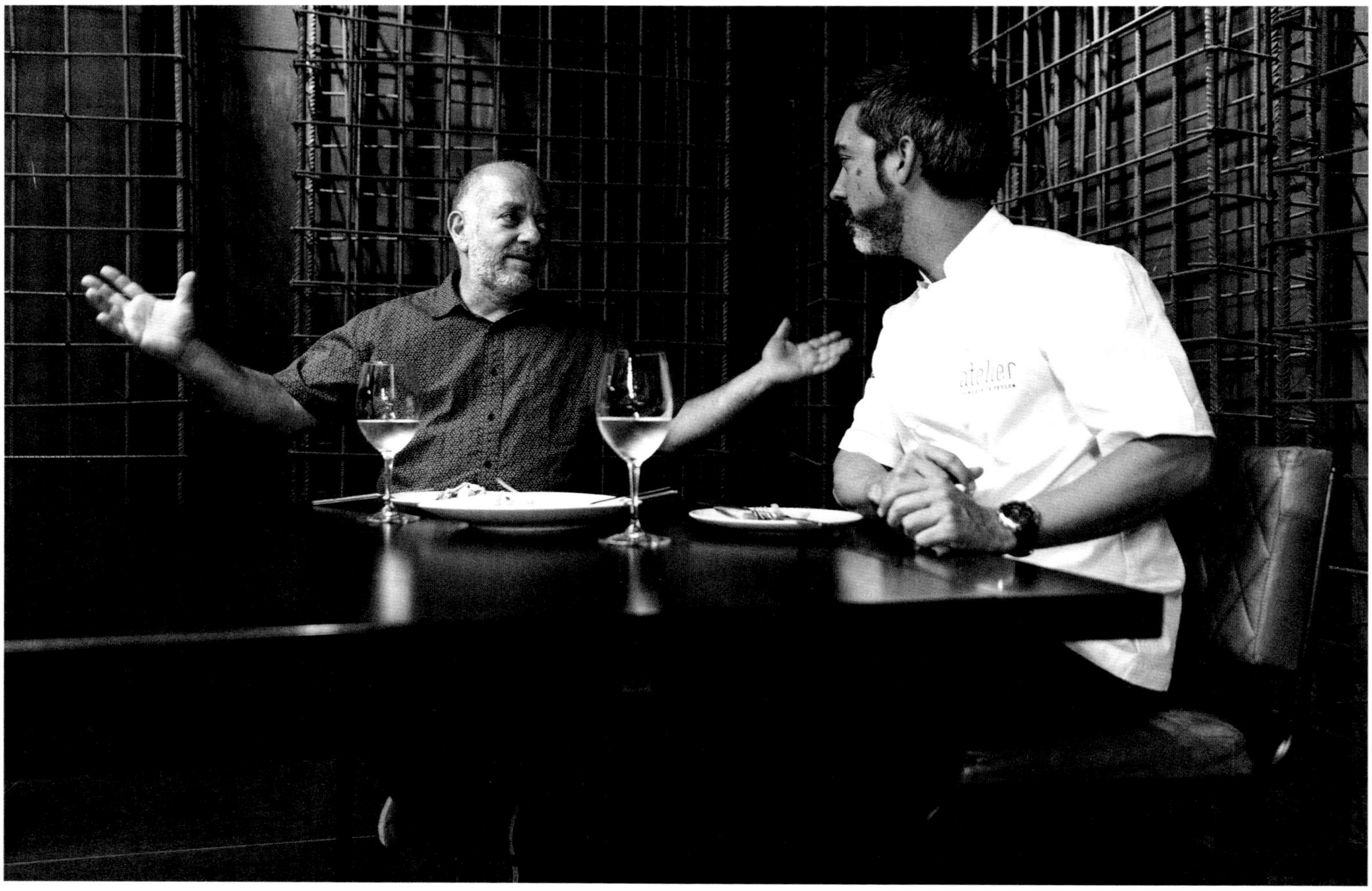

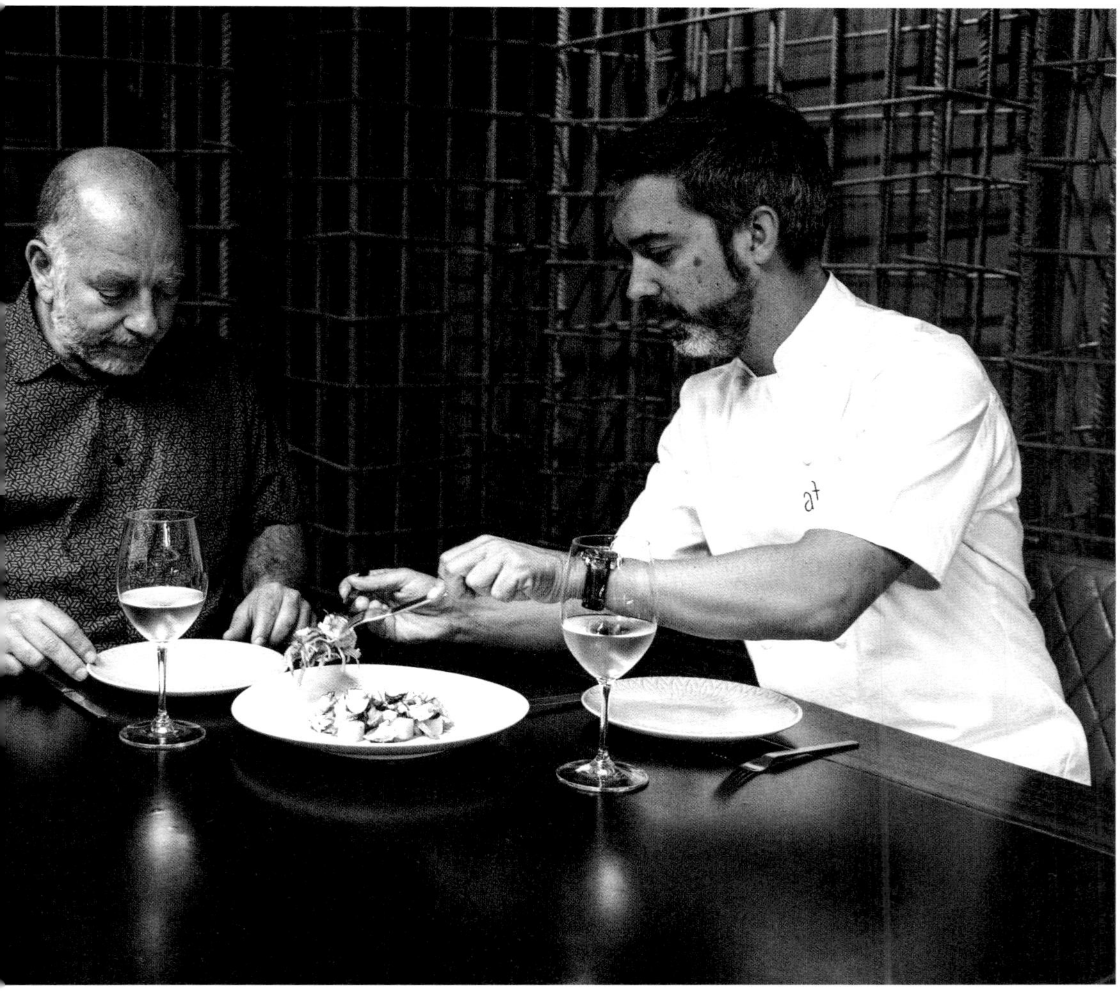

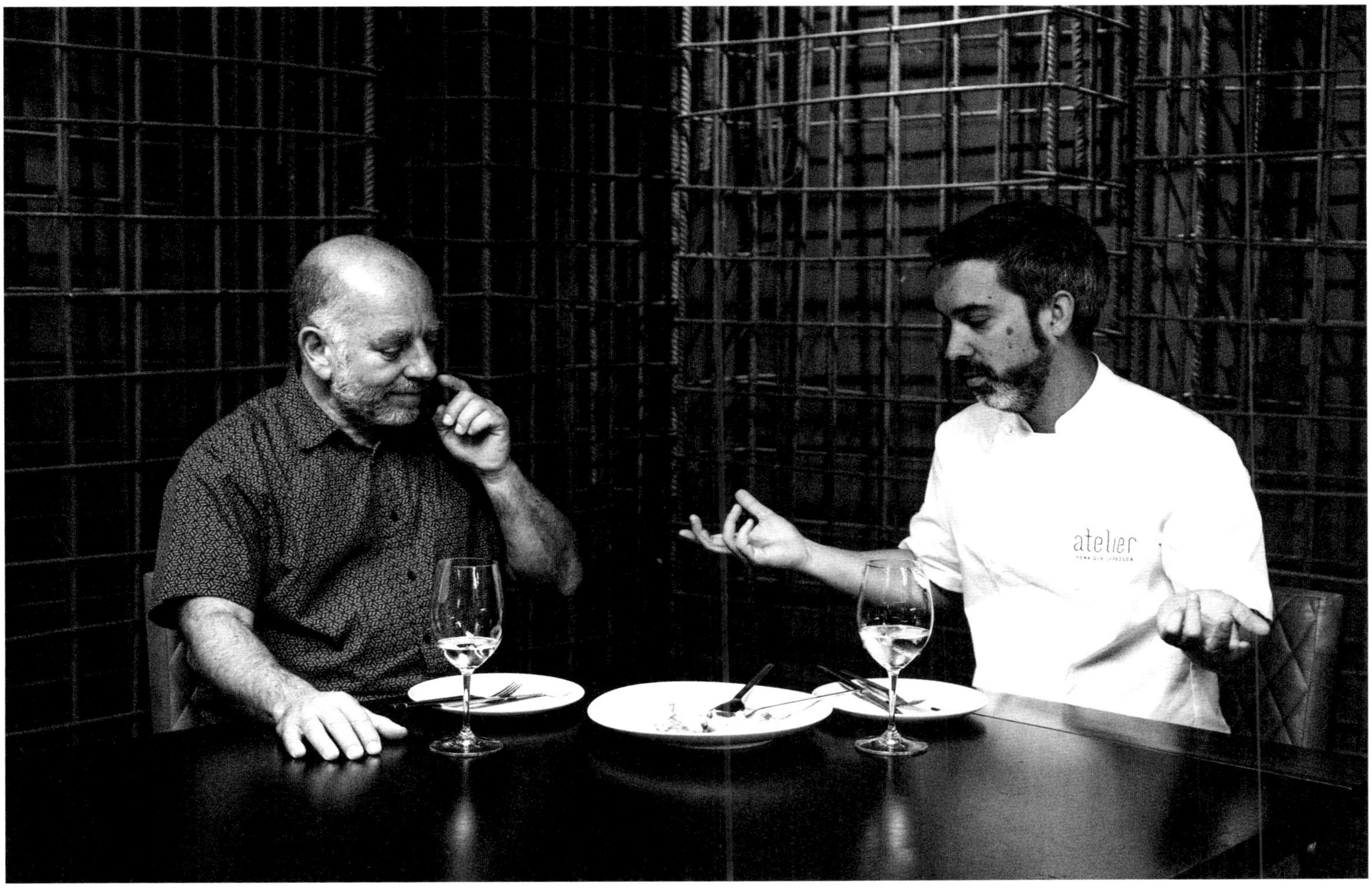
atelier

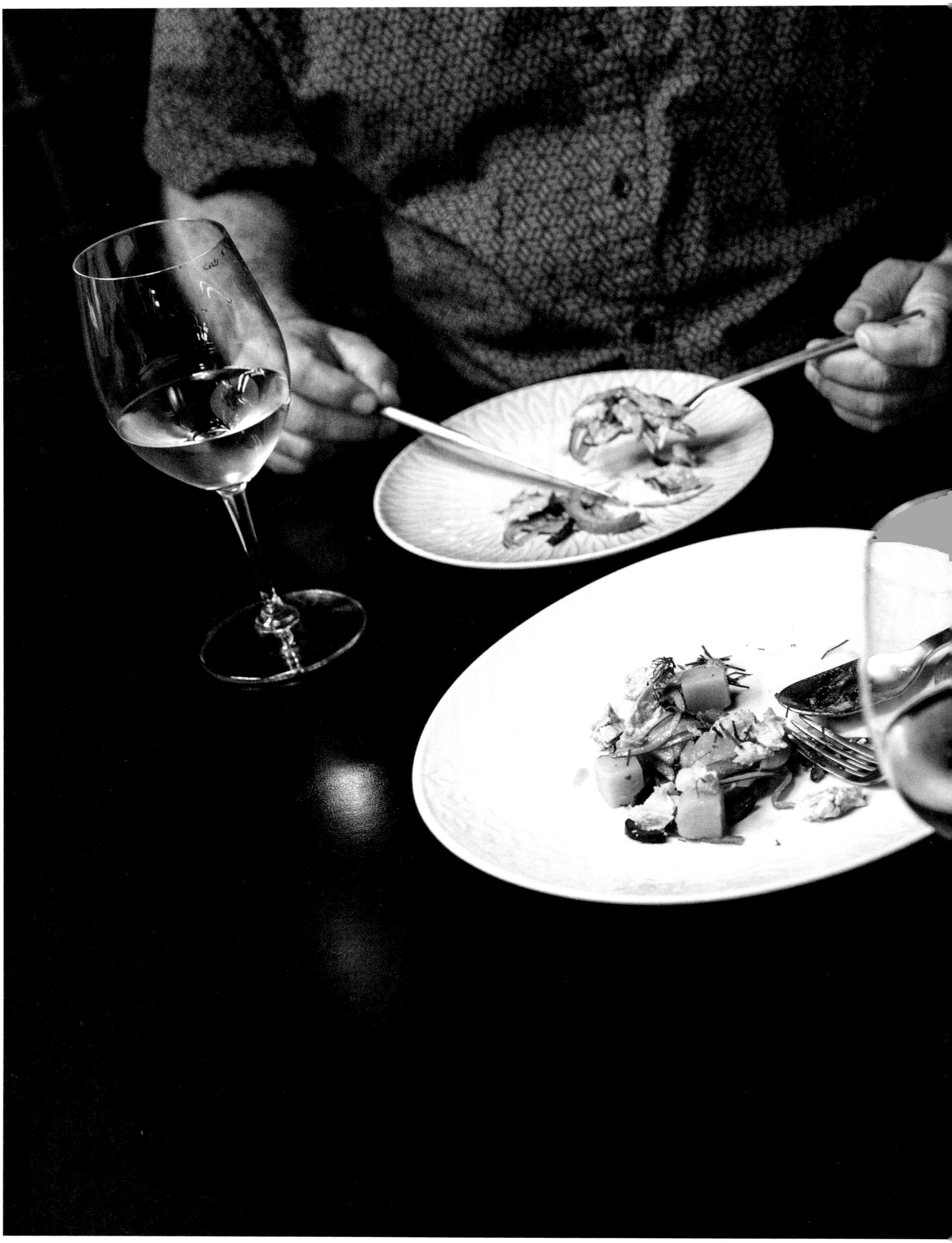

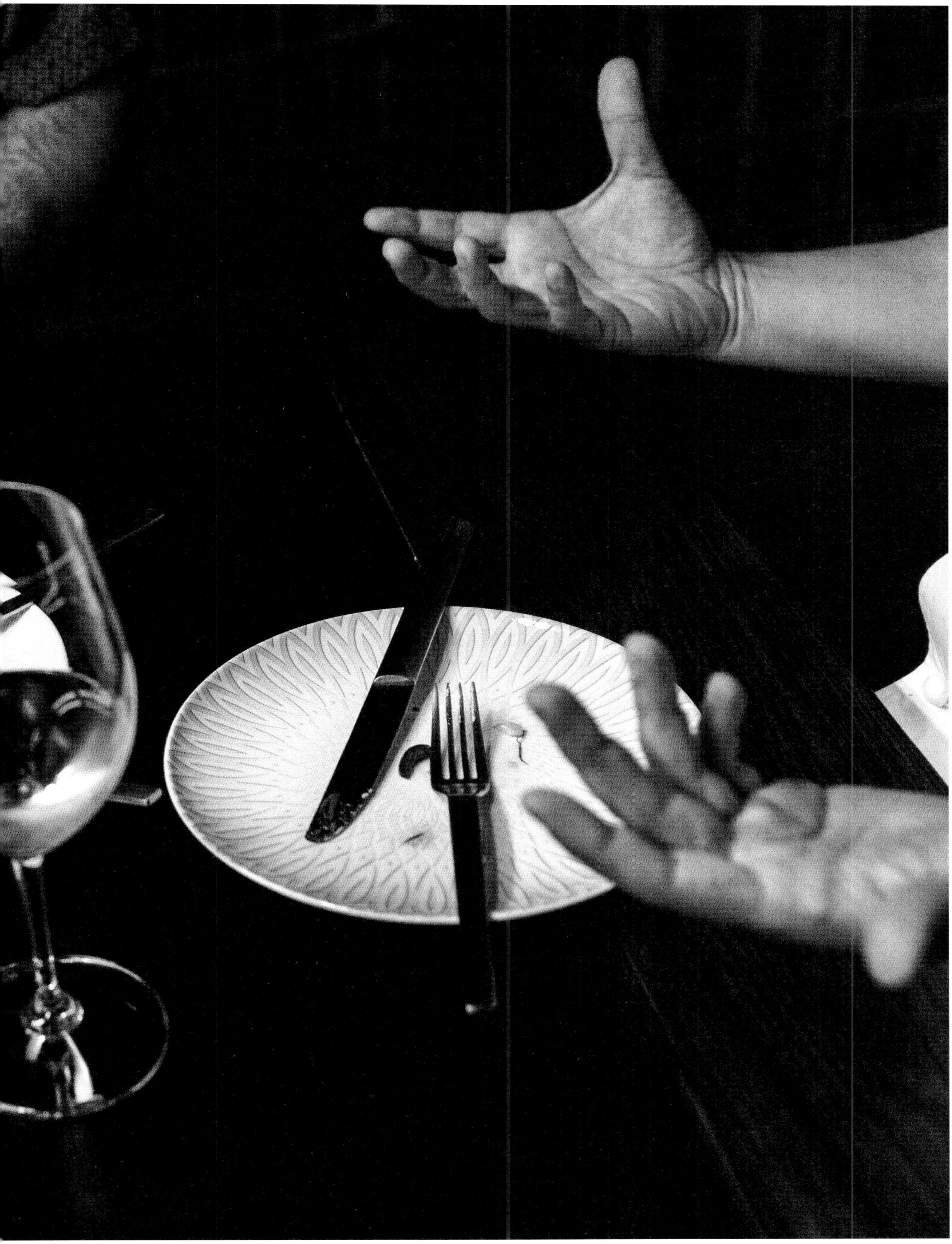

HENRIQUE SÁ PESSOA

SALAD OF
SMOKED SALMON
IN OLIVE OIL

SMOKED SALMON
IN OLIVE OIL
BRAND JANUS

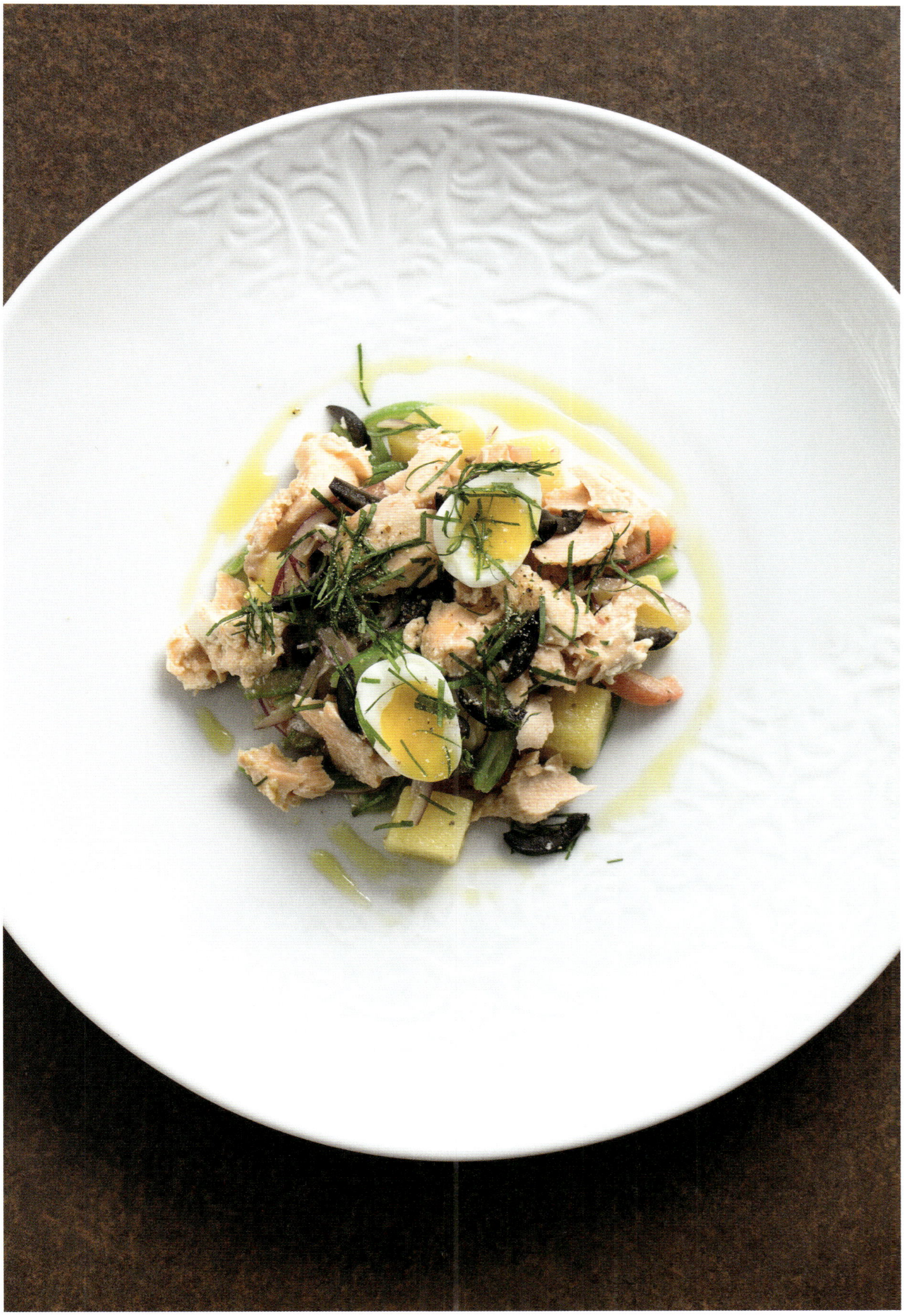

PACKED BY

2018

M I G

U E L

PRESSED CAN, METAL
CHAIN AND ACRYLIC BOX

P A L

M

10 × 21 × 30 CM

A

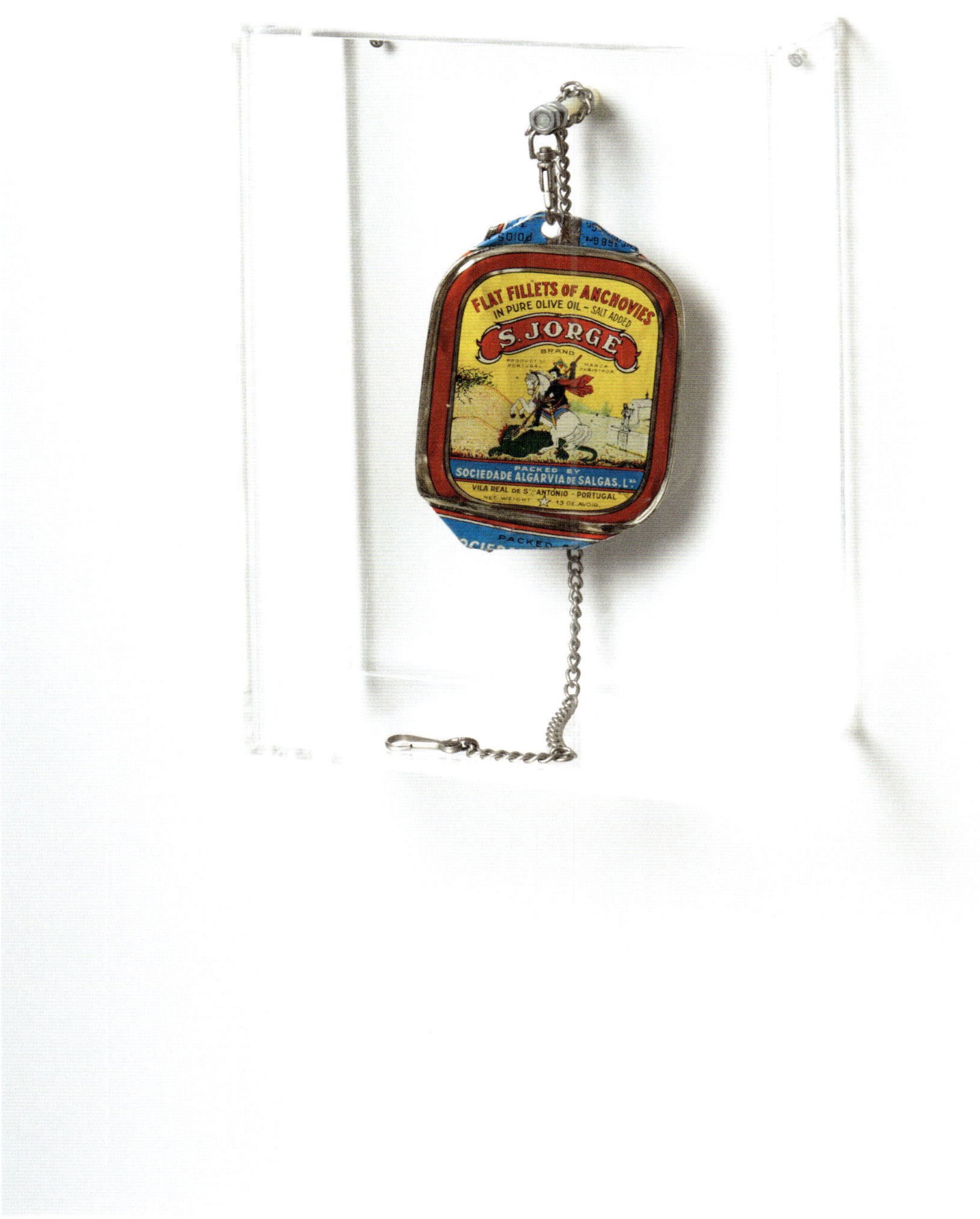
FLAT FILLETS OF ANCHOVIES
IN PURE OLIVE OIL – SALT ADDED
S. JORGE
BRAND
PACKED BY
SOCIEDADE ALGARVIA DE SALGAS, L.DA
VILA REAL DE S.TO ANTONIO - PORTUGAL

LEONEL
PEREIRA

PEDRO
GOMES

PEDRO
GOMES

LEONEL
PEREIRA

FLAVOUR COMES FROM TRADITION

The Algarve always announces itself by smell, something hard to explain but easy to understand. The car doors open and it invades us – something vegetable, citrus, tropical and African at the same time. It's holiday time, it's childhood, it's the Algarve.

Chef Leonel Pereira welcomes us to his Algarve restaurant São Gabriel and takes us to the table. The dish is ready and there's no time to lose – in Algarve it's high season almost all year round. We move on to the photos and it's Leonel who chooses the perspective. We can see the professionalism and care; nothing is left to chance.

The meeting between Pedro and Leonel is a duplicate: the first one likes to cook and the chef confesses to some abstract painting and "doodles" with the pen.

While the tuna *sangacho* poses for the photographer Jorge Simão, the conversation moves on. Pedro begins. "I started drawing early," he says. "I didn't know if I wanted to be an artist or an architect, so I did both courses."

And Leonel follows. "Well, with me it was the opposite," says the chef. "Until the age of 18 I didn't even know that men cooked. I applied to work in a bar because I wanted to have blonde, Swedish friends. Here, we start to enjoy nightlife very early – everyone had foreign girlfriends and I wanted one too. On the day I was due to start my job I was late – I used to do motocross and had been watching a race. They told me they already had a substitute but there was a job in the kitchen pantry. I said okay and I went down to the dungeons. I didn't think it would be for me, but I put up with it for a week, then more, then more. And there I still am."

"These days I wonder if I could have been an architect," says Leonel. "Architecture is the foundation for cooking."

And the inspiration? The method?

"I believe that flavour comes from tradition," says Leonel. "The rest is creativity. You know, I don't value recipes at all. My clients and my cooks are the ones with my recipes, I'm the chef without recipes!"

Now Pedro gives us his. "I have an idea, I think about the work and I let it sit for a few months, 'canned'. Then I come back and see if it's worth it."

Leonel laughs. "Your work lasts," he says. "Ours ends up in the toilet after a few hours."

"But the memory remains," offers Pedro.

"Just the memory, which fades and changes," says Leonel.

"On the other hand, ours isn't useful," says Pedro. "Yours is."

"Yes, but I'm not an artist," says Leonel. "Only sometimes, when I draw."

"Fair enough," replies Pedro. "My doodles are really a profession."

"In the kitchen, I'm zero artist," says Leonel. "But I'm creative. I just see myself as a cook after 15 years in the kitchen."

The conversation is coming to an end. A lot has been said and a lot remains to be said. Pedro and Leonel embrace and exchange contacts. A sentence remains: provocative, disenchanted. It's Leonel who says it.

"You know, this world isn't really art. It's a difficult, unstable world. But it's *a la mode*. In truth, if you need to wait 15 or 20 years to get this far only to see those kids setting themselves up as stars, well, fuck cooking!"

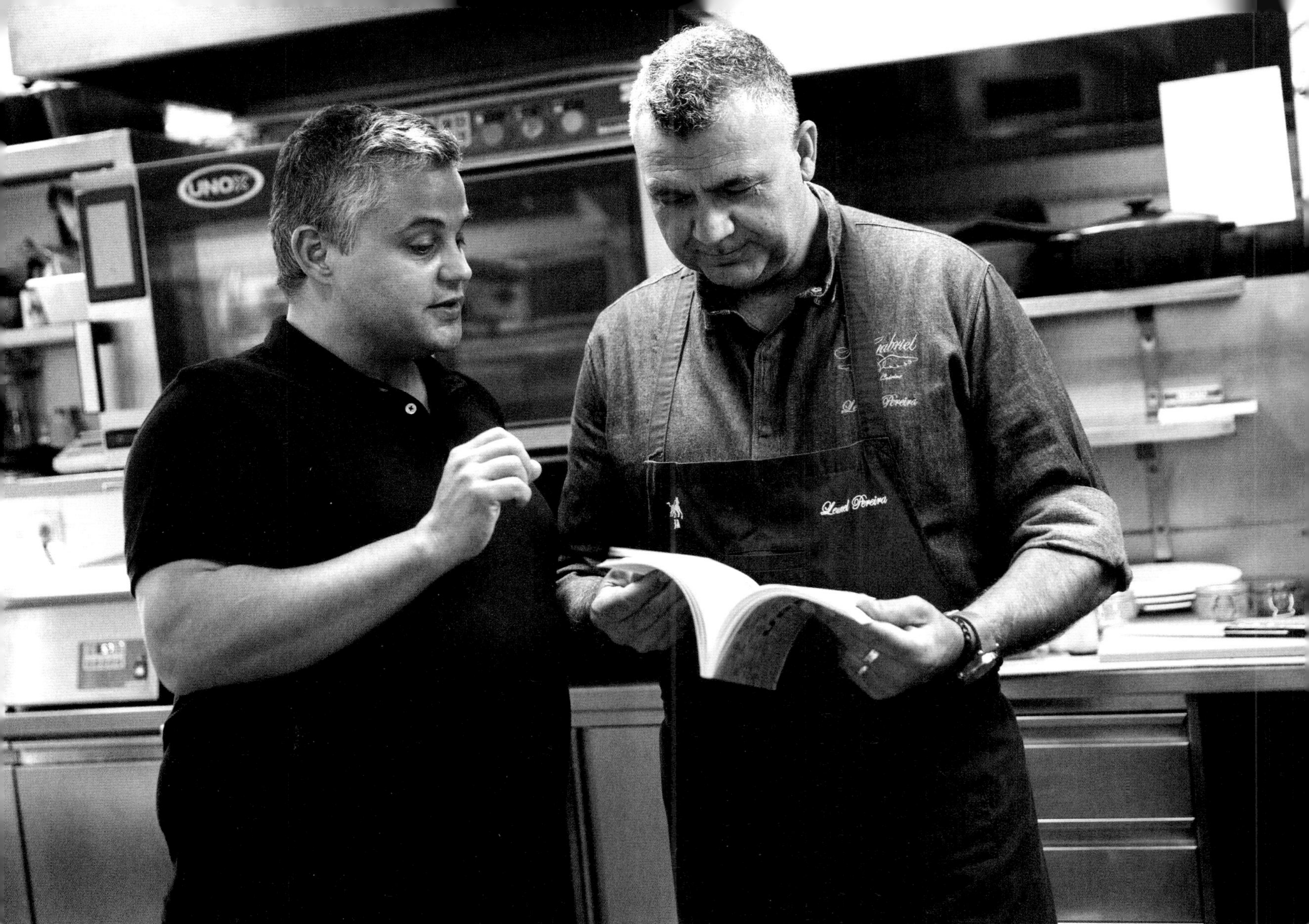
UNOX

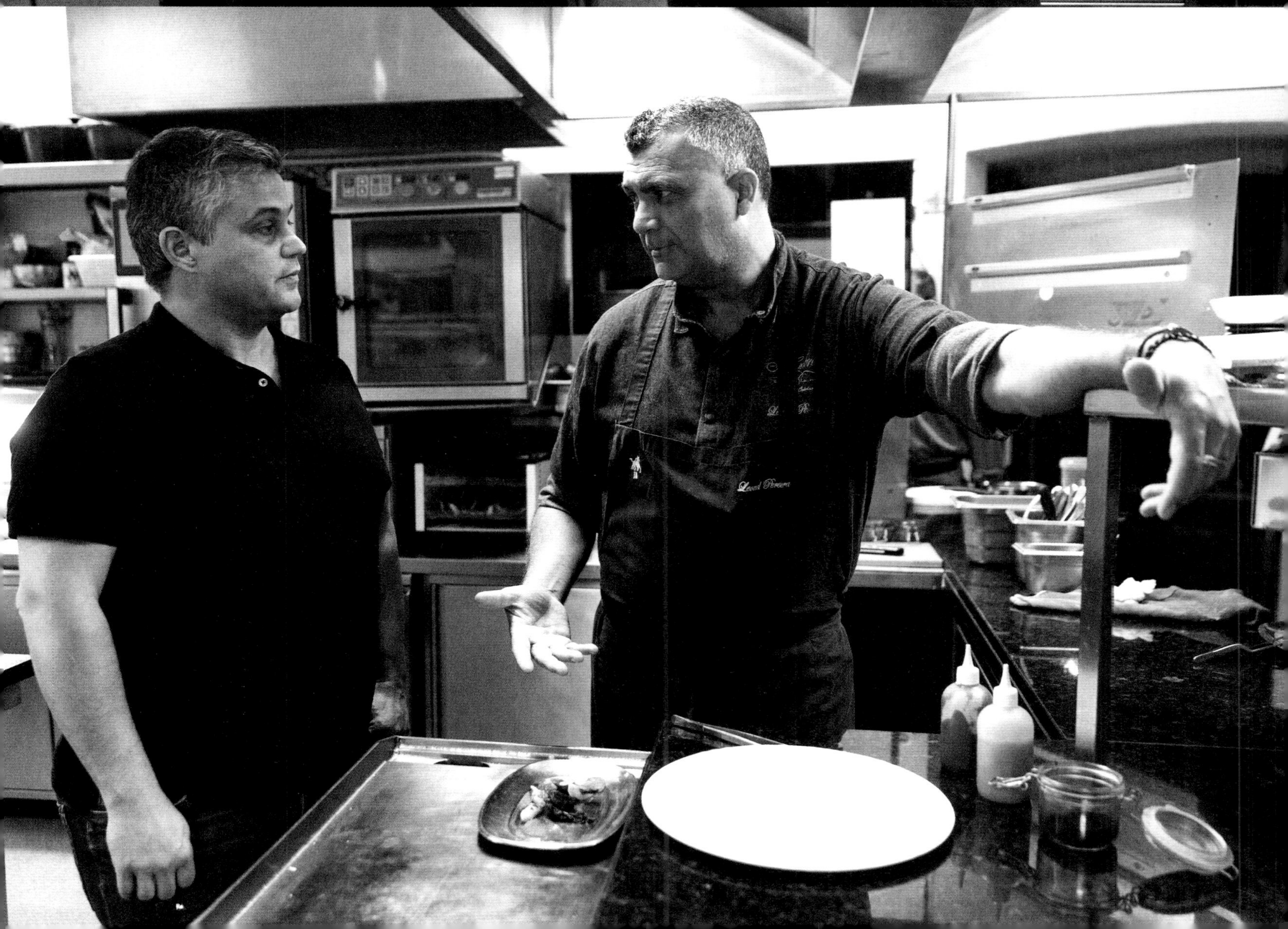

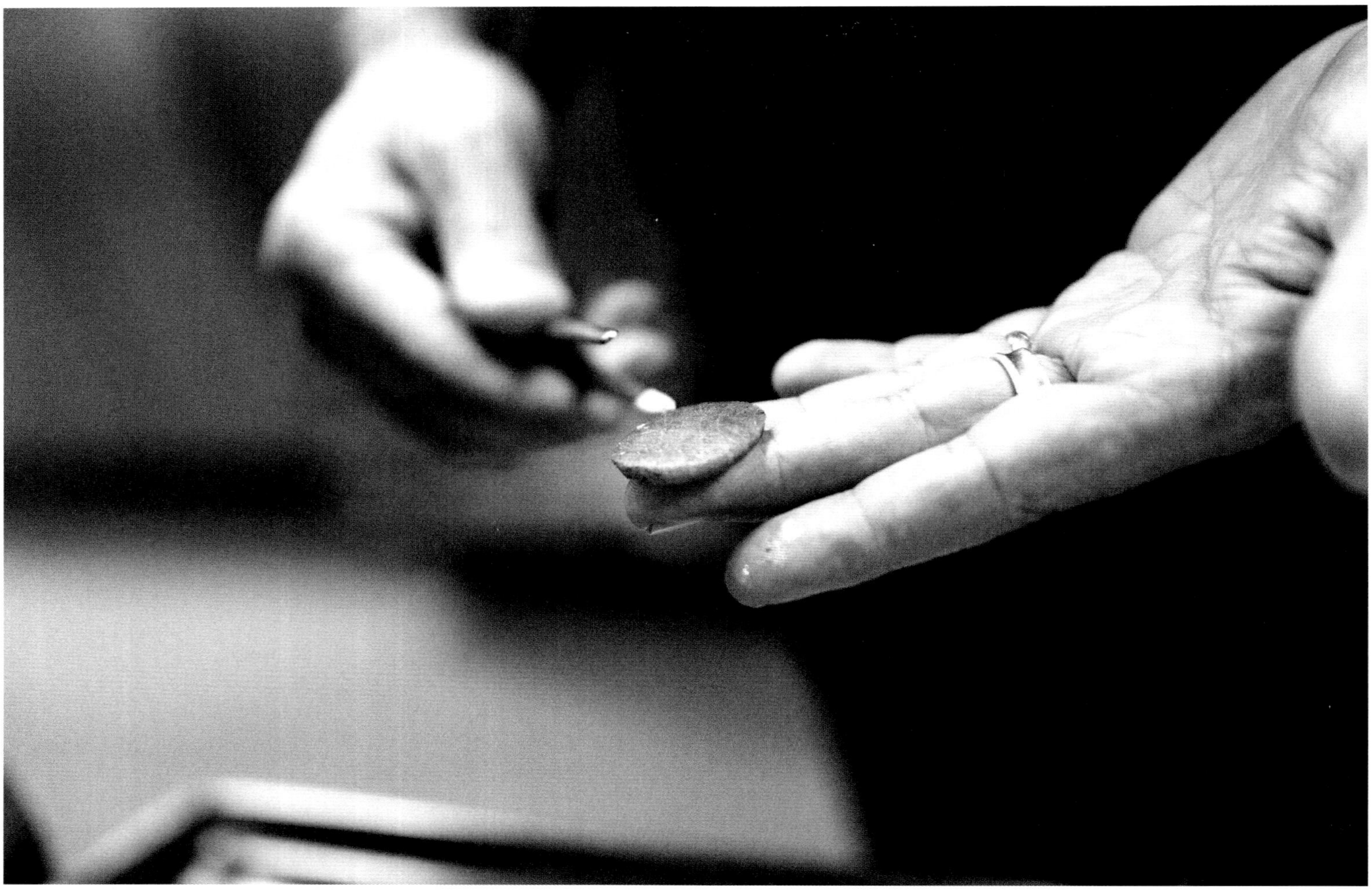

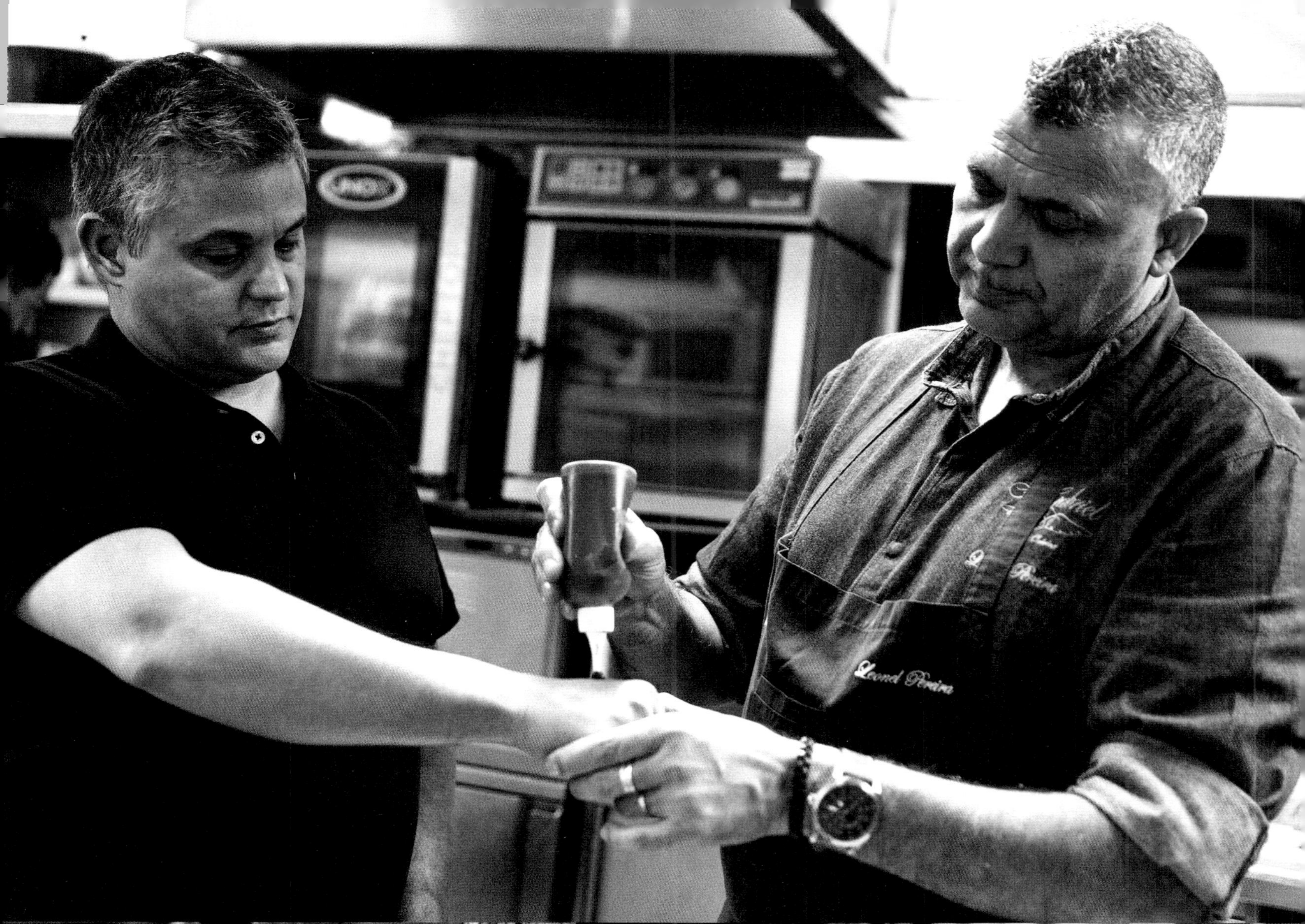
Leonel Pereira

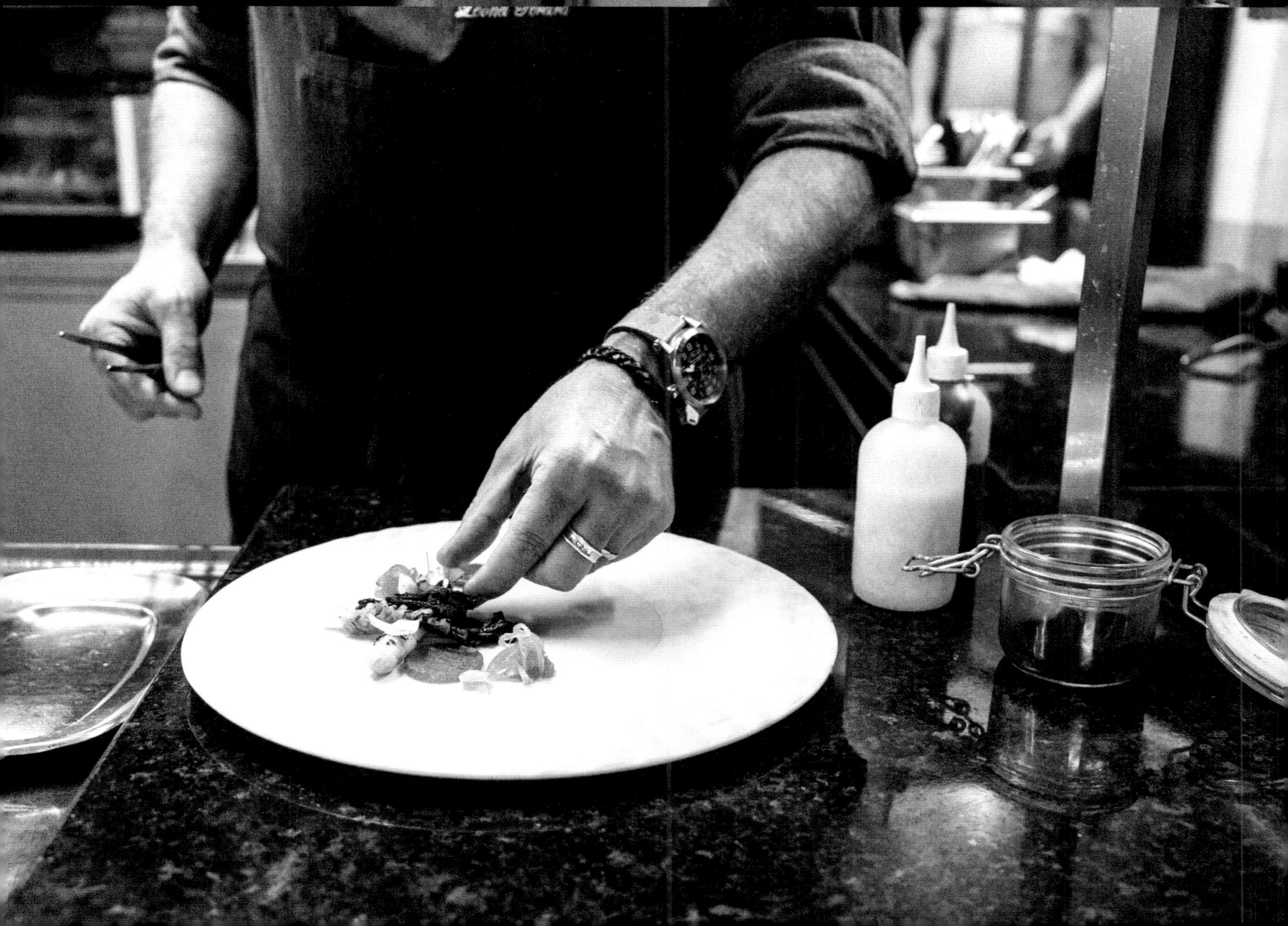

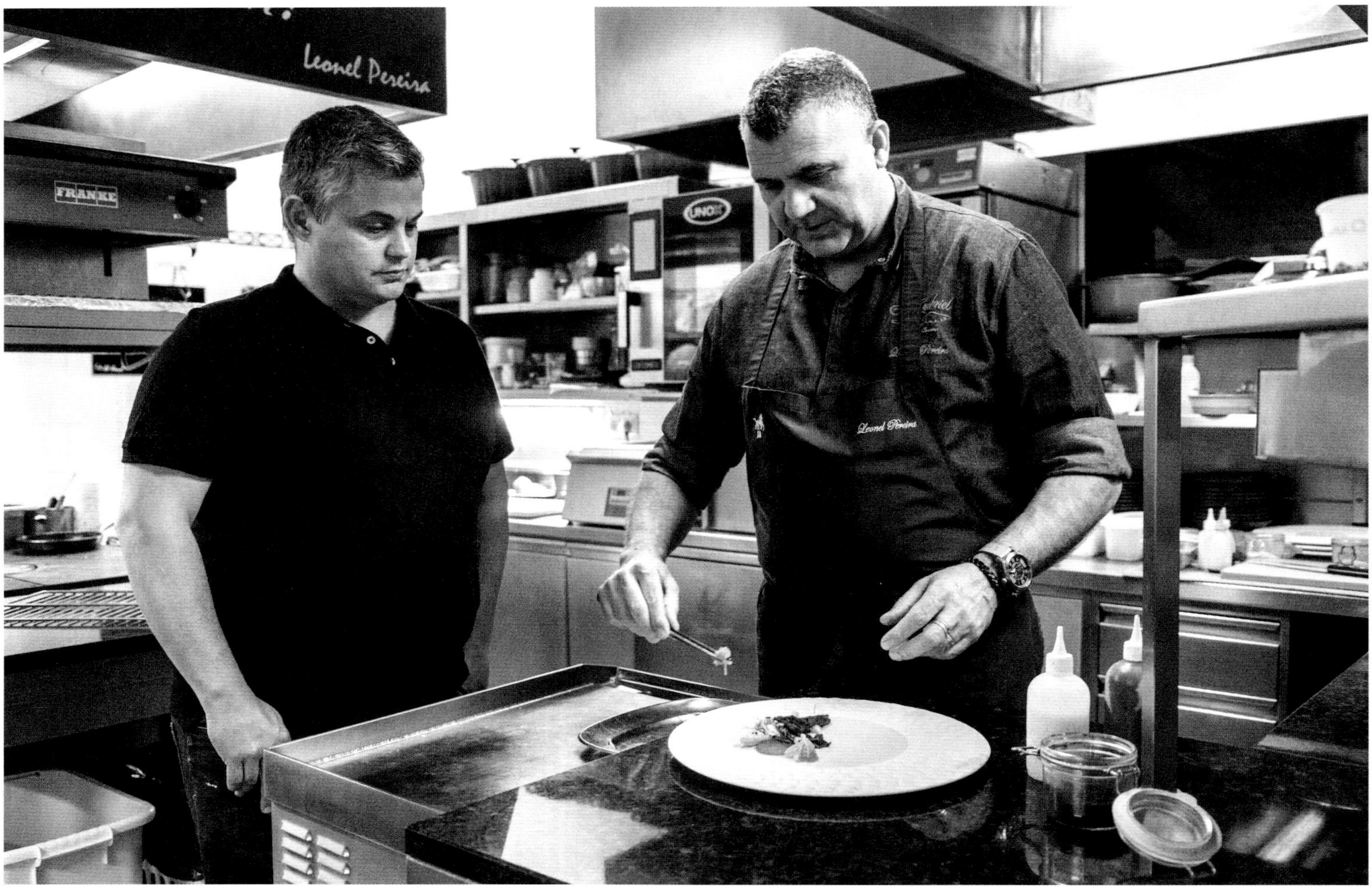
Leonel Pereira
FRANKE
Leonel Pereira

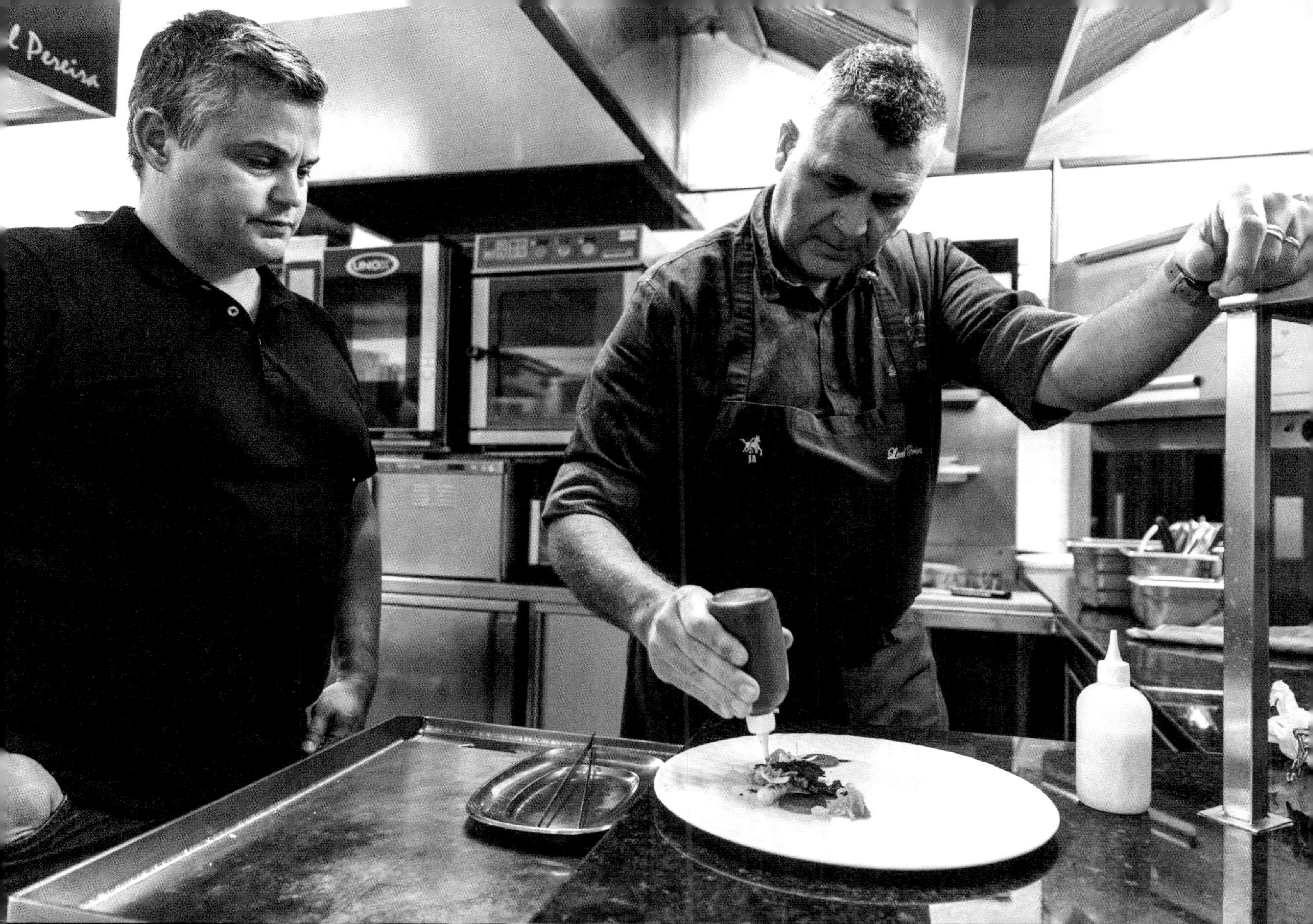
Pereira
UNOX

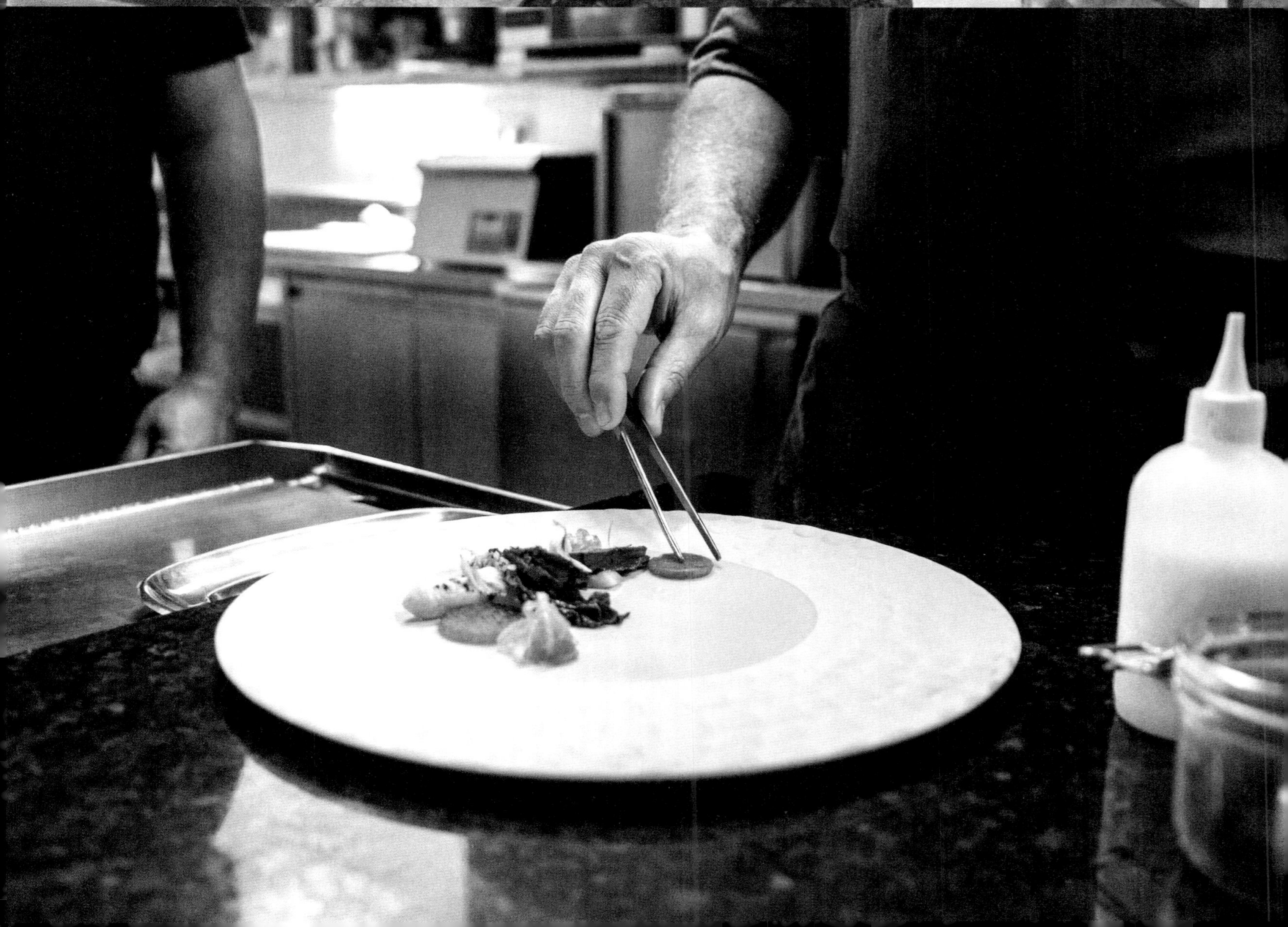

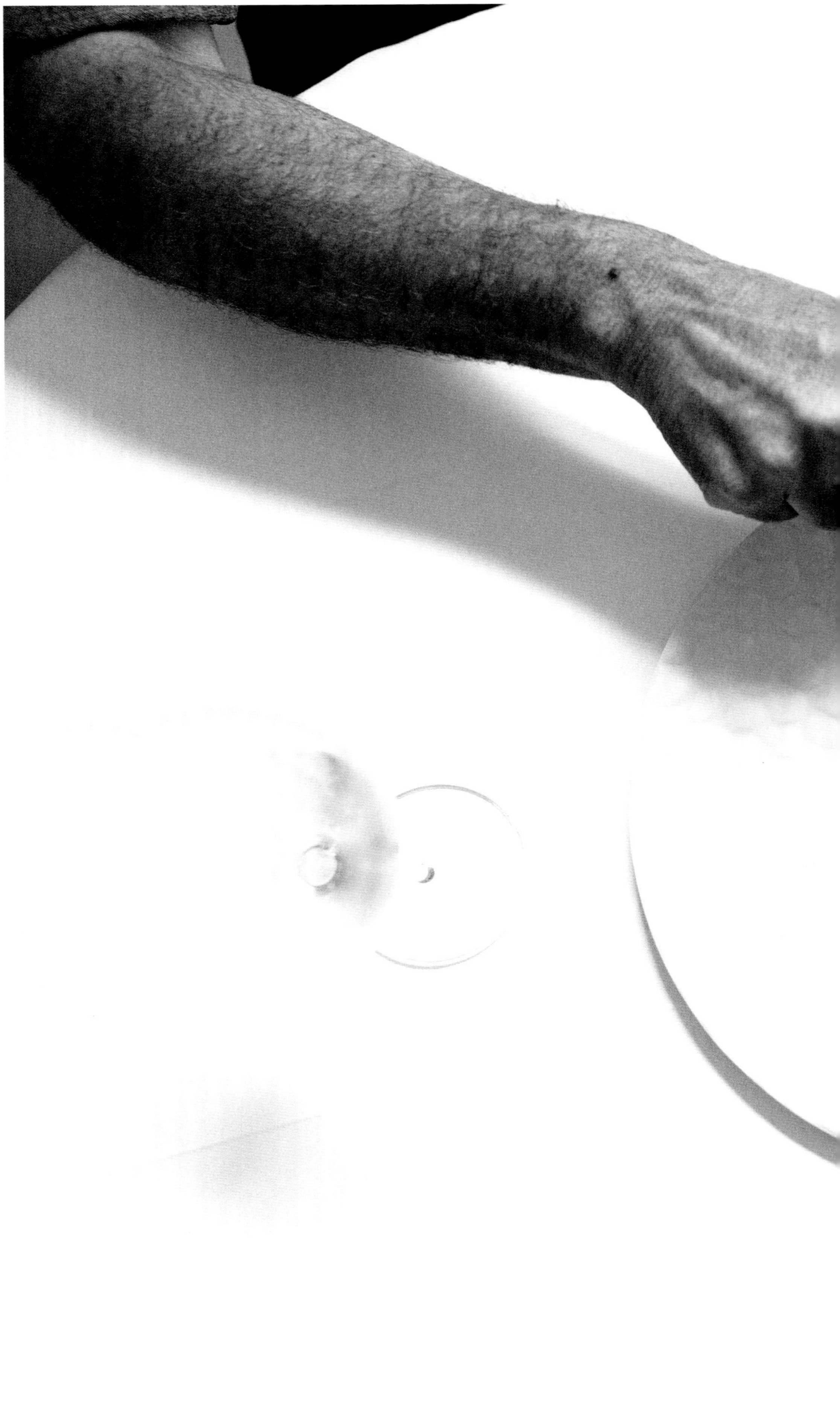

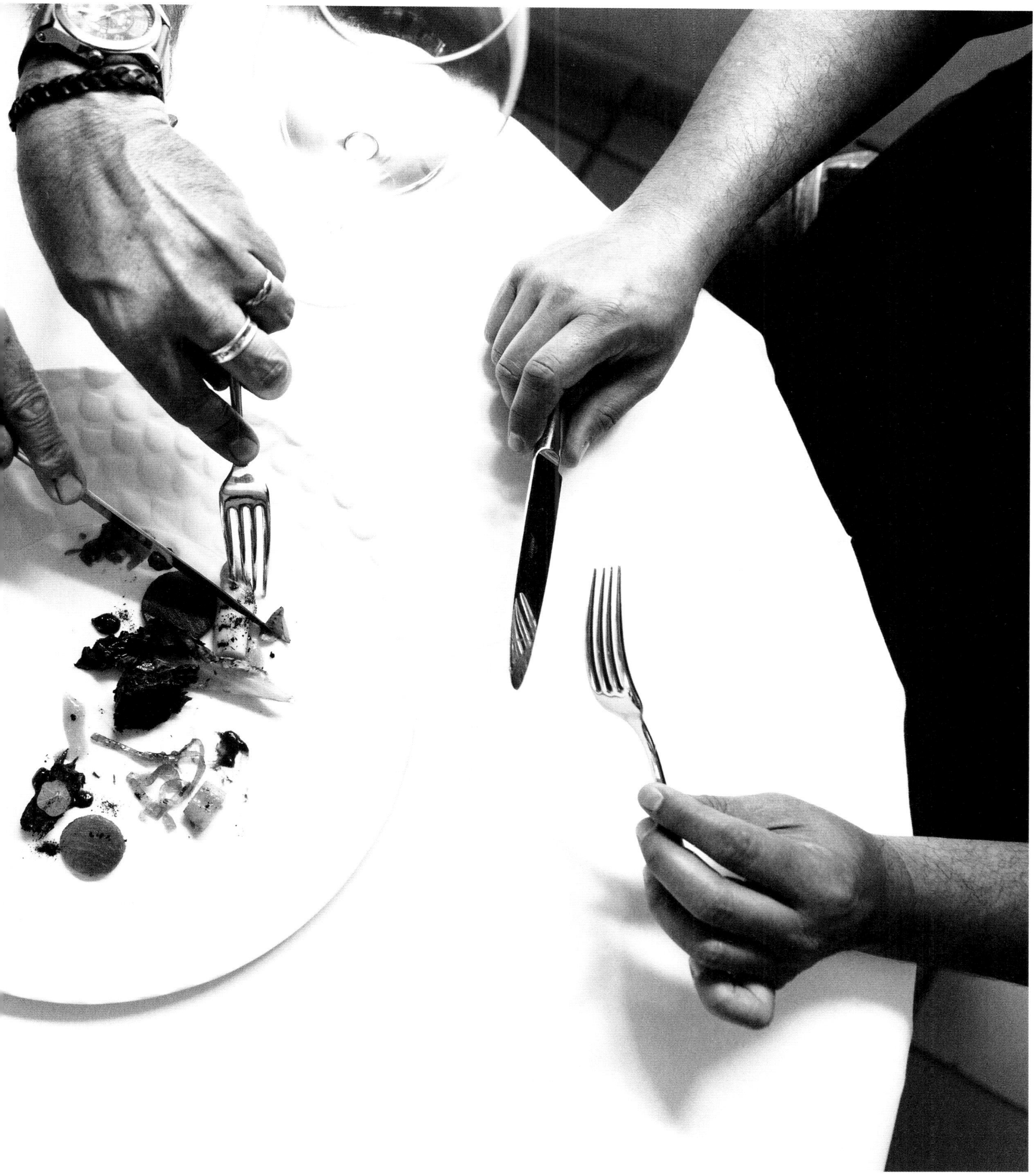

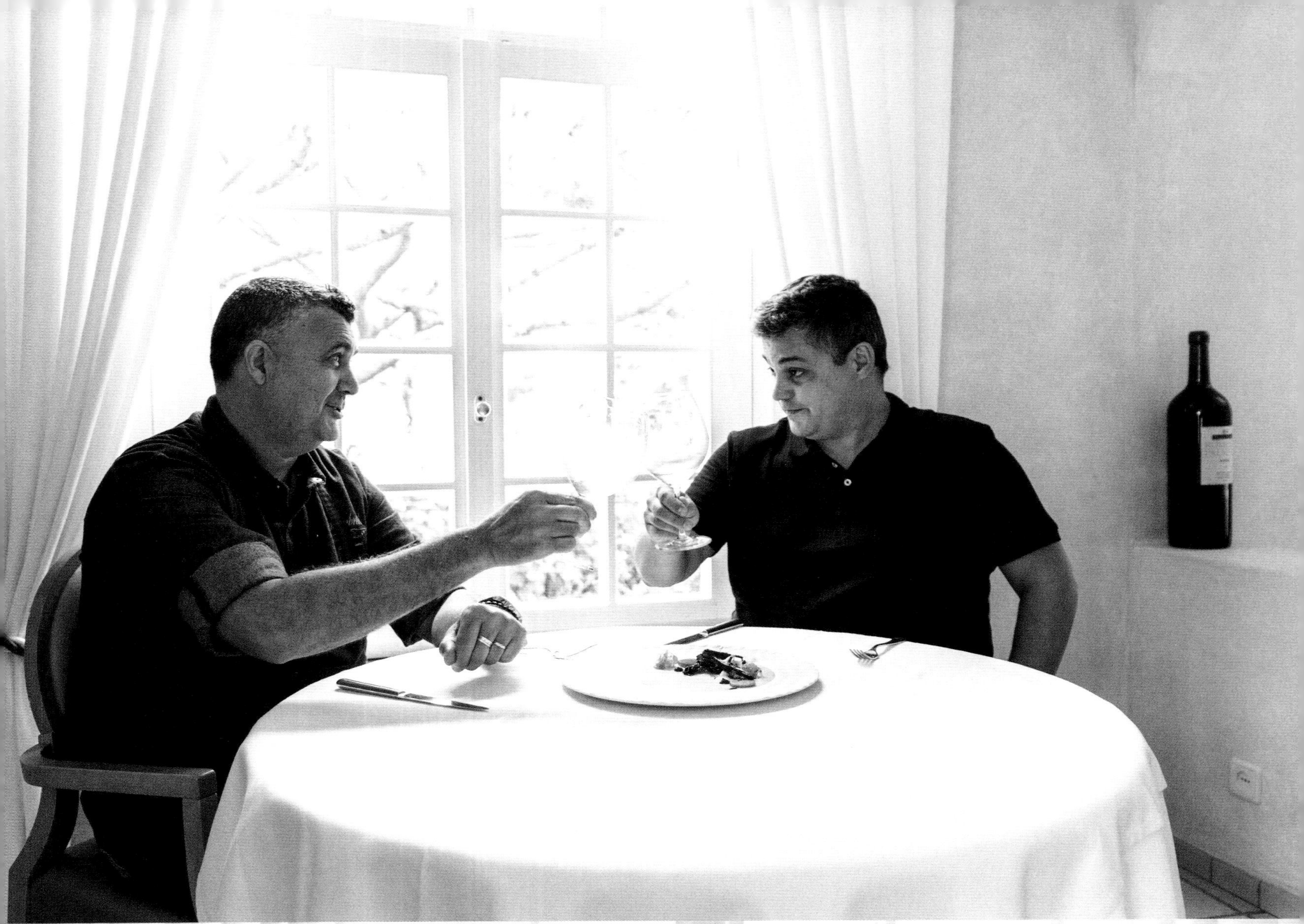

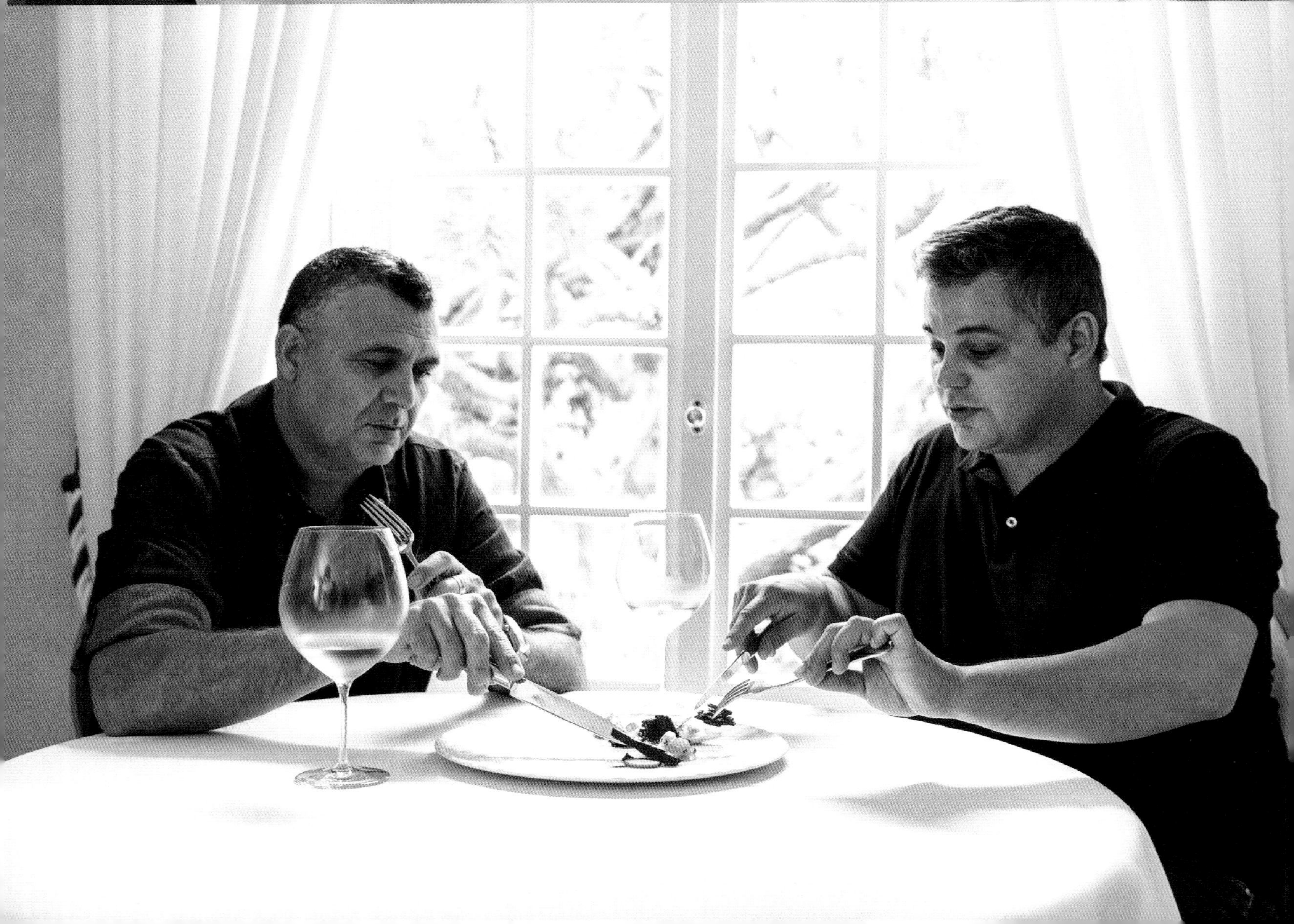

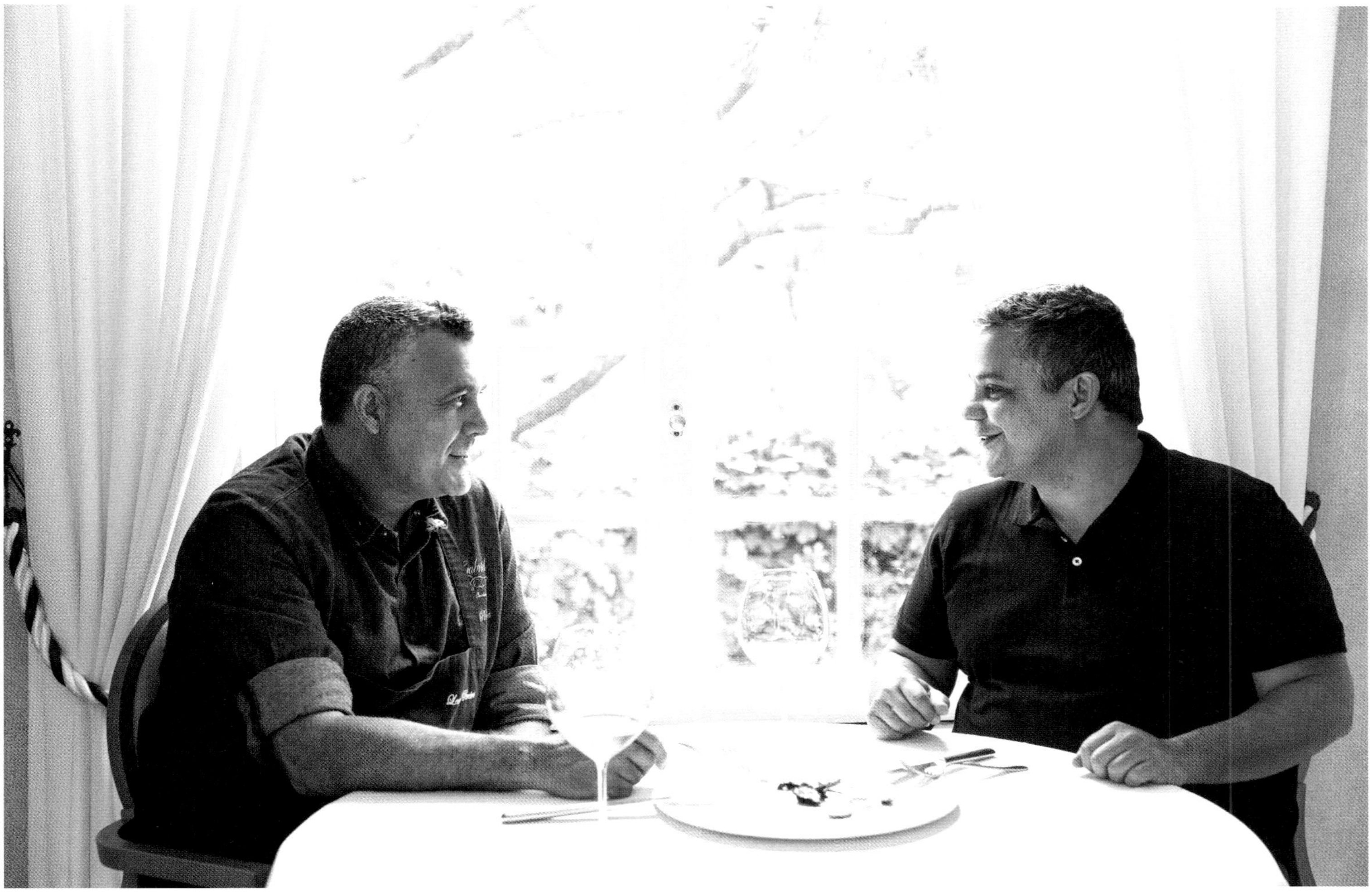

LEO NEL

TUNA SANGACHO WITH
BEETS, CRYSTALLIZED ONION
AND CUCUMBER GEL

PER EIRA

TUNA SANGACHO
BRAND SANTA CATARINA

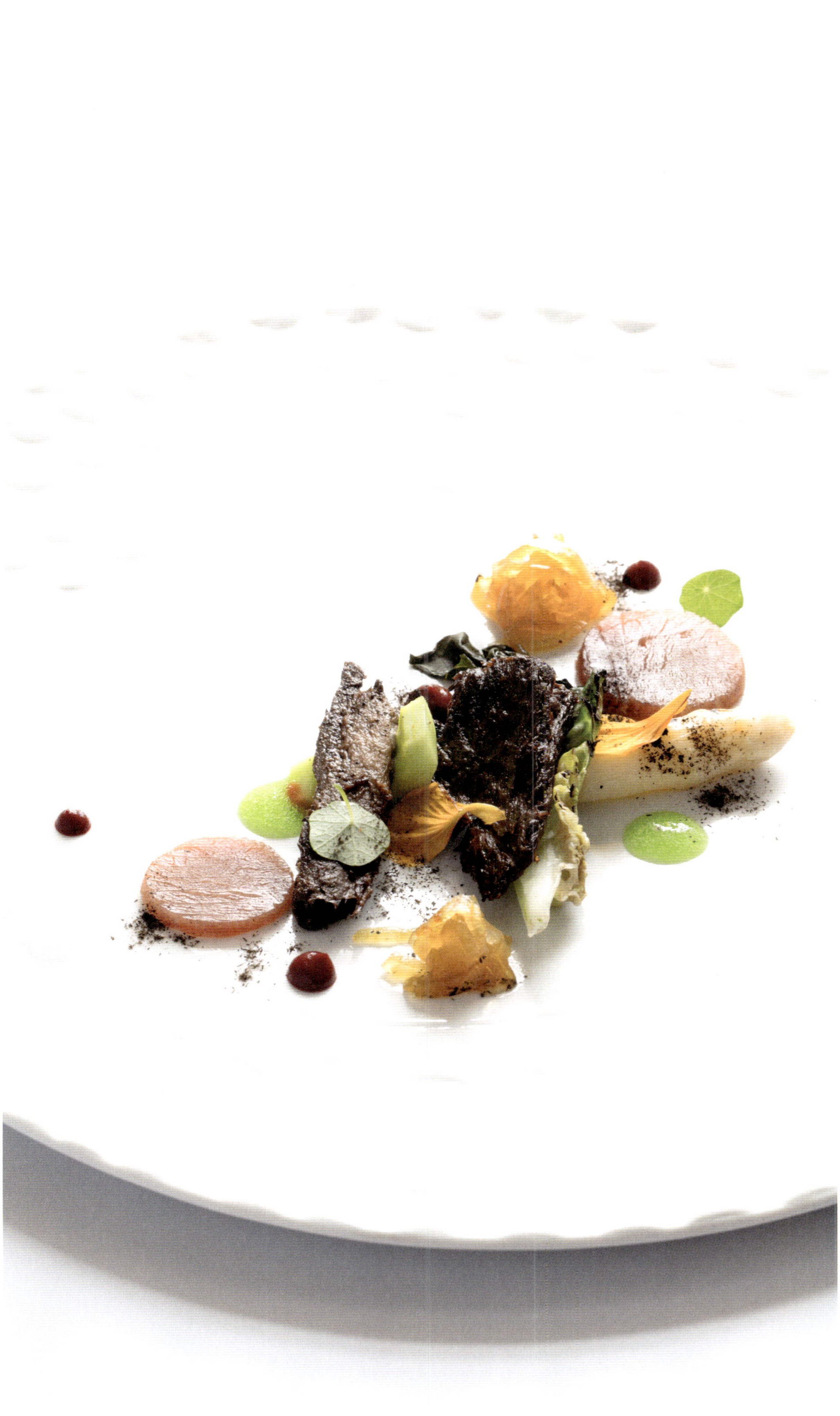

PEDRO GOMES

POLVO

2018

286

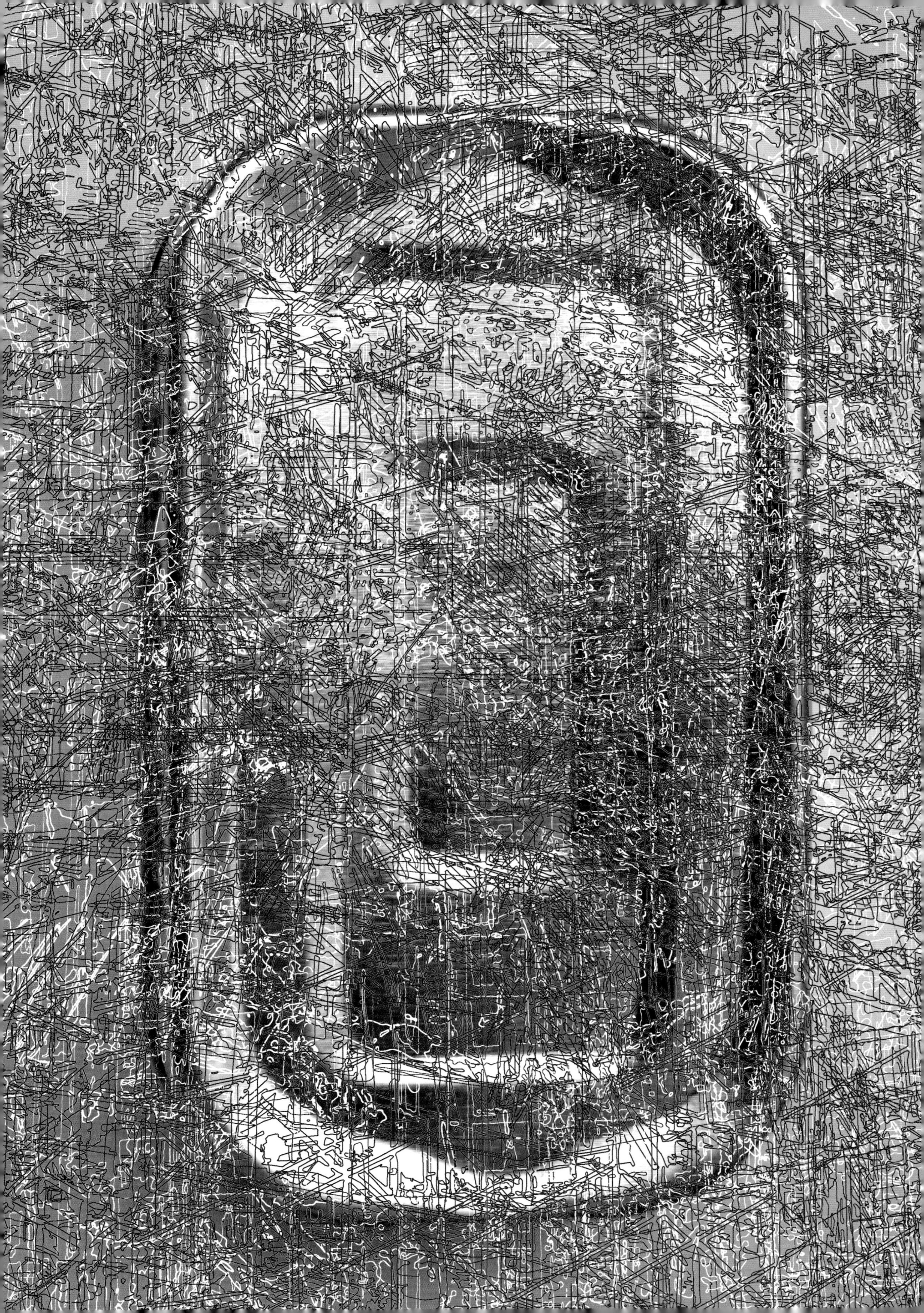

JOSÉ
JÚLIO
VINTÉM

ANTÓNIO
NEVES
NOBRE

ANTÓNIO
NEVES
NOBRE

JOSÉ
JÚLIO
VINTÉM

JOSÉ JÚLIO VINTÉM
ANTÓNIO NEVES NOBRE

FINALLY, AN ARTIST WHO EATS AND DRINKS

Portalegre is situated in the interior of Portugal, in a rural area where there is still much to explore – the landscape, the people, the products. And, above all, the Tomba Lobos restaurant of José Júlio Vintém – known as 'Zé' – where you can taste his delicacies, listen to his stories and drink his wines.

In the end, you can find everything in Portalegre. It's Zé who says it. "I've been here for 46 years now and I don't plan to leave," he says. "This place wants for nothing."

We discover that the artist António Neves Nobre has origins in Portalegre. The town is bigger than it seems.

As sauces and local sausage arrive, Zé asks: "So, do you like it? If you don't, it's because you're not hungry." But we do like it. A lot.

António is earning Júlio's respect. "Finally, an artist who eats and drinks."

The small plates arrive in their own time: eggs with truffles, bacon petals, little cheeses that taste like big cheeses, pork belly, ears and other temptations. All with a wickedly divine refinement. We eat, we drink and we talk. The talk is between artists, so we talk about art.

"The artist begins in doubt," Zé says. "There's nothing more beautiful than witnessing the insecurity of the human being. You know, every time I've felt certain and overconfident, things have gone wrong."

And inspiration?

António says it comes from everything that gives him pleasure, an infallible criterion. "Then, I don't know," he says. "I try to communicate an idea made of many ideas."

And subjectivity? "If I chew to the left side, it might taste like pepper," says Zé. "If I chew to the right, it will taste like good sausage."

António thinks, drains another glass and answers. "I try to practise an art that has the maximum possibilities for those who see it," he says. "That's why I don't give titles to my work."

Things are becoming more complex. We move on to ambitions, first Zé, then António:

"My dream is to invent a technique," says Zé.

"Mine is to invent a dish without technique," says António.

"Almost everything has been invented..." says Zé.

"I'm not so sure," says António.

Silence, complicit smiles, superficial disagreements sit atop a deeper understanding.

And books?

For Zé it is *Perfume*, by Patrick Süskind. António talks of the Austrian poet and novelist Rainer Maria Rilke.

"At the age of 14, I had to fight against Rilke to settle myself," says António. "I rebelled and faced life. Either you are an artist or you're not. I made my move, I wanted to be one."

Many hours pass. We are full, we have surrendered to so many flavours and ideas. Zé saves a final stab. A firewater liquor, to chop finely.

Then, before we leave, coffee, water and fresh air for everyone. Zé grasps António's shoulder and asks, defiant: "But, in the end, how many people value me and how many value you? How do you combat that?"

"We don't fight," replies António. "We don't need to fight."

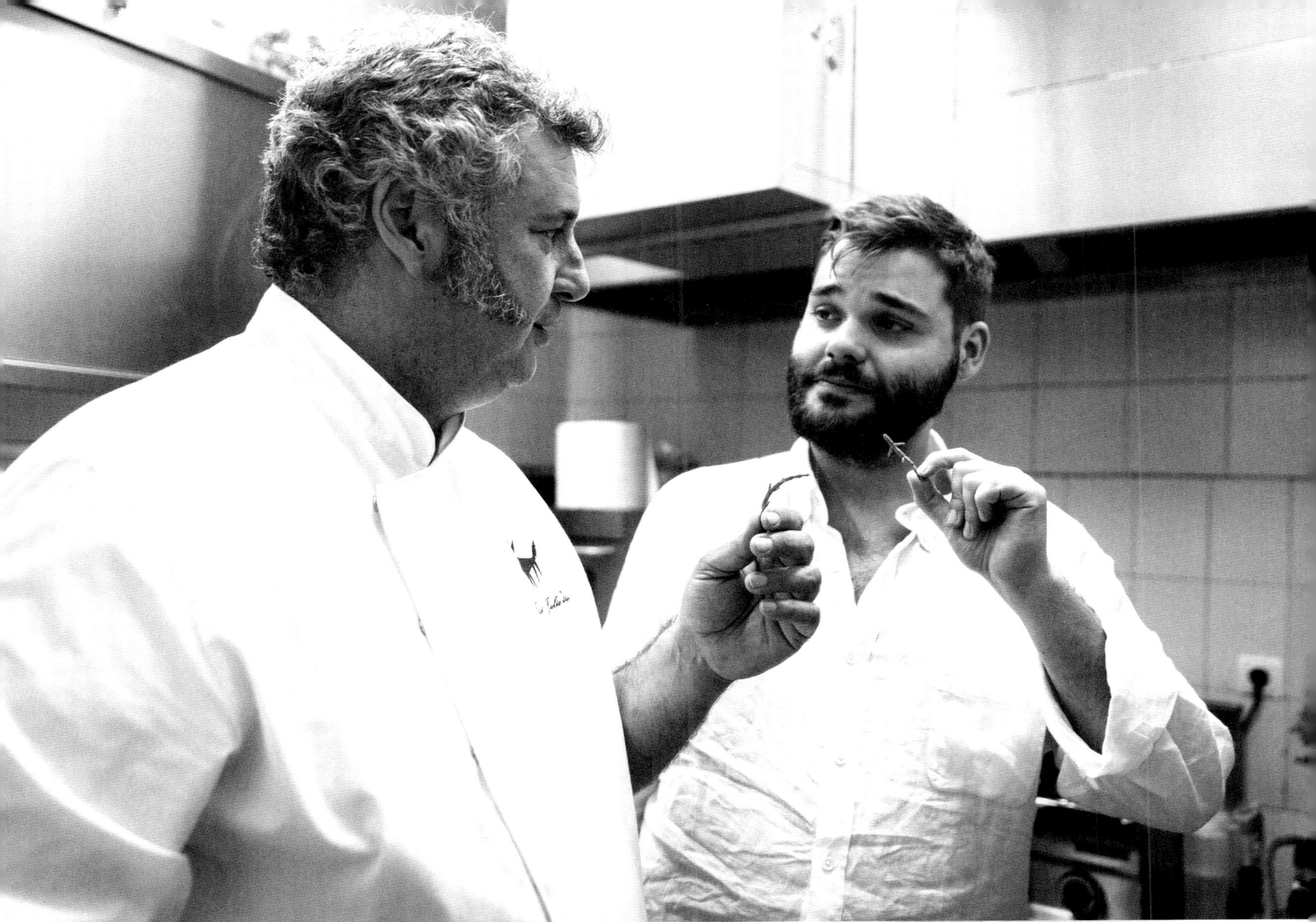

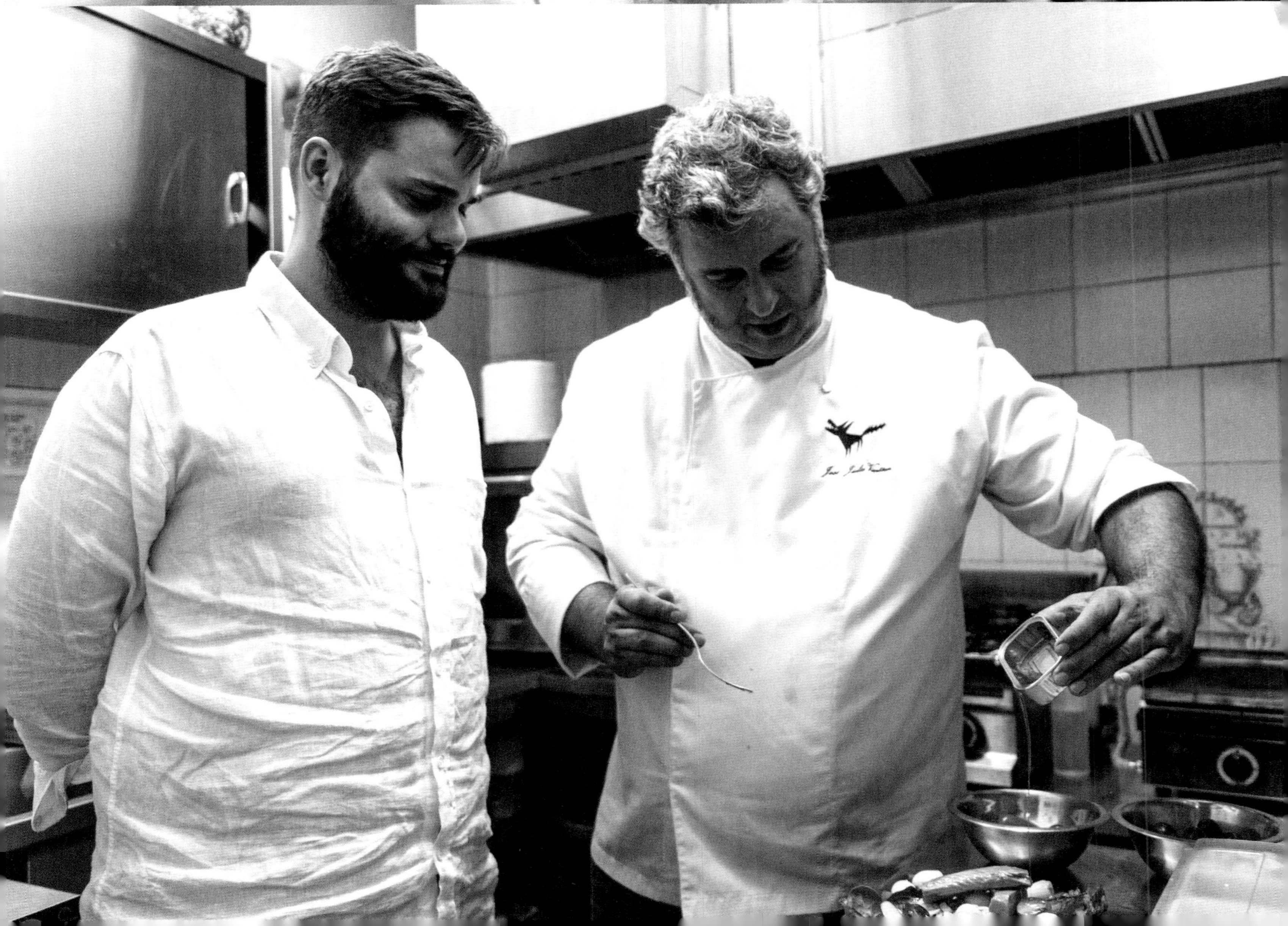

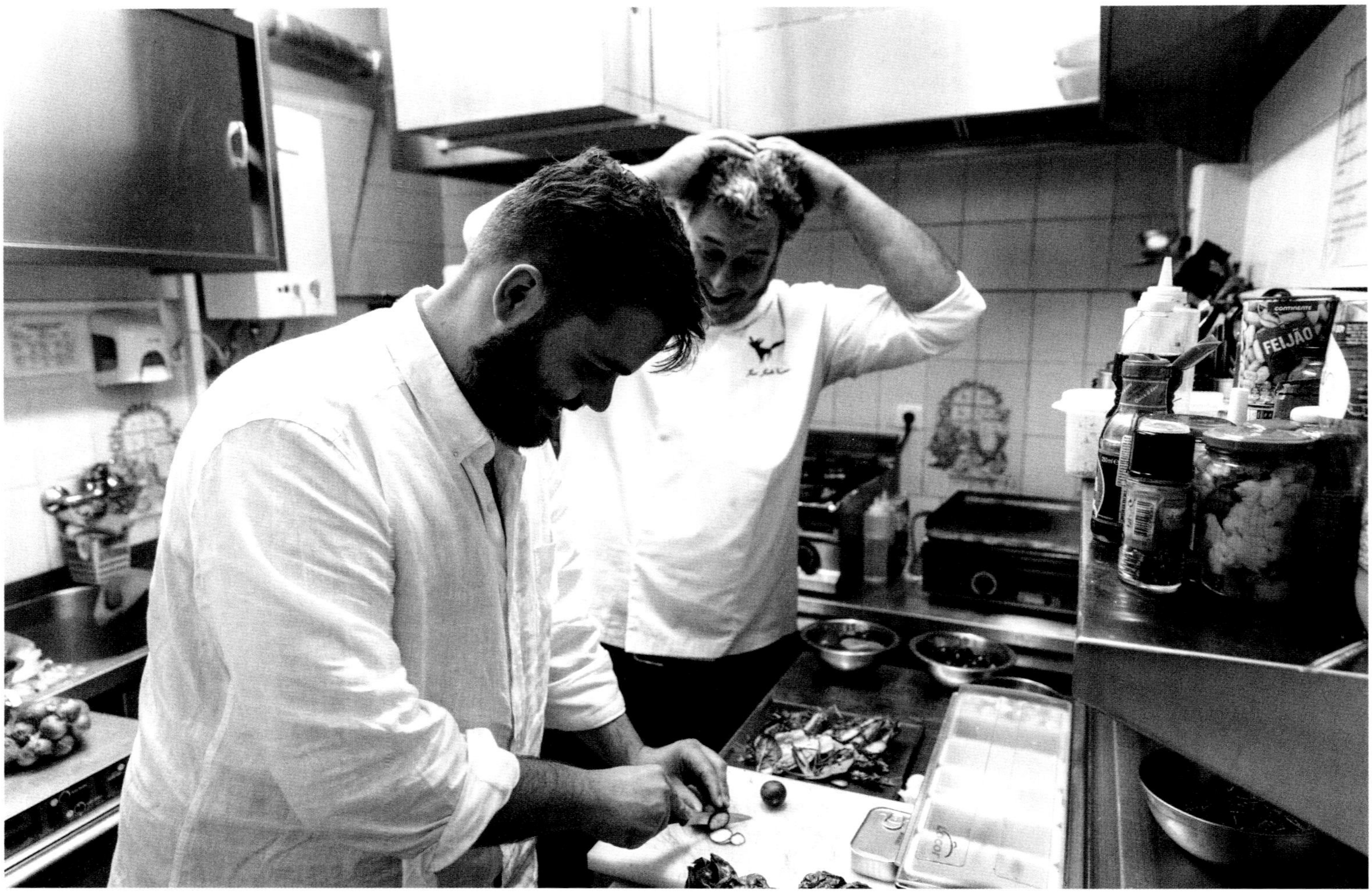
FEIJÃO

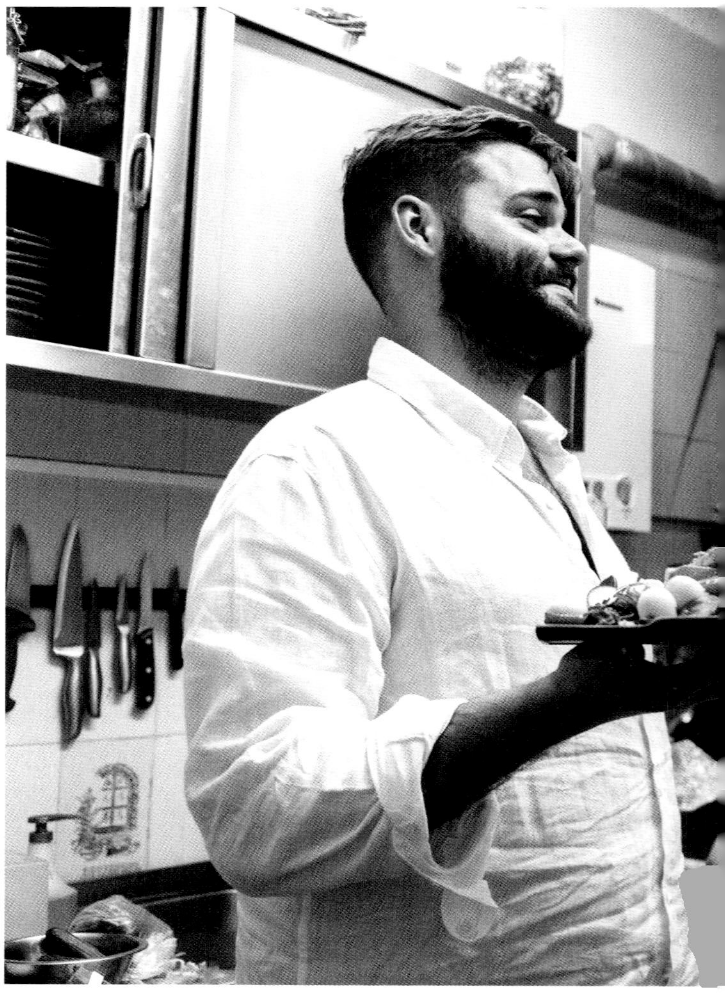

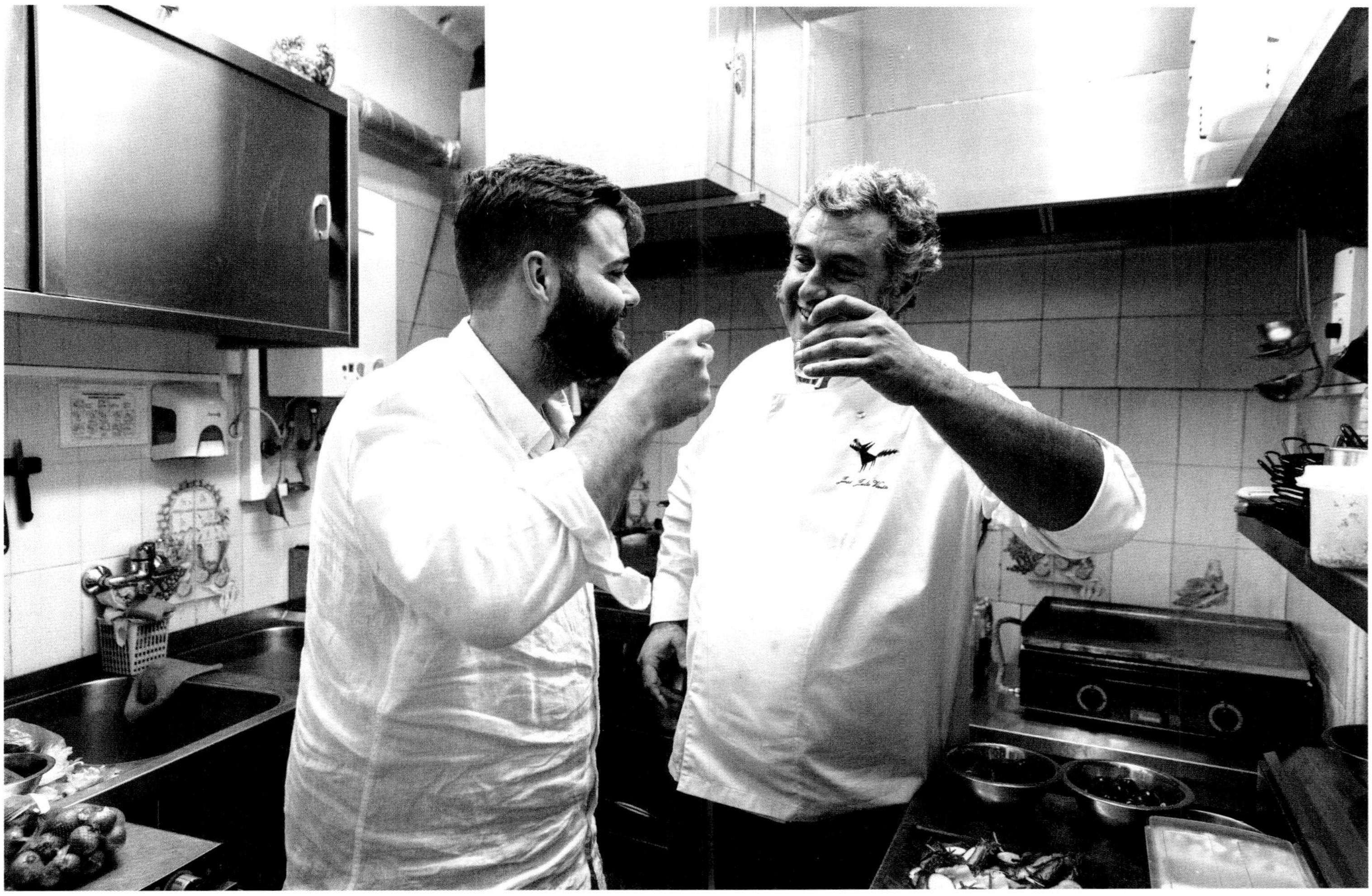

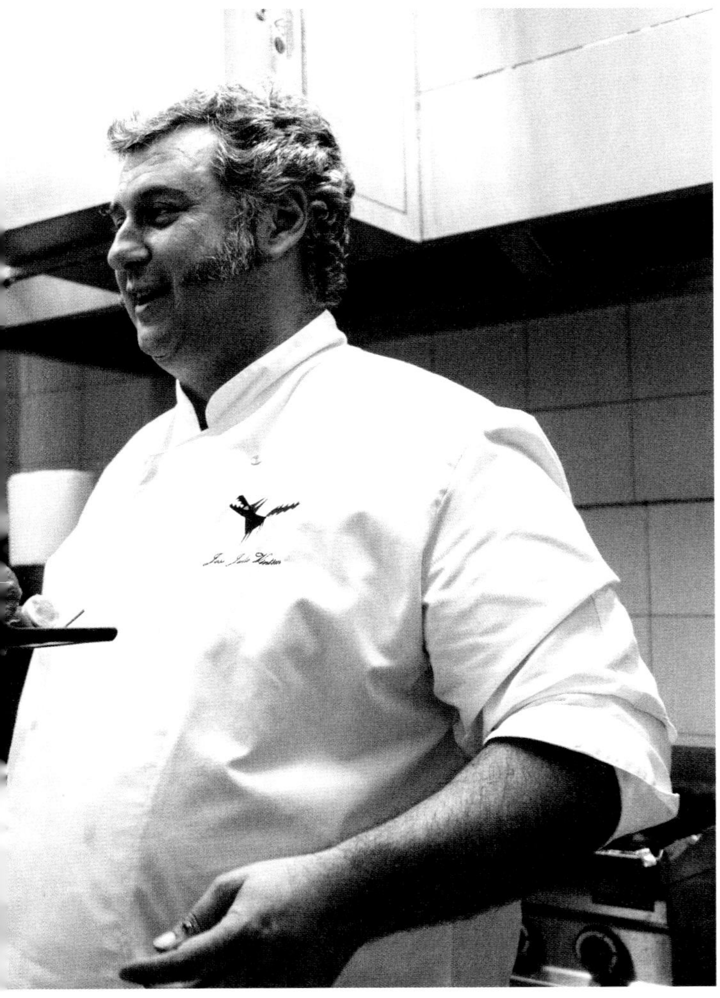

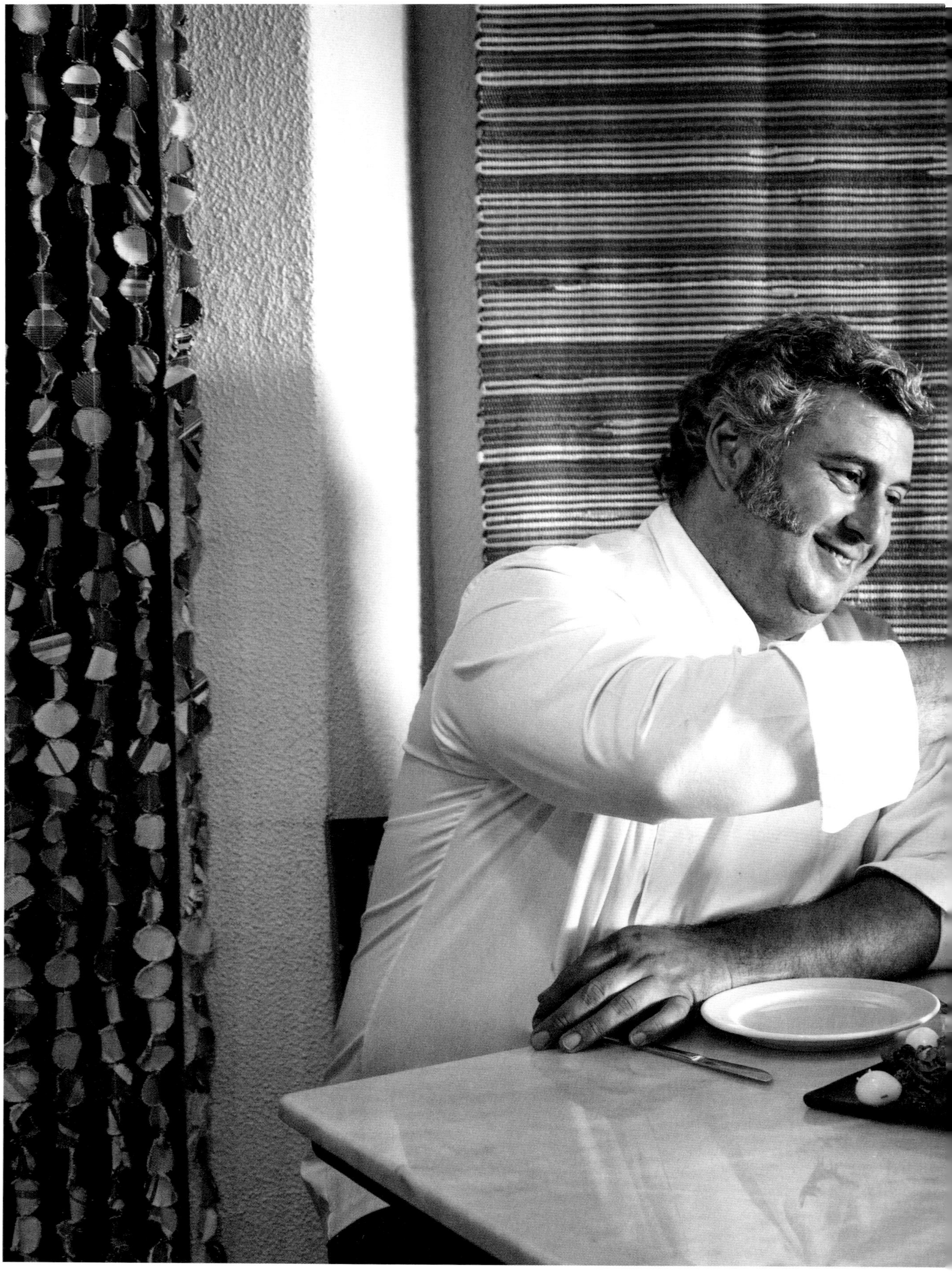

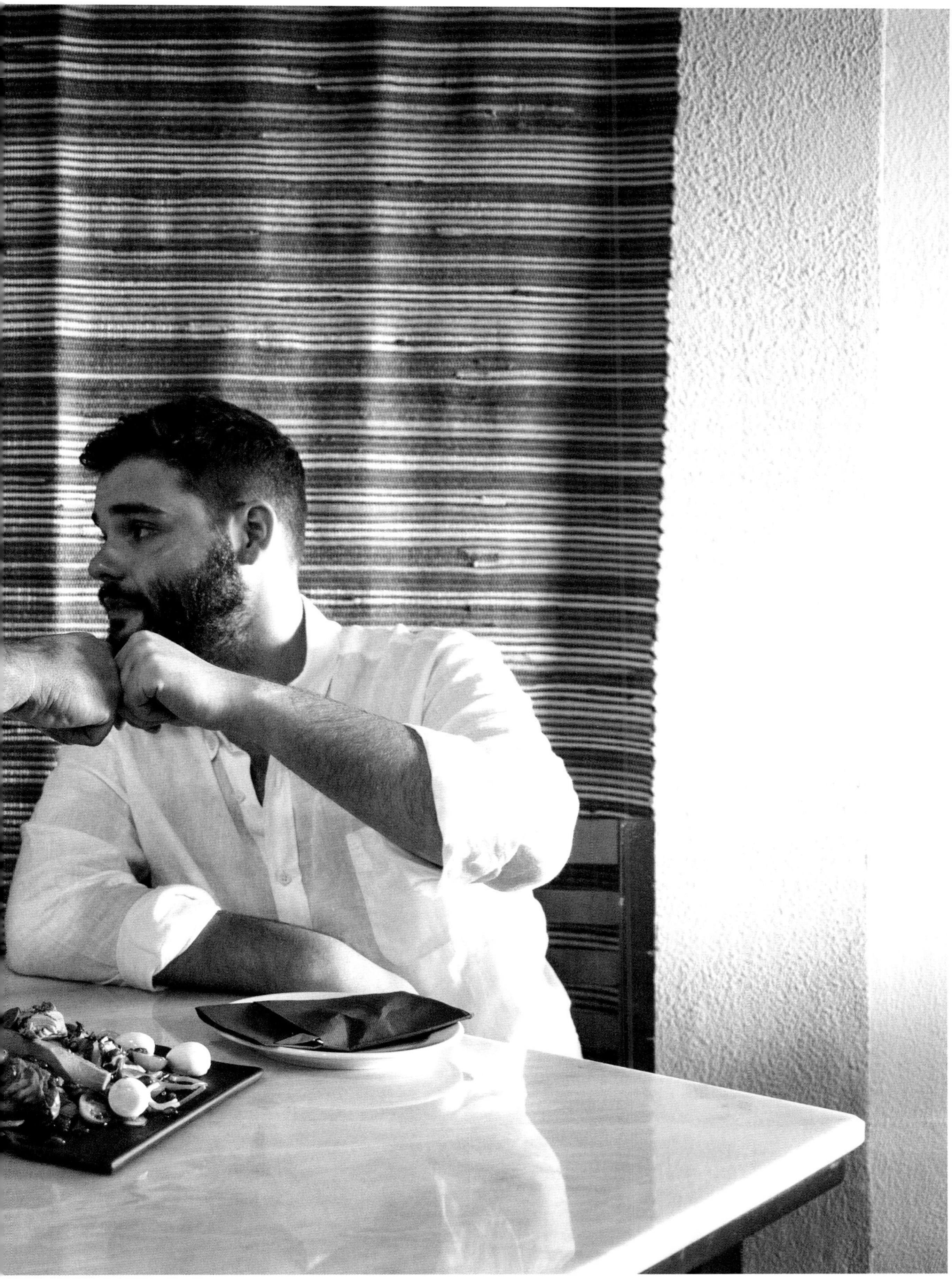

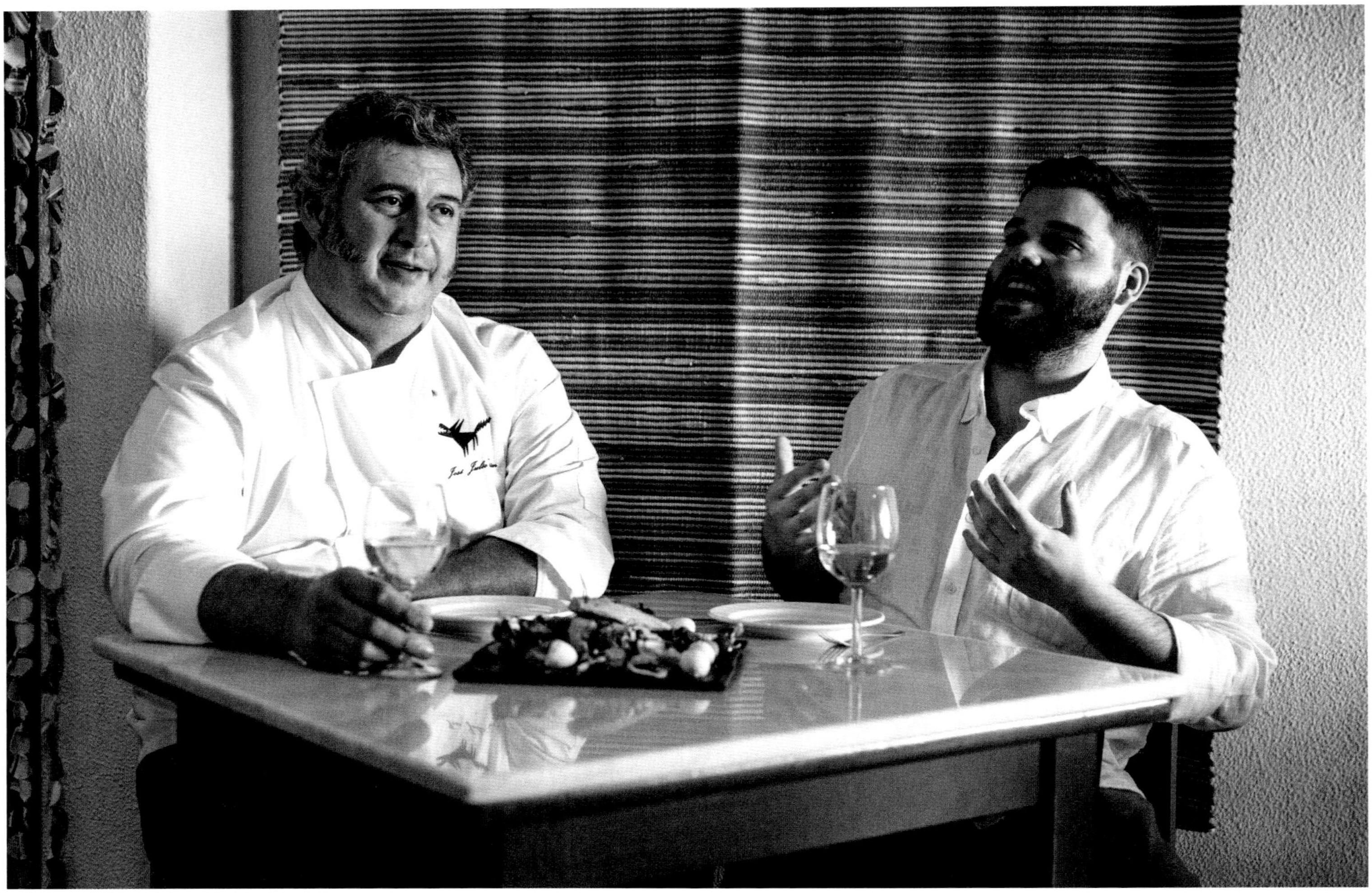

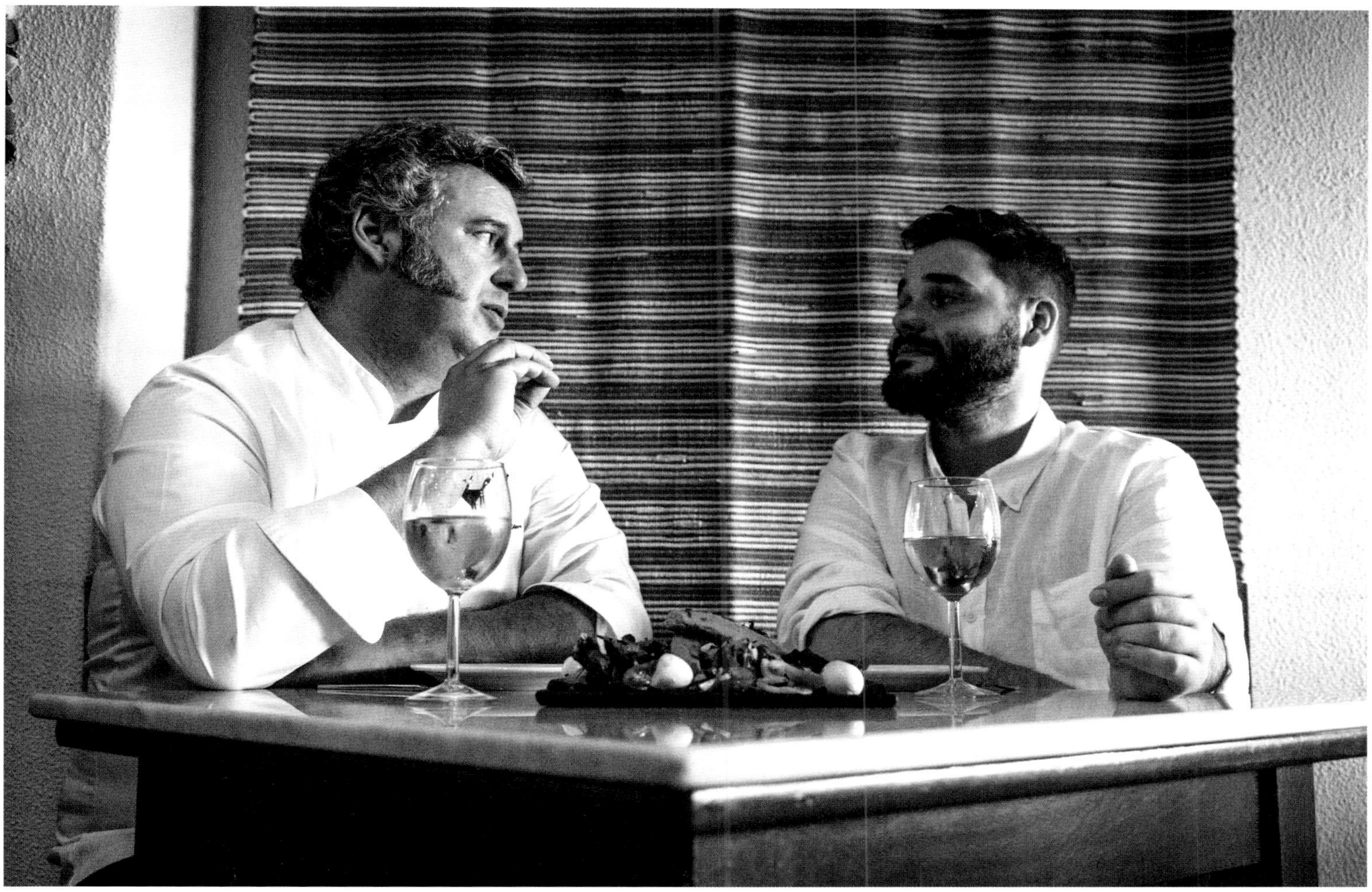

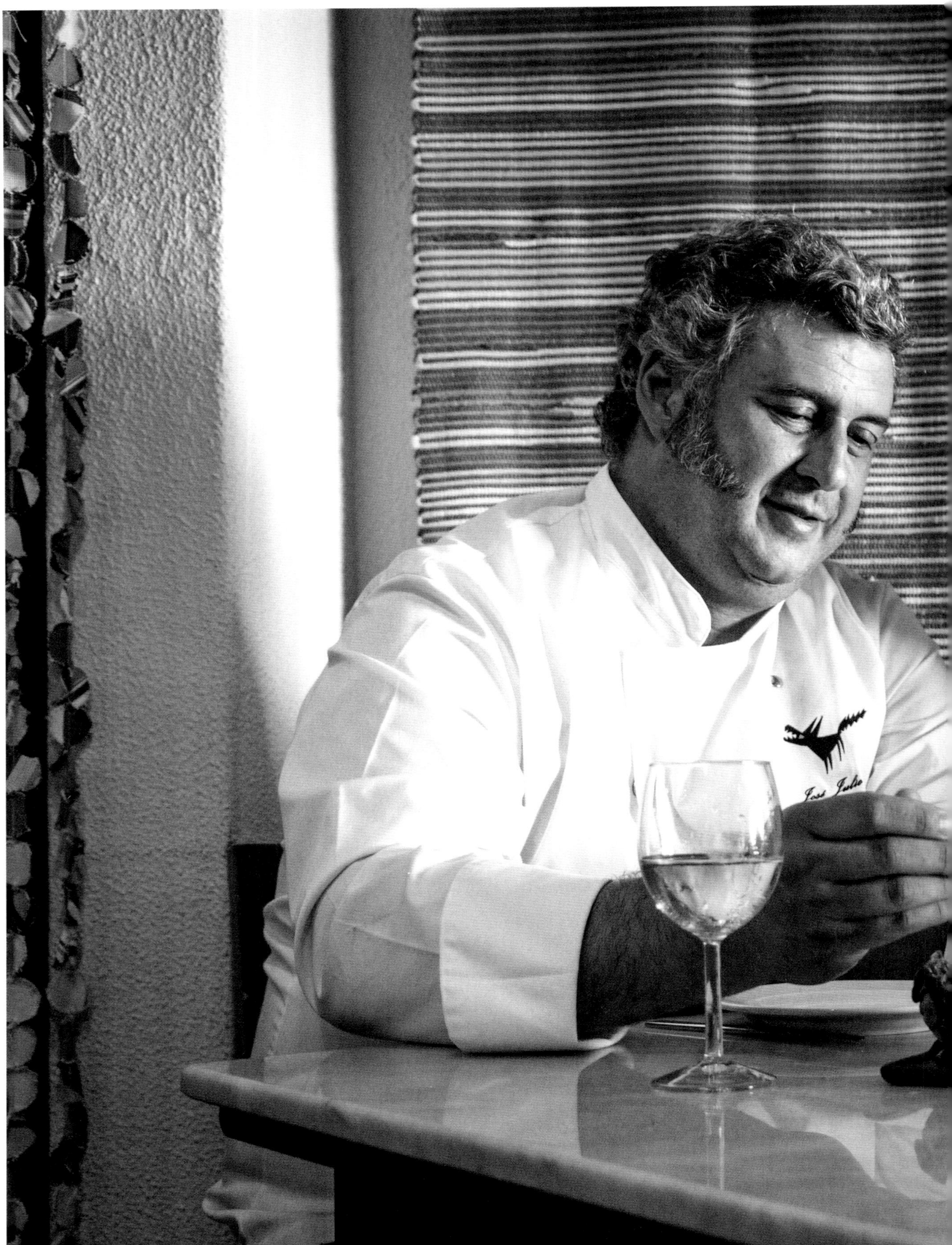

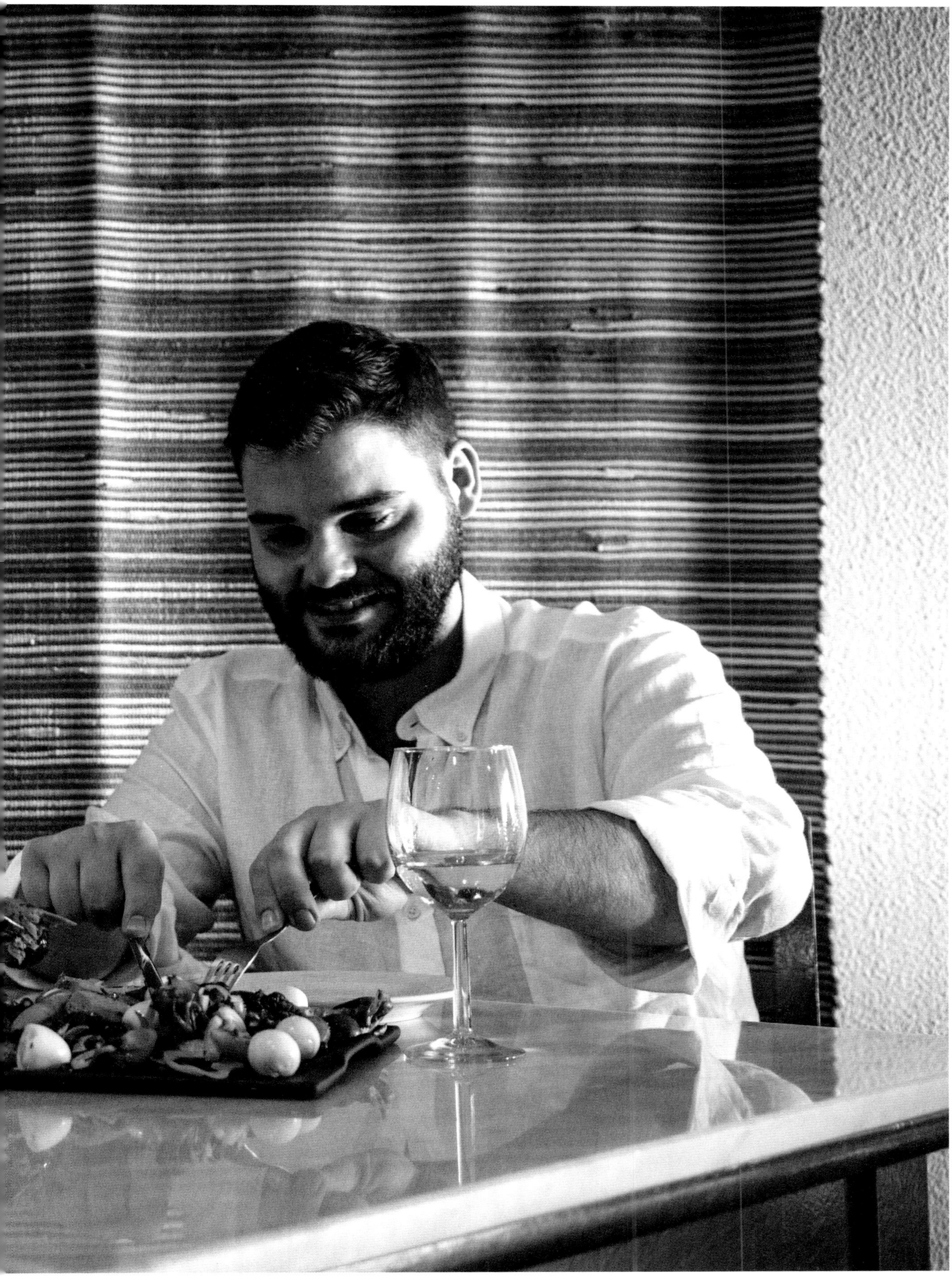

JOSÉ
JÚL
IO
VIN
TÉM

SALAD OF TUNA LOINS IN OLIVE OIL, QUAIL EGGS, LEAVES AND POMEGRANATE

TUNA FILLETS IN OLIVE OIL
BRAND CORRETORA

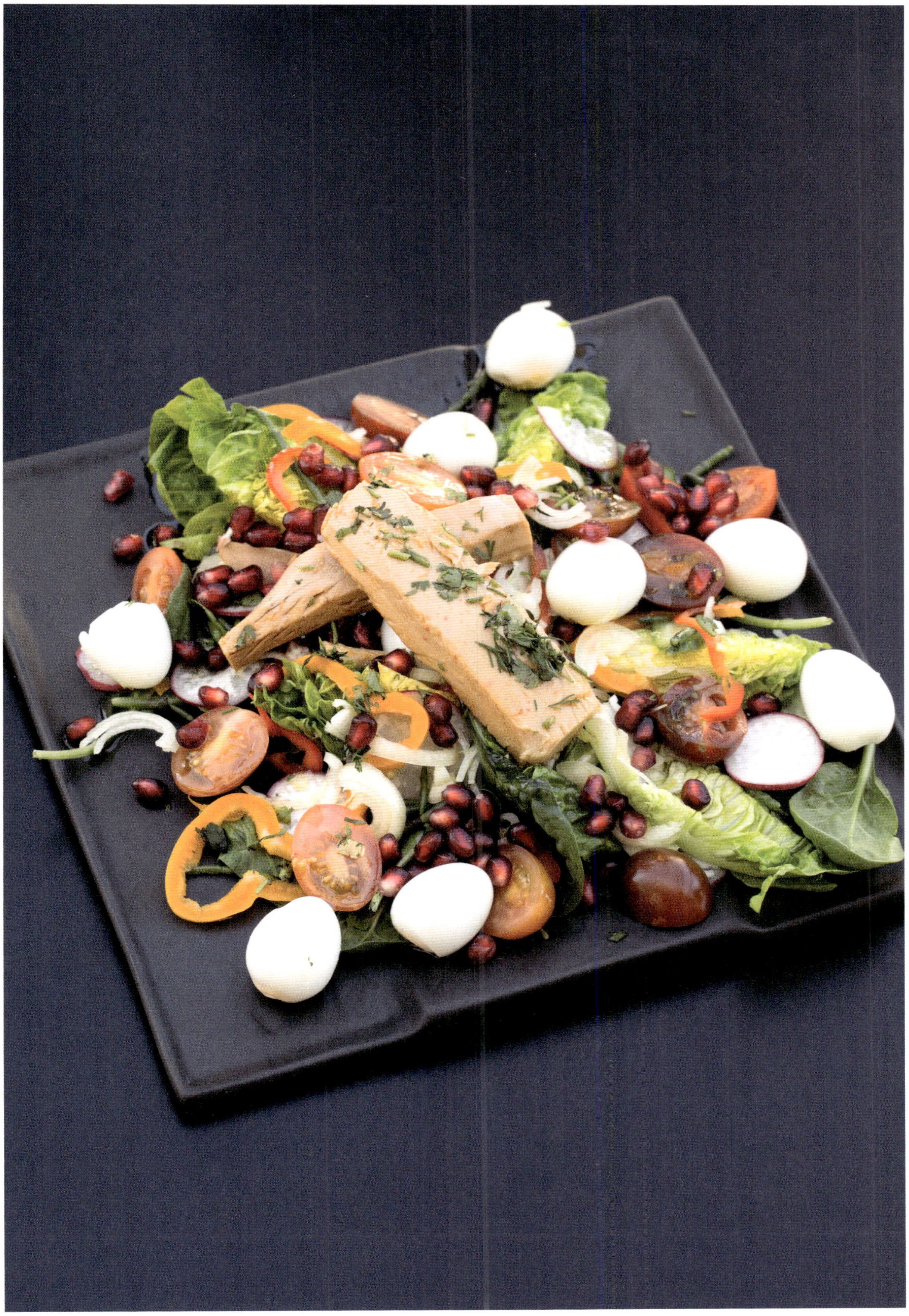

ANTÓNIO NEVES NOBRE

OILED

2018

OIL ON CANVAS

30 × 50 CM

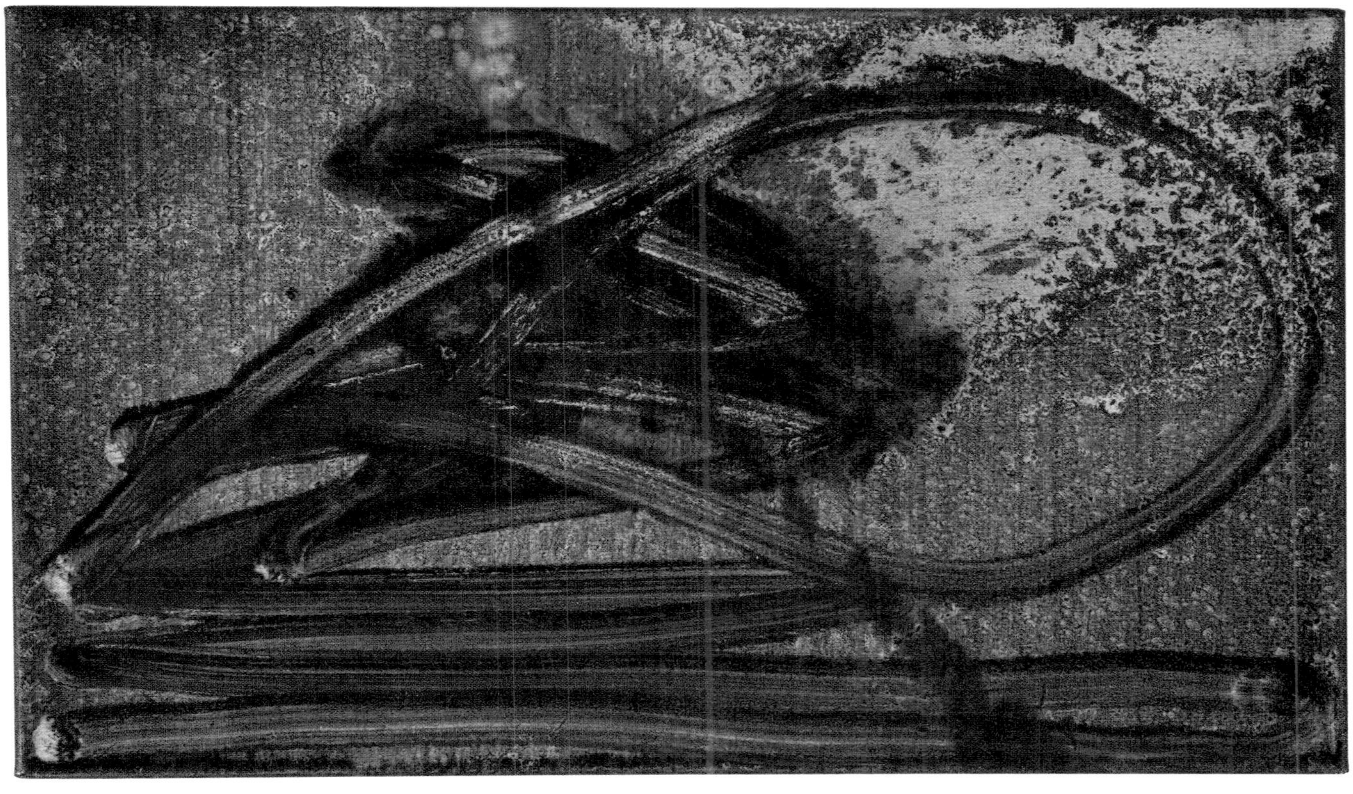

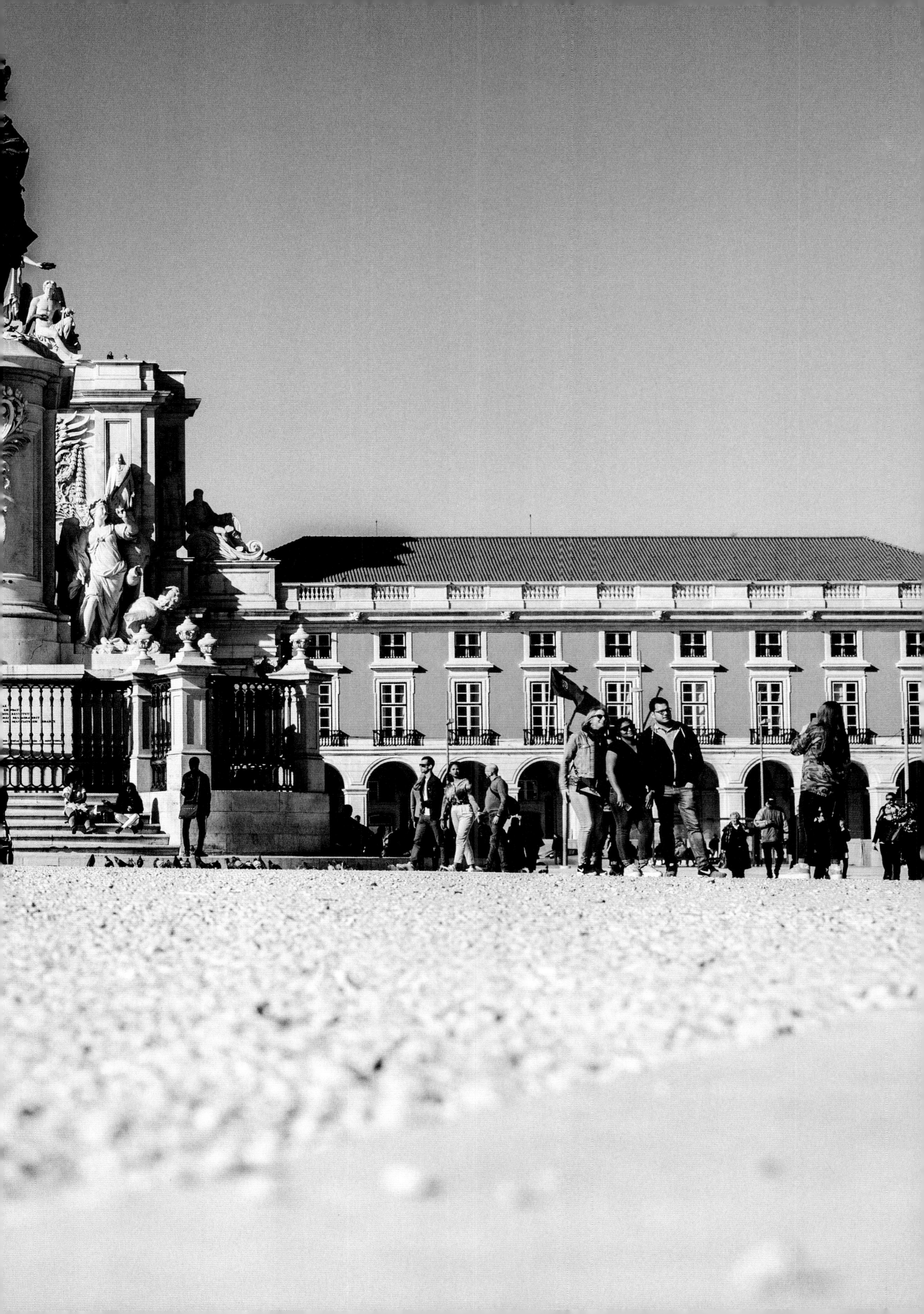

TIME

TIME

LINE

LINE

I've always liked timelines. They allow us to see historical events in an easier, more visual way. This timeline displays, in chronological order, some major events in the fields of art and gastronomy, and their major periods.

We strive for accuracy and fairness, but we do not pretend to include all events, just some of the important ones in both fields. We hope it provides an easy way of understanding some of what was happening in both areas over time.

TIMELINE

FOOD

C. 4.5 MILLION YEARS AGO
Earliest hominins diet: fruit, leaves, flowers, bark, insects and meat

C. 4.4 MILLION YEARS AGO
Australopithecines appear. First human ancestors to live on the savannah

C. 2.5 MILLION YEARS AGO
Homo habilis appears. Some hominids develop meat-rich diets as scavengers

1.6 MILLION YEARS AGO
Possible first **sporadic use of fire**

C. 1 MILLION YEARS AGO
Oldest evidence of **controlled fire use**

290,000 – 4,000 BCE
First complex **stone blades and grinding stones**

400,000 – 350,000 BCE
Early humans begin to hunt with spears

C. 150,000 YEARS AGO
Humans possibly capable of **speech**

50,000 BCE
Cave dwellers left wild date seeds and evidence of pine nuts, walnuts, acorns or chestnuts, North Iraq

C. 50,000 – 30,000 BCE
General use of fire started

C. 35,000 BCE
Fruits, nuts and roots were being gathered for food. No cultivation

C. 35,000 YEARS AGO
Palaeolithic hunter-gatherers use mammoth tusks and bones to support hide-covered tents

C. 33,000 YEARS AGO
The Neanderthals vanish; modern humans are the only surviving members of our species

C. 29,000 YEARS AGO
Paleolithic people cook animals in cooking pits, Central Europe

TIMELINE MARKERS

6 MILLION BCE

PREHISTORIC ART TIMELINE (2.5 MILLION – 500 BCE)

STONE AGE ART (FROM C. 2.500,000 BCE)

1 MILLION BCE

100,000 BCE

30,000 BCE

PALAEOLITHIC ART (C. 2.500,000 – 10,000 BCE) – STONE AGE ART

ART

C. 6 MILLION YEARS AGO
Various species of ape develop the habit of **walking upright on two feet**

C. 4.5 MILLION YEARS AGO
Certain primates, in Africa, sufficiently like humans to be classed as **hominids**

C. 4.4 MILLION YEARS AGO
Ardi, earliest known individual of partially human type, Ethiopia

C. 3.2 MILLION YEARS AGO
Lucy, female of the species Australopithecus afarensis, Ethiopia

C. 2.5 MILLION YEARS AGO
Chipped stone tools made by hominids at Gona

C. 2.2 MILLION YEARS AGO
Creatures of the **genus Homo** living in east Africa

C. 2.2 – 1.4 MILLION YEARS AGO
Homo habilis, east Africa

C. 1.8 MILLION YEARS AGO
Homo erectus east Africa

C. 1.7 MILLION YEARS AGO
Homo erectus moves out of Africa and begins to spread through Europe and Asia

1.6 MILLION YEARS AGO
Humans in coastal areas of South Africa eat shellfish and other marine sources of food

1.4 MILLION YEARS AGO
Hand axe in volcanic rock, Tanzania

C. 1 MILLION YEARS AGO
Elementary speech may go back a million years

C. 800,000 YEARS AGO
Humans living in Britain, making stone tools

700,000 – 290,000 BCE
Bhimbetka's rock shelters, India

C. 500,000 YEARS AGO
Fire is used in China by Peking Man

400,000 – 350,000 BCE
Pigments and paint grinding equipment, Twin Rivers, Zambia

290,000 – 4,000 BCE
Petroglyphs, prehistoric rock carvings

C. 230,000 YEARS AGO
Humans evolve to be classified as **Homo sapiens**

230,000 – 50,000 BCE
Venus of Berekhat Ram

C. 150,000 YEARS AGO
Possible second migration from Africa

C. 130,000 YEARS AGO
Neanderthal man established in Europe and Asia

110,000 BCE
Beads made from shells of a sea snail in Israel

82,000 BCE
Tiny shells coated in red clay, human ornamentation or a currency, Morocco

70,000 BCE
Blombos Cave rock art

C. 60,000 YEARS AGO
First human inhabitants of Australia make the crossing from Southeast Asia

60,000 BCE
Engraved ostrich eggshells – **Diepkloof rock shelter**

C. 50,000 BCE
Neanderthals decline in numbers, first in Asia and then in Europe

C. 45,000 YEARS AGO
Divje Babe Flute, Neanderthals carve a flute from the leg bone of a bear

C. 40,000 BCE
Ostrich-shell beads found in Kenya

Sulawesi cave art, Indonesia, oldest hand stencil painting

C. 35,000 BCE
Venus of Hohle Fels, from the tusk of a woolly mammoth, Germany

C. 31,000 YEARS AGO
Representational painting was invented, **Chauvet-Pont d'Arc**

C. 30,000 – 6,000 BCE
Aboriginal rock art from **Ubirr**

C. 30,000 BCE AGO
The rock shelters and caves of **Bhimbetka**

C. 29,000 YEARS AGO
Hand print, **Cosquer Cave**, near Marseille

C. 27,000 YEARS AGO
Humans at **Dolní Věstonice** model figures in burnt clay

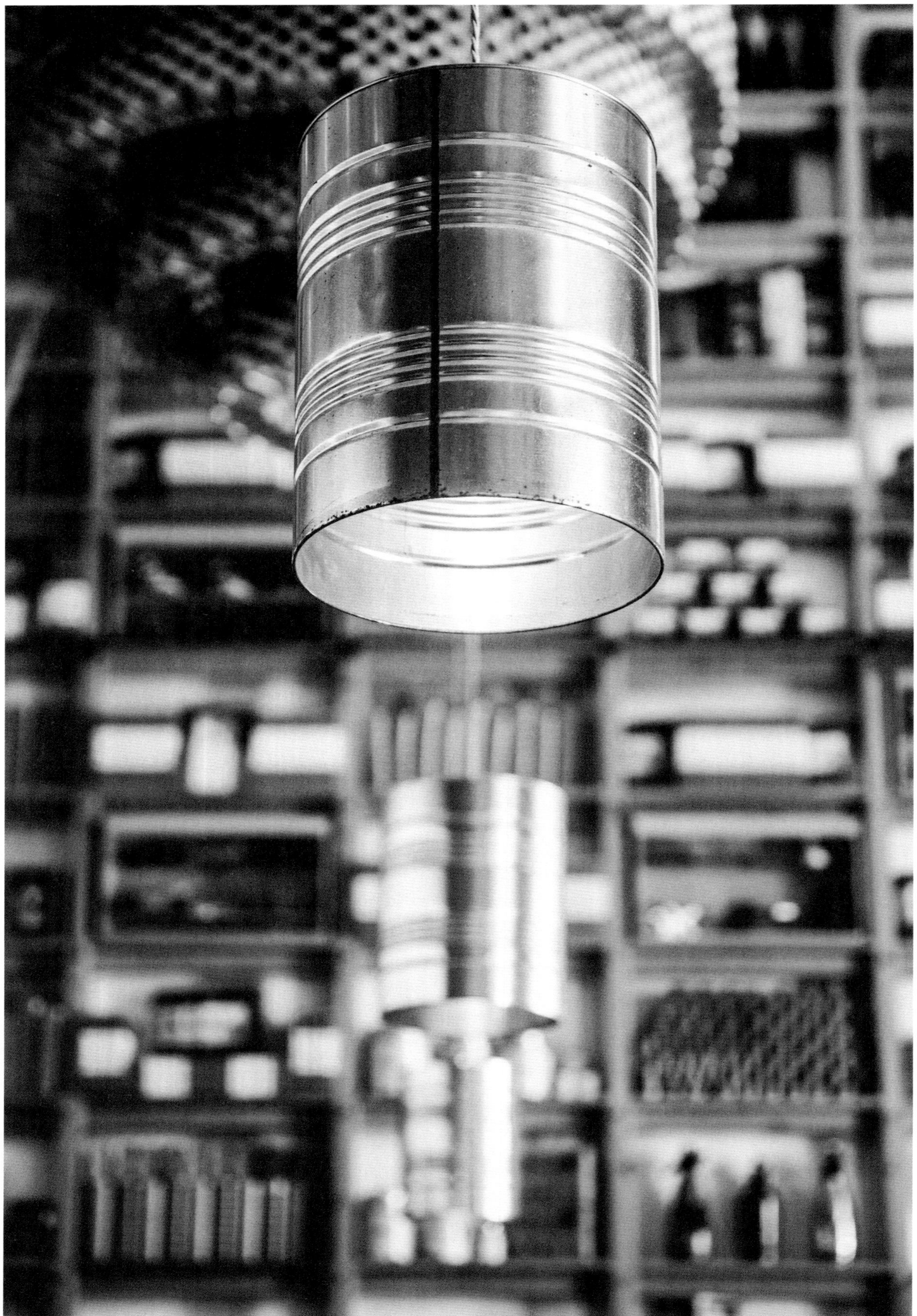

FOOD

15,000 BCE
Apparent marks of **cutting on animal fossils** in LA suggest human activity
The principle of the **bow and arrow** is developed
Needles of bone or ivory are now fine enough to take a thread as thin as horse hair
Central plains of North America have a widespread human population

15,000 – 10,000 YEARS AGO
Hunter-gatherers gradually extend their territory far into South America

14,000 BCE
During the **Mesolithic period** humans continue to improve their tool-making skills but are still nomads and hunter-gatherers

12,000 BCE
Einkorn may have been the first domesticated grain

11,500 BCE
Holocene Epoch start, end of glacial period

11,000 BCE
Figs trees may have been domesticated in the Near East
Flint-edged wooden sickles are used to gather wild grains

10,000 BCE
Brewing of beer in Sumer, southern Mesopotamia
Goats domesticated in the Near East
Crude forms of flatbread were being made
Emmer emerged as the second domesticated grain, Egypt

9,800 BCE
Evidence suggests that **wheat had been domesticated**

9,300 BCE
Evidence of **systematic storage** of wild grains, discovered in Jordan

9,000 BCE
Plant cultivation begins in the Fertile Crescent region, Middle East
Wheat, barley, sheep, goats and **elephants** domesticated, Indian subcontinent

8,700 BCE
Maize was domesticated from its wild grass ancestor

8,500 BCE
Humans raised **domesticated goats, sheep** and **cereal grains,** Mesopotamia

8,000 BCE
Domestication of potatoes around **Titicaca Lake**, border of Peru and Bolivia
Egyptians dried fish and poultry on the lower Nile using the hot desert sun
Pigs domesticated in China
Barley grown in the Near East, used for bread and for beer

7,500 BCE
Apples cultivated in southwestern Asia, evidence for **domestication of corn**

7,000 BCE
The **first beer in the world**, known as *kui*, brewed by the ancient Chinese
Pigs and sheep domesticated and used extensively in China and Africa
Neolithic Revolution, the first agricultural revolution, consolidating the transition from hunting and gathering to agriculture and settlement in Mesopotamia

6,950 – 6,440 BCE
Bananas deliberately planted at Kuk Swamp, highlands of New Guinea

6,500 BCE
Cattle domesticated by this time

6,000 BCE
Semi-nomadic people in Pakistan domesticated **wheat, barley, sheep and goat**
Lima beans were being cultivated and cattle was domesticated in Peru
Fava beans were being used in the eastern Mediterranean region
Chilli peppers and **squash** were part of the Mesoamerican diet

5,900 BCE
Earliest evidence for **millet consumption** in western China

5,500 BCE
Chinese were eating **domesticated chickens**, originally from Thailand

5,000 BCE
Maize was being cultivated in the Andes
Aniseed elixir mentioned as remedy for plague and cholera, *Book of Genesis*
Rice villages arise in China around the Yellow River
Dates cultivated in the Middle East
The Egyptians begin **irrigating crops** and **organised farming**
Sumerians using the herbs **thyme and laurel** as medicine
Cultivation of **peas** in Europe
Evidence of **avocado** use in Mexico

4,000 BCE
Grapes cultivated in the region of the Caspian Sea
Some writings suggest that **garlic** was grown in China
Egyptians using **yeast** as a leavening agent

TIMELINE

20,000 BCE
10,000 BCE
8,000 BCE
NEOLITHIC REVOLUTION OCCURRED 7,000 BCE
5,000 BCE

JŌMON PERIOD (14,000 – 1,000 BCE)
PALAEOLITHIC ART (C. 2,500,000 – 10,000 BCE) – STONE AGE ART
MESOLITHIC ART (C. 10,000 – 4,000 BCE) STONE AGE ART
THE NEOLITHIC ERA OR NEW STONE AGE (10,200 – 4,500 AND 2,000 BCE)
MESOPOTAMIAN ART (C. 4,500 – 539 BCE)

ART

C. 25,000 YEARS AGO
Venus of Willendorf found near the town of Willendorf in Austria
Dame de Brassempouy, Venus figurine with facial features
Abri du Poisson, rock shelter adorned with an engraved salmon
The Dappled Horses of Pech-Merle by Gravettian artists

C. 24,000 YEARS AGO
Decorated **female figurine** carved from limestone, **Kostenki**, Russia

C. 23,000 YEARS AGO
Figure of a flying bird, carved in mammoth ivory, Siberia

22,000 – 20,000 BCE
Prehistoric rock art site of the **Côa Valley**, Portugal

20,000 BCE
Bison Licking Insect Bite, prehistoric carving from the Upper Palaeolithic, France

C. 15,330 – 15,050 BCE
The Great Hall of the **Lascaux Caves**

JŌMON PERIOD (14,000 – 1,000 BCE)
Rich in tools and jewellery made from bone, stone, shell and antler; pottery figurines and vessels; and lacquerware

14,000 BCE
Cave painting of a bison at **Altamira Cave**

13,000 – 9,500 BCE
Cueva de las Manos, Argentina

12,000 BCE
Canine jaw, Mesopotamia, earliest evidence of **dog domestication**

11,000 BCE
Flint-edged wooden sickle and **Clovis point** made

THE NEOLITHIC ERA (10,200 – 4,500 AND 2,000 BCE)
Rich in tools and jewellery made from bone, stone, shell and antler; pottery figurines and vessels; and lacquerware

10,000 BCE
Artworks by Mesolithic hunter-gatherers

9,300 BCE
Antrea Net is the oldest known fishing net

9,000 BCE
Jericho is one of the earliest continuous settlements

8,000 BCE
Ice Age ends and enables humans to develop permanent settlements
Cave of **El Charco del Agua Amarga**, *Archer Chasing a Wild Hog*
Cuevas de la Araña, honey-gathering painting

6,500 BCE
Fish traps used to catch eel, perch, pike and carp, Netherlands

5,000 BCE
Thinker of Cernavoda and Women of Hamangia, terracotta sculptures
Beginning of the **Egyptian Empires**

4,600 – 4,200 BCE
Varna civilisation, first culture to have developed goldsmithing

NEOLITHIC ART (4,000 – 2,000 BCE)
Influenced by the development of agriculture, and animal husbandry, Neolithic people responsible for more portable art and less rock/cave painting

4,000 BCE
Papyrus, the precursor to paper, was invented by the Egyptians
Wandjina paintings by Aboriginal Australians

FOOD

3,500 BCE
People on the steppes of Kazakhstan achieve **riding and milking horses**

Pomegranate was one of the first cultivated fruits

Bread making probably originates in Egypt

Sumerians using **wild mushrooms** as a food

Edible olive was grown on the island of Crete

3,100 – 30 BCE
Egyptian art. First civilisation with a recognisable style of art

3,000 BCE
Olive tree cultivated in Crete for exporting

Potatoes being cultivated in the Andes Mountains

Flaxseed was being cultivated by the Babylonians

Chinese eat noodles and cultivate soybeans, rice, wheat, barley and millet

Musa acuminata **banana** introduced into eastern Africa and South Asia

Sorghum cereal grain cultivated in sub-Saharan Africa, Sudan and Guinea

Farmers of Mesopotamia grow crops of onions, turnips, beans, leeks, lettuce and garlic

Lentils discovered at a settlement site in Lake Biel, Switzerland

Non-bitter almonds appeared in the eastern Mediterranean

2,900 BCE
Edible figs, Middle East and, eventually, the Mediterranean

2,853 BCE
Emperor Shennong of China declared **five sacred plants**: rice, wheat, barley, millet and soybeans

2,737 BCE
Legend has it that Chinese Emperor Shen Nung **discovers tea**

2,700 BCE
Wine in the Nile Delta, Egypt

Chinese herbal encyclopedia list 365 medicinal plants

2,600 BCE
Drinking scene from a cylindrical seal shows **people drinking beer through straws**

2,558 – C. 2,532 BCE
Beer was often used throughout Egypt as compensation for labour

2,200 BCE
Mesopotamian tablet has the **oldest recipe for beer**

2,400 – 1,900 BCE
Bone forks found in archaeological sites of the Bronze Age Qijia culture

2,000 BCE
Olives, peaches and apricots cultivated in Eastern Mediterranean

Wine made in Portugal. Tartessians plant vines in the Sado and Tagus valleys

People using pepper in India where it's native

Development of technology for **butter production**

Art of distillation, perfumes and flavourings, ancient Mesopotamia

Water-treatment knowledge

1,000 – 2,000 BCE
Arab traders carried **banana** suckers from Southeast Asia back home

1,800 BCE
Sumerian poem *Hymn to Ninkas*, song of praise to the goddess of beer, Ninkasi

1,750 BCE
Kanasu Broth, clay tablet from ancient Mesopotamia describing **recipe for mutton and vegetable broth**

1,600 BCE
Pomegranate was brought to Egypt from Syria during the rule of the Hyksos

Figs were grown in Crete

1,500 BCE
Coriander being used as a culinary herb in Egypt

Sausages made by stuffing spiced meat animal intestines, Babylonia

Horseradish is used in both culinary and medical applications in Egypt

1,325 BCE
Tutankhamen's tomb contained seeds and plant products including watermelon, lentils, almonds, date palm, cumin and coriander

1,100 BCE
Soybeans appear

1,000 BCE
Maize spreads to Peru

Incas **froze potatoes** in the snow for preservation

People ate **pork in the Middle East** until 1,000 BCE

Geese known to have been popular in Germany

Chinese thought to be producing a type of **alcohol spirit from rice**

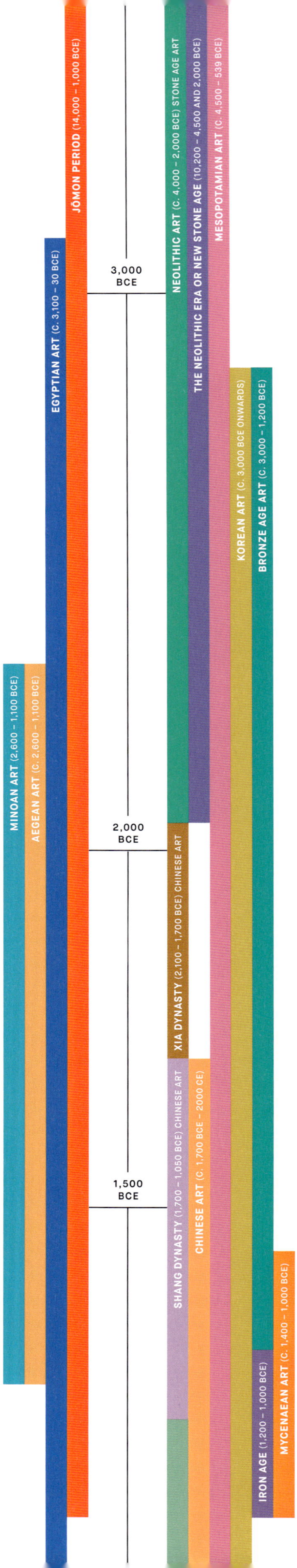

ART

3,500 BCE
Wheel created to serve as potter's wheels in Mesopotamia

The **earliest cities** are built in Mesopotamia

3,400 BCE
Thet **writing system**, invented by the Sumerians, emerged in Mesopotamia

3,200 BCE
Newgrange, Neolithic monument built by Stone Age farmers

EGYPTIAN ART (3,100 – 30 BCE)
First civilisation with a recognisable style of art

3,100 BCE
Stonehenge was created

3,000 BCE
Bronze invented in Mesopotamia

Egyptians paint **tomb walls with pictures** of gardens, fish ponds and fruit trees

2,630 BCE
Step Pyramid of Djoser is built

2,600 BCE
Standard of Ur, box showing animals and other provisions being brought in procession to a banquet

2,558 – C. 2,532 BCE
The **Great Sphinx** of Giza

2,500 BCE
Maikop Gold Bull, Russia

2,000 BCE
Glass invented in Ancient Egypt

Maya developed their **first civilisation** in the Preclassic period

2,125 – 1,975 BCE
Food for the afterlife, wooden model of brewers and butchers' tomb of Sebekhetepi, Egypt

1,958 BCE
The Mysterious Tomb of Het Heru Priestess Senet, wall painting showing the process of making **flatbread**

1,750 BCE
Knossos palace built by the **Minoans**

1,650 BCE
Fisherman, fresco of a young fisherman with his catch, detail of a fresco in Akrotiri, Thera, Greece

1,550 BCE
Ebers Papyrus lists hundreds of medicinals, including anise, saffron, fenugreek, mustard, fennel, cardamom, garlic, thyme and poppy seeds

1,500 BCE
Bull's Head Rhyton, Minoan art

Rise of **Olmec culture**, Mesoamerica

Temples of **Karnak and Luxor**, in ancient Thebes

1,425 BCE
Minoan civilisation collapses and is conquered by the Mycenaeans

1,345 – 1,335 BCE
Painted limestone ***Akhenaton Presenting a Duck to Aten***

1,250 BCE
Ramses II creates a spectacular temple in his own honour at **Abu Simbel**

1,100 BCE
Phoenician sailors use the **Pole Star** for navigational purposes

1,200 – 900 BCE
Olmec colossal heads, Mexico

1,000 – 500 BCE
Lamassu from the citadel of Sargon II, Dur Sharrukin, modern Iraq

FOOD

883 – 859 BCE
Mobile kitchen Assyrian war camp, wall relief Palace of Ashurnasirpal II

800 BCE
Germans were brewing beer (which they called ale)

A native of Mexico, **the tomatillo** was cultivated before the tomato

776 BCE
A cook, **Coroibus of Elis**, first recorded winner in the ancient Olympics in a foot race

700 BCE
Aubergines being cultivated in China

600 BCE
Assyrian king **Sardanapalus** introduced the **first cooking competition**

The **Accidental Coagulation Theory** states that tofu was developed by accident, probably in northern China

500 BCE
Hebrews, Greeks and Romans were known to use snow in storage pits, and Egyptians placed jars out overnight to cool

Sugar cane cultivated in India

Soy sauce's origin in China

499 – 449 BCE
Greco-Persian Wars

350 BCE
Poem ***Hedypatheia*** (Pleasant Living or Life of Luxury) by **Archestratus**, who was the first to approach cooking as an art

327 BCE
Alexander the Great found **bananas** in India

221 – 207 BCE
First known cooking apparatus that completely enclosed a fire, built from clay, Qin dynasty

200 BCE
Flour milling introduced into China during the Han era

Book of Rites, a Chinese history book compiled in the Western Han Dynasty

2ND CENTURY BCE
Athenaeus writes ***Deipnosophistai*** (The Learned Banquet), dialogue between two banqueters who discuss, for several days, food and recipes

179 – 122 BCE
Liu An Theory, tofu was developed by Liu An, King of Huai-nan, China

168 BCE
In Ancient Rome, ***pistores*** was the name given to the slaves who ground the corn in the mortar, the actual bakers

138 – 125 BCE
Pomegranates first came to China from the Middle East via the Silk Road

130 – 100 BCE
Greek philosopher **Alexander of Aphrodisias** describes the process to get drinking water

95 BCE
Sergius Orata was probably the first to lay out **artificial oyster beds** at Lake Lucrine

CLASSICAL GREEK ART (500 – 323 BCE)
HELLENISM (323 – 331 BCE)
CELTIC ART (C. 500 BCE – C. 17 CE)
INDIAN, CHINESE AND JAPANESE ART (653 BCE – 1900 CE)
ETRUSCAN ART (C. 700 – 90 BCE)
ART OF CLASSICAL ANTIQUITY (800 BCE – 400 CE)
EGYPTIAN ART (C. 3,100 – 30 BCE)

500 BCE

QIN EMPEROR AND 3-YEAR DYNASTY (221 - 206 BCE)

SIX DYNASTIES PERIOD (220 BCE – 589 CE)

HAN DYNASTY (206 BCE – 220 CE) CHINESE ART

ROMAN ART OF THE LATE EMPIRE PERIOD (C. 200 – 400 CE)

ZHOU DYNASTY (1,050 – 221 BCE) [INC. WARRING STATES PERIOD 475 – 221 BCE] CHINESE ART
CHINESE ART (C. 1,700 BCE – 2000 CE)
MESOPOTAMIAN ART (C. 4,500 – 539 BCE)
ROMAN ART (C. 500 BCE – 476 CE)
KOREAN ART (C. 3,000 BCE ONWARDS)
GREEK ART (C. 650 – 27 BCE)
ROMAN ARCHITECTURE (C. 400 BCE – 400 CE)

ART

957 BCE
Pillars in Solomon's temple, Jerusalem, decorated with pomegranates

ART OF CLASSICAL ANTIQUITY (800 BCE – 400 CE)
Greek idealism: balance, perfect proportions, architectural orders (Doric, Ionic, Corinthian)

753 BCE
The legendary **founding date of Rome**

750 BCE
First use of **Greek alphabet**

GREEK ART (650 – 27 BCE)
Parthenon, Myron, Phidias, Polykleitos, Praxiteles

645 – 635 BCE
Wall panel relief showing the so-called ***Ashurbanipal's Banquet Scene***, North Palace in Nineveh

575 – 550 BCE
Hunting a Wild Boar with Dogs, wine-bowl from Corinth with the names of six of the hunters on it, in Greek

563 BCE
Birth of **Gautama Buddha**, the founder of Buddhism

520 BCE
Picture from a large jar shows people **harvesting olives**

500 BCE
Roman Republic starts

Encaustic paints, invented by Greek artists, mixing coloured pigments and wax

Buddhas of Bamiyan, Afghanistan

490 BCE
Athens defeats Persia at Marathon

480 BCE
The *Kritios Boy* reveals a Greek sculptor's first attempts to achieve a new degree of naturalism

478 – 474 BCE
Charioteer of Delphi, naturalistic bronze statue made in ancient Greece

475 – 221 BCE
Winged cup with geometric designs, Eastern Zhou dynasty, Warring States period

460 BCE
Start of **democracy in Athens**

C. 431 – 404 BCE
Peloponnesian Wars fought between Athens and Sparta

C. 450 – 440 BCE
Greek sculptor **Polykleitos** develops a posture in which the statue stands in an asymmetrical pose with the body's weight on one leg

447 – 432 BCE
The Parthenon, dedicated to the goddess Athena, is built as the primary temple on the Acropolis

ROMAN ARCHITECTURE (C. 400 BCE – 400 CE)
Arch, dome vault, use of concrete. Greatest public buildings in the history of architecture: temples, basilicas, amphitheatres, triumphal arches, monuments, public baths

C. 336 – 323 BCE
Reign of **Alexander the Great**

2ND HALF OF 3RD CENTURY BCE
Terracotta *lekanis* (dish) with lid and finial

220 BCE
Marble sculpture of ***The Dying Gaul***

C. 210 BCE
Chinese Terracotta Army

206 BCE – 220 CE
Woodblock printing is invented in Han dynasty, first print culture

Court eunuch **Cai Lun** invented the pulp papermaking process in **105 CE**

206 BCE – 1911 CE
Chinese calligraphy

200 BCE
Silver ***patera*** (saucepan-shaped vessel), Late Roman

3RD – 1ST CENTURY BCE
Rattle bowl, trophy-head deity, Peru, Ica Valley, Paracas culture

2ND CENTURY BCE
Still life from a villa at Tor Marancia, Rome, shows fish, fowl and vegetables common in Roman kitchens

130 – 100 BCE
Venus of Milo granted to **Alexandros of Antioch**

100 BCE
Mosaic-makers of Pompeii, pictures with millions of small marble pieces

C. 80 BCE
Fish Mosaic: **Pompeii – Ocean/Sea Life scenes**

C. 75 BCE
Ancient Rome's greatest amphitheatre, the **Colosseum** is built

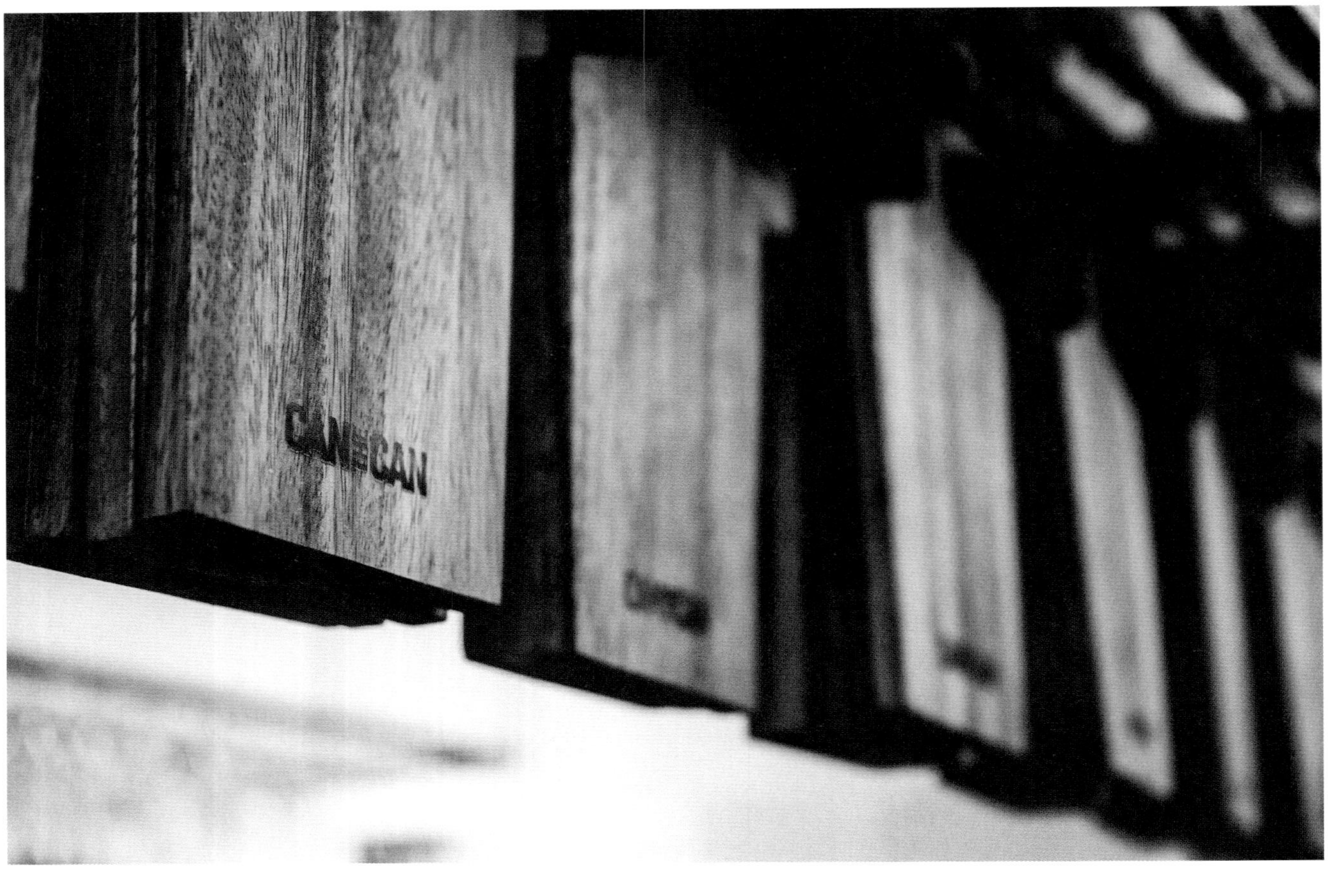

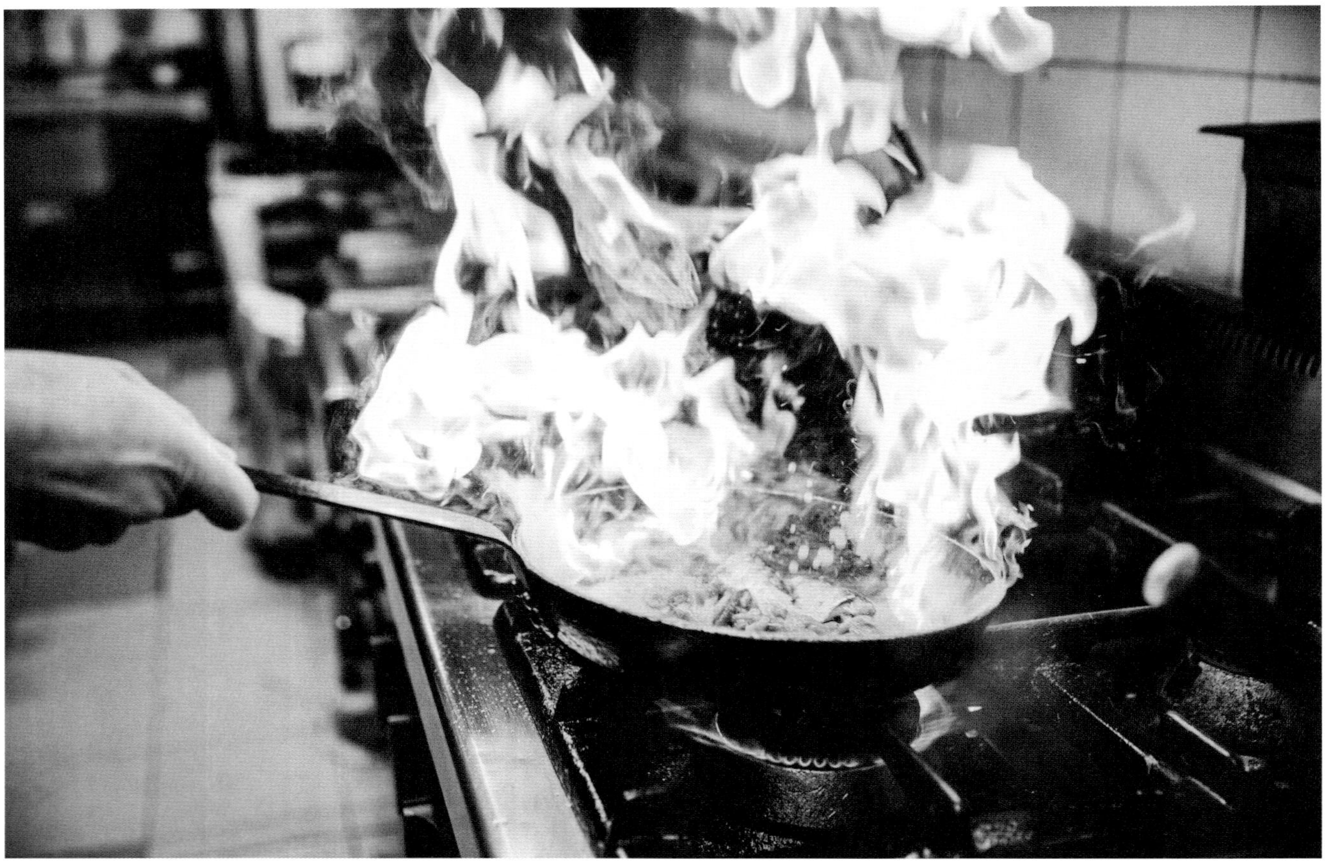

FOOD

50 BCE
Broccoli being cultivated in Europe

Pepper introduced to Java by Hindu settlers and into Europe by Arab Traders

45 BCE
Julian Calendar, New Year celebrated for the first time on 1 January

44 BCE
Ancient Roman cuisine changed by the influence of Greek culture

5 BCE
Palm sugar being used by the Chinese

Woks being used in China

4 BCE
Sushi originated in Southeast Asia as a method for preserving fish

Chinese codified the **five basic taste sensations**: sweet, sour, briny, spicy and bitter

3 BCE
Street vendors hawked fried fish and grilled meats, Sumerian capital of Ur

In Egypt, small **raw birds** were pickled in brine and eaten cold

1 CE
Roman poets **Virgil and Ovid** referenced **strawberry** as an ornament

Garum, fermented fish sauce, used as a condiment

Mary or Marianne, Alexandria's alchemist, discovered the properties of the bain-marie, and originated its name: **Mary's bath**

The most famous of all meals: **the Last Supper of Christ**

25 – 200 CE
One of the first applications of metals was to build a **stove**

54 CE
Tiberius Claudius Drusus Nero Germanicus poisoned with mushrooms by his wife Agrippina

79 CE
Carbonised loaf of bread stamped *Property of Celer, Slave of Q. Granius Verus*, Pompeii

100 CE
Emperor Trajan created a **guild of bakers** who were to supply bread to the public at the state's expense

Written record of distilling by Greek philosopher **Alexander of Aphrodisias**

De Re Coquinaria by **Apicius**, collection of Roman cookery recipes

220 CE
Recipe for tofu and soy milk, discovered on a stone in northern China

250 CE
Mesoamerican culture discovers the **cacao bean**

408 CE
Visigoths attacked Rome and asked for 3,000 pounds of pepper as part of the city's ransom

6TH CENTURY CE
Industrial activity in **Tróia**, Setúbal, Portugal, centred on fishing and manufacture of preserved fish supplied to the rest of the Roman Empire

500 – 1000 CE
Knowledge of distillation spread to Europe with the travelling Moors

511 – 526 CE
De observatione ciborum (On the Observance of Foods) by **Anthimus**

536 CE
A **fog** blankets the Earth for almost two years, causing a global famine

7TH CENTURY CE
The **patron saints of cooks** lived in this century: **Fortunat**

Royal courts of the Middle East began to **use forks at the table** for dining

Arab traders brought the **banana** to the Middle East and Africa

647 CE
The earliest record of **spinach** found in China, from Nepal

718 CE
Earliest reference to **sushi** in Japan, in the Yōrō Code

760 CE
Chinese Cha'an (**Zen**), Buddhist monk **Lu Yu** writes *The Book of Tea*

HELLENISM (331 – 323 BCE)
CELTIC ART (C. 500 BCE – C. 17 CE)
INDIAN, CHINESE AND JAPANESE ART (653 BCE – 1900 CE)
ART OF CLASSICAL ANTIQUITY (800 BCE – 400 CE)
EGYPTIAN ART (C. 3,100 – 30 BCE)
SUI DYNASTY (589 – 618) CHINESE ART
THE DARK AGES (450 – 1050)

THREE KINGDOMS PERIOD (C. 57 BCE – 668 CE) KOREAN ART

1ST CENTURY CE

2ND CENTURY CE

MIDDLE AGES (OR MEDIEVAL PERIOD) 5TH CENTURY CE

8TH CENTURY CE

CHINESE ART (C. 1,700 BCE – 2000 CE)
ROMAN ART (C. 500 BCE – 476 CE)
KOREAN ART (C. 3,000 BCE ONWARDS)
GREEK ART (C. 650 – 27 BCE)
ROMAN ARCHITECTURE (C. 400 BCE – 400 CE)
BYZANTINE AND ISLAMIC ART (476 – 1453)

ART

50 BCE
Tomb of the baker Eurysaces, mausoleum of Marcus Vergilius Eurysaces

44 BCE
Julius Caesar was assassinated by a group of Roman senators

30 BCE
Death of Cleopatra VII and end of Egypt's dynastic period

27 BCE – 180 CE
The Pax Romana allowed further advances in art, culture and technology

1 CE
Buddhism entered Han China via the Silk Road

Multigenerational banquet depicted on a mural from Pompeii

Baker's Shop, fresco in Pompeii

C. 5 – 25 CE
The Portland Vase, cameo glass

64 CE
The Great Fire of Rome begins on 18 July and burns for a week

97 CE
Rome had nine **aqueducts** and a great **sewer** known as *Cloaca Maxima*

100 CE
Part of a silver drinking set, a board from Arcisate, Italy

160 – 170 CE
Signboard for a well-stocked **poulterer's shop** from Ostia

250 CE
The **Maya classical period** begins

292 CE
Diocletian splits Roman Empire

4TH CENTURY CE
Celtic art, Carolingian Renaissance, Romanesque, Gothic

350 CE
Mosaic depicting banquet during a hunting trip, **Villa Romana del Casale**, Sicily

320 CE
***Adam and Eve* fresco**, catacombs of Saints Marcellinus and Peter, Rome

336 CE
First recorded **celebration of Christmas** on December 25

5TH CENTURY CE
Buddhism spreads to Japan

Middle Ages (or Medieval period) lasted from the 5th to the 15th century

C. 500 – 1450 CE
Collapse of Rome and rise of Byzantine art

565 CE
Greek cup depicting Arcesilaus II, King of Cyrene, weighing silphium

7TH CENTURY CE
Murals in caves in the Bamiyan Valley, Afghanistan, **the world's first oil paintings**

610 CE
Islam was a religion founded by Muhammad, Arabian merchant from Mecca

TANG DYNASTY (618 – 906 CE)
True porcelain is manufactured in northern China

632 – 732 CE
First **Arab Muslim conquests**, after the death of the Islamic prophet **Muhammad**

ICONOCLASM CONTROVERSY (726 – 843 CE)
Use of religious images and icons were strongly opposed by both Church figures and state officials within the empire.

742 CE
Charlemagne was born, starting a period which saw the flowering of scholarship, literature, art and architecture, known as the **Carolingian Renaissance**

FOOD

800 CE
Coffee beans consumed in North Africa, not yet used to brew a beverage

812 CE
Charlemagne ordered imperial farms to grow anise, fennel and fenugreek

850 CE
Legend that **coffee** was discovered by Ethiopian goat herder, **Kaldi**

500 – 1000 CE
Kitab al-tabikh, book of cookery written by **Ibn Sayyar al-Warraq**

10TH–13TH CENTURIES
Forks were fairly common among the wealthy in Byzantium

900 CE
Earliest-known **windmills** developed in Persia

Farm-raised fish in China

Bananas make their way to Europe from maritime trade routes

11TH CENTURY CE
Small forks used for eating first appeared in Tuscany

Venetian *Doge*, **Domenico Selvo**, marries a Greek princess who brings to his court the **practice of eating with forks**

1000 CE
Coffee spreads to Yemen from Ethiopia

Distillation of whisky by monks coming from Europe to Scotland and Ireland

12TH CENTURY CE
Caviar was known in Russia

1100
Spinach reaches Spain, brought from North Africa by the Moors

1135
King Henry I of England died from indigestion caused by eating lampreys

1137
Louis VI, **'Louis the Fat'**, dies

1170
Okra cultivated in Egypt

1200
Anonymous *Andalusian Cookery Book*

1206
The Mongol Empire emerged under the leadership of **Genghis Khan**

1250
Earliest records of **wine distillation** appear in Italy

1274
King Edward I of England coronation feast included 278 bacon hogs, 450 pigs, 440 oxen, 430 sheep and 22,600 hens and capons

1300
The Important Things to Know About Eating and Drinking by **Huou**, chef at the court of Kublai Khan

Earliest version of *Le Viandier* written, about 10 years before Guillaume Tirel's birth. Unknown original author

The **strawberry** was cultivated in Europe

1307
Swiss patriot **William Tell** shot an apple off his son's head

1315 – 1317
The **Great Famine** in Ireland

1364 – 1380
Forks are listed in inventory of plate during the reign of Charles V, France

1375
Le Viandier by Guillaume Tirel, alias **Taillevent**

1389
The four seasons of the House of Cerruti, Tacuinum Sanitatis, by **Ibn Butlan of Baghdad**

1390
The Forme of Cury, an extensive collection of **medieval English recipes**

1393
Le Ménagier de Paris, or *Le Ménagier* (The Parisian Household Book)

15TH CENTURY
O Livro de Cozinha da Infanta D. Maria de Portugal, the **first Portuguese cookbook**

Chinese are believed to have invented the first **natural bristle toothbrush**

1400s
Portuguese and Spanish developed important templates for later **New World plantation sugar** production on their Atlantic islands

1403
Charles VII of France was born. His mistress, **Agnès Sorel**, was a celebrated cook who created several dishes, and had numerous culinary creations named in her honour

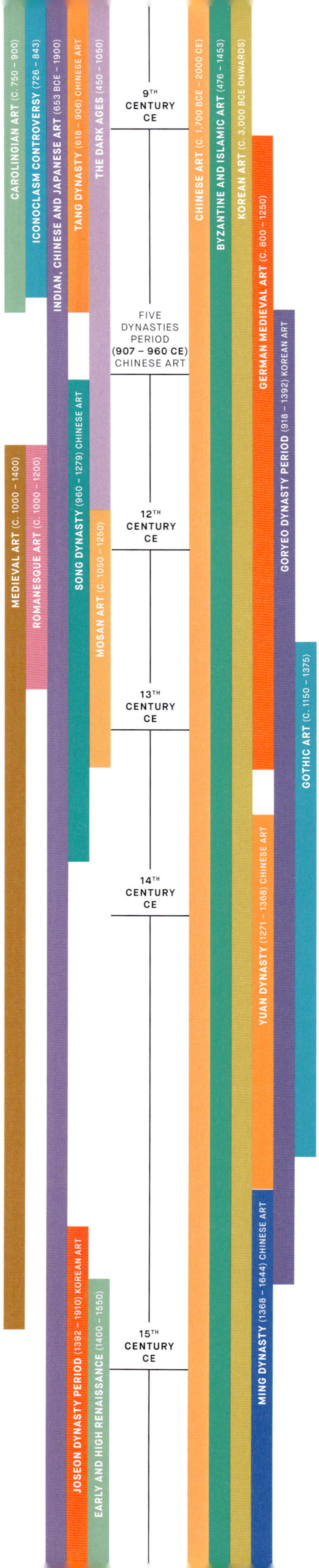

ART

770 CE
Woodblock printing in Japan (*mokuhanga*)

793 CE
Viking raids by seaborne Scandinavian pirates on sites in Britain

868 CE
Earliest dated printed book known, ***Diamond Sutra***, printed in China

11TH CENTURY CE
Concept of the **camera obscura** was understood by ancient scholars and formally developed by Islamic polymath **Ibn al-Haytham**

12TH CENTURY CE
Scholars meeting in a garden, painting attributed to **Emperor Huizon**

1100
Angkor Wat temple complex in Cambodia

1170
Bayeux Tapestry depicts the tale of the conquest of England in 1066

1200
Inca civilisation arose from the Peruvian highlands

1275
Medieval jug from France, found at Lesnes Abbey near London

14TH CENTURY CE
Canvas was introduced in Italy as a cheaper alternative to wood panel

1321
Trois Dames de Paris from **Couvin de Watriquet's** tale

1325 – 1330
The Last Supper by **Ugolino da Siena**

1337
Beginning of the **Hundred Years War**

1340
Dining room scene from the ***Luttrell Psalter***, by anonymous scribes and artists

1347
Black Death (bubonic plague) killed some 20 million people in Europe

1389
Gaston III, Count of Foix-Béarn, commissioned *The Book of the Hunt*

FOOD

1404
The word **brioche** first appeared

1411
Charles VI of France gave sole rights to the ageing of **Roquefort cheese** to the village of Roquefort-sur-Soulzon

Armagnac's name has been recorded, the oldest known wine spirit

1414
Coffee was known in Mecca

1425
There were around 4,000 **taverns in Paris**

1430
Bananas brought to Europe from Africa by voyages promoted by **Prince Henry the Navigator**

1444
Any merchant selling **adulterated saffron** in Bavaria was burned alive

1449
Evidence of coffee drinking in Yemen's Sufi monasteries

1450
Forks were first used in Portugal at the time of **Infanta Beatrice**

1453
Coffee was being grown in the Yemeni district of Arabia

1465
Liber de arte coquinaria was published by **Martino de Rossi**, the first Italian celebrity chef

1470
De honesta voluptate et valetudine, the first cookbook ever printed, by Bartolomeo Sacchi aka **Bartolomeo Platina**

1488
Portuguese explorer **Bartolomeu Dias**, first European mariner to round the southern tip of Africa

1490
Predecessor of the **modern oven** first appeared in Alsace, France

1493
Christopher Columbus returned from his first voyage

1494
Arawak Indians use Jamaican pepper to season and smoke meat, foundation of **Jamaican Jerk**

1495 – 1498
Portuguese, Norman, Breton and English fishermen, the first to adopt the **cod salt-based curing technique** from Basque fishermen in Newfoundland by the late 1400s

1494
Distilling of whisky in Scotland is fully underway

1497
Vasco de Gama left Lisbon to search for a sea route to India

1498
Portuguese vessels reached **Calicut in India** for the purpose of spice trading

16TH CENTURY CE
Aztecs invented ***guacamole***, word derived from *ahuaca-mulli* (avocado sauce)

Coffee was known in Persia, Egypt, Syria and Turkey

Cashews and **peanuts** introduced to Europe by Portuguese traders from the Americas

Kidney beans and **vanilla pods** introduced to Europe from the Americas

Cauliflowers introduced to France from Italy

Rice and **limes** introduced to Mexico by Spanish traders

Forks were widely adopted in Italy

1500
Native Americans utilised and cultivated **wild pecans**

C. 1500
Madeira's wine industry on the island supplied ships travelling to the East Indies with wine

1512
Swans were a common **Christmas dish** on the rich man's table

1513
The first Portuguese ship to reach a Chinese port in Canton

1519
Spanish explorers became the first Europeans to eat **avocados**

1520
Large quantities of **sugar** were being shipped from Brazil to Lisbon

Corn imported into Spain from West Indies by **Hernán Cortés** and **Christopher Columbus**

1521
Spanish missionaries brought the **pomegranate** to the New World

1524
Italian explorer **Giovanni da Verrazano** found **Muscadine grapes** (big white grapes) growing on the North Carolina coast at Cape Fear

VENETIAN AND NORTHERN RENAISSANCE (1430 – 1550)

INDIAN, CHINESE AND JAPANESE ART (653 BCE – 1900 CE)

JOSEON DYNASTY PERIOD (1392 – 1910) KOREAN ART

EARLY AND HIGH RENAISSANCE (1400 – 1550)

1430

1450

1470

1490

16TH CENTURY CE

1510

CHINESE ART (C. 1,700 BCE – 2000 CE)

BYZANTINE AND ISLAMIC ART (476 – 1453)

VENETIAN PAINTING (C. 1450 – 1800)

KOREAN ART (C. 3,000 BCE ONWARDS)

MING DYNASTY (1368 – 1644) CHINESE ART

ART

1430 – 1580
Fine art printing established during the German Renaissance

The Hours of Catherine of Cleves, illuminated manuscript, Gothic style

1447
The Last Supper by **Andrea del Castagno**

Johannes Gutenberg invents the printing press with replaceable wooden or metal letters

1449
Birth of **Lorenzo de Medici** the Magnificent, sponsor of many artists

1450
Madonna and Child Surrounded by Angels by **Jean Fouquet**

1452
Leonardo da Vinci, the epitome of a 'Renaissance man', was born

1453
Fall of Constantinople

1470
Bathhouse in **Valerius Maximus'** *Facta et Dicta Memorabilia*

1480
Domenico Ghirlandaio's *Herod's Banquet*, fresco in the Cappella Tornabuoni, Florence

1482 – 1483
La Primavera by **Botticelli**

C. 1487
Madonna of the Pomegranate by **Sandro Botticelli**

1495 – 1498
The Last Supper by **Leonardo da Vinci**

1500
The Lady and the Unicorn, **tapestry** illustrating the five senses

C. 1500
The Seven Deadly Sins and the Four Last Things by **Hieronymus Bosch**

1501 – 1504
David by **Michelangelo**

1503 – 1506
Mona Lisa, also known as *La Gioconda*, by **Leonardo da Vinci**

1505 – 1508
Benedictine monks depicted in a fresco by **Sodoma**

1510 – 1518
The Virgin and Child with St Anne, altarpiece by **Gerolamo dai Libri**

1513
The Sistine Madonna by the Urbino master **Raphael**

1517
Martin Luther nails a piece of paper containing the 95 revolutionary opinions that would begin the Protestant Reformation

1519
Portuguese navigator **Ferdinand Magellan** discovered the Strait of Magellan

1522
The fleet returned home three years later with spices from the East; only 18 of the original 270 man crew returned, and only one ship out of five. Magellan was killed on the voyage

1524
Golden Age of Venetian Painting: Giorgione, Titian, Tintoretto and Veronese

MANNERISM (1527 – 1580)
Art that breaks the rules; artifice over nature. Golden Age of Venetian Painting with Giorgione, Titian, Tintoretto and Veronese

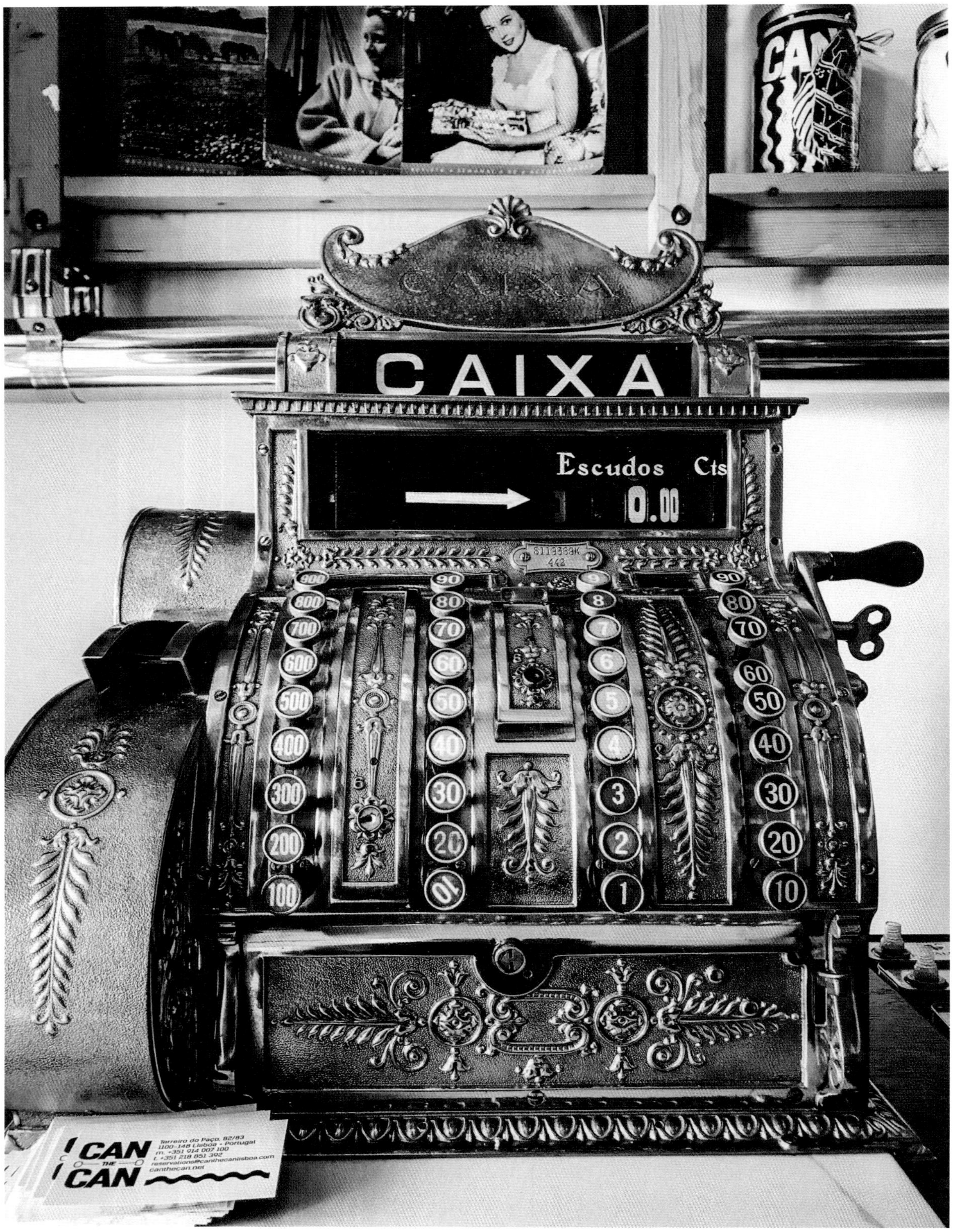
CAIXA
Escudos Cts
CAN THE CAN

FOOD

1532
Caviar is first mentioned as an *hors d'œuvres* in *Pantagruel*, the first of five comic novels by **François Rabelais**

1533
Forks were brought from Italy to France by **Catherine de Medici**

1536
To deceive the Inquisition, the inhabitants of Mirandela, Portugal, created a **sausage made with bread and chicken**, which resembled traditional pork sausages: the ***alheira***

1539
Hernando de Soto arrived at Tampa Bay, Florida, with America's first 13 **pigs**

1542
Historia Stirpium by **Leonhard Fuchs**, German botanist and physician

1544
Hernán Cortés introduced **chocolate as a drink** to Spain

1550
The **first café** in the world supposedly opened in Constantinople

1551
A New Herball by **William Turner**, known as the Father of English Botany

1552
Mal Cozinhado a place in Lisbon with ten porches 'where there's always someone with fire braziers grilling sardines and fish'

Treatise on the majesty, magnitude and abundance of Lisbon town by **J. Brandão**

GRANDE CUISINE (1553 – 1898)
Cooking style defined by attention to detail, fancy dishes and rich food

1553
Calvados brandy mentioned in the diary of **Gilles de Gouberville**, a gentleman of the Cotentin, France

1554
Tomatoes from South America cultivated in Europe

1555
Istanbul introduced to **coffee** during the reign of Sultan Suleiman

Nostradamus published the *Traité des fardemens et confitures*

1564
William Shakespeare was born, many references to food in his works

1568
Alexander Nowell, the Dean of St. Paul's Cathedral, developed a method to **bottle beer**

1569
Law in France forbidding bakers to wear breeches other than on Sundays

1570
Opera dell'arte del cucinare, book by **Bartolomeo Scappi**

1573
Potatoes brought back from the Americas and cultivated in Spain

1574
Corporation of Pasta Makers is founded in Genova, Italy

1577
The Regolazione dell'Arte dei Maestri Fidelari, Savona, Italy

1580s
Ritrato e Riverso del regno di Portogallo, Italian, anonymous

1581
Ein new Kochbuch by **Marx Rumpolt**: large-format, illustrated cookery book is published

1582
La Tour d'Argent restaurant is founded in Paris

1586
Sir Thomas Harriot brought the first **potatoes** to England, from Colombia

1588
Julien Le Paulmier lists in his *Traité du Sidre*, dozens of apple varieties

1590
The Florentine Codex, ethnographic research study in Mesoamerica by the Spanish Franciscan friar **Bernardino de Sahagún**

1591
First appearance in English print of the **word caviar** originated from the Turkish *khavyar*

LATE 16TH CENTURY
Production and sale of confectionery by convents, Lisbon

VENETIAN AND NORTHERN RENAISSANCE (1430 – 1550)
INDIAN, CHINESE AND JAPANESE ART (653 BCE – 1900 CE)
JOSEON DYNASTY PERIOD (1392 – 1910) KOREAN ART
EARLY AND HIGH RENAISSANCE (1400 – 1550)
GRANDE CUISINE (1553 – 1898)

1530
1540
1550
GRANDE CUISINE 1553 – 1898
1560
1570
1580
1590

CHINESE ART (C. 1,700 BCE – 2000 CE)
VENETIAN PAINTING (C. 1450 – 1800)
KOREAN ART (C. 3,000 BCE ONWARDS)
MING DYNASTY (1368 – 1644) CHINESE ART
MANNERISM (1527 – 1580)

ART

1527
Birth of **Giuseppe Arcimboldo**, Italian painter best known for creating imaginative portrait heads made entirely of objects such as fruits, vegetables, flowers, fish and books

1530 – 1550
The Legend of the Baker of Eeklo by **Jan van Wechelen**

1536
The Last Judgement, fresco at Sistine Chapel by **Michelangelo**

1543
Copernicus proves the Earth revolves around the Sun

1551
Butcher's Stall with the Flight into Egypt by **Pieter Aertsen**

1559
The Cook by **Pieter Aertsen**

1560
First **wood-encased carpentry pencil** by **Simonio** and **Lyndiana Bernacotti**

1562
The Wedding Feast at Cana by **Paolo Veronese**

1565
Marten van Cleve I, *Kitchen Scene*, Verona, Castelvecchio

1567
The Vegetable Market by **Joachim Beuckelaer**

The Peasant Wedding by **Pieter Bruegel**

1569
The Four Elements: Water and Earth by **Joachim Beuckelaer**

1570
The Four Elements: Fire and Air by **Joachim Beuckelaer**

1573
The Feast in the House of Levi by **Paolo Veronese**, a man with a fork

1576
The Supper at Emmaus by **Jacopo dal Ponte**, called Bassano

1580s
An Elderly Couple by **George Flegel** and **Lucas van Valckenborch**

1580
The Kitchen by **Vincenzo Campi**

1580 – 1590
The Butcher's Shop by **Annibale Carracci**

Mangiafagioli (The Beaneater) by **Annibale Carracci**

1581
Chicken Vendors by **Vincenzo Campi**

1590
Vertumnus, a portrait by **Giuseppe Arcimboldo** depicting Rudolf II, Holy Roman Emperor painted as Vertumnus, the Roman God of the Seasons

A Small Celebration by **George Flegel** and **Lucas van Valckenborch**

1591
Metal Plate with Peaches and Vine Leaves by **Giovanni Ambrogio Figino**

1592
The Last Supper by **Tintoretto**

Cannibalism Among the Brazilian Natives by **Théodore de Bry**

1593
Boy with a Basket of Fruit by **Caravaggio**

1595
Bacchus by **Caravaggio**

1596
Fruitmand by **Caravaggio**

LATE 16TH CENTURY
The Cook, by Renaissance painter **Bernardino Campi**

FOOD

17TH CENTURY
Manuscript 142 do Arquivo Distrital de Braga, assigned to **Frei Luís de Távora**

Chocolate houses were the social meeting places of the day

First made in Holland, **gin** spread quickly throughout Europe

Parsley introduced to America by British colonists

Jerusalem artichoke introduced to Europe from its native North America

1600
Ice cream is said to have come from France

Virginia strawberries of North America reached Europe

British merchants formed the **East India Company** and introduced **teas** into England and the American colonies

1602
The **Dutch East India Company** is founded

Massachusetts Bay Colony introduced to **clams** by the native Indians

1611
Englishman **Thomas Coryate** brought the **first forks to England**

1615
Venetian merchants, acquainted with **coffee** in Istanbul, carried it back to Italy

The first **tea** is imported to the West

Ann of Austria introduces **drinking chocolate** to the French Court

1623
Wild turkeys found by the Pilgrims in the New World

Coffee forbidden by the Sultan of the Ottoman Empire, Murad IV

Use of **celery** as food was first recorded in France

1626
Claude Lorrain, painter, credited with the invention of **puff pastry**

1630
Louis de Béchameil (Béchamel) was born

Massachusetts Bay governor introduced the fork to American dining

1633
Bananas were displayed in the storefront of **Thomas Johnson**, probably the first time they were seen in Great Britain

1634
Dijon in France granted the exclusive rights to make mustard

Samuel Cole supposedly opened the **first tavern in Boston**

1637
Coffee was first introduced as a drink to Oxford by a Turk

Cardinal Richelieu 'created' the **table knife** when he had the points rounded on all knives to be used at his table. Presumably so no one could stab him

C. 1640
Birth of **Louis XIV** of France. A gourmet, gourmand and many say, a glutton. During his reign food began to be served in **courses, and forks came into widespread use**

1644
First coffee beans arrived in Marseille with French ambassador **Jean de la Roque**

1645
First coffee house in Italy after coffee previously being sold on the street by lemonade vendors

1646
l'Art de trancher la viande et toutes sortes de fruits à la mode italienne et nouvellement françoise by **Jacques Vonte**

1650
Some claim that the **first café** opened in Oxford

MIDDLE 17TH CENTURY
There were over **300 coffee houses in London**

UKIYO-E[A] (C. 1600 – 1900)
BAROQUE ART (C. 1600 – 1700)
INDIAN, CHINESE AND JAPANESE ART (653 BCE – 1900 CE)
JOSEON DYNASTY PERIOD (1392 – 1910) KOREAN ART
GRANDE CUISINE (1553 – 1898)

17TH CENTURY CE
1610
1620
1630
1640
1650

CHINESE ART (C. 1,700 BCE – 2000 CE)
VENETIAN PAINTING (C. 1450 – 1800)
KOREAN ART (C. 3,000 BCE ONWARDS)
MING DYNASTY (1368 – 1644) CHINESE ART
QING DYNASTY (1644 – 1911) CHINESE ART

ART

BAROQUE ART (1600 – 1700)
A new found splendour, richness and exuberance in art, which was used as a weapon in the religious wars. Rubens, Rembrandt, Caravaggio, Palace of Versailles

UKIYO-E [A] (1600 – 1900)
Literally, the term *ukiyo* means 'floating world'

1600
Still Life by **Osias Beert**

A Chinese Dish with Artichokes, a Rose and Strawberries by **Giovanna Garzoni**

1602 – 1603
Supper at Emmaus by **Caravaggio**

1602
Still Life with Game, Vegetables and Fruit by **Juan Sánchez Cotán**

Banquet of the Chevaliers of the Holy Spirit by **Abraham Bosse**

1610
The Feast of Antony and Cleopatra by **Leandro Bassano**

1610 – 1625
The Chef by **Alejandro de Loarte**, kitchen scene of Bodegón

1611
Still Life with Wine Cooler by **Frans Snyders**

1614
Still Life with Dead Game, Fruits, and Vegetables in a Market by **Frans Snyders**

1615
Still Life with Cheese by **Floris van Dyck**

1618
Old Woman Frying Eggs by **Diego Velázquez**

Three Men at a Table by **Diego Velázquez**

Allegory of Taste by **Jan Bruegel the Elder and Peter Paul Rubens**

1618 – 1648
Thirty Years War between Catholics and Protestants

1618 – 1688
The Hunt Picnic by **Gaston Fébus**, *livre de chasse*

1620
Novum Organum Scientiarum, philosophical work by **Francis Bacon**

Still Life with Fruit and Flowers by **Balthasar van der Ast**

1623
Still Life with Fruit and Vegetables by **Juan van der Hamen y León**

1626
Paysage by **Claude Lorrain**, born Claude Gellée, dit Claude Lorrain

Poultry Vendor by **Alejandro de Loarte**

1627
Still Life with a Turkey Pie by **Pieter Claesz**

1630
Still Life with Grapes, Flowers and Shells by **Juan de Espinosa**

Still-Life with Bread and Confectionery by **Georg Flegel**

1633
Still Life with Lemons, Oranges and a Rose by **Francisco de Zurbarán**

Galileo was forced by the Inquisition to renounce his theory of Earth revolving around the Sun

1634
Still Life with a Gilded Beer Tankard by **Willem Claesz**

1638
Great Meal, Still Life with Lemons Featured Prominently by **Georg Flegel**

C. 1640
Still Life with a Bowl of Chocolate by **Juan de Zurbarán**

Still Life with Servant by **Paul de Vos**

1635 – 1640
Still Life with Fish, Crustaceans, Onions, Oranges and Cat by **Baltazar Gomes Figueira**

1644
Kitchen Scene by **David Teniers**

Banquet Still Life by **Adriaen van Utrecht**

Still Life of Glasses in a Basket by **Sebastien Stoskopff**

1645
Still Life with Glass, Glass Stand and Musical Instruments by **Jan Davidsz Heem**

Still Life with Game, Fish, Fruit, Vegetables, Animals and Figures by **Adriaen van Utrecht**

1646
Breakfast Piece by **Pieter Claesz**

1648
The Father in the Kitchen by **Adrien van Ostade**

1649
Fruit Stall with a Couple by **Peter van Boucle**

1625 – 1650
Dish with Jasmine and Hazelnuts by **Giovanna Garzon**

1650
Still Life with Fruit, Plates and Dishes on a Turkey Carpet by **Francesco Fieravino**

MIDDLE 17TH CENTURY
Fruit and Vegetable Stall by **Frans Snyders**

FOOD

1651
Le Cuisinier François by **Pierre François de la Varenne**

1653
Le Pâtissier François by **Pierre François de la Varenne**

1654
Queen's Lane Coffee House established in Oxford, which still stands today

Nicolas de Bonnefons publishes *Les Délices de la Campagne*

1656
Le Cuisinier by **Pierre de Lune**

1657
Opening of the **first chocolate house in London**

1660
Asser Levy from Portugal, applied for a license to sell **kosher meat**

1662
Tea was officially introduced to England by **Catarina de Bragança**

1668
Experiments on the Generation of Insects by **Francesco Redi**

Drowned ring bread appears on several paintings

1669
Paris was introduced to coffee by Hoşsohbet Nüktedan Süleyman Ağa

1670
The Sensible Cook, or Careful Housekeeper by **Marcus Doornick**

At Cologne Cathedral, the choirmaster makes sugar sticks to give to the young singers in the choir, **the first candy canes**

Coriander cultivated for the first time in the USA, in Massachusetts

1671
François Vatel was responsible for a banquet for 2,000 guests, in honour of Louis XIV, when he committed suicide

1673
The White Horse Tavern in Rhode Island was built

1674
L'Art de Bien Traiter by **L.S.R.**, probably a cook named Robert

1675
The Accomplish'd lady's delight in preserving, physick, beautifying, and cookery by **Hannah Woolley**

1676
Compagnie de Limonadiers was formed in Paris. Vendors sold lemonade from tanks they carried on their backs: **the first commercial soft drinks**

1679
'**Steam Digester**' pressure cooker by **Denis Papin**

1680 – 1691
Hans Sloane mixed bitter Jamaica chocolate beverage with milk to improve its taste. **Chocolate milk was invented**

1680
Arte de Cozinha by **Domingos Rodrigues** cook of the Royal House of Portugal

1683
Legend says **croissants** were created in Vienna, Austria to celebrate defeating the Turks

Bagels were created by a Vienna baker

1686
Opening of **Paris's first coffee shop** called **Le Procope**

1691
Le Cuisinier Royal et Bourgeois by **Massialot**

1692
Nouvelle Instruction Pour les Confitures, les Liqueurs et les Fruits by **Massialot**

1693
Dom Perignon supposedly discovers the process for making **champagne**

1696
The **first coffee house** was set up in New York, named **The King's Arms**

1700
Salted cod become a staple food for the Portuguese, nicknamed 'the loyal friend'

Cesare Spadaccini designed a bronze machine to make pasta

1703
Mount Gay Estate, the oldest existing brand of rum, began **distilling rum**

1709
Daniel Gabriel Fahrenheit invents the **alcohol thermometer**

AMERICAN COLONIAL ART (C. 1670 – 1800)
UKIYO-E[A] (C. 1600 – 1900)
BAROQUE ART (C. 1600 – 1700)
INDIAN, CHINESE AND JAPANESE ART (653 BCE – 1900 CE)
JOSEON DYNASTY PERIOD (1392 – 1910) **KOREAN ART**
GRANDE CUISINE (1553 – 1898)

1660
1670
1680
1690
18TH CENTURY CE

CHINESE ART (C. 1,700 BCE – 2000 CE)
VENETIAN PAINTING (C. 1450 – 1800)
KOREAN ART (C. 3,000 BCE ONWARDS)
QING DYNASTY (1644 – 1911) **CHINESE ART**
ROCOCO ART STYLE (18TH CENTURY)

ART

1651
'Bodegón' with Dead Bird by **Juan de Espinosa**

1653
Still Life with Lobster, Drinking Horn and Glasses by **Willem Kalf**

Still Life with Oysters and Grapes by **Jan Davidsz**

1655
Slaughtered Ox by **Rembrandt**

1655 – 1665
Boy with a Basket of Bread and Pastries by **Evaristo Baschenis**

1656
Still life Ode to the Herring by **Joseph de Bray**

1657
The Milkmaid by **Johannes Vermeer**

1658
The Baker Arent Oostwaard and his Wife Catharina Keizerswaard by **Jan Havicksz**

1659
Fruit by **Theodoor Aenvanck**

1660
Still Life with Beer Glass and Nuts by **Georg Hainz**

Still Life with Fruit and a Beaker on a Cock's Foot by **Abraham Mignon**

1665
Still Life with Beer Glass by **Johann Georg Hinz**

1667
Venetian Banquet for Queen Christina of Sweden by **Pierre Paul Sevin**

1668
Bodegón by **Tomás Hiepes**

1600 – 1670
Stil Life with Cakes by **Josefa de Óbidos**

1670 – 1684
Agnus Dei Sacrificial Lamb by **Josefa de Óbidos**

A Poulterer's Shop by **Gerrit Dou**

Earliest success of **ukiyo-e** with **Hishikawa Moronobu's** paintings

1674
Revelry at an Inn by **Jan Steen**

1676
Still Life with Flowers, Candies and Cherries by **Josefa de Óbidos**

1680 – 1691
Still Life near a Fountain by **Pieter Gijsels**

1681
The Baker by **Job Adriaensz Berckheyde**

1684
The Riches of the Sea with Neptune, Tritons and Two Nereids by **Guiuseppe Recco** and **Luca Giordano**

1685 – 1815
European politics, philosophy, science and communications were radically reoriented as part of the Age of Reason movement, or the Enlightenment

1690
Mangia Bene, a trump card from a pack by **Giuseppe Maria Mitelli**

1694
The Apotheosis of St Ignatius by **Pozzo**

1696
A Bowl of Strawberries on a Stone Plinth by **Adriaen Coorte**

1697
Still Life with Asparagus by **Adriaen Coorte**

1699
Carrot by **Willem Frederik van Royen**

ROCOCO ART STYLE (18TH CENTURY)

EARLY 18TH CENTURY
Salty Easter Meal by **Tommaso Realfonso**

1700
Still Life with Fried Eggs, Lemon, Bread and a Flask of Wine by **Cristoforo Munari**

Still Life with Fruit by **Jan van Huysum**

The Banquet of Cleopatra by **Gerard Hoet**

1706
Giant Cauliflower by **Bartolomeo Bimbi**

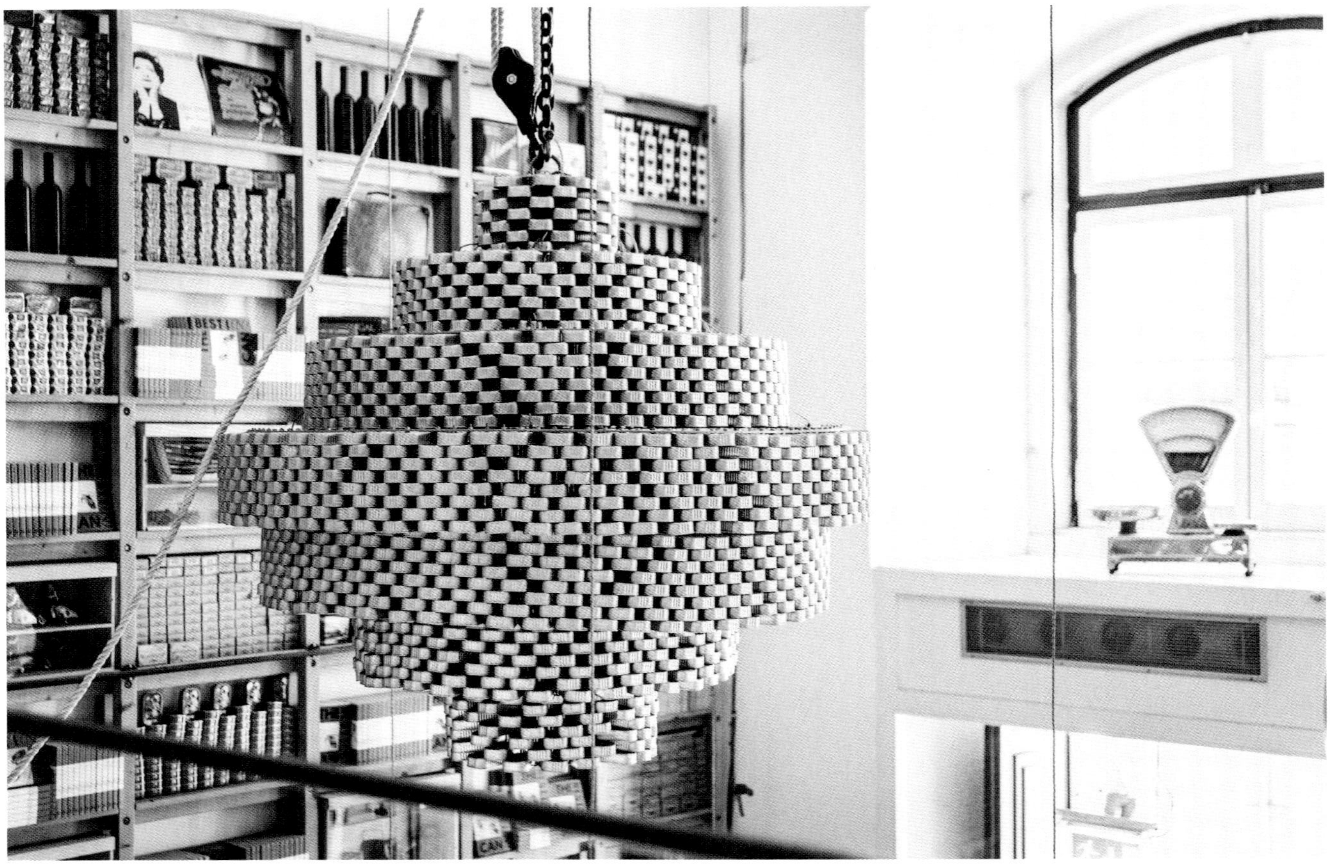

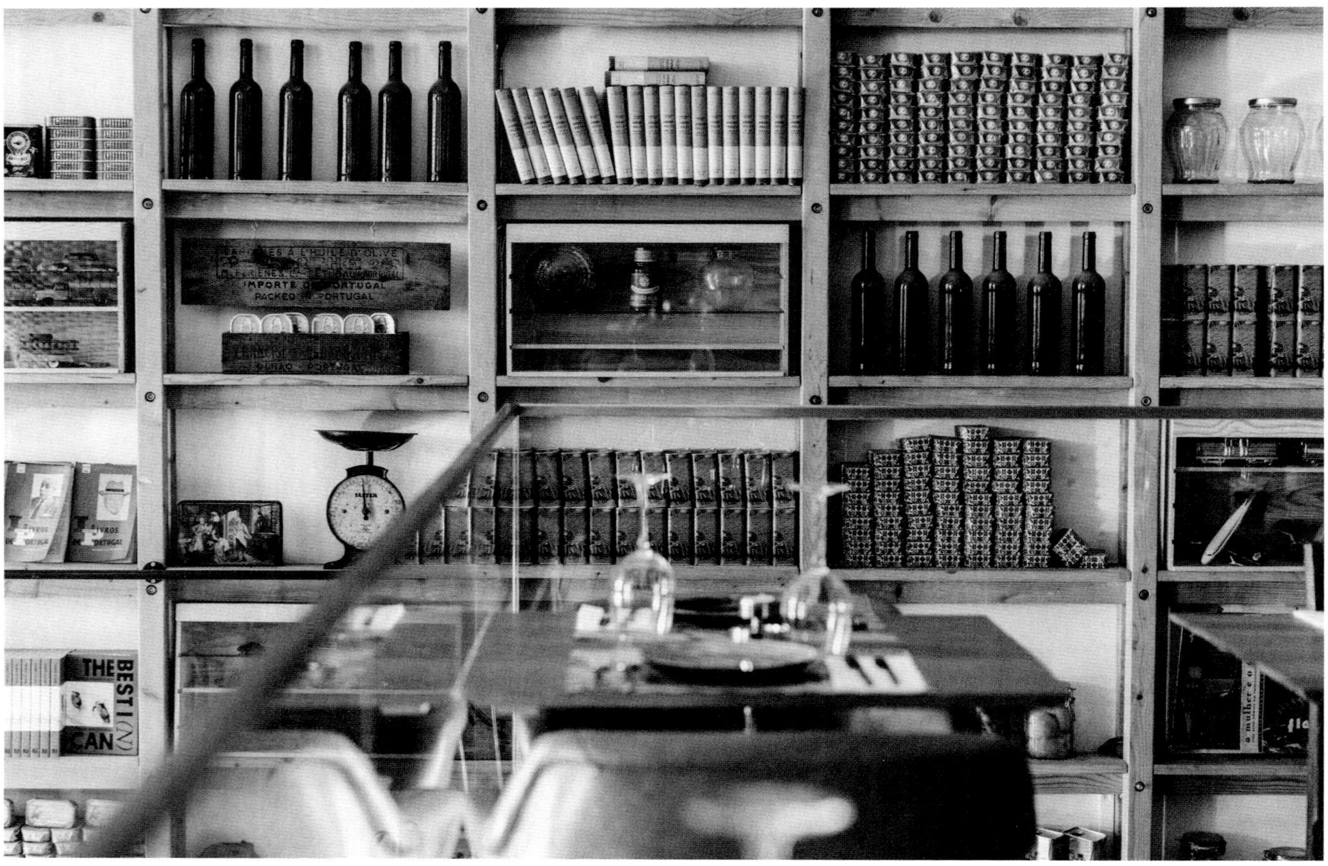
THE BEST I(N) CAN
SALTER

FOOD

1717
Thomas Twining opens **Golden House**, world's first dry tea and coffee shop

1718
John Montagu, 4th Earl of Sandwich is born. His butler and cook is credited with the invention of the **sandwich**

1720
Invention of **meringue** is attributed to **Gasparini**, a Swiss pastry chef

1723
First **glassworks specialising in wine bottles** sets up in Bordeaux

1727
Portuguese sailor named **De Mello Palheta** introduced **coffee to Brazil**

1729
Literary, epicurean and gastronomic society founded in Paris by **Piron**, **Gallet**, **Collé and Crébillon fils** at **Le Caveau**

1732 – 1733
Compleat City and Country Cook by **Charles Carter**

1733
The Modern Cook by **Vincent La Chapelle**

1735
French architect François de Cuvilliés invented the **castrol (or stew) stove**

1736
The Country Housewife and Lady's Director in the Management of a House, and the Delights and Profits of a Farm by **Richard Bradley**

1740
Venice issues a licence to **Paolo Adami** to open the **first pasta factory**

1741
Anders Celsius developed the **centigrade temperature scale**

1742
Benjamin Franklin invented the **Franklin stove**

The Compleat Housewife, **first American cookbook**

1745
Drambuie liqueur formula given to Mackinnon family by Prince Charles Edward

1747
Art of Cookery by **Hannah Glasse**

1748
La Cuisinière Bourgeoise by **Menon**

Worcester Royal Porcelain Company is founded in England

First form of artificial refrigeration, invented by **William Cullen**

1755
Marie Antoinette was born. 'If they have no bread, let them eat cake'

One of Europe's most powerful **earthquakes struck Lisbon**

1756
Marquis of Pombal established bouncaries and regulations for the production of authentic Douro **port wine**

1758
Benjamin Jackson advertised mustard for sale for the first time in America

1759
First historical mention of a **mère** dates back to **Mère Guy**

1760
Foundation of **Lombart Chocolate** or Chocolaterie Lombart

Restaurants invented in Paris in the 1760s began to serve *restaurants*, a type of soup

1763
Stefano Lucciardi wins the right to a 10-year monopoly for **production of Genova-style dried pasta**

1764
Lawrence's Hotel is established in Sintra, Portugal

1765
The first ***pâté de foie gras*** created by Norman chef **Jean-Joseph Close**

1765
Opening of the **Boulanger's Restaurant** by Monsieur Boulanger, first in history

1768
Le Cannameliste français ou Nouvelle instruction pour ceux qui désirent d'apprendre l'office, rédigé en forme de dictionnaire by **Joseph Gilliers**

1770s
Keiller's marmalade, first commercial brand of marmalade in Great Britain

1770
Earliest known design for a **weighing scale** by **Richard Salter**

1771
Antoine-Augustin Parmentier won an contest with potato voted as the best substitute for regular flour

1772
The Frugal Housewife by **Susannah Carter**, first published in London

1773
The café **Cadran Bleu** opened in Paris

AMERICAN COLONIAL ART (C. 1670 – 1800)
UKIYO-E[A] (C. 1600 – 1900)
INDIAN, CHINESE AND JAPANESE ART (653 BCE – 1900 CE)
JOSEON DYNASTY PERIOD (1392 – 1910) KOREAN ART
GRANDE CUISINE (1553 – 1898)
INDUSTRIAL REVOLUTION (1760 – 1840)

1720
1730
1740
NEOCLASSICAL 1750 – 1850
1760
1770

CHINESE ART (C. 1,700 BCE – 2000 CE)
VENETIAN PAINTING (C. 1450 – 1800)
KOREAN ART (C. 3,000 BCE ONWARDS)
QING DYNASTY (1644 – 1911) CHINESE ART
ROCOCO ART STYLE (18TH CENTURY)
AMERICAN REVOLUTION (1765 – 1783)
NEOCLASSICAL ART (FLOURISHED 1770 – 1830)
ROMANTIC ART STYLE (C. 1770 – 1920)

ART

1710
Ichikawa Danjūrō I in the role of Takenuki Gorō by **Torii Kiyomasu**

1716 – 1780
Manchego Cheese, Pears and an Earthenware Jug by **Luís Meléndez**

1727
Suplicio dos Doces, book written by a Jesuit priest and master of theology, **Silvestre Aranha**

1728
La Raie by **Jean-Baptiste-Siméon Chardin**

1732 –1733
Tavern Scene or *The Orgy* by **William Hogarth**

1735
Engravings by **Martin Engelbrecht**

1740
Le Garçon Cabaretier by **Charles-Nicolas Cochin**

1744
A Lady Pouring Chocolate by **Jean-Étienne Liotard**

The Sense of Taste by **Philippe Mercier**

1745
Charles Edward Stuart's travelling canteen by Edinburgh goldsmith **Ebenezer Oliphant**

Taking the Evening Cool by Ryōgoku Bridge, Western-style graphical perspective (uki-e) and increased use of printed colour by **Okumura Masanobu**

1754
Sculptor **Franz Anton Bustelli** employed at Porzellan Manufaktur Nymphenburg

1755
Earthquake by **João Glama Stöberle**

1760
Le Panier de Fraises des Bois by **Jean-Baptiste-Siméon Chardin**

1763
The Dancing Couple by **Jan Steen**

1764
Catherine the Great established the **Hermitage Museum** in **St Petersburg**

1768
Foundation of the **Royal Academy of Arts** in London

NEOCLASSICAL (1770 – 1830)
Art that recaptures Greco-Roman grace and grandeur

ROMANTIC ART STYLE (1770 – 1920)
The triumph of imagination and individuality

1770s
Still Life with Fruit by **Jan van Huysum**

1770
Still Life with Chocolate Service by **Luis Meléndez**

1771
White Soup Bowl by **Anne Coster Vallayer**

Still Life with Pomegranates, Apples, Azaroles and Grapes in a Landscape by **Luis Meléndez**

1772
Still Life with Oranges and Walnuts by **Luis Meléndez**

FOOD

1776
Book of Cookery, Pastry, Preserving, Pickling and Medicinal Recipes by **Hannah Wilson**

1780
The Modern Cook or The Art of Cuisine by **Lucas Rigaud**

1782
Café Martinho da Arcada opens in Lisbon by **Julião Pereira de Castro**

La Grande Taverne de Londres is founded in Paris by **Antoine Beauvilliers**

1783
Johann Jacob Schweppe founded the **Schweppes** Company in Geneva

C. 1783 – 1888
Abolitionism, also called the abolition movement, started

1784
Tavares Rico, Lisbon's oldest restaurant, by the Italian **Nicolau Massa**

1788
Arte Nova e Curiosa para Conserveiros, Confeiteiros e Copeiros, first Portuguese confectionery book – undocumented author

1789
First national **Thanksgiving Day** celebrated in the US

1793
First American hotel, **The Union Public Hotel**, built by **Samuel Blodget Jr.**

1794
La Cuisinière Républicaine, first potato cookbook, by **Madame Mérigot**

1795
Prize offered by French government for the **invention of a method to keep food safe for troops**

1796
American Cookery by **Amelia Simmons**

1797
Dubied Père et Fils, manufacturer of the **absinthe liqueur**, later Pernod Fils

1799
Physicist **Sir Benjamin Thompson** stumbled on the method of **sous-vide**

Honoré de Balzac was born, French author of some repute for his gluttony

EARLY 1800s
Beginnings of **large-scale candy making**, especially in England

1800
Chicken Marengo was supposedly created by Napoleon's Swiss chef to commemorate victory over the Austrians in the Battle of Marengo

Pastry cook **Jean Avice** is said to have been the creator of the **madeleine**

The Champeaux restaurant, immortalised by **Émile Zola**, was founded

First **soup kitchens** in London opened to serve the poor

1801
Joseph Berchoux invents the word **gastronomy** by publishing *La Gastronomie*

1802
Thomas Moore created an icebox and patented the **refrigerator**

The Café Anglais opened in the Boulevard des Italiens

1803
Almanach des gourmands by **Alexandre Balthazar Laurent Grimod de La Reynière**

1804
First bananas marketed in the United States were brought from Cuba

1805
Pernod Fils company is founded in Pontarlier, France by **Henri-Louis Pernod**

1806
First definition of the word **cocktail** appeared in the New York publication *The Balance and Columbian Repository* of Hudson newspaper

Boston Exchange Coffee House opened

1808 – 1812
Le Manuel des amphitryons by **Grimod de La Reynière**

1809
Nicolas Appert invents the **canning process for food**

1810
Prince Borisovitch Kourakine invented the ***service à la Russe***

Sir John Leslie, a Scot, was the first to **freeze water artificially**

Peter Durand was granted the first patent for **preserving food in tin cans**

1814
L'Art du Cuisinier by **Antoine Beauvilliers**

1815
The world's **first commercial cheese factory** established in Switzerland

---

INDUSTRIAL REVOLUTION (1760 – 1840)
AMERICAN COLONIAL ART (C. 1670 – 1800)
UKIYO-E[A] (C. 1600 – 1900)
INDIAN, CHINESE AND JAPANESE ART (653 BCE – 1900 CE)
JOSEON DYNASTY PERIOD (1392 – 1910) KOREAN ART
GRANDE CUISINE (1553 – 1898)

1785
1795
19TH CENTURY CE
1805
1810
1815

CHINESE ART (C. 1,700 BCE – 2000 CE)
VENETIAN PAINTING (C. 1450 – 1800)
KOREAN ART (C. 3,000 BCE ONWARDS)
QING DYNASTY (1644 – 1911) CHINESE ART
AMERICAN REVOLUTION (1765 – 1783)
FRENCH REVOLUTION (1789 – 1799)
NEOCLASSICAL ART (FLOURISHED 1770 – 1830)
ROMANTIC ART STYLE (C. 1770 – 1920)

ART

1778
The Wards at Saint John's Hospital by **Jan Beerblock**

First historically recorded **samovar-makers** by the **Russian Lisitsyn brothers, Ivan Fyodorovich** and **Nazar Fyodorovich**

1779
Still Life with Fruits, Knife and Pencil by **Jan Brandes**

1782
Le Restaurant by **Nicolas Lavreince**

1785
Still Life with Watermelon, Grapes, and Figs by **Morgado de Setúbal**

1794
Louvre opened as a public museum in Paris

1795
Still Life with Pea and Plums by **Mateusz Tokarski**

1798
First successful model of a practical paper machine invented by **Nicholas Louis Robert**

1799
Invention of lithography by the Austrian printer, **Alois Senefelder**

1800
Iron-framed lever press, by **Lord Stanhope**

The Pasta-eater, unknown author

1803
Machine-made paper begins to replace hand-made paper

1804
Napoleon crowned emperor of France

Fungi Austriaci, iconibus illustrati by **Leopoldus Trattinnick**, Austrian botanist

1808 – 1812
A Butcher's Stall by **Francisco de Goya**

1810
Rice Cakes and Bonito by **Toyota Hokkei**

1812
Pomona Britannica, work on fruit and flowers by **George Brookshaw**

1814
Frederich Koenig's steam printing machine marks the beginning of the mechanical printing with the production of *The Times*

1815
Beef by **James Ward**

L'intérieur d'une cuisine by **Martin Drölling**

FOOD

1816
The **umami taste** was identified by French cuisine and referred to as '**osmazone**' by the chemist **Louis Jacques Thénard**

1819
François-Louis Cailler opens the **first Swiss chocolate factory** near Vevey

1820
António Marrare opens **Café Marrare 'do Polimento'**, Lisbon

1822
Dish **Chateaubriand** created by chef Montmireil, for Vicomte **François-René de Chateaubriand**

1824
Pierre-Joseph Colin opens in Nantes, the **first canning factory**

The Virginia Housewife cookbook by **Mary Randolph**

Jean-Jacques-Régis de Cambacérès died, who famously said: 'a country is governed by good dinner parties'

1825
Ezra Daggett and Thomas Kensett granted the first US patent for **food storage in tin cans**

Brillat-Savarin's book *La Physiologie du goût* is published

1826
British inventor **James Sharp** patented the **first successful gas stove**

1827
John Morrel & Co founded in Bradford, England

Café and restaurant **Aurea Peninsular** opens in Lisbon, by **José Joaquim da Nobrega**

1828
Le Cuisinier parisien, ou l'art de la cuisine française by **Marie-Antoine Carême**

Van Houten invented cocoa pressing method and then **cocoa powder**

The word **cupcake** is first found in *Receipts* by **E. Leslie**

Le Gastronome Français ou l'Art de Bien Vivre by **Honoré de Balzac**

1829
Balthazar Roiz Castanheiro opens **Confeitaria Nacional**, Lisbon

1830
Physiologie Gastronomique by **Honoré de Balzac**

Béarnaise sauce made by **Collinet** in Pavillion Henri IV restaurant

1831
Jonathan Dodgson Carr starts producing **Carr's biscuits**

1832
Opening of **Restaurante Irmãos Unidos** in Lisbon

1833
Jordan Mott invented the **first practical coal oven**, the baseburner

Marie-Antoine Carême died in Paris, 'the cook of kings and the king of cooks'

1834
José Maria da Fonseca, Portuguese wine company is founded

Jacob Perkins patented the **first ice-making machine**

1835
Opening of **Fábrica de Cerveja Trindade** in Lisbon

1837
John Lea and **William Perrins** of Worcester create **Worcester Sauce**

Pastéis de Belém production starts in Antiga Confeitaria de Belém, Lisbon

1839
Marie, Vicomte de Botherel installed kitchens on buses

1840
Gas was first used for cooking

Ginjinha Espinheira opens in Lisbon

French writer and critic **Émile Zola** was born, also known as a gourmand

1840s
The first **iceboxes** were made in wood, lined with tin or zinc

1841
The Hotel Braganza opens its doors in Lisbon

1843
Manual device cranked by a handle to produce **ice cream** is made by **Nancy Johnson**

1844
First successful refrigeration machine developed by **John Gorrie**, USA

1845
The Modern Cook by **Charles Elmé Francatelli**

1846
Mathis Ferrari opens the pastry shop **Casa Ferrari**, Lisbon

The Gastronomic Regenerator by chef and food writer **Alexis Benoît Soyer**

Gâteau St-Honoré originated by pastry chef **Fauvel**

1847
J. S. Fry & Sons, Ltd, produced the **first solid chocolate bar**, England

INDUSTRIAL REVOLUTION (1760 – 1840)
VICTORIAN ART (1840 – 1900)
UKIYO-E[A] (C. 1600 – 1900)
INDIAN, CHINESE AND JAPANESE ART (653 BCE – 1900 CE)
JOSEON DYNASTY PERIOD (1392 – 1910) KOREAN ART
GRANDE CUISINE (1553 – 1898)

1825
1830
1835
1840
1845

CHINESE ART (C. 1,700 BCE – 2000 CE)
QING DYNASTY (1644 – 1911) CHINESE ART
KOREAN ART (C. 3,000 BCE ONWARDS)
NEOCLASSICAL ART (FLOURISHED 1770 – 1830)
ROMANTIC ART STYLE (C. 1770 – 1920)

ART

1816
Silver service, **known as the Baixela da Victoria**, designed by the Portuguese painter **Domingos António Sequeira**

Photography was invented by **Joseph Nicéphore Niépce**

1819
Inauguration of the **Prado Museum**, with **Maria Isabel de Bragança** as the great promoter of the project

1823 – 1826
Still Life with Lemon and Cut-Glass Wine Goblet by **Maria Margaretha van Os**

Founding of **Vista Alegre** porcelain factory, in Portugal

1824 – 1826
Still Life with Fruit, Bottles, Breads by **Francisco Goya**

1826
View from the Window at Le Gras by **Joseph Nicéphore Niépce**, earliest surviving photograph of a real-world scene

1826 – 1827
Still Life with Lobster and Trophies of Hunting and Fishing by **Eugène Delacroix**

1829
The Great Wave off Kanagawa, woodblock print by **Katsushika Hokusai**

1830
Liberty Leading the People by **Eugène Delacroix**

1832
Joseph Nicéphore Niépce snapped the **first reported food photograph**

1836
Our Dining Room at York by **Mary Ellen Best**

1840
Mount Edgcumbe Estate Workers in a Kitchen Interior by **Nicholas Condy**

1841
American portrait painter **John Goffe Rand** invented the **paint tube**

1842 – 1846
Chef and writer **Alexis Benoît Soyer**, opens art gallery Soyer's Philanthropic Gallery in memory of his wife, **Elizabeth Emma Jones**

1846
Isabella by **John Everett Millais**

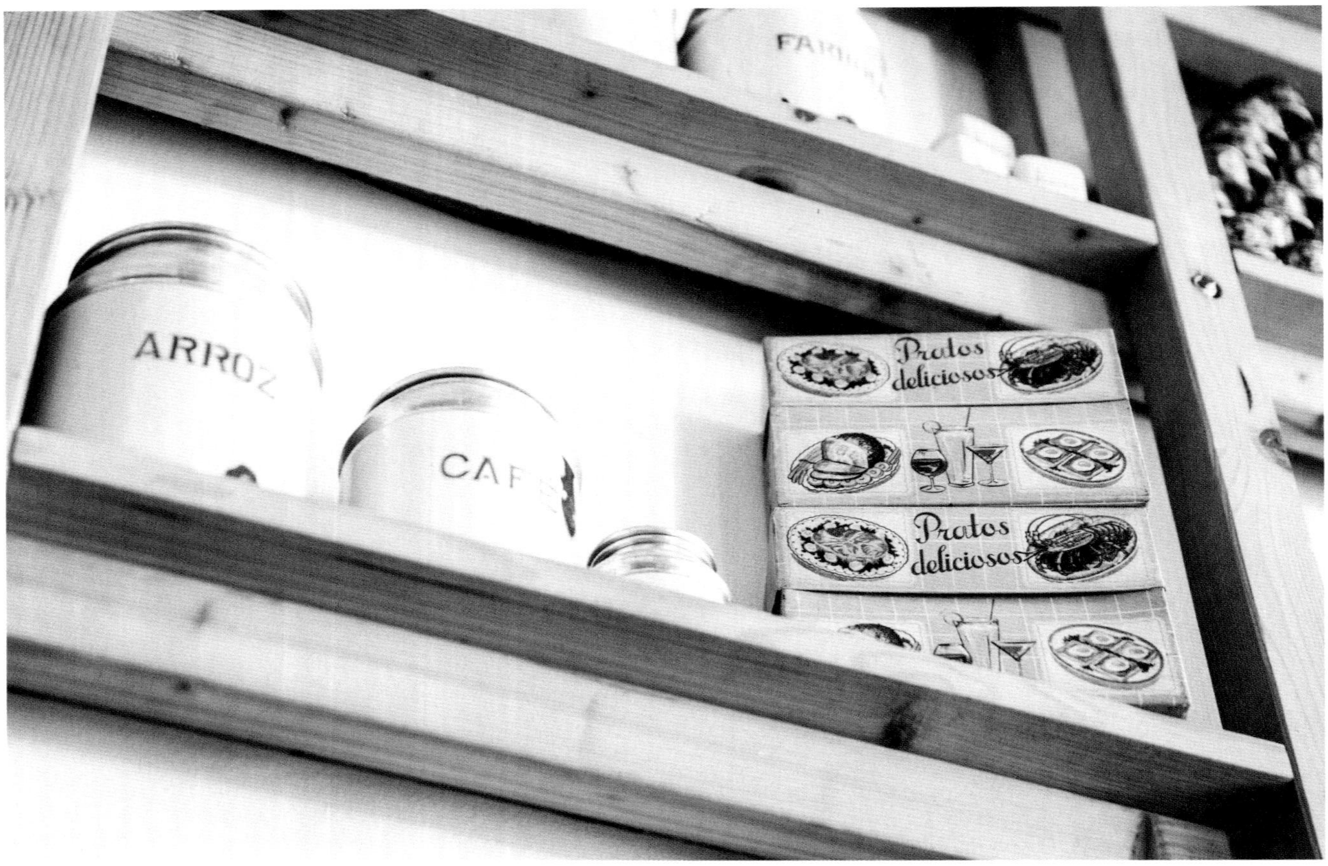
ARROZ
Pratos deliciosos
Pratos deliciosos

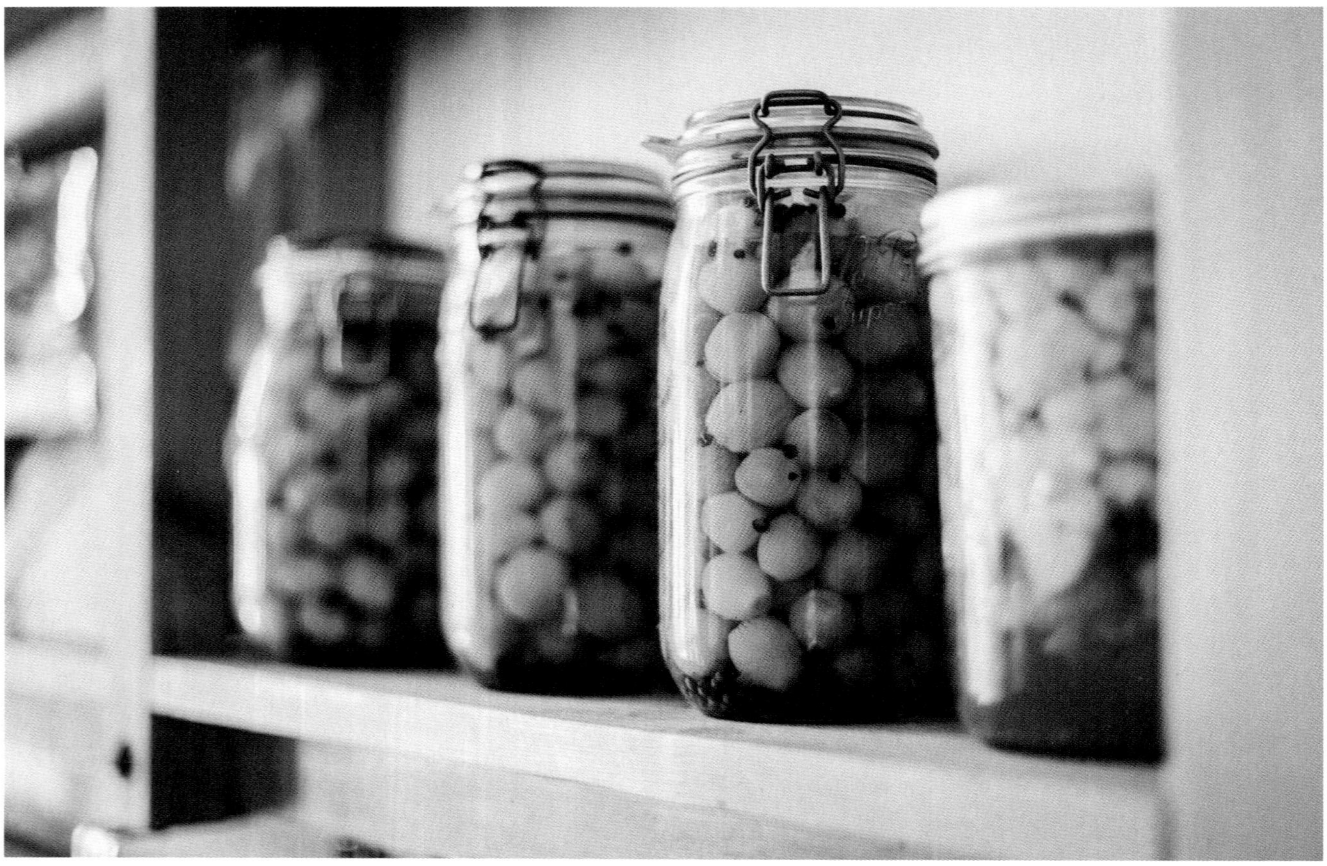

FOOD

1847
Louis Bignon bought the **Café Riche**, founded in 1785 by Madame Riche

1849
Cadbury introduced his brand of chocolate bars

1850
Opening of **Hotel Universal** in Lisbon

Edmond Carré developed the first **absorption refrigerator**

1851
Lorenzo Delmonico joined his uncles in **Delmonico's**, NY

Ice cream became an industry in the USA, pioneered by **Jacob Fussell**

1852
The publishing house **Larousse** is founded

Tavares Pobre restaurant is founded in Lisbon by **Vicente Marques Caldeira**

The Pantropheon or History of Food, book by **Alexis Benoît Soyer**

1853
Ramirez & Cª, Ltd, founded in Vila Real de Santo António by **Sebastian Ramirez**

1854
Le Cuisinier Praticien by **Charles Reculet**

George Speck invented potato chips at Moon's Lake House, 'Saratoga chips'

Manuel José Neto, associated with Feliciano António da Rocha, established a small unit of sardine cans in Setúbal, Portugal

1856
Jean Naigeon, a merchant from Dijon, creates **Dijon mustard**

La cuisine classique by **Urbain Dubois**

1858
Agapito Fernandes opened **Estrela da Sé** restaurant, Lisbon

1859
Nellie Melba born, operatic soprano for whom Escoffier named **Peach Melba**

Great Atlantic and Pacific Tea Company (A&P) was founded

1860
Louis Pasteur discovers microorganisms and their role in food spoilage

1861
Mrs Beeton's Book of Household Management by **Isabella Beeton**

1862
Ferdinand Carré exhibited an ice machine with 200 kg output per hour

Almanach des Gourmands by **Charles Monselet**

1863
Written reference to the **word *finocchio*** as gay slang appears in Tuscany

1864
The Hotel Nunes, owned by **João Nunes**, opens in Sintra, Portugal

The **Bofinger** was founded by Alsatian **Frédéric Bofinger**

1866
Adolphe Dugléré became the head chef of the **Café Anglais**

Anglo-Swiss Condensed Milk Company is founded, beginning of **Nestlé**

1867
Henri Nestlé brought an infant formula (**Nestlé's Milk Food**) to the market

Traitement Pratique des Vins by **Raimond Boireau**

Café Anglais served '**Three Emperors Dinner**' for three royal guests during the Universal Exposition of Paris

1868
La Cuisine Classique by **Émile Bernard** and **Urbain Dubois**

Élie Benard opened a pâtisserie with his own name in Lisbon

Edmund McIlhenny introduces his **Tabasco** sauce to the world

The 366 Menus of Baron Brisse by **Baron Léon Brisse**

1869
Hippolyte Mège-Mouriès created **margarine** in France

Le Livre des Conserves by **Jules Gouffé**

Joseph A. Campbell started Anderson & Campbell Preserve Company

1870
O Cozinheiro dos Cozinheiros by **Paul Plantier**, dedicated to Portuguese writer **Júlio César Machado**

Escoffier mobilised as a **cook in the French army**

Nantucket Receipts by **Margaret Cook** was published in Boston

French **Chef Choron** was serving dishes at the **Voisin Restaurant**, which included exotic animals. During the Siege of Paris the zoo became a source of food

1872
Franciscus Bresiers grew the **first Belgian endives**

Grand Dictionnaire de la Cuisine by **Alexandre Dumas**

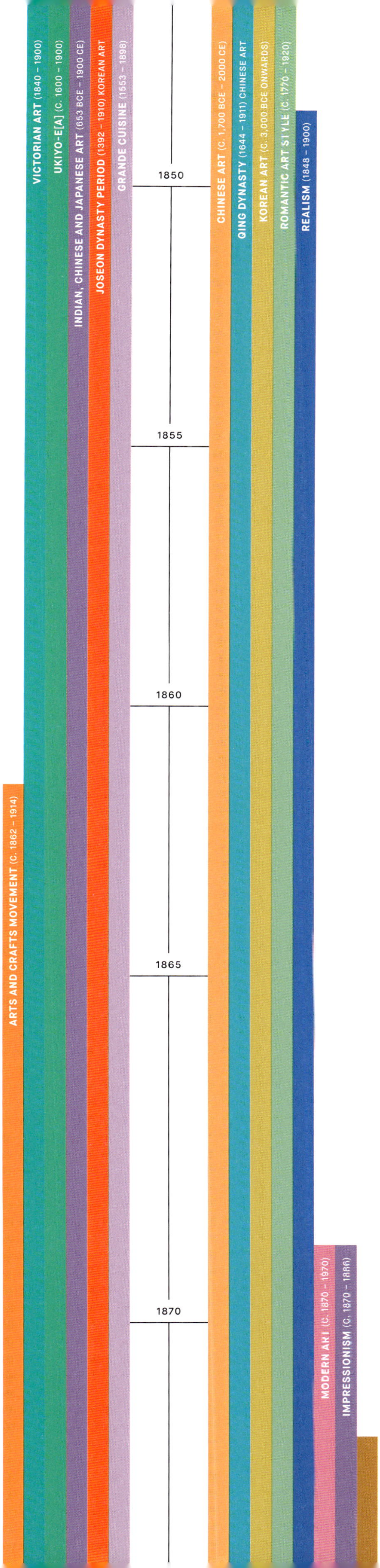

ART

REALISM (1848 – 1900)
Celebrating working class and peasants; en plein air rustic painting – Corot, Courbet, Daumier, Millet

1850
Ludwig Passini, *Artists at the Caffé Greco in Rome*

Mushroom by **Victor Hugo**

1854
Breakfasting at the Café Ledoyen, Paris, *on Salon Opening Day* by **Hugo Birger**

La Salle à manger de la princesse Mathilde, rue de Courcelles by **Sébastien Charles Giraud**

1856
Kiss Me and You'll Kiss the Lasses by **Lily Martin Spencer**

1859
The Absinthe Drinker by **Édouard Manet**

1860
George Wyndham 1st Lord Leconfield and Sir Reginald Graham at Breakfast by **Percy Wyndham**

1861
Colour photography invented by physicist **James Clerk Maxwell**

1862
The Luncheon on the Grass by **Édouard Manet**

Oysters by **Édouard Manet**

1863
Still Life with Oranges by **Antonio Mensaque**

1864 – 1935
Still Life with Oysters by **Luciano Freire**

1864
Still Life, Piece of Beef by **Édouard Manet**

1866
In a Roman Osteria by **Carl Bloch**

Wine Glasses by **Antonio Salviati**, **Venetian glass** manufacturer

1867
Cherettes posters by **Jules Chéret**

1868
'QWERTY' keyboard was patented by American inventor **Christopher Sholes**

The Luncheon by **Claude Monet**

1869
Paul Alexis Reading to Émile Zola by **Paul Cézanne**

IMPRESSIONISM (1870 – 1886)
Capturing fleeting effects of natural light – Monet, Manet, Renoir, Pissarro, Cassatt, Morisot, Degas

1870
Japonism became a prominent trend and had a strong influence on the early Impressionists

Invention of **flat-bottomed paper bag** by **Margaret E. Knight** and **Charles B. Stilwell**

Les Confitures 149, lithographic plate by **Émile Deyrolle**

1870 – 1871
Franco-Prussian War

THE BELLE ÉPOQUE (1871 – 1914)
Optimism, regional peace, economic prosperity, an apex of colonial empires, and technological, scientific and cultural innovations

1871 – 1972
Still Life with Apples by **Gustave Courbet**

FOOD

1873
Henry Schacht founded the American caviar business, Delaware River

Le Livre de Pâtisserie by Jules Gouffé, illustrated by **E. Ronjat**

1874
Margarine was introduced into the United States

1875
Opening of **Restaurant Club, O Silva**

1876
Bananas formally introduced at the Centennial Exposition in Philadelphia

Arte de Cozinha, a book by **João da Mata**, with recipe 'Amêijoas à Bulhão Pato'

With his brother and cousin as partners, **Henry J. Heinz** formed the partnership of F & J Heinz. **Ketchup** was added to the product line

1877
Grande Hotel de Paris opened its doors in Oporto, Portugal

Joseph Favre launched the journal *La Science Culinaire* in Geneva

1879
The canned tuna industry was set up in Vila Real de Santo António by **Parodi & Roldan**, who founded the factory Santa Maria

1880
Mary Anerley by R.D. Blackmore mentions **rat pies** in England

The **Tarte Tatin** is created at the **Hôtel Tatin** in Lamotte-Beuvron, France

Opening of **Restaurante Faz Frio** in Lisbon

Spanish industrialist **Tenório** founds the factory S. Francisco, Portugal (tuna)

1881
First Algarve sardine canning factory, **Établissements F. Delory**

1882
Chinese artichokes cultivated in Crosne, France, by **Pailleux**

The first ***concours culinaire*** was held in Paris

1884
First recorded use of the word ***bistro*** in the French language

Evaporated milk is patented by **John Mayenberg** from St Louis, USA

1885
Pastry shop **Pastelaria Baltresqui**, founded by **Rodolfo Baltresqui**, moves to Chiado, Lisbon

Establishment of **J. Lyons and Co.** of restaurants, catering and hotels

Set up of **Grupo do Leão** (Lion's Group), Portuguese artists who met at Leão de Ouro Cervejaria in Lisbon (1881 – 1889)

1886
Atlanta pharmacist **Dr John S. Pemberton** creates **Coca-Cola**

Le Traité sur L'art de Travailler les Fleurs en Cire by **Auguste Escoffier**

1887
Development of milk chocolate around the world by **Daniel Peter**

1888
Pasteur Institute was inaugurated

Ai Cula Ni Bokola, cannibal fork from Fiji Islands

CLASSIC CUISINE (1889 – 1970)
Simplification of Grande Cuisine founded by Auguste Escoffier

1889
Brothers André and **Édouard Michelin** founded **Michelin tyre company**

Chef Raffaele Esposito of Pizzeria Brandi and his wife created a pizza resembling the colours of the Italian flag, naming it after the Queen Margherita of Savoy - **Pizza Margherita**

The Savoy opens, built by **Richard D'Oyly Carte**

French nightclub, **Moulin Rouge**, opened its doors

1890
Dr John H. Kellogg develops processes for producing **wheat flakes**

L'Heure Enchantée by **Gabriel Vicaire**

Auguste Escoffier was given the direction of the kitchens of the **Savoy Hotel**

La Tour d'Argent presented a numbered certificate to each person who ate the restaurant's signature dish, **pressed duck**

1891
Carpenter Electric Heating Manufacturing Co. invented an **electric stove**

La Scienza in Cucina e L'Arte di Mangiare Bene by **Pellegrino Artusi**

ART

1873
Gargantua and 'Pilgrims eaten in salads', illustration by **Gustave Doré**

1875 – 1885
Mound of Butter by **Antoine Vollon**

1876
In a Café, also called *Absinthe* by **Edgar Degas**

1877
Affecting Farewell – The Crab Pot by **Ernest Griset**

Luther at the Diet of Worms, by **Von Werner**

1877 – 1878
Édouard Manet, *A corner of the Café-Concert*

1878
Toast rack designed by **Christopher Dresser**

1879
After the Luncheon by **Pierre-Auguste Renoir**

POST-IMPRESSIONISM (1880 – 1905)
A soft revolt against Impressionism – Van Gogh, Gauguin, Cézanne, Seurat

1880
Bunch of Asparagus by **Édouard Manet**

Apples and Biscuits by **Paul Cézanne**

New Map of France According to the Last Discoveries of the Savants and the Explorers by French illustrator **Albert Robida**

Samovar by **K.E. Makowsky**

1881
At the Bistro by **Jean-Georges Béraud** (precise date unknown)

Luncheon of the Boating Party by **Pierre-Auguste Renoir**

1882
Nature Morte by **James Ensor**

Chef Père Paul by **Claude Monet**

1883 – 1885
Lady at the Tea Table by **Mary Cassatt**

1884
At the Café by **Federico Zandomeneghi**

Fábrica de Faianças das Caldas (faience), **Bordallo Pinheiro**, Portugal

Still Life by **Victoria Duborg**

Asphyxia by **Angelo Morbelli**

1885
The Potato Eaters by **Vincent van Gogh**

Interior of the Osteria di Ponte Mammolo by **Mario De Maria**

The 'Grupo do Leão' by **Columbano Bordalo Pinheiro**

1886
Breakfast in the Green by **Anders Zorn**

Funghi by **Giovanni Segantini**

1887
Under the Lamp by **Marie Bracquemond**

Girl with Peaches, Portrait of Vera Mamontova by **Valentin Serov**

The Soldier Drinks by **Marc Chagall**

1888
Restaurant in Arles by **Vincent van Gogh**

The White Slave by **J.J. Lecomte de Nouy**

Hip, Hip, Hurrah! by **Peder Severin Krøyer**

1889
Still Life with Peaches by **Paul Gauguin**

Still Life by **Estêvão Silva**

Exposition Universelle, Paris

EXPRESSIONISM (1890 ONWARDS)
Emotion distorting form

1890
Still Life with Peaches and Pears by **Paul Cézanne**

Bread and Water by **Jacob Collins**

Cake, Lemon, Strawberries and Glass by **John Frederick Peto**

Illustration by **Frédéric Delair**, unknown artist

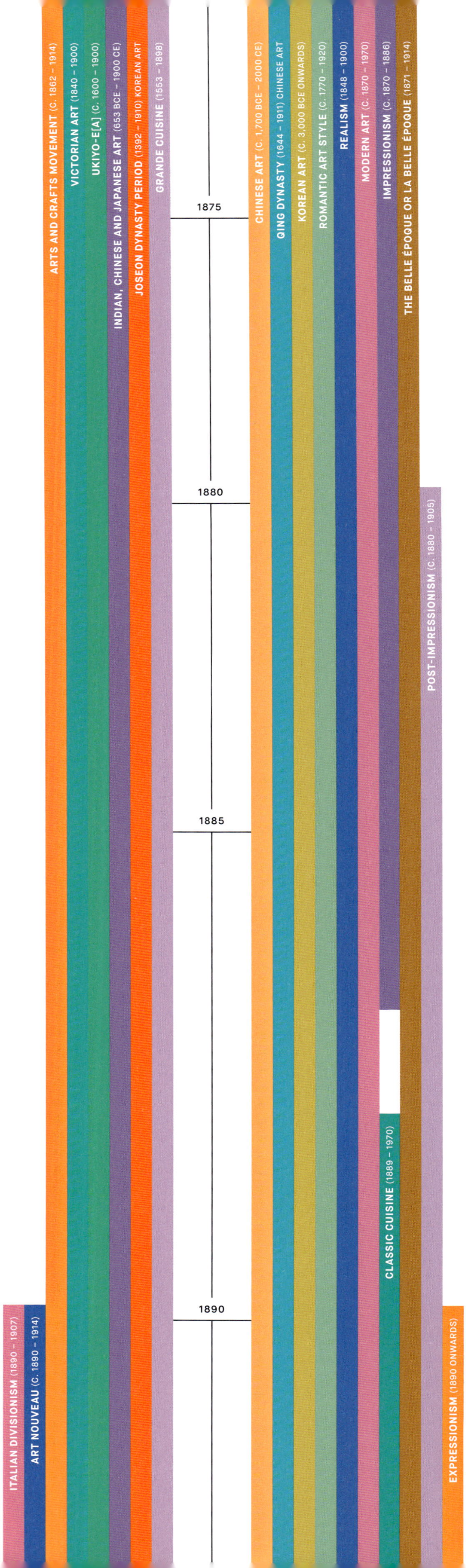

FOOD

1892
Thomas Ahearn patented the invention of an **electric oven**

Júdice Fialho opens his canned fish factory, **Fábrica São José**, in Portimão, Portugal

1893
Sir Thomas Lipton officially established the **Thomas J Lipton Co.**

Coffee from Brazil introduced into Kenya and Tanzania, not far from its place of origin in Ethiopia, 600 years prior

Eclipse Toaster, **first electric toaster** invented by **Alan MacMasters**

1894
Canned fish factory **Conservas Brandão, Gomes & Cia**, Espinho, Portugal

The Epicurean, cookbook by **Charles Ranhofer**

O Cozinheiro Indispensável, book by **Ernest Chardron**

1895
The Cordon Bleu cooking school in Paris, founded by **Marthe Distell**

1896
First US patent for an electric stove granted to **William S. Hadaway Jr.**

Nabisco used a boy in a yellow raincoat in its advertisements to emphasise the **moisture barrier**

First canning factory using salt, Matosinhos, Portugal, by **Joaquim Ferreira Pedro (Luças)**

1897
Waldorf Astoria Hotel was completed on Fifth Avenue in New York, USA

1898
Caleb 'Doc' Bradham developed a beverage called **Brad's Drink**. Later **Pepsi-Cola**

César Ritz and **Escoffier** opened the **Hotel Ritz** in Paris

1899
The Carlton opens, run by **César Ritz** with **Auguste Escoffier** as head chef

Campbell produced the **first canned condensed soups**

Grand Restaurant Augusto moves to Rua Garret in Lisbon

1900
O cozinheiro prático, by **Maria Sofia P. da Silva**, the first cookbook published in Portugal to include vegetarian recipes

First Michelin Guide was created by the Michelin brothers

Mères Lyonnaises began to open their own restaurants serving homemade food

Double seamed cans, invented by **Max Ams** in 1888, now developed in Europe, providing an **airtight seal** to the tin can

Ellsworth Statler established a chain of middle-class hotels with restaurant recipes standardised

1901
François Bise joined his wife Charlyne's restaurant, **L'Auberge**

César Ritz and **Escoffier** team broke up when Ritz had a nervous breakdown

1902
Feu Brothers founded the canned fish factory S. Francisco, Portimão, Portugal

Opening of hotel and restaurant **Esperança**, in Setúbal, Portugal

À la Mode Cookery by **Harriet Anne de Salis**

1903
Le Guide Culinaire, manual of classic cuisine by **Auguste Escoffier**

First english edition *The Complete Guide to the Art of Modern Cookery* by **Auguste Escoffier**

Willow Tea Rooms opens in Glasgow, designed by **Charles Rennie Mackintosh**

1904
Real Confeiteiro Português e Brasileiro book by **Sofia de Sousa**

Ernest Hamwi created the first **conical-shaped edible ice cream cone**

Tratado Completo de Cozinha e de Copa by **Carlos Bento da Maia**

David Evans Strickler invented the **banana split sundae**

Iced tea is attributed to the merchant **Richard Blechynden**

Thomas Sullivan, New York tea merchant, invented the **tea bag**

1905
London **Jewish Bakers' Union** was formed

Brazileira do Chiado, founded by the Portuguese company **Teles & Cª**

ITALIAN DIVISIONISM (1890 – 1907)
ART NOUVEAU (C. 1890 – 1914)
ARTS AND CRAFTS MOVEMENT (C. 1862 – 1914)
VICTORIAN ART (1840 – 1900)
UKIYO-E[A] (C. 1600 – 1900)
INDIAN, CHINESE AND JAPANESE ART (653 BCE – 1900 CE)
JOSEON DYNASTY PERIOD (1392 – 1910) KOREAN ART
GRANDE CUISINE (1553 – 1898)
CLASSICAL REVIVAL IN MODERN ART (C. 1900 – 1930)
GERMAN EXPRESSIONISM (C. 1905 – 1935)
FAUVISM (PARIS C. 1905 – 1907)

1895

20TH CENTURY CE

CLASSICAL REVIVAL IN MODERN ART (C. 1900-1930)

1905

CHINESE ART (C. 1,700 BCE – 2000 CE)
QING DYNASTY (1644 – 1911) CHINESE ART
KOREAN ART (C. 3,000 BCE ONWARDS)
ROMANTIC ART STYLE (C. 1770 – 1920)
REALISM (1848 – 1900)
MODERN ART (C. 1870 – 1970)
CLASSIC CUISINE (1889 – 1970)
THE BELLE ÉPOQUE OR LA BELLE ÉPOQUE (1871 – 1914)
POST-IMPRESSIONISM (C. 1880 – 1905)
EXPRESSIONISM (1890 ONWARDS)

ART

1892
At the Moulin Rouge by **Henri de Toulouse-Lautrec**

Diminution du gaz... Nouvelle cuisinière universelle, commission Chabrier jeune... poster by **Jules Chéret**

1893
Absinthe Robette poster by **Henri Privat-Livemont**

In the Kitchen, Preparations for Christmas Eve Dinner in a Paris Restaurant by **Gustave Henri Marchetti** in *L'Illustration*

1894
Moulin de la Galette by **Paul Hoeniger**

1895
Quinquina Dubonnet, Apéritif, Dans tous les Cafés poster by **Jules Chéret**

The Children's Meal by **Pierre Bonnard**

At the Table by **Louis Valtat**

1896
Ice Cream Cone by **Italo Marchioni**

Pollet et Vittet, Chocolaterie de Pepinster by **Henri Meunier**

Lithographic poster for Lefèvre-Utile Biscuits (LU), by **Alphonse Mucha**

1897
National Gallery of British Art opened, renamed **Tate Gallery** in 1932

1898
Bibendum mascot by French cartoonist **Marius Roussillon**

October (Study of Mushrooms) by **Ed Koning**

1899
The Cook by **Édouard Vuillard**, in *Landscapes and Interiors* magazine

The First Thanksgiving 1621 by **Jean Leon Gerome Ferris**

Moët & Chandon: Dry Imperial, poster by **Alphonse Mucha**

Tropon, the most concentrated nourishment, poster by **Henry Clemens van de Velde**

1900
Express Dairy milk cart – Guaranteed Absolutely Pure, poster

Group portrait of the staff in the Cinotto Restaurant, Turin by **V. Persico**

A Roman Feast by **Roberto Bompiani**

Still Life with Bottles and Fruit by **Alexej von Jawlensky**

Advertising board for Tuborg beer by **Erich Henningsen**

1901
The Gourmet by **Pablo Picasso**

Family Eating Soup by **Vasili Nikolaevich**

Bitter Campari advertisement by **Adolf Hohenstein**

1902
Terrace of Restaurant Jacob in Nienstedten on the Elbe by **Max Liebermann**

First neon lamp invented by French engineer **Georges Claude**

Supper by **Leon Bakst**

1903
The Blind Man's Meal by **Pablo Picasso**

Tea-Drinking by **Andrey Ryabushkin**

Wright Brothers' first flight

FAUVISM (1905 – 1907)
Harsh colours and flat surfaces

1905
Strawberries by **Pierre-Auguste Renoir**

Young woman of the Samovar by **Igor Grabar**

An Elegant Lady in the Famous Paris Restaurant, Vatel by **Maurice Millière**

An Evening of Prizes at the Armenonville Pavilion by **Henri Gervex**

Still Life with Fried Eggs in Frying Pan by **Paula Modersohn-Becker**

1906
Woman at a Table (The Procuress) by **Georges Rouault**

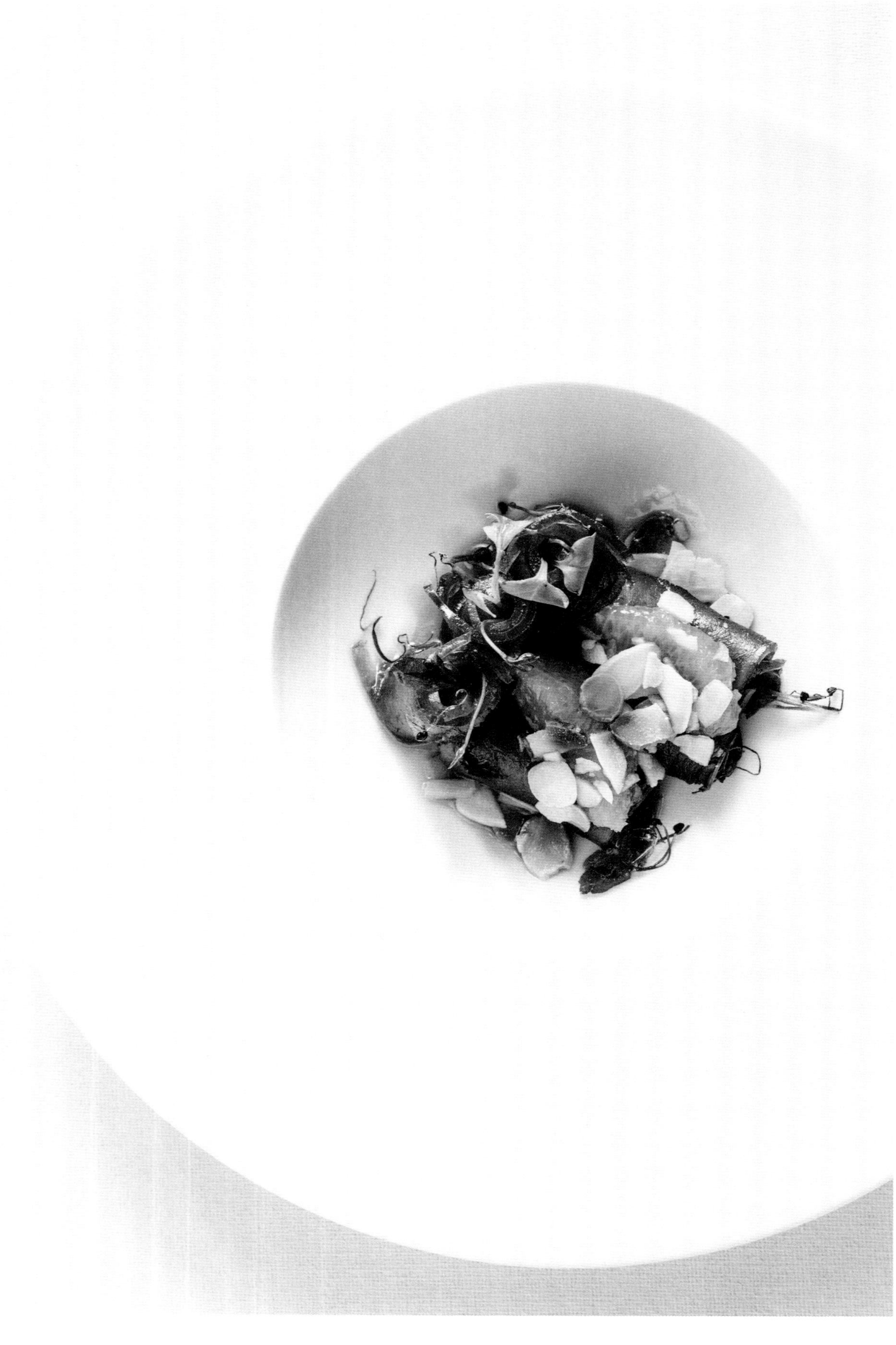

FOOD

1906
Will Keith Kellogg creates **Kellogg's Corn Flakes**

1908
Umami, coined by Japanese **Kikunae Ikeda** from a nominalisation of *umai* (delicious)

Opening of **Maxim's** by **José Nunes Ereira**, in Restauradores, Lisbon

Houdini introduced his own original act, *Milk Can Escape*

Melitta Bentz invented the **coffee filter**

1909
Frank Shailor patented his idea for the **'D-12' electric toaster**

1910
William Hadaway built the **first oven toaster** for **Westinghouse Corporation**

First Michelin Guide for Spain and Portugal

Sturgeon was nearly extinct in American waters due to over-fishing

Tradition of the **American bars** began in Paris

1911
Auguste Escoffier started publishing the magazine *Le Carnet d'Épicure*

Mars chocolate began as the **Mar-O-Bar Co.** by Frank C. Mars of Tacoma

Café Brazileira do Rossio opens in a old cloakroom shop dating from 1820

1912
The Club des Cent (Club of Hundred) founded by **Louis Forest**

Le Livre des Menus, book by **Auguste Escoffier**

The Terrail family bought the **La Tour d'Argent** restaurant

1913
First Michelin guide for Portugal

Opening of **Leitaria Luso Central**, in Rossio, Lisbon

Domelre, **automatic electric refrigeration unit** by **Fred W. Wolf Jr.**

Harry MacElhone takes over as owner of **Harry's Bar** in Paris

1914 – 1918
Die Gulaschkanone (The Goulash Cannon) German army mobile soup kitchen

1914
Cuisine by **Louise Saulnier**

Gerhard Behrend, coffee maker, the Silex Company Boston

1915
The Imperial Hotel in Tokyo, designed by **Frank Lloyd Wright**

1916
Opening of **Café Chave d'Ouro** in Rossio, Lisbon

First store designed as a self-service opened in Memphis by **Clarence Saunders**

1917
Rendez-Vous de l'Avenue, later **Café Abadia**, opens in Lisbon

1918
Restaurant **Chic** opens in Lisbon, famous for chicken shanks and Chic-style steaks

William C. Durant started the **Frigidaire Company**

Canned fish company **Paschoal, Nero & Company**, Sesimbra, Portugal

1919
Closing of **Hotel Central**, Lisbon, restaurant frequented by Jules Verne

Portuguese olive oil brand **Gallo** registered by **Victor Guedes & C.A.**

1920
Conserveira Pinhais & Cª Lda founded in Matosinhos, Portugal

Clarence Birdseye perfected a **method of ultra rapid freeze**

A new **Michelin Guide** was launched, on sale for the first time

Pavlova dessert created during or after one of **Anna Pavlova's** tours to Australia and New Zealand

Cellophane manufacture opened the era of transparent wrappings

After the First World War, **domestic refrigerator** began to displace the icebox

Mère Bourgeois is the first chef awarded by **Club des Cent**

Escoffier became the first chef to receive the **Legion of Honour**

1921
Café Majestic opens in Oporto, Portugal, with Art Nouveau decoration

Decoration for **Bal Tik-Tak**, a futurist-style ballroom, by **Giacomo Balla**

Fernand Point renamed his father's restaurant **La Pyramide**

1922
Opening of **Pastelaria Versailles**, Lisbon

Opening of **Casa Suissa**, later **Pastelaria Suiça**, Rossio, Lisbon

AGA cooker invented by Swedish Nobel prize-winner **Nils Gustaf Dalén**

First aerial crossing of South Atlantic by **Gago Coutinho** and **Sacadura Cabral**

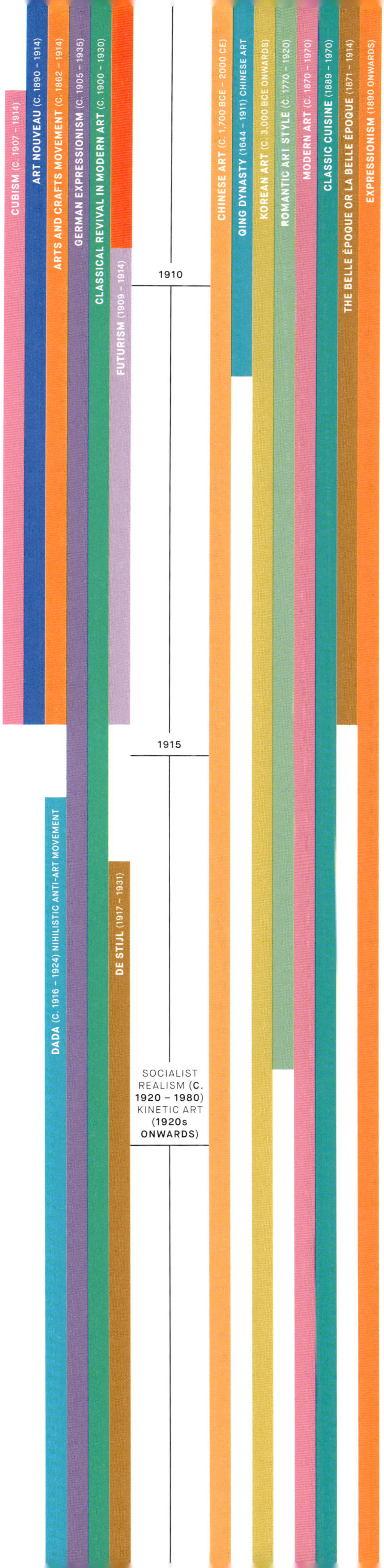

ART

1907
Celebrating S. Martinho by **José Malhoa**

1908 – 1914
Still Life with Fruit Basket by **Maurice de Vlaminck**

1908
Oysters by **Ernst Heilemann**

Promotional posters for **Harry Houdini's** *Milk Can Escape*

Red Room (Harmony in Red) by **Henri Matisse**

1909
Wilhelm Mozer by **Ludwig Hohlwein**

1910
Herbata Marka Herbatnik, lithograph by **Paul Leni**

Still Life with Onions and Herring by **Isidre Nonell**

Still Life by **Adriano de Sousa Lopes**

Lee Newman patented a **felt-tipped marking pen**

In a Restaurant, Paris by **Elena Andreevna Kiseleva**

1911
Jar, Bottle and Glass by **Juan Gris**

Carnival/Porto Wine by **Leonetto Cappiello**

The Lunch by **Manuel Jardim**

1912
Post card with inside view of the Graben café by **Josef Hoffmann**

Kandinsky and Erma Bossi at the Table by **Gabriele Münter**

1912 – 1913
Dessert by **Auguste Herbin**

1913
Bodegón by **Juan Gris**

Armory Show, major exhibition of modern art, is held in America

Bilz Brause poster by **Fritz Boscovits**

1914 – 1918
First World War

1914
The Bottle Rack by **Marcel Duchamp**

The First Thanksgiving at Plymouth by **Jennie Augusta Brownscombe**

1915
The Merchant Wife's Tea by **Boris Kustodiev**

DADA (C. 1916 – 1924)
Avant-garde precursor of modern art

1916
Garden Path with Chickens by **Gustav Klimt**

The Coffee Mill by **Juan Gris**

Be Patriotic, Sign Your Country's Pledge to Save The Flood, U.S. Food Administration poster by **Paul Stahr**

1917
Russian Revolution

Fountain by **Marcel Duchamp**

Eat More, Eat Less by **L.N. Britton**

1918
Advertising for Rendez-Vous de l'Avenue by **Rodrigues Castañe**

Comical Repast (Banquet of the Starved) by **James Ensor**

The Table in Front of the Building by **Juan Gris**

1919
Bauhaus, German school of design founded by **Walter Gropius in Weimar**

1920
Coachman at Traktir (Pub) by **Boris Kustodiev**

Vermouth Martini liqueur advertisement

Design for advertising poster, *Even the Sun is Happy to Eat Our Chocolate*

National Confectionery Industry issues adverts in press, encouraging women to take up home baking as a source of extra income

Advertisement for **Baker's Cocoa**, Walter Baker Company, Massachusetts

The Table (Still Life with Rabbit) by **Joan Miró**

Baker by **Boris Kustodiev**

Plums by **Georgia O'Keeffe**

1921
Kitchen Table by **Paul Outerbridge Jr.**

The Chef of Hotel Chatham, Paris by **William Orpen**

Bitter Campari advertisement by **Leonetto Cappiello**

1922 – 1923
Plate XII from Ecce Homo by **George Grosz**

1922
First exhibition of Portuguese photographer **Américo Augusto Ribeiro**, Setúbal

Food Grinder by **John H. Lickert**

FOOD

1923 – 1948
Foundation of **Companhia das Cervejas Estrella**, in Lisbon

1924
La Teca, la Veritable Cuina Casolana de Catalunya by **Ignasi Domènech**

1925
Toy cooker with kitchen box by **Attilio Mussino**

Inauguration of **Cervejaria Portugália** in Lisbon

Doces e Cosinhados: Receitas Escolhidas book by **Isalita**

1926
Michelin Guide began to award single **stars** for fine dining establishments

Kuchnia (The Kitchen) book by **Vladimir Izenberg**

Grete Lihotzky, ***Frankfurt Kitchen***, Ginnheim-Höhenblick Housing Estate

Birth of **Godiva chocolate**

Les Plaisirs de la Table by **Édouard Nignon**

Arte de Bem Comer book by **Alinanda**

1927
Charles Lindbergh achieves the world's **first non-stop transatlantic flight**

Le Riz (Rice) book by **Auguste Escoffier**

General Electric introduced the **Monitor-Top**, a million units were produced

1928
Culinária by **Olleboma** alias **António Maria de Oliveira Bello**

Marguerite and Marius Bise opened **Auberge du Père Bise**, France

1929
Demolition of the famous **Waldorf Astoria Hotel**, New York

João Fernandes do Pinho opens the restaurant **A Floresta**

Licor Beirão is named, invented by **José Carranca Redondo**

La Morue (Codfish) book by **Auguste Escoffier**

1930
Nestlé makes the **first white chocolate**, named **Galak**

The Savoy Cocktail Book by **Harry Craddock**

Opening of **Conserveira de Lisboa**, canned fish conserves shop

1931
Colonel Harland Sanders takes over a Shell filling station in small-town Kentucky – the begining of **Kentucky Fried Chicken**

Michelin Guide criteria for starred rankings (from 0 to 3) was published

The Futurist Kitchen Manifesto, written by **Filippo Tommaso Marinetti** and **Fillia**

Joy of Cooking, **Irma Starkloff Rombauer** and **Marion Rombauer Becker**

1932
Café Palladium opens in Lisbon by **Tavares & Ferreira**

Alexandre Dumaine buys the **Hostellerie de la Côte d'Or**

La Bonne Cuisine de Chez Nous by **Madame Germaine** (Germaine Deloge)

A cozinheira das cozinheiras, book by **Rosa Maria**

1933
Nicolasa Pradera published the cookbook *La Cocina de Nicolasa*

Bragard, brand of kitchen outfits by **Henri Bragard**

Eugénie Brazier or **Mère Brazier**, first woman to earn three Michelin stars

A Cozinha Ideal book by Portuguese **Chef Manuel Ferreira**

Frigidaire (General Motors division) first talked about **induction cooking**

1934
Mestre João Ribeiro, referred to as the best Portuguese chef of the 20th century, worked at the famous **Aviz Hotel**

My Cuisine by **Auguste Escoffier**

1935
Magic Chef stove by American Stove Company

Initiation of the **Consórcio Português de Conservas de Peixe**, Portugal

'To drink wine is to feed one million Portuguese', **slogan of Estado Novo**, Portugal

1936
Instituto Português de Conservas de Peixe replaces the Consórcio Português de Conservas de Peixe

Opening of restaurant **Gambrinus** in Lisbon

Il Doppio Quattrova, ovvero La Cucina Elegante, book by **Emma Vanzetti**

Little Tramp (Charlie Chaplin) fed by the **automated feeding machine** in *Modern Times* movie

First issue of ***Conservas***, Portuguese magazine about the canning industry

1937
Xavier Marcel Boulestin, first TV chef, in *Cook's Night Out* on BBC

1938
Nestlé introduced their brand of instant coffee, **Nescafé**

Flex-seal speed cooker, first saucepan-style pressure cooker by **Alfred Vischler**

ART DECO (C. 1925 – 1940)
SURREALISM (C. 1924 – 2004)
GERMAN EXPRESSIONISM (C. 1905 – 1935)
CLASSICAL REVIVAL IN MODERN ART (C. 1900 – 1930)
DE STIJL (1917 – 1931)
SOCIAL REALISM (C. 1930 – 1945)

1925
1930
1935

CHINESE ART (C. 1,700 BCE – 2000 CE)
KOREAN ART (C. 3,000 BCE ONWARDS)
MODERN ART (C. 1870 – 1970)
CLASSIC CUISINE (1889 – 1970)
EXPRESSIONISM (1890 ONWARDS)

ART

1923 – 1948
L'Autarca table by **Angelo Fasce**

The Table Piled with Food, plate XXXV (supplementary suite) by **Marc Chagall** in *Les Âmes Mortes* (Gogol)

1923
Butcher, Rue Christine by **Eugène Atget**

1924
First Thing Every Morning, Eno's Fruit Salt ad by **E. McKnight Kauffer**

Newtown Pippin Apples by **H.H. Blakesly**

Painted silk banner of the **London Jewish Bakers' Union**

1926
Eggplant and Tomatoes by **Charles Demuth**

Around the Fish by **Paul Klee**

Still Life by **Preston Dickinson**

Banana Skirt, costume by **Josephine Baker**

First fluorescent lamp invented by **Edmund Germer** in Germany

1927
Automat by **Edward Hopper**

Red Snapper, design for H.P. (Horsepower) by **Diego Rivera**

Advertising postcard for *tortellini* manufactured by **Zambelli Bassi**

1928
Scatole d'Amore in Conserva by **Filippo Tommaso Marinetti**

Konditor by **August Sander**

1929
Still Life #2 by **Louis Lozowick**

Bar – Paris, watercolour by **Carlos Botelho**

Wasp and Pear by **Gerald Murphy**

1930
Tables for Ladies by **Edward Hopper**

Adega do Galo by **José Dominguez Alvarez**

Cointreau poster by **Charles Loupot**

1931
Still Life with Lamprey by **Abel Abrantes Manta**

Still Life on White by **Elizabeth V. Blackadder**

Menu for Taverna Futurista Santopalato, Torino, by **Nicola Diulgheroff**

Speakeasy by **Glenn Coleman**

1932
Fried Egg on the Plate without the Plate by **Salvador Dalí**

Marinetti published *The Futurist Cookbook*, a provocative work about art

Dubonnet poster by **A.M. Cassandre**

1933
Plucked Goose by **Chaim Soutine**

Gilbey's Invalid Port poster by **E. McKnight Kauffer**

Maison Prunier restaurant poster by **A. M. Cassandre**

Dining Room on the Garden by **Pierre Bonnard**

1935
The Arts Club's Woman Chef by **Francis Edwin Hodge**

Gum Ball No. 10: 'Sugar Daddy' by **Charles Bell**

Wine list for the Hotel Algarve in Praia da Rocha, Portugal by **Maria Keil**

The Portrait by **René Magritte**

1936
This is a Piece of Cheese by **René Magritte**

Sardines La Rose, advertisement by **Antonio Gómez Feu**

ETP – Estúdio Técnico de Publicidade founded by designer **João Rocha**

Fur Breakfast, fur-covered cup, saucer and spoon by **Meret Oppenheim**

Lobster Telephone by **Salvador Dalí**

1937
Guernica by **Pablo Picasso**

How to Cook Portuguese Canned Sardines, leaflet by **Fred Kradolfer**

C. 1937 – 1943
Hopi Woman Grinding Corn by **Carl Moon**

1938
The Golden Book of Portuguese Fish Canning by **Leitão de Barros**

Fruits of the Earth by **Frida Kahlo**

Nescafé's first launch campaign advert, featured in a Swiss newspaper

FOOD

1938
Larousse publishing house published *Larousse Gastronomique* by **Pierre Athanase Larousse**

Tupperware foundation was established by chemist **Earl S. Tupper**

1939
Advertisement ***Coca-Cola goes along*** was launched and used in the 1940s

Maison Pic earned the prestigious three Michelin stars with **André Pic** as chef

Ministry of Food, a wartime department was established to ensure population receives proper nutrition

Pressure cooker 'Presto' unveiled at New York World's Fair

C. 1940
Restaurante Espelho de Água, project by **António Lino** for the **Exposição do Mundo Português**, Lisbon

Volúpia - A Nona Arte: a Gastronomia by **Albino Forjaz de Sampaio**

M&M's created, 'Melts in your mouth, not in your hands'

American army includes **chocolate bars in soldiers' 'D-Ration'**

1941
Gourmet, magazine devoted to food and wine, published by **Condé Nast**

General Mills introduced **Cheerioats** breakfast cereal, later **Cheerios**

Beltsville small white turkey developed

1942
Fernando van Zeller Guedes created **Mateus Rosé wine**

Frying pan by **Corning Glass Works**

René Lasserre transforms his establishment into a small luxury townhouse where he organises festive galas with parades of models

1944
On **D-Day**, troops landed with the **Michelin Guide's 1939** edition in hand

Variações sobre a Gastronomia, book by **Paulo Duarte**

1945
Raymond Thuillier opens his restaurant **l'Oustau de Baumanière**

Opening of restaurant **Fialho** in Évora, Alentejo, Portugal by **Manuel Fialho**

Plastic bottles and **aerosols** were first introduced

The Book of Pantagruel by **Bertha Rosa Limpo**

1946
Opening of ice cream shop **Santini**, Tamariz beach, Estoril, Portugal

First issue of ***Conservas de Peixe***, a magazine about the Portuguese fish canning industry

1947
American Raytheon Corporation built **Radarange microwave oven**

1948
Raymond Oliver purchased **Le Grand Véfour**

Tupperware home parties started

1950
Idea of a **Mediterranean cuisine** originated by **Elizabeth David's** book, *A Book of Mediterranean Food*

Diner's Club issued the first 'general purpose' **credit card**

1951
Tesouro Das Cozinheiras book by **Mirene**

1952
Jean Delaveine received the title *Meilleur Ouvrier de France en Pâtisserie*

Time magazine called **Michelin Guide** the 'tourist's Bible'

A Arte de Bem Saborear, book by **Auronanda**

1953
Burger King was initially called **Insta-Burger King**

1954
Khrushchev and his entourage were served Cantonese speciality **'A Battle of the Dragon and the Tiger'**, with snake and cat, during a trip to China

Opening of **Pique-Nique**, one of the first snack bars in Lisbon

1955
Diamante coffee machine by **Bruno Munari** and **Enzo Mari** for **La Pavoni**

As Melhores Receitas de Cozinha, book by **Libânia de Sousa Alves**

1956
António and **Manuel Paramés** open **Restaurante Cervejaria Solmar**

1957
NY magazine *Culinary Review* qualifies **João Ribeiro** as 'Portugal's most eminent culinarian'

Hôtel Moderne became **Les Frères Troisgros**

1957 – 1962
Peanut butter and fried banana sandwich, the favourite of **'The King' (Elvis)**

1958
Chupa Chups® (lollipops) founded by **Enric Bernat Fontlladosa**

Charles Barrier wins, in his first paticipation, *Meilleur Ouvrier de France*

1959
L'Art des Mets, book by **Francis Amunategui**

Ritz Hotel in Lisbon, by **Porfírio Pardal Monteiro** with the collaboration of several artists **Almada Negreiros, Sarah Afonso, Barata Feyo, Carlos Botelho**

Insta-Burger King was renamed **Burger King**

ART DECO (C. 1925 – 1940)
SURREALISM (C. 1924 – 2004)
SOCIAL REALISM (C. 1930 – 1945)
ART INFORMEL (1940s – 1950s)
ABSTRACT EXPRESSIONISM (1940s – 1950s)
POP ART (C. 1955 – 1970)

1940

1945

1950

1955

CHINESE ART (C. 1,700 BCE – 2000 CE)
KOREAN ART (C. 3,000 BCE ONWARDS)
MODERN ART (C. 1870 – 1970)
CLASSIC CUISINE (1889 – 1970)
EXPRESSIONISM (1890 ONWARDS)

ART

1939
Costume Design by Salvador Dalí for Dream of Venus by **Horst P. Horst**

Museum of Non-Objective Painting, Solomon R. Guggenheim Foundation

Try cooking cabbage this way, leaflet from the UK government in the Second World War

Bones on the Table by **Kurt Roesch**

Doctor Carrot, the Children's Best Friend, poster by unknown artist

Still Life, Table with Bowl of Fruit by **Pierre Bonnard**

ABSTRACT EXPRESSIONISM (1940s – 1950s)
Post-Second World War: pure abstraction and expression without form; popular art absorbs consumerism

C. 1940
Supper Time by **Horace Pippin**

Advertising for canning companies like Feu Hermanos, Portimão, Portugal by **Antonio Gómez Feu**

Streamliner meat slicer (model 410) by **Egmont Arens** and **Theodore C. Brookhart**

1940 – 1943
Sardines, photograph by **Wols**

1940 – 1947
Alexey N. Tolstoj by **Pyotr Petrovich Konchalovsky**

1941
Delicious Dishes poster by **Frederick H. K. Henrion**

A Better Home, Rural Electrification Administration's poster by **Lester Beall**

Two Mullets by **Georges Braque**

1942
Mice Foul Food poster by **Herbert Tomlinson**

Grow Your Own Food poster by **Abram Games**

Nighthawks by **Edward Hopper**

1943
Freedom from Want by **Norman Rockwell**

The Bride Frightened at Seeing Life by **Frida Kahlo**

1944
Food Needs Transport, Don't Waste It poster by **Jan Lewitt**, **George Him**

Julia Côta has worked with clay since she was nine years old. Her grandfather **Domingos Côto** created the first Barcelos' cock

1945
Tupperware food storage container by **Earl S. Tupper**

The Queue at the Fish Shop by **Evelyn Dunbar**

Universal Pressure Cooker by **William J. Russell**

1946
Mural paintings at Gare Marítima da Rocha do Conde de Óbidos, Lisbon, by **Almada Negreiros**

Still Life of Fruit in a Bowl by **Manuel Bentes**

1947
Dining Room on the Garden by **Pierre Bonnard**

1948
Melon Eaters by **Renato Guttuso**

Duck Fight by **Karl Knaths**

1949
Lobsters and Fish by **Pablo Picasso**

1950
Sunday on the Banks of the Marne by **Henri Cartier-Bresson**

The Bricklayer's Lunch by **Júlio Pomar**

Bowl, Eggs and Lemons by **William Scott**

1951
Healthy and good with butter poster by **Donald Brun**

French Prawn by **Leonard Baskin**

1952
Eucharistic Still Life by **Salvador Dalí**

Barilla, La pasta del buon appetito advert by **Erberto Carboni**

1953
Poultry Market by **Walter Williams**

1954
Figure with Meat by **Francis Bacon**

Spanish Still Life by **Grace Hartigan**

1955
Bella Notte, spaghetti scene from *Lady and the Tramp* by **Walt Disney**

Meuble Cuisine Atelier Le Corbusier Type 1, **Le Corbusier**

1957
Hotel Royal's flatware designed by **Arne Jacobsen**

1957 – 1962
Still Life with Glass Under the Lamp by **Pablo Picasso**

1958
PH Artichoke Lamp designed by **Poul Henningsen**

1959
Sculpture-Morte by **Marcel Duchamp**

Unverkennbar Bols poster by **Michael Engelmann**

Solomon R. Guggenheim Museum by **Frank Lloyd Wright**, opens in New York

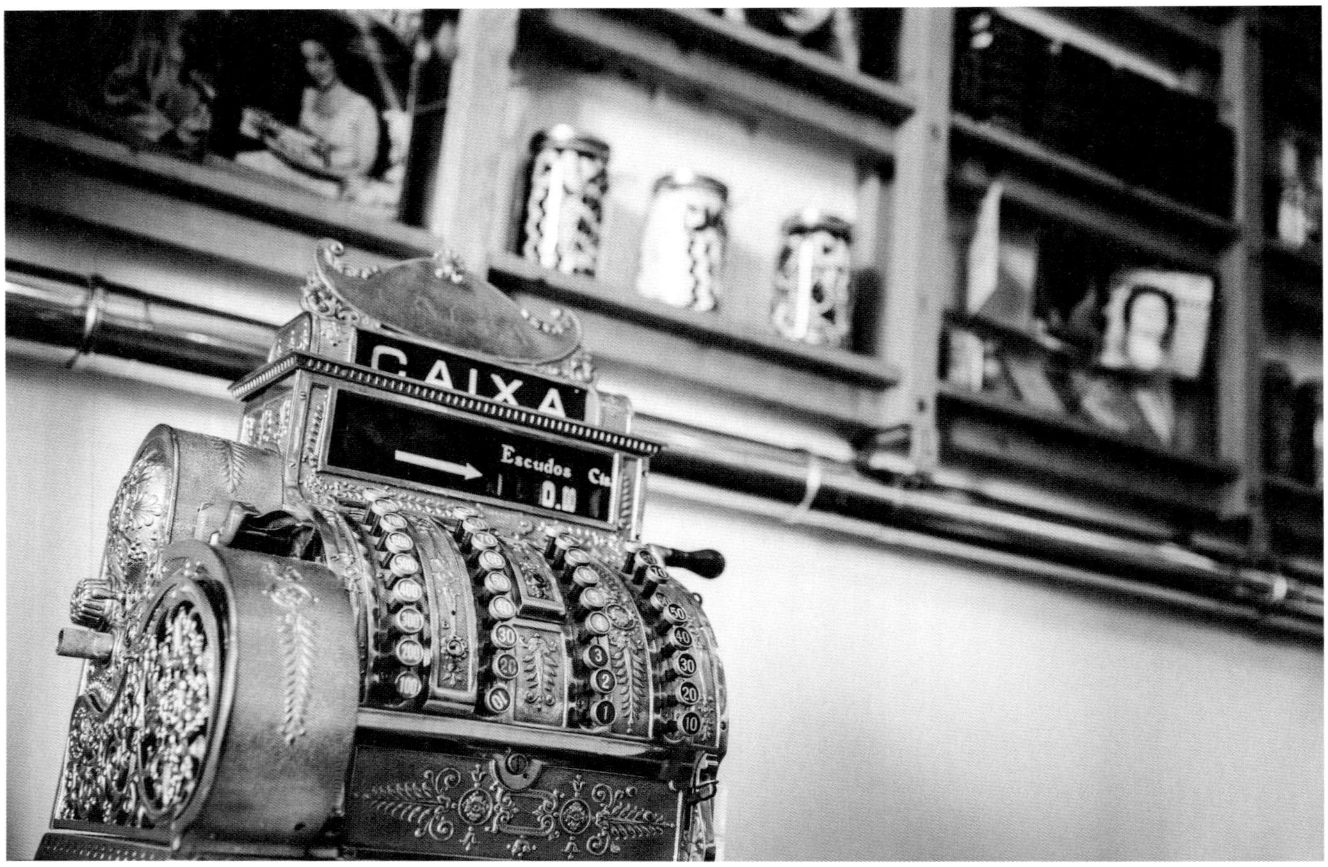
CAIXA
Escudos

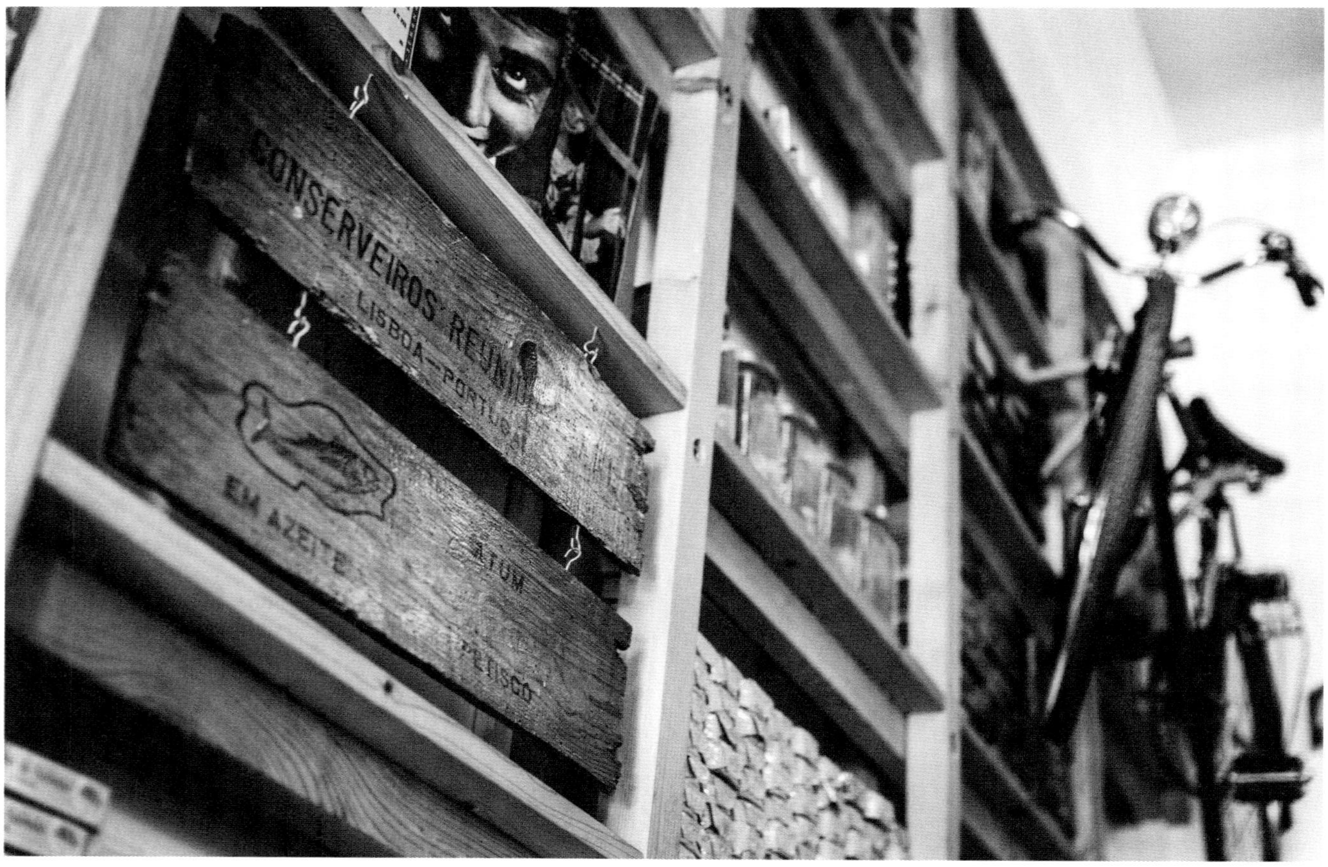
CONSERVEIROS
LISBOA—PORTUGAL
ATUM

FOOD

1960

Albrecht von Goertz cesigned the **Starmix MX3 food processor**

Invention of heat-stable **vacuum pouches**

Alex Humbert at **Maxim's** anticipated the Nouvelle Cuisine movement with his *saddle of lamb Callas*

1961

Soviet cosmonaut **Yuri Gagarin** becomes the **first man in space**

An Anecdoted Topography of Chance, book by **Daniel Spoerri**

Mastering the Art of French Cooking written by **Simone Beck, Louisette Bertholle and Julia Child**

First English Edition of **Larousse Gastronomique**

1962

Opening of **Restaurant Aviz**, Lisbon

Churrasqueira do Campo Grande opening in Lisbon

A Voir et à manger by **Christian Bourgois**, first Paris guide, éditions Julliard

1963

The French Chef, television cooking show created and hosted by **Julia Child**

Ermal Cleon 'Ernie' Fraze invented the **pull-tab opener** for beverage cans

Robot-Coupe invented the food processor **Magimix**

Martin Luther King delivers his 'I have a dream' speech

1964

Comidas Meu Santo by **Guilherme Figueiredo**

1965

Henri Gault and **Christian Millau** founded **Gault & Millau**

US astronaut **John Young** made an attempt to eat a corned beef sandwich on-board Gemini III

The Immigration Act led to an appetite for new spicy flavours from Thailand and Vietnam

Peter Buck and **Fred DeLuca** open **Subway**, the world's largest restaurant chain

1966

Opening of **Galeto** restaurant, Lisbon

English edition of *The Art of Cuisine*, with recipes by **Henri de Toulouse-Lautrec**, first published in 1930 with **Maurice Joyant**

1967

Raytheon Corporation acquired **Amana Refrigeration Inc.** and introduced a **countertop microwave**

La Cuisine, detailed technical cookbook by **Raymond Oliver**

Auberge de l'Ill, a classical French restaurant by the **chef Paul Haeberlin**, was first awarded a three-star Michelin rating

Albert and Michel Roux, the **Roux Brothers**, opened Le Gavroche in London and are still regarded as the godfathers of modern restaurant cuisine in the UK

1968

Make the greatest cooking discovery since fire, **Amana Radarange microwave oven's** advertising

Restaurant Spoerri was opened in Düsseldorf by **Daniel Spoerri** with an art gallery above it

Alain Senderens opened L'Archestrate, a seven-table restaurant in Paris

1969

Neil Armstrong and Buzz Aldrin take the first steps on the moon

Allen Ruppersberg installed a temporary restaurant, **Al's Café** in LA

New Paris guide, the **Guide Julliard**

Ma Gastronomie first published in French, 200 recipes based on **Fernand Point's** notes

Louis Outhier, one of the few chefs in history to simultaneously earn three Michelin stars (1969 to 1988) and four toques in the Gault & Millau guide

Luís Sttau Monteiro created, under the pseudonym Manuel Pedrosa, in the newspaper *Diário de Lisboa*, a section called ***A Melga no Prato*** (The Mosquito on the Plate), which had general articles on gastronomy and restaurants

Roger Vergé opened his Michelin three-star restaurant **Moulin de Mougins**, Cannes

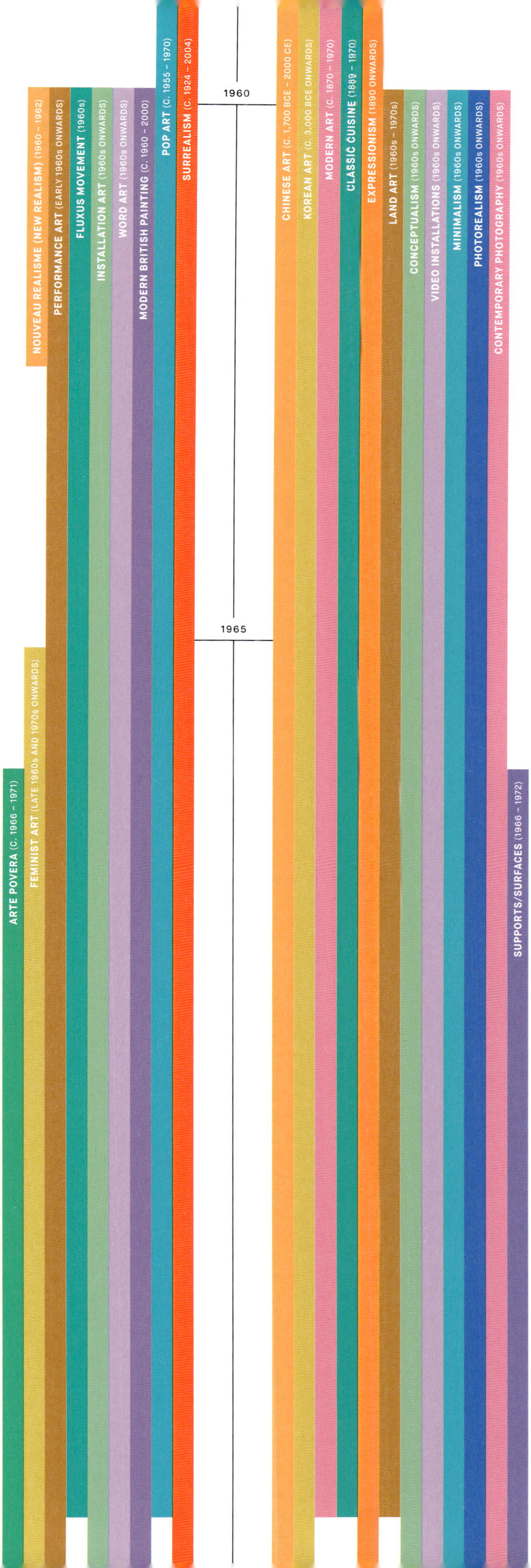

ART

1960

Barbecue by **Archibald Motley**

Le Plein (Full Up) by **Arman**

Kichka's Breakfast by **Daniel Spoerri**

1961

Artist's Shit artwork by **Piero Manzoni**

I Love You with My Ford by **James Rosenquist**

Nevera nueva by **Antonio López**

1962

Campbell's Soup Cans by **Andy Warhol**

Salads, Sandwiches and Desserts by **Wayne Thiebaud**

Floor Burger by **Claes Oldenburg**

Green Coca-Cola Bottles by **Andy Warhol**

1963

Cakes by **Wayne Thiebaud**

Dinner Date by **Marisol Escobar**

Mystery Food by **Ben Vautier**

Tupperware advertisement from the January 25 issue of *LIFE* magazine

1964

Sombras projetadas by **Lourdes Castro** (with **René Bertholo**)

Hot Dog by **Roy Lichtenstein**

Última Ceia by **Malangatana**

Casserole et moules fermées by **Marcel Broodthaers**

1965

Tableau piège – Restaurant de la City Galerie, Zurich by **Daniel Spoerri**

Ample Food for Stupid Thought by **Robert Filliou**

1964 – 67 *Cylinda Ice Bucket* by **Arne Jacobsen**

Cold War and **Vietnam War**

1966

Opening of the **Whitney Museum of American Art**

False Food Selection by **Claes Oldenburg**

Annie, Poured From Maple Syrup by **Ed Ruscha**

1967

Flux Mystery Food, printed can by **Ben Vautier**

Toaster by **Richard Hamilton**

Red Stripe Kitchen from the series House Beautiful: Bringing the War Home by **Martha Rosler**

The Dramatic Tale of an Egg – 5 by **António Areal**

Andy Warhol's print of a banana becomes the cover artwork for the debut album of **The Velvet Underground**

1968

The Identical Lunch with Ay-O by **Alison Knowles**

Everness II 1 by **Joseph Beuys**

Wheel of Delights by **Lygia Pape**, an invitation to taste the different colours, created with water colouring, porcelain, anilins, flavours and droppers

1969

Still Life #2 Homage to David by **Gabriel Laderman**

Meals from Al's Café by **Allen Ruppersberg**

Let It Bleed, album cover for **The Rolling Stones** at Decca Records, created by **Robert Brownjohn**, with food styling by **Delia Smith**

Esquire magazine, issue no. 426 cover by **George Lois**

Literature Sausage by **Dieter Roth**

Calouste Gulbenkian Foundation and **Museum** were inaugurated

Photo-Fry by **Gordon Matta-Clark**

FOOD

1970

First induction stove by Westinghouse Electric Corporation

Roger Vergé founded **l'École de Cuisine du Soleil Roger Vergé** in Mougins

Villeroy & Boch's avant-garde picnic set La Bomba by **Helen von Boch** and **Frederigo Fabbrini**

1971

Thermomix VM 2000, launched by Vorwerk Corporate Group

FOOD, artist-run restaurant in SoHo, New York, was founded by artists **Carol Goodden, Tina Girouard** and **Gordon Matta-Clark**

Gaston Lenôtre started a school in the town of Plaisir, in Yvelines, Paris

1972

Marc Meneau received his first Michelin star at the restaurant **L'Espérance**

Gault & Millau's first independent guide to French restaurants

1973

Claude Peyrot awarded three stars in the Michelin Guide

Joseph Rostang took over **La Bonne Auberge** in Antibes

Jacques Pic, son of André Pic, restored the third Michelin star to **Maison Pic**

Jesús Oyarbide opens his restaurant **Zalacaín** in Spain

Les Diners de Gala, cookbook by **Salvador Dalí**

The **Concorde** made its first transatlantic crossing

1974

First Michelin Stars attributed to Portuguese restaurants in Portugal: **O Pipas** in Cascais, **Aviz** and **Michel** in Lisbon and **Portucale** in Porto

Georges Pralus incorporated **sous-vide** into a commercial kitchen

Michel Guérard invented *cuisine minceur*, a form of healthy cooking

Michel and **Maryse Trama** inaugurate their first restaurant **On the Thumb**

1975

Friedman Paul Erhardt, aka **Chef Tell**, was the inspiration for the *Muppet Show*'s Swedish Chef

Pedro Subijana Reza started out in **Akelare** restaurant, Spain

1976

Marc Haeberlin joins his father **Paul** and his uncle **Jean-Pierre**, the fourth generation of Haeberlins in the kitchen

José Quitério founded the gastronomic column of the *Expresso* newspaper, which lead the way for the criticism and appraisal of restaurants in printed form

Yves Thuriès was twice named *Meilleur Ouvrier de France*

1977

Paul Bocuse's *French Cooking* book, Pantheon Books

Im Schiffchen restaurant was founded in Düsseldorf by **Jean-Claude Bourgueil**

Pierre Koffman opened his first restaurant, **La Tante Claire**, Chelsea

Gualtiero Marchesi opened his first restaurant in Via Bonvesin de la Riva, Milan

Constitution of **ANICP-National Association of Canned Fish Industry**

1978

Disappearance of the **Portuguese Gastronomy Society**, founded in 1933

Patrick O'Connell and **Reinhardt Lynch** opened **The Inn at Little Washington** in an abandoned gas station

1979

Peter Doyle sets up **Turrets restaurant** at the Castlereagh Hotel, Sydney

Karl and his brother **Rudolf Obauer** open **Restaurant Obauer**, in Werfen

Marijuana in Cucina, book by **Luigi P. Esposito** and **Marino Sinibaldi**

Jean-Louis Palladin opened his first restaurant in USA, **Jean-Louis**, Watergate

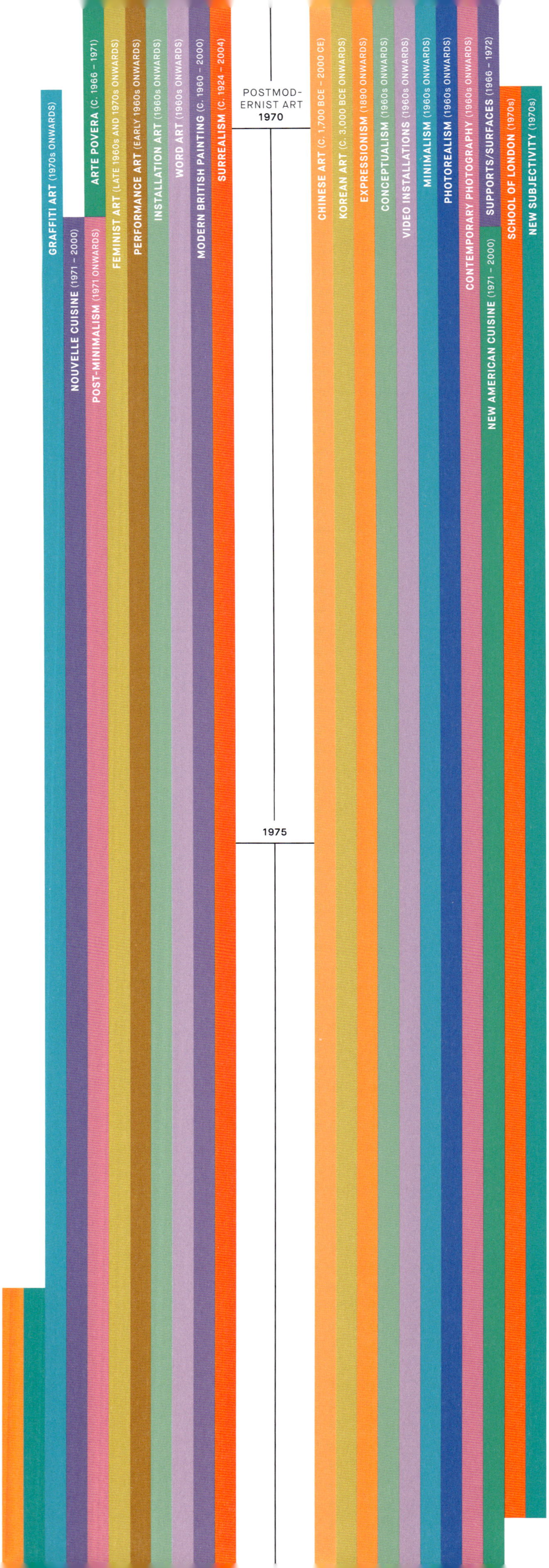

ART

1970

Gas Stove by **Marcel Broodthaers**

Four-colour Meal, performance by **Antoni Miralda** and **Dorothée Selz**

Insertions into Ideological Circuits: Coca-Cola Project by **Cildo Meireles**

Supermarket Shopper, hyperrealistic sculpture by **Duane Hanson**

1971

The Origin of Table Manners, installation by **Lothar Baumgarten**

No Gas Café from *No Gas* series by **Red Grooms**

1971 – 1980

The Dinner by **Antonio López García**

1972

Food, documentary by **Gordon Matta-Clark**

The Gourmet Cat by **Ronald Searle**

Shigeko Kubota's video *Marcel Duchamp and John Cage*

Some Living American Women Artists / Last Supper by **Mary Beth Edelson**

1973

French Cooking by **Allen Jones** in *Homage to Picasso* (various artists)

Breakfast, Trail's End Restaurant, Kanab, Utah, August 10, 1973 by **Stephen Shore**

Blue Fish by **Roy Lichtenstein**

Still Life With Crystal Bowl by **Roy Lichtenstein**

Delphic Kitchen Utility Blades designed by **Harry V. Cremonese**

Kitchen Knife and Cutting Board designed by **Maria Benktzon** and **Sven-Eric Juhlin**

Landscape Table by **Ana Vieira**

La Grande Bouffe, French-Italian film directed by **Marco Ferreri**

1974

Rubik's Cube by **Ernö Rubik**

The Dinner Party, installation by **Judy Chicago**

1975

Madonna of Peas by **Joe Brainard**

Street Trader, photograph by **Paul Trevor**

Semiotics of the Kitchen by **Martha Rosler**

1976

Weeping Willow, lacquer tea caddy by **Mutsumi Suzuki**

Le Déjeuner Sur l'Herbe 77 by **Ana Vieira**

Snak Shak, Montezuma, Georgia by **William Eggleston**

1977

Can opener designed by **Harvey J. Finison**

Centre Georges Pompidou, Paris

Hot Dogs, from the portfolio *Manhatttttan* by **Antoni Miralda**

1978

From Northeast to Coimbra by **Túlia Saldanha**

Purple Woman/Kitchen/Second View, plastic figures by **Laurie Simmons**

Knork Fork, designed by **Maria Benktzon** and **Sven-Eric Juhlin**

LOWBROW ART MOVEMENT
(1979 ONWARDS)
Cultural roots in underground comix, punk music, tiki culture and hot-rod cultures of the street. Often known by the name Pop Surrealism

1979

Screwpull Corkscrew designed by **Herbert Allen**

At the Carpet Shop by **Peter Fischli** and **David Weiss**

Arroz e Feijão (Rice and Beans) by **Anna Maria Maiolino**

Breakfast in America, **Supertramp** album cover by **Mike Doud**

FOOD

1980

Ferran Adrià began his career as a dishwasher at the Hotel Playafels, Castelldefels, Spain

Emanuela and **Fulvio Pierangelini** opened restaurant **Gambero Rosso** in San Vincenzo

1981

Fernando Fernandes and **José Miranda** opened **Pap'Açorda** restaurant, at Bairro Alto in Lisbon

Quique Dacosta restaurant opened its doors under the name of **El Poblet**

Heinz Winkler at 32 years old is the youngest chef to receive three Michelin stars

Chef **Jean Louis** and his Spanish wife **Evelyn Fuertes** opened **Neichel's Restaurant** in the residential Pedralbes district of Barcelona

Luisa Valazza opens **Al Sorriso** with her husband **Angelo Valazza**

1982

Manuel Reis opens **Frágil** nightclub in Lisbon

Cozinha Tradicional Portuguesa by **Maria de Lourdes Modesto**

1983

Bachus, bar and restaurant founded in Lisbon by the brothers **José**, **Joaquim** and **Belmiro Costa**, together with **Arménio Fernandes** and **Antero Jacinto**

Gérard Boyer moved to **Les Crayères**, château on the outskirts of Reims

Geert Van Hecke opened his restaurant De Karmeliet in Bruges

1984

Francis Mallmann, specialist in Patagonian cuisine, published his first book, *La Cocina al instante*

Frédy Girardet published *The Cuisine of Frédy Girardet*

El Internacional Tapas Bar & Restaurant, an artistic project and social experiment, by **Antoni Miralda** and **chef Montse Guillén**, NY

Keith Floyd started his first **BBC TV series** *Floyd on Fish*

1985

Noélia opens, with her husband, the restaurant **Noélia & Jerónimo**, in Cabanas, Portugal

At the age of 20 **Martín Berasategui** took over his parents' restaurant, **Bodegón Alejandro**, and earned his first Michelin star there by the age of 25

Portuguese **Chef Michel da Costa** organised the banquet commemorating Portugal's accession to the European Economic Community (EEC)

Kiyomi Mikuni opened **Hôtel de Mikuni** restaurant in Tokyo

1986

Pastry chef **Lucien Peltier** creates the cake **Ambre**

Maria Paola Porru opens **Casanostra**, an Italian restaurant in Lisbon

Bernard Pacaud opened his first restaurant, **Ambroisie**, in Paris

Three brothers - **Joan** as the chef, **Jordi** as pastry chef and Josep as sommelier, created **El Celler de Can Roca**, in Girona, Spain

1987

Paul Bocuse conceived the idea of a culinary competition, the **Bocuse d'Or**

Alain Senderens introduced an innovation in **Lucas Carton** restaurant menus suggesting wines by the glass to accompany each dish

La Cuisine, une passion de père en fils, by **Michel** and **Jean-Michel Lorain**

Michel Rostang, the first Parisian chef to create a *bistro*, **Le Bistrot d'à Côté Flaubert**

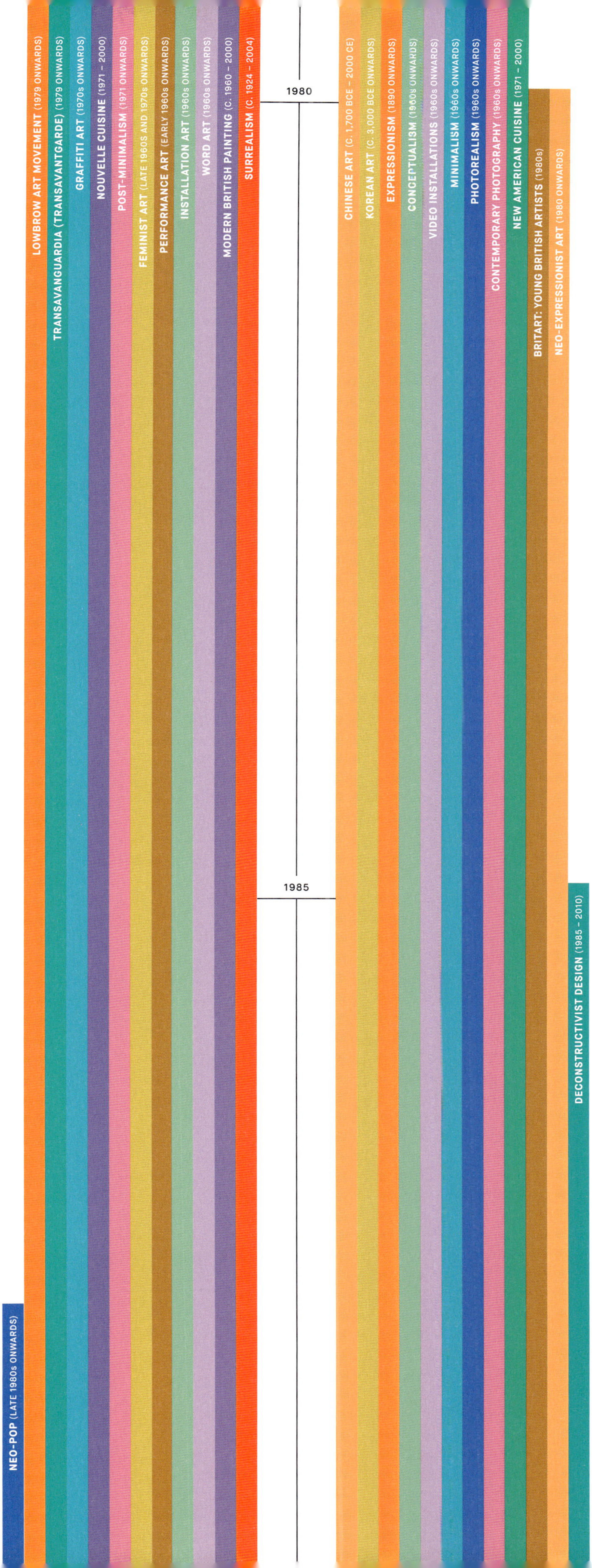

ART

1980

La Boucherie by **Eduardo Luiz**

Vegetables, Seward County, Seward, Nebraska photograph by **Ronald R. Geibert**

Cafe Deutschland (Style War) from the series Cafe Deutschland (1977 – 1982) by **Jörg Immendorff**

Cover for Bob James's album *H* by **Paula Scher** and **John Paul Endress**

1981

In early 1980s, **Adobe**, **Aldus**, **Apple** and **Hewlett-Packard** each produced key technologies that allowed professional desktop publishing to overtake package printing

Enigma 3 by **Regina Silveira**

Cézanne Still Life #4 by **George Segal**

Ricard Bottle by **Alan Byrne**

Homage to Cézanne by **Joan Ponç**

1982

First edition of **ARCO, International Contemporary Art Fair of Madrid**

Crystal Louisiana Hot Sauce by **Akira Inada**

Cafe Assistants, Compass Cafe, Colsterworth, Lincolnshire from the portfolio A1: The Great North Road photograph by **Paul Graham**

1983

Soupe du Jour by **Bill Woodrow**

White Food, video by **Stephen Laub**

Macintosh 128K Home Computer by **Apple Inc., Steve Jobs** and **Jerry Manock**

1984

Foundation of **Novodesign**, Portuguese Design Company by **Carlos Coelho, Paulo Rocha and Victor Moura Vicente**

1985

Capri Battery, installation by **Joseph Beuys**

Bronze by Gold by **Richard Hamilton**

Fish by **Valentin Khrushch**

Tampopo, Japanese film by **Jûzô Itami**

1986

Nomos Dining Table designed by **Norman Foster**

Boîte de sardines (Can of Sardines) by **Miquel Barceló**

Adjustable spoons designed by **Ergonomi Design Gruppen, Maria Benktzon, Håkan Bergkvist, Sven-Eric Juhlin**

Infant's fork and spoon, designed by **Michael Wilson**

1987

Shark Food from the series *Aquarellen (Watercolors)* by **Thomas Schütte**

Max le Chinois colander by **Philippe Starck**

Still Life, Vegetables and Jug by **Maria Toscano Rico**

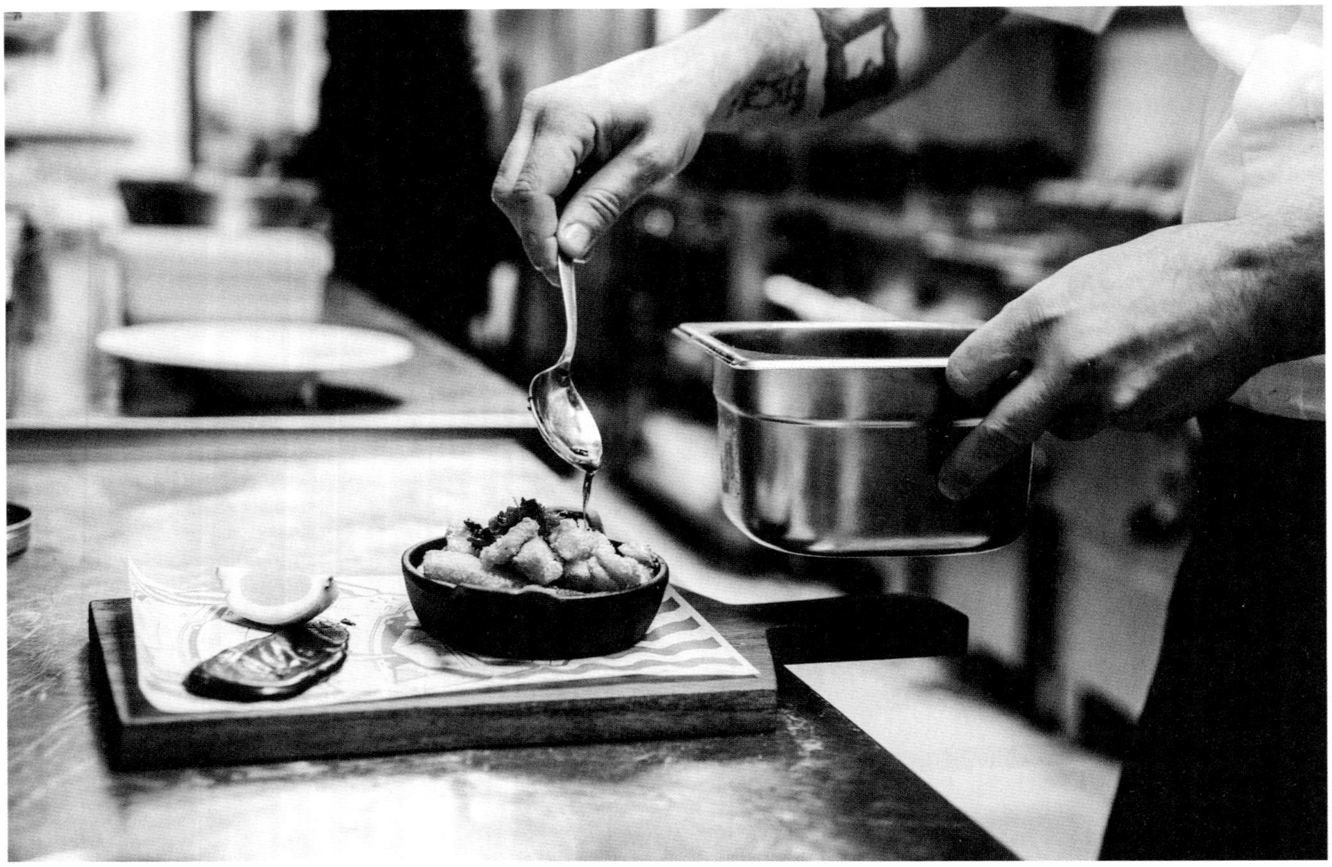

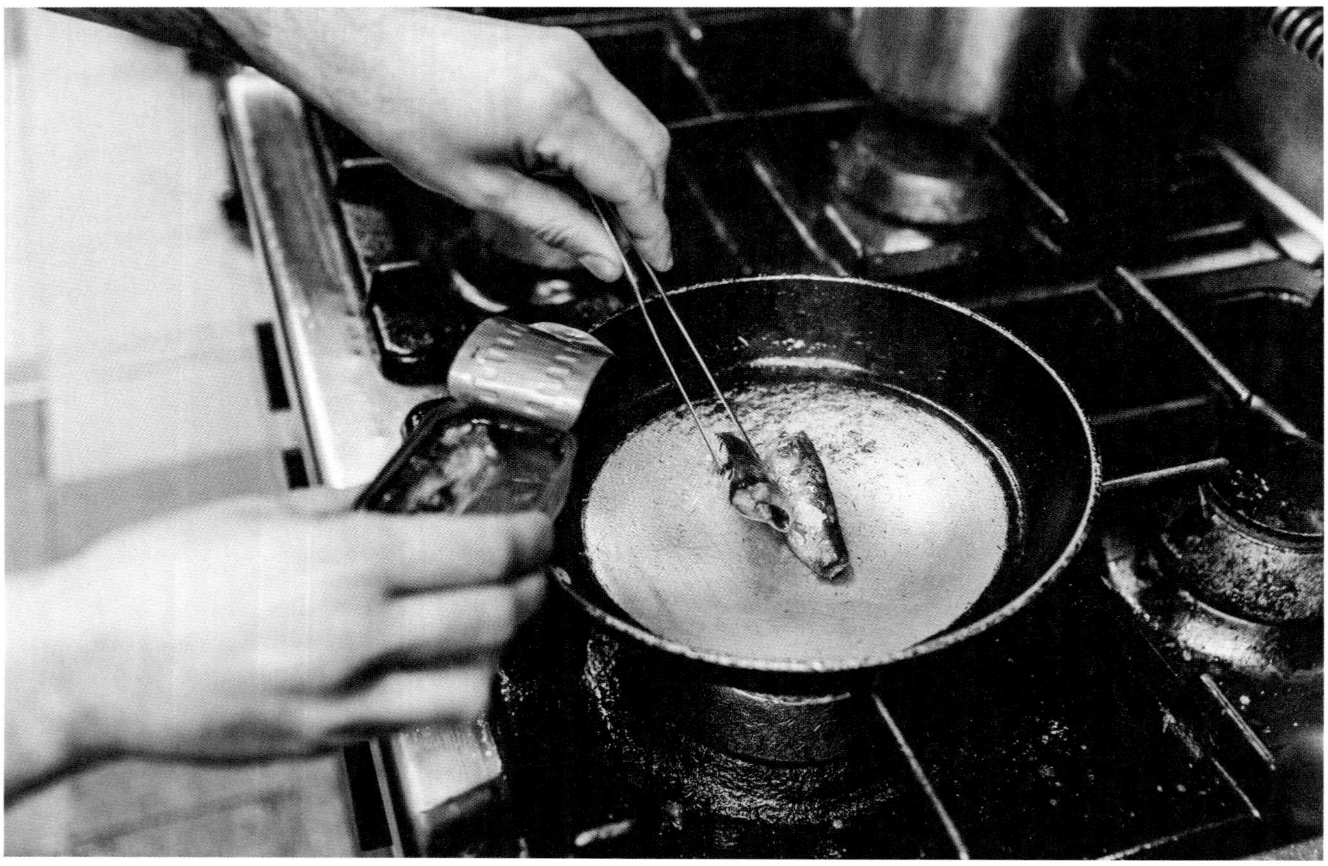

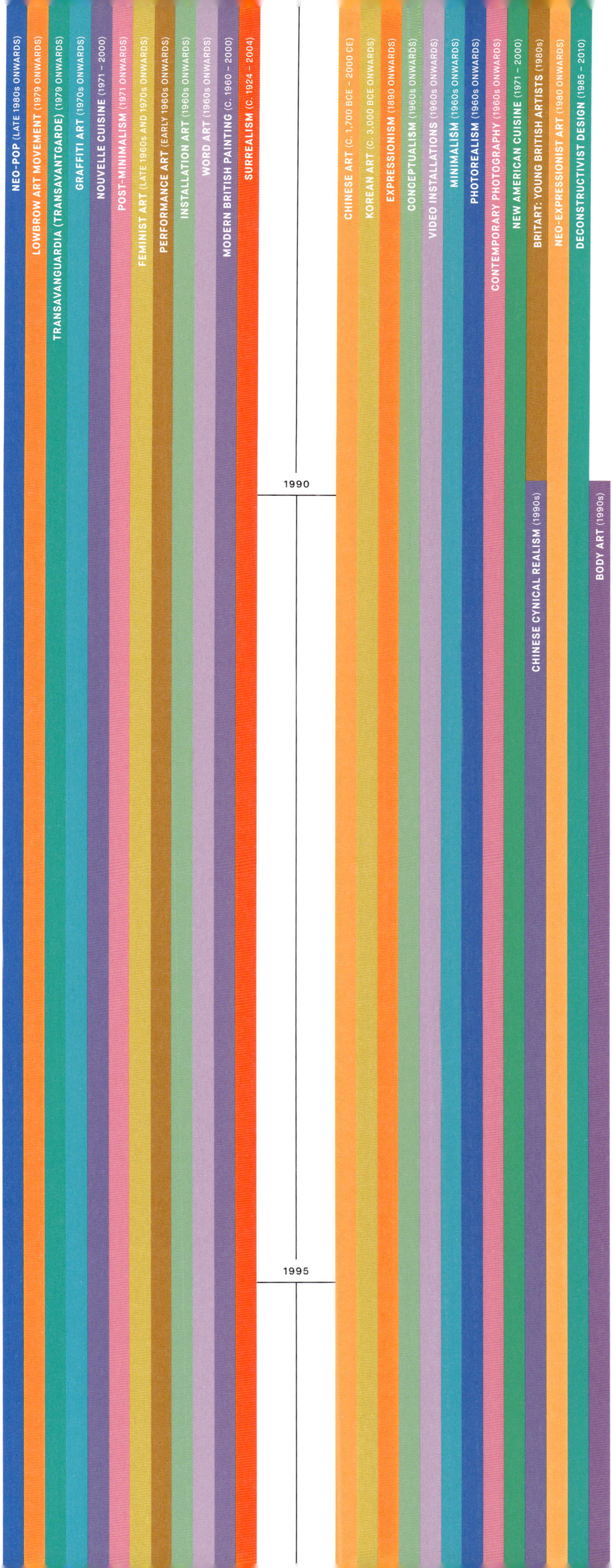

FOOD

1987

Jean Bardet organised the meal of the **G7 Summit** in Versailles

Charlie Trotter's most well-known restaurant, **Charlie Trotter**, opens in Chicago

1988

Therm **molecular gastronomy** coined by **Nicholas Kurti** and **Hervé This**

Twins **Jacques** and **Laurent Pourcel** opened **Le Jardin des Sens** in Montpellier

1989

Portuguese chef **Luís Baena** worked with **Paul Bocuse** at **Le Saint Honoré** restaurant at Méridien Hotel, Rio de Janeiro

Limited **private internet connections** to parts of the internet by commercial entities emerged in several American cities

Gordon Ramsay was trained under **Guy Savoy**, and described him as his culinary mentor

1990

Justa Nobre and her husband **José Nobre**, opened the restaurant **O Nobre** in Ajuda, Lisbon

Georges Blanc, son of Paulette Blanc, creates the **Ancienne Auberge**

Zagat Guide asked its 7,000 diners, "Where would you eat the last meal of your life?" Respondents overwhelmingly chose **Bouley**, flagship restaurant of **David Bouley**

Joël Robuchon was awarded *Cuisinier du Siècle*, becoming the **most starred chef**

Research at CERN in Switzerland by British computer scientist **Tim Berners-Lee** resulted in the **World Wide Web**

1992

4 Estações na Casa da Comida - Cozinha em Portugal by **Jorge Vale**

EU introduction of the system **Appellation d'Origine Protégée (AOP)**

Annie Féolde won her third Michelin star at **Enoteca Pinchiorri**

Jonnie Boer and **Thérèse** purchased the restaurant **De Librije**

Sydney Morning Herald's **Good Food Guide** awarded **Tetsuya Wakuda's** restaurant, **Tetsuya's**, Three Hats

1993

Hilario Arbelaitz gets the prize of *Best Chef in the Basque Country*

Miguel Castro e Silva started the **Miguel Restaurant**, in Foz do Douro, Portugal

On Cooking by **Sarah R. Labensky** and **Alan M. Hause**

Michel Jr. (Michel Albert Roux) took over his father's restaurant, **Le Gavroche** in London

1994

José António Inácio de Sousa Quitério created and directed the collection of gastronomy books *Coração, Cabeça e Estômago* (Heart, Head and Stomach)

Marco Pierre White became the first British chef to be awarded three Michelin stars and also the youngest in Michelin history

Eckart Witzigmann received the award *Chef of the Century* by Gault & Millau

1995

Sukiyabashi Jiro opens his restaurant located in Ginza subway station, Tokyo

Heston Blumenthal bought a run-down pub in Bray, Berkshire, called **The Ringers** and re-opened it as **The Fat Duck**

Massimo Bottura opened Osteria Francescana in Modena, Italy

ART

1988

Bedsit cooker designed by **Andy Pollock** of Teeside Polytechnic

Mackerel by **Sir Kyffin Williams**

1989 – 1991

Communism collapses in Eastern Europe and the USSR

1989

The Cook, the Thief, His Wife & Her Lover, film written and directed by **Peter Greenaway**

Igloo del pane by **Mario Merz**

Fall of **Berlin Wall**. Much of the artwork was not claimed by artists and remains anonymous

1990

Black Supper by **Andres Serrano**

Tuna, Little Horse Mackerel and Pomegranate by **Michiko Kon**

Anthro/Socio (Rinde Facing Camera), video installation by **Bruce Nauman**

1991

Bossy Burger, video by **Paul McCarthy**

1992

Untitled (Red, Yellow, Green Curry), by **Rirkrit Tiravanija**

Apple Core by **Claes Oldenburg**

Mister Meumeu cheese grater, designed by **Philippe Starck**

The Cocktail Party, installation by **Sandy Skoglund**

Like Water for Chocolate, movie by **Alfonso Arau**, based on Laura Esquivel's book

1993

Slim-Fast: Délice de Fraise by **Sylvie Fleury**

5 o'clock Tea by **Licio Passon**

Tom's Diner by **Ralph Goings**

1994

Untitled, no. 58 of 69, from the illustrated book *Album* by **Louise Bourgeois**

Pom'patate by **Nelly Trumel**

The Feast by **Bertrand Joliet**

1995

Eggplants and Cauliflowers by **Hervé Di Rosa**

Fourth Detail March 25th by **David Hockney**

A-1 Sauce by **Ralph Goings**

Use It Containers designed by **Constantin Boym** and **Laurene Leon Boym**

Cake by **Jeff Koons**

Donut by **Ralph Goings**

Untitled (Rock Novelty) from the series *British Food*, by **Martin Parr**

FOOD

1995

Seeing many of his peers die of stress and heart attacks, **Joël Robuchon** retired at the age of 50

The Art of Cooking With Steam by **Jacques Manière**

Norman Van Aken opened **Norman's** in Coral Gables, Florida

1997

The Michelin Guide introduced the **Bib Gourmand**

Gianfranco Vissani achieved television fame for his participation in several RAI broadcasts with *Uno Mattina*

Frédéric Anton became the chef of the restaurant **Le Pré Catelan**

1998

Daní García inaugurated his first restaurant **El Tragabuches**, in Ronda

Andoni Luis Aduriz founded his own restaurant, called **Mugaritz**

Pierre Hermé created **Maison Pierre Hermé** in Paris, with **Charles Znaty**

Chef **Christian Bau** became the Chef de Cuisine at **Victor's Fine Dining** in Schloss Berg castle

Antoine Westermann starts to oversee the kitchen operations at **Fortaleza do Guincho** in Cascais, Portugal, alongside executive chef **Vincent Farges**

Bernard Loiseau's culinary group was listed on the stock exchange

Damien Hirst opens the restaurant **Pharmacy** in Notting Hill

1999

Brazilian Chef **Alex Atala** opens restaurant **D.O.M.** in São Paulo

Opening of **Denis Martin** research laboratory

2000

Ma Cuisine: Des Landes au Carré des Feuillants by **Alain Dutournier**

Combal, restaurant opened by **Davide Scabin** in 1994, in Turin, moved to Castello di Rivoli Museum of Contemporary Art and became **Combal.Zero**

Enrique Olvera redefines Mexican food and opens **Pujol** in Mexico City

Kitchen Confidential: Adventures in the Culinary Underbelly by **Anthony Bourdain**

2001

José Júlio Vintém opens the restaurant **Tomba Lobos**, Portalegre, Portugal, with typical cuisine from Alentejo

Parkheuvel, owned by **Cees Helder**, became the first Dutch restaurant to hold three Michelin stars

Alain Passard introduced, for the first time in a three-star restaurant, menus that put vegetables at the centre of the plate, banning meat

Joachim Wisslers collected three Michelin stars at **Vendôme** restaurant between 2001 and 2005

Alain Ducasse prepared a multi-course gala dinner for Prince Albert, his bride Charlene Wittstock, and their 500 A-list guests at their royal wedding

2002

Yotam Ottolenghi and **Noam Bar** founded **Ottolenghi**, Notting Hill, London

Jean-Georges Klein earned his third Michelin star

2002 – 2003

Bawabet Dimashq established the largest restaurant in the world

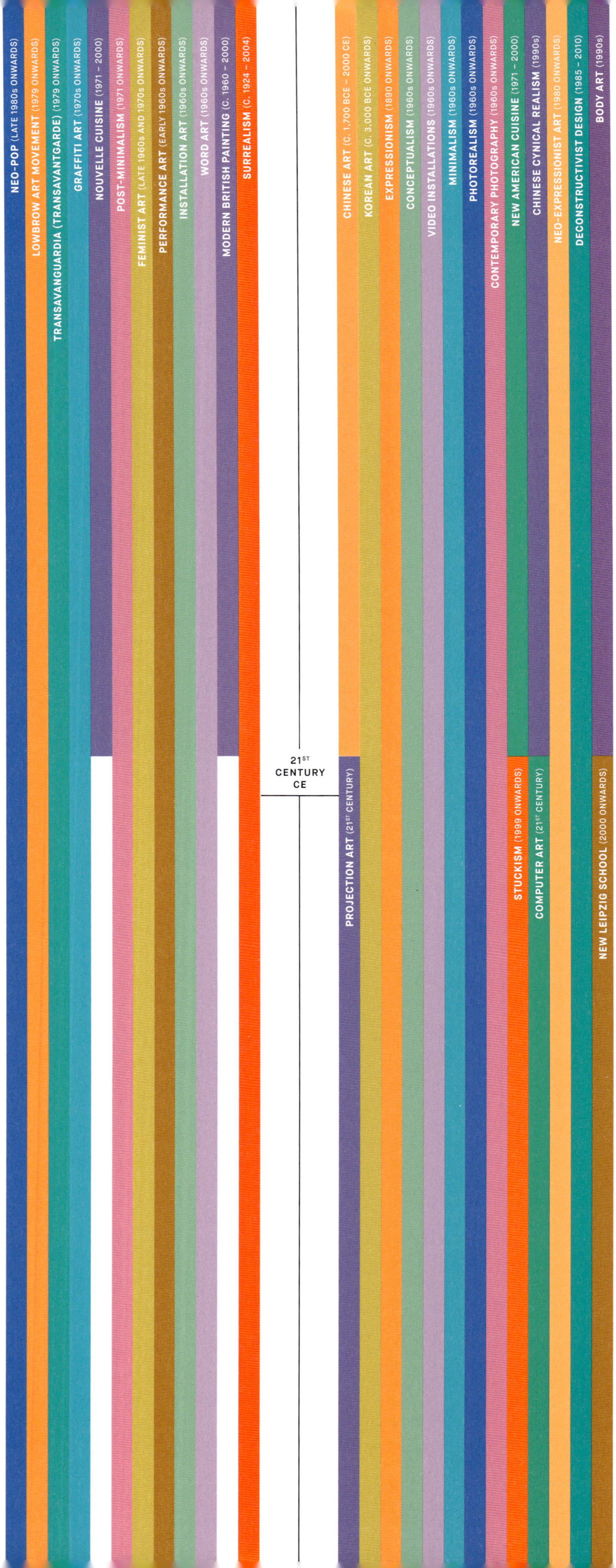

ART

1996

Wrecked by **Sam Taylor-Johnson**, modelled on Leonardo da Vinci's *Last Supper*

1997

Sleeping Dogs by **Dennis Oppenheim**

Chicken Knickers by **Sarah Lucas**

On the Verge of Visibility by **Wolfgang Tillmans**

1998

Carbon Oven by **Los Carpinteros**, collective of Cuban artists **Alexandre Arrechea, Dagoberto Rodriguez** and **Marco Castillo**

Florida by **Martin Parr**

Gardener's Square (set of 7) by **Andreas Siekmann**

The Chromatic Diet by **Sophie Calle**

Carcasses (Baalbeck) by **Mona Hatoum**

Old Man's Cloth by **El Anatsui**

1999

Double Mona Lisa (Peanut Butter and Jelly), After Warhol series by **Vik Muniz**

Lips from *To Kiss Your Lips* (set of 4) by **Julia Jacquette**

2000

Emigre 49, the Everything is for Sale issue from **Emigre Inc**

TaTa Ma Chance, from the portfolio *Break the Silence!* by **Giselle Baillie**

Untitled (Apple and pear, nylon filament and screws) by **Urs Fischer**

One More Bread by **Juan Hidalgo**

Sandwiches by **Jeff Koons**

Champagne and Chocolate by **Maira Kalman**

2001

Street Trader Waiting to Sell Food to Construction Workers from 93 Grayston Office Park, Sandton by **David Goldblatt**

Still Life with Chicken by **Jacinto Luís**

Homage to V. Van Gogh from the series *Vita Brevis* by **Maria Beatriz Cascas**

Nutsy's McDonald's by **Tom Sachs**

Still Life, single-screen projection by **Sam Taylor-Johnson**

2002

Dream Cakes by **Riiko Sakkinen**

Tea and coffee service *Future Systems* designed by **Officina Alessi**

2002 – 2003

The Greater (Grater) Divide by **Mona Hatoum**

FOOD

2003

Anthony Bourdain's world-travel television show *A Cook's Tour*

It is widely believed that **Bernard Loiseau** killed himself because his restaurant, **La Côte d'Or**, in Burgundy, was in danger of losing its third star

Yamamoto opened his own small restaurant **Nihonryori Ryugin** in Tokyo

Carlos Braz creates 'The Best Chocolate Cake in the World'

Wylie Dufresne opened **wd~50** restaurant at 50 Clinton Street, in Manhattan

The **millionth duck** was eaten in 2003 at **La Tour d'Argent** restaurant

2004

Gérard Rabaey publishes his first book, *Le Pont des Délices*

Roger Souvereyns said "I do not want to get old being sick. I hope that I die in the kitchen, on the street, in the opera. I've worked so much out of the ground that I would never be able to be at home. (...)"

Jacques Torres opened **Jacques Torres Chocolate Haven**, in Manhattan

Juan Amador opened his own restaurant **Amador** in Langen, near Frankfurt

The restaurant **Noma** was opened with **Redzepi** as the head chef

2005

Michelin produced its **first American guide** concentrating on New York City

Jamie Oliver embarked on his *School Dinners* (documentary) campaign to improve the quality of food fed to pupils in schools

Enrico Crippa opens his restaurant **Piazza Duomo** in Alba, Italy

Didier Courten settled at **Le Terminus** in Sierre, Switzerland

Creation and opening of **Alexandre Bourdas**' restaurant **Sa.Qua.Na** in Honfleur, France

Schwarzwaldstube restaurant maintained three Michelin stars for 25 consecutive years, under the leadership of **Harald Wohlfahrt**

Grant Achatz opens **Alinea** in Chicago's Lincoln Park, with **Nick Kokonas**

Cristeta Comerford, chef from Manila, becomes the **Executive Chef of the White House** and the first woman in history to hold this position

Bertílio Gomes led the gastronomy of the restaurant **VirGula**, Lisbon

Subtilezas Gastronómicas - Receitas à Volta de um Vinho by **José Manuel Bento dos Santos**

2006

Heston Blumenthal and **Harold McGee** published a *Statement on the 'New Cookery'* in the *Observer* to summarise the tenets of molecular gastronomy

Thomas Keller is awarded three stars in the inaugural Michelin Guide to the San Francisco Bay Area, for **The French Laundry** restaurant

2007

In the second reissue of the **Larousse Gastronomique**, **Joël Robuchon** invited **Miguel Castro e Silva** to participate in the publication with three of his recipes. To this day he is the only Portuguese chef with recipes at Larousse

Antoine Westermann gives up his three stars to turn to new culinary adventures

The American food critic **Jonathan Gold** became the first food critic to win the Pulitzer Prize for Criticism

Anne-Sophie Pic recovers the third star that **Maison Pic** had lost in 1995

Peter Goossens operates a brasserie at the **Museum of Fine Arts** in Brussels with only typical Belgian dishes

NEO-POP (LATE 1980s ONWARDS)
LOWBROW ART MOVEMENT (1979 ONWARDS)
TRANSAVANGUARDIA (TRANSAVANTGARDE) (1979 ONWARDS)
GRAFFITI ART (1970s ONWARDS)
POST-MINIMALISM (1971 ONWARDS)
FEMINIST ART (LATE 1960s AND 1970s ONWARDS)
PERFORMANCE ART (EARLY 1960s ONWARDS)
INSTALLATION ART (1960s ONWARDS)
WORD ART (1960s ONWARDS)
SURREALISM (C. 1924 – 2004)

2005

PROJECTION ART (21ST CENTURY)
KOREAN ART (C. 3,000 BCE ONWARDS)
EXPRESSIONISM (1890 ONWARDS)
CONCEPTUALISM (1960s ONWARDS)
VIDEO INSTALLATIONS (1960s ONWARDS)
MINIMALISM (1960s ONWARDS)
PHOTOREALISM (1960s ONWARDS)
CONTEMPORARY PHOTOGRAPHY (1960s ONWARDS)
STUCKISM (1999 ONWARDS)
COMPUTER ART (21ST CENTURY)
NEO-EXPRESSIONIST ART (1980 ONWARDS)
DECONSTRUCTIVIST DESIGN (1985 – 2010)
NEW LEIPZIG SCHOOL (2000 ONWARDS)

ART

2003

Fish Tail film by **Joaquim Pinto** and **Nuno Leonel**

Meatballs with Chocolate by **Riiko Sakkinen**

Apple and Teacup by **Michael Spano**

Wedding Cake by **Bruno Pacheco**

Vb 52, 166, Nt by **Vanessa Beecroft**

Two Cows by **Subodh Gupta**

Portuguese design studio **Silvadesigners** uses the sardine as a branding for ***Festas de Lisboa***

2004

Micro and Soft on Macintosh Apple, video by **Marco Maggi** and **Ken Solomon**

Dry Food by **Ryoko Aoki**

Tools, Raskolnik House, Siberia, photograph by **Mark de Fraeye**

Water Textures series by **Hans Gissinger**

House of Bread by **Urs Fischer**

2005

Museum of Food and Drink (MOFAD), Brooklyn, NY

Manufacturing 17, Deda Chicken Processing Plant, Dehui City, Jilin Province, China, photograph by **Edward Burtynsky**

Cracked Eggs and Milk by **Janet Fish**

Rougets (Two little fish) by **Julian Merrow-Smith**

Apples by **Andrey Aranyshev**

Tazzina da Caffé (Coffee Cup) by **Stefania Russo**

Kitchen Suprematism by **Blue Noses**

Brioix al vapor by **Francesc Guillamet**

Sharing Dinner, a project by **Marije Vogelzang**

2006

Dressing the Meat of Tomorrow, model by **James King**, Royal College of Art

Elizabeth Taylor and Hershey's Syrup Can by **Paul McCarthy** and **Damon McCarthy**

2007

Ratatouille, American computer-animated comedy film produced by Pixar, has its roots in **Chef Bernard Loiseau's** life story

Strawberries and Ostrich Egg by **Sharon Core**

Daddies Tomato Ketchup Inflatable by **Paul McCarthy**

Apple unveils iPhone, a phone that reinvented the 'phone'

Spills by **Subodh Gupta**

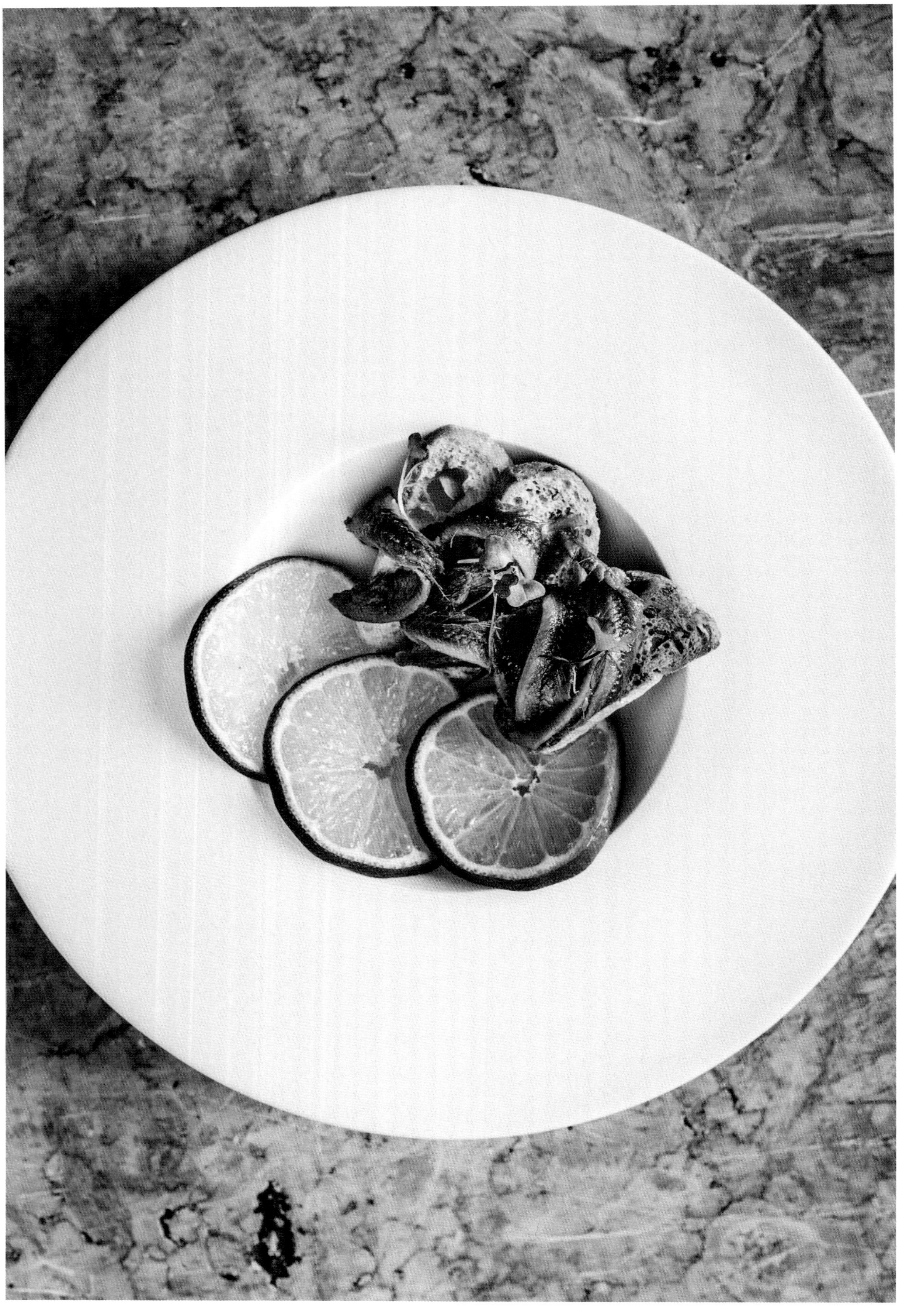

FOOD

2008

Chef **Jacques Decoret** and his wife **Martine** opened **Maison Décoret**

Massimiliano Alajmo worked with master perfumer Lorenzo Dante Ferro, studying the sense of smell as it relates to the dining experience

Juan Mari Arzak received the Universal Basque Prize

Jonnie Boer and his wife Thérèse Boer open **Librije's Hotel** in a restored women's prison

Opening of **Hotel Le Clos des Cîmes** restaurant by chef **Régis Marcon**

Yannick Alléno, 'Prince of the Palaces', launched the Group **Yannick Alléno**

Santiago Santamaria i Puig, aka **Santi Santamaria**, *La Cocina al Desnudo*

Manfred Kohnke, editor-in-chief of the German edition of Gault & Millau, threatens to lower the ratings of even top chefs, if they use too many additives in their practice of molecular gastronomy

2009

Andrea Volpato and **Young-Mi Park-Snowden** opened **Kimchi Princess** in Berlin

Philippe Rochat won three Michelin stars at **Restaurant de L'Hôtel de Ville**, in Crissier, Switzerland

Heinz Beck opened his first restaurant in London, **Apsleys – A Heinz Beck Restaurant**, at the Lanesborough Hotel

Simon Rogan and **Penny Tapsell** run a farm just outside Cartmel, which provides the ingredients for the plates of restaurant **L'Enclume**

Eyvind Hellstrøm announced he would leave Bagatelle after 27 years

Vitor Sobral opens its first restaurant, **Tasca da Esquina**, in Lisbon

Edward Voon is the executive chef of the restaurant **Le Pan** in Kowloon Bay, Hong Kong

Chef **Pedro Lemos** opens a restaurant with his name in Oporto, Portugal

Henrique Sá Pessoa opens **Alma** restaurant in Lisbon

Pote do Rei restaurant opens in São Paulo, Brazil, with **Chef William Ribeiro** and his famous dish, **Bacalhau à Moura Encantada**

2010

Ricardo Costa becomes head chef of **Yeatman's** restaurant, Vila Nova de Gaia

Les parfums de l'enfance from ***Voyages aux pays des Merveilles*** by **Olivier Roellinger**

Dieter Müller open a gourmet restaurant on board cruise ship MS *EUROPA*

Guy Martin chosen to prepare the celebratory meal of the annexation of Savoie to France cooking for French President Nicolas Sarkozy himself

Gualtiero Marchesi became the first celebrity chef to design two hamburgers and a dessert for McDonald's

José Andrés formed the **World Central Kitchen**, which provides healthy food to families and individuals touched by disasters

2011

Thomas Keller is first American male chef to be designated a **Chevalier of the French Legion of Honour**

Gordon Ramsay made an appearance on **The Simpsons** episode *The Food Wife*

Alfonso Laccarino, interviewed for Andy Whyler's restaurant guide: "There are some dishes I am proud of. One of them is the Vesuvius of Rigatoni..."

Maguy Le Coze and **Chef Eric Ripert** redesigned the restaurant **Le Bernardin**

Alain Roux developed new menus for the Business Premier class on board Eurostar trains

elBulli restaurant in Spain, established by **Ferran Adrià**, closes on 30 July

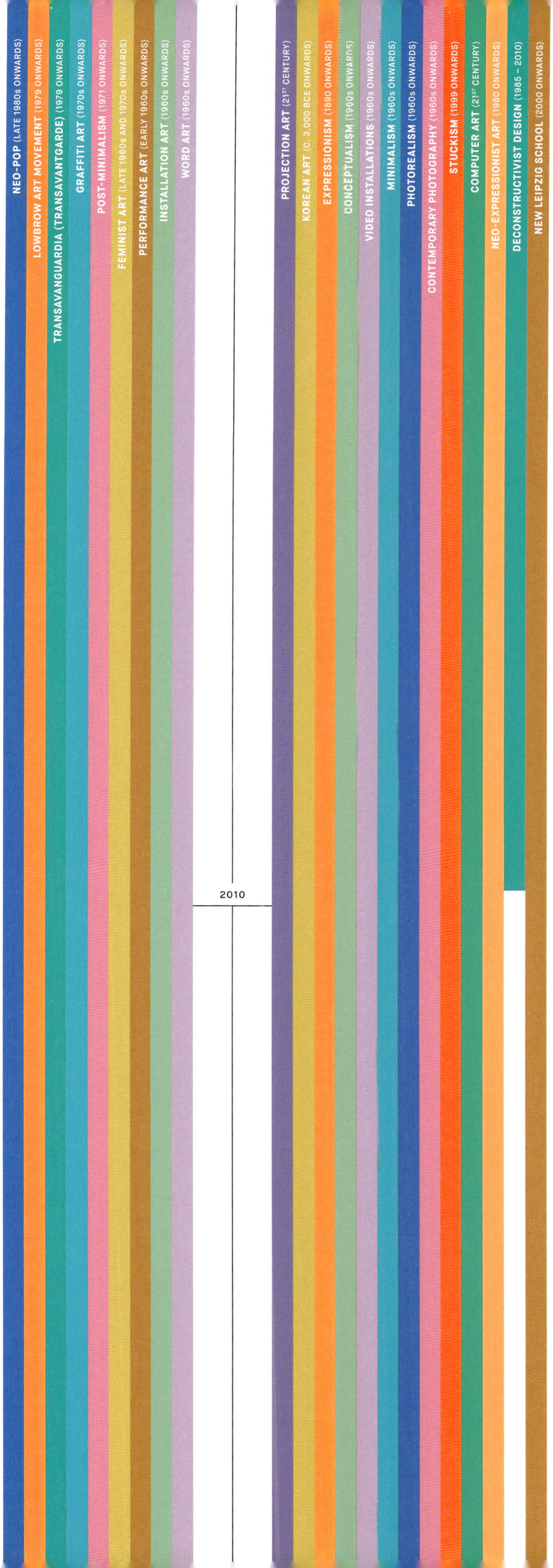

ART

2008

Kefir Ivó (Drinking Kefir) by **Székely Beáta**

Bread, Grapes and Walnuts by **Josep Santilari Perarnau**

Leonardo's Last Supper, multimedia project by **Peter Greenaway**

Self Portrait As Cucumber by **Erwin Wurm**

Caso by **Vìctor Guadalajara**

2009

La Comilona by **Cesar Flores**

Toaster Deluxe Study VII, collage by **Richard Hamilton**

Fried Egg by **Tjalf Sparnaay**

Apple (Apfel) (for Parkett no. 87) by **Katharina Fritsch**

Green Peppers, Shiitake by **Elad Lassry**

Oats by **Jani Leinonen**

The Breakfast by **Milan Rubio**

Matinée, digital video by **Liliana Porter** and **Ana Tiscórnia**

2010

Puente Almendrado, Chocolate con Almendras by **Los Carpinteros**

Project for the Life of a Tin series by **Cristina Castañeda Granja**

Enviropig, screenprint by **Nathan Meltz**

Beets by **Elad Lassry**

How Not to Cookbook: Lessons Learned the Hard Way, book by **Aleksandra Mir**

Atlanta by **Martin Parr**

2011

Bread and Water by **Jacob Collins**

Flesh painting (on sensualism) by **Marc Quinn**

Lunch with Cows by **Kultivator**, an experimental co-operation of organic farming and visual art practice

Fiesta by **Aleksandar Basic**

Dom Pérignon and Empty Glasses by **Noel Bensted**

L'Art del Menjar: De la Natura Morta a Ferran Adrià, an exhibition in Barcelona which celebrates artists' views of the act of eating

One Third (Cherries; Strawberries; Octopus; Cheese), photograph by **Klaus Pichler**

Serie Conservas by **Franco Aceves Humana**

FOOD

2012

Tacopedia, book by **Deborah Holtz** and **Alejandro Escalante**

The Edible Metaphor by **Peter Kubelka** at the (S8) Mostra de Cinema Periférico, in Spain

José Avillez reopens **Belcanto**, founded in 1958 by **Jaime Gonzalez**

Can the Can restaurant opens in Lisbon, in Terreiro do Paço, with a new and unique **concept of cooking using Portuguese canned fish**

2013

Chef Julio Biosca returned the Michelin star held by his restaurant, **Casa Julio**, in Valencia, Spain

Having spent much of his professional life abroad, **Leonel Pereira** opens **São Gabriel**, his first co-owned restaurant in Quinta do Lago, Algarve

The new **Sang Hoon Degeimbre's** restaurant **L'Air du Temps** is inaugurated

François Rabelais University in Tours awarded an honorary doctorate to **Martín Berasategui** in Culinary Studies

In the Australia Day Honours List, **Neil Perry** was made a Member of the Order of Australia in the General Division

Thierry Marx conducts research at the **French Culinary Innovation Centre** at Orsay University, exploring how food will evolve between now and 2030 – 2050

Exhibition at **London's Somerset House** called *elBulli: Ferran Adrià and The Art of Food*

After 17 successful years, **Agneta Green** and **Magnus Ek** closed the **Oaxen Skärgårdskrog** restaurant in Stockholm

2014

Chef Frederick Dhooge, in East Flanders, Belgium, returned his star because he wanted to be able to cook simpler food, like fried chicken

Sergio Herman and **Nick Bril** opened their restaurant, The Jane, in Antwerp, in a former chapel with the kitchen located on the altar because they say "Food is our religion"

Christian Le Squer became the head chef at restaurant **Le Cinq** at the Four Seasons Hotel George V, in Paris

Philippe Chevrier gave his mother's name, Denise, to one of his flagship restaurants: **Denise's Art of Burger** in Geneva

Marlene Vieira opens her restaurant at Time Out market in Lisbon

Carlo Cracco founded a *bistro* in Milan called **Carlo e Camilla in Segheria**

Barack Obama dined at **Sukiyabashi Jiro** with Japanese Prime Minister Shinzō Abe

Will Goldfarb and his wife opened Room 4 Dessert in Ubud (Bali), Indonesia

Miguel Laffan wins his first Michelin star, and the first for Alentejo region in Portugal, at **L'AND Vineyards** restaurant

2015

Chef Alain Ducasse sent meals to astronauts orbiting Earth aboard the International Space Station

Alexandre Silva opens restaurant **LOCO**, in Lisbon

João Oliveira joined **Vista** restaurant in Portimão, Algarve

João Rodrigues was rewarded with the award of Chef de L'Avenir by the International Gastronomy Academy

Pierre Gagnaire won a Best Chef in the World award

Jean-François Piège opens **Le Grand Restaurant** in Paris

Heston Blumenthal's most elaborate project was probably the **space menu** he prepared for British astronaut Major Tim Peake

Cláudia and **João Mácara** opened the traditional Portuguese restaurant **Cantinho Português** in São Paulo, Brazil

- **NEO-POP** (LATE 1980s ONWARDS)
- **LOWBROW ART MOVEMENT** (1979 ONWARDS)
- **TRANSAVANGUARDIA (TRANSAVANTGARDE)** (1979 ONWARDS)
- **GRAFFITI ART** (1970s ONWARDS)
- **POST-MINIMALISM** (1971 ONWARDS)
- **FEMINIST ART** (LATE 1960s AND 1970s ONWARDS)
- **PERFORMANCE ART** (EARLY 1960s ONWARDS)
- **INSTALLATION ART** (1960s ONWARDS)
- **WORD ART** (1960s ONWARDS)

2015

- **PROJECTION ART** (21st CENTURY)
- **KOREAN ART** (C. 3,000 BCE ONWARDS)
- **EXPRESSIONISM** (1890 ONWARDS)
- **CONCEPTUALISM** (1960s ONWARDS)
- **VIDEO INSTALLATIONS** (1960s ONWARDS)
- **MINIMALISM** (1960s ONWARDS)
- **PHOTOREALISM** (1960s ONWARDS)
- **CONTEMPORARY PHOTOGRAPHY** (1960s ONWARDS)
- **STUCKISM** (1999 ONWARDS)
- **COMPUTER ART** (21st CENTURY)
- **NEO-EXPRESSIONIST ART** (1980 ONWARDS)
- **NEW LEIPZIG SCHOOL** (2000 ONWARDS)

ART

2012

2012 by **Paulina Mitek**

The Head Chef, An American Success Story by **John Carroll Doyle**

Studio Cookbook II by **Hato Press**

2013

Lobster Roll by **Gina Beavers**

4 eggs by **Alberto Macone**

Last Supper (after Leonardo) by **Yinka Shonibare MBE**

Only Want You to Love Me by **Miles Aldridge**, by Rizzoli New York

Big Big Mac by **Tom Friedman**

Blood Orange is the New Kale by **Nate Lowman**

Aperitif by **Roeland Kneepkens**

Feast by **Helen Masacz**

2014

The In Vitro Meat Cook Book, **Koert van Mensvoort** and **Hendrik-Jan Grievink**

Contemporary Pieces, a project by **Rebecca Rütten**

Artisanal confectionery shop **LIQ NYC** creates **lollipops**, infusing famous paintings into the hard-candy orbs.

Stove by **Thomas Demand**

Bittersweet Symphony by **Condiment Junkie**

Sushi Pleats Please, set of travel accessories by **Issey Miyake**

Man with Banana by **Juss Piho**

Table Manners, movies by **Zina Saro-Wiwa** (2014 – 2016)

The Last Supper by **Ken** and **Julia Yonetani**

2015

Energy: Cocktails to Get You UP, a collaboration book between artist/ photographer **Pete Deevakul** and bartender **Steph Russ**

Crossed Confections by **Torbjørn Rødland**

Dear Data: Week 17 (Food Preferences/A Week of Food Preferences) by **Giorgia Lupi, Stefanie Posavec**

Food Porn XX, ceramic installation: 400 sculptures by **Beatriz Albuquerque**

Chanda Mama Door Ke (From Far Away Uncle Moon Calls) by **Subodh Gupta**

Deep Fried Gadgets series by **Henry Hargreaves**

Crossing the Wild Line installation by **Dana Sherwood**

FOOD

2016

Benoît Violier, chef of **Restaurant de l'Hôtel de Ville**, which boasts Michelin's highest rating, died in an apparent suicide

Manolo de la Osa opens his new restaurant, **Adunia**, with the 'Infinite Table'

Opening of **Moments Restaurant** in the Hotel Mandarin Oriental in Barcelona, managed by chef **Carme Ruscalleda** and her son **Raül Balam**

Opening of **Enigma** project, the latest gastronomic expression of **Albert Adrià**

Paolo Lopriore opened **Il Portico**, Appiano Gentile, in the province of Como

Danyel Couet and **Melker Anderson's** latest restaurant, **Mother**, in Stockholm

Chan Hon Meng, first street food chef in the world to achieve a Michelin star

Miguel Vieira wins his first Michelin star in Portugal, at **Fortaleza do Guincho**, in Cascais

Cinco Séculos à Mesa by **Guida Cândido**, 500-year-old Portuguese recipe book

Luís Lavrador is the head chef of the Portuguese **National Football Team**, responsible for the athletes' meals during the UEFA European Championship, which saw Portugal as winners

2017

Michel Bras, whose restaurant had been rated three stars in the Michelin Guide since 1999, chose to voluntarily give up his rating

Mathias Dahlgren creates next-generation vegetarian cuisine at **Rutabaga**

Miguel Laffan becomes creative Chef at **Can the Can**

2018

Pedro Pena Bastos becomes head chef at **Ceia**, fine dining restaurant, Lisbon

Jay Fai became a national celebrity as the first **Thai street food chef** to be awarded a Michelin star

José Avillez is distinguished with the International Academy of Gastronomy's greatest award, the *Grand Prix de l'Art de la Cuisine*

Tiago Bonito won the first star of his career at **Largo do Paço**, Amarante, Portugal

Lisbon welcomes for the first time, the **Portugal** and **Spain Michelin Guide's Gala** in 2019

Portugal has one new two-star restaurant with chef **Henrique Sá Pessoa** at Alma (Lisbon), and three new single-star restaurants, with chef **Pedro Almeida** at **Midori** (Sintra), chef **Óscar Geadas** at **G Pousada** (Bragança) and chef **António Loureiro** at **A Cozinha** (Guimarães)

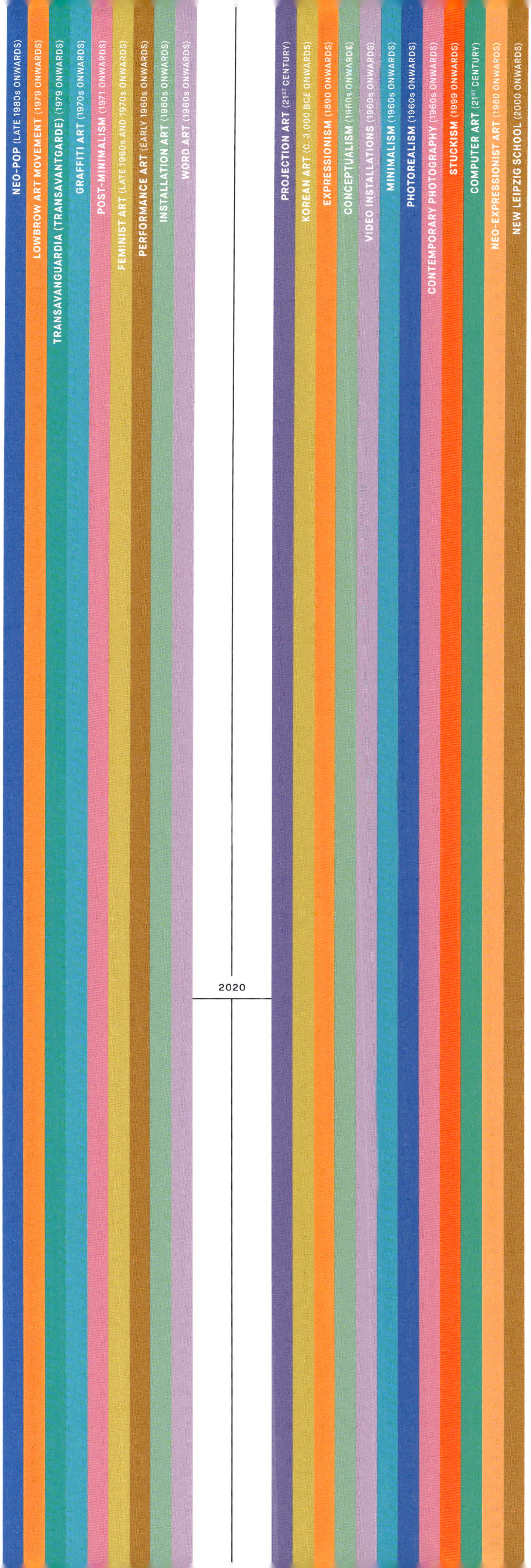

ART

2016

Extreme Beauty, Spa Days series by **Aleksandra Kingo**

The Photographer's Cookbook, book by **Lisa Hostetler**

Serving Suggestions by **Patricia Tobin**

Herod's Banquet by **Justin Bradshaw**

The Best I(n) Can, first book by **Can the Can**

The Battle for Humankind by **Luis Geraldes**

2017

Gluten Freedom by **Chloe Wise**

Invasion of the Kitchen Bots, illustration by **Gabriel Silveira** for *Wired* magazine

La Torta Apetitosa II by **Robert Romanowicz**

Dinner Party by **Zoey Frank**

2018

Prelude by **Mar Gasca Madrigal**

Tomato Spray, street art by **Thierry Guetta** aka **Mr. Brainwash**

Desserts by **Annie Collinge**

The Aviary Cocktail Book by **Grant Achatz, Nick Kokonas, Allen Hemberger**

2020

Eat & Art book by **Can the Can**

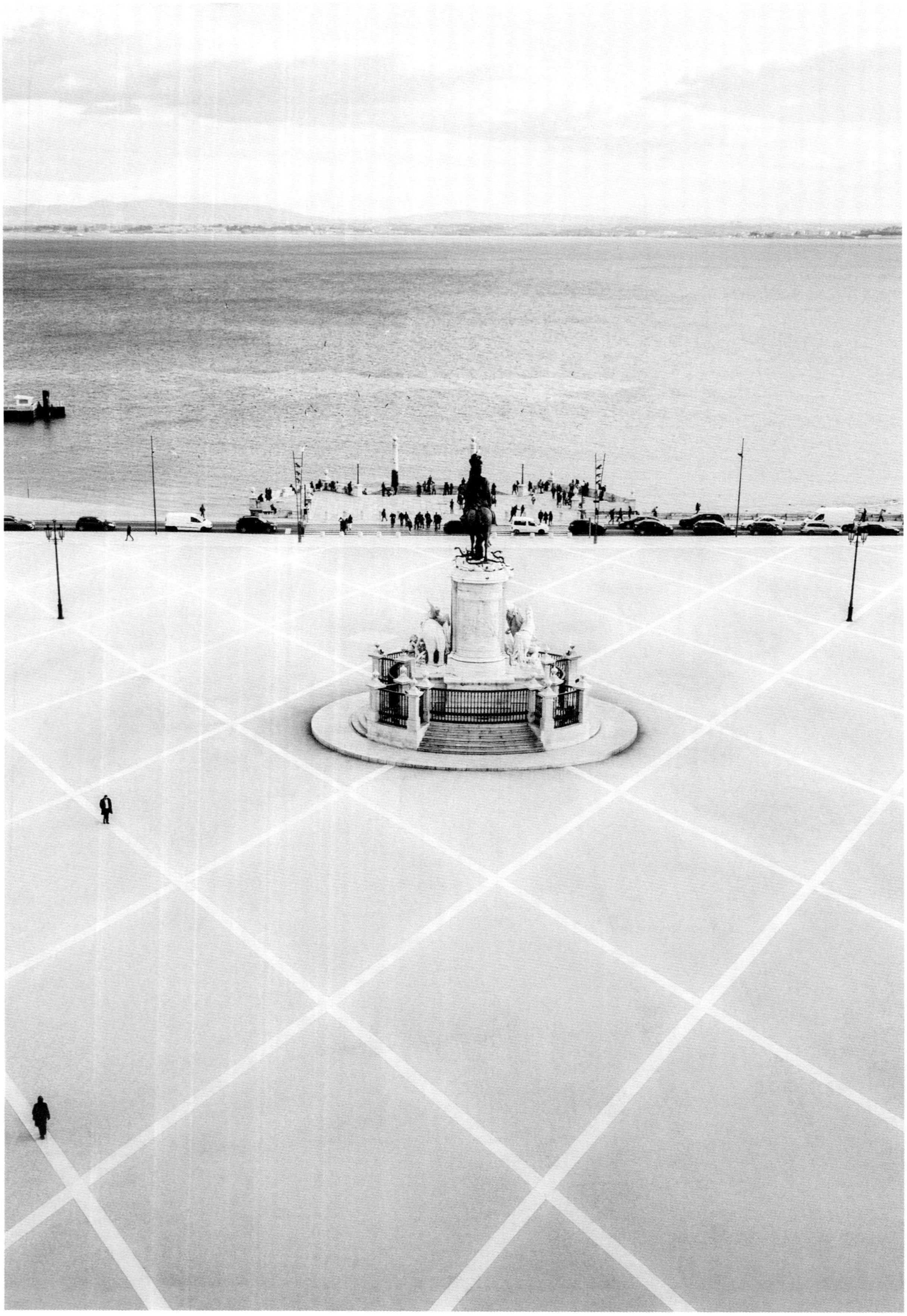

Books

À LA TABLE DE L'HISTOIRE
Marion Godfroy – Xavier Dectot
Flammarion – 2011

À MESA COM EÇA DE QUEIRÓS
Maria Antónia Goes
Colares Editora – 2016

À MESA COM RAMALHO ORTIGÃO
Maria Antónia Goes
Colares Editora – 2018

ALIMENTOS AO SABOR DA HISTÓRIA
Fortunato da Câmara
Colares Editora – 2011

ARTE DE COZINHA
Domingos Rodrigues
Relógio de Água – 2017

ARTS & FOODS: RITUALS SINCE 1851
Germano Celant – Random House Espanol – 2018

BEM COMER & CURIOSIDADES
José Quitério – Documenta – 2015

CAFÉS DE LISBOA
Marina Tavares Dias – Quimera – 1999

DALÍ. LES DÎNERS DE GALA
Salvador Dalí – Taschen – 2016

ESCRITORES À MESA (E OUTROS ARTISTAS)
José Quitério – Assírio & Alvim – 2010

EXPERIMENTAL EATING
Tom Howells, Leanne Hayman
Black Dog Publishing – 2014

FOOD & DRINK INFOGRAPHICS. A VISUAL GUIDE TO CULINARY PLEASURES
Simone Klabin, Julius Wiedemann
Taschen – 2018

FOOD IN ART FROM PREHISTORY TO THE RENAISSANCE
Gillian Riley – Reaktion Books – 2014

FOOD: A CULINARY HISTORY (EUROPEAN PERSPECTIVES: A SERIES IN SOCIAL THOUGHT AND CULTURAL CRITICISM)
Jean-Louis Flandrin, Massimo Montanari – Columbia University Press – 2013

FOOD: A HISTORY
Dr. Felipe Fernandez-Armesto
Pan Books – 2001

FOOD: THE HISTORY OF TASTE
Paul Freedman – Thames and Hudson 2007

HISTÓRIA DA COZINHA E DOS COZINHEIROS
Edmund Neirinck e Jean-Pierre Poulain
Colares Editora – 2007

HISTOIRE DE LA TABLE
Pierre Ennès, Gérard Mabille, Philippe Thiébaut – Flammarion – 1994

L'ART DEL MENJAR. DE LA NATURA MORTA A FERRAN ADRIÀ
Fundació Caixa Catalunya – 2011

MEMÓRIAS E RECEITAS CULINÁRIAS DOS MAKAVENKOS
Francisco de Almeida Grandela
Colares Editora – 2010

MILESTONES IN THE HISTORY OF EMPIRICAL SCIENCES
Heitor Matallo Junior – lulu.com – 2013

NEW LAROUSSE GASTRONOMIQUE
Hamlyn – Octopus Publishing Group 2019

O LIVRO DE MESTRE JOÃO RIBEIRO
José Quitério – Assírio & Alvim – 1996

OBRA DE MIGUEL TORGA
Dina Fernanda – Ferreira de Sousa
Colares Editora – 2017

OH! SARDINHA LINDA
Carlos Consiglieri, Marília Abel
Colares Editora – 2000

ON COOKING: A TEXTBOOK FOR CULINARY FUNDAMENTALS
Global Edition – Sarah R. Labensky, Priscilla A. Martel, Alan M. Hause, Steven Labensky – 2014

OS MISTÉRIOS DO ABADE DE PRISCOS
Fortunato da Câmara
A Esfera dos Livros – 2013

SABORES DA MESA NA THE ILLUSTRATED ENCYCLOPEDIA OF FRUITS, VEGETABLES & HERBS
Deborah Madison – Chartwell Books – 2017

THE MORDERN ART COOKBOOK
Mary Ann Caws – Reaktion Books – 2013

Documents

HISTORY OF COOKING
Maria Cecilia Metran

Online

alexandrepomar.typepad.com
all-art.org
artistsnetwork.com
artsy.net
britannica.com
centrepompidou.fr
design-is-fine.org
foodreference.com
foodtimeline.org
garfadasonline.blogspot.com
guggenheim.org
gulbenkian.pt
hermitagemuseum.org
metmuseum.org
moma.org
museuartecontemporanea.gov.pt
restosdecoleccao.blogspot.com
rijksmuseum.nl
sammlung-boros.de
surfacemag.com
tate.org
useum.org
vads.ac.uk
widewalls.ch

A BEST I(N) CAN collection book
by CAN THE CAN Lisbon, Portugal
www.canthecan.net

CONTENTS
CAN THE CAN

CREATED BY
Victor Moura Vicente

EDITOR
Victor Moura Vicente

PRODUCER
Maria da Luz

FOOD PHOTOGRAPHY
Jorge Simão

PHOTOGRAPHY
Jorge Simão and Mariana Motta Veiga

IMAGE TREATMENT
Mariana Motta Veiga

GRAPHIC DESIGN
Silvadesigners

WRITER
Nuno Camarneiro

INTRODUCTION
André Quiroga

TIMELINE
Victor Moura Vicente

TIMELINE TECHNICAL SUPERVISION
Professor Eduardo Duarte, Faculdade de Belas-Artes da Universidade de Lisboa and Professor José Luís Pimentel Lavrador, Higher Education Teacher

ENGLISH TRANSLATION
Isabel Mota and Vera Freitas

COPY EDITING AND ENGLISH REVISION
David Roberts

PROOFREADING
Helena Soares and Black Dog Press

List of ANICP associated fish canning companies (ANICP – the National Association of Manufacturers of Canned Fish)

A POVEIRA – MINERVA brand
Sardine roes in olive oil

BRIOSA – BRIOSA brand
Garfish in spiced olive oil

COFACO AÇORES – PITÉU brand
Anchovy fillets in olive oil

COFISA – VASCO DA GAMA brand
Mackerel fillets in olive oil

COMUR – COMUR brand – Smoked eels

CONSERVEIRA DO SUL SA – MANNÁ brand – 'Ventresca' tuna in olive oil

CORRETORA – CORRETORA brand
Tuna fillets in olive oil

ESIP – EUROPEAN SEAFOOD INVESTMENTS PORTUGAL, S.A.
MARIA ELISABETH brand
Sardines in olive oil

EXPOCONSER – EXPORTADORA DE CONSERVAS S.A. – CÂNTARA brand – Smoked lamprey loins

GENCOAL S.A. – JANUS brand
Smoked salmon in olive oil

LA GONDOLA – LA GONDOLA brand
Octopus in olive oil

LUÇAS & Cª. LDA – LUÇAS brand
Black swordfish fillets

RUBEN AUGUSTO LARANJEIRA MAIA, LDA – MARINA brand
Sardines in olive oil with lemon

PINHAIS & Cª LDA – PINHAIS brand – Horse mackerel in olive oil

PORTUGAL NORTE, LDA
PORTHOS brand – Tuna fillets in hot vegetable oil

RAMIREZ & Cª FILHOS, S.A.
RAMIREZ brand – Mussels in pickled sauce

SANTA CATARINA INDÚSTRIA CONSERVEIRA, S.A. – SANTA CATARINA brand – Tuna sangacho

VIANAPESCA – OP COOPERATIVA DE PRODUTORES DE PEIXE DE VIANA DO CASTELO, CRL
VIANA PESCA brand – Mackerel fillets in smoked olive oil

ACKNOWLEDGEMENTS

I would like to offer my special thanks to Jorge Simão, who made the introductions to all the Portuguese chefs participating in this book.

I am deeply grateful to Portuguese artist Ana Vidigal, who liked the idea from the very start and encouraged me to pursue it, introducing me to all the artists.

My great appreciation goes to José Avillez, the first chef we invited, who, without knowing me or my background, accept the invitation without a blink and helped with the list of chefs. Also to all the chefs for believing in this project and agreeing to participate amid their busy lives. Thanks to all the artists who agreed to create a special piece of art for this project.

Thanks to André Quiroga for writing the introduction to the book. Thanks also to Isabel Mota and Vera Freitas, who translated texts with the greatest commitment and energy, and also Isabel Soares, the best proofreader of texts. Many thanks to my dear friend David Roberts, who made the texts sound truly native.

On the design front, I would like to express my thanks to the Silvadesigners team, especially the principal designers of the book, Catarina Marques, Luís Alexandre and Jorge Silva.

On the research side, thanks to Professor Eduardo Duarte and Professor Luís Lavrador, whose knowledge was invaluable, and who patiently endured many rounds of emails about our timeline.

It is impossible not to mention and thank the Can the Can team, who give life to this project every day, especially our incredible, unsurpassable manager, Elsa Henriques.

Can the Can is associated with ANICP, the National Association of Manufacturers of Canned Fish, whom we thank for their support in making our project an integral part of Lisbon's touristic offering to lovers of great gastronomy and culture.

The work and travelling to put this book together has been intense and extensive, but very enjoyable. It was a pleasure and I would like to thank this optimistic team: Mariana Motta Veiga, Jorge Simão and Nuno Camarneiro. We met amazing people and made friends – what more can you ask for?

Above all, I could never done this without the inspiration, ideas (and contrariness when necessary) I received from my wife, Maria da Luz.

I would like to dedicate this project to my father, who always made me believe everything is possible.

Victor Moura Vicente was born in Lisbon and studied photography and design. In 1984 he founded Novodesign together with Carlos Coelho and Paulo Rocha, a Portuguese design company that become sector leader for 20 years. Victor developed the Can the Can concept and project in 2012, with the aim of making the historic canned fish industry an integral part of the national tourist offering, establishing it as something that fits perfectly with the pursuit of leisure for lovers of gastronomy and culture.

BLACK DOG PRESS LIMITED
298 Regents Park Road
London N3 2SZ
United Kingdom

+44 (0) 20 8371 4047
office@blackdogonline.com
www.blackdogonline.com

ISBN 978-1-912165-23-0

British Library Cataloguing-in-Publication Data. A CIP record for this book is available from the British Library.

Printed by Kopa, Lithuania

black dog press

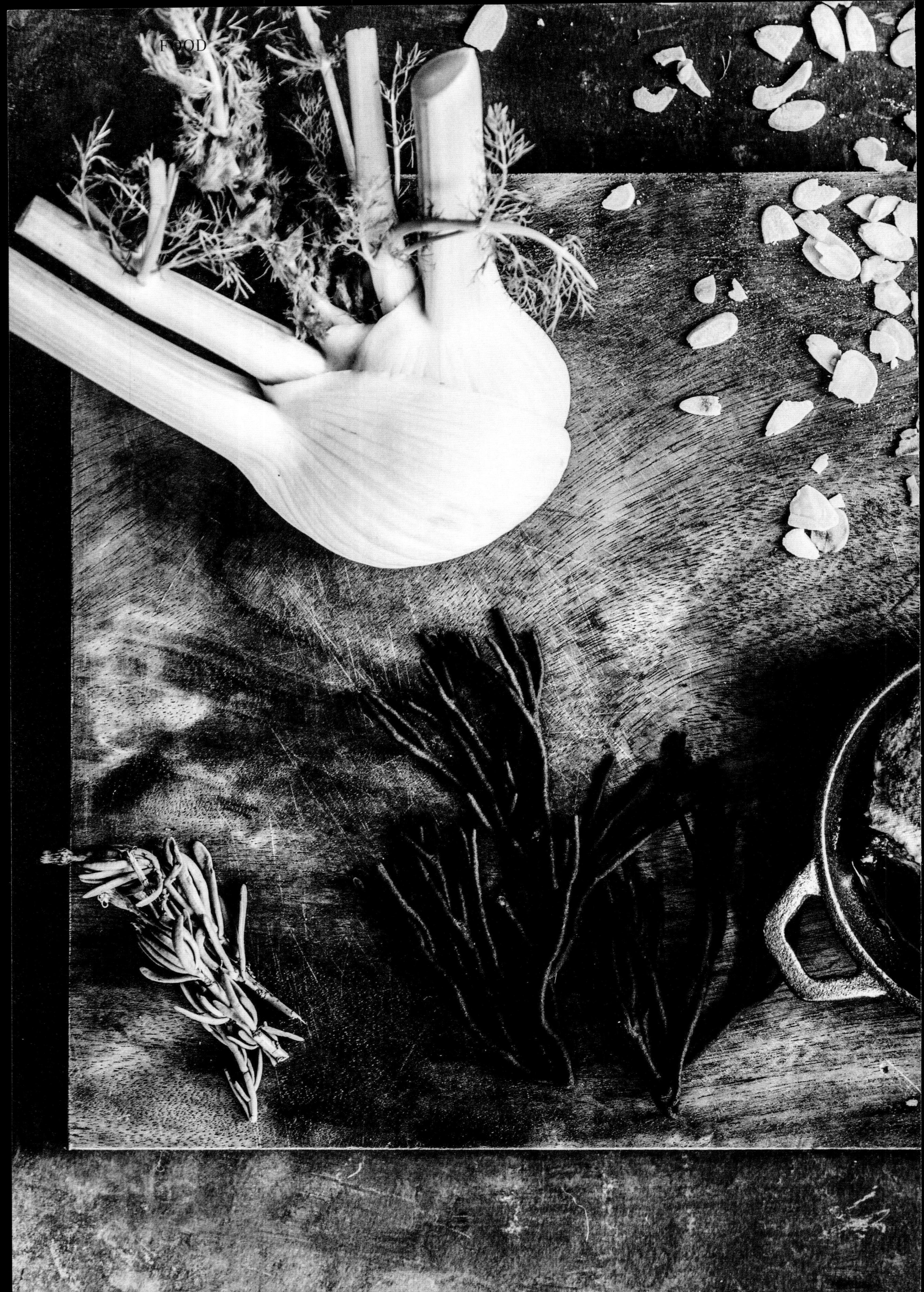

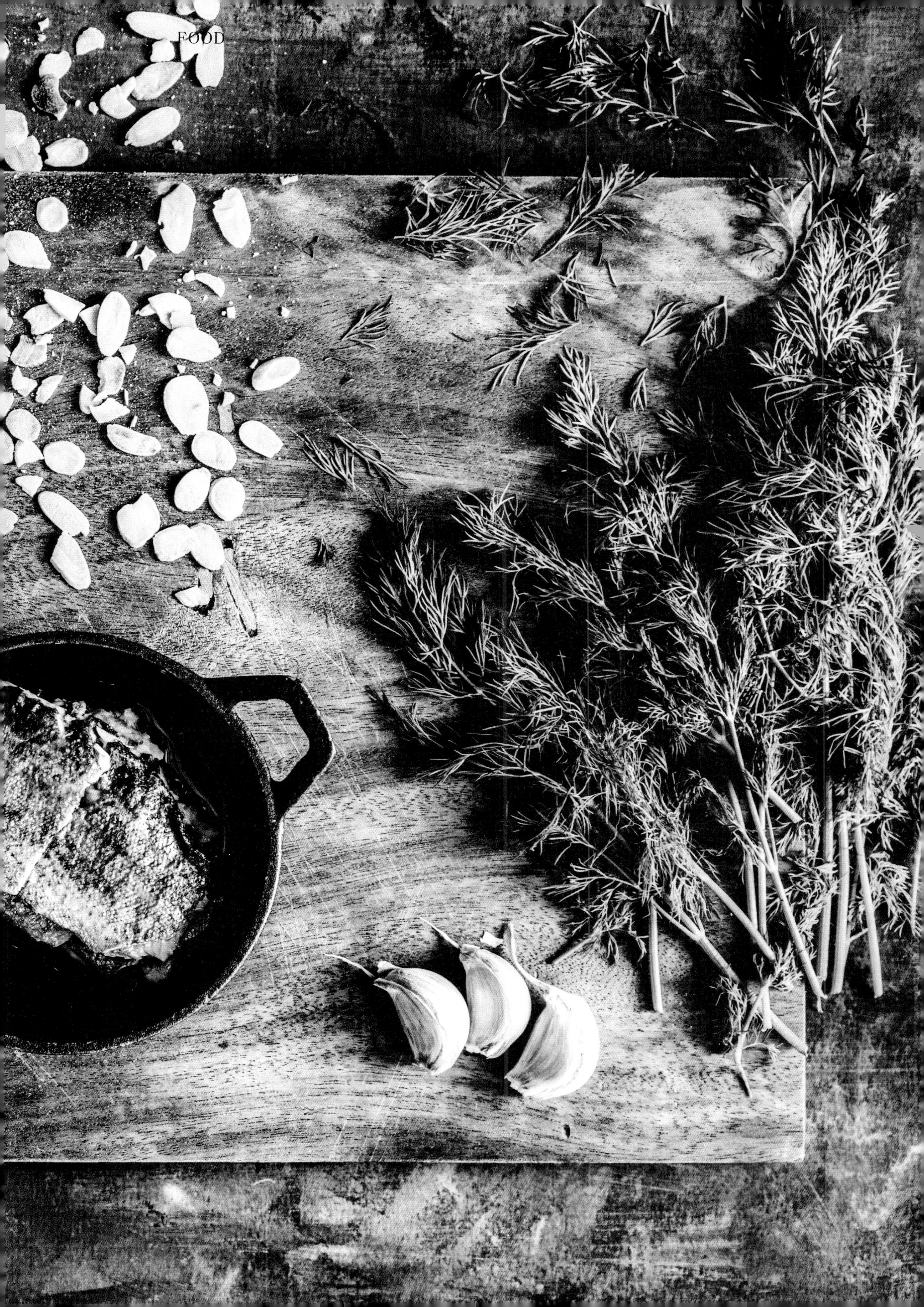